POW! WOW!

First Edition
February, 2020
Edition of 3000
ISBN: 978-1-7327980-7-6

Paragon Books
929 Camelia Street
Berkeley, CA 94710-1419
paragon-books.com

Principal: Ken Harman Hashimoto
Producer: Jennifer Rizzo
Design & Layout: Shaun Roberts

This book was designed in San Francisco, California. The text was composed using 'Post Grotesk' from Sharp Type Co.

Printed in South Korea

USD $44.95
ISBN 978-1-7327980-7-6
54495
9 781732 798076

POW! WOW!

PARAGON BOOKS

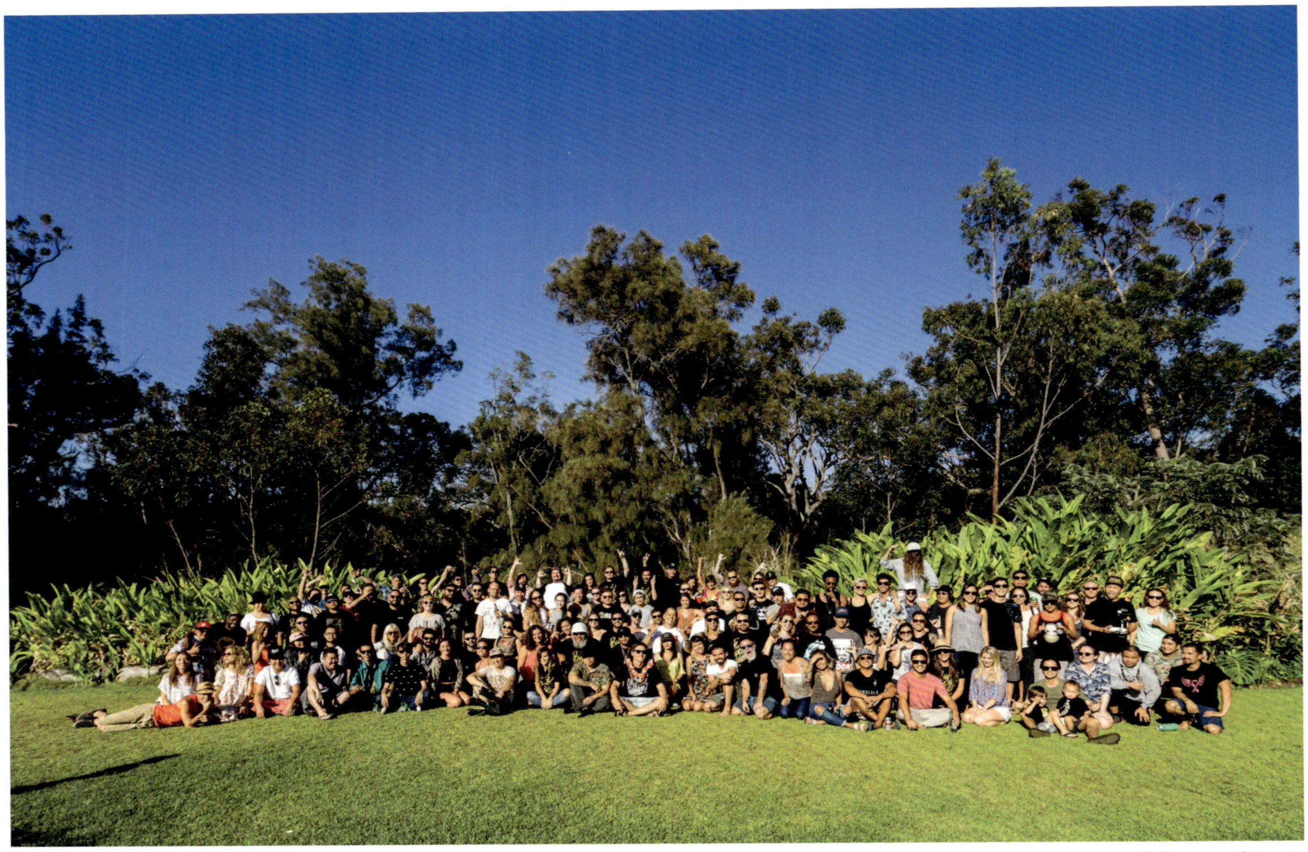

To Amy, Ella, Stella, and
my mother Tammy.

— Jasper Wong

To Shanna, Nova, Ever and
my parents Nodie & Lulik.

— Kamea Hadar

To Noelle & Neila, and
my mom Joyce.

— Jeff Gress

Contents

A city can't be great without world-class art, and Long Beach has always been proud of its museums, galleries, and local artists. But we really took it to the next level when POW! WOW! arrived in 2015. With more than 40 murals now spread throughout nearly every neighborhood, Long Beach has undeniably taken its place among the great art cities of the world, thanks to an amazing and unique group of muralists and street artists who bring their passion and creativity to the walls of Long Beach every summer.

With outposts in Japan and the US, POW! WOW! is surely the premier international street art event in the world, and Long Beach could not be prouder to host it. The excitement, style and beauty that these incredibly talented artists bring has elevated the Long Beach art scene and become one of the most important parts of experiencing this city from the street level. Pow!Wow! is one of my favorite events, and I know that countless residents and visitors feel the same.

Turning walls into canvases not only brings color and vitality to parking lots, alleys, neighborhoods, and even the LA River, it stimulates creativity and inspiration in all who encounter these larger-than-life murals.

Our thanks to Jasper Wong, all the artists, & the whole POW! WOW! team for continuing to produce this outstanding event and for bringing art into the daily lives of so many Long Beach residents.

Mayor Robert Garcia
Long Beach, CA

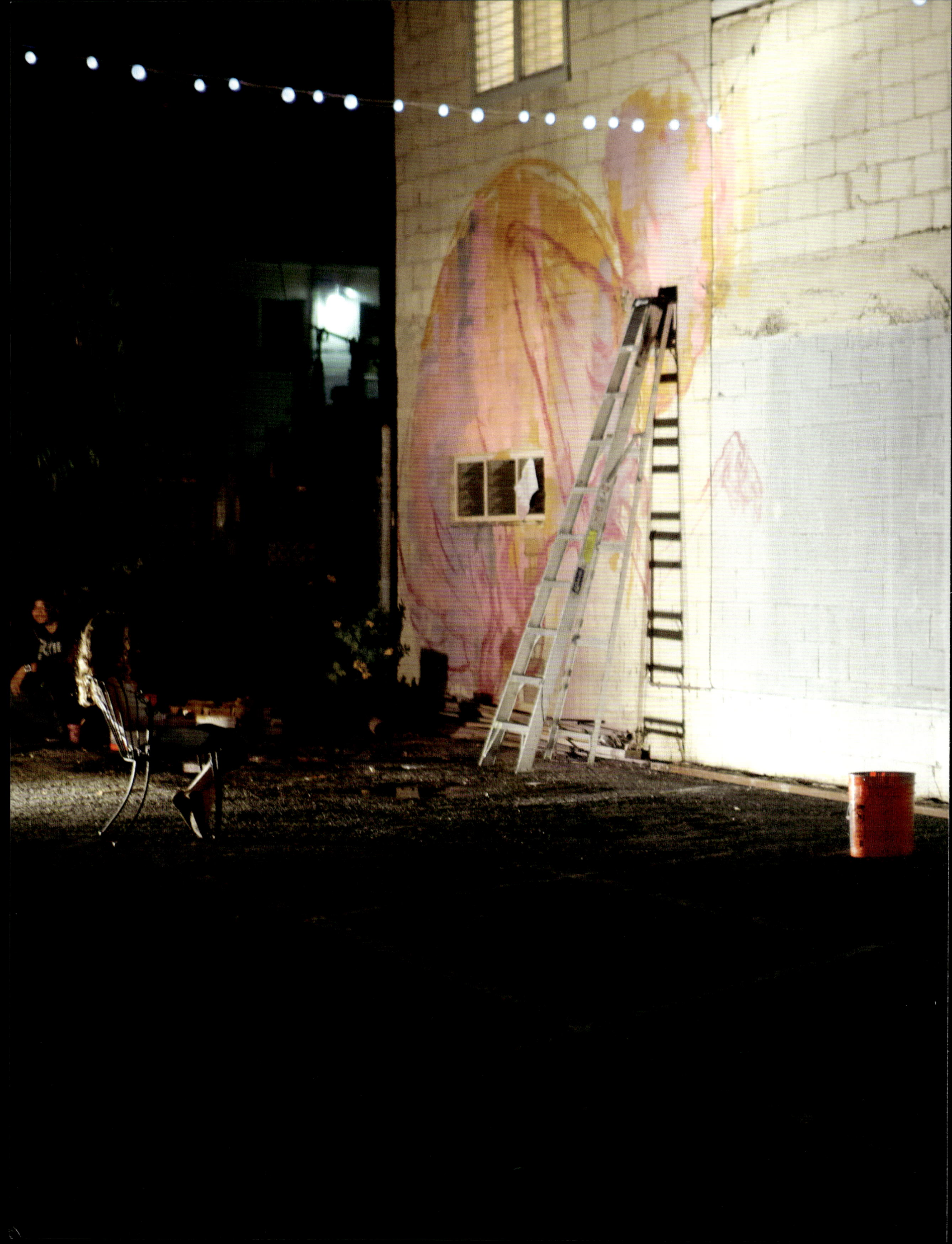

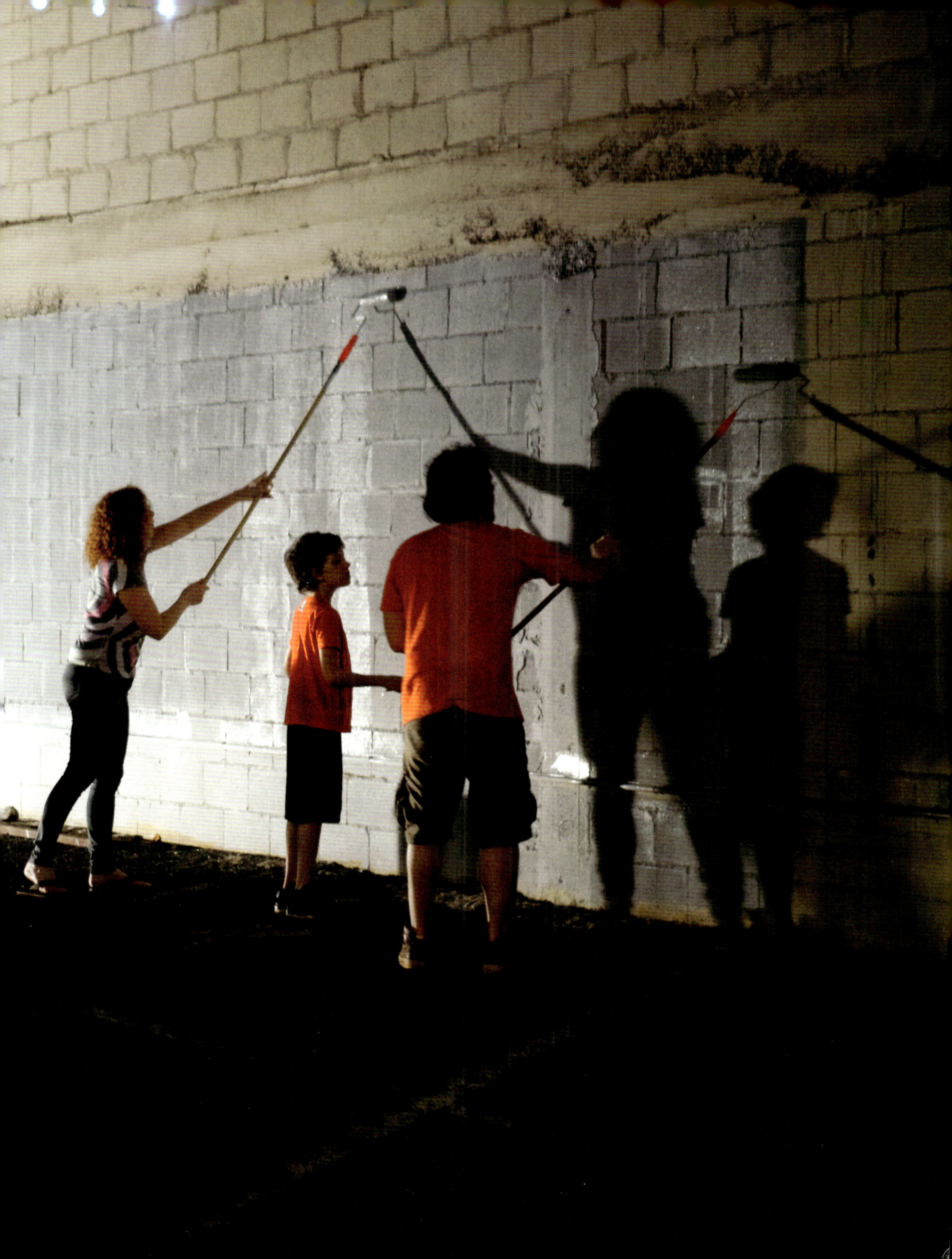

Foreword

Jeff Hamada

I feel lucky to have been part of the first POW! WOW! Hawai'i that Jasper Wong and Kamea Hadar organized in 2011. This was the second POW! WOW!, Jasper organized the first in Hong Kong the year before. The event was small enough that the invited artists and media could stay together in Kamea's parent's house on the North Shore, and everyone had a real bed. I only mention the beds because the event would quadruple in size over the next two years with upwards of 40 people staying on the property at one time—there would be a pillow and a blanket and someone sleeping on every inch of that floor. It was a far cry from the Waikiki hotels that have sponsored the event in recent years but it was also a big part of what made it special. Foodland for breakfast, Zippy's for dinner. It was family style and it all came from a very earnest and naive desire to bring people together—not just to paint walls and go home, but to actually get to know each other, share stories, and form real friendships.

When I think about the first POW! WOW! Hawai'i, I think of Scien and Klor, the legendary French graffiti artists who founded 123Klan. They brought their two kids, Tom and Cleo, along on the trip, and I spent a lot of time with all four of them.

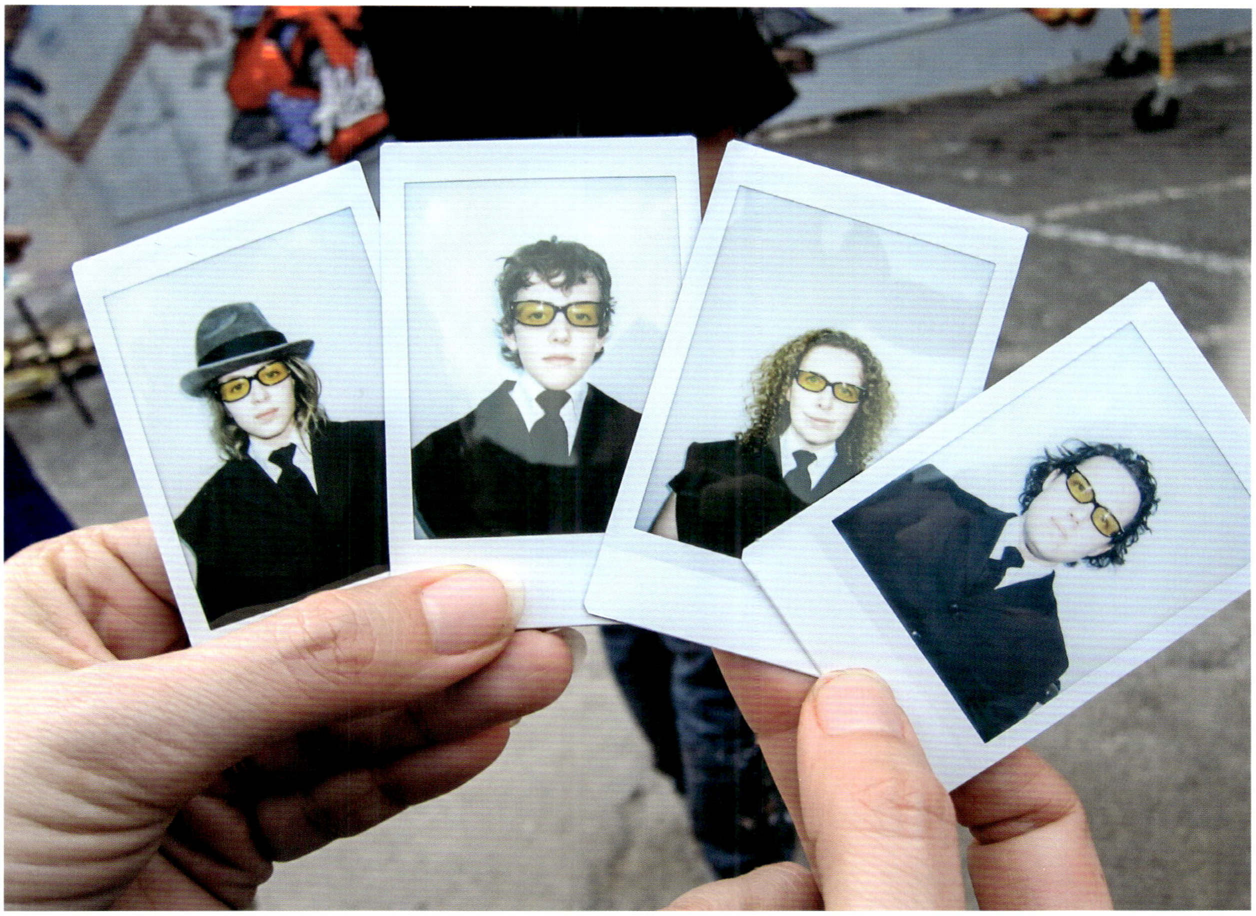

Portraits taken by Suitman as part of his photography project at POW! WOW! Hawaii, 2011 © Jeff Hamada

The neat thing was they planned to collaborate on a mural together, as a family, for the very first time. Tom sketched a skull warrior and Cleo drew a Mr. Chocolate Bar guy (still one of my all-time fav characters). Scien helped Tom, and Klor helped Cleo re-sketch their drawings on the wall. Just thinking about this kind of makes me a little bit emotional. It was a beautiful thing to watch. At one point I saw them all pose for a photo and all four of them threw up their middle fingers.

I remember Scien told me that the kids might miss a bit of school coming on a trip like this, but he and Klor felt it was a really important thing for them to experience—being surrounded by art and artists, and travelling. And they didn't want to force them to be artists, if they decided they wanted to be lawyers, great, at least they'd get to see what this was like first.

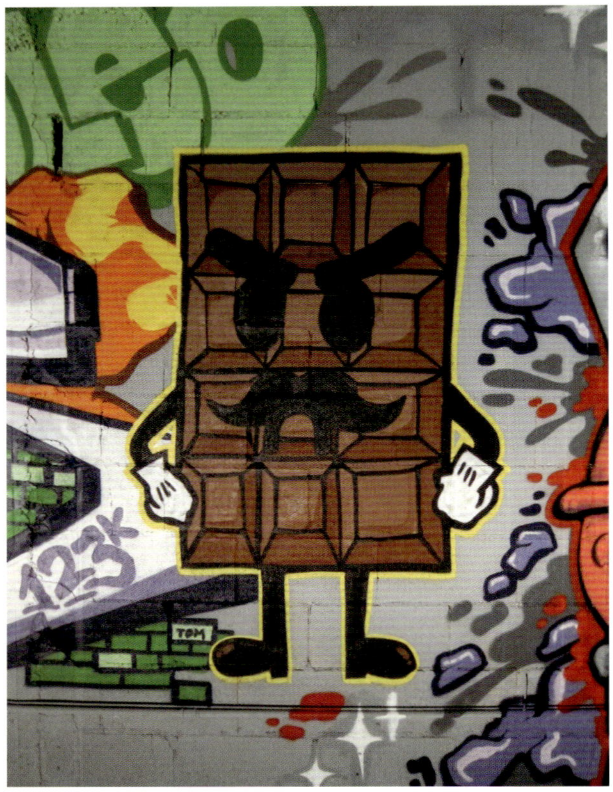

Mr. Chocolate Bar © Jeff Hamada

I was 28, an adult (or at least the age of an adult), and the whole POW! WOW! experience was giving me a whole new perspective on what I wanted to spend my life doing. I tried to imagine what it would have been like to see it all at Tom and Cleo's age. I don't think they were even in high school yet. Two weeks surrounded by people from all different parts of the world, none of whom had "normal" jobs, all figuring out their own paths and creating ways to live doing what they loved. I'd been running Booooooom for three years at this point and I think this was the first time where I felt like there were a bunch of other people like me out there, making it up as they went. It was reassuring.

At some point during the trip, Tom and Cleo caught a lizard (I think it was a lizard) and it kind of became their pet. One afternoon we had a party at Jasper's mom's place and a lot of people came over to barbecue and hang out. The house and the yard were full of people having a great time, laughing and talking, and then someone noticed the kids were crying in the backyard. Scien ran out to see what was going on. I think Klor or someone said that the lizard had died. Scien hugged the kids and tried to comfort them, he was in full-on dad mode. And so in the middle of this big party, surrounded by all these happy people, the three of them walk to the far end of the yard and they have this little funeral service for their pet. I think that's when I felt like '*I actually really know these people*'.

This memory really stuck with me. Maybe it was because I'd been to lots of events where artists had big egos, and they were just too cool, and they didn't want to really get to know anyone. This was the complete opposite of that. This was an honest moment and the kind of thing that only happens when people are being themselves. What I'm trying to say is when you look at all the photos in this book—a book celebrating the 10th anniversary of what is now a massive arts festival that has expanded across the United States, and brought art and artists to cities in Japan, Taiwan, Israel, Guam, The Netherlands, Korea, Italy—just remember, the spirit of POW! WOW! is a party where a guy can have a lizard funeral for his kids.

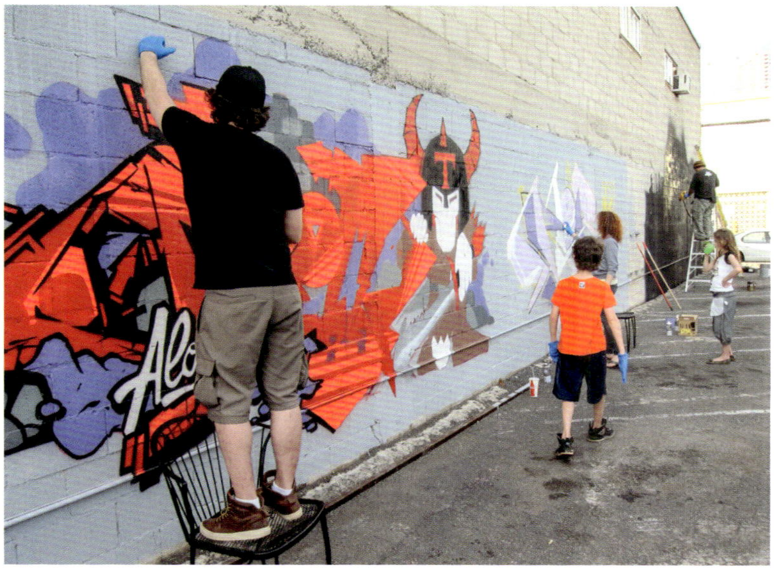

© Jeff Hamada

Jeff Hamada is a Japanese Canadian artist based in Vancouver, Canada. In 2008 he created Booooooom, which quickly became one of the largest online arts publications on the Internet and firmly established itself as an authoritative voice in contemporary arts and culture. Over the past decade, he's helped launch the careers of hundreds of young emerging artists and photographers, and has collaborated with brands like Uniqlo, Converse, Red Bull, and WeTransfer.

Jeff has also spoken on the topics of curation, creativity, and community-building at creative conferences and festivals including: IAM (Barcelona), 180 CREATIVE CAMP (Portugal), POW! WOW! (Taipei), CREATIVE MORNINGS (Vancouver), CARBON (Melbourne).

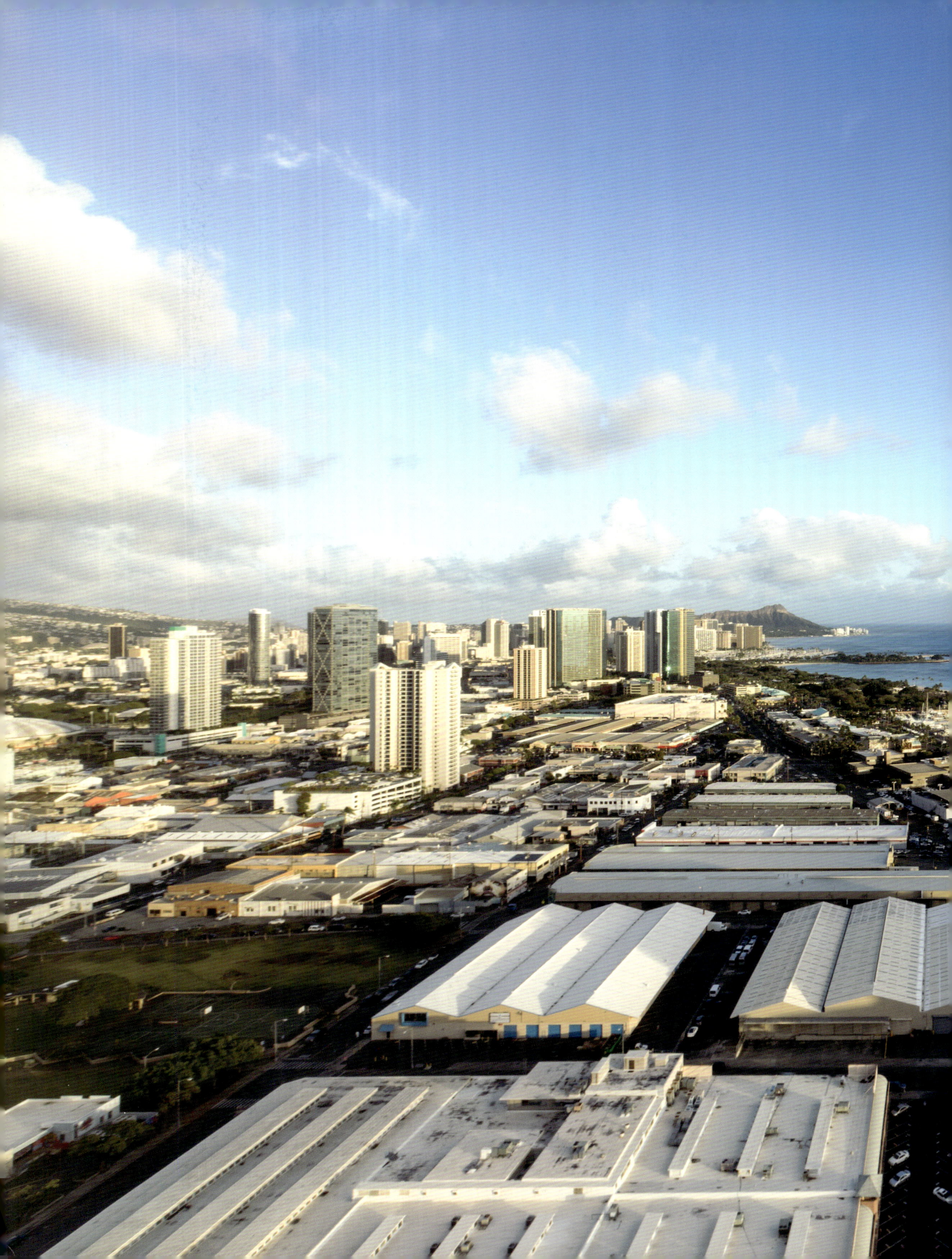

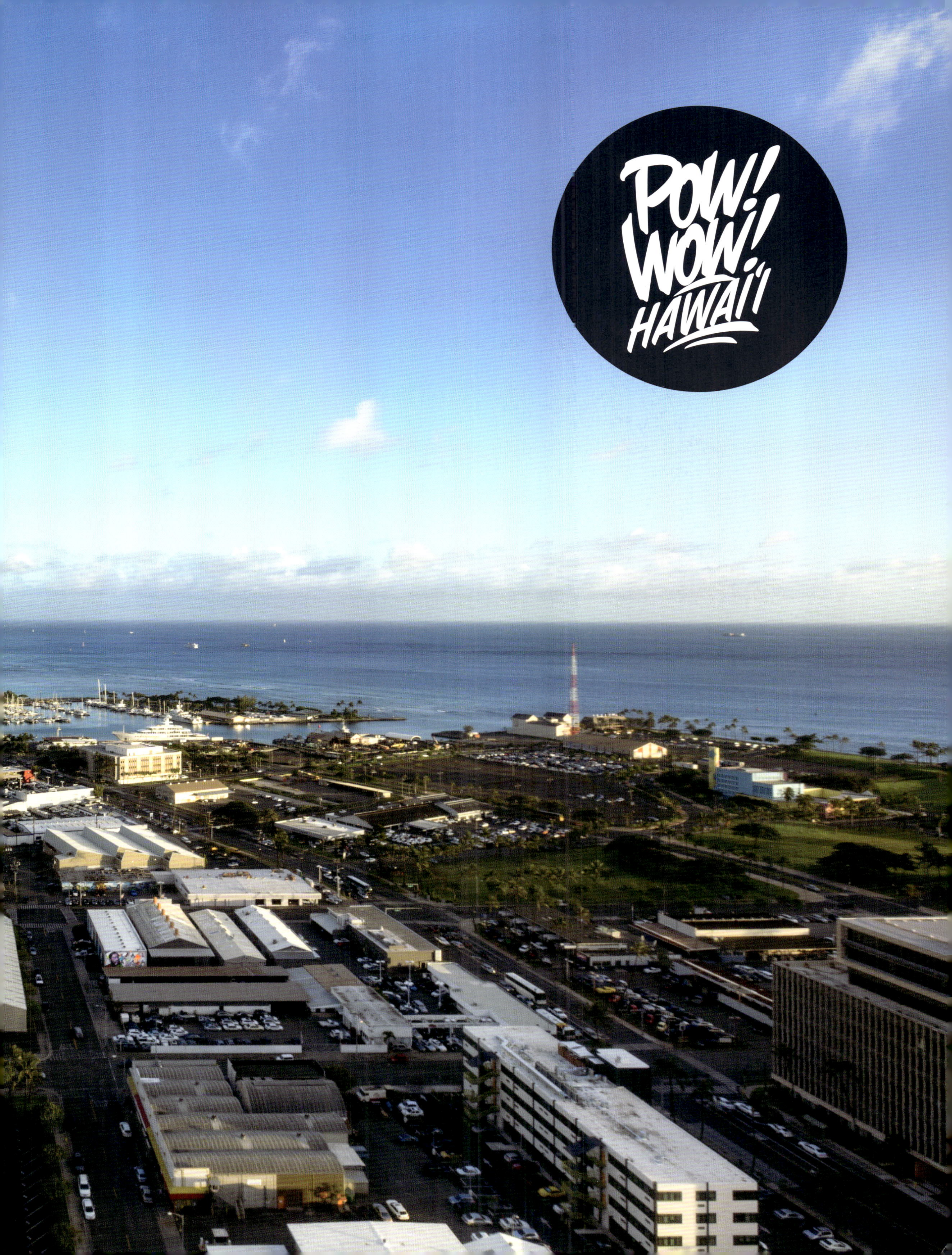
POW!
WOW!
HAWAI'I

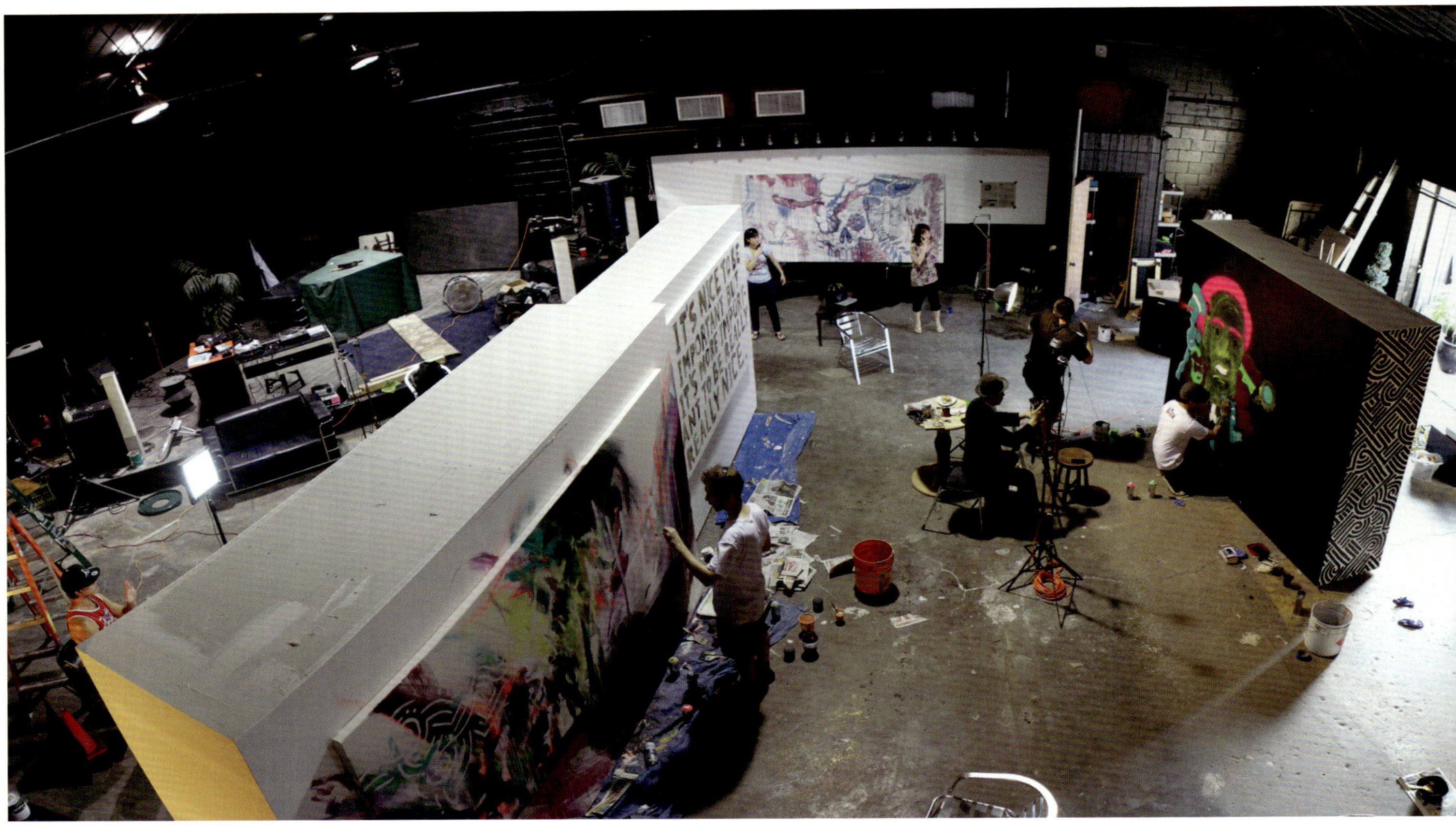

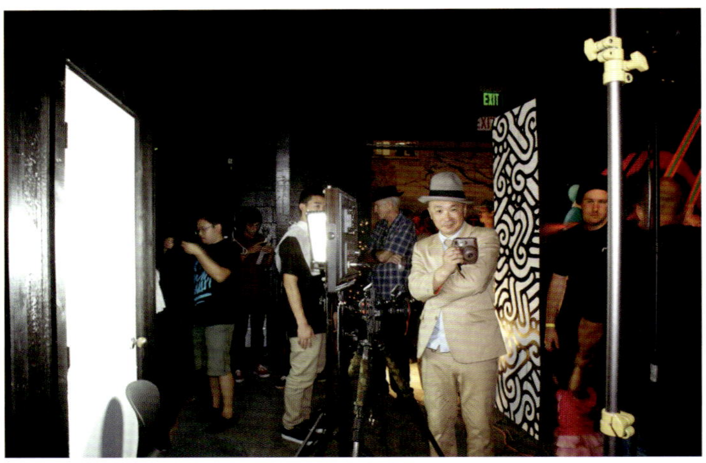

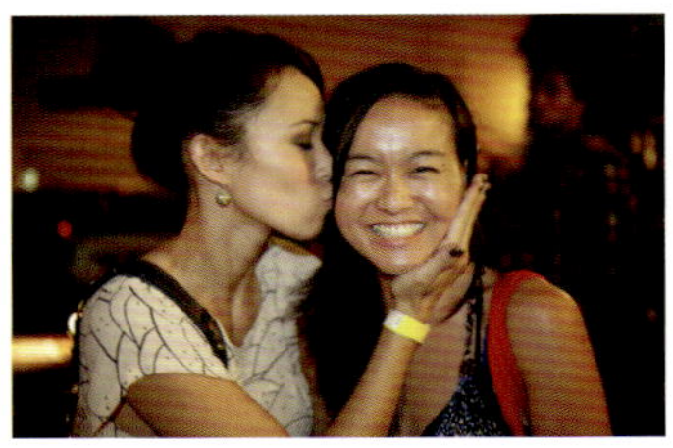

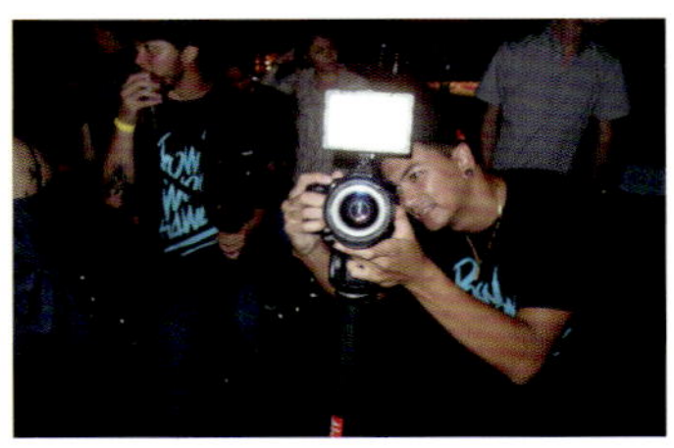

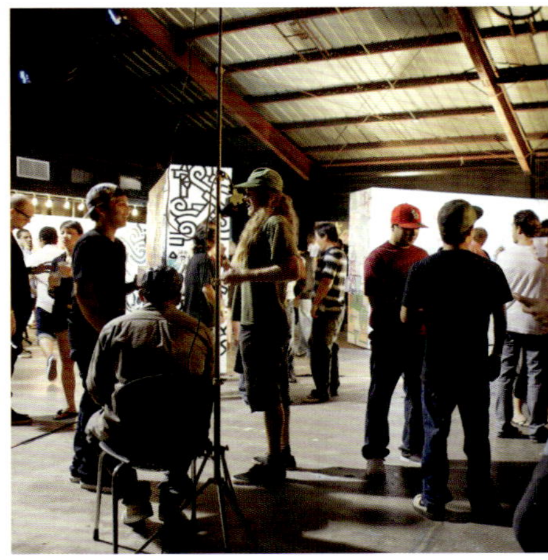

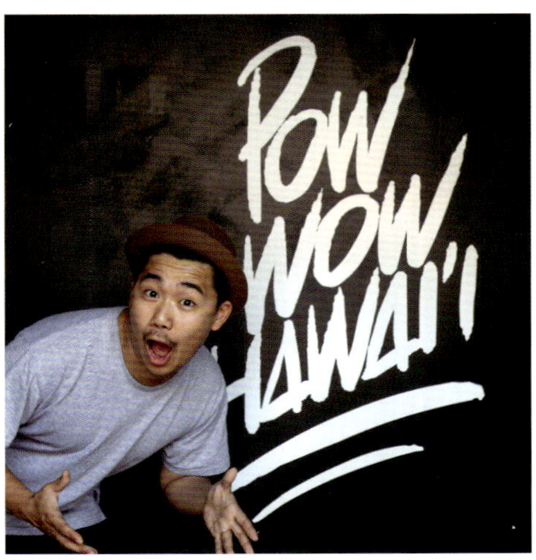
Pow Wow Hawai'i

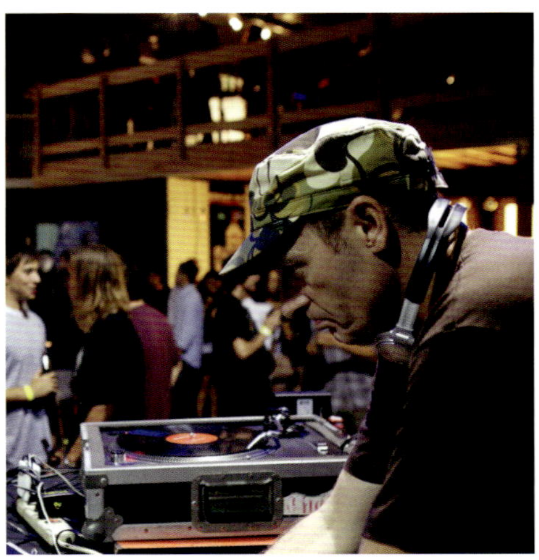

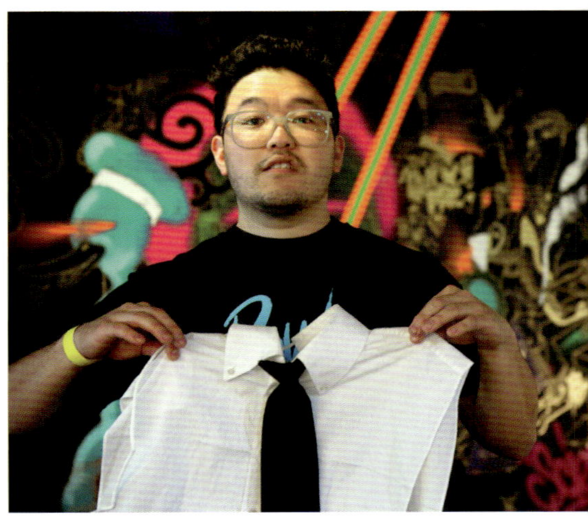

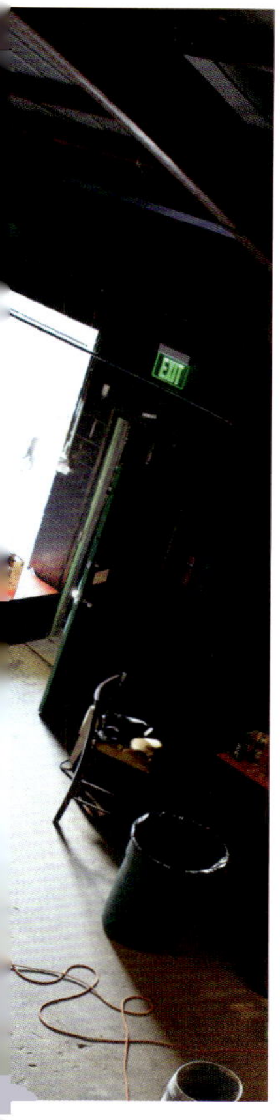

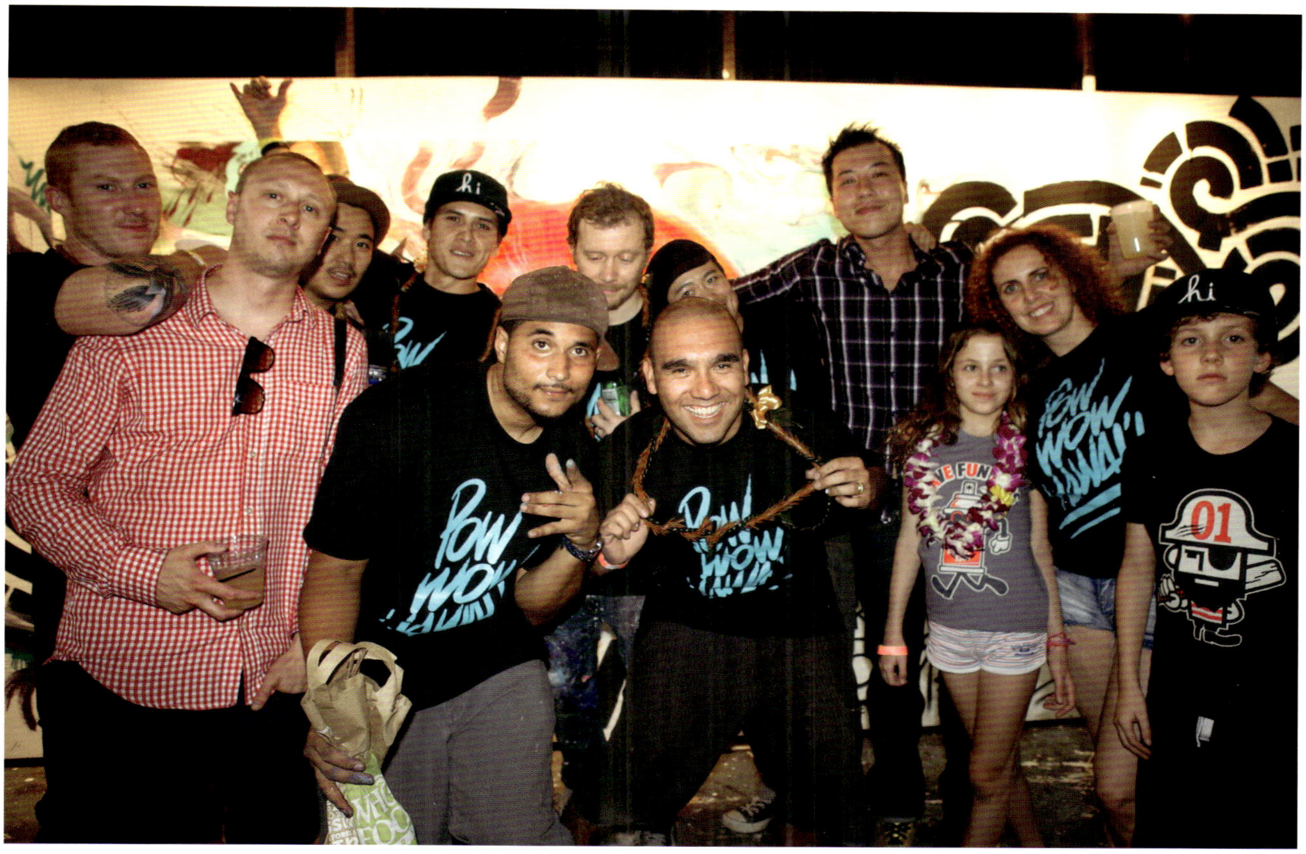

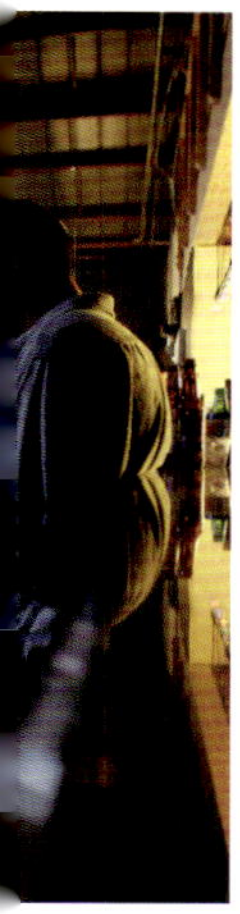

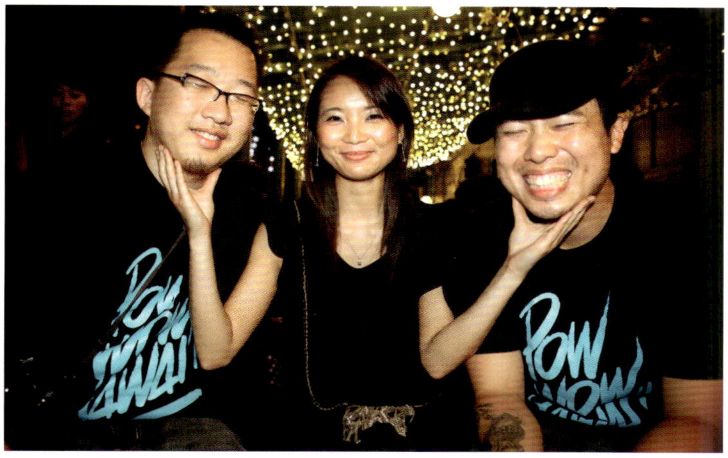

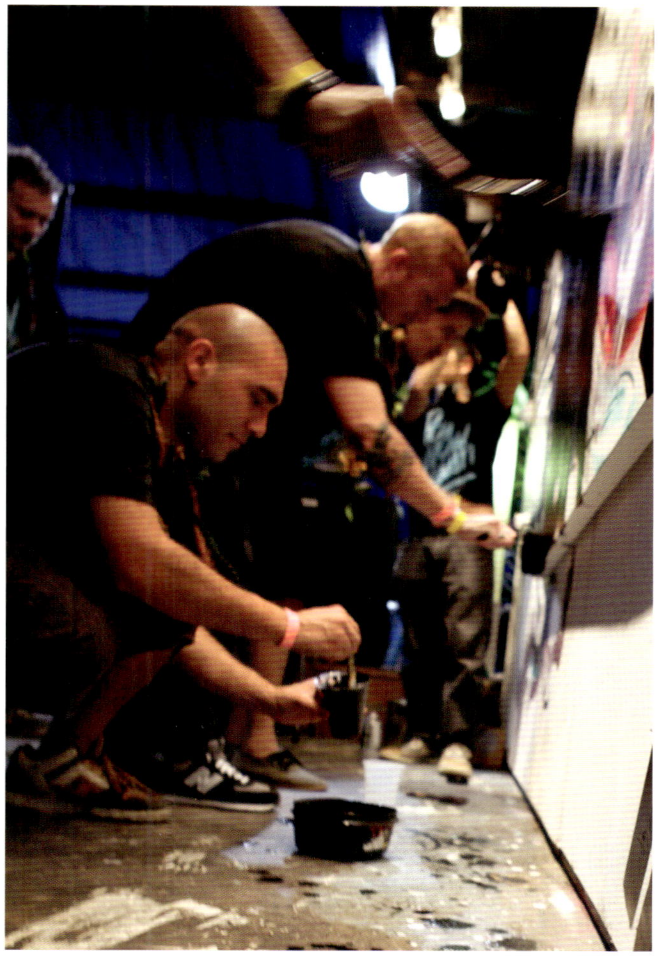

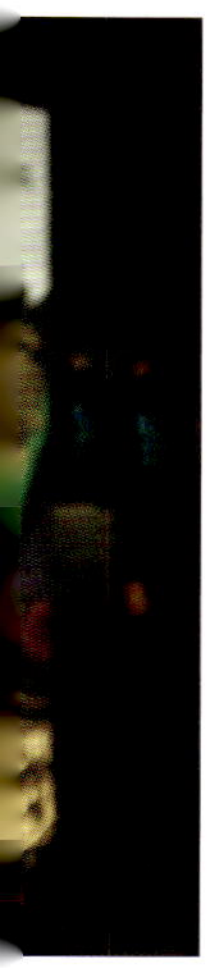

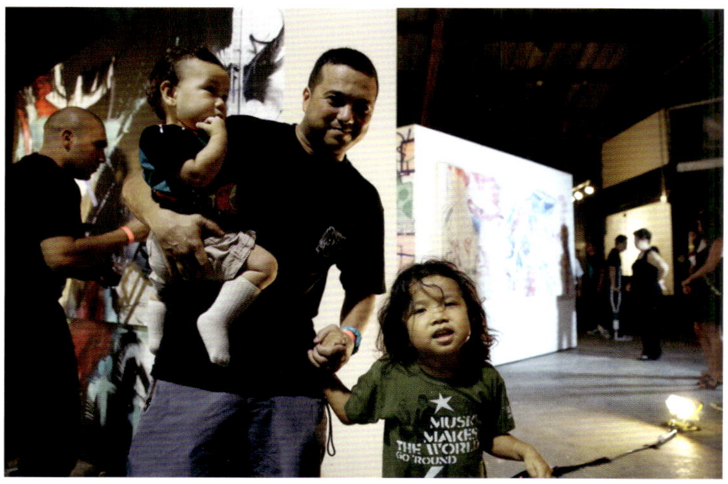

MUSIC MAKES THE WORLD GO 'ROUND

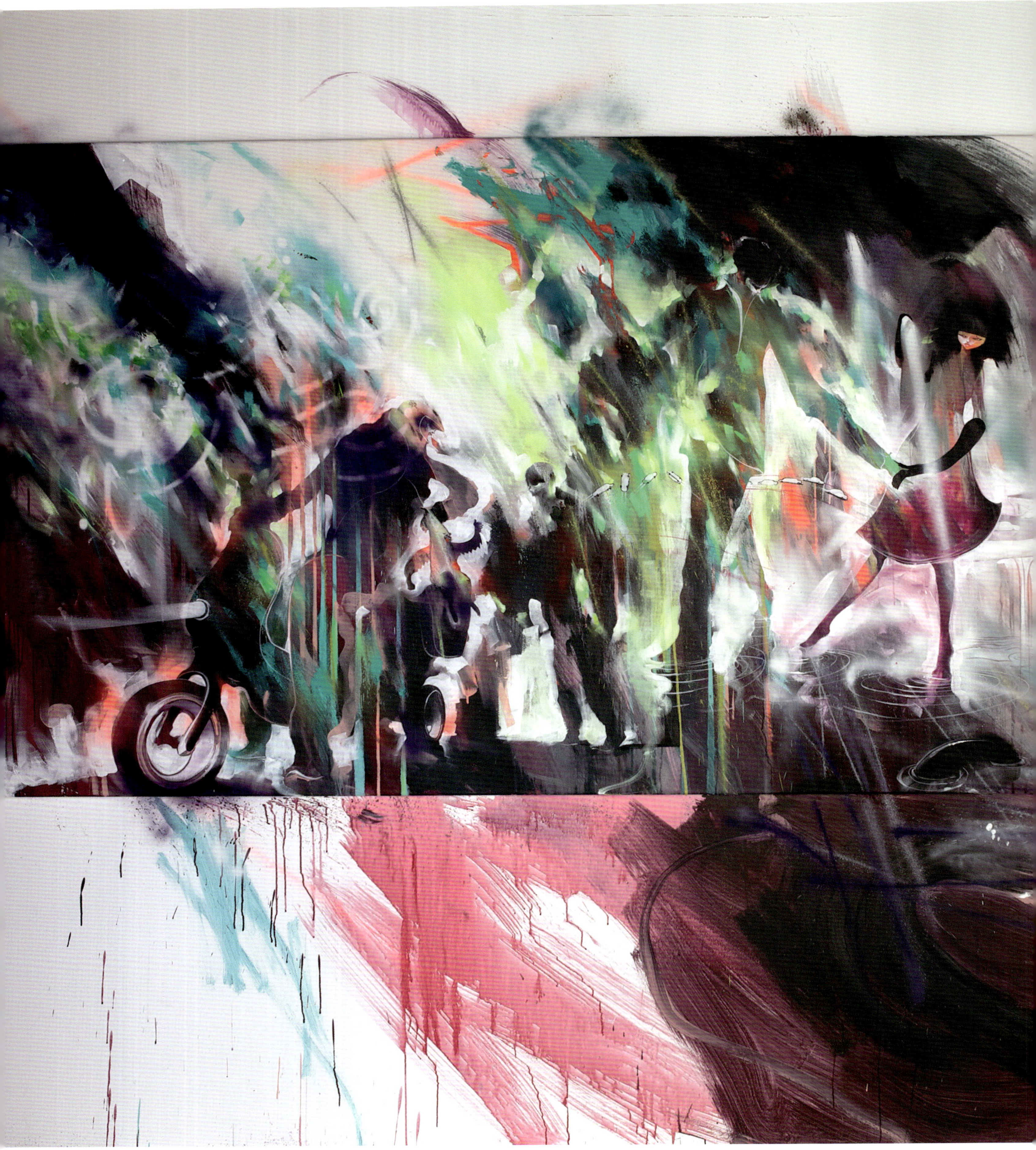

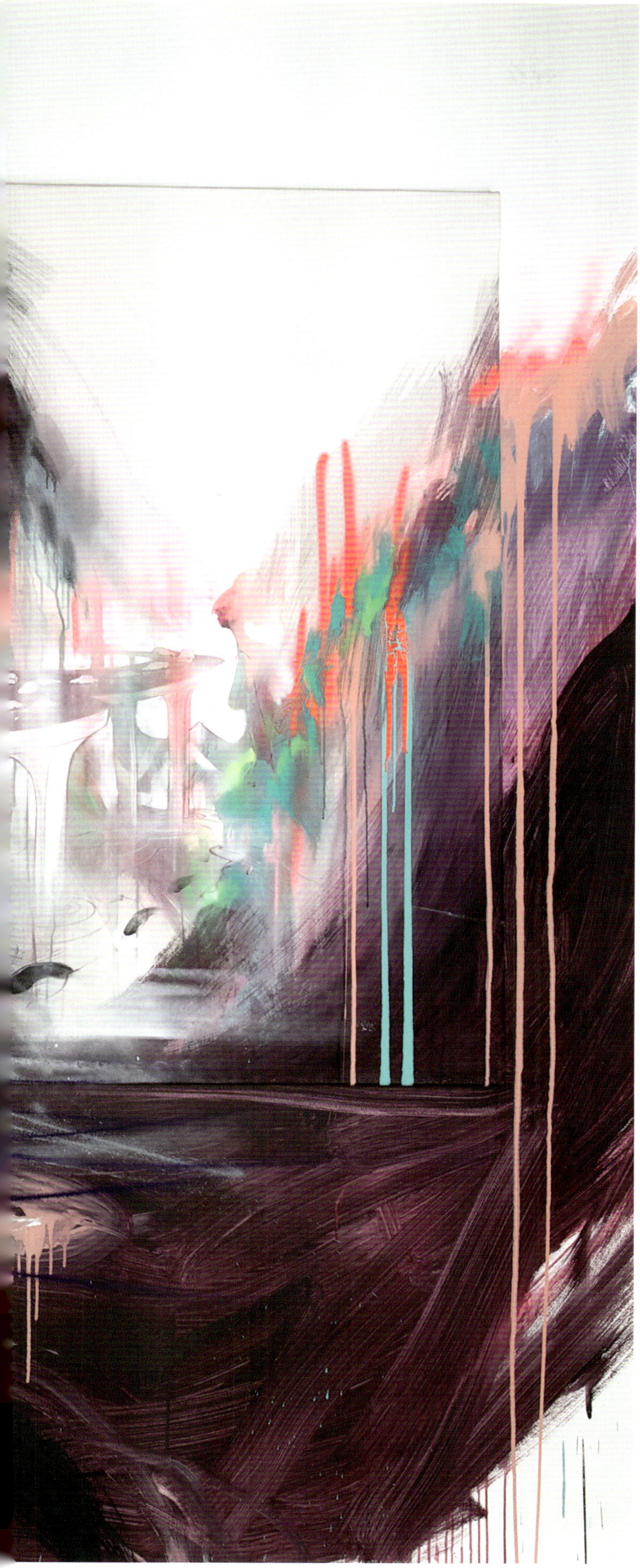

Hawaii 2011

Will Barras

@WILL__BARRAS

Will Barras' composition and fluid lines provide poignant detail in liquid abstraction. The subject matter is readily familiar, but capatured in a manner that seems to jar time and space with psychedelic abstraction. It is his way of expressing the emotional movements of this labour. It is therapy and pleasure and necessity. Though Will is more passionate about cricket, and even the art of the poached egg than he is of skate or snowboarding, he is hailed as one of the visual artists who best represents these influential creative movements. This is not only an indicator of his prolific work rate and good nature, his artwork being featured on all types of boards, clothes, and mural campaigns, but more so of his unique voice, technical competency & sense of exploration.

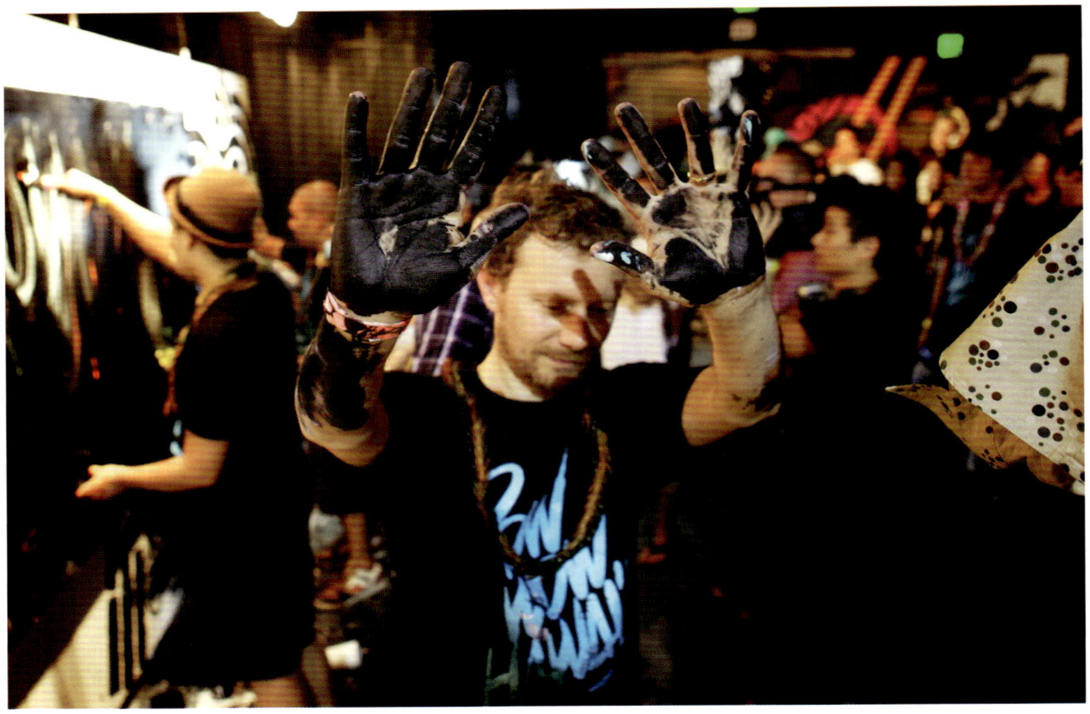

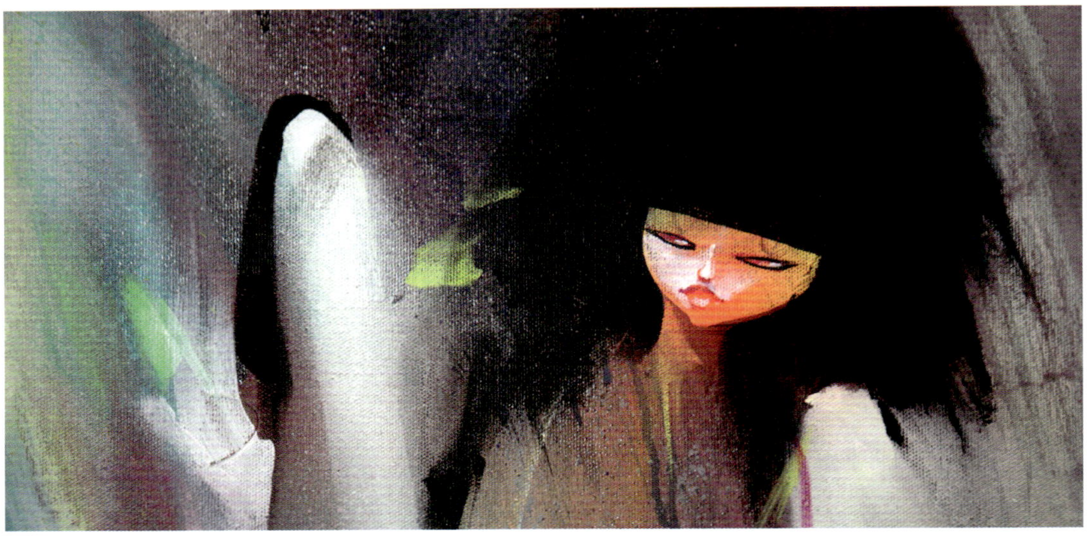

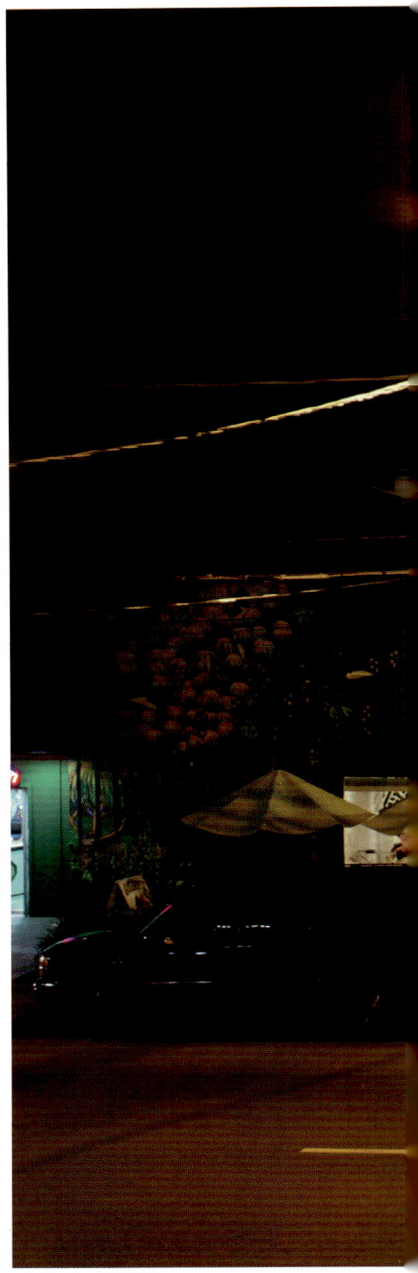

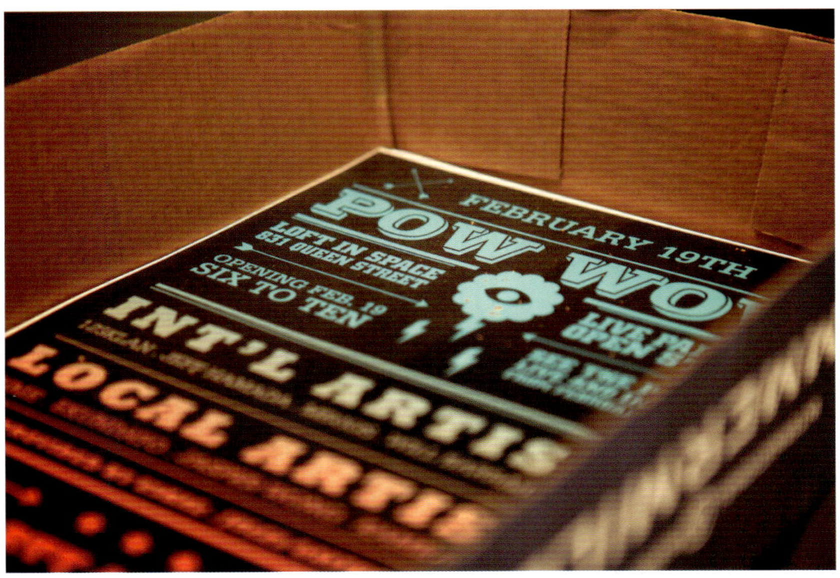
FEBRUARY 19TH
LOFT IN SPACE
831 QUEEN STREET
OPENING FEB. 19
SIX TO TEN

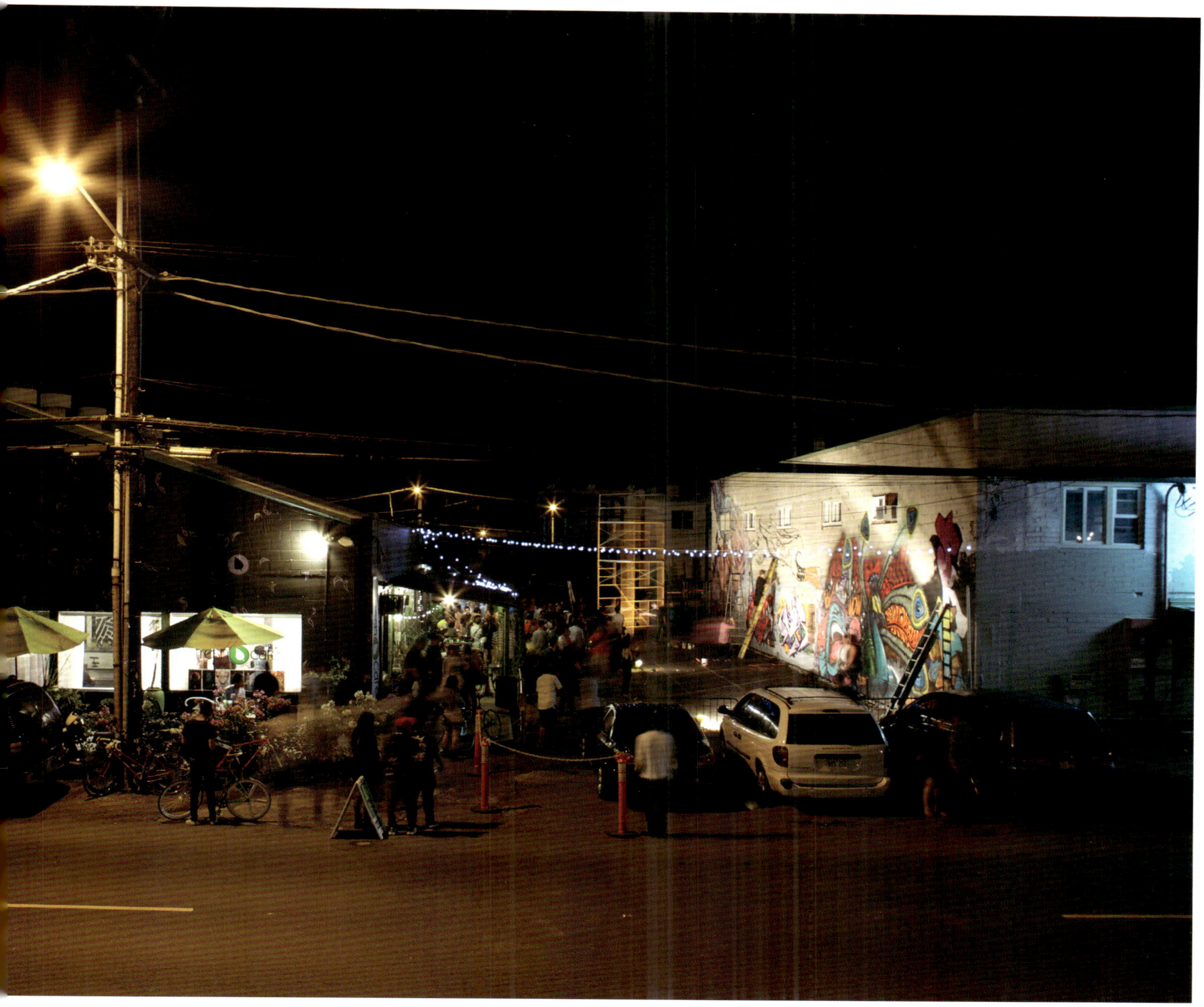

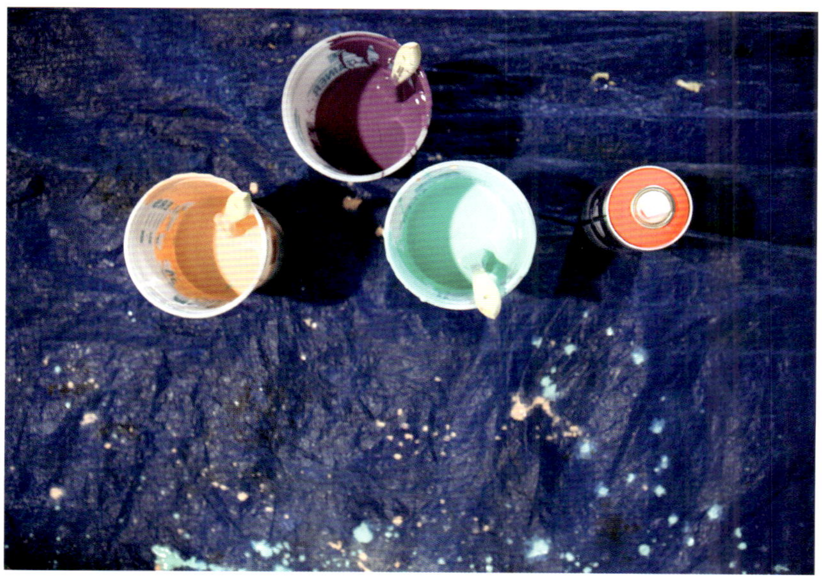

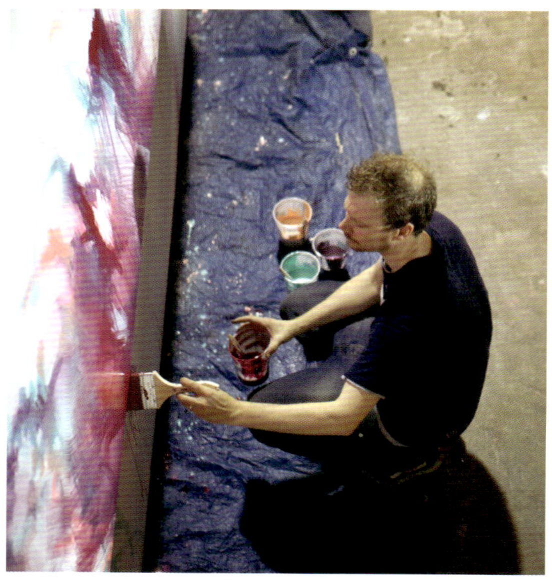

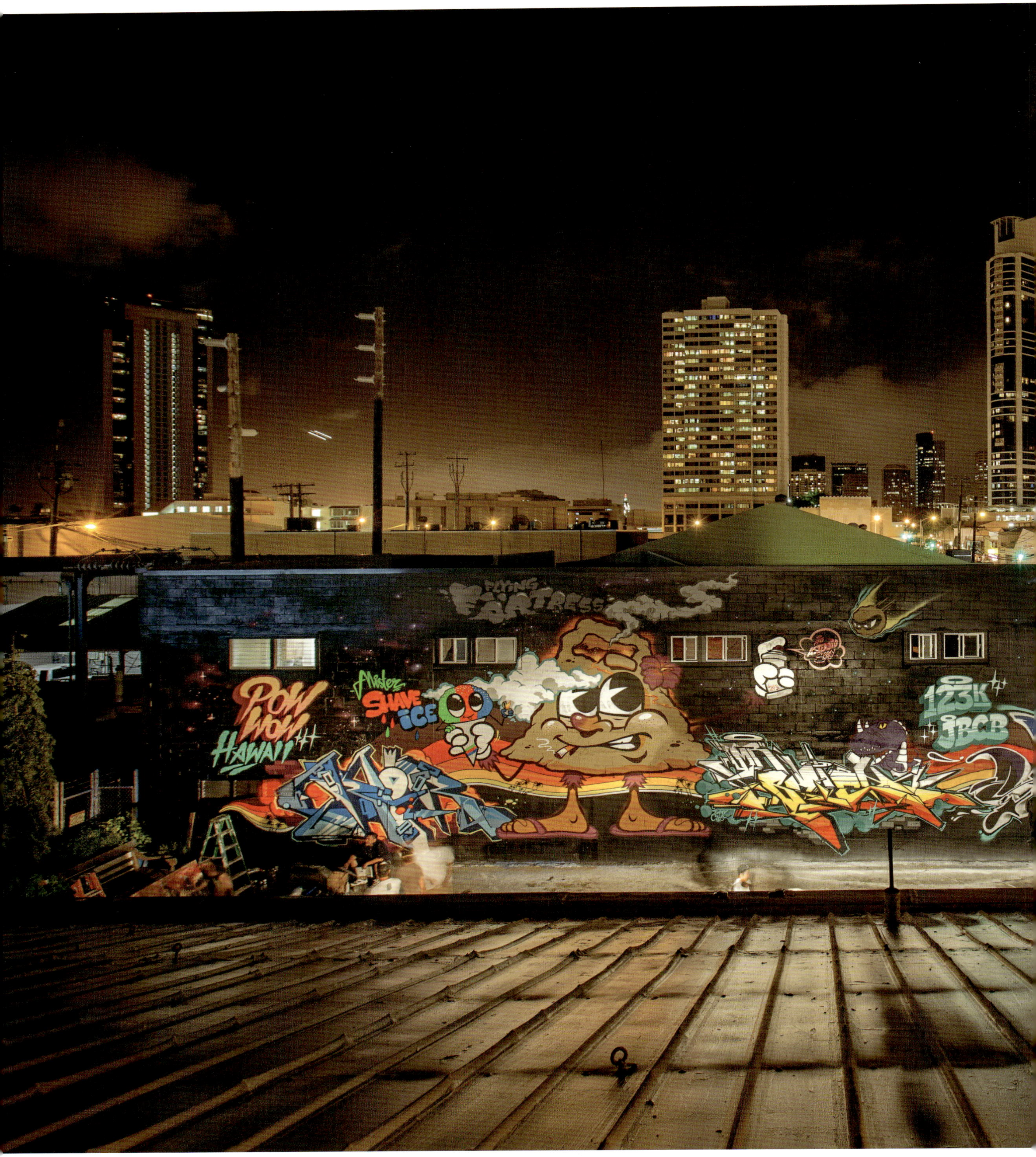
FLYING FARTRESS
POW WOW HAWAII
SHAVE ICE
123K
JBCB

Hawaii 2012

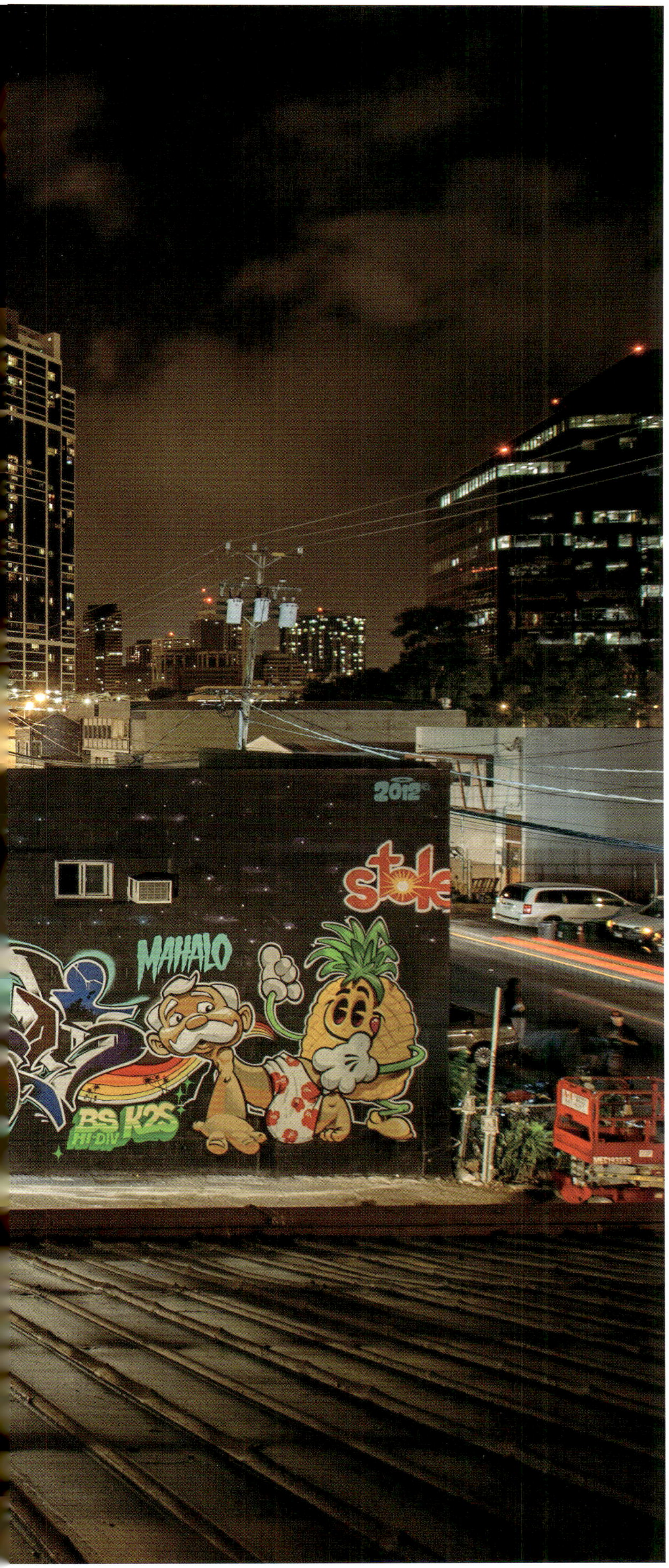

OG Slick 123Klan & Flying Fortress

@OG_SLICK @123KLAN @FLYINGFORTRESS243

Slick's rise to the top can be traced back to the mid '80s, from painting on the streets of Honolulu to the mean streets of Los Angeles. Slick spent his early years attending ArtCenter College of Design during the day and doing graffiti at night.

Slick has designed graphics for the likes of Stussy, X-Large, Adidas, Obey, Disney and the list goes on. His graphic design aesthetic has influenced an entire generation of artists / designers. He pioneered a movement called "street wear" long before the term was even coined.

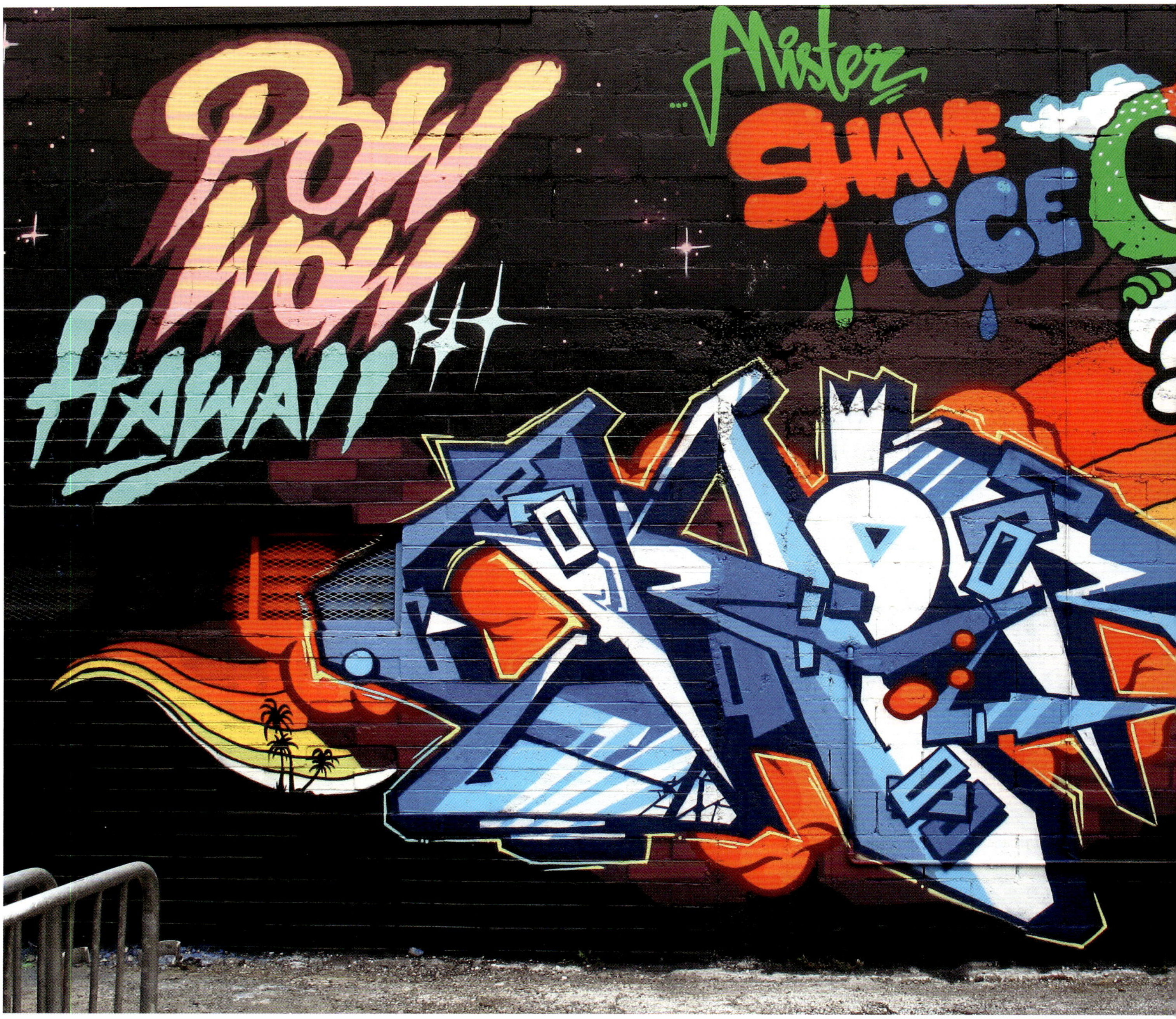
POW WOW
HAWAII
Mister
SHAVE
ICE

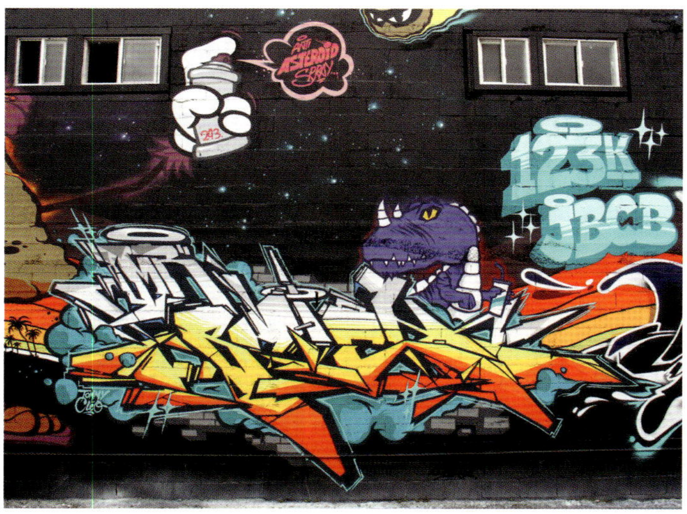
123K
JBCB

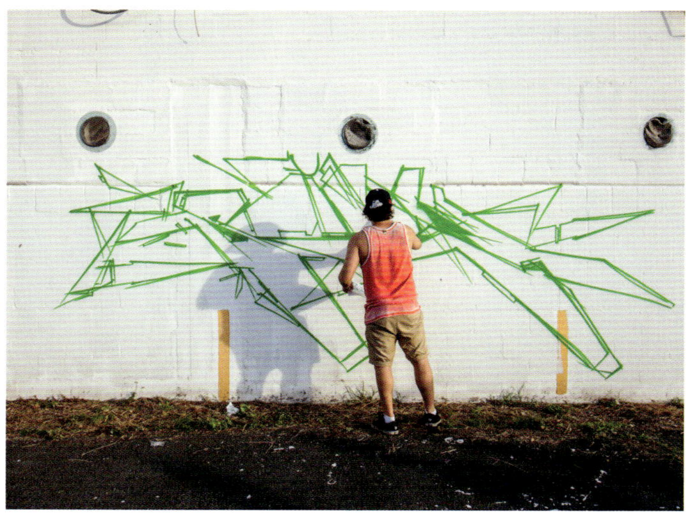

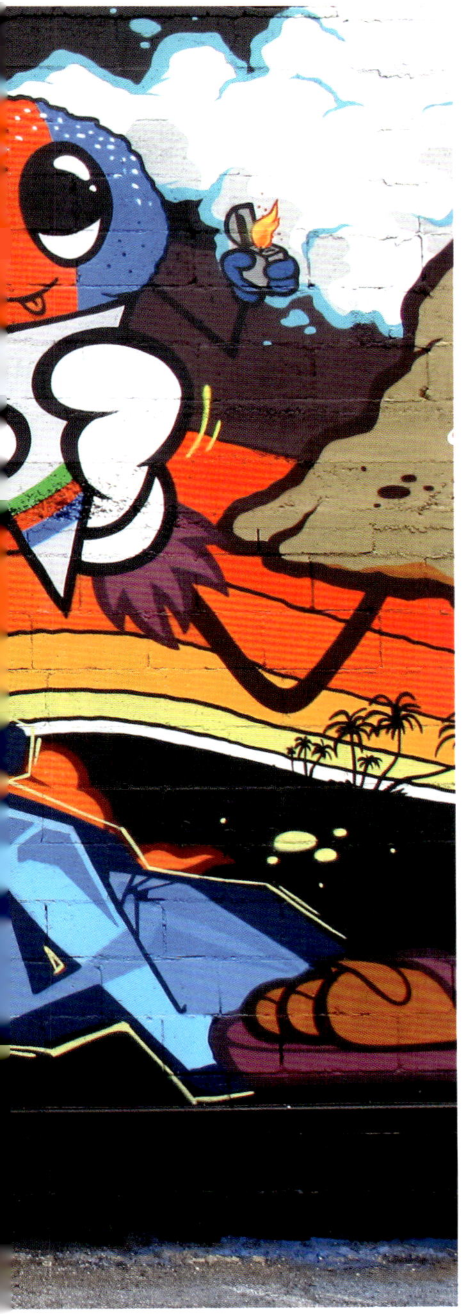

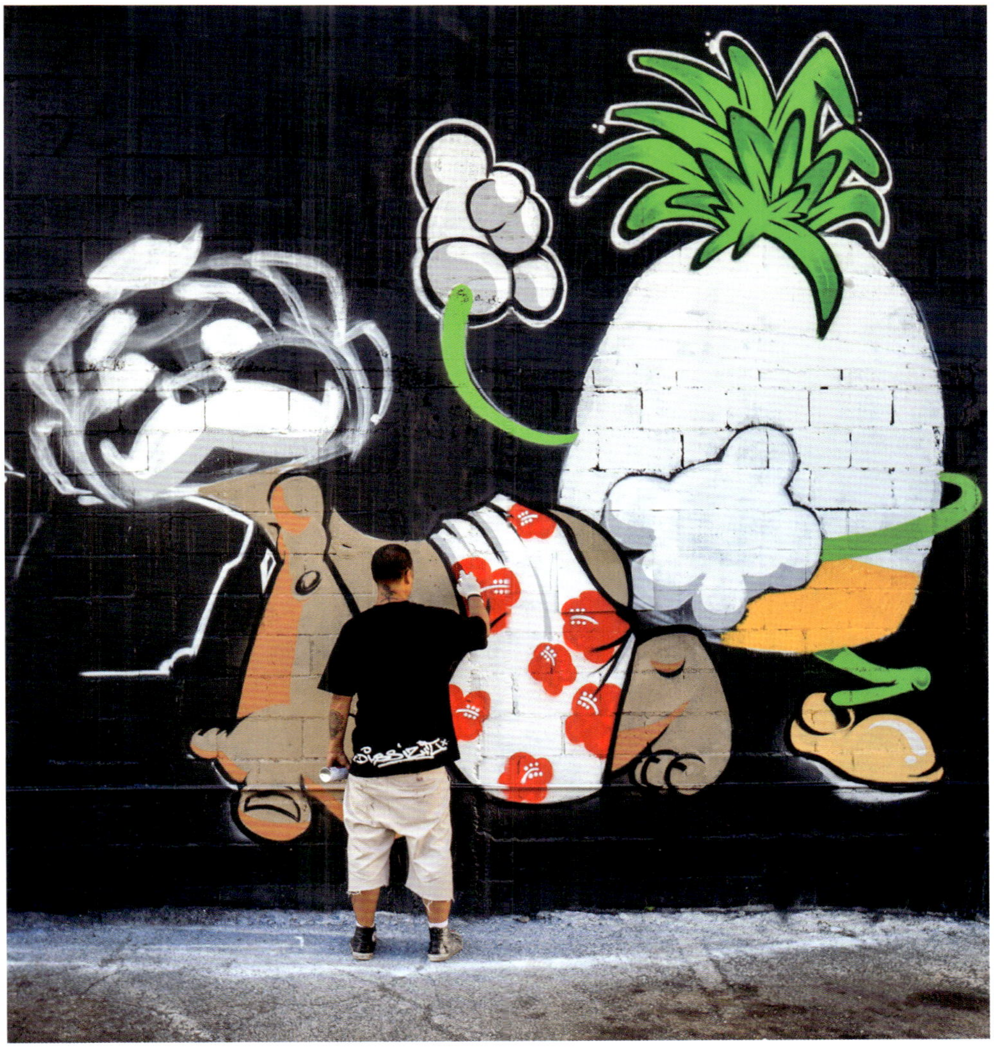

123Klan is a creative studio founded in France in 1992 by the most famous French couple in the country, Scien and Mrs. Klor. They have currently been based in Montreal since 2007.

They specialize in logos, character designs, illustrations, typefaces and of course, their first love, graffiti.

They have worked on different kinds of projects and mediums that range from: street wear, video games, motion design, web, print, toys, skateboards, and sport wear lines... This hyper-active French couple is unstoppable!

Matthias took the name **Flying Fortress** from a World War II bomber. He has became famous for his "Teddy Trooper", now found on every imaginable surface. A skateboarder since the end of the eighties, Matthias discovered the works of Jim Philips and Andy Howell and New York's graffiti scene during its golden era. Flying Fortress, like numerous artists committed to the urban scene and skateboarding culture, encounter and link the universes of skateboarding and graffiti via their work. His compositions have been used by several skateboard brands like Hessenmob, Rockawaybear and Grave skateboards, and he has collaborated with Element and DVS on other artistic projects. Adfunture also produces his "Teddy Troopers" as urban vinyl toys.

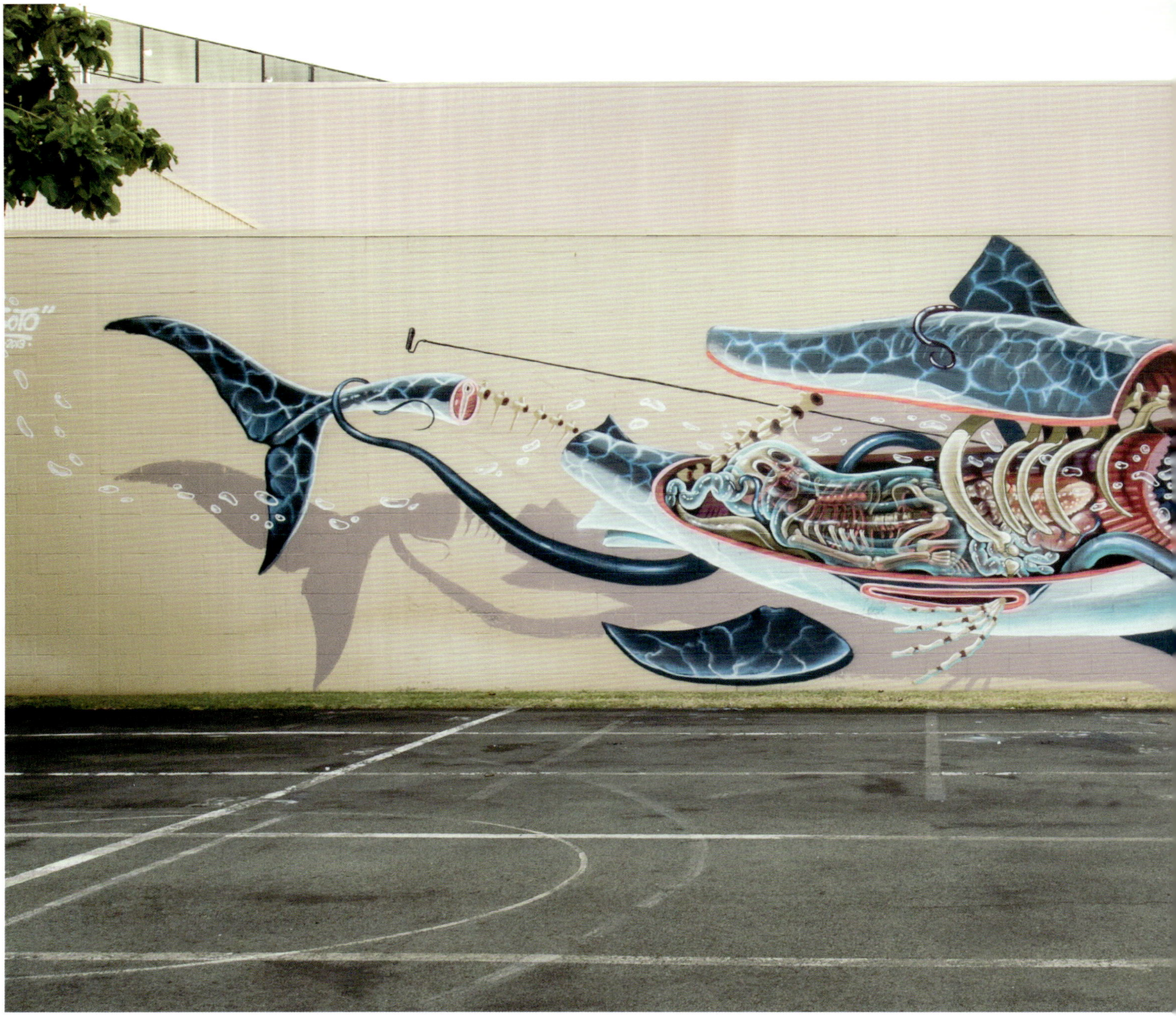

Hawaii 2013

Nychos & Jeff Soto

@NYCHOS @JEFFSOTOART

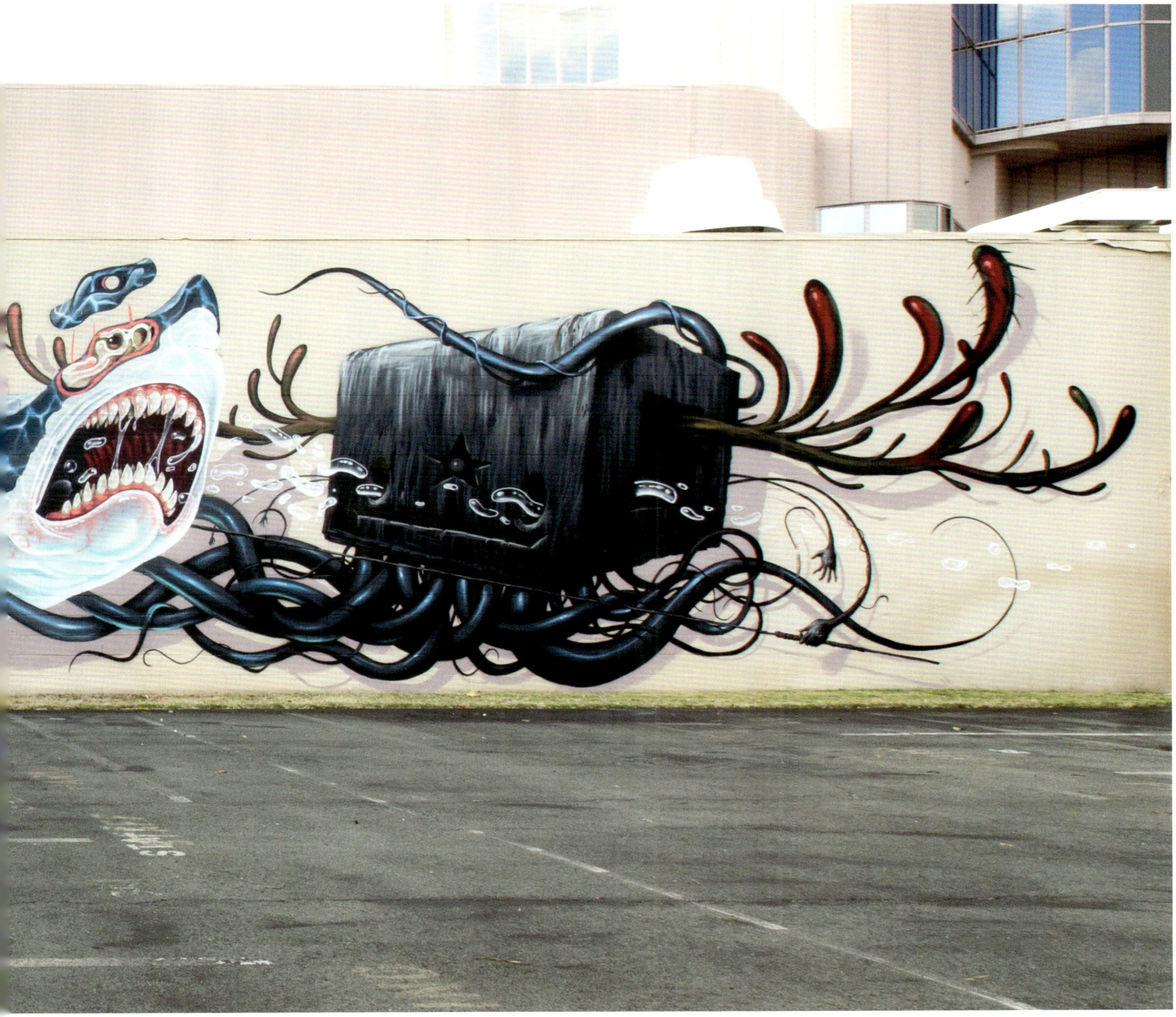

The urban art and graffiti illustrator **Nychos** was born in 1982 in Styria, Austria where he grew up in a hunting family. Getting confronted by the anatomy of dead animals at an early age and being an '80s kid with an interest for cartoons ended up being some of the ingredients which inspired him when he started graffiti and painting at the age of 18. Over the years he developed a distinctive style which stands out—his dissections and cross sections of human and animal bodies are easily recognized.

Jeff Soto is a painter, illustrator and muralist who has exhibited in galleries and museums around the world. When he was 13, he simultaneously discovered both traditional painting and illegal graffiti, and ever since, both worlds have informed his work. The artist's distinct color palette, subject matter and technique resonate with a growing audience and bridge the gap between pop surrealism and street art.

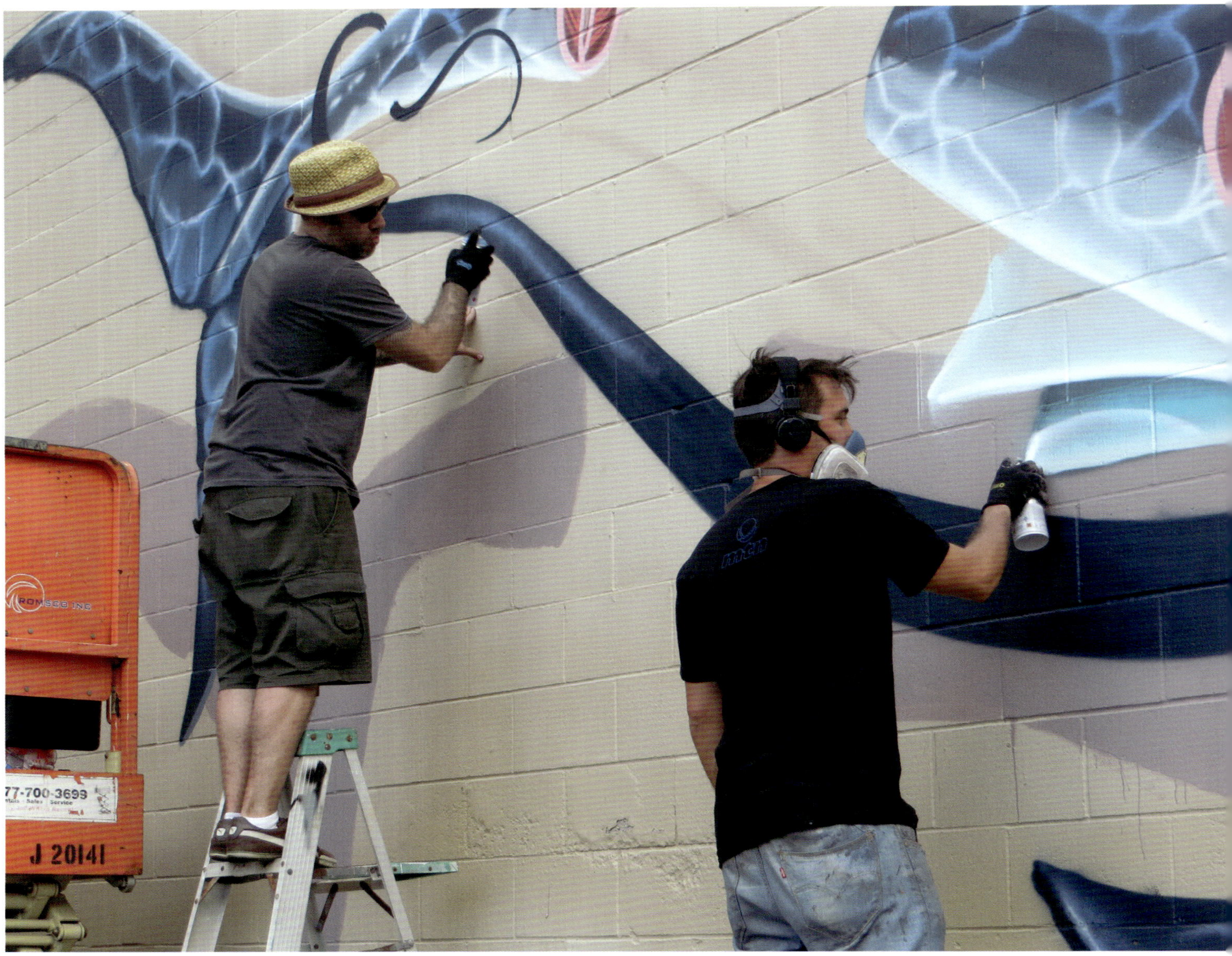
77-700-3698
J 20141

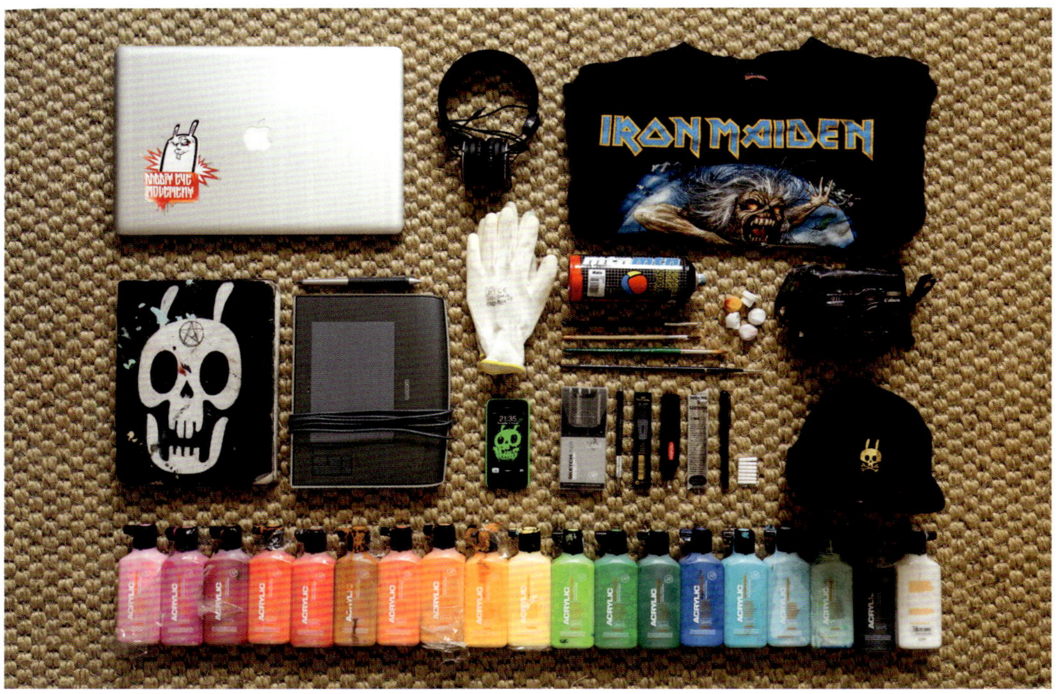
IRON MAIDEN

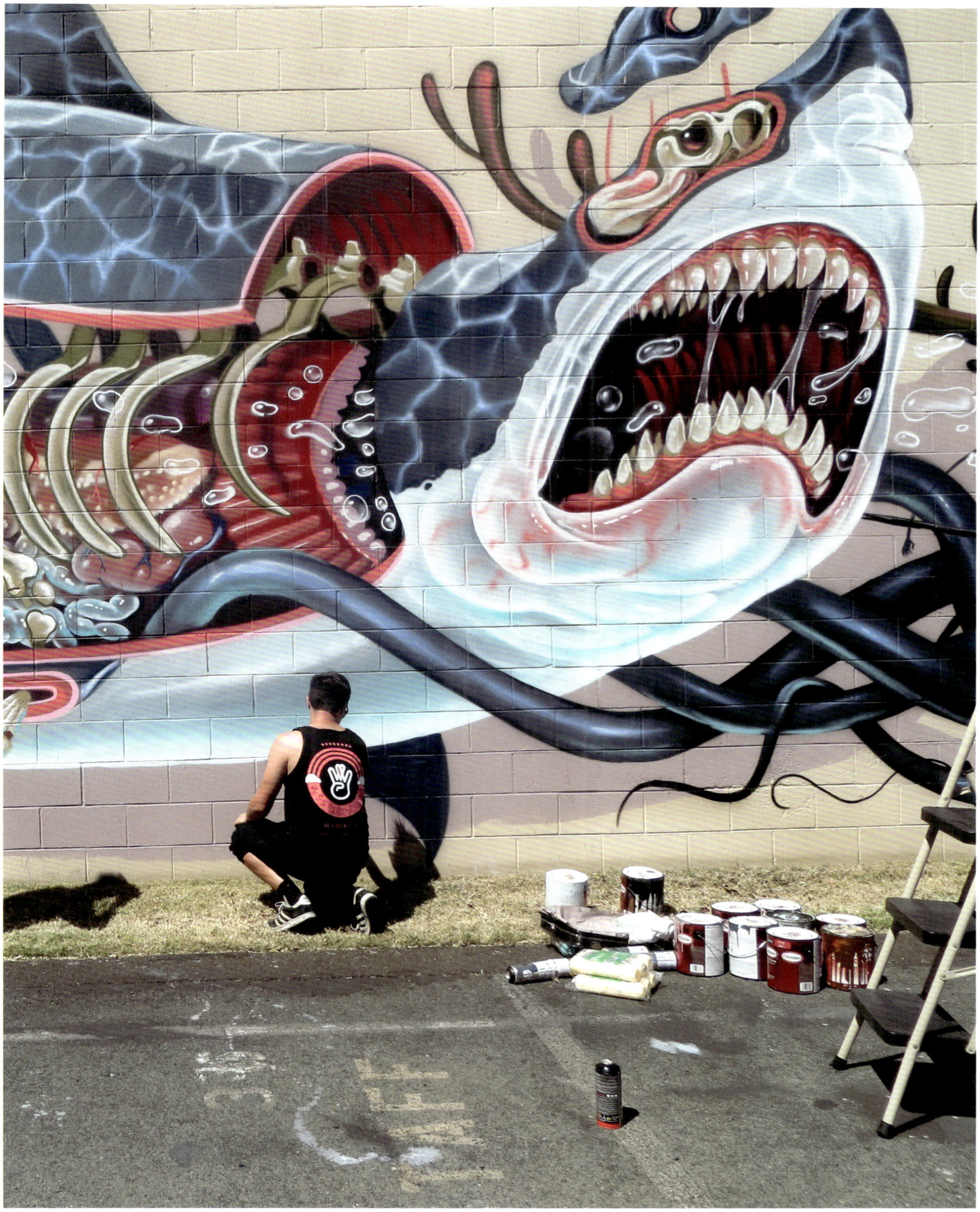

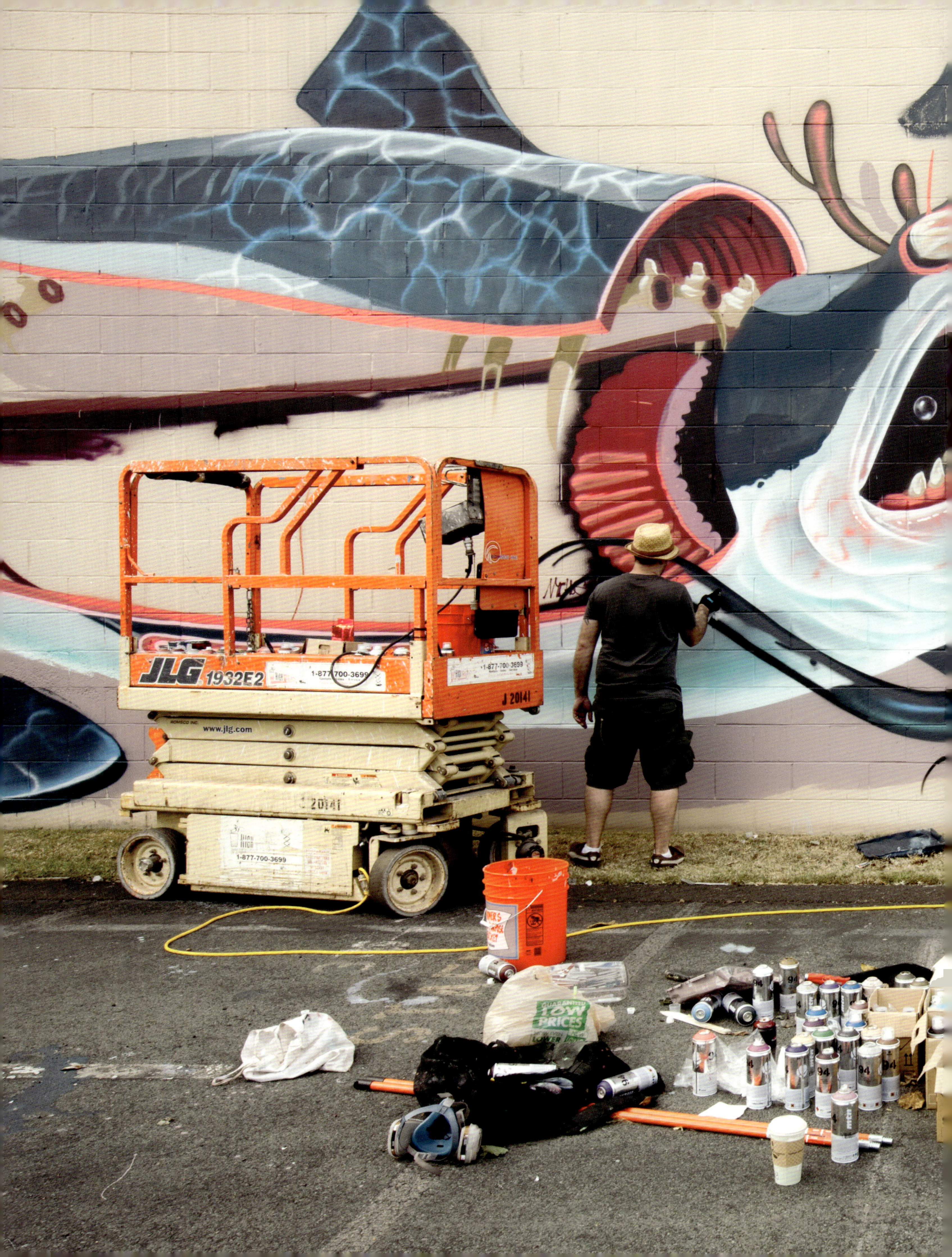
JLG
1932E2
1-877-700-3699
J 20141
www.jlg.com
20141
1-877-700-3699

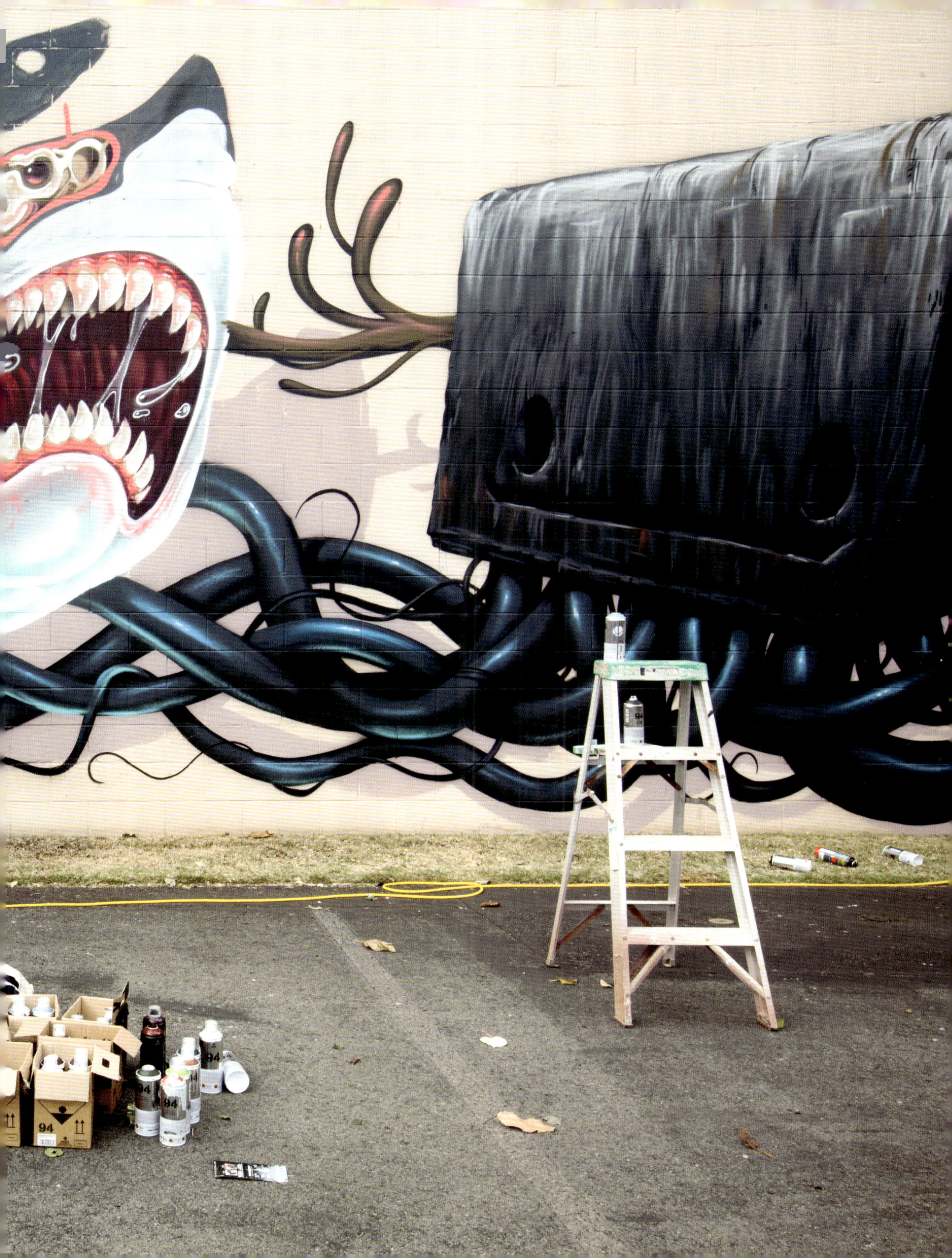

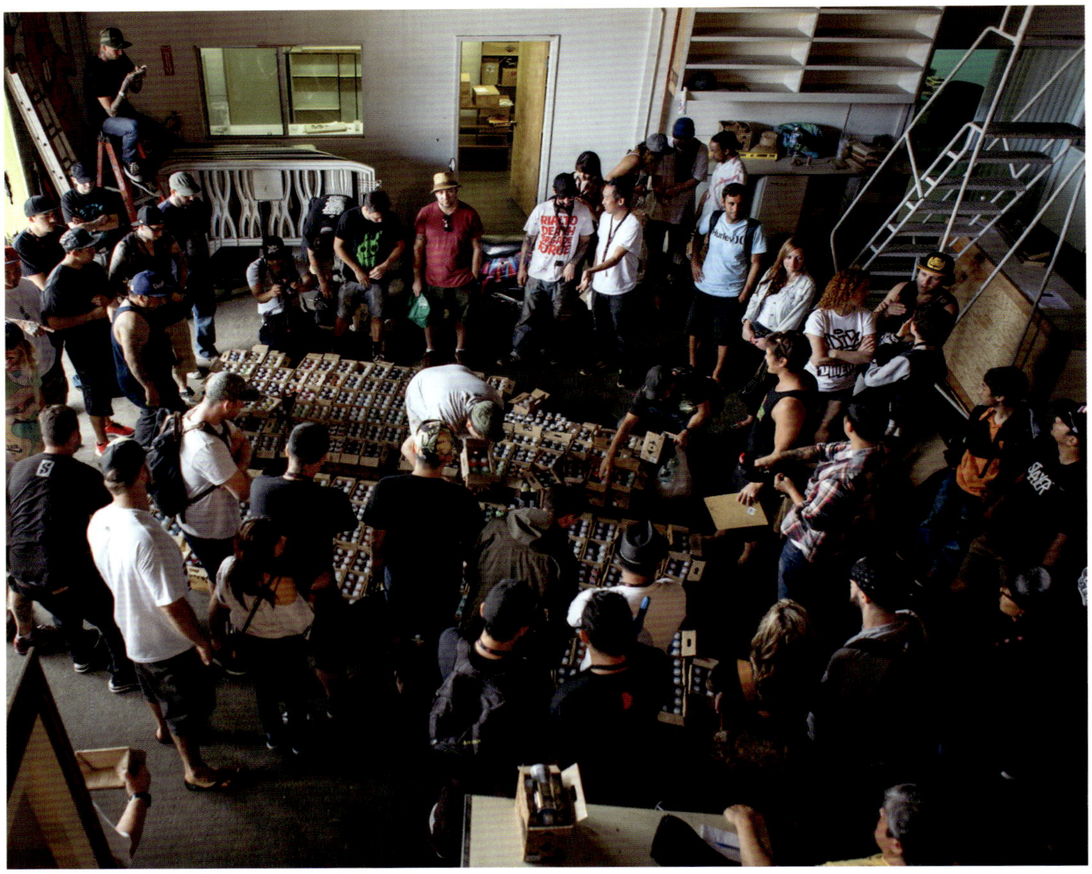

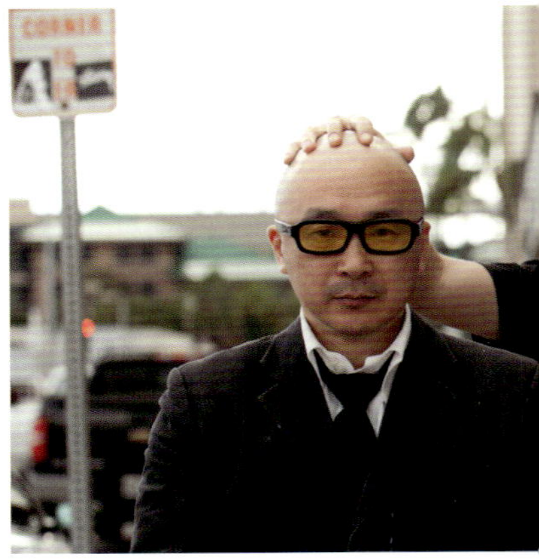

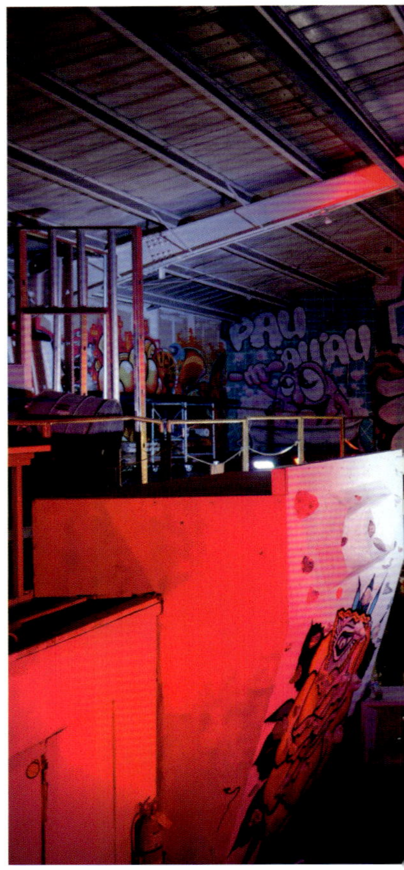

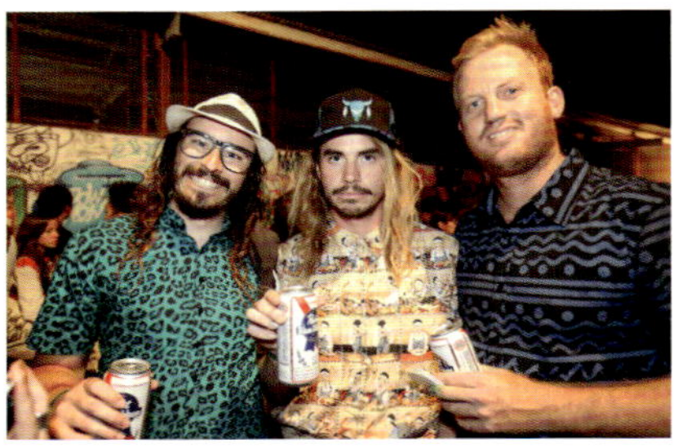

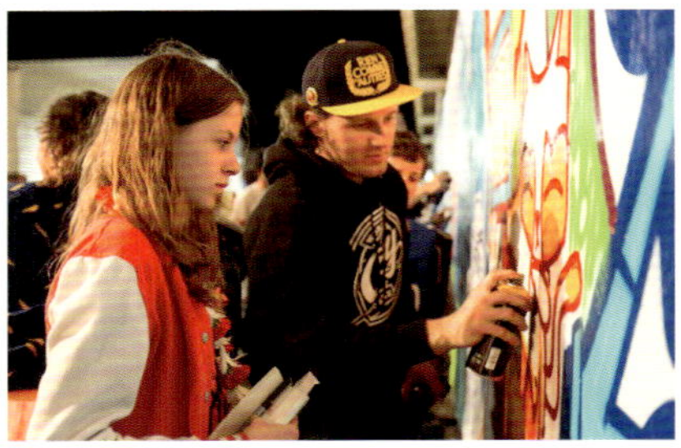

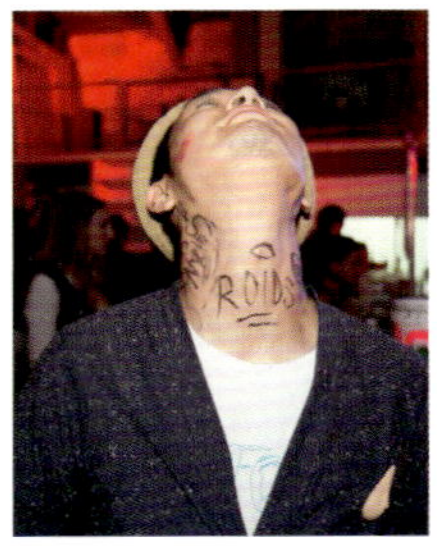

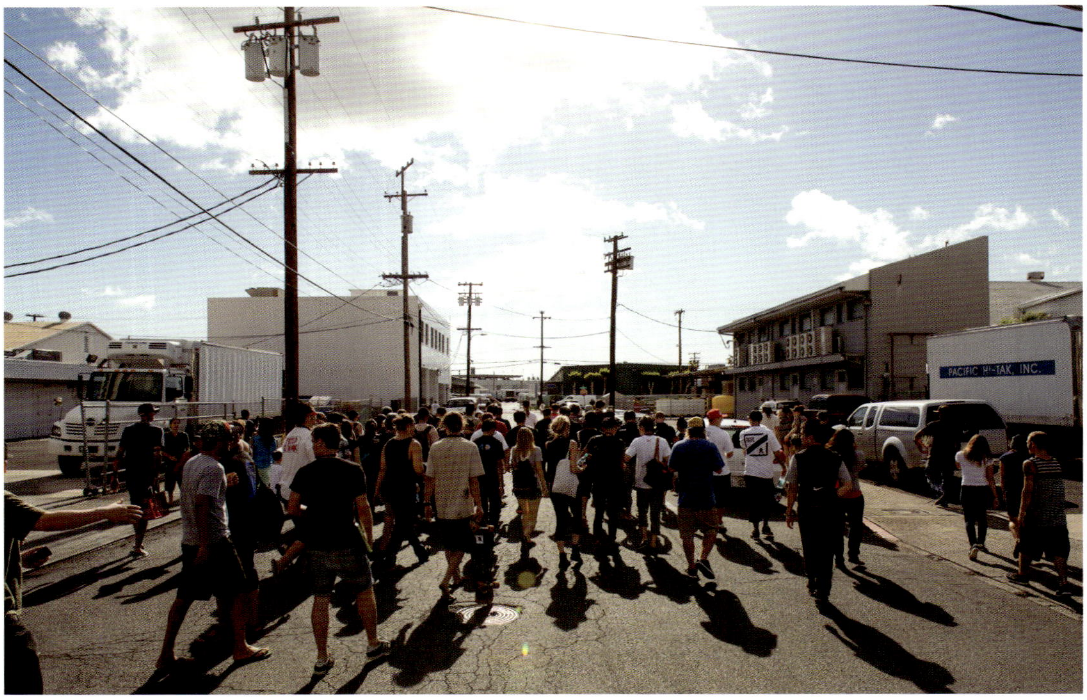
PACIFIC HI-TAK, INC.

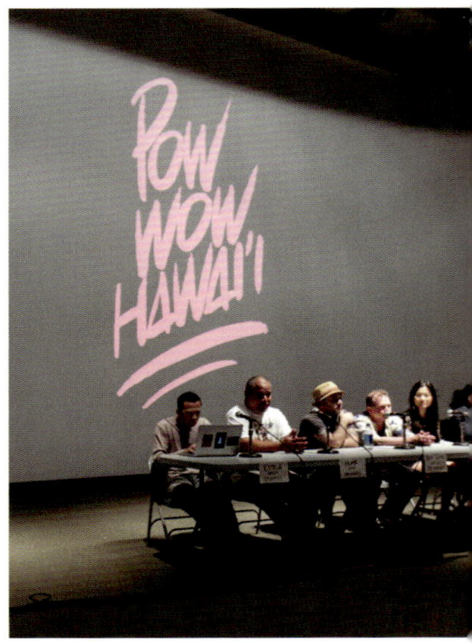
Pow Wow Hawai'i

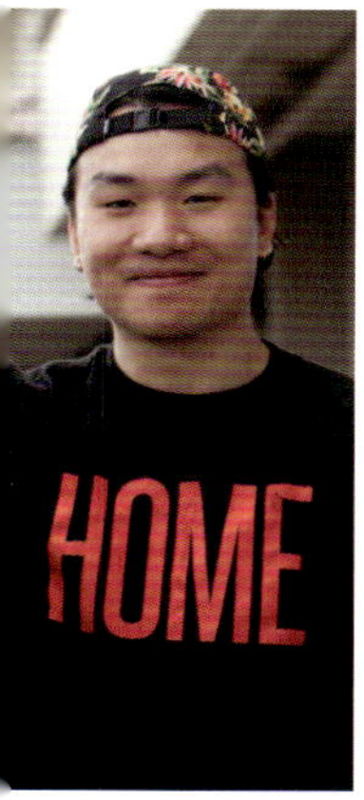
HOME

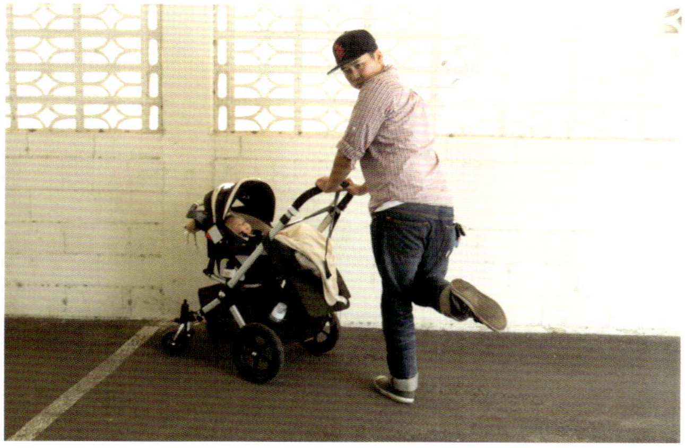

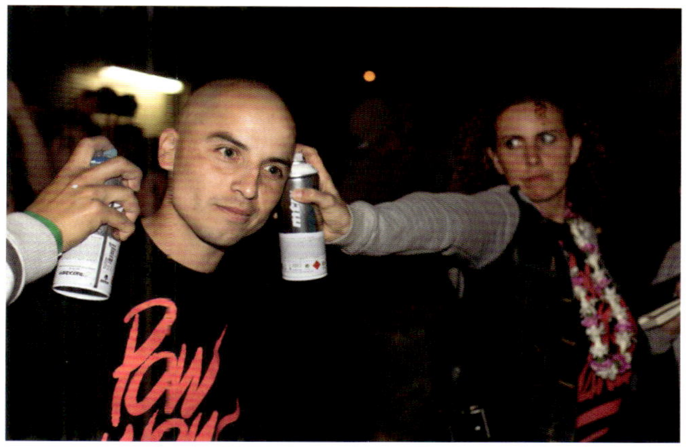

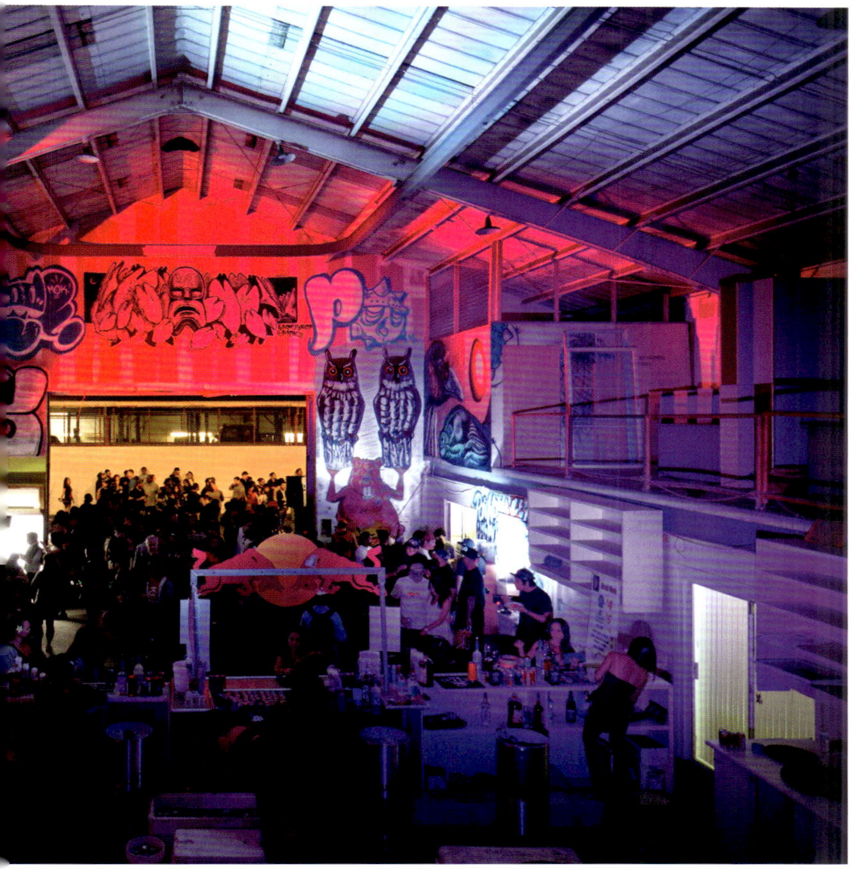

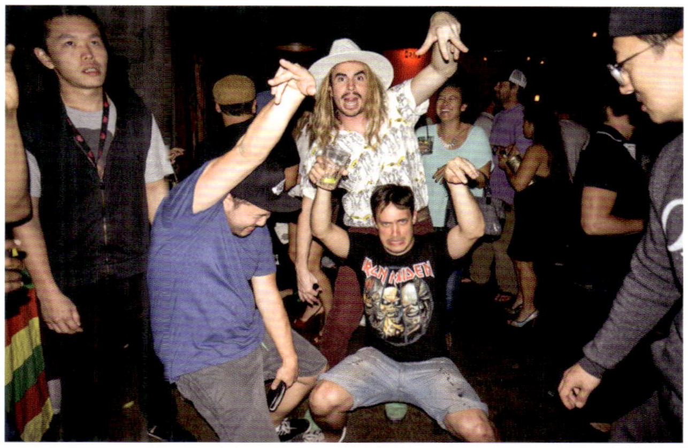

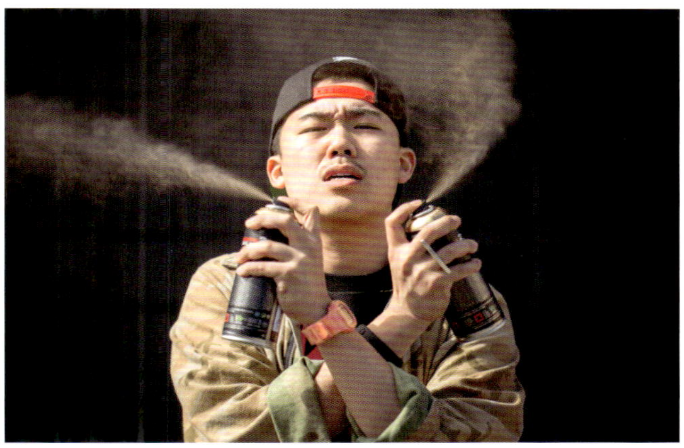

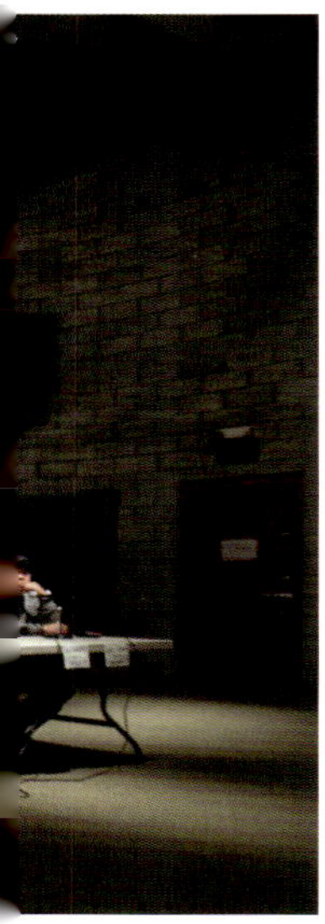

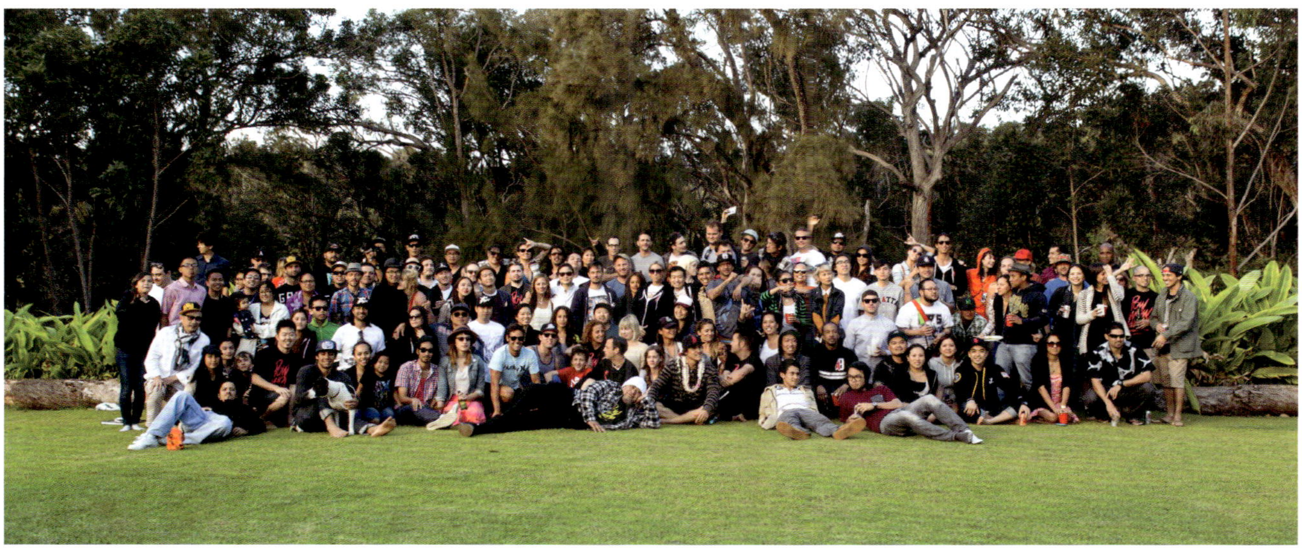

James Jean

@JAMESJEANART

James Jean is a Taiwanese American visual artist, known for both his commercial work and fine art gallery work. He is known in the American comics industry as a cover artist for various books published by DC Comics, as well as for his work for Prada, ESPN and Atlantic Records. His work, which has been collected in numerous volumes, has been compared by The New York Times to that of Maxfield Parrish.

Dana Jennings of The New York Times says of Jean's work: "And, as with his Fables work, the paintings and illustrations are often suffused with a dreamy romanticism and lyricism worthy of Maxfield Parrish, even as Mr. Jean subverts those and other isms."

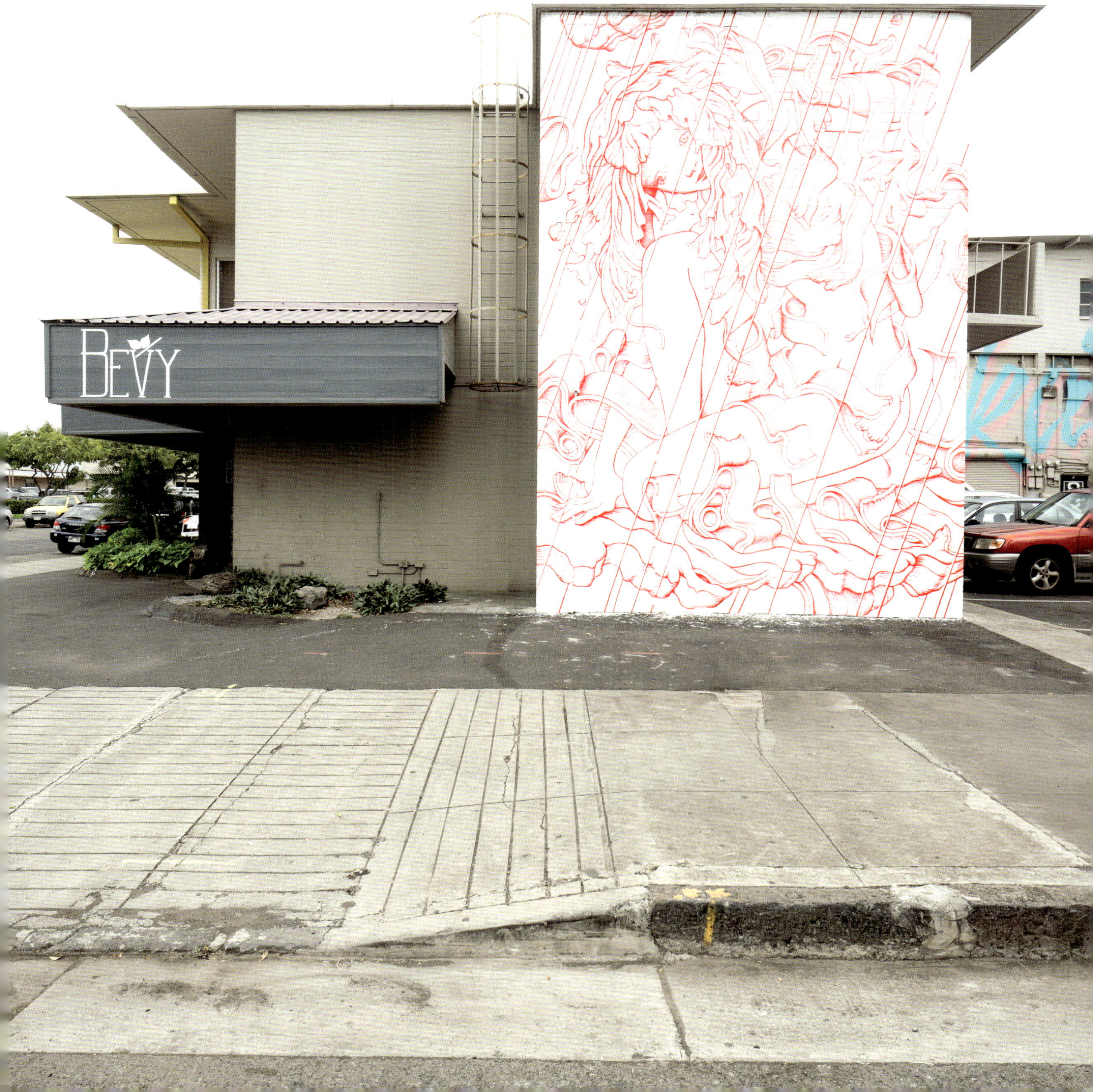
BEVY

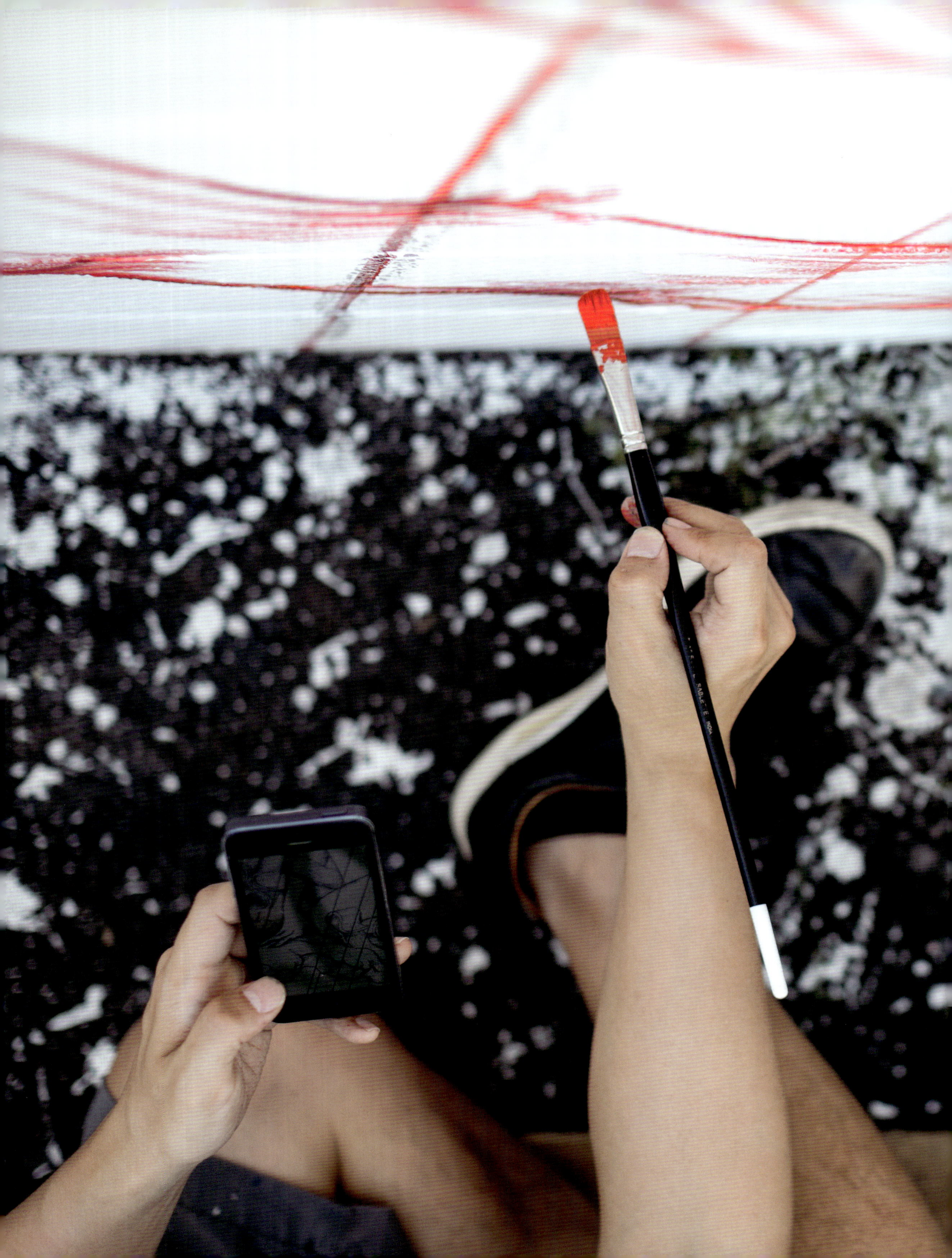

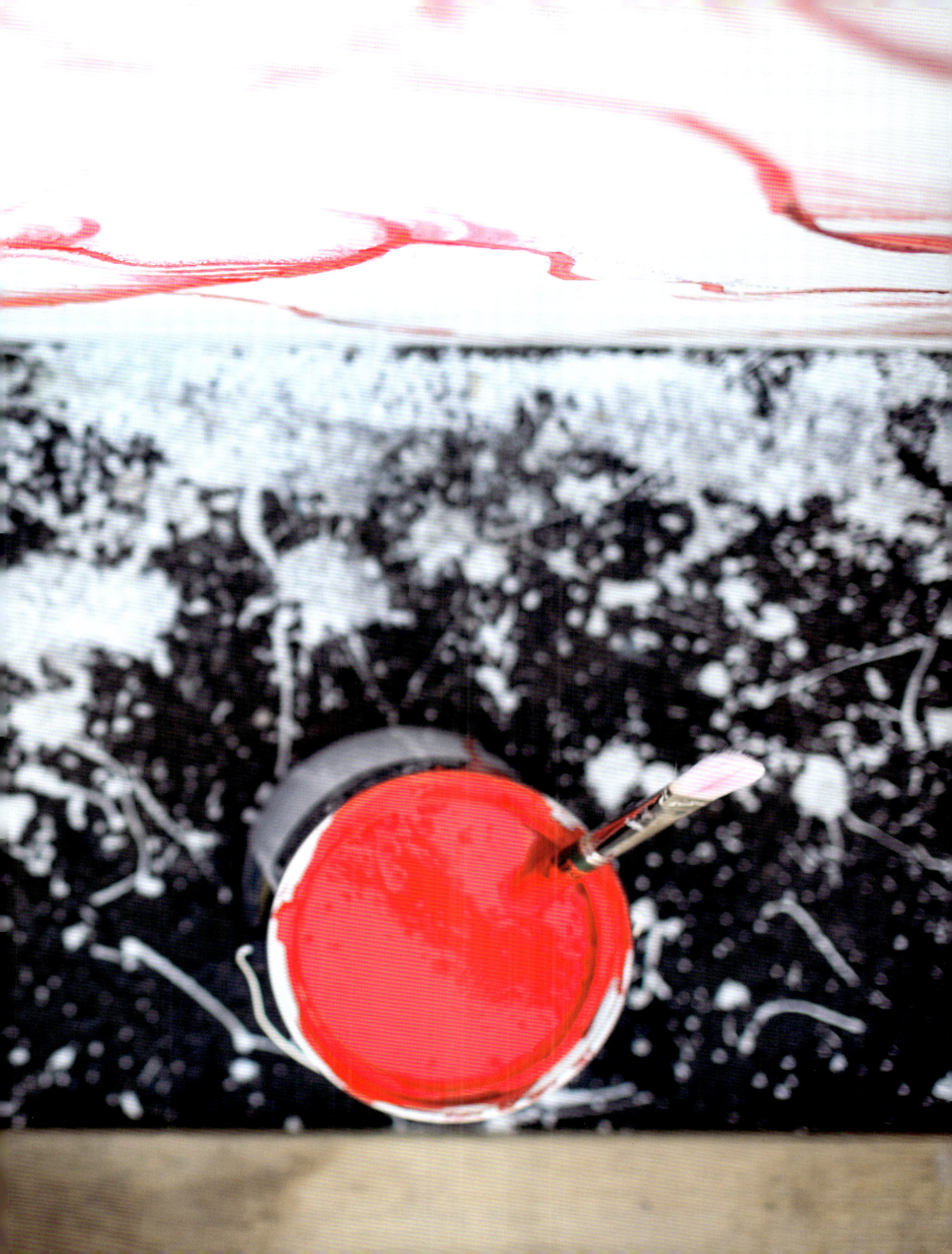

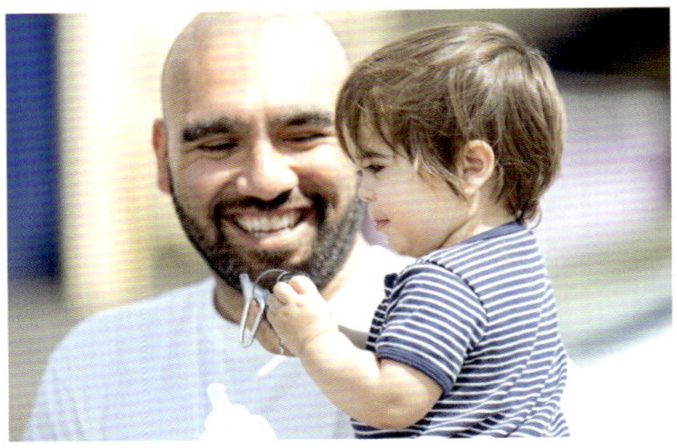
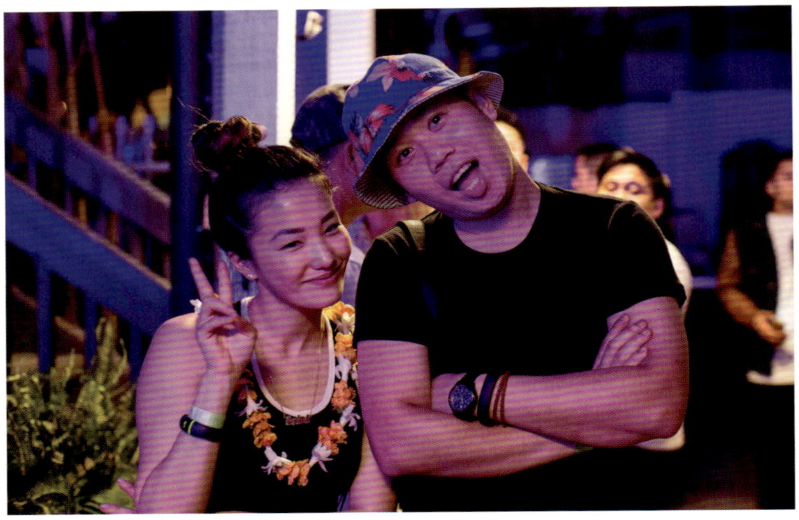
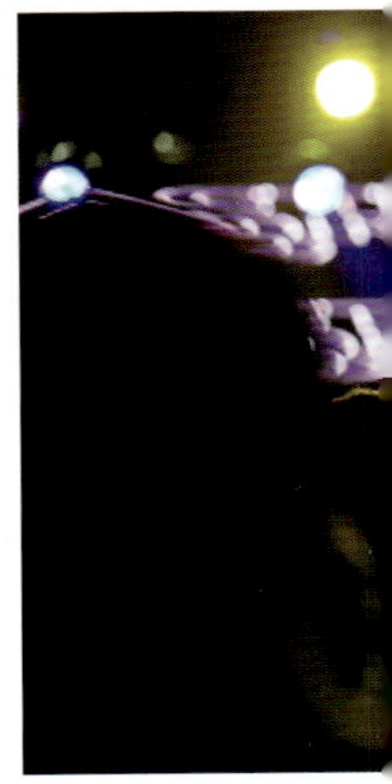
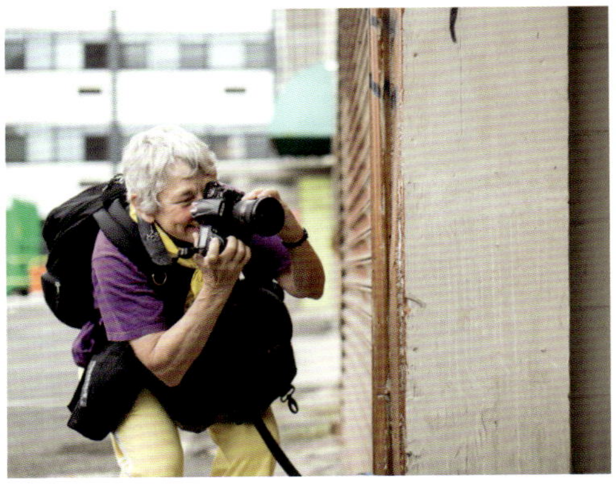
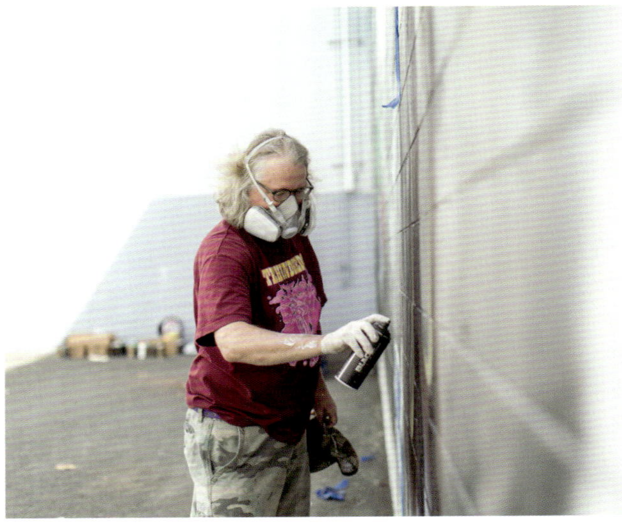
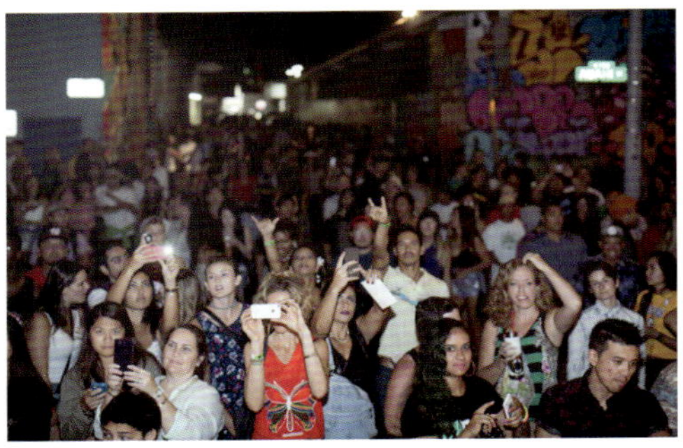
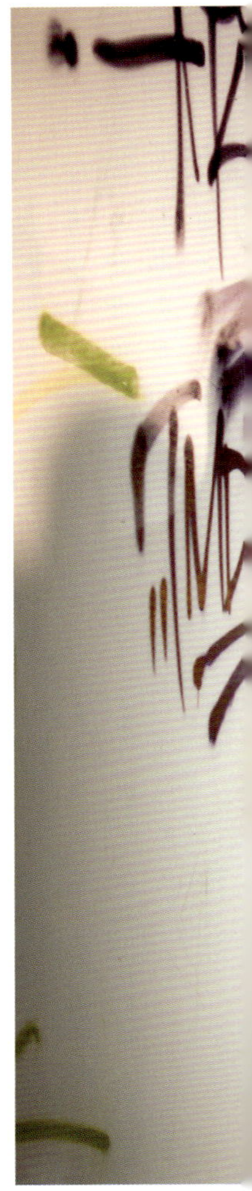
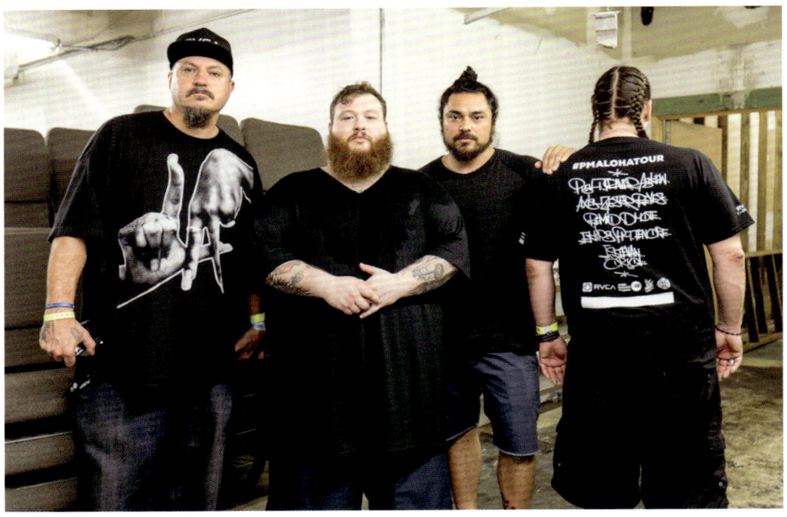
#PMALOHATOUR
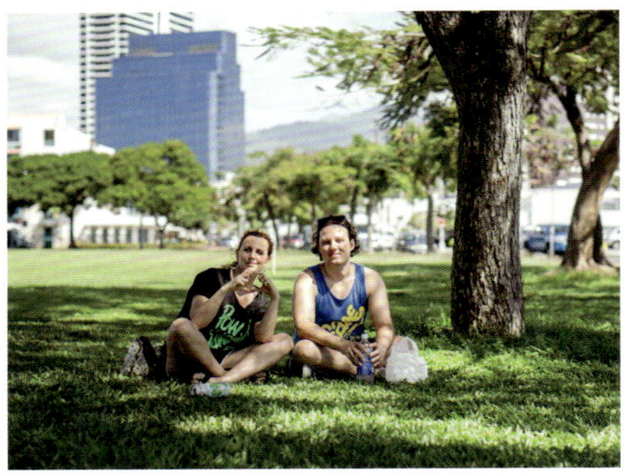
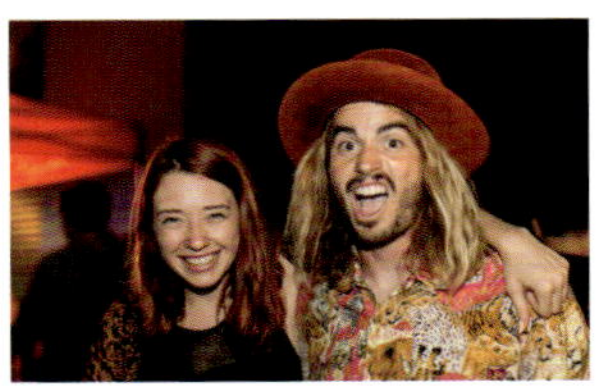
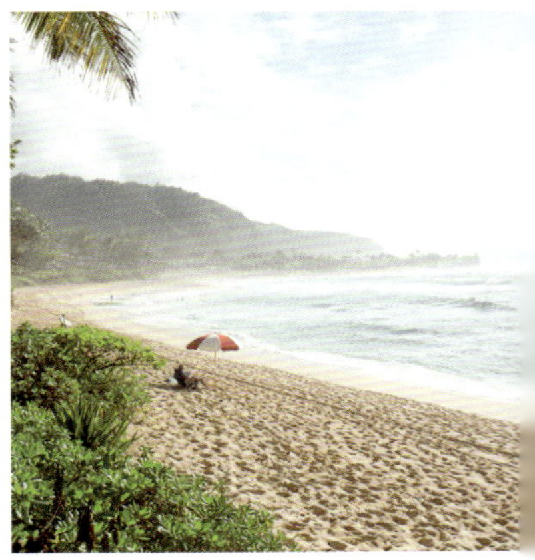
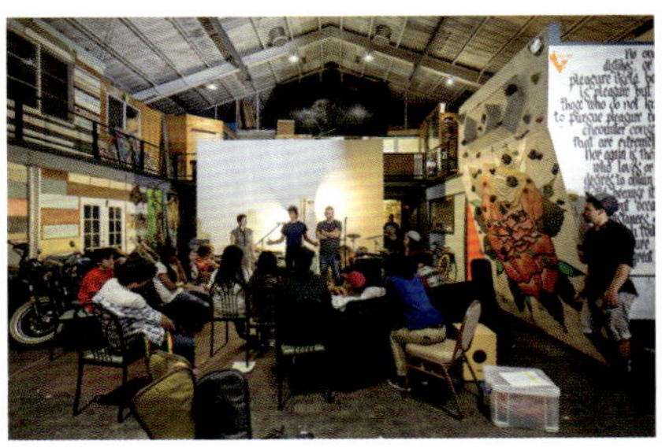
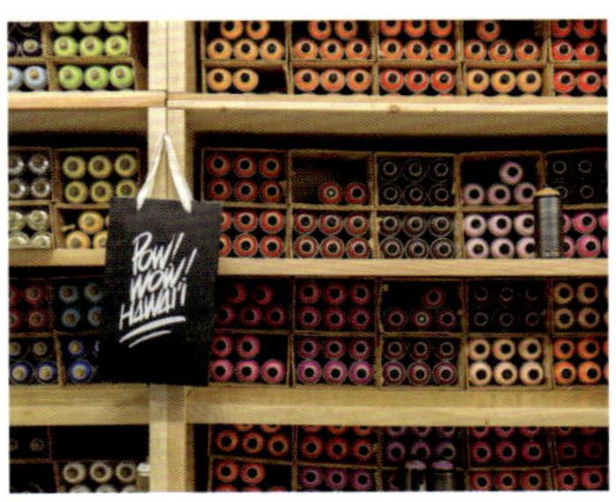
Pow! Wow! Hawaii
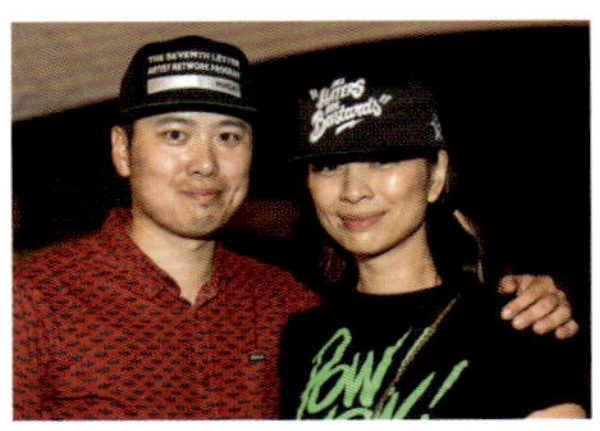

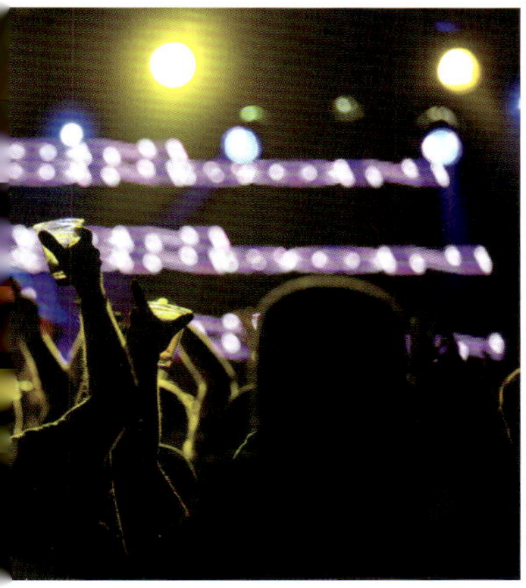
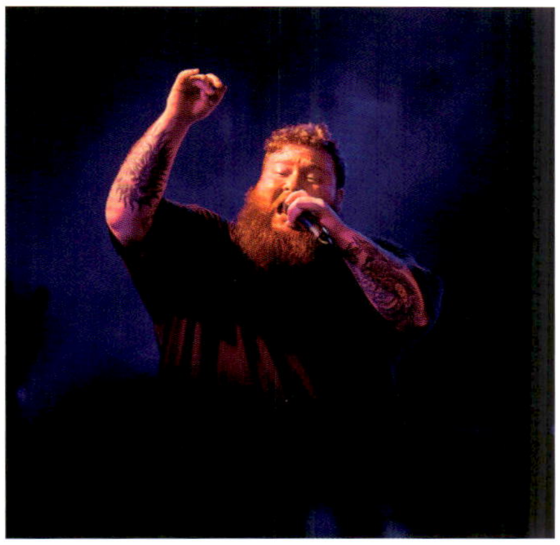
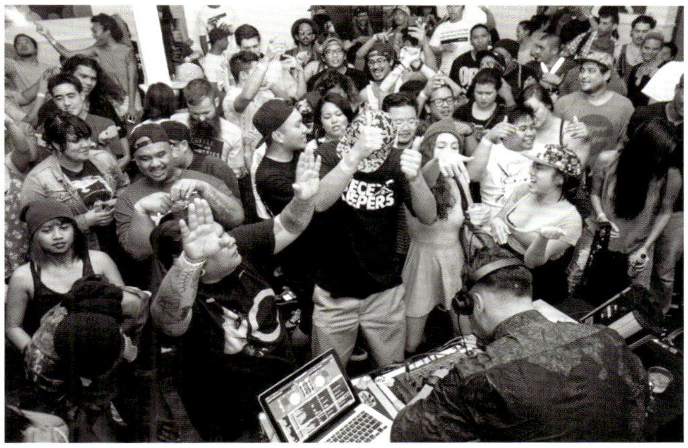
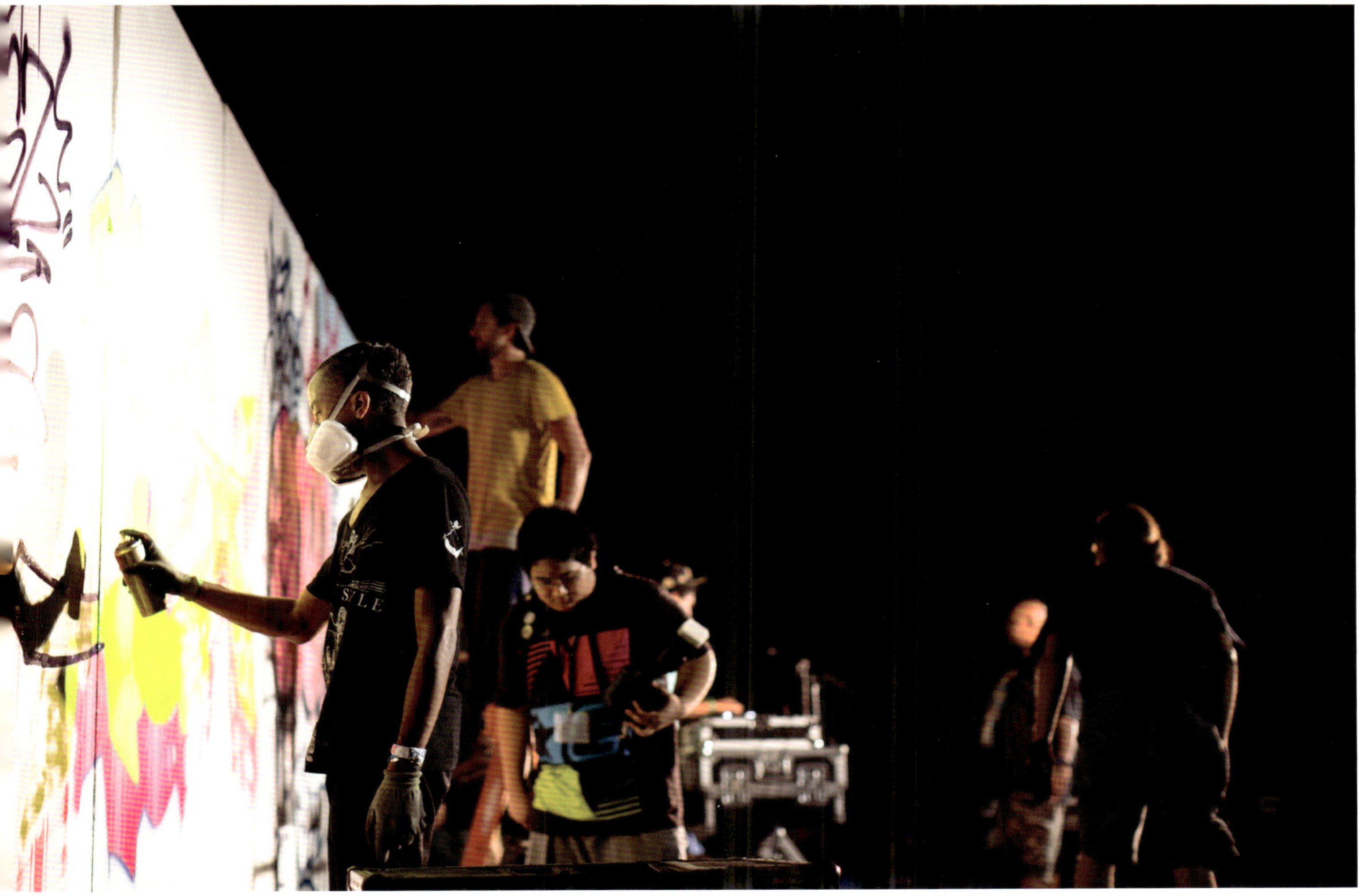

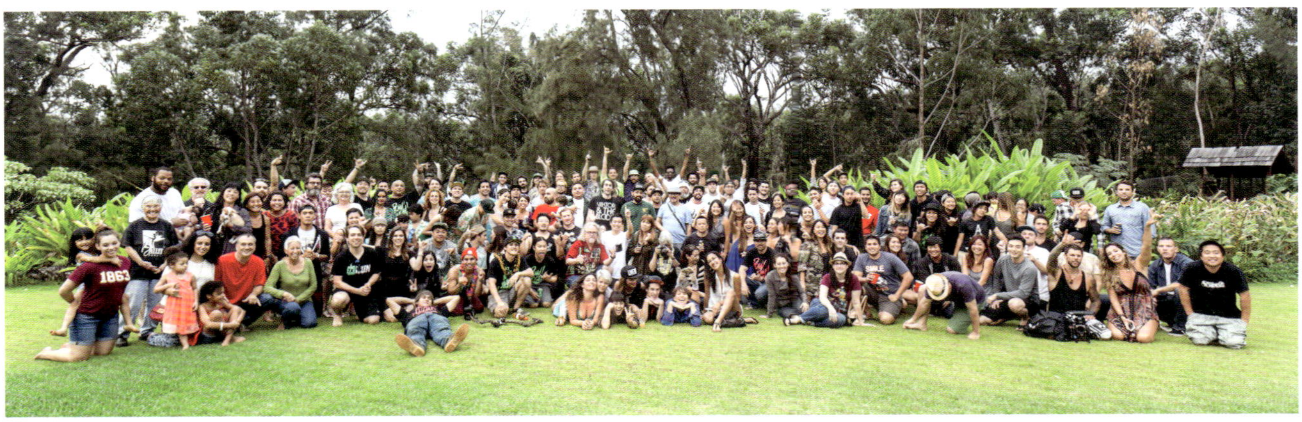

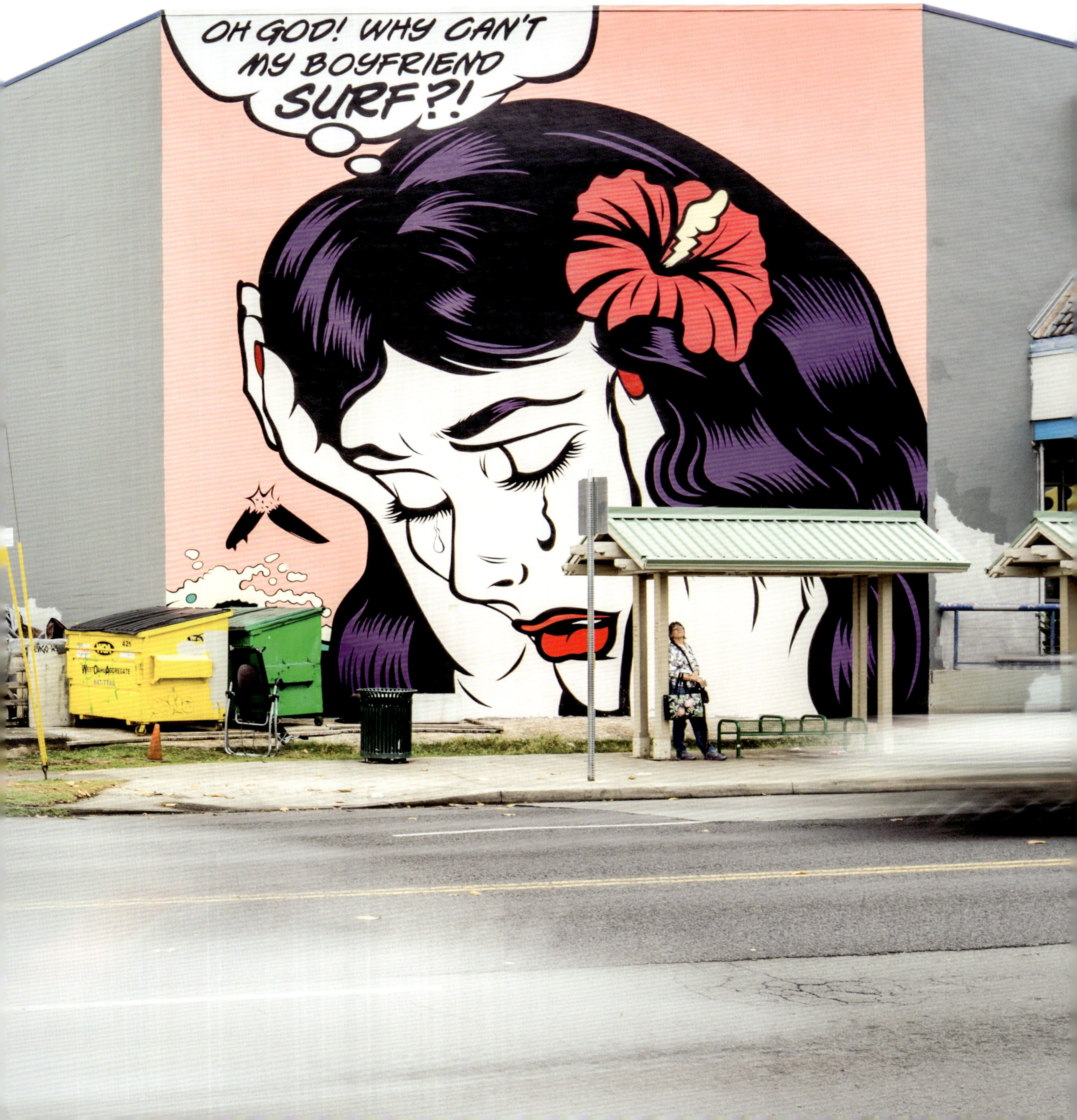
OH GOD! WHY CAN'T MY BOYFRIEND SURF?!

Hawaii 2015

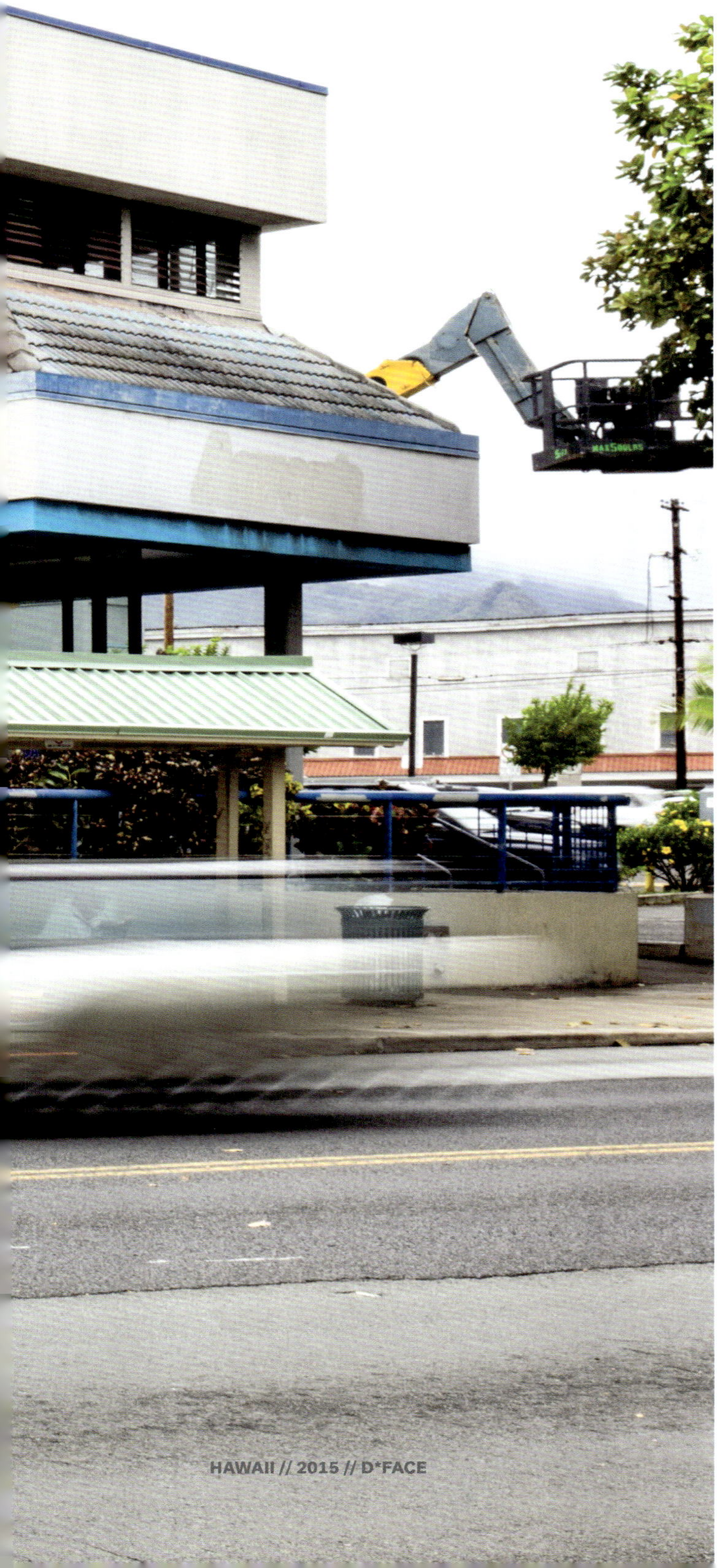

D*Face

@DFACE_OFFICIAL

D*Face is one of the most prolific contemporary urban artists of his generation. Working with a variety of mediums and techniques, he uses a family of dysfunctional characters to satirise and hold to ransom all that falls into their grasp a welcome jolt of subversion in todays media saturated environment.

D*Face uses the term—aPOPcalyptic—to define his work, a metaphorical backdrop for the corruptive persuasive consumerist folly that has been force fed into our society, a blend of 'pop art' spliced with fragility of life, his work reflects our popular culture encompassing the American dream and the false ideal of 'good' triumphing over 'evil', no longer relevant in todays society. His imagery delivers the viewer a moral dilema embrace or reject, laugh or deny.

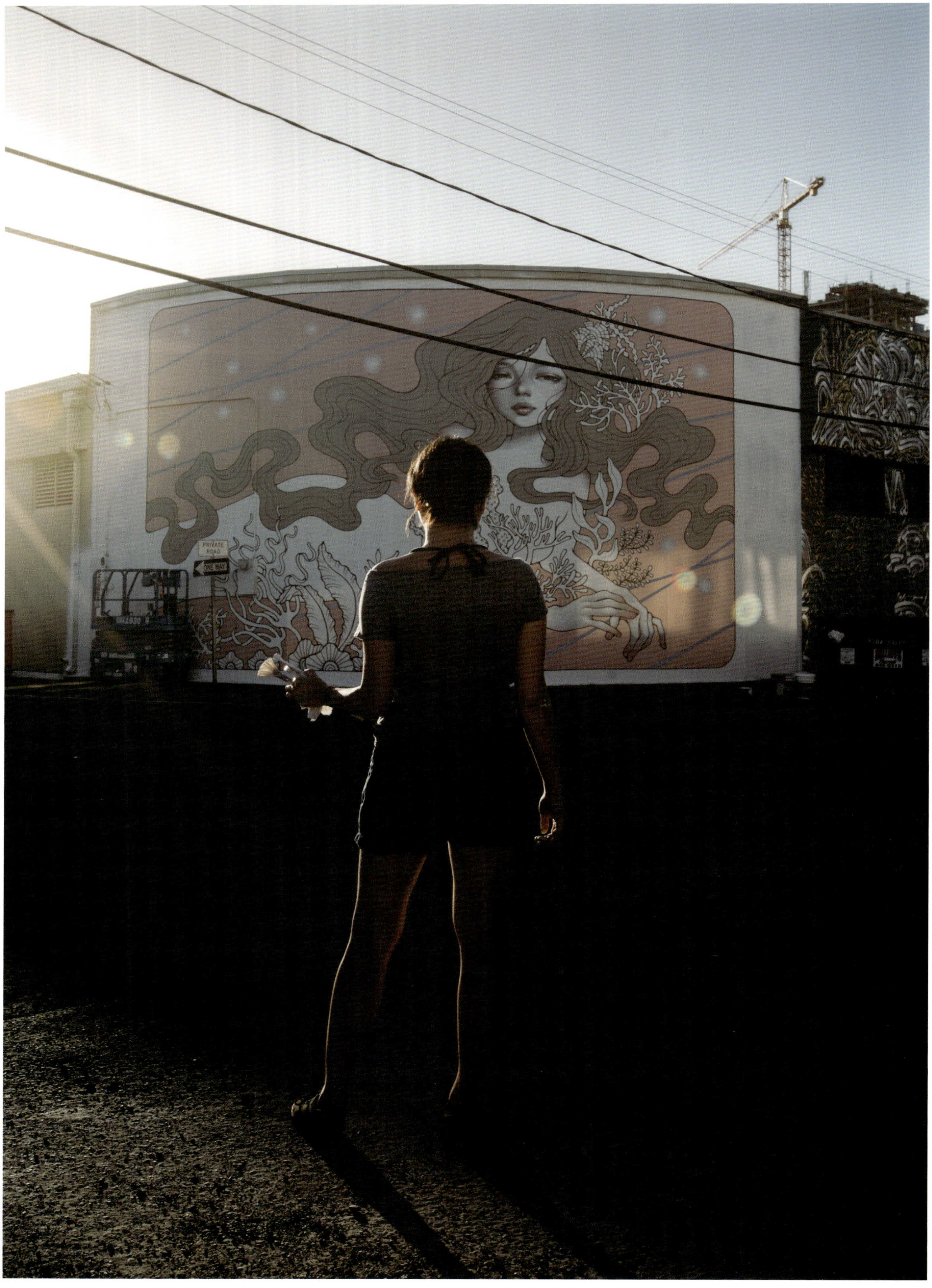
PRIVATE ROAD
ONE WAY

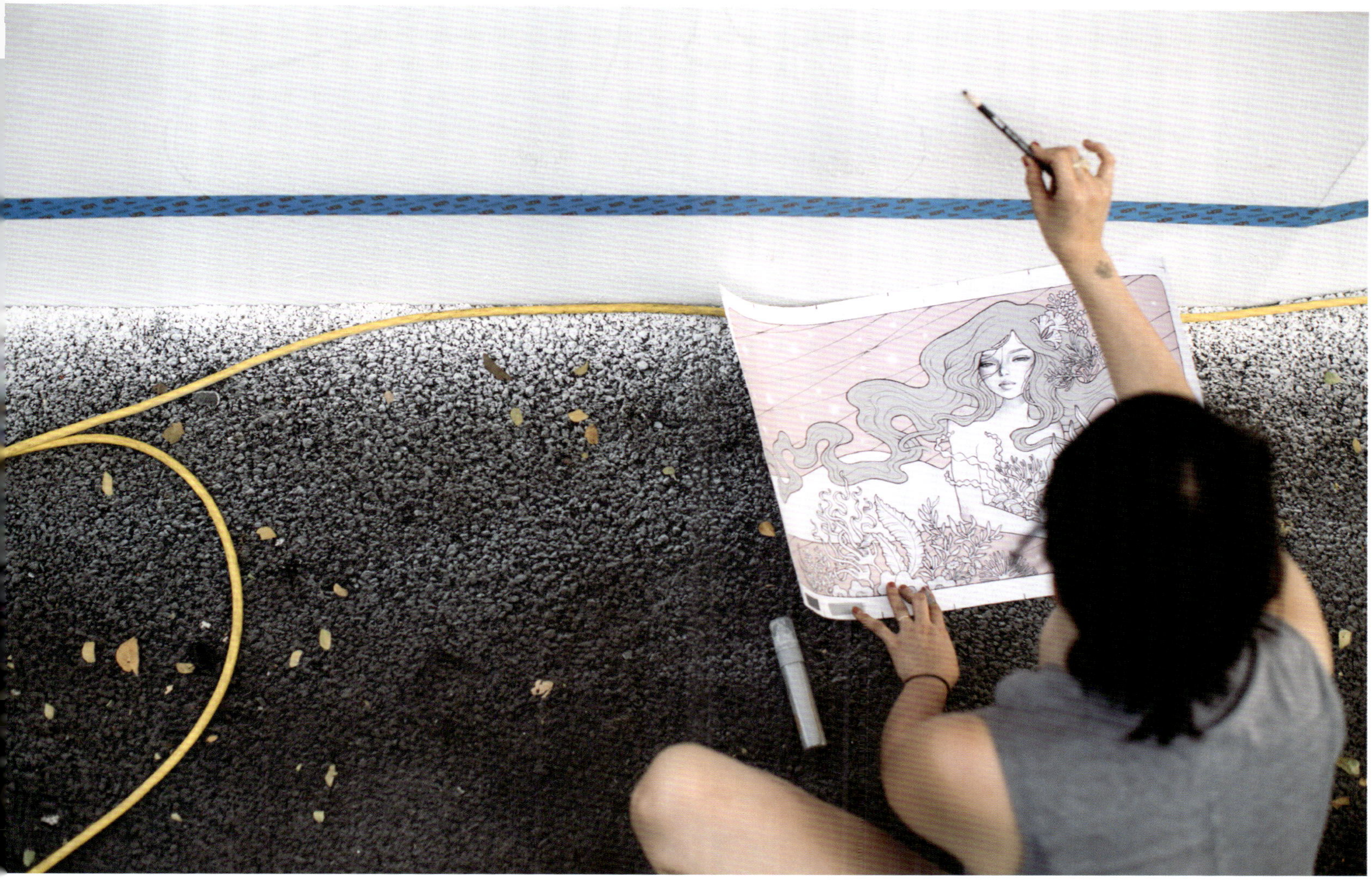

Hawaii 2016

Audrey Kawasaki

@AUDKAWA

Audrey Kawasaki is a Japanese-American artist known for her oil and acrylic paintings of women on wood panels. Her work contains contrasting themes of innocence and eroticism, conveying the mysterious intrigue of female sensuality. Kawasaki's art is a personification of femininity and the juxtaposition of emotions that this entails. She paints sultry, seductive and uninhibited subjects with delicate beauty and a provocative gaze directed at the viewer. Their graceful gestures and ghost-like features carry mysterious expressions of melancholy and longing which belies the strength and power that resides in each of these girls. Pulling inspiration from Art Nouveau and manga comics, Kawasaki's art has, in turn, inspired and empowered a new generation of artists. Born and raised in Los Angeles where she currently lives and works, Audrey enjoys noodles, seafood, anything citrus, video games, audio books, dancing, and white wine spritzers.

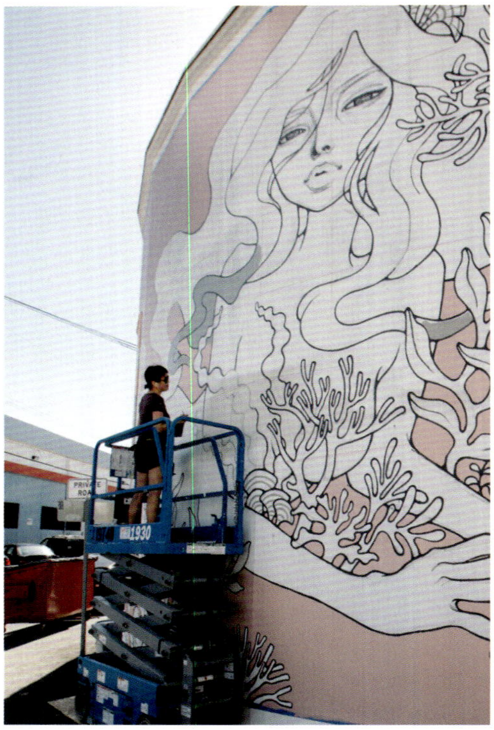

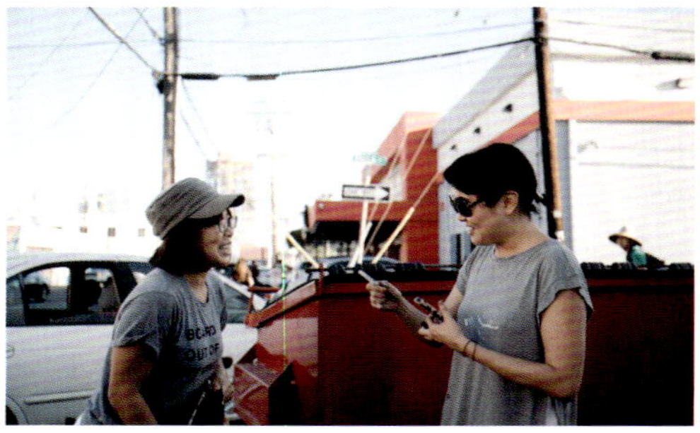

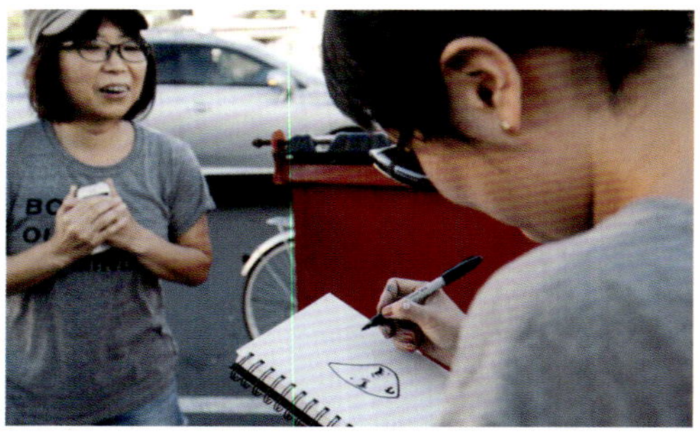

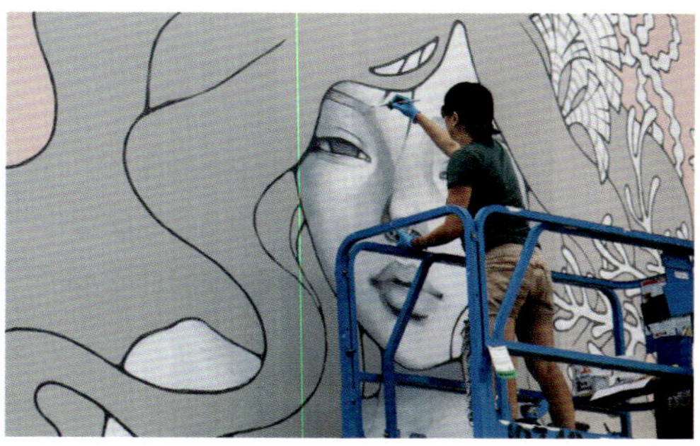

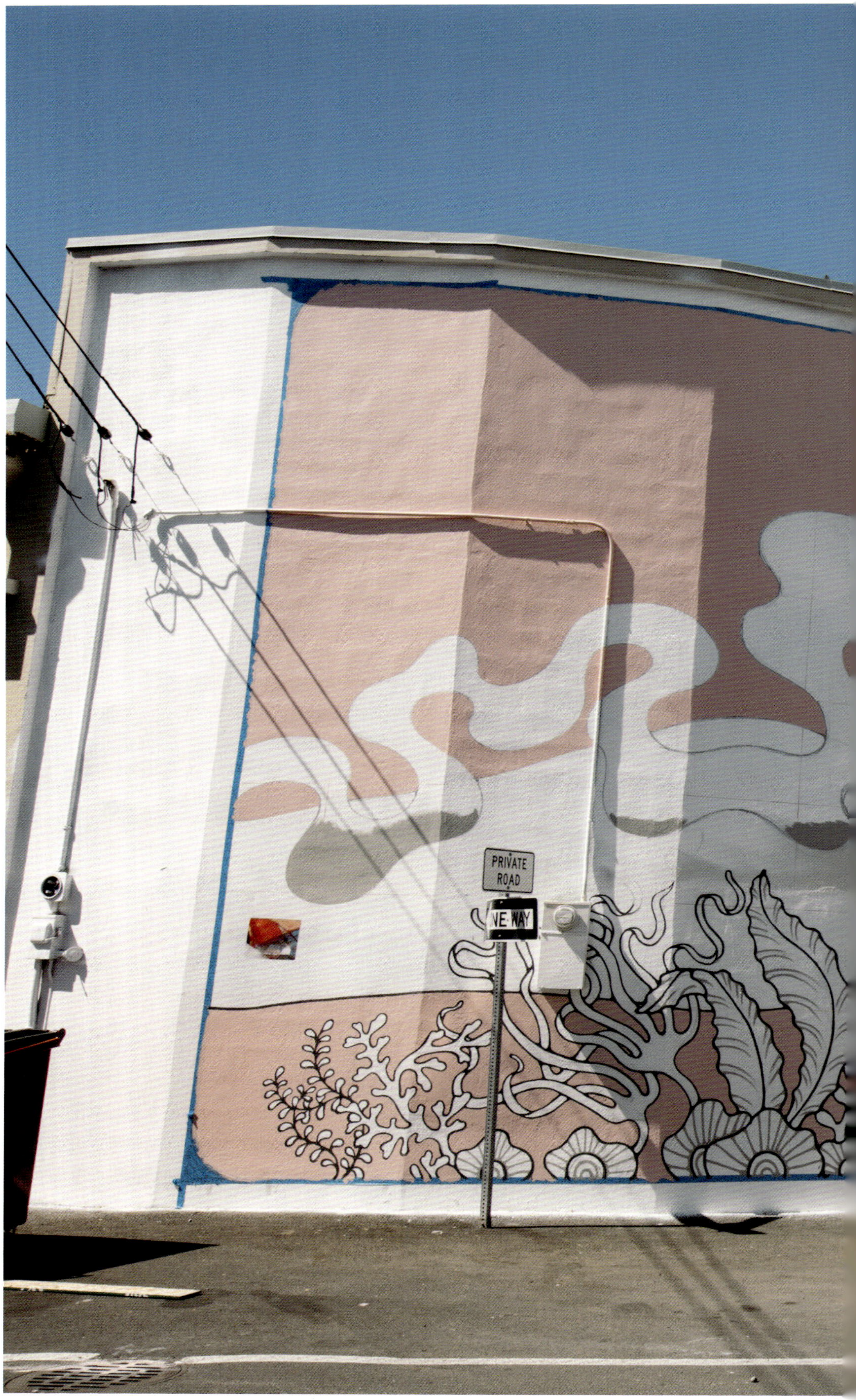
PRIVATE
ROAD

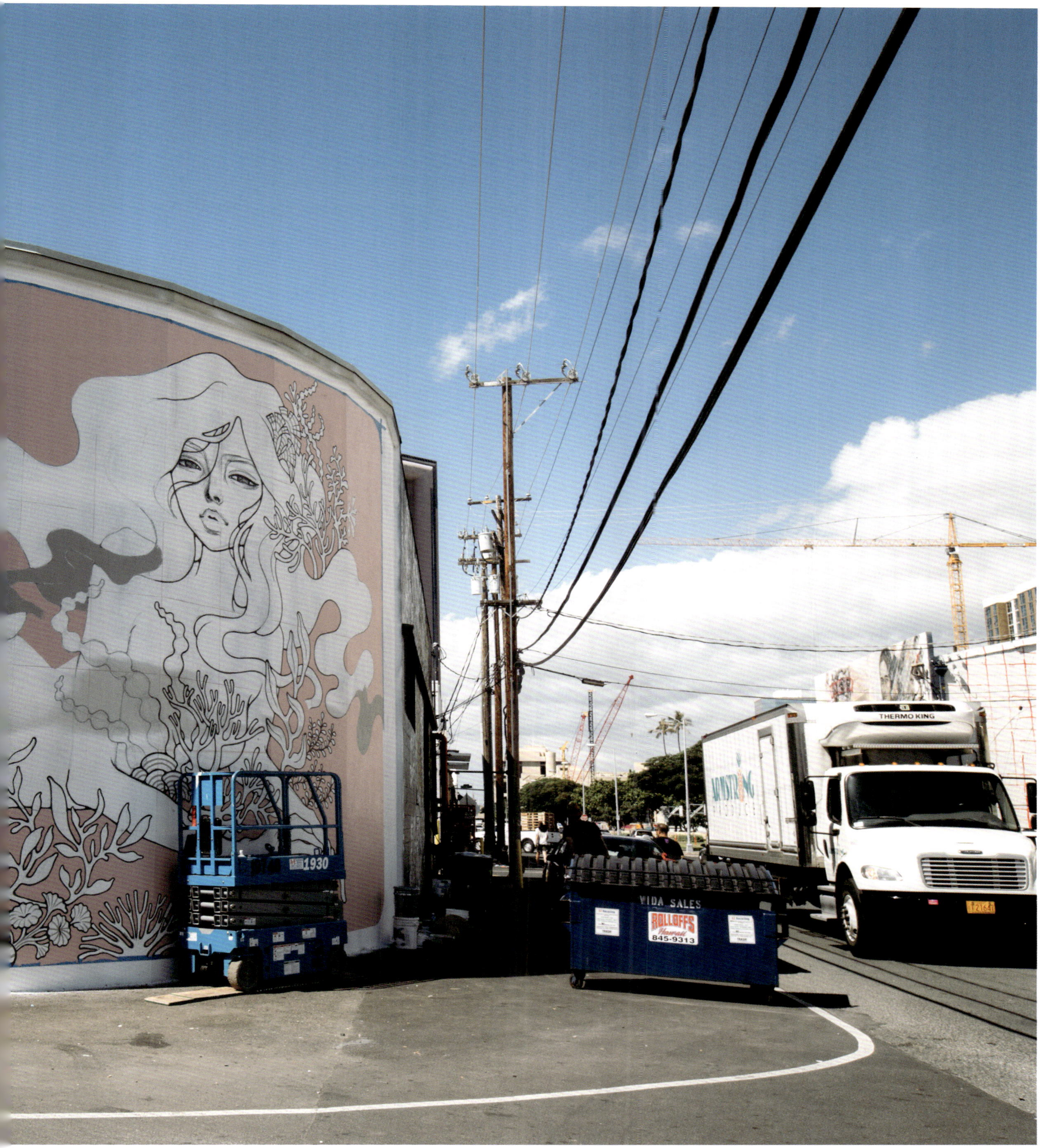
THERMO KING
1930
VIDA SALES
ROLLOFFS
845-9313

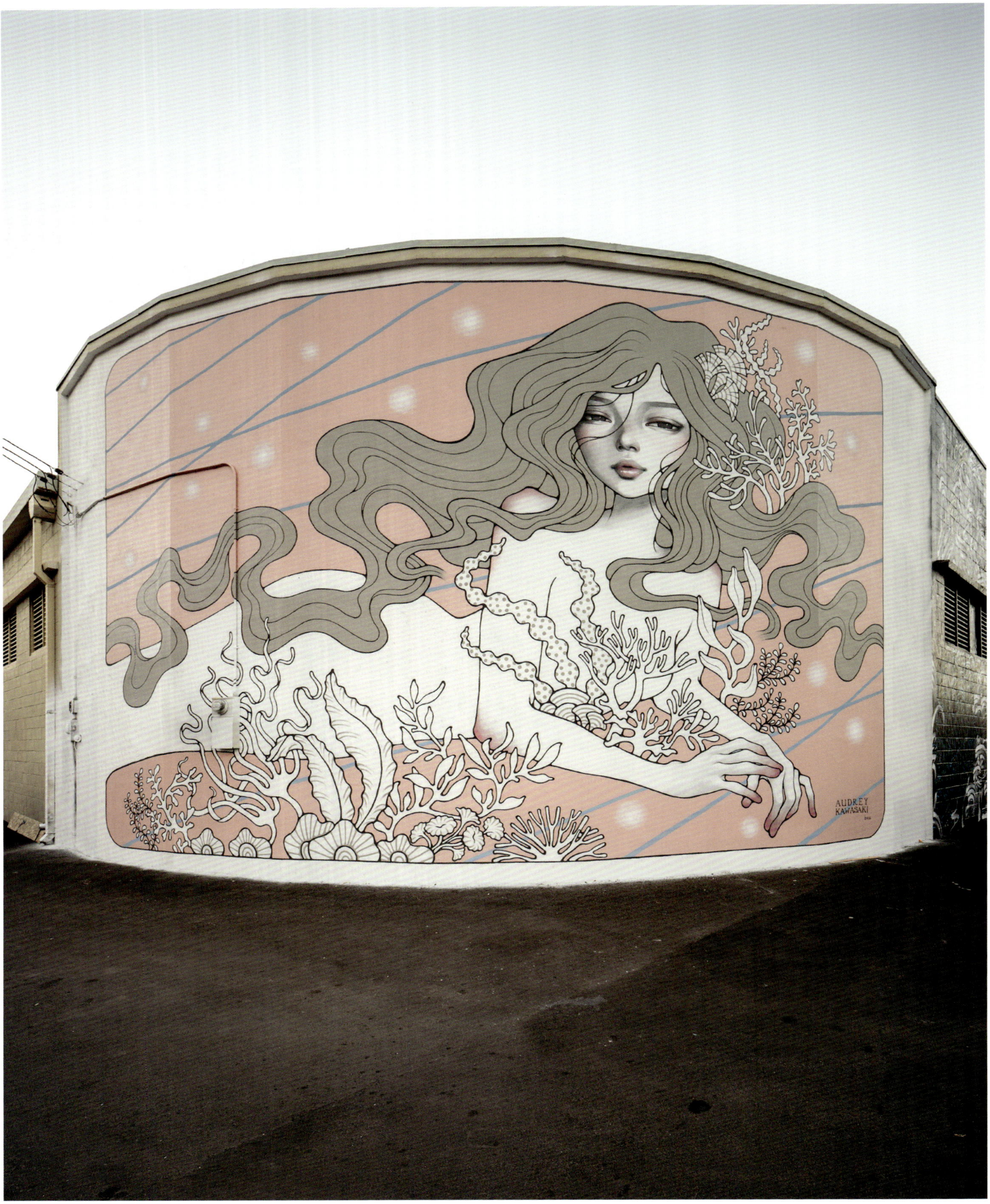
AUDREY
KAWASAKI

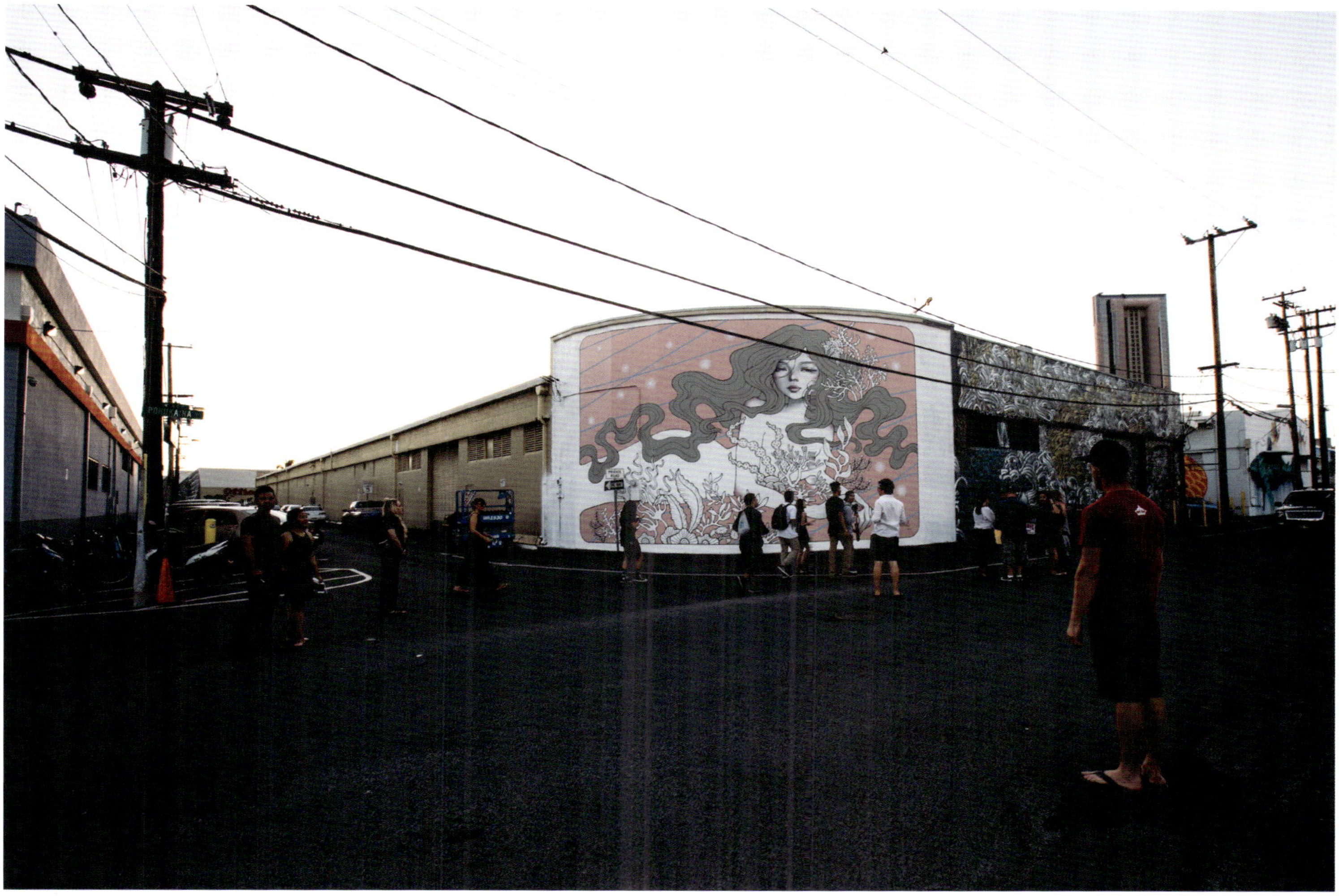

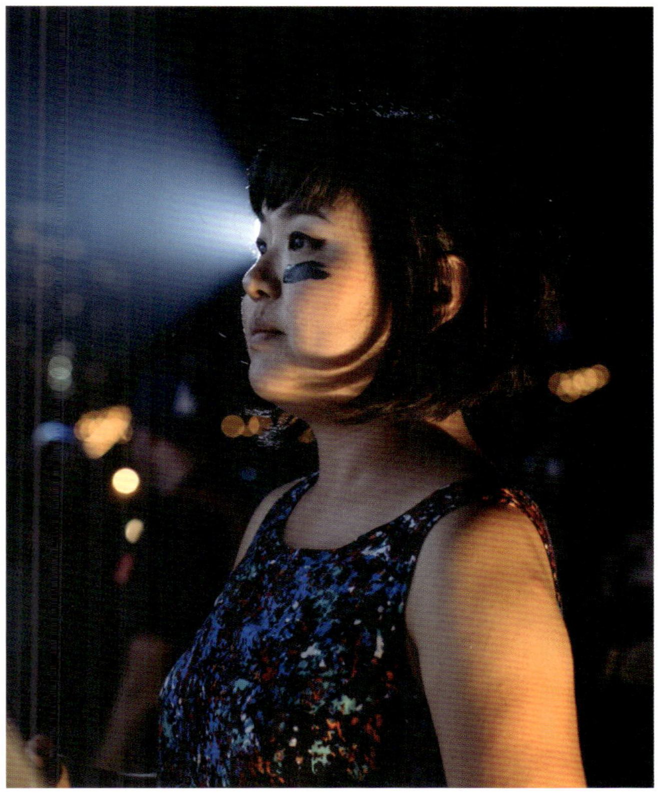

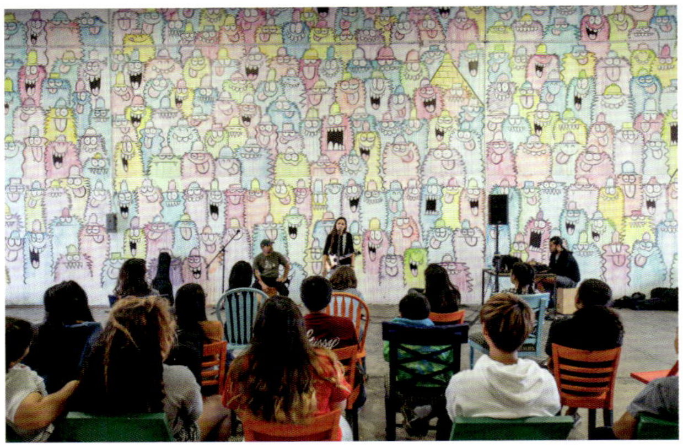
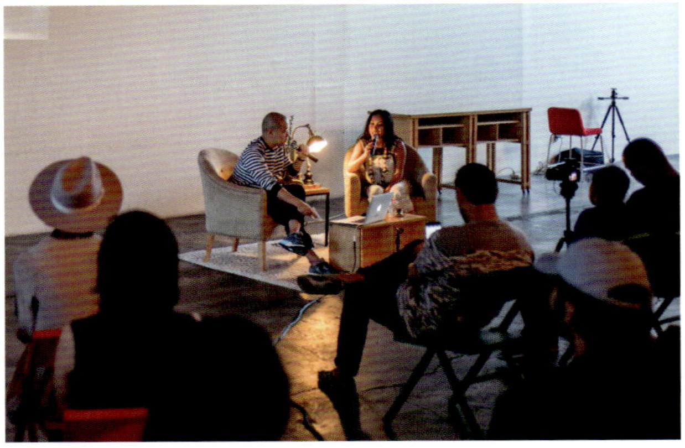
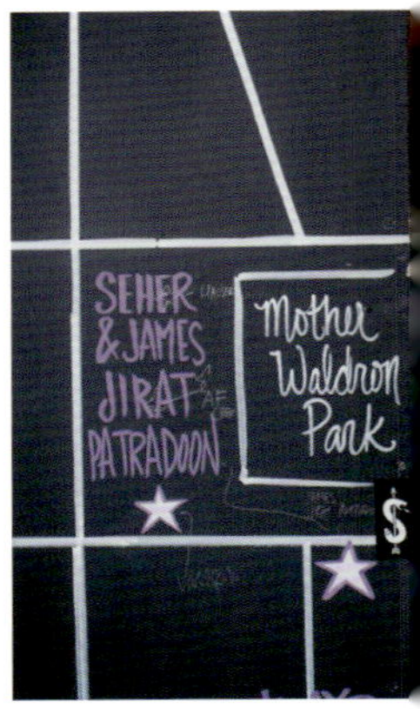
SEHER
& JAMES
JIRAT
PATRADOON
Mother
Waldron
Park
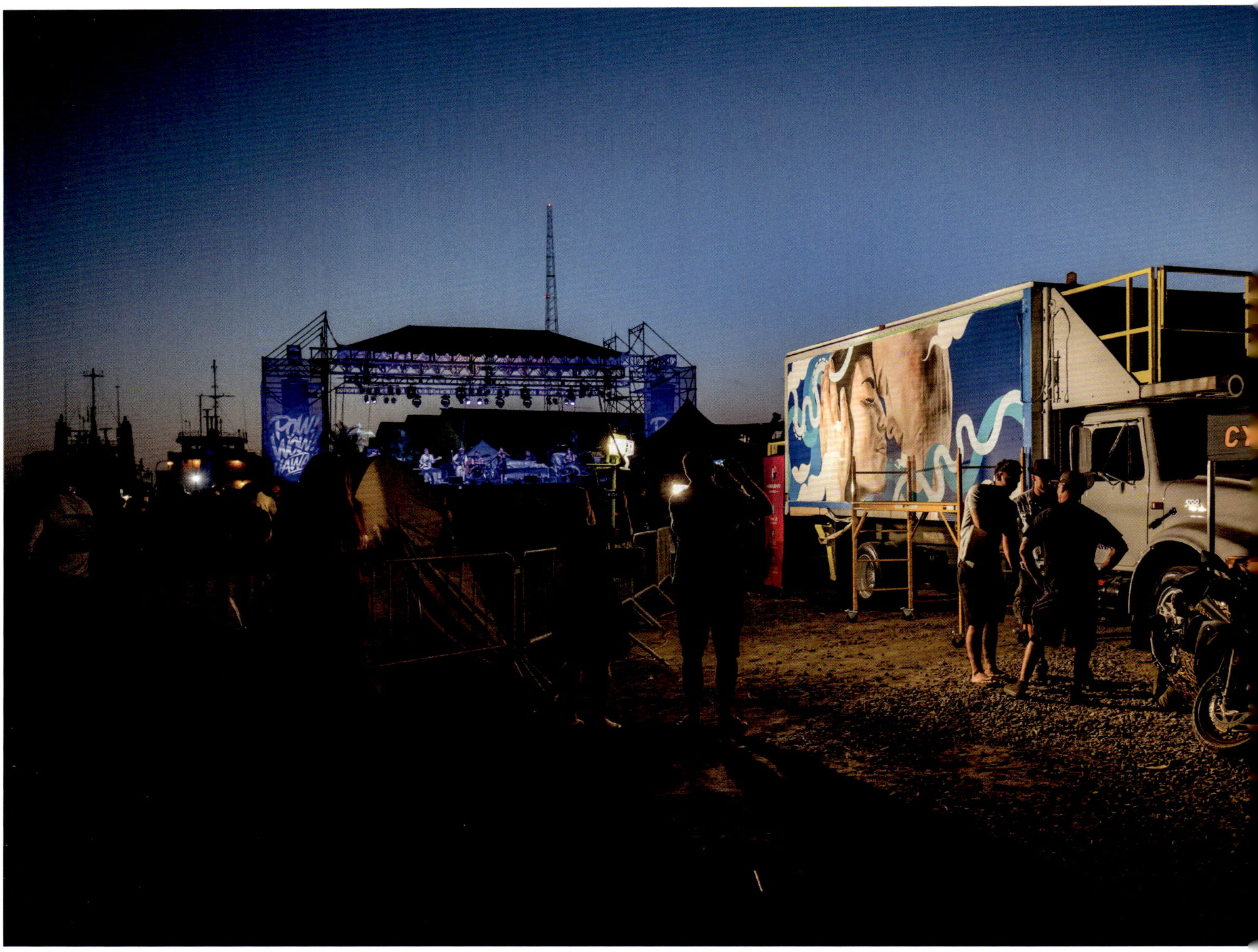
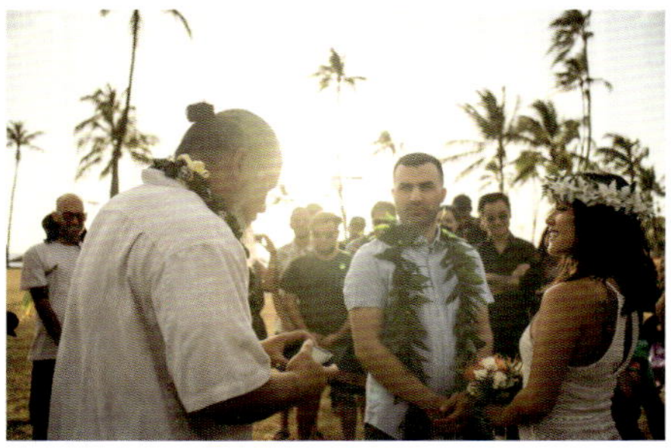
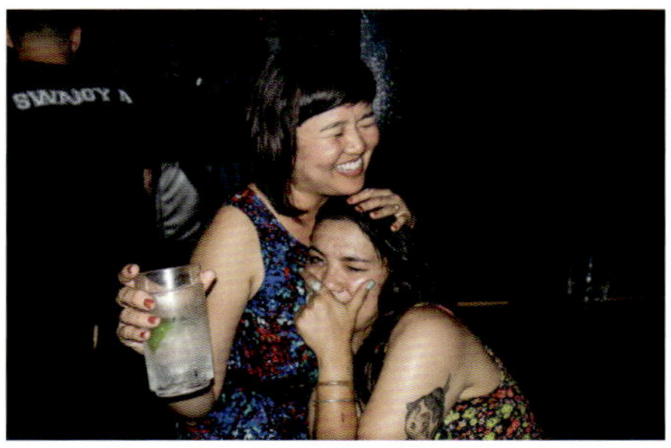
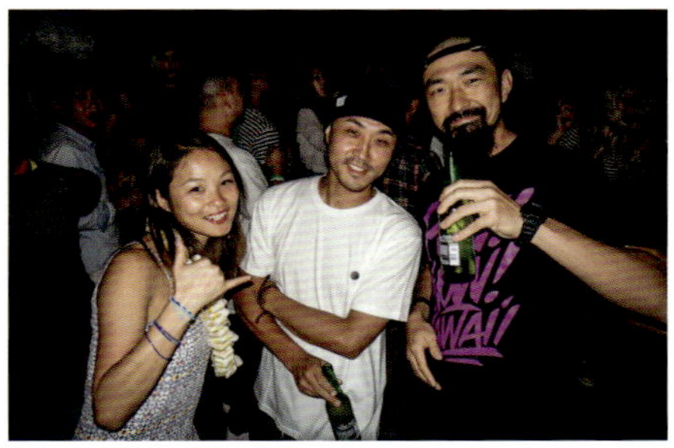
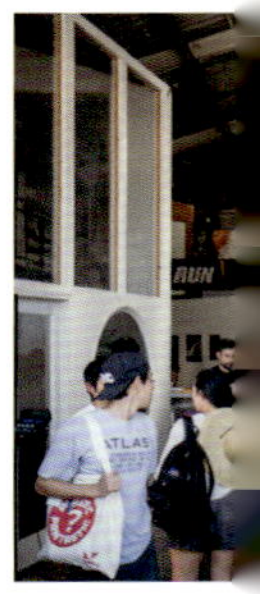

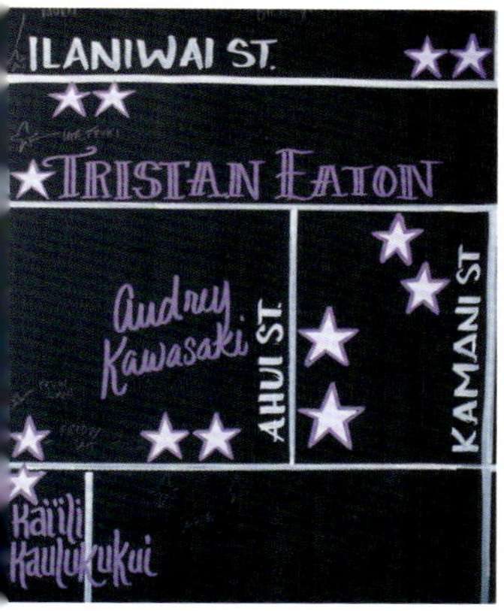
ILANIWAI ST.
TRISTAN EATON
Audrey Kawasaki
AHUI ST.
KAMANI ST
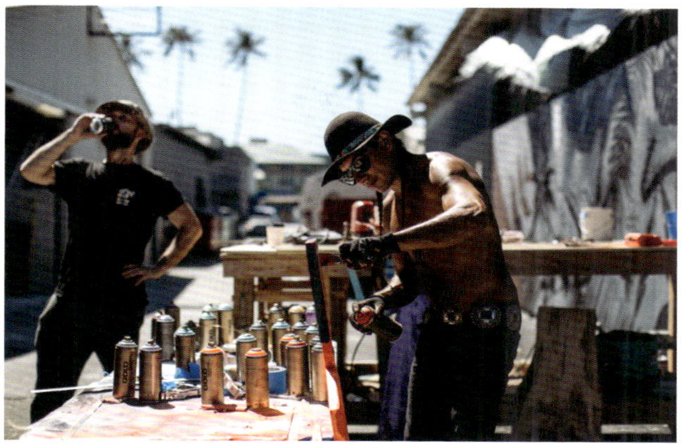
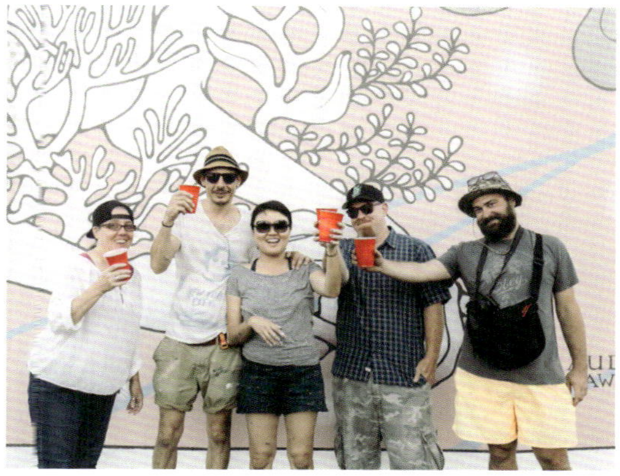
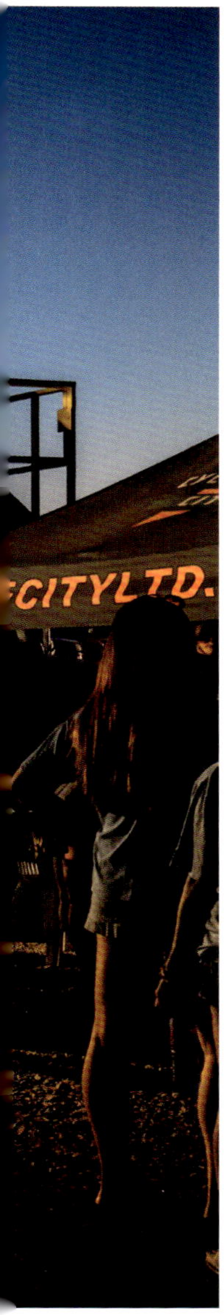
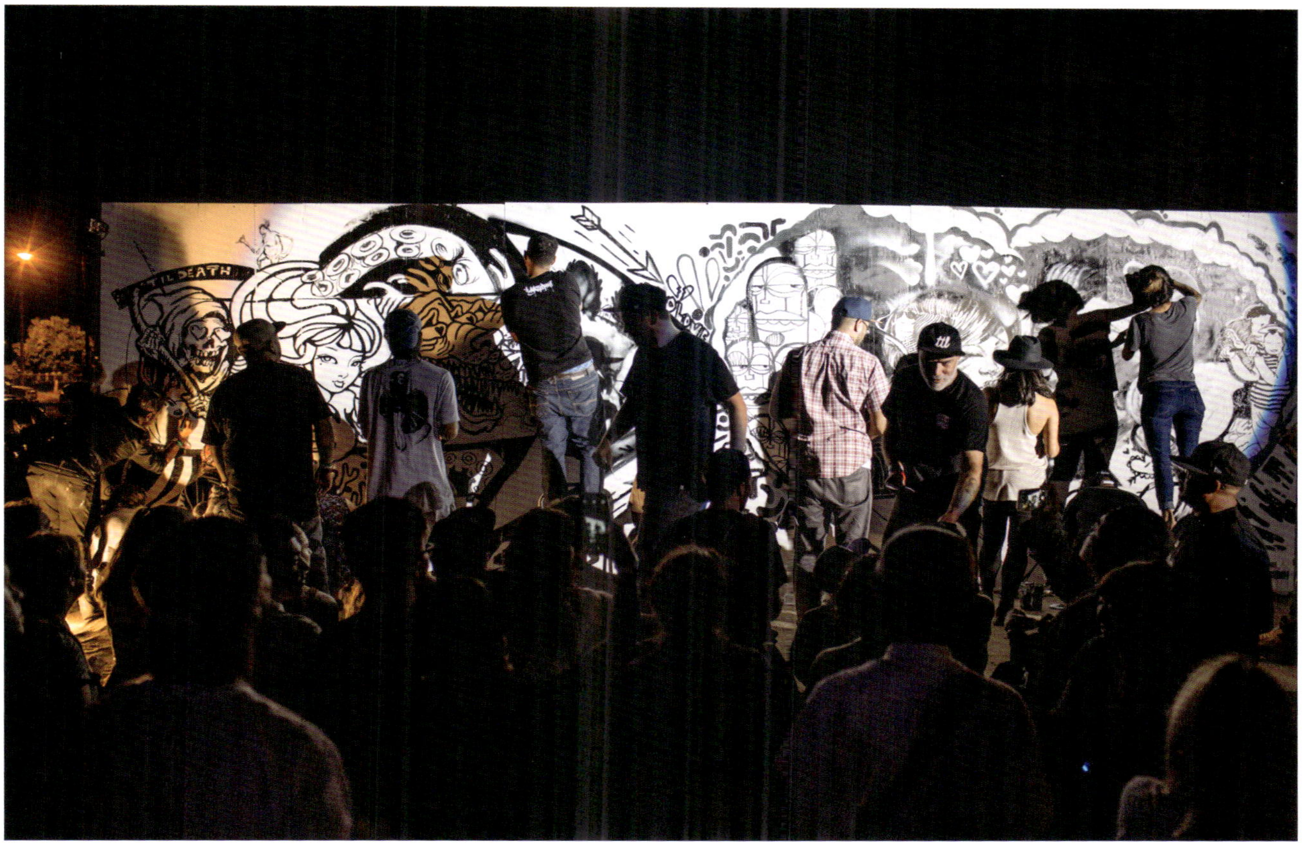
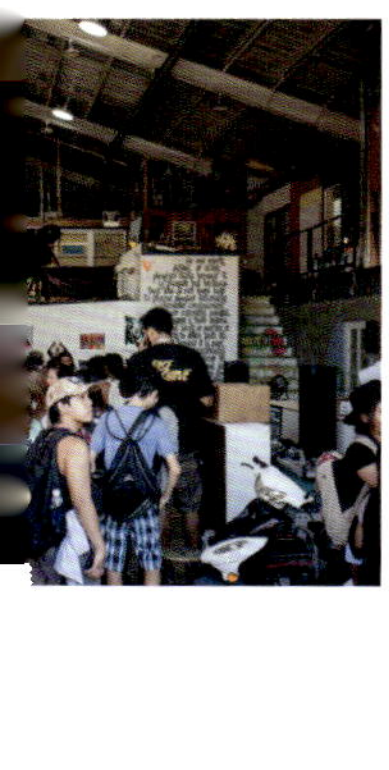
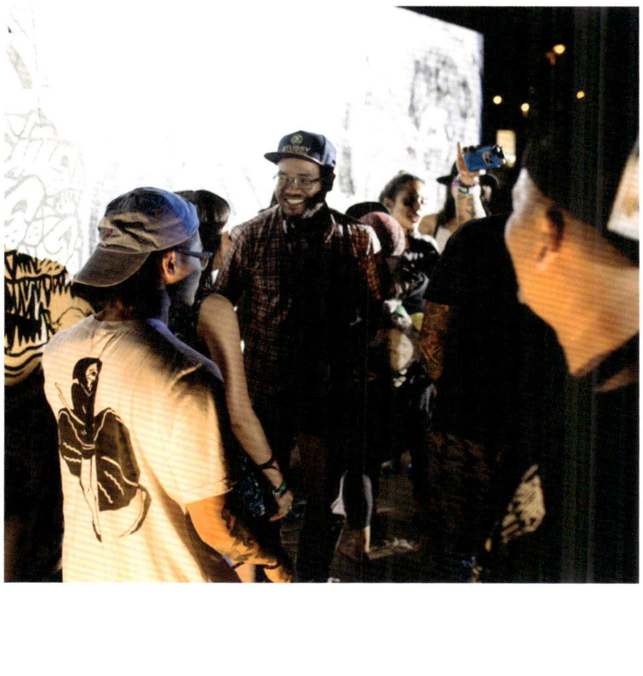
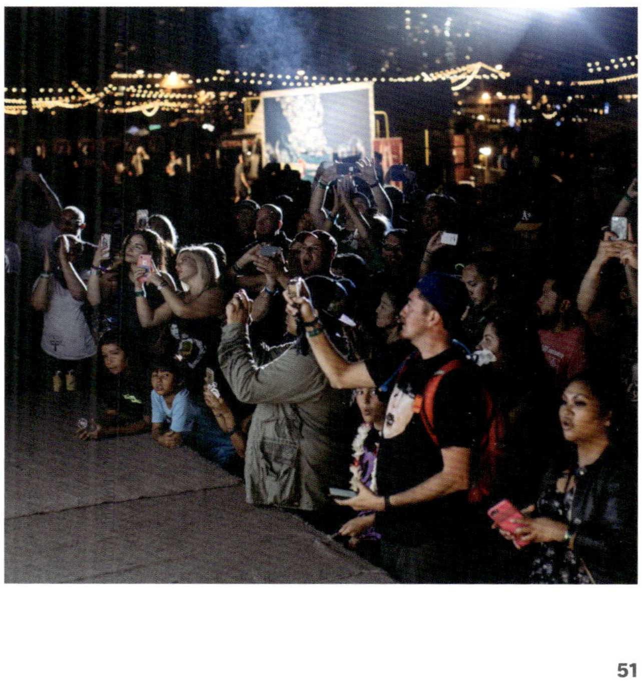

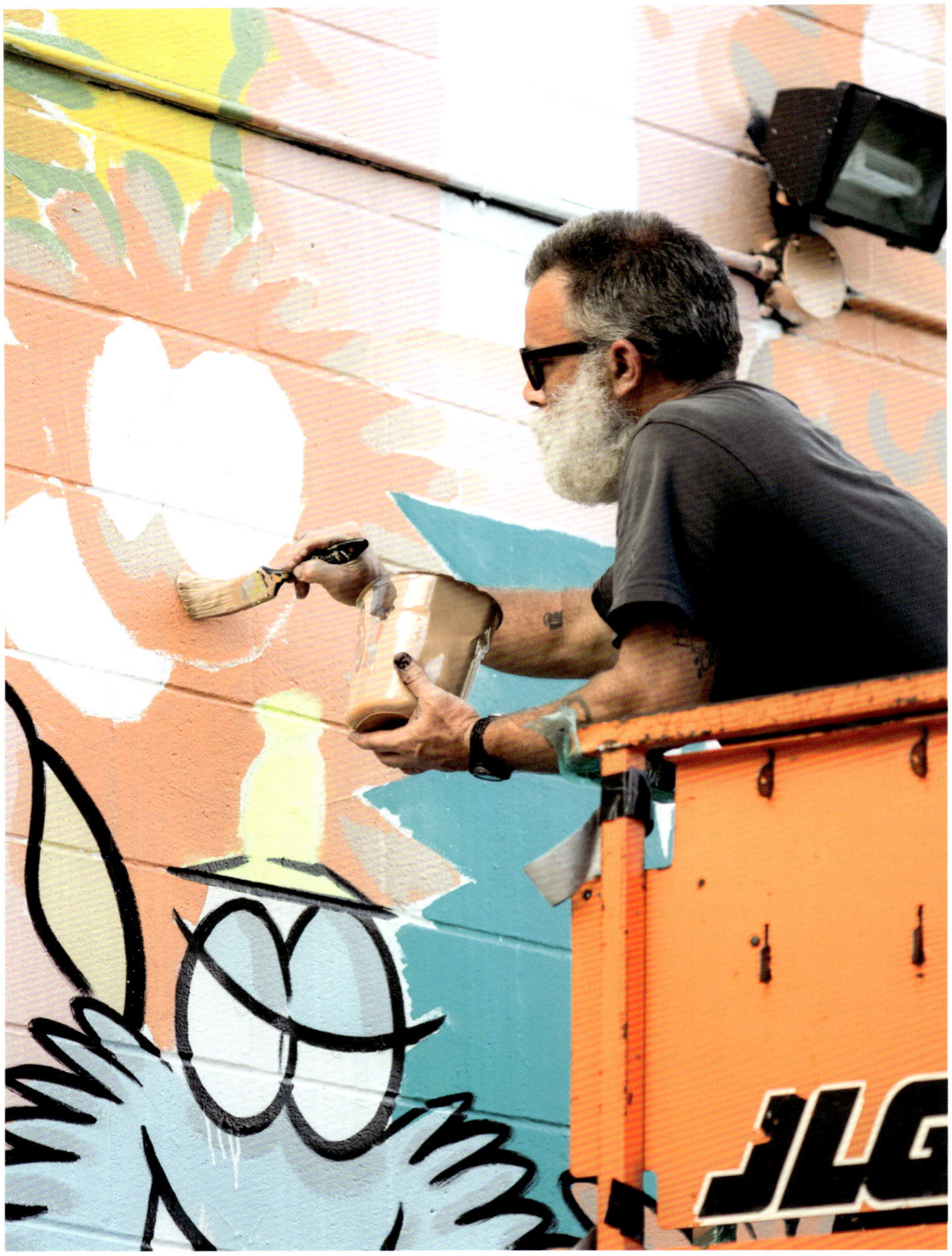

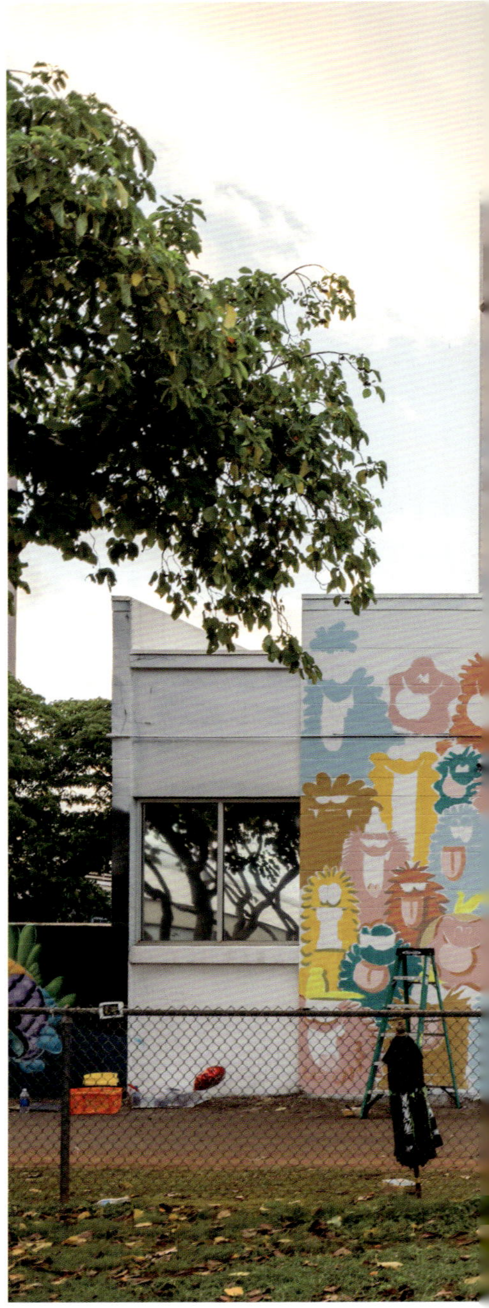

Hawaii 2017

Kevin Lyons

@KLYONSNATBORN

Kevin Lyons has worked with such clients as Nike, Converse, Umbro, Coca-Cola, American Express, among others. In 2010, he won an Emmy for title design for Eric Ripert's PBS series, Avec Eric, and also won a Cannes Golden Lion for his campaign for Diesel while Managing Partner at Anomaly NYC.

Kevin served in a variety of diverse roles including, Design Director at Stussy Worldwide; Art Director for Spike Jonze's Girl Skateboard Company; US Art Director for Tokion Magazine & Senior Designer for Nike Inc., where he was responsible for branding several big-time college & pro sports franchises.

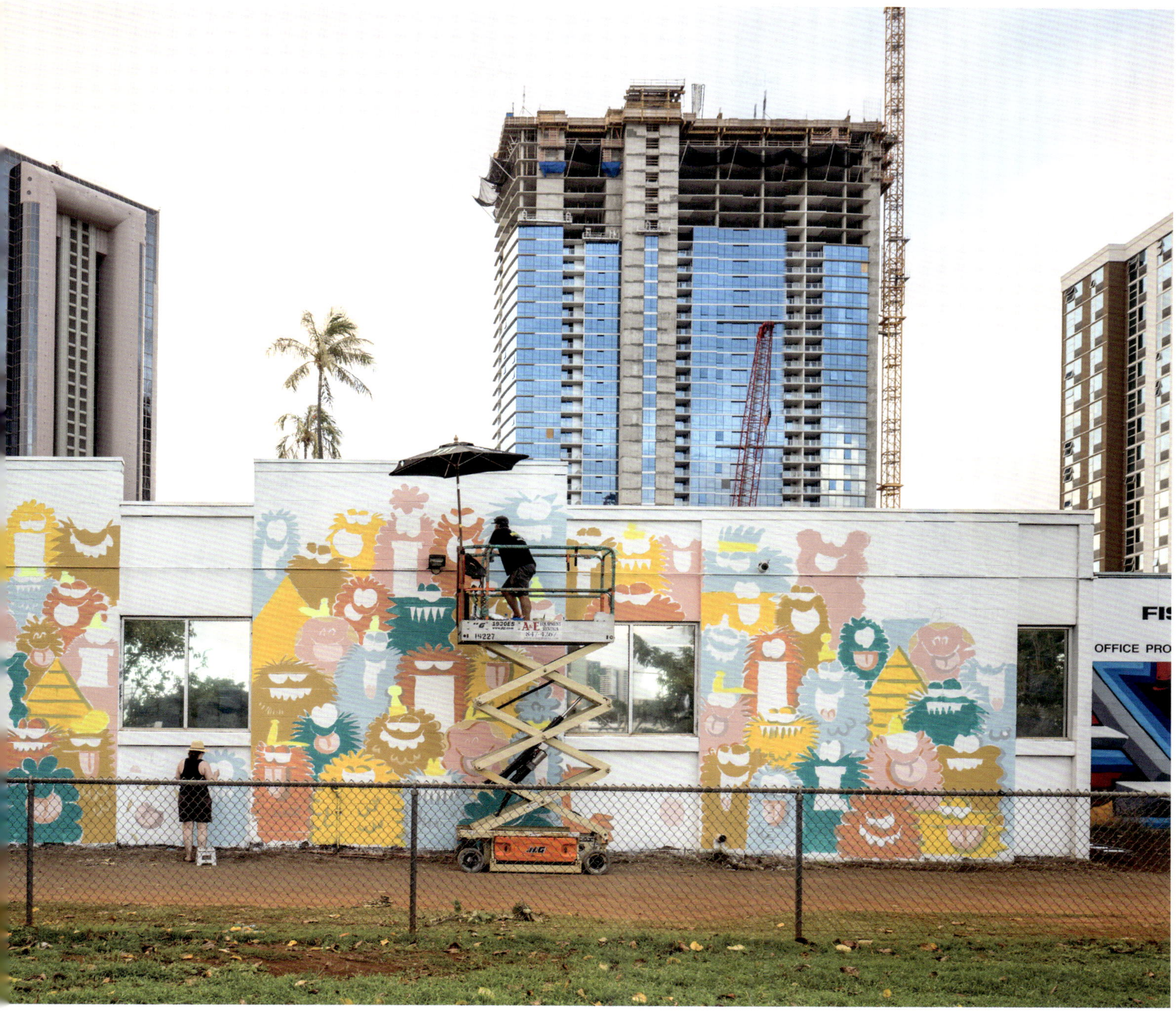

In 2001, Kevin was named to "The Top Forty Designers Under Thirty" by ID Magazine. He has written articles for the AIGA Journal, as well as addressing the AIGA twice including once as a published recipient of its Fresh Dialogues Series. He has held teaching assistant positions at both RISD and CalArts, and has been a visiting critic at the Yale Graduate School of Design. He was an Assistant Professor of Typography at the Pratt Institute from 2000-2002.

Kevin produces two clothing lines; one for 2K, called Atlantis and the other under his personal namesake, NATURAL BORN—both are distributed globally. His own work has been published worldwide from Thrasher, The Face, Lodown, The New York Times Magazine, Arkitip, Anthem and Refill. He has shown worldwide including solo shows in Paris, Philadelphia, Los Angeles, San Francisco, and Tokyo. His books and zines are available from And Press and Nieves.

Kevin Lyons is a graduate of the Rhode Island School of Design where he received a degree in film and has a Masters Degree from CalArts.

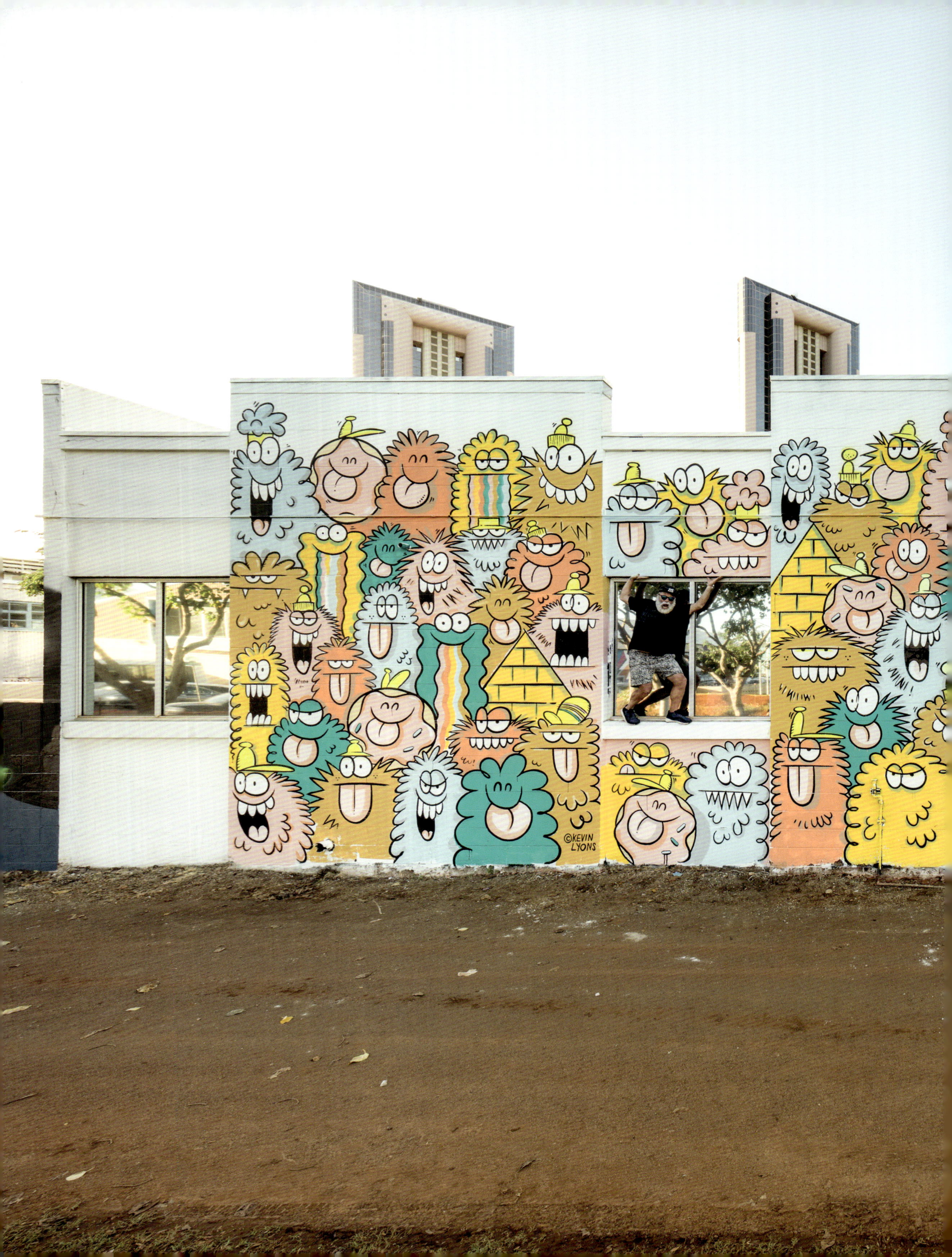
©KEVIN
LYONS

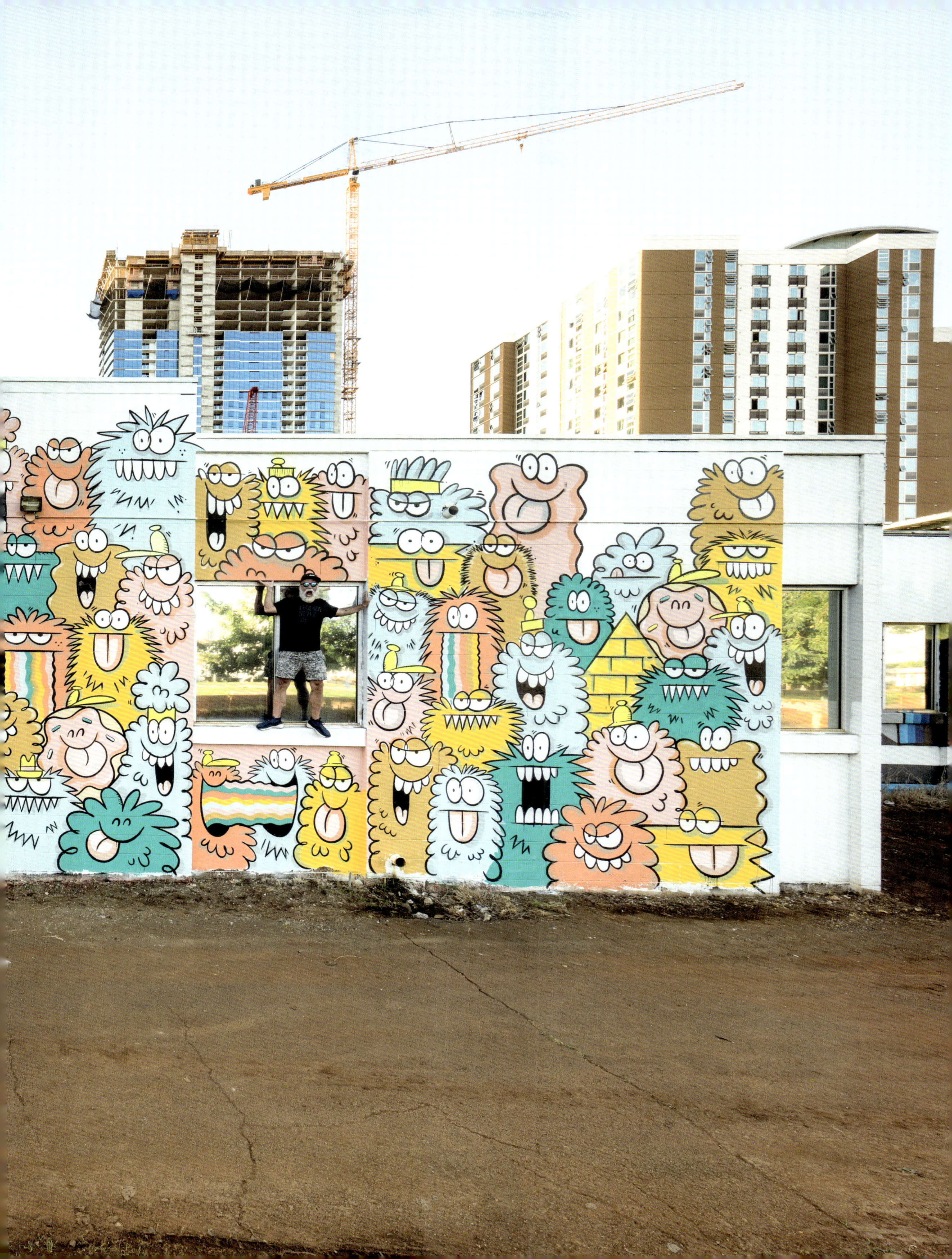

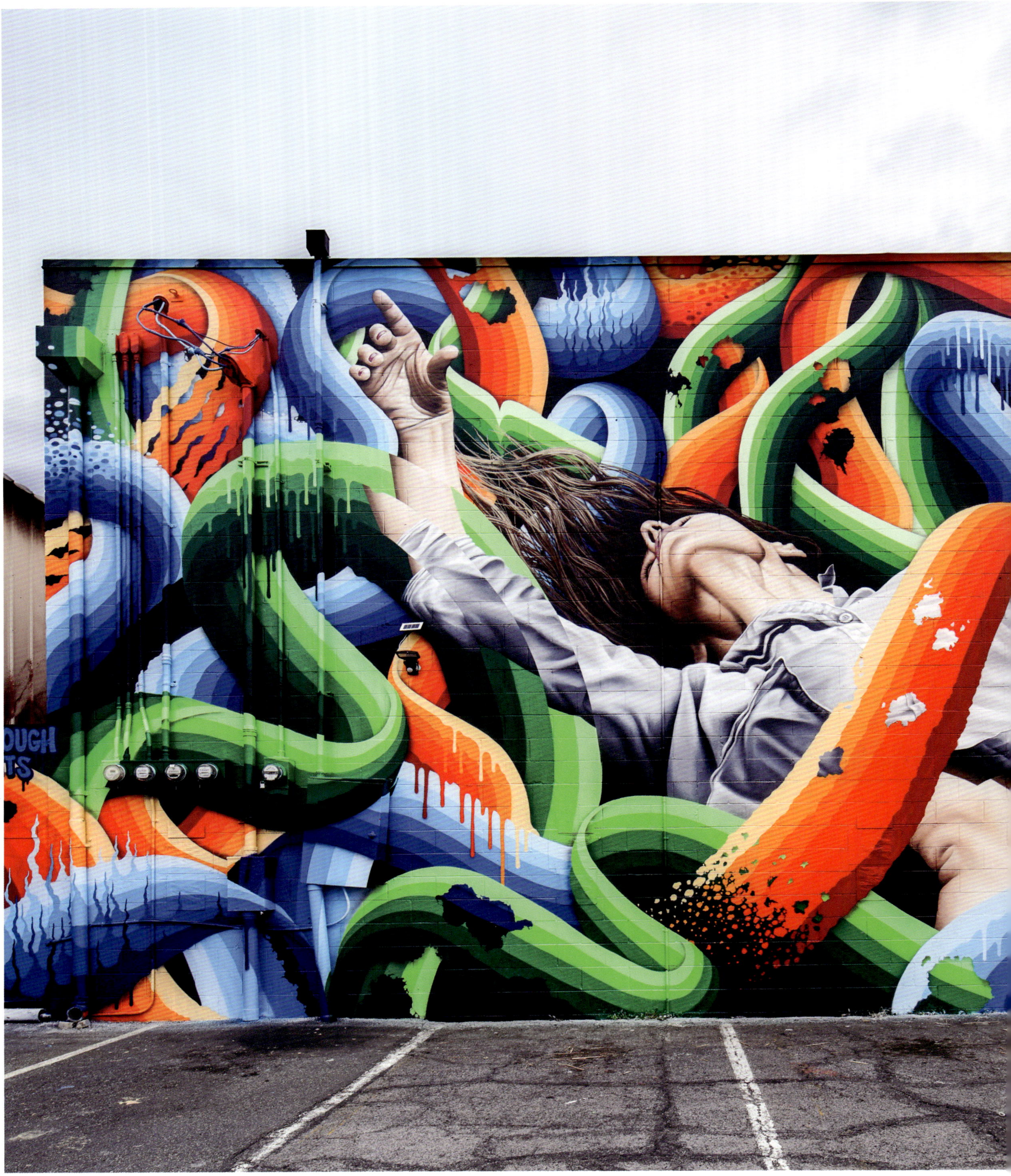

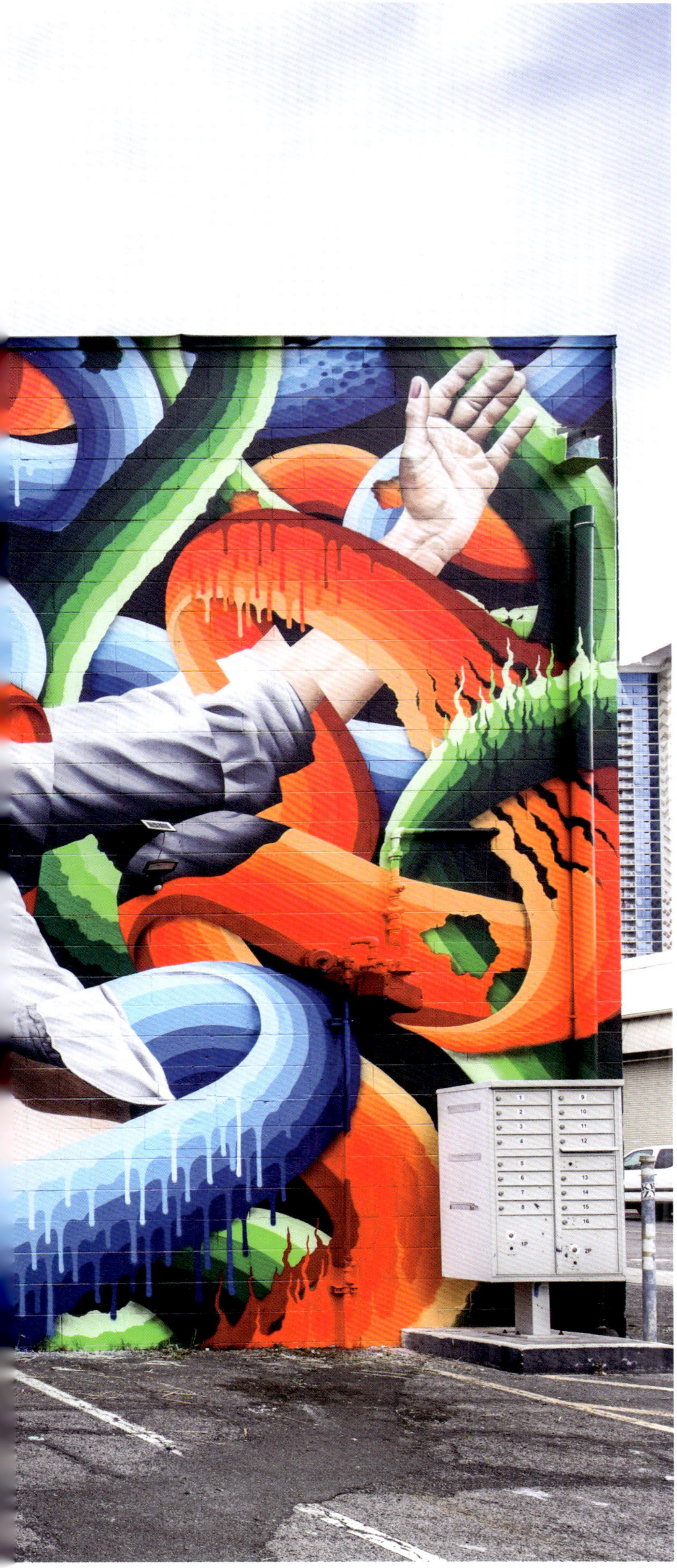

James Bullough & Ricky Watts

@JAMES_BULLOUGH @RICKYWATTS

James Bullough is an American born artist living and working in Berlin, Germany. His studio paintings, and huge monumentally scaled site-specific murals combine delicately handled realistic portraiture with harsh graphic distortion and abstraction. Inspired by the gritty urban graffiti he saw as a youth growing up in Washington, DC, Bullough harnessed it's energy and edge while teaching himself more traditional realistic oil painting techniques by studying the Old Masters. Combining the momentum of the one and the technical precision of the other, his work is about staging compelling contrasts and juxtapositions. Whether working with spray paint on massive facades or oils in his studio, Bullough's work strikes a delicate balance between realistic portraiture and stylized distortions, straddling the space between traditional and contemporary.

Richard "Ricky" Watts is most notably recognized for his abstract works of fluid shapes and psychedelic color patterns. Watts' self-taught techniques derive from his younger graffiti years in Northern California. A versatile artist with range across multiple mediums, Ricky's large-scale murals and intricate paintings on canvas can be seen throughout the United States. His commissions list includes projects for major technology, fashion and automotive companies.

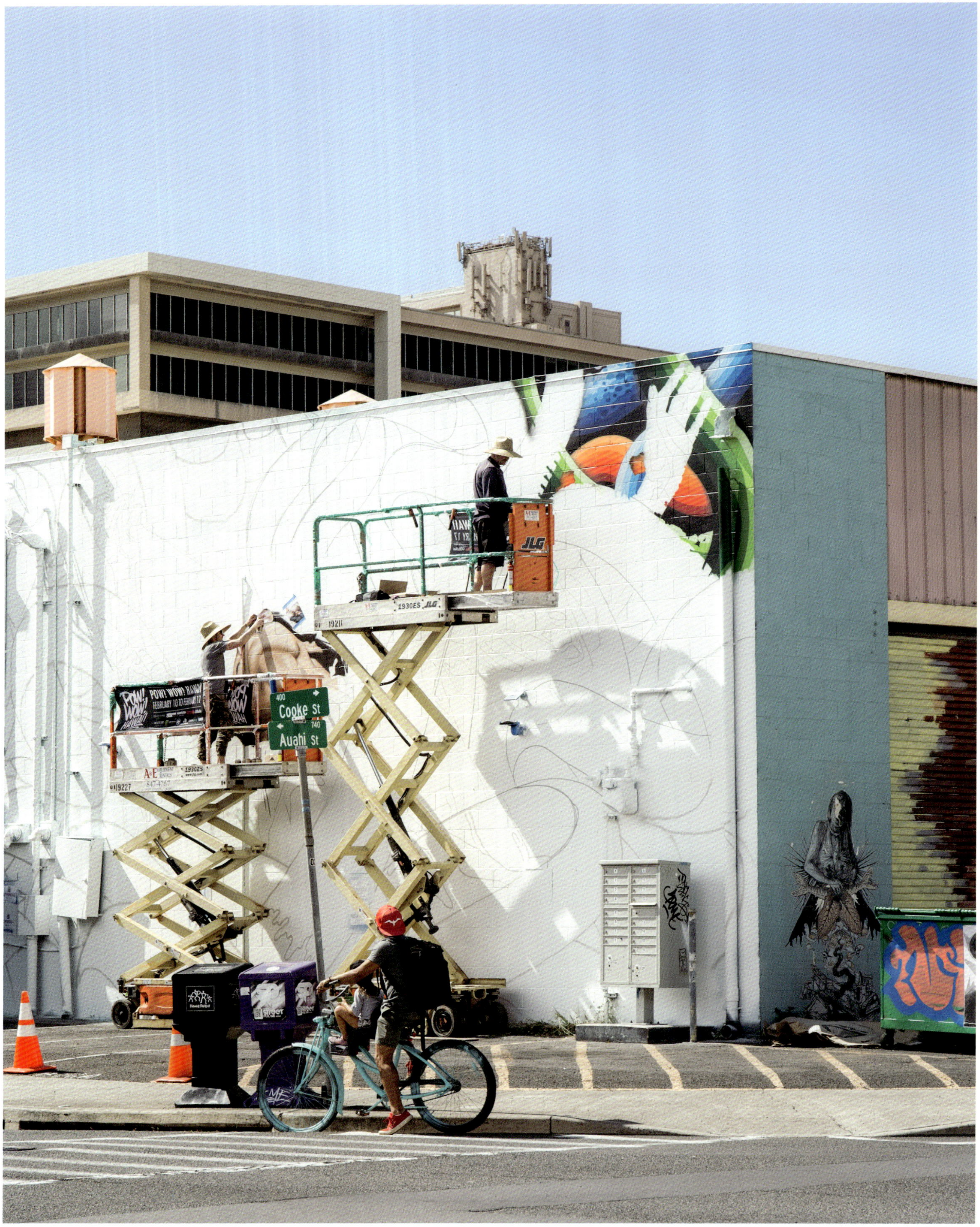
400
Cooke St
740
Auahi St
JLG
1930ES
POW! WOW! HAWAII
FEBRUARY 10 TO FEBRUARY 17

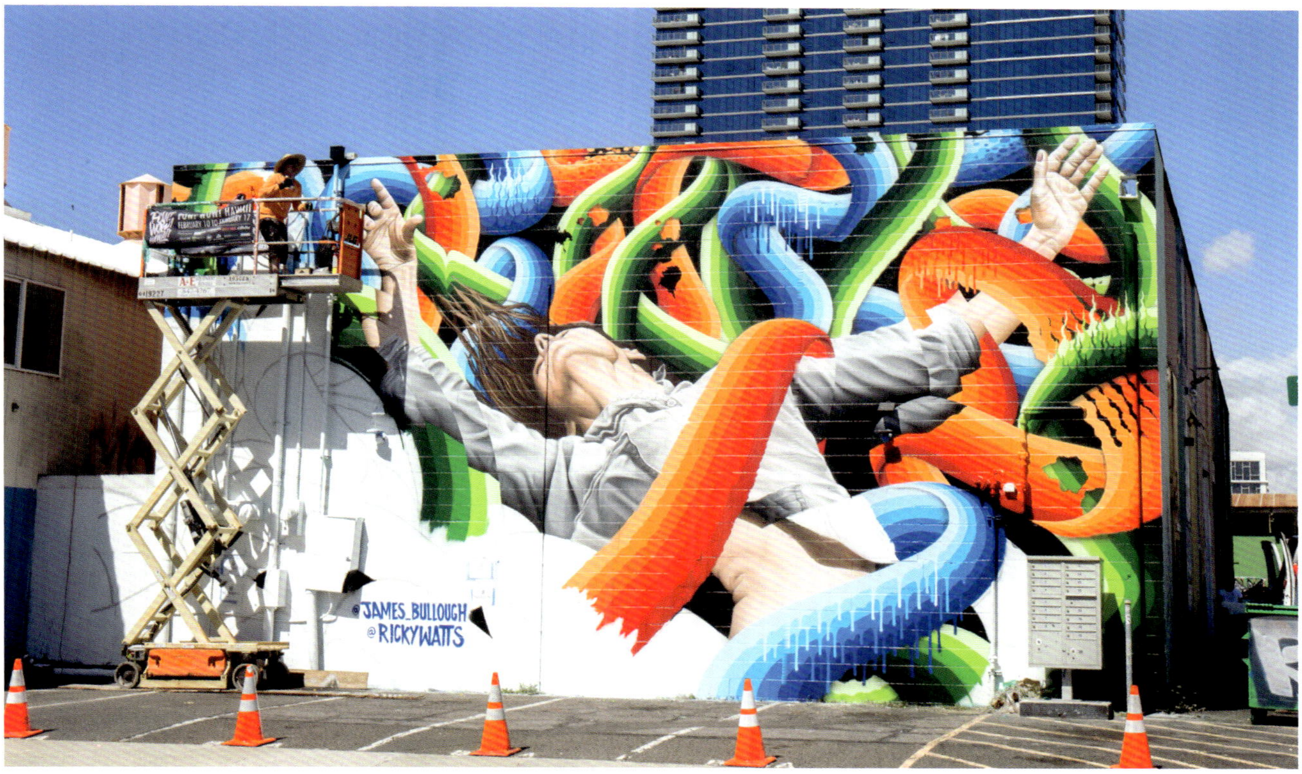
@JAMES_BULLOUGH
@RICKYWATTS

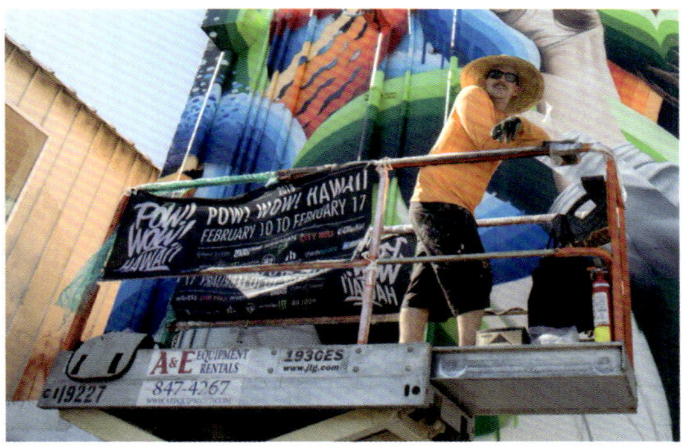
POW! WOW! HAWAII
FEBRUARY 10 TO FEBRUARY 17
A&E EQUIPMENT RENTALS
847-4267
1930ES

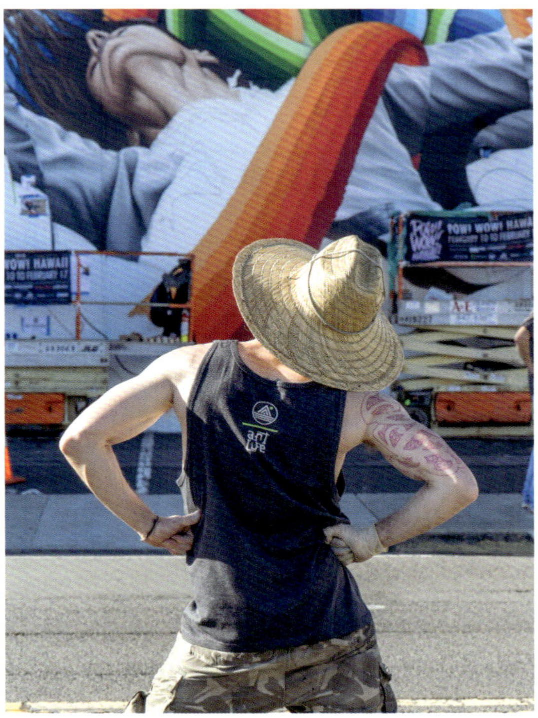

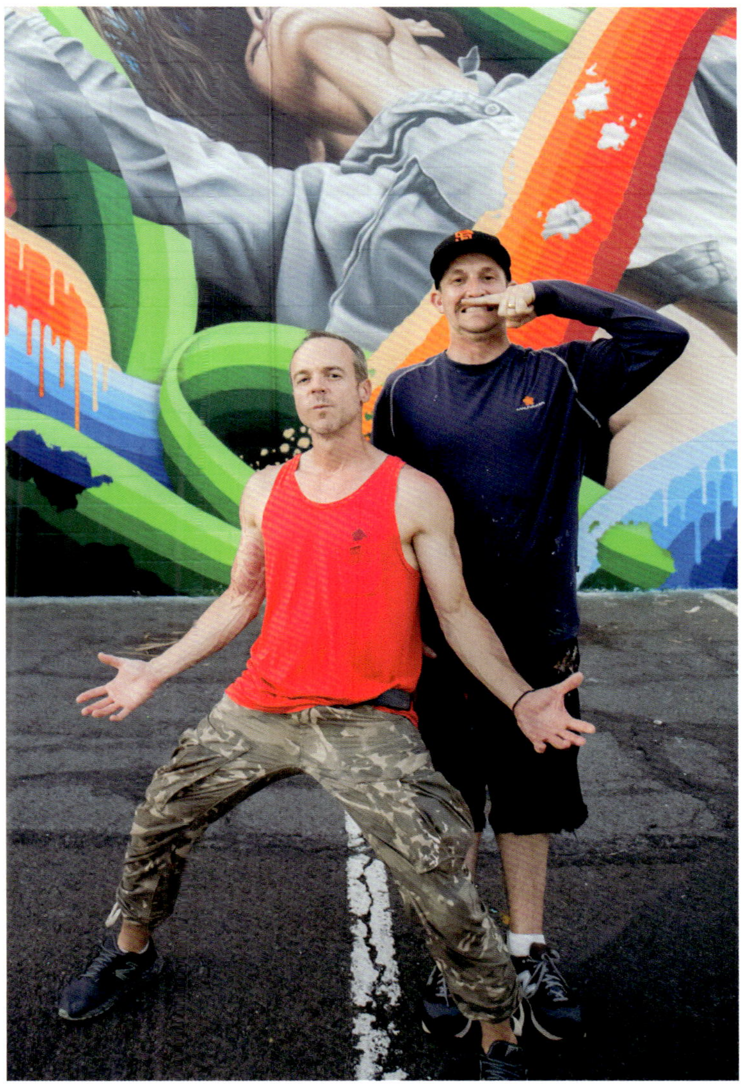

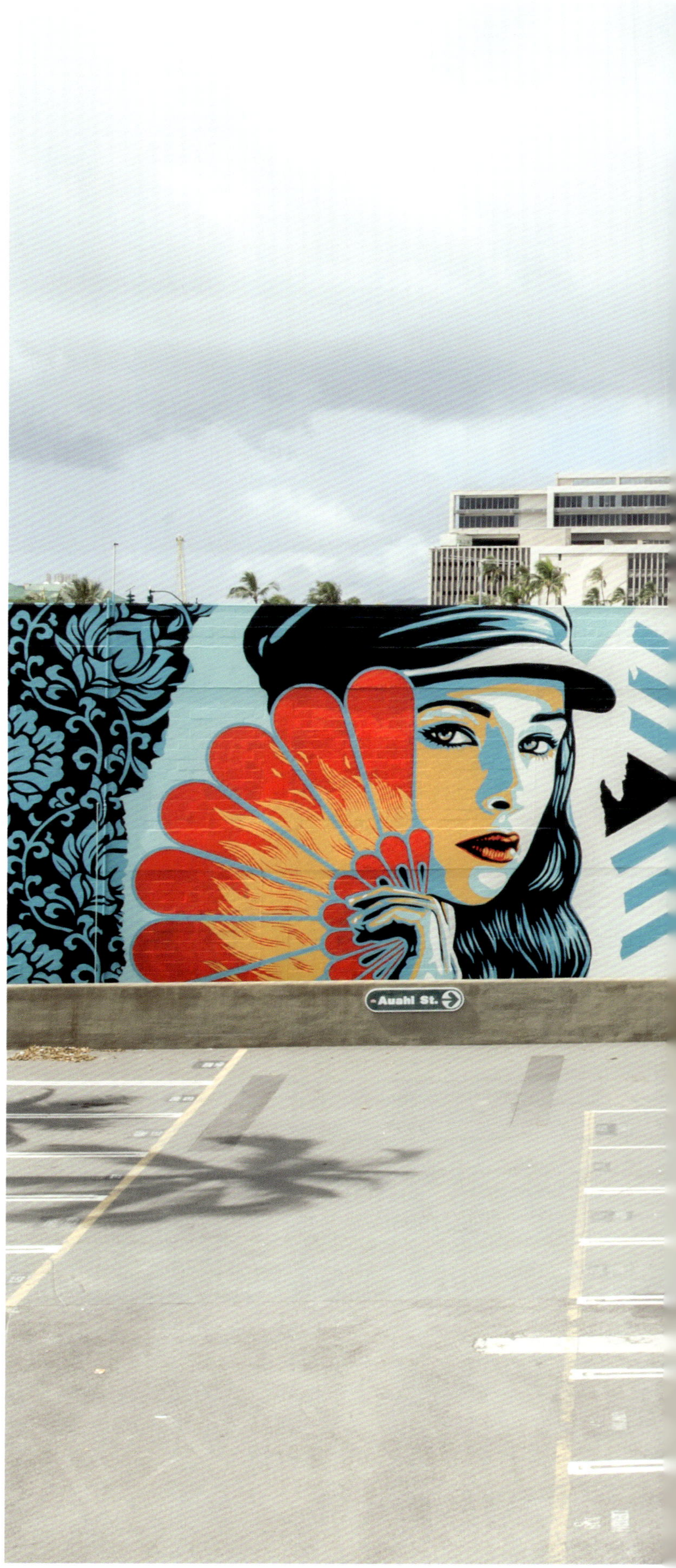

Shepard Fairey

@OBEYGIANT

Shepard Fairey is an American contemporary street artist, graphic designer, activist, illustrator and founder of OBEY Clothing who emerged from the skateboarding scene. He first became known for his "Andre the Giant Has a Posse" and OBEY sticker campaign while attending the Rhode Island School of Design (RISD), which appropriated images from the comedic supermarket tabloid Weekly World News.

He became widely known during the 2008 U.S. presidential election for his Barack Obama "Hope" poster. The Institute of Contemporary Art, Boston has described him as one of the best known and most influential street artists. His work is included in the collections at The Smithsonian, the Los Angeles County Museum of Art, the Museum of Modern Art in New York City, the Museum of Contemporary Art San Diego, the National Portrait Gallery in Washington, D.C., the Virginia Museum of Fine Arts in Richmond, and the Victoria and Albert Museum in London.

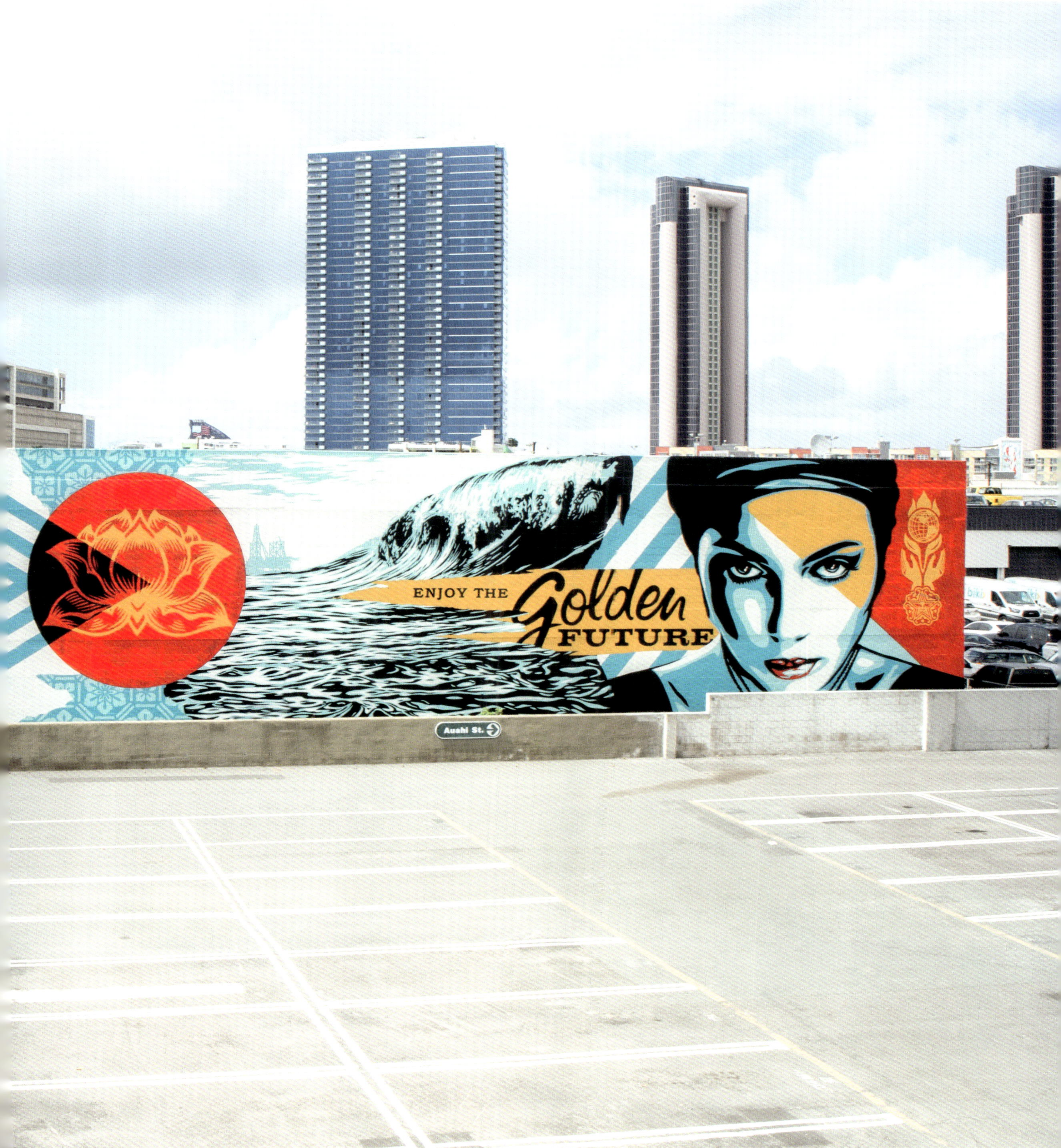
ENJOY THE
Golden
FUTURE
Auahi St.

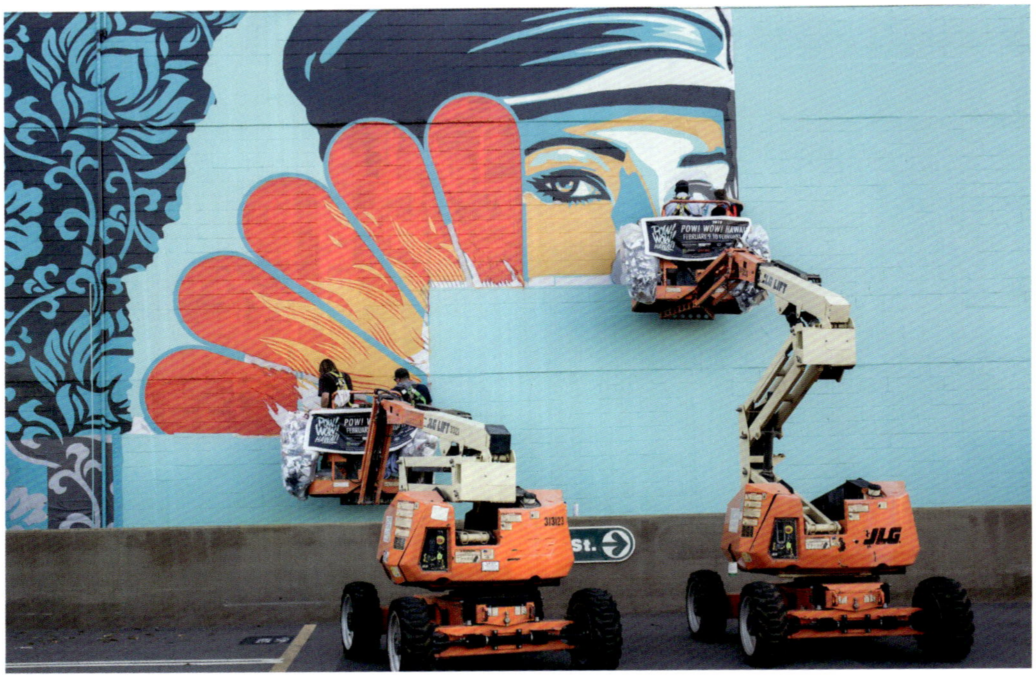
JLG

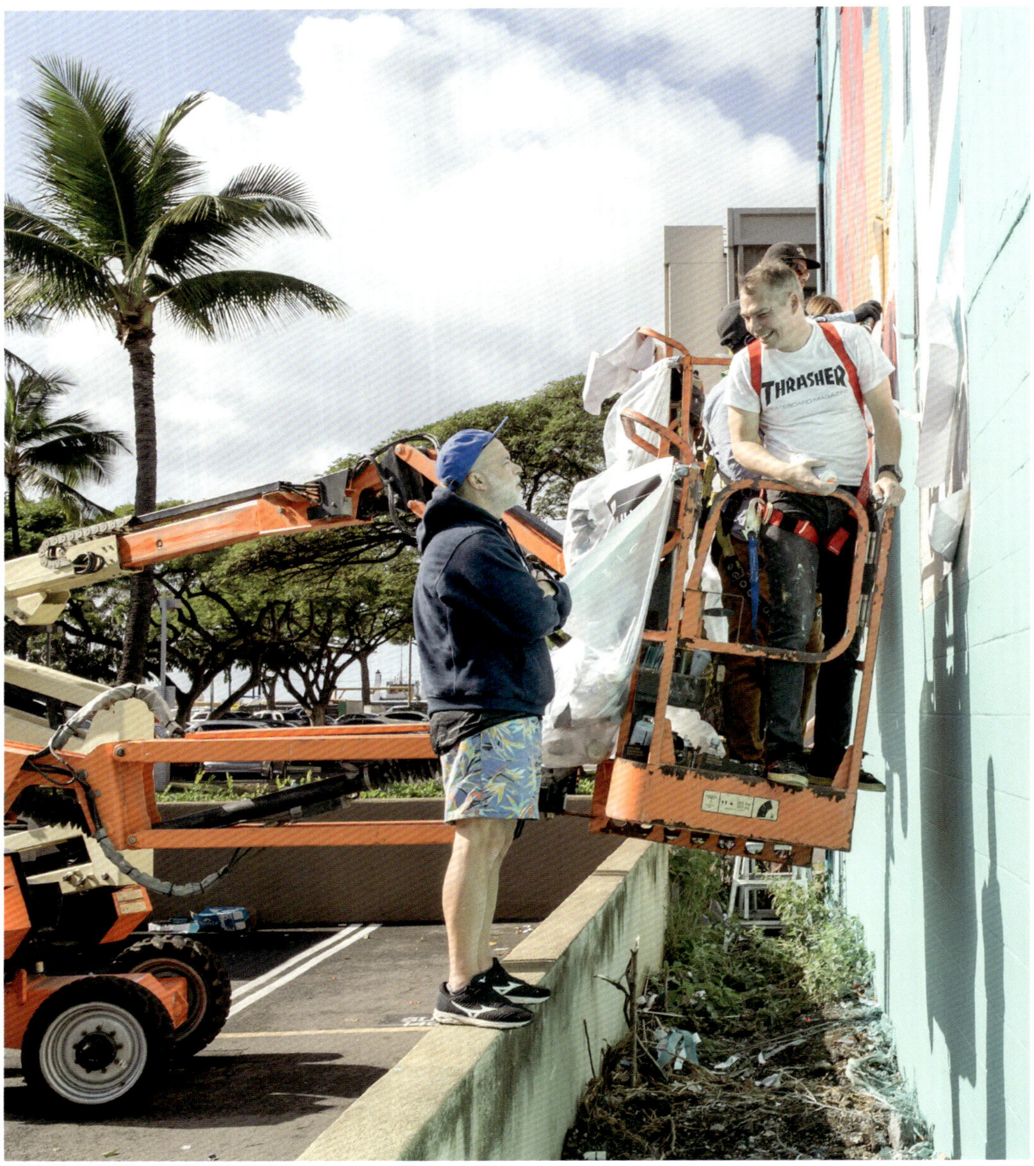
THRASHER

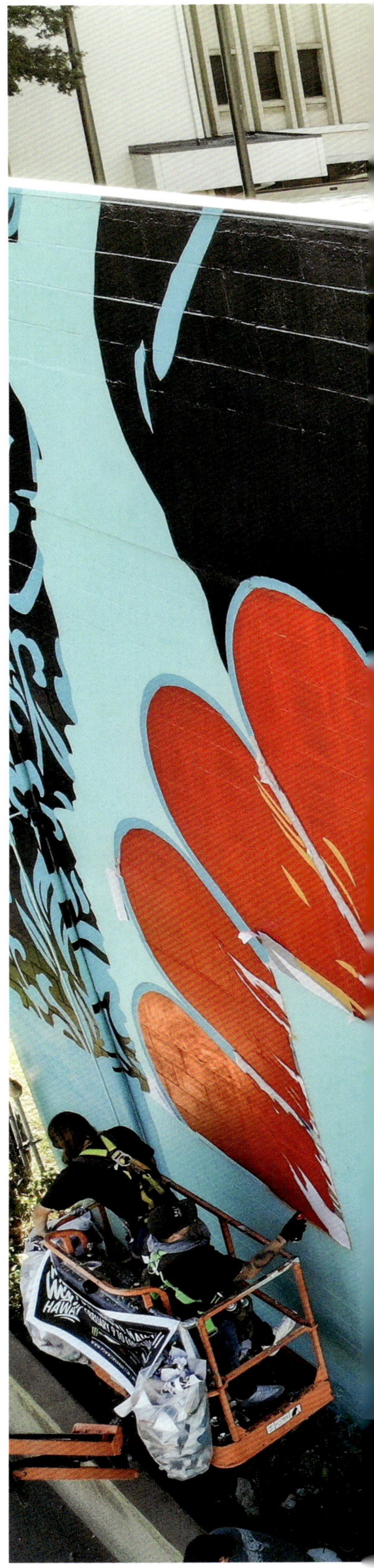

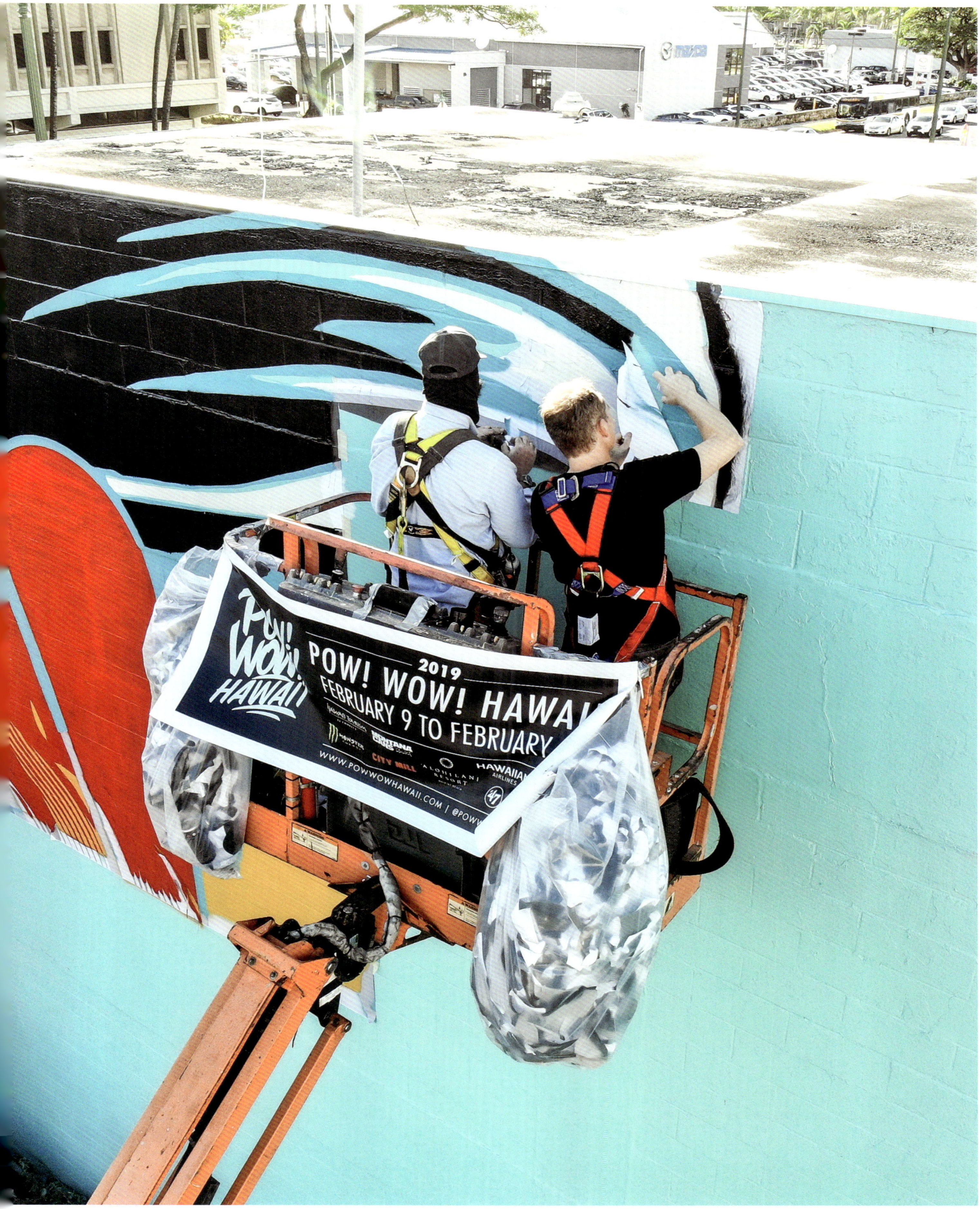
POW! WOW! HAWAII
2019
POW! WOW!
FEBRUARY 9 TO FEBRUARY
CITY MILL
HAWAIIAN AIRLINES
WWW.POWWOWHAWAII.COM

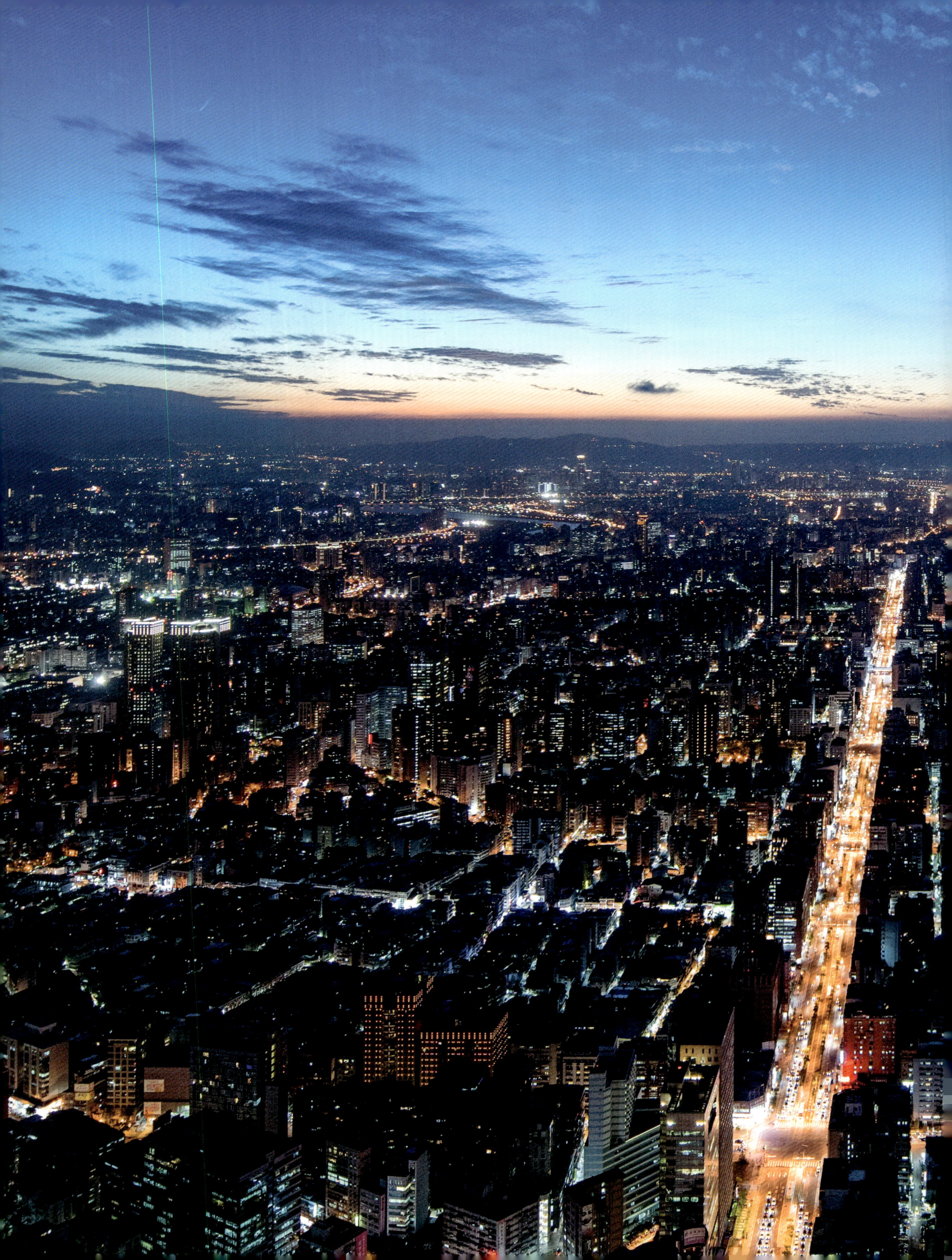

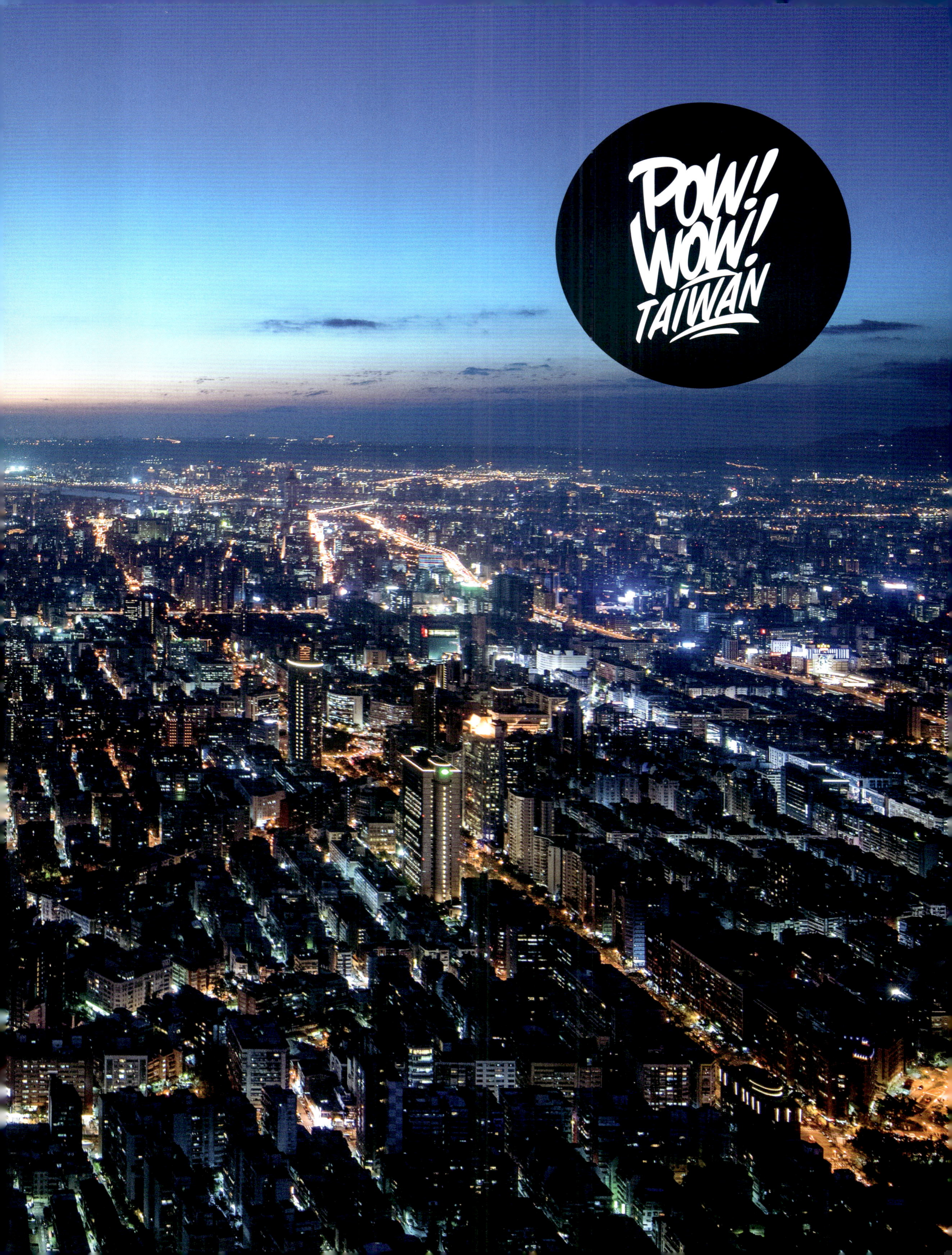
POW! WOW! TAIWAN

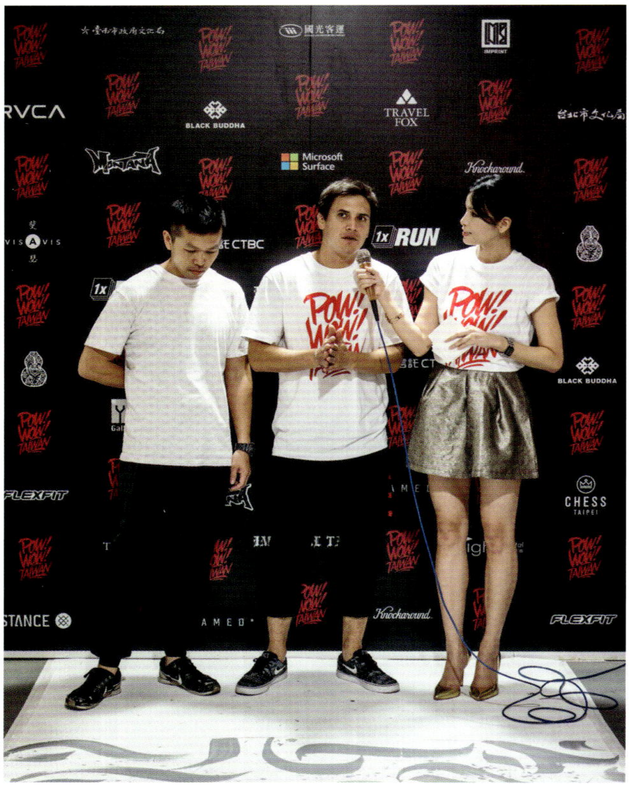
POW! WOW! TAIWAN
RVCA
BLACK BUDDHA
TRAVEL FOX
Microsoft Surface
1x RUN
CTBC
FLEXFIT
CHESS TAIPEI
STANCE

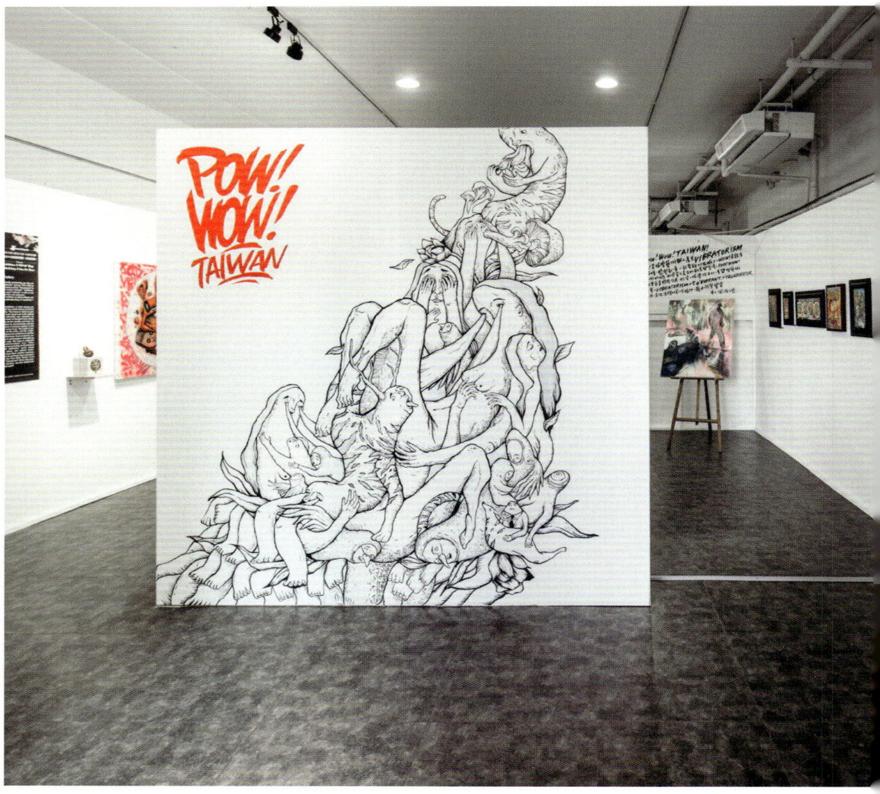
POW! WOW! TAIWAN

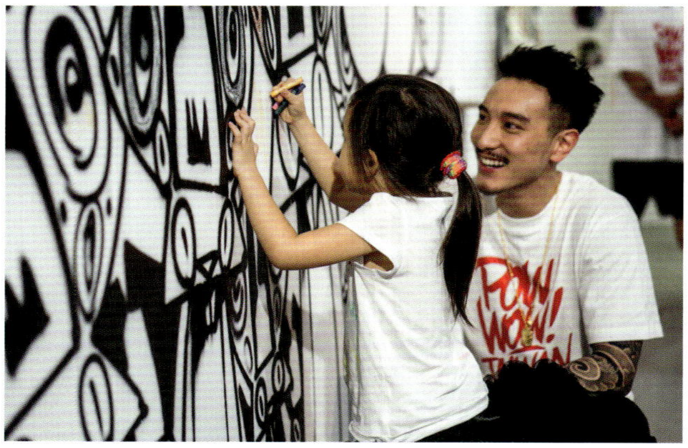
POW! WOW! TAIWAN

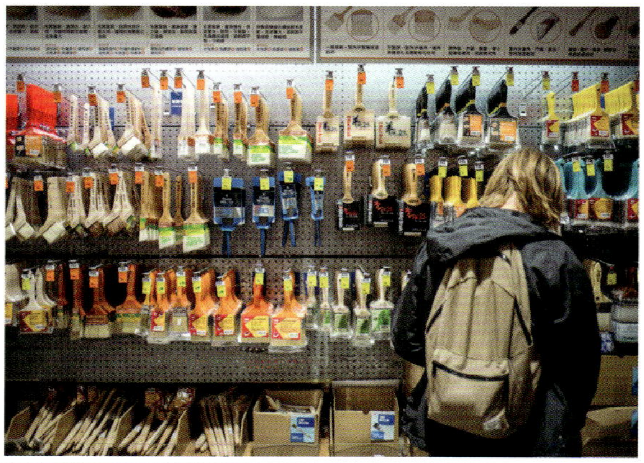

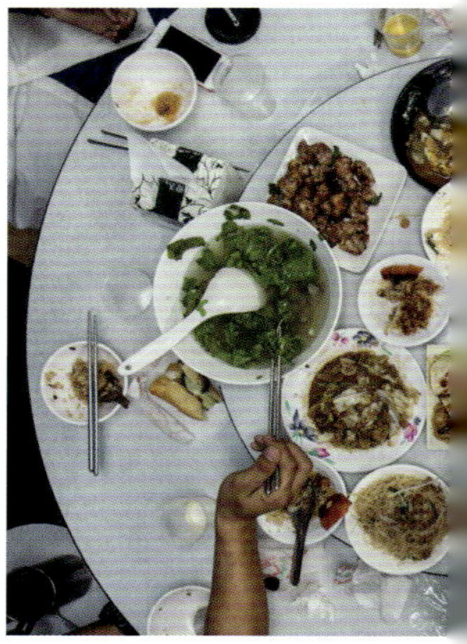

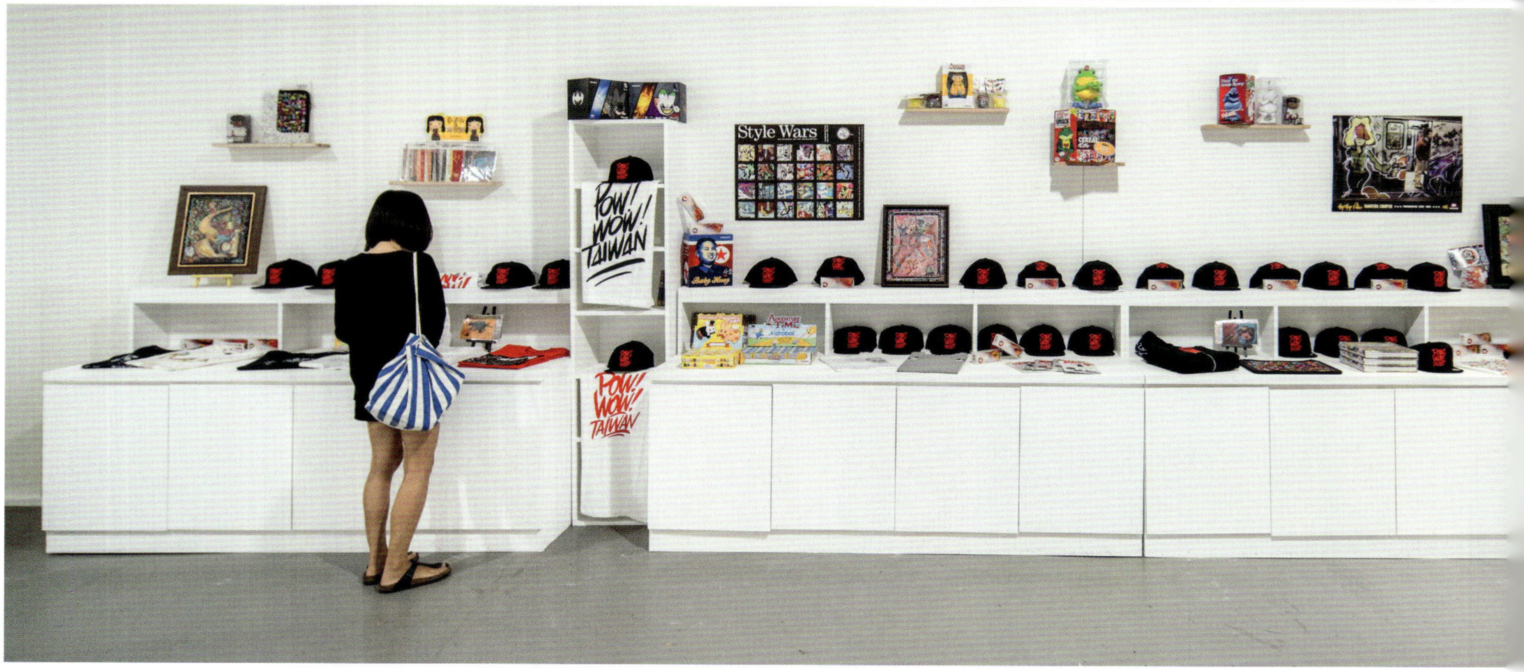
Style Wars
POW! WOW! TAIWAN

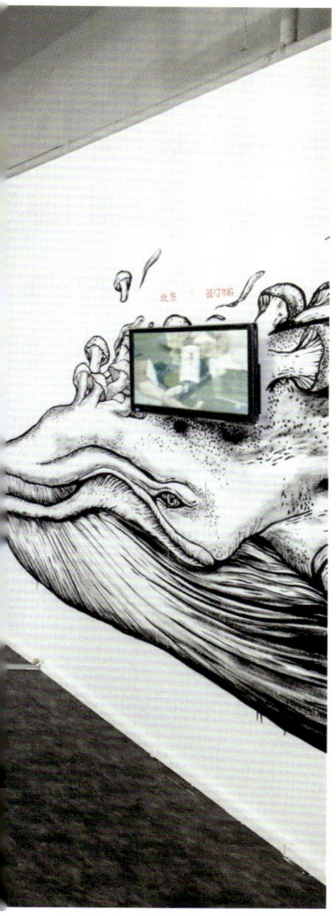

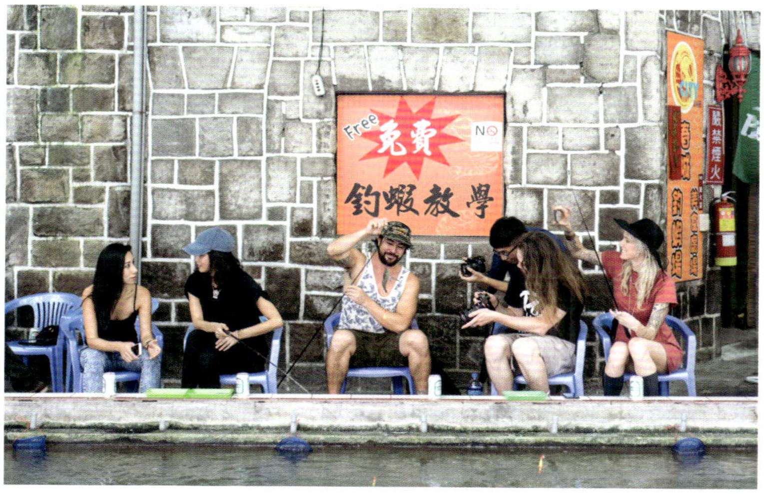

Free
免費
釣蝦教學

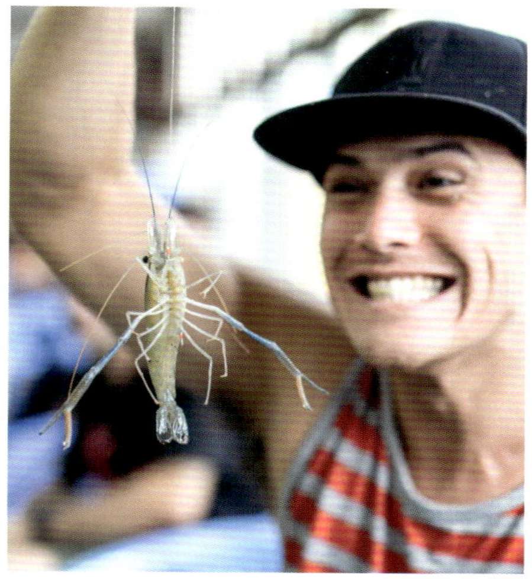

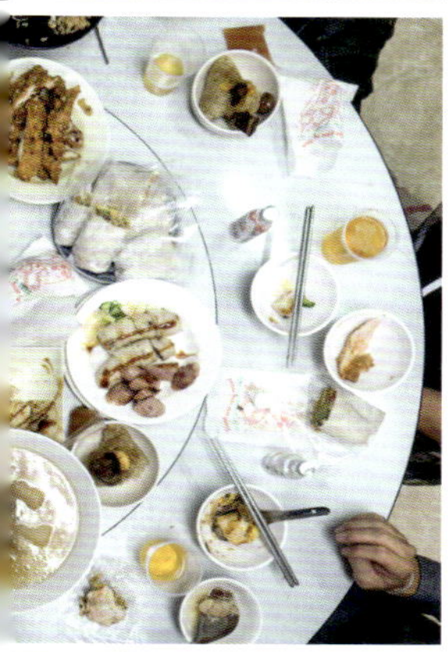

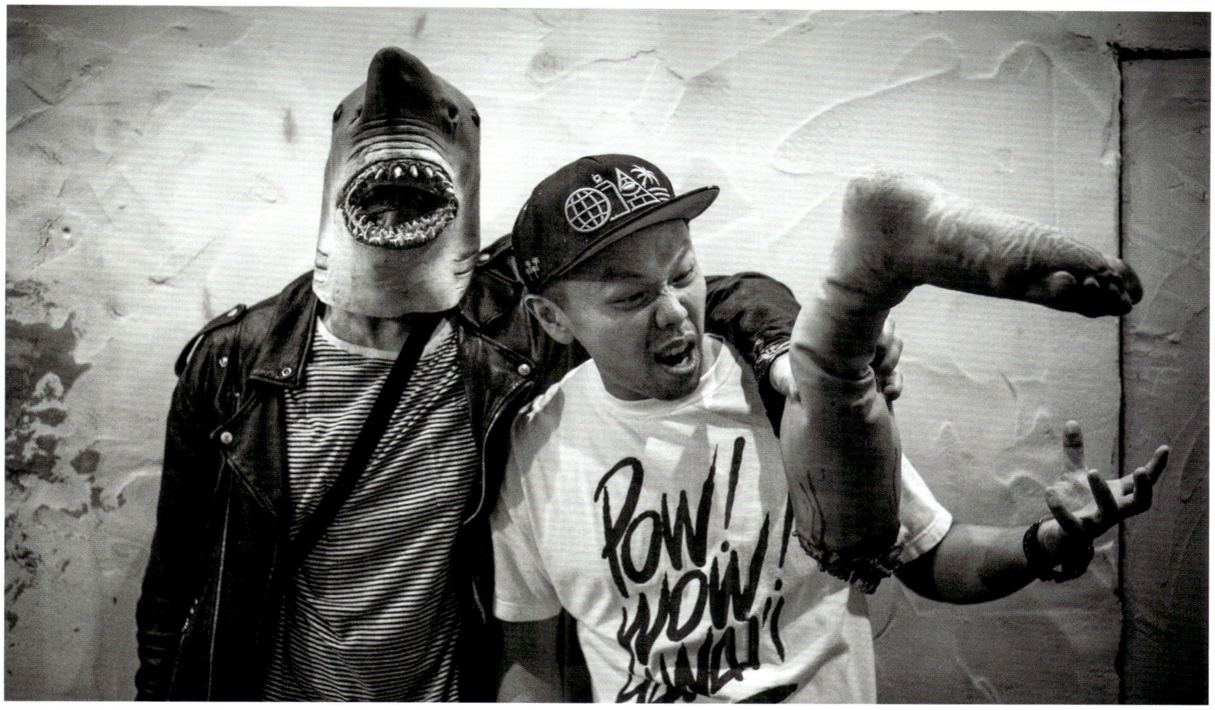

POW!
WOW!

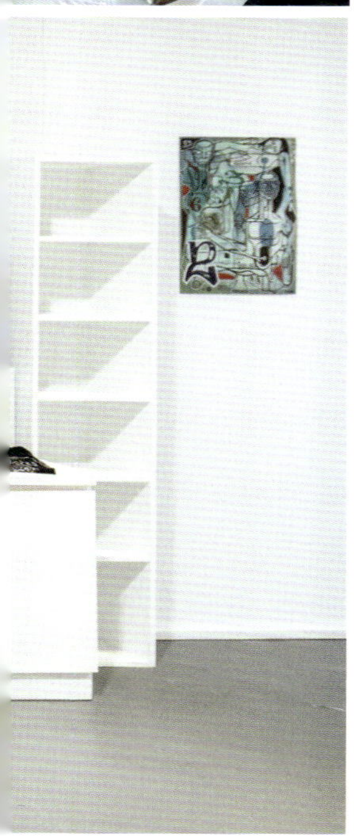

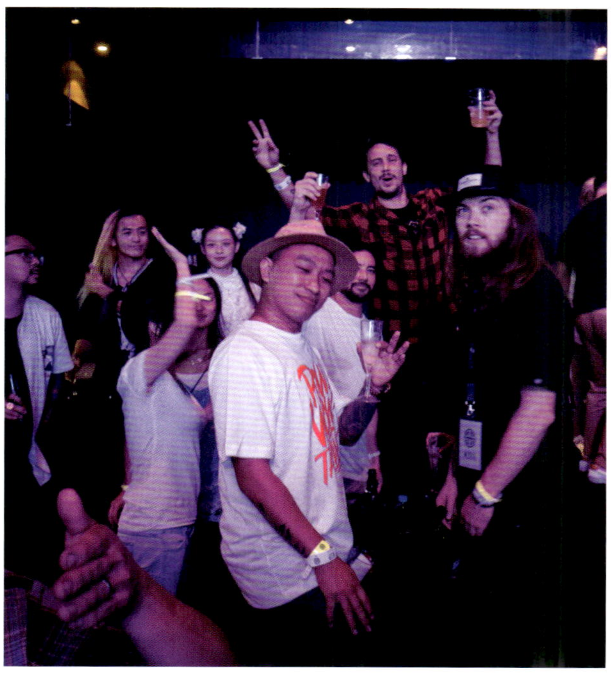

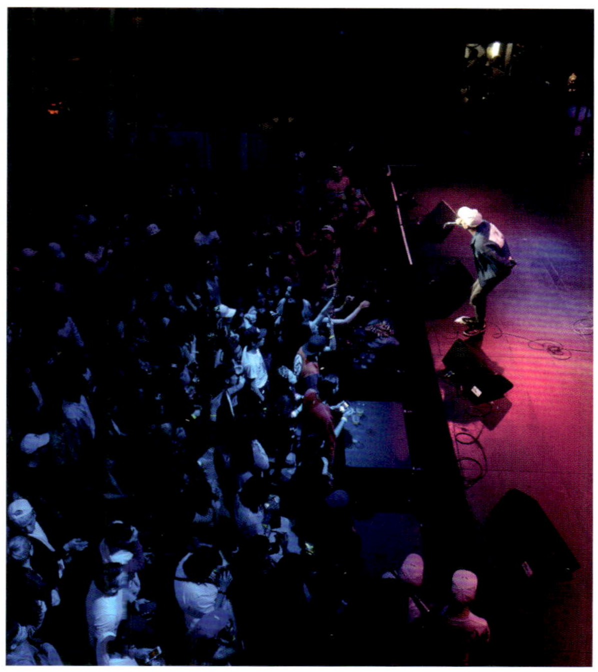

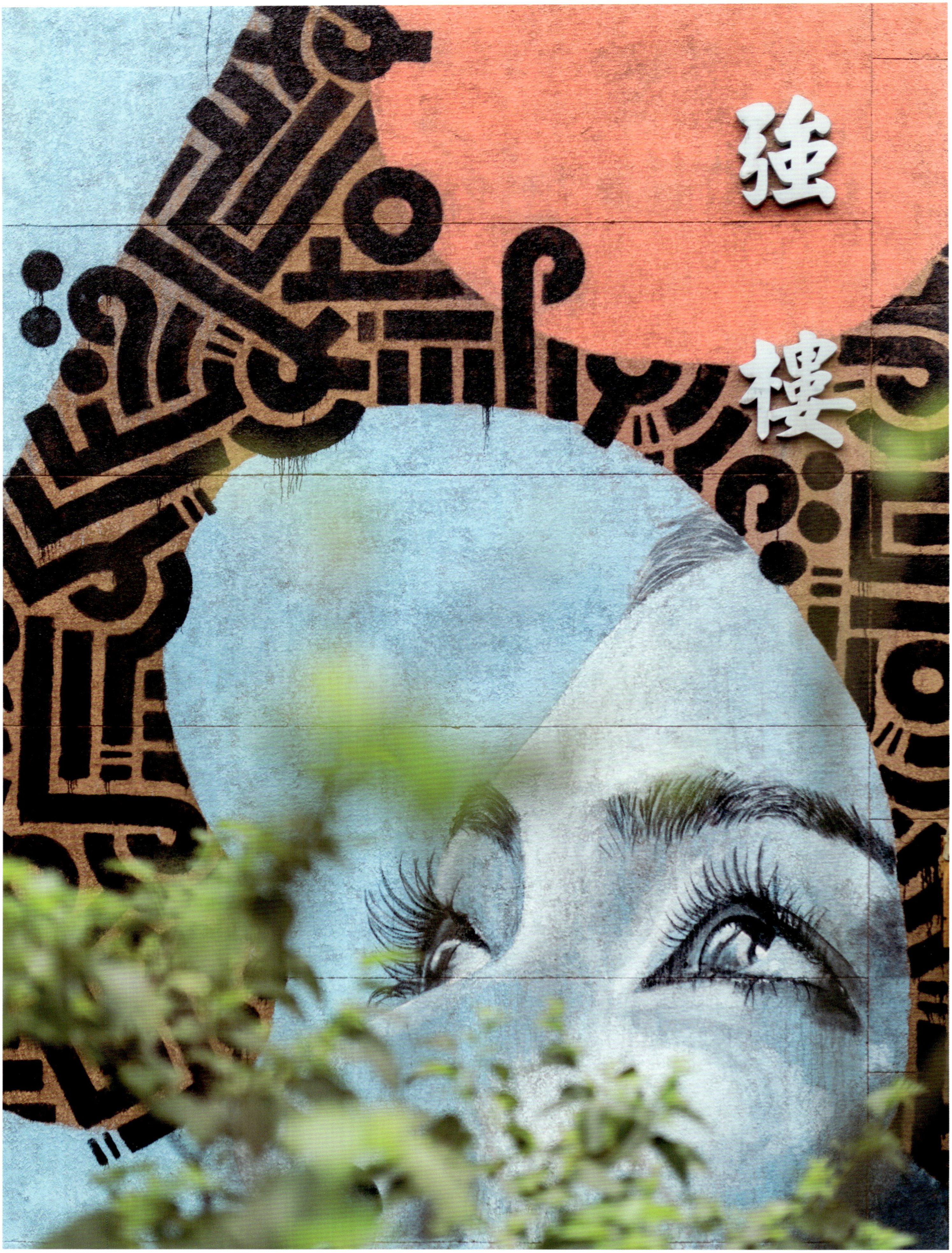
強
樓

Rone & Aaron de la Cruz

@R_O_N_E @ AARONDELACRUZ

Famous for his sumptuous paintings of glamorous women, in particular an often recurring image of his so-called Jane Doe, **Rone's** work attempts to locate the friction point between beauty and decay, the lavish and despoiled, creating an iconic form of urban art with a strongly emotional bent. Producing many of his early works either through a process of stenciling or screen-printing however, like fellow Everfresh member Meggs, Rone's movement toward a more freehand style of practice has enabled a certain amount of openness and looseness to seep into his images, a rawness which can perhaps be seen to have enhanced the affective quality they contained. A key individual in the Melbourne street art scene then, Rone's images have not only appeared all over his city itself but have increasingly began to appear all around the world too, his trademark figures, his heroic, alluring, cinematic icons manifesting themselves in ever larger, more elaborate and emotive forms.

Aaron De La Cruz's work, though minimal and direct at first, tends to overcome barriers of separation and freely steps in and out of the realms of design, graffiti, and illustration.

Sometimes a simple mark etched on a tree is as powerful as a masterpiece in a museum. It is this minimalist nature and his need to create with the least possible amount of mediums that makes Aaron De La Cruz's work so unique. He constantly battles for perfection with every mark he makes and that often leads to the misperception that it is machine made. To the contrary, his work is a free flow of ideas on surface that streams at a constant pace from his skilled hands. The goal of his work is to make the biggest mark on society with the bare minimum of mediums. A simple mark etched on the world.

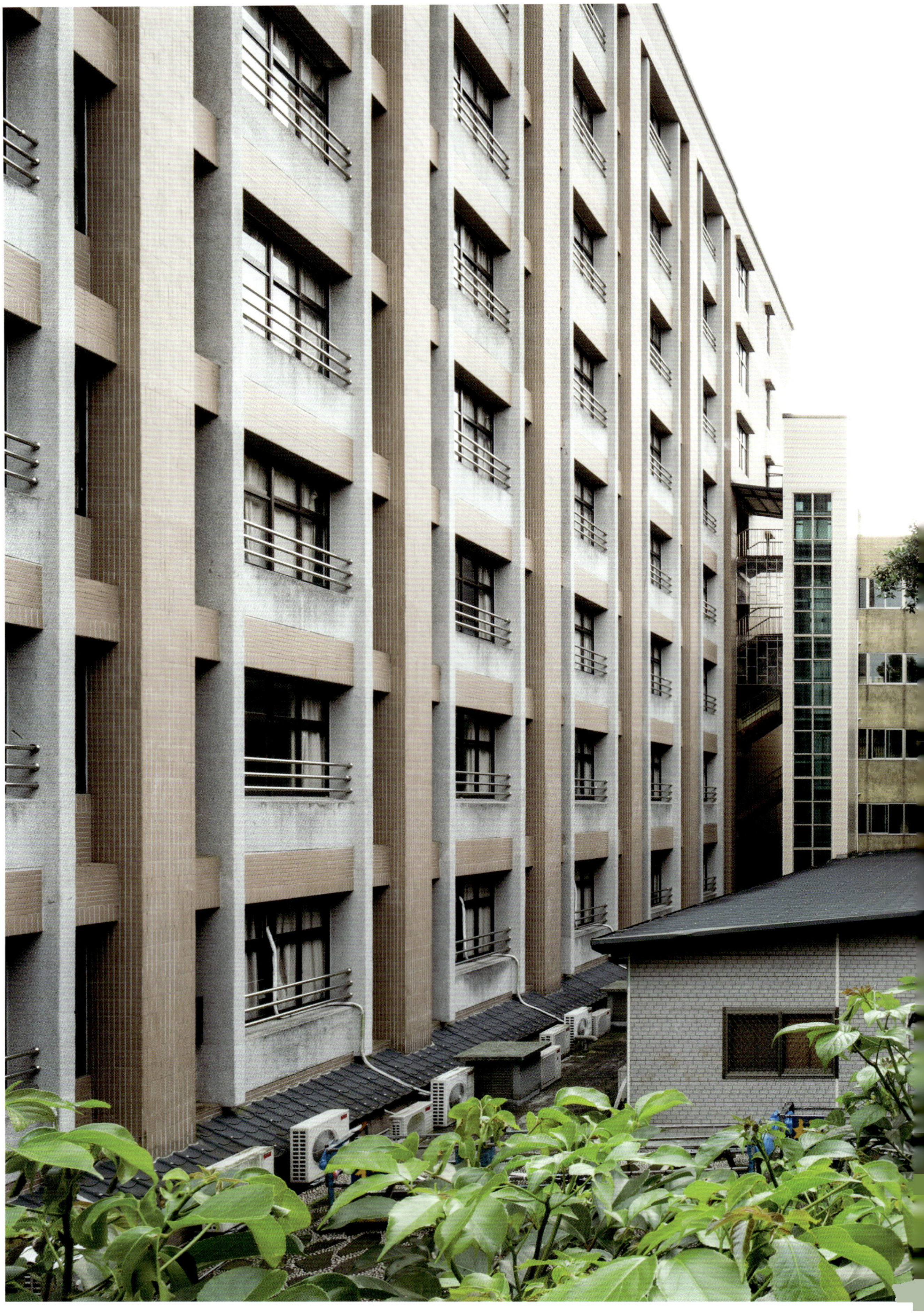

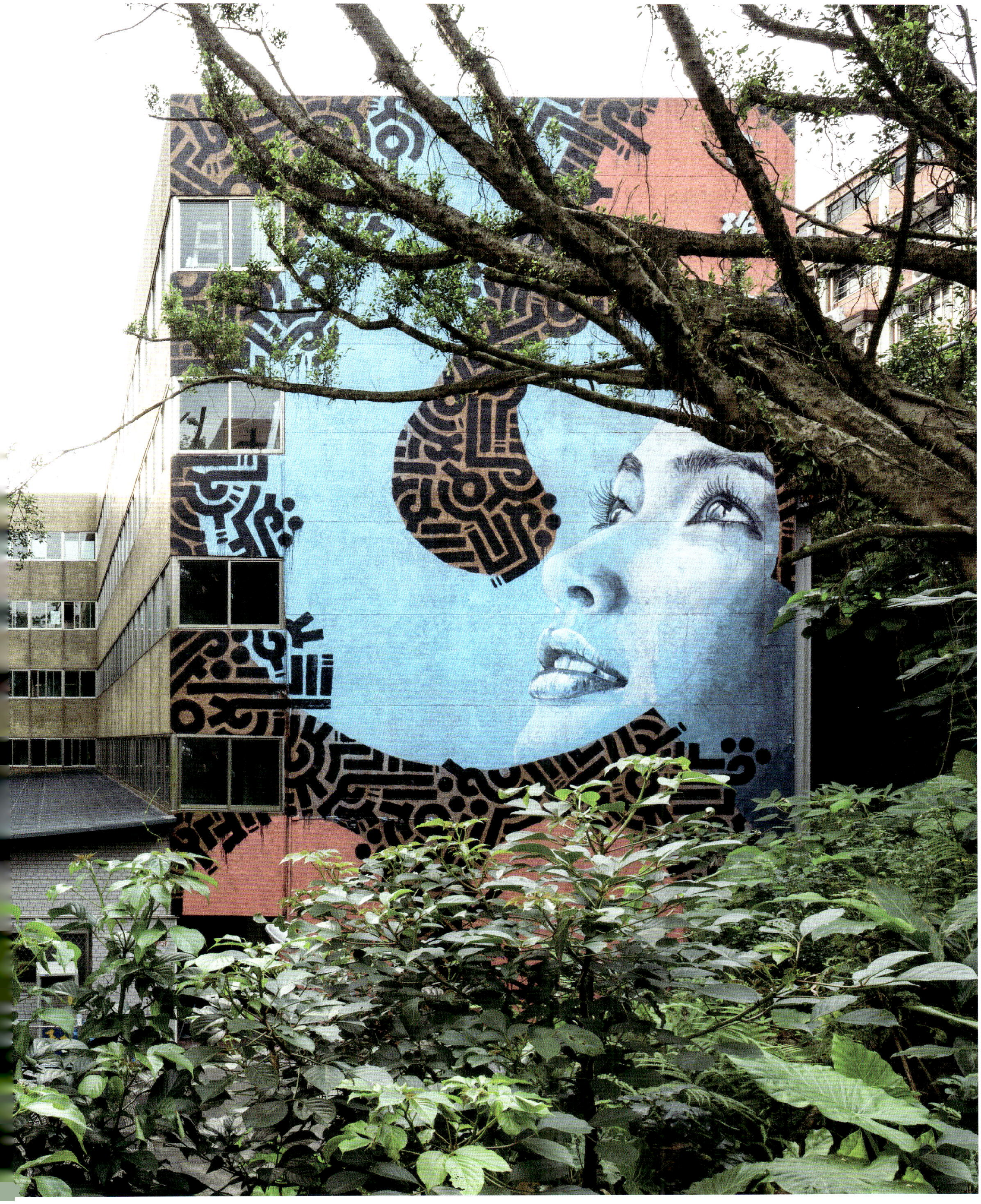

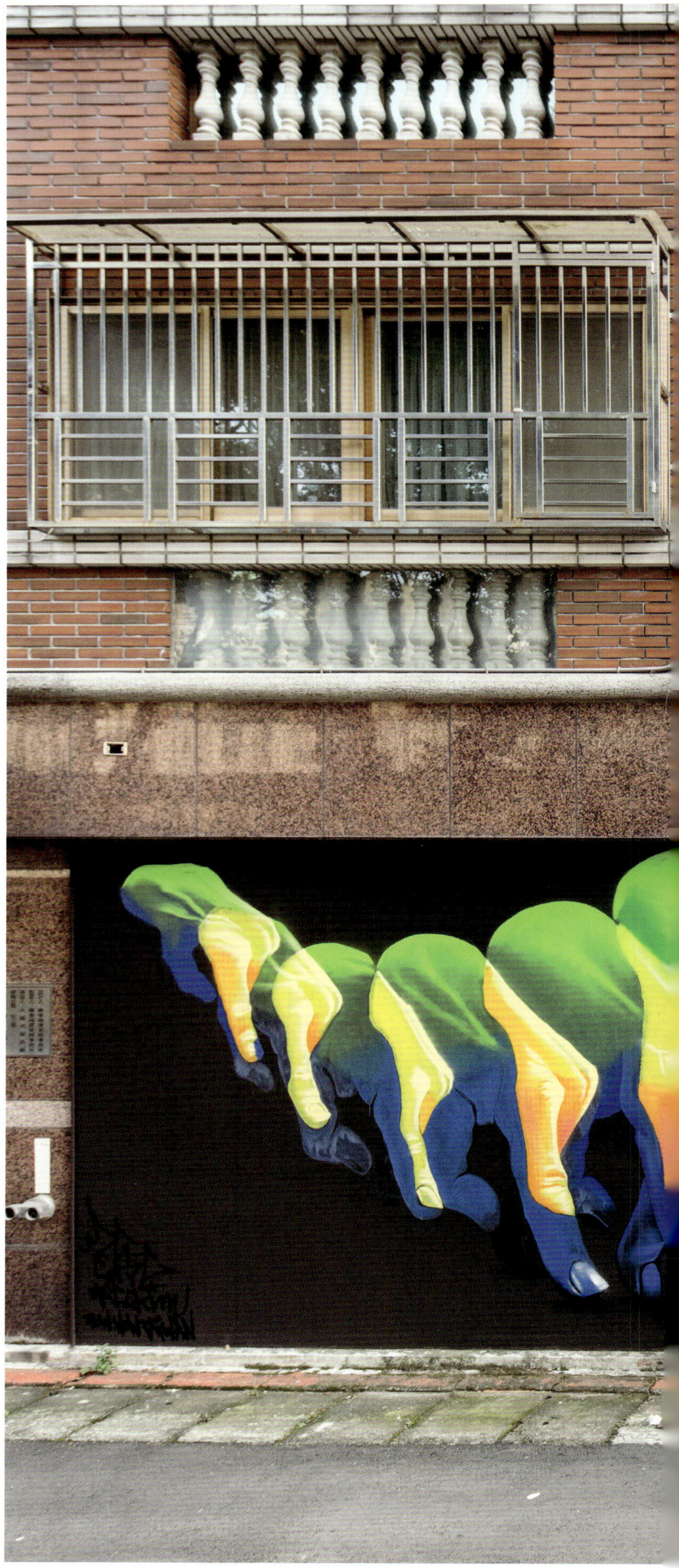

Case Maclaim

@CASE_MACLAIM

Case Maclaim is a German Graffiti Artist living in Frankfurt. His images are based on the re-presentation of body shapes and photo-realistic portraits. He is one of the four members of the "Maclaim Crew", which was founded in 2000 and is considered as pioneers in photo-realistic representation within the graffiti scene. He focuses on the body which he abstracts from its human origin to give way for narrative, monstrous, animalistic or mythic elements. The usual ideal of beauty is replaced by bizarre-controversial characteristics, vexing but simultaneously fascinating. Also the world of emotions is traced perpetually: Uncertainty, melancholy and the constant fight of being a human are broached as the issue. The figurative subjects impress by their perfect execution and their excellent mixture of pictorial pureness and high narrative value.

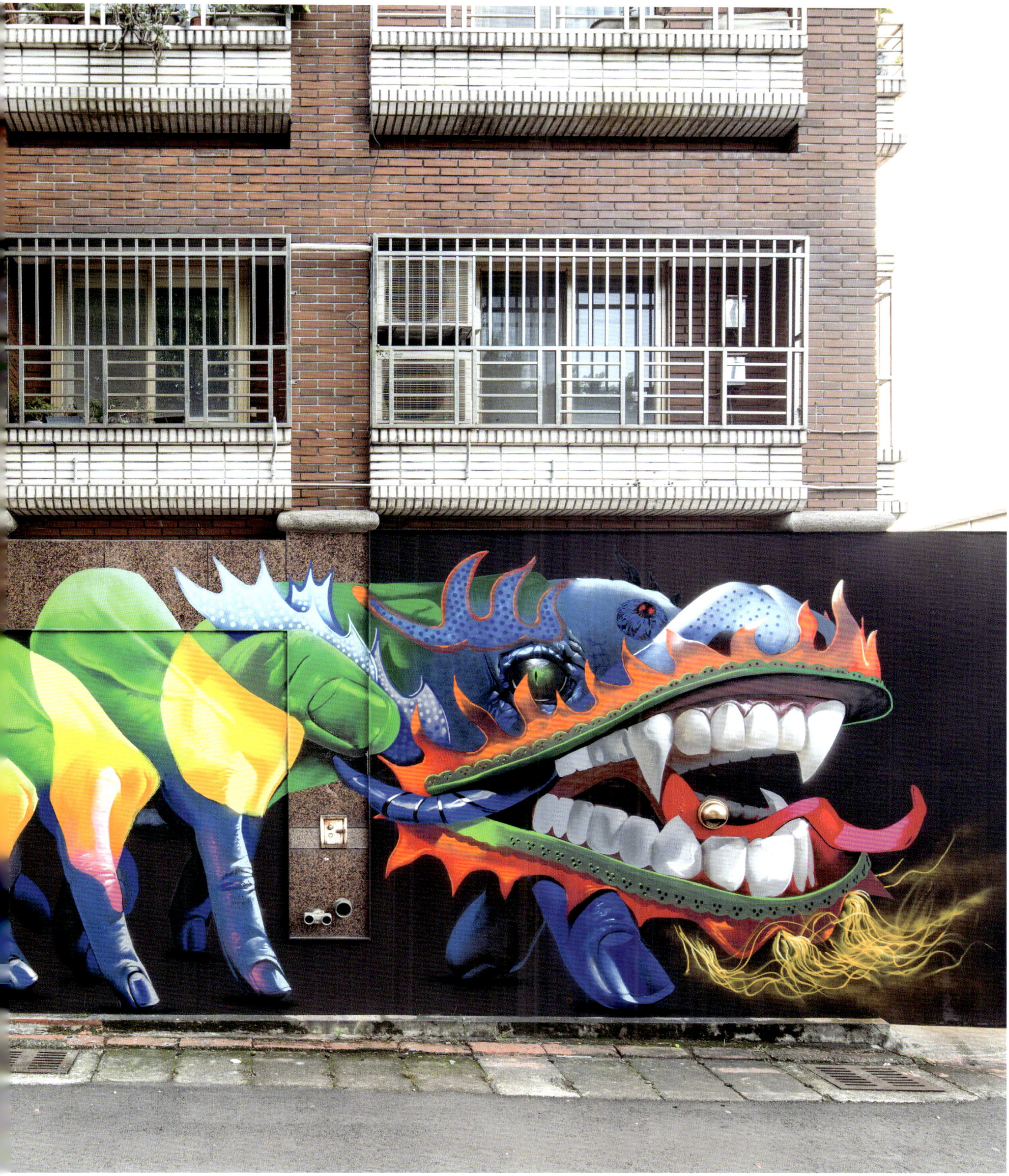

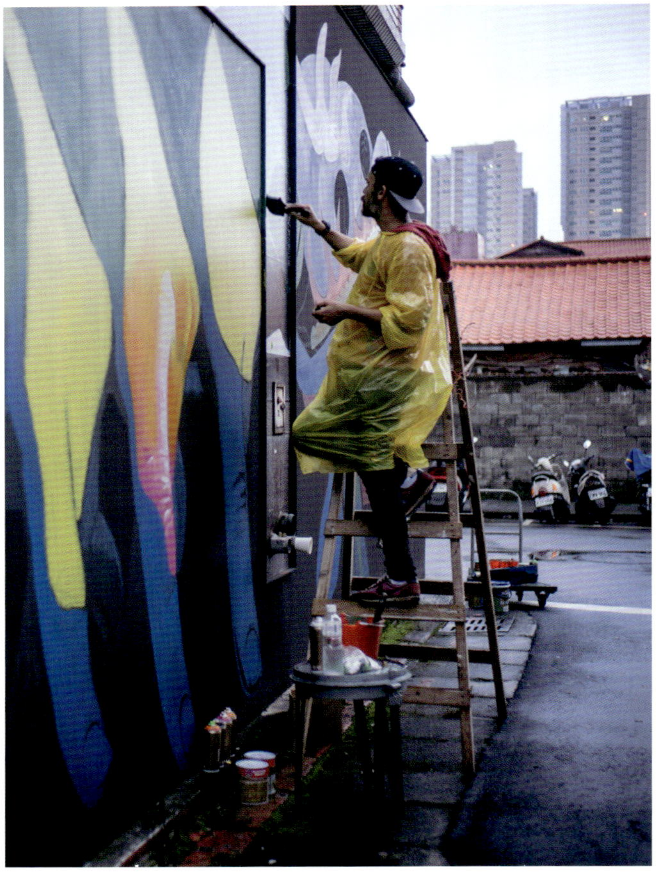

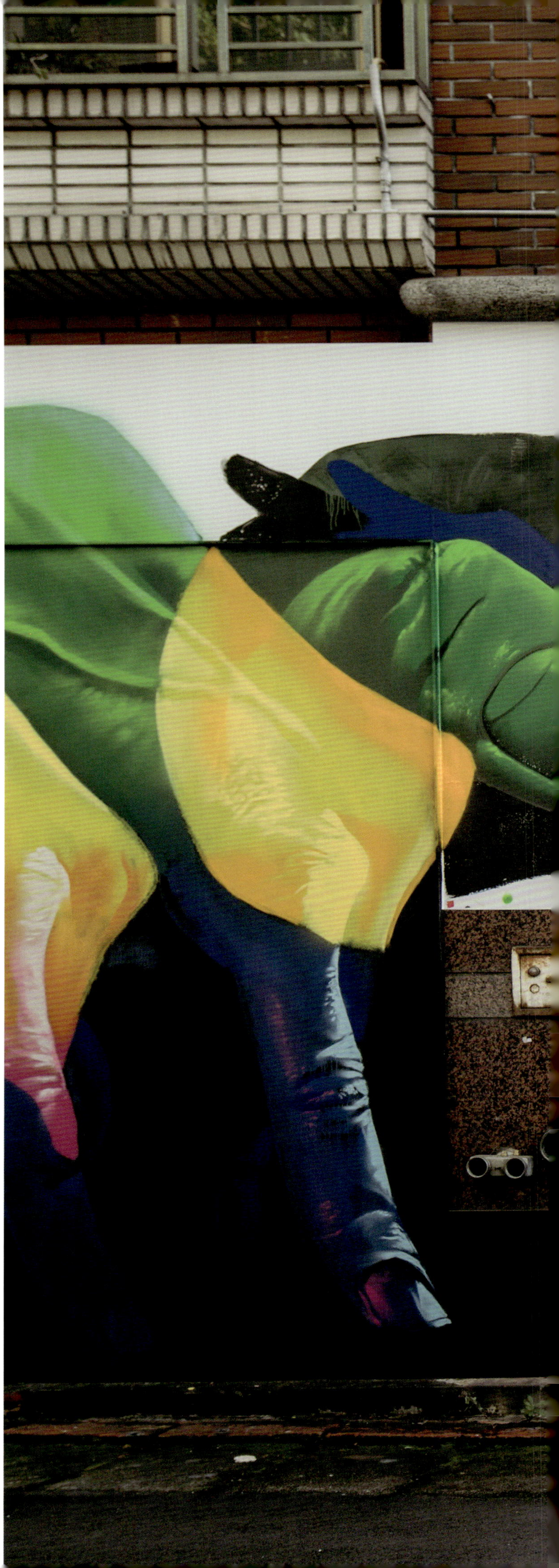

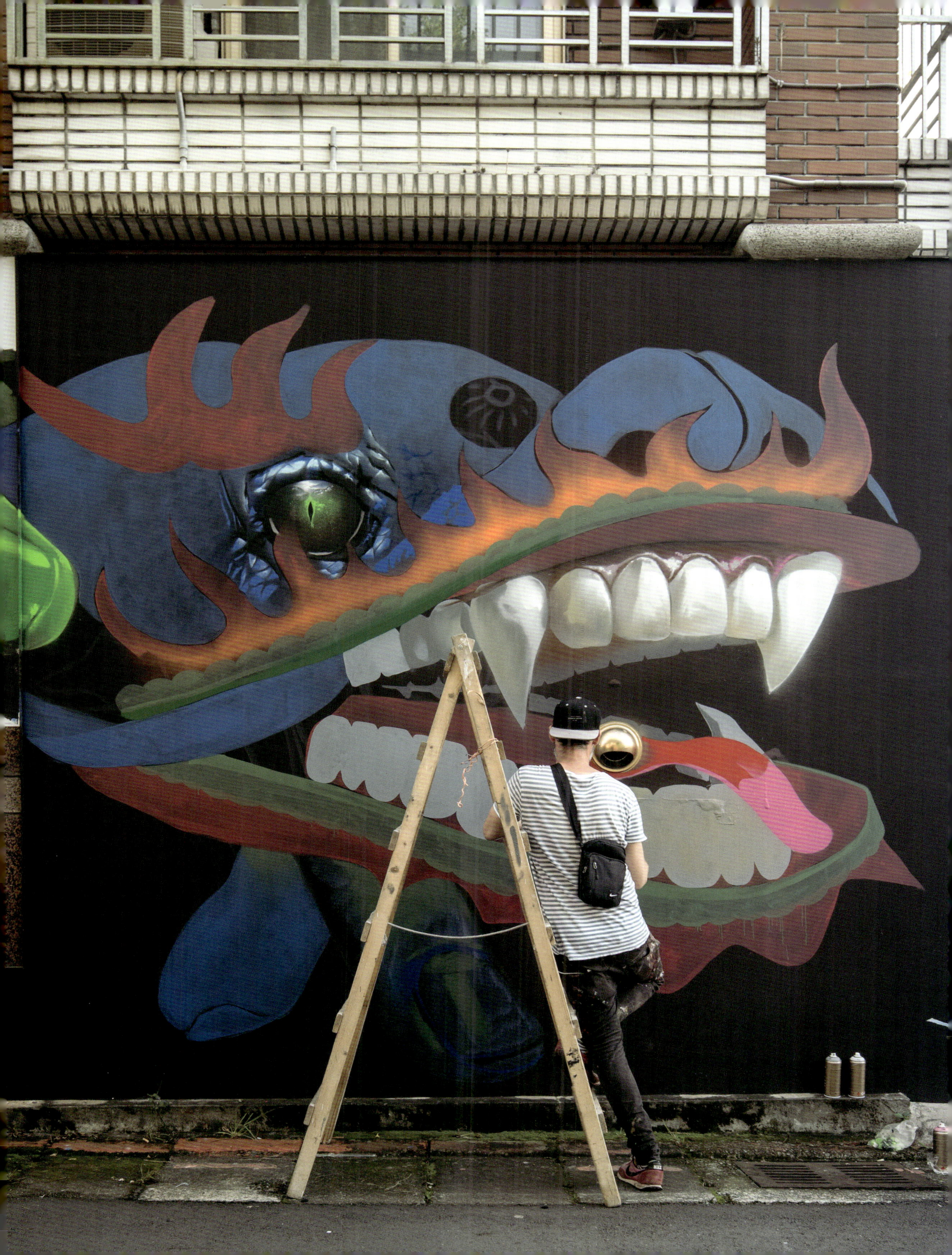

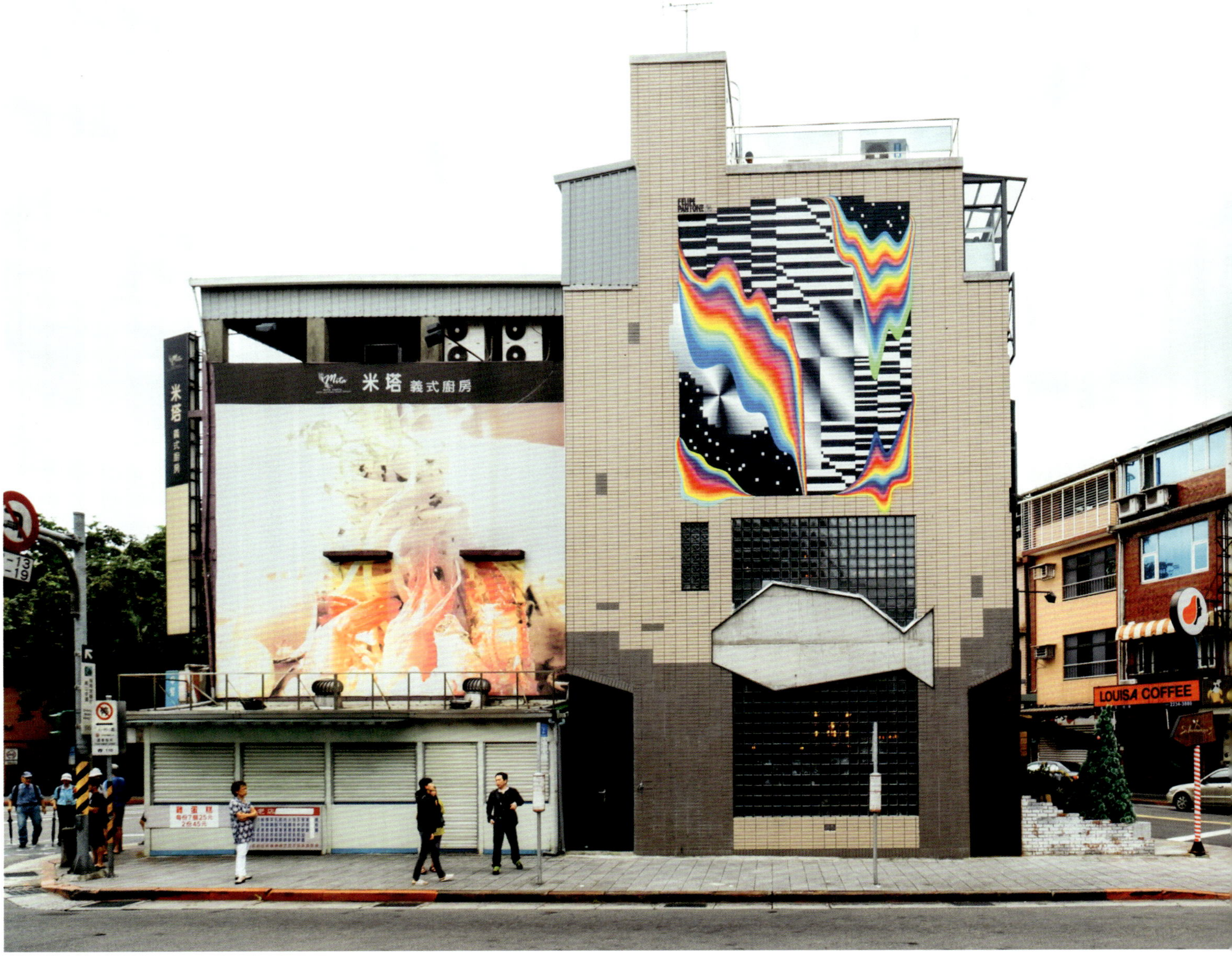

Taiwan 2016

Felipe Pantone

@FELIPEPANTONE

Felipe Pantone evokes a spirit in his work that feels like a collision between an analog past and a digitized future, where human beings and machines will inevitably glitch alongside one another in a prism of neon gradients, geometric shapes, optical patterns, and jagged grids.

Based in Spain, Pantone is a byproduct of the technological age when kids unlocked life's mysteries through the Internet. As a result of this prolonged screen time, he explores how the displacement of the light spectrum impacts color and repetition.

"Color only happens because of light, and light is the only reason why life happens," Pantone says. "Light and color are the very essence of visual art. Thanks to television, computers, and modern lighting, our perception of light and color has changed completely."

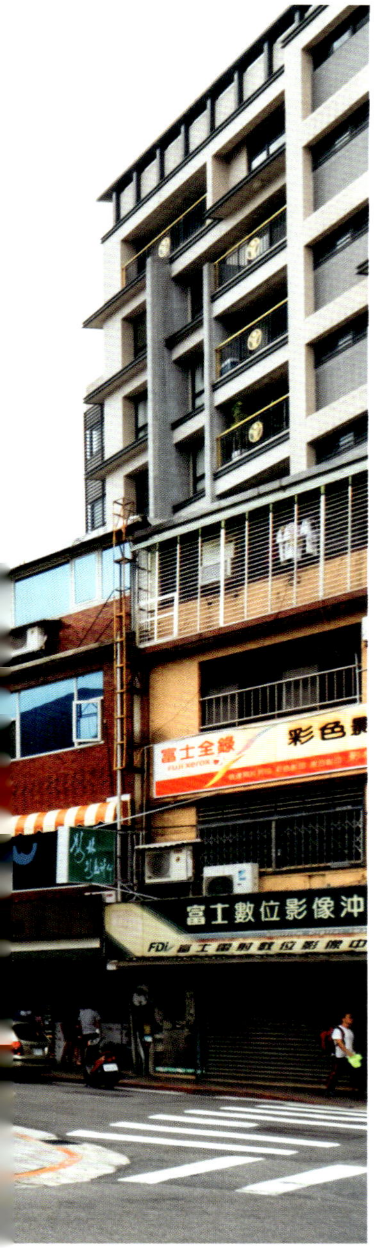

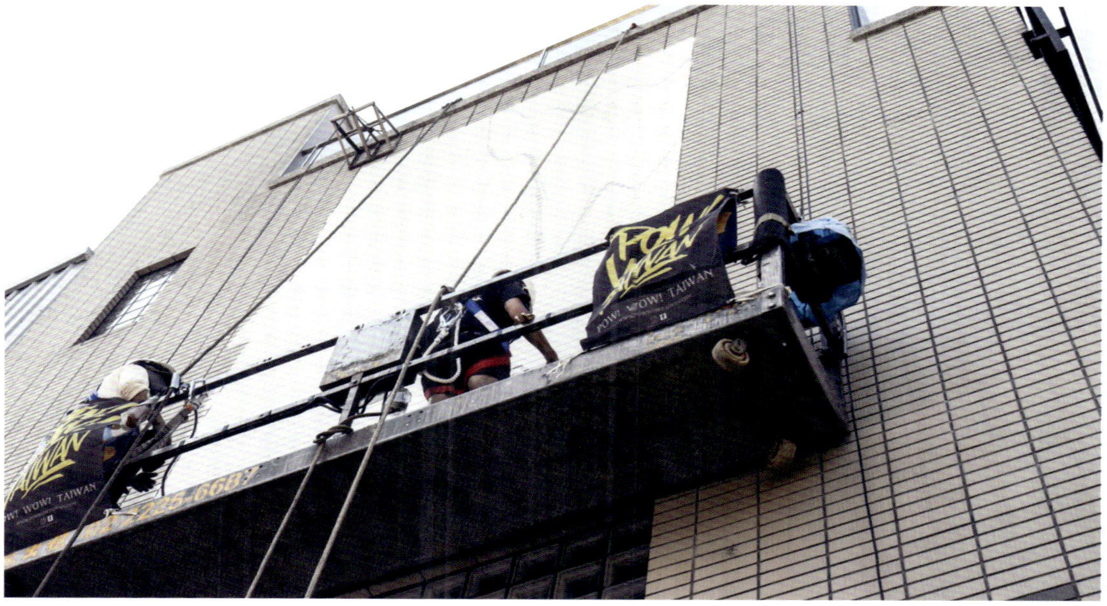

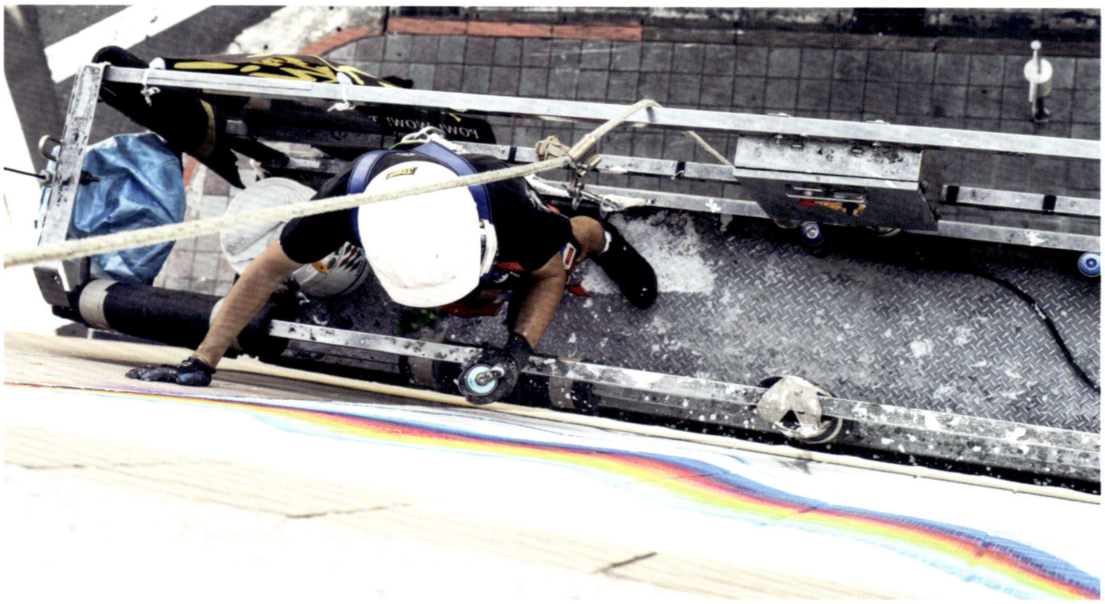

For Pantone, his art is a meditation on the ways we consume visual information. Drawing inspiration from kinetic artist like Victor Vasarely and Carlos Cruz-Diez — who both utilized the moiré effect (in which lines of contrasting color give the impression of movement) — his contemporary work produces the sensation of vibration as the viewer's position changes in relation to the work.

To achieve the desired effect, Pantone utilizes modeling software which allows for 3D insights into a project, which then can be translated into frescoes, murals, paintings, and sculptures which give tactile merit to what is occurring in the digital world.

"I grew up as a simple painter, trained as a painter, and now my biggest goal is to get clear of all the academic training and to be able to make art freely, with the tools that work best," he says.

Whether it's exhibiting in galleries around the world, transforming a 1984 Chevrolet Corvette into something futuristic, or painting the largest mural in Portugal, Pantone's diverse applications are united by the intersection of technology and fine art.

"I try to create things that are not supposed to be where they are," he says. "To bring awareness of certain things, to move people's thoughts elsewhere."

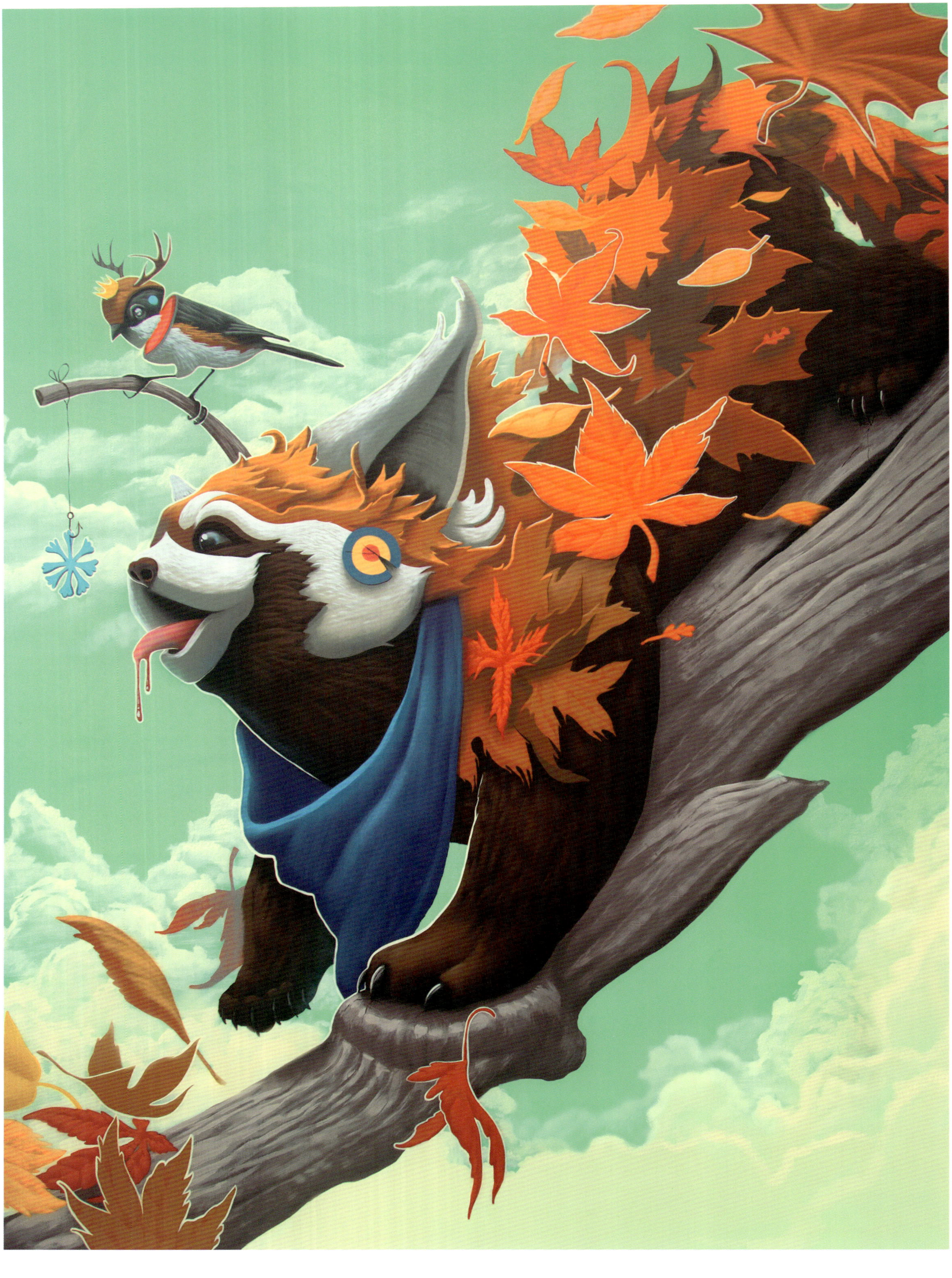

Dulk

@DULK1

Antonio Segura (Dulk) was born in Valencia where he still lives. Dulk is an all-purpose artist. Between urban art, drawing, painting, sculpture, each medium is a challenge that he takes up with pleasure and determination. His art has evolved in a remarkable way in recent years but its essence has always been the same. His naturalistic worlds show us a tragi-comic and surrealistic themed landscape full of details, sometimes real sometimes fiction but always inviting us to dive on them. His compositions recreate biological environments involved in antagonistic concepts. With a soft chromatic palette, Dulk creates a oneiric narrative scenario full of characters, which is the first visualization transmits beauty and calm but that will lead us to a deeper meaning in the following observations. The artistic evolution of the work is projected beyond the perfection of the technique and the detail that invite you to get lost or the spaces where you can get carried away. The study has led to subsequent incorporation into a plastic language, endowing creations with the autonomy that allows the viewer to be free in the dialogue with the work and share with it an open story.

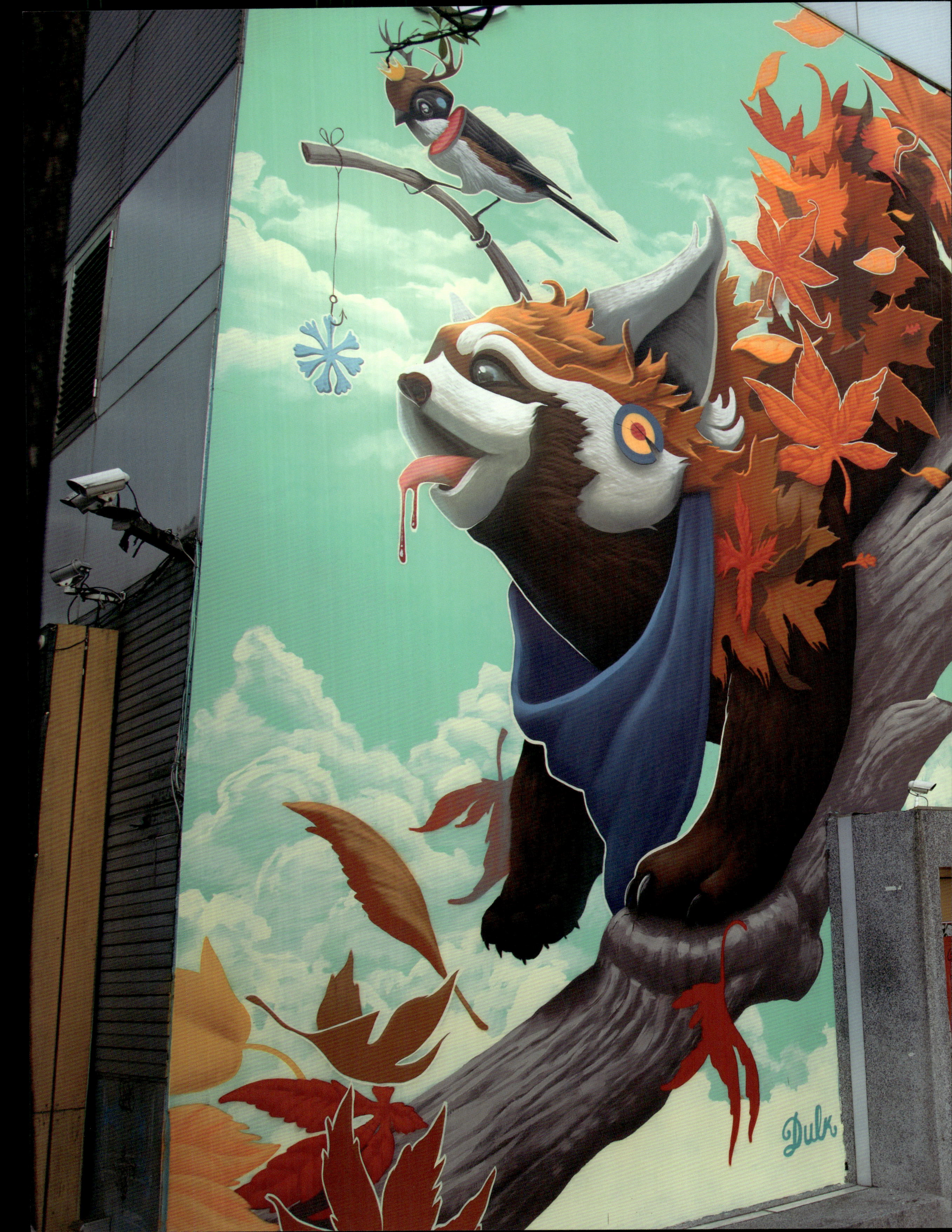
Dulk

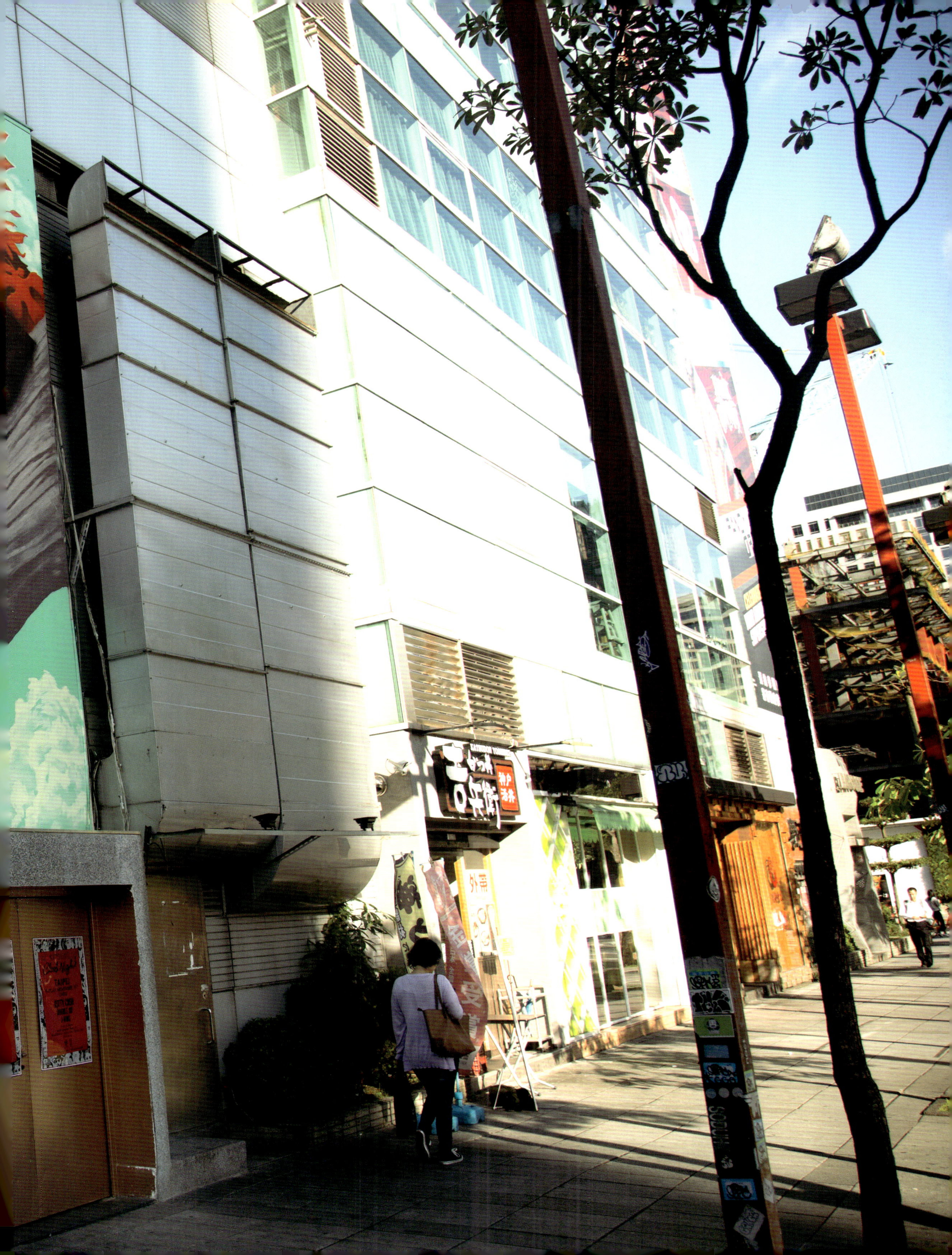
かつ丼
吉兵衛
外帶
TAIPEI

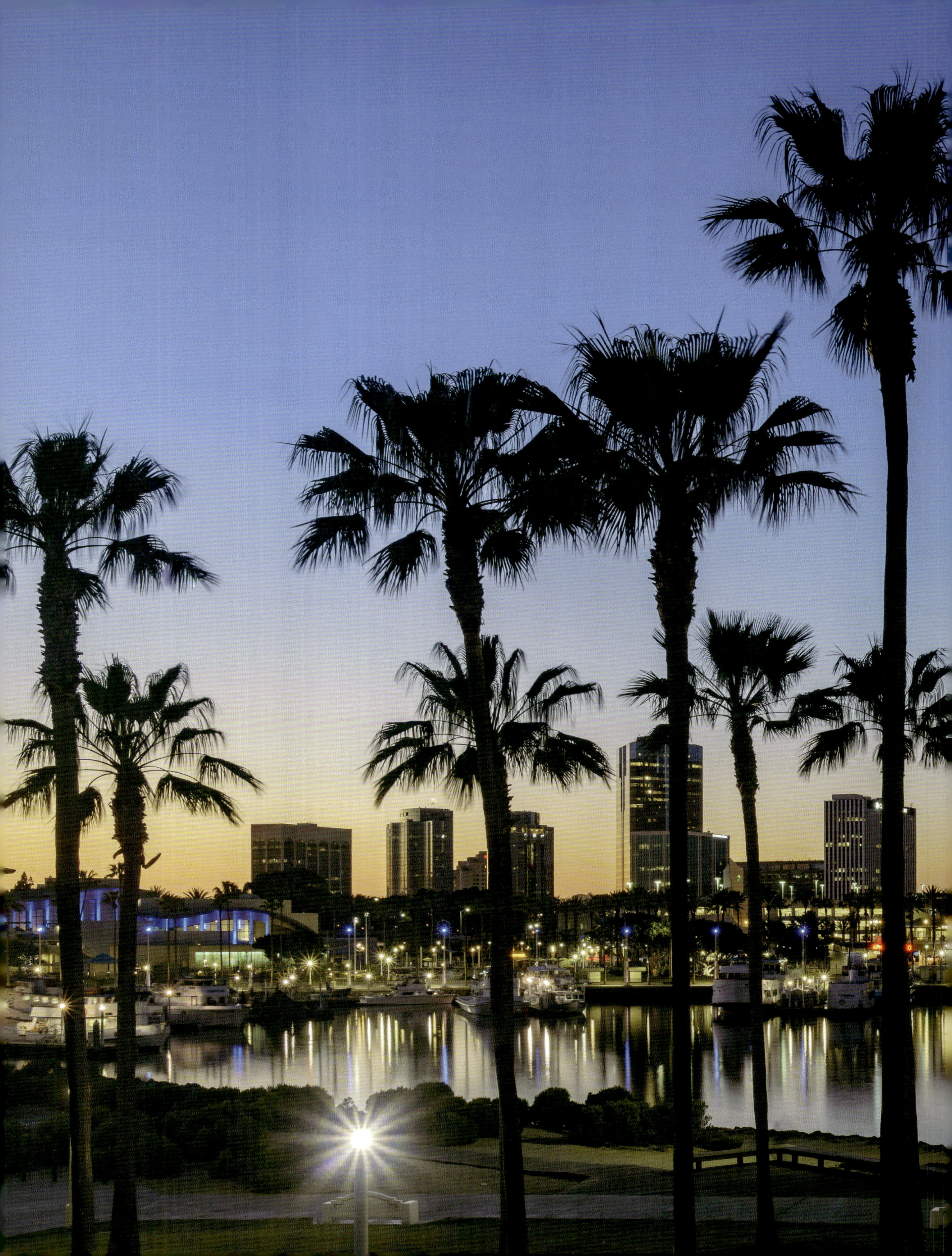

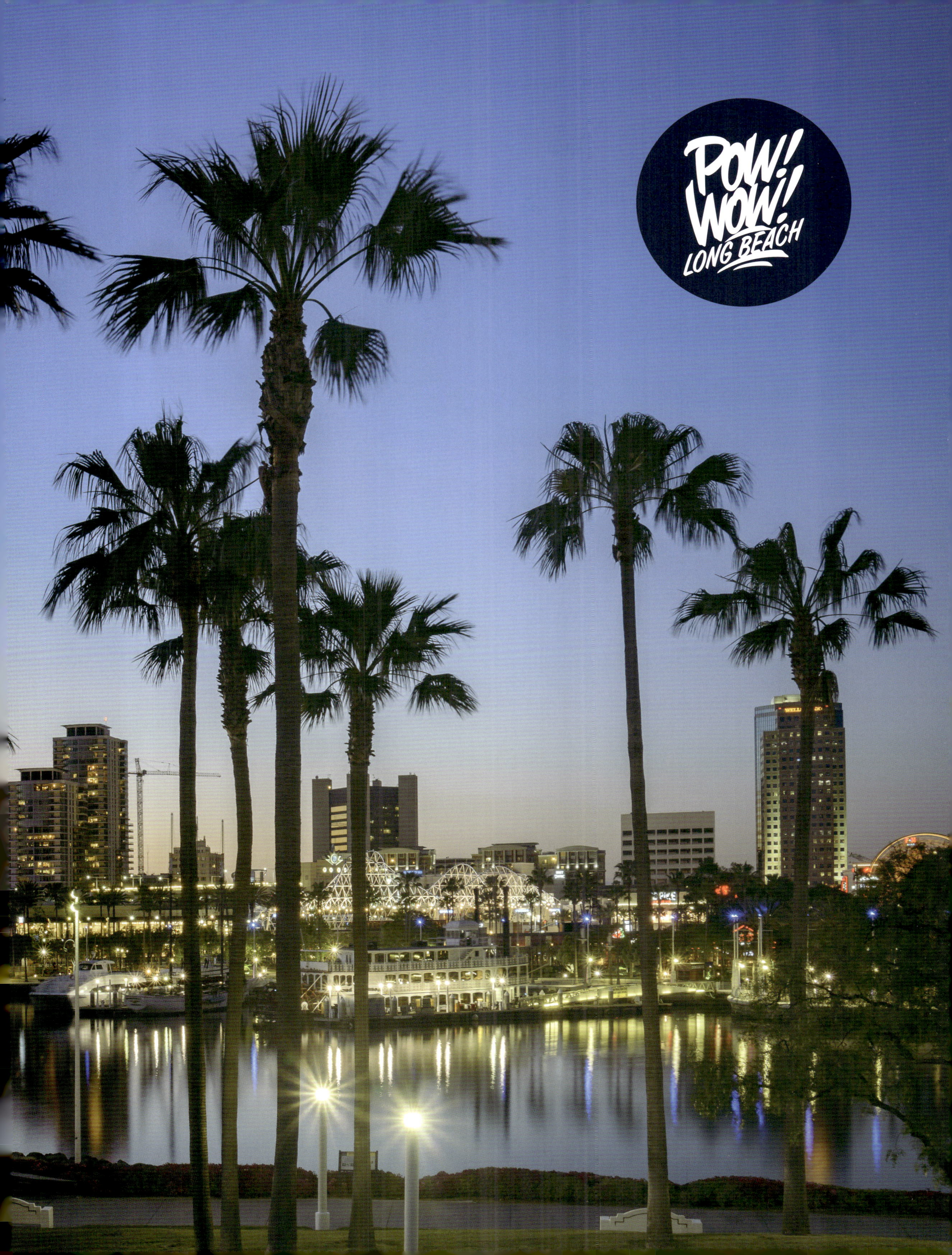
POW! WOW!
LONG BEACH

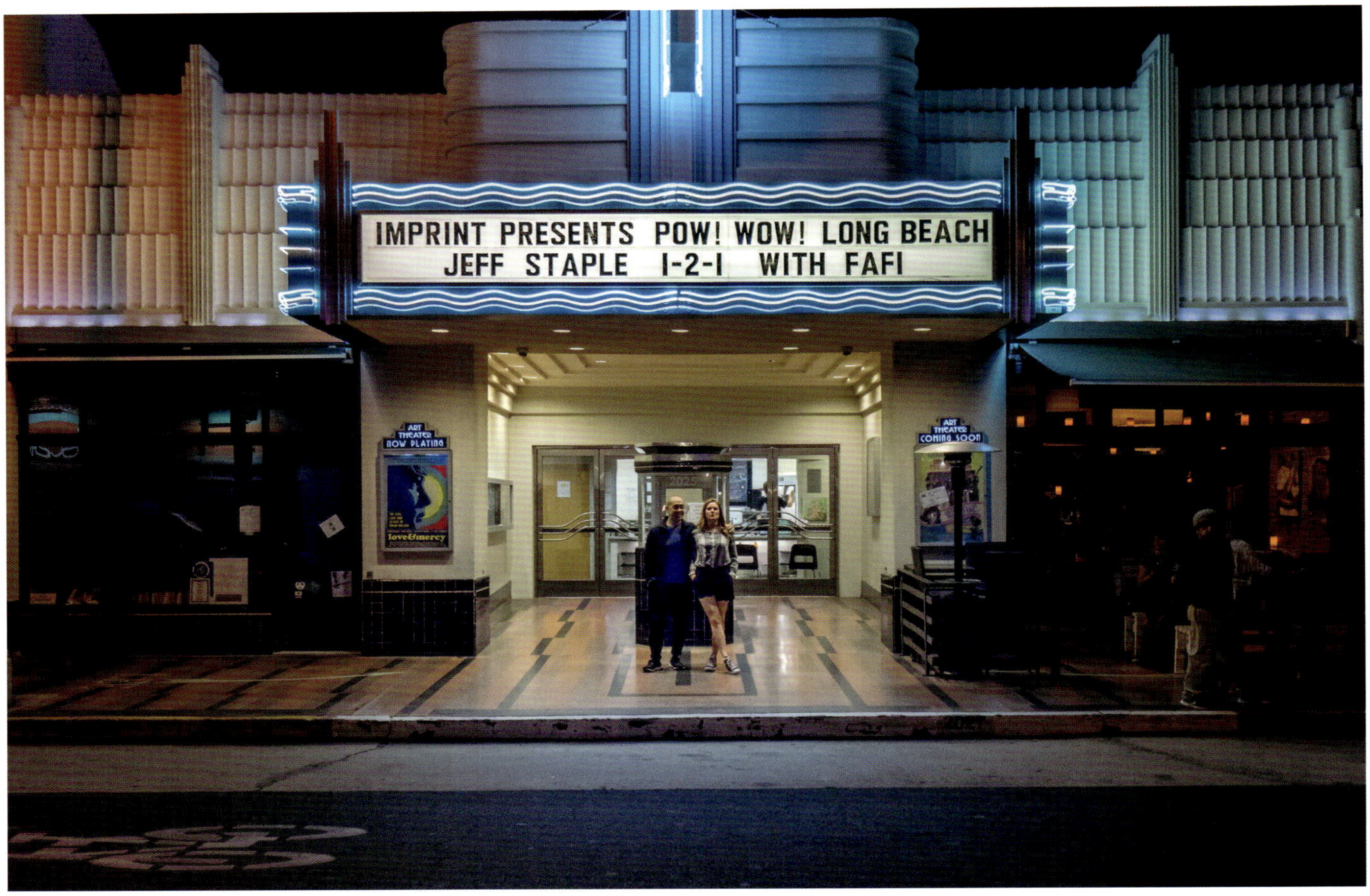
IMPRINT PRESENTS POW! WOW! LONG BEACH
JEFF STAPLE 1-2-1 WITH FAFI
ART THEATER NOW PLAYING
ART THEATER COMING SOON

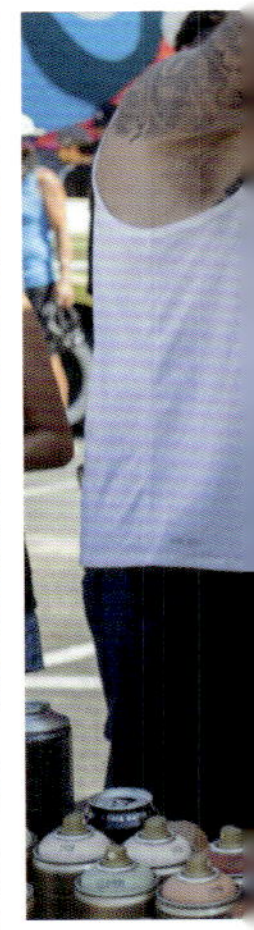

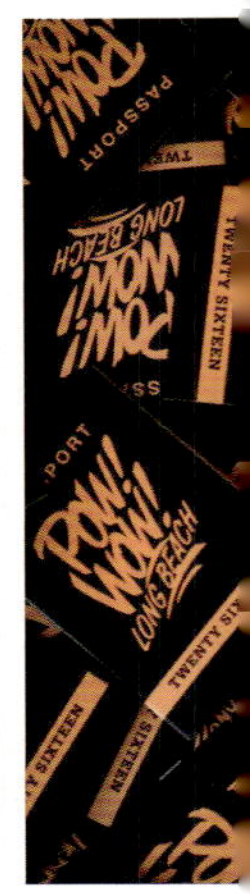
POW! WOW! LONG BEACH
PASSPORT
TWENTY SIXTEEN

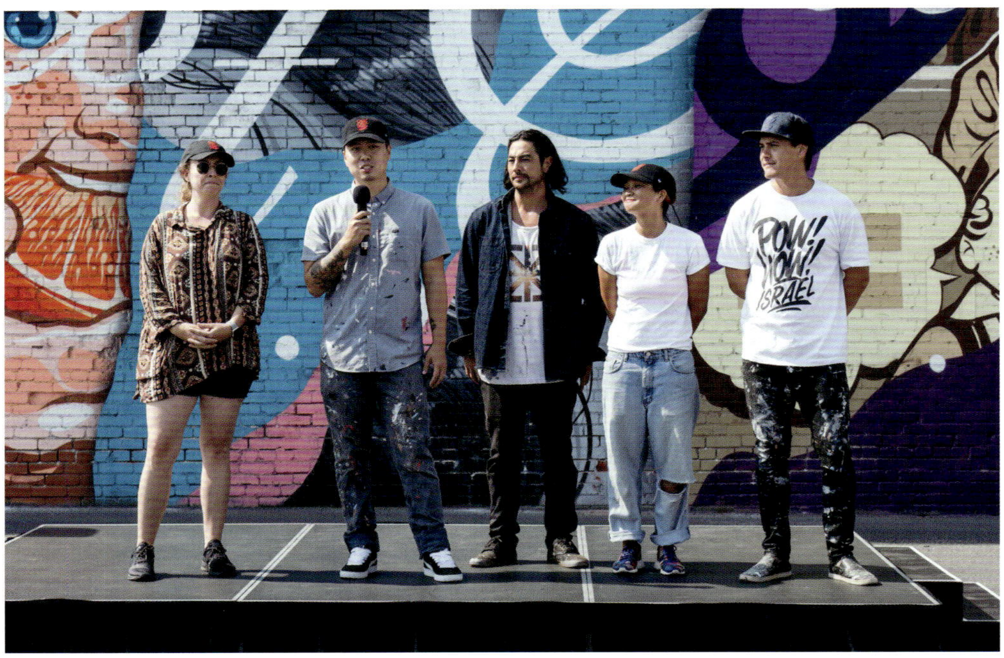
POW! WOW! ISRAEL

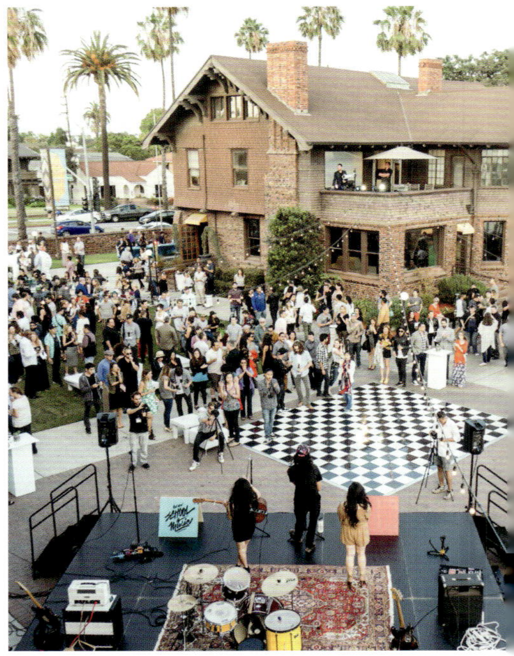

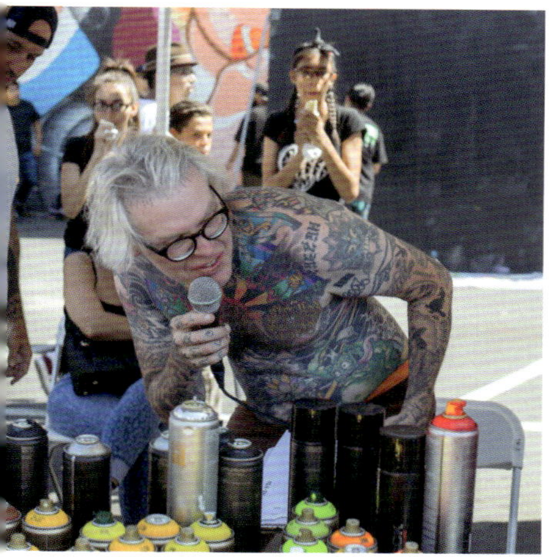
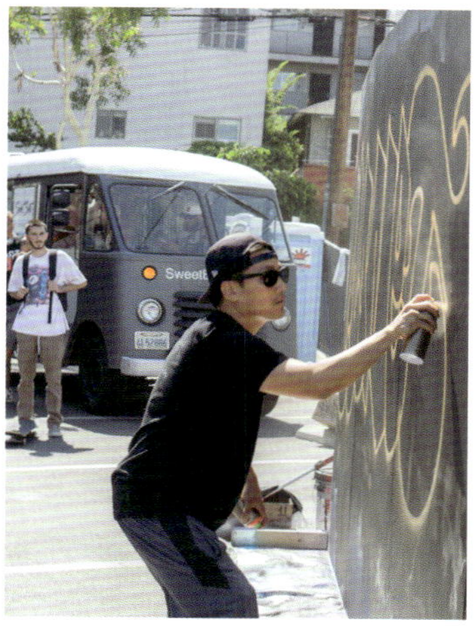
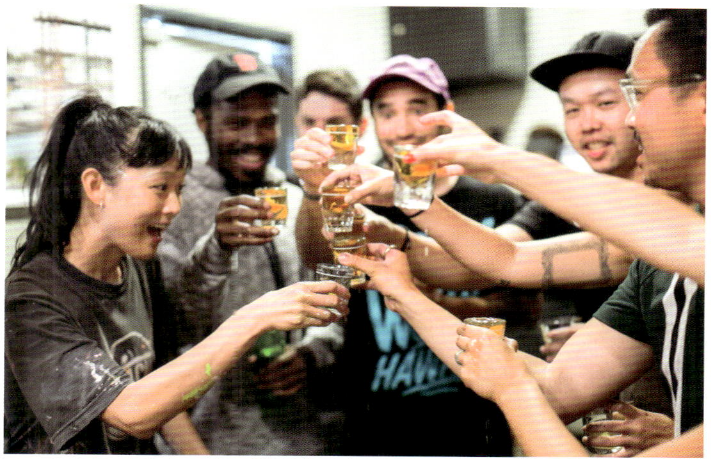
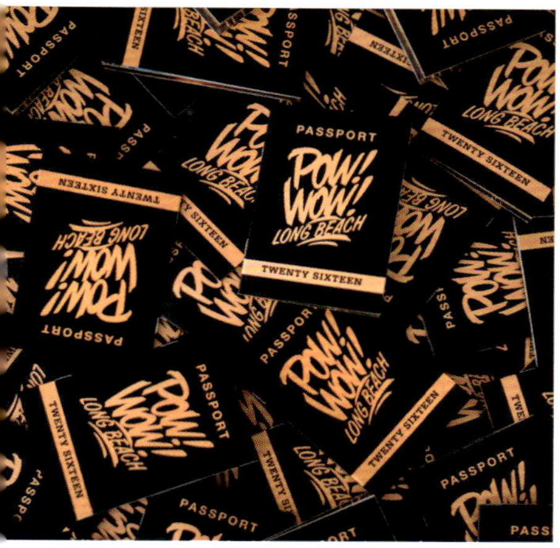
PASSPORT
POW! WOW! LONG BEACH
TWENTY SIXTEEN
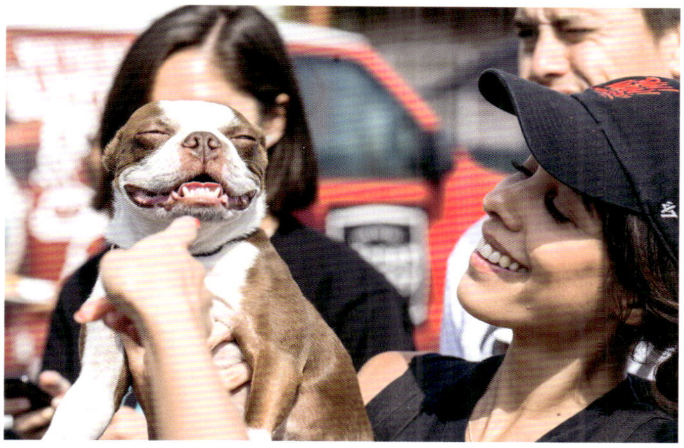
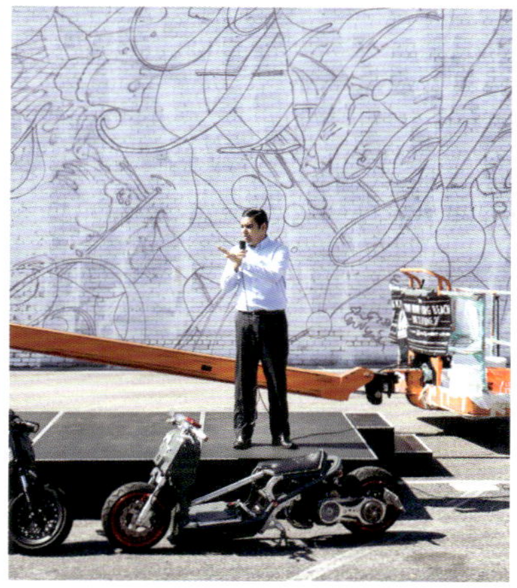
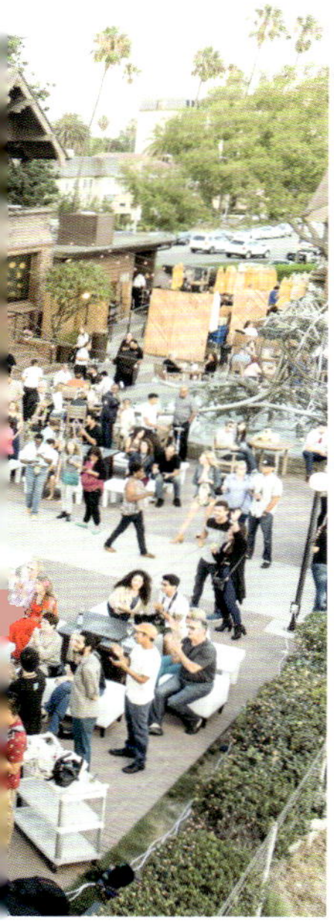
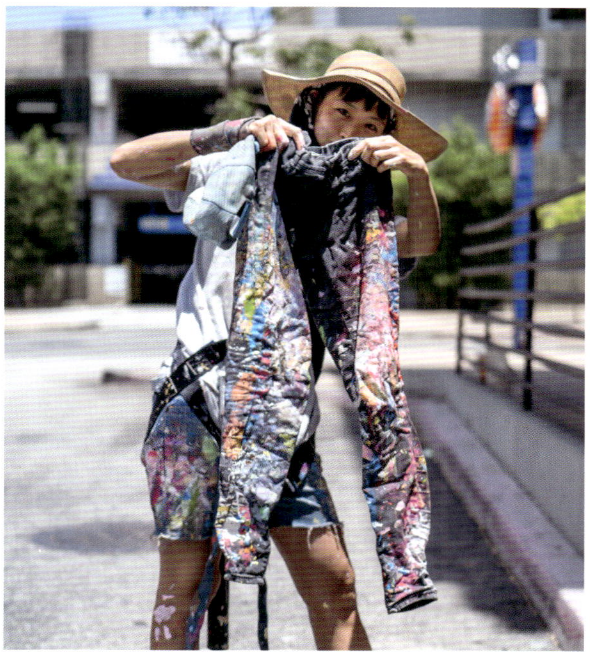
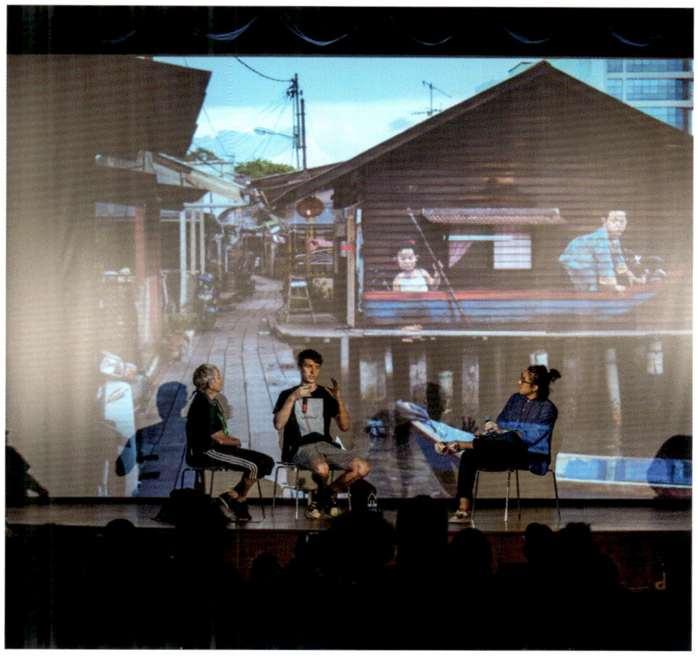

Long Beach
2015

Tristan Eaton

@TRISTANEATON

Born in L.A. in 1978, **Tristan Eaton** started pursuing street art as a teenager, painting everything from billboards to dumpsters in the urban landscapes of the cities where he lived, be it London, Detroit, or New York. He designed his first toy for Fisher-Price at 18 years old and soon became a driving force in the world of designer toys. Eaton's work for Kidrobot, including the famous Dunny and Munny art toys, helped him achieve international renown and an ever-growing fan base. After forming his Creative Agency Thunderdog Studios in New York City in 2004, Eaton became a leader in the advertising and commercial-art spheres, and is regularly commissioned by a roster of clients that includes Nike, Versace, and even Barack Obama.

These days, Eaton is one of the most prominent street artists working today. Eaton's large scale mural work features a meticulous, visual collage of pop imagery mixed with his unique personal style, all executed with freehand spray paint on a colossal scale. Eaton now focuses on his Fine Art and large-scale mural work full-time, which can be found in dozens of cities across the globe from Paris to Shanghai. Eaton's work can also be seen in the Museum of Modern Art's (MoMA) permanent collection.

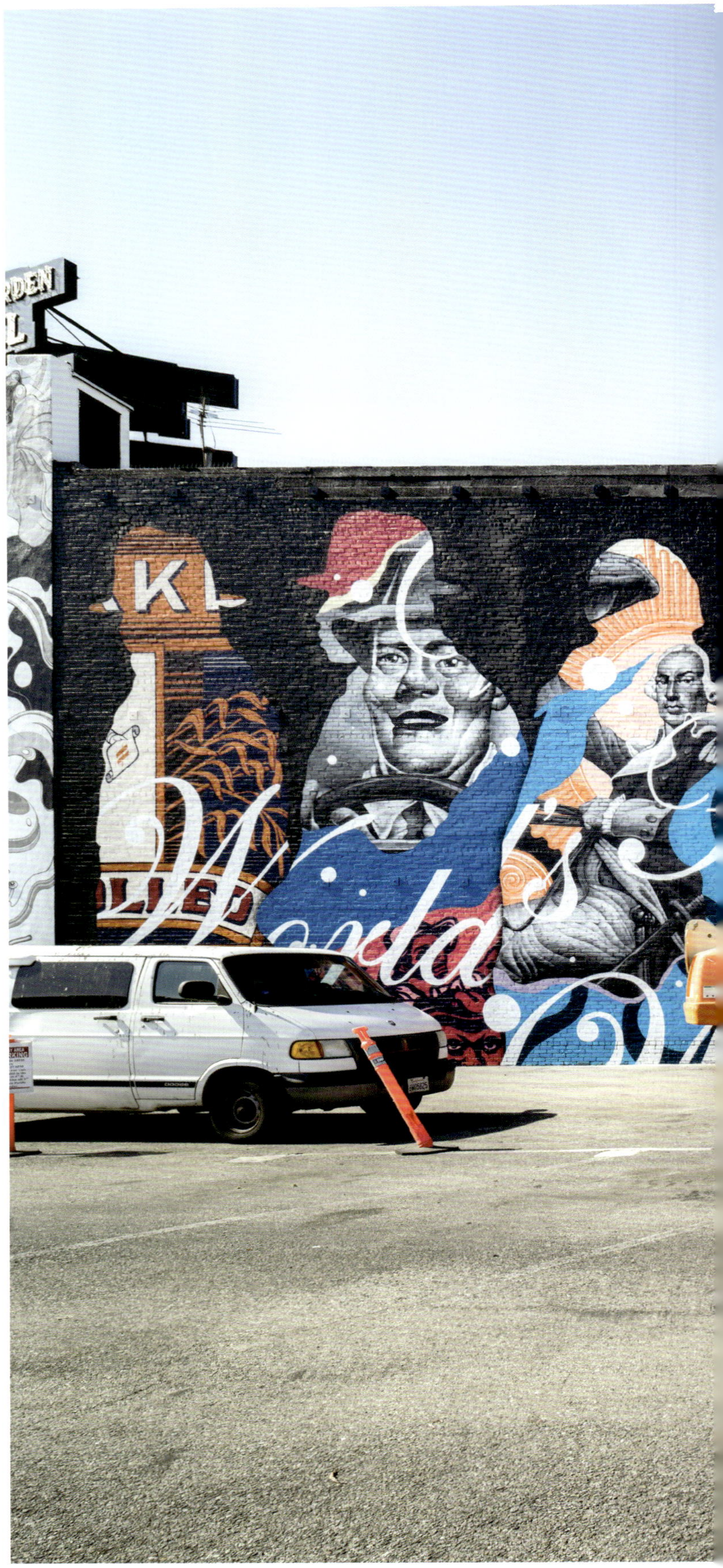

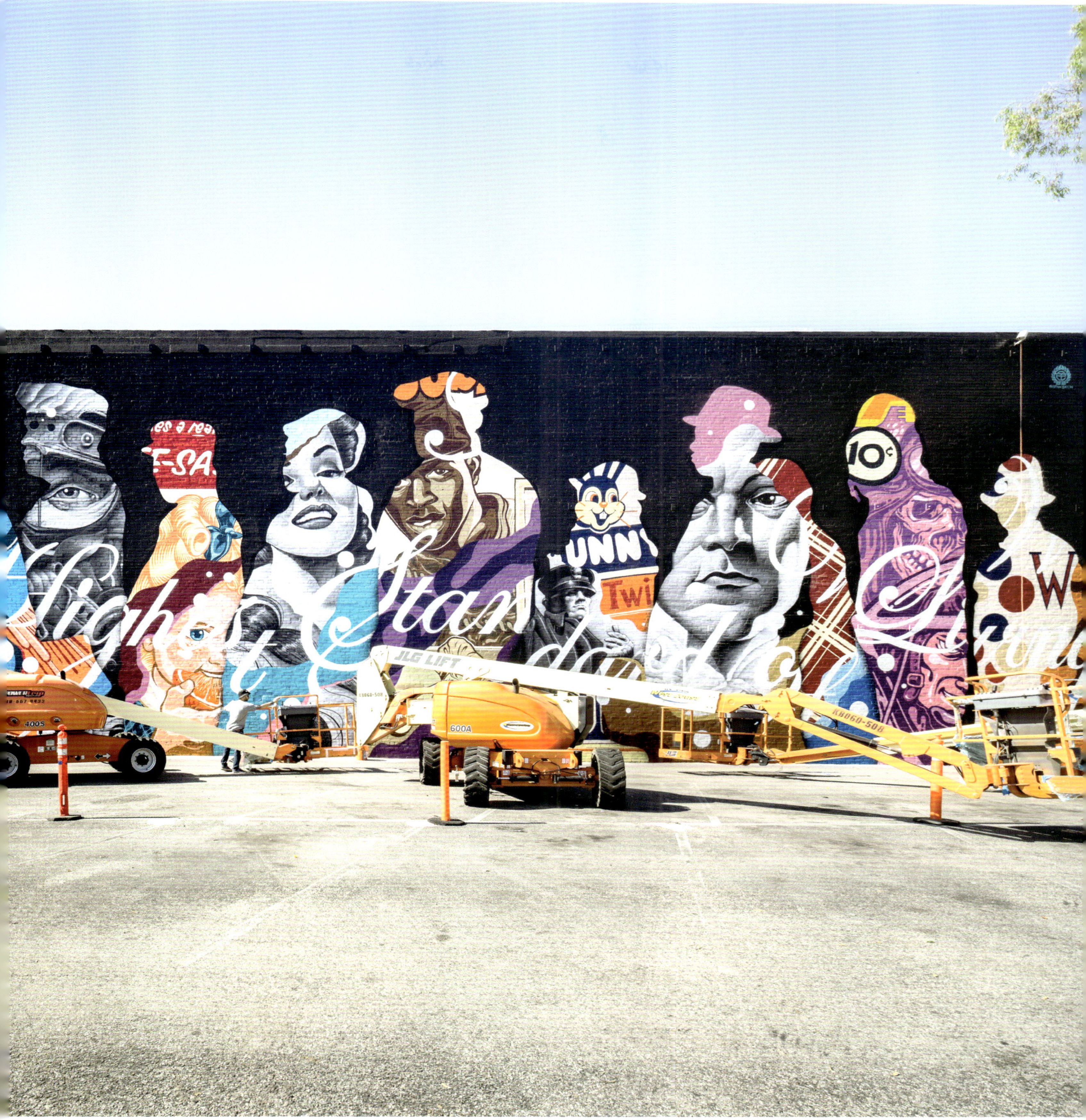

JLG LIFT
600A
10¢

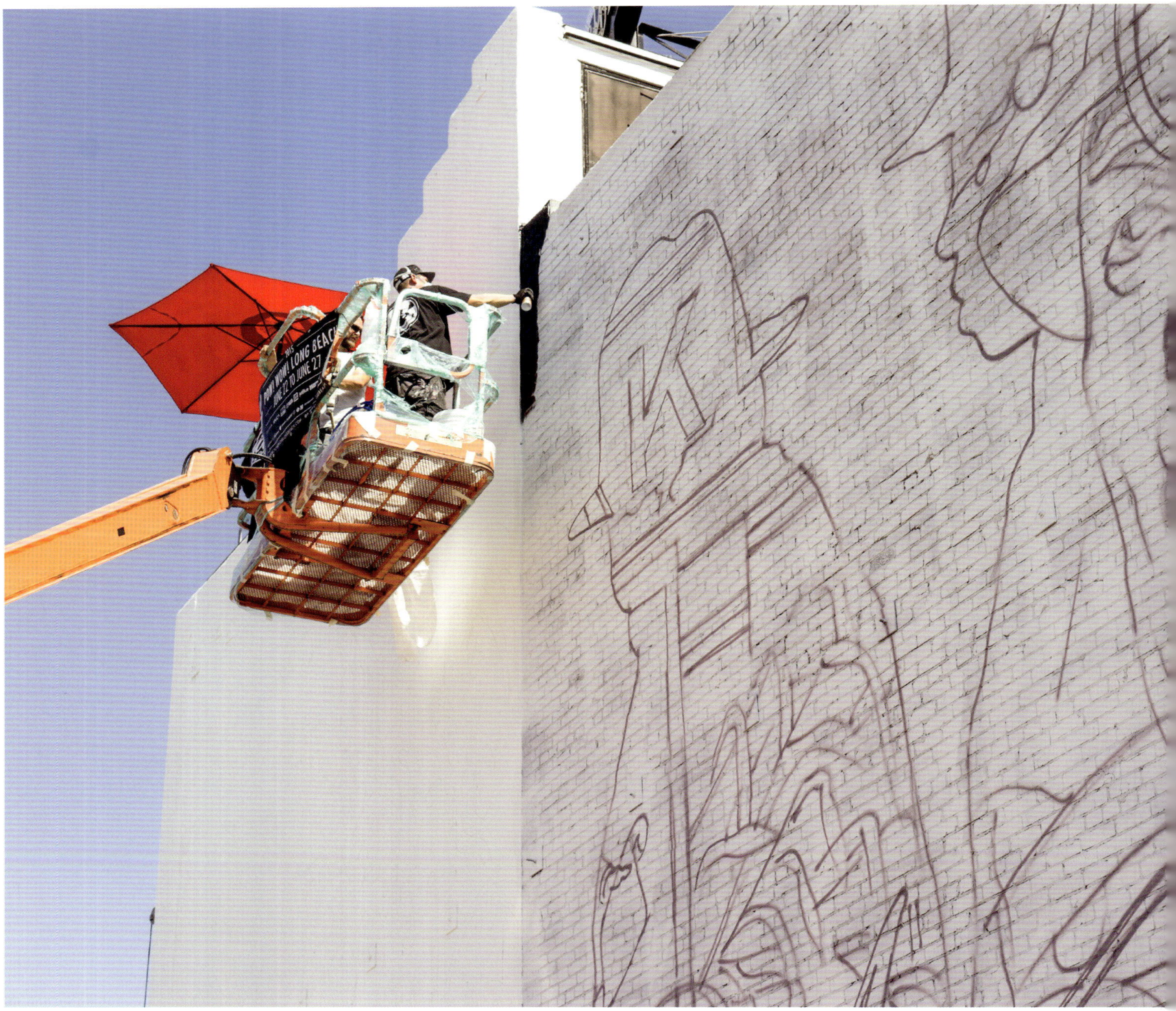
2015
POW! WOW! LONG BEAC
UNE 22 TO JUNE 27

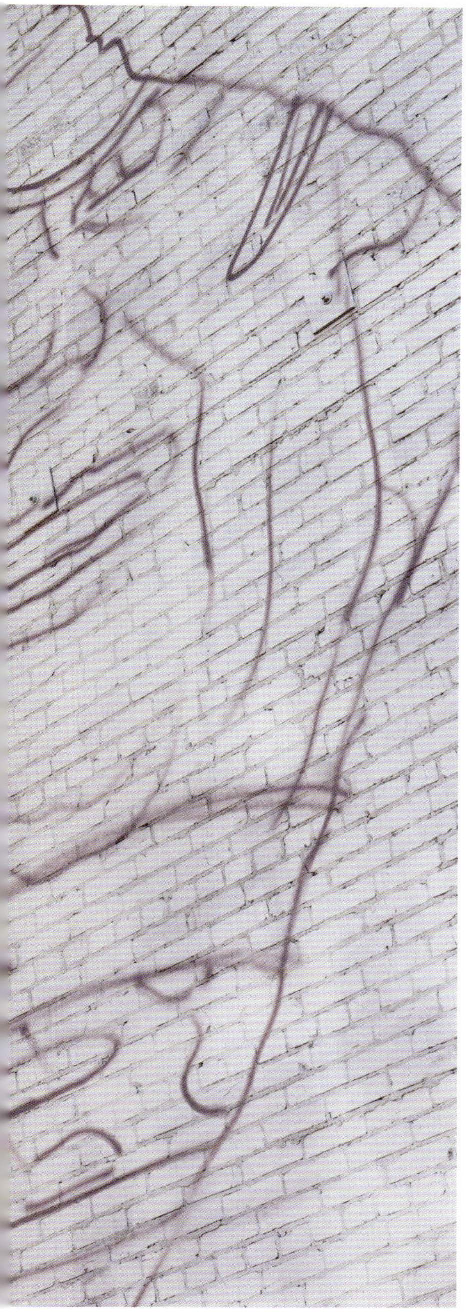

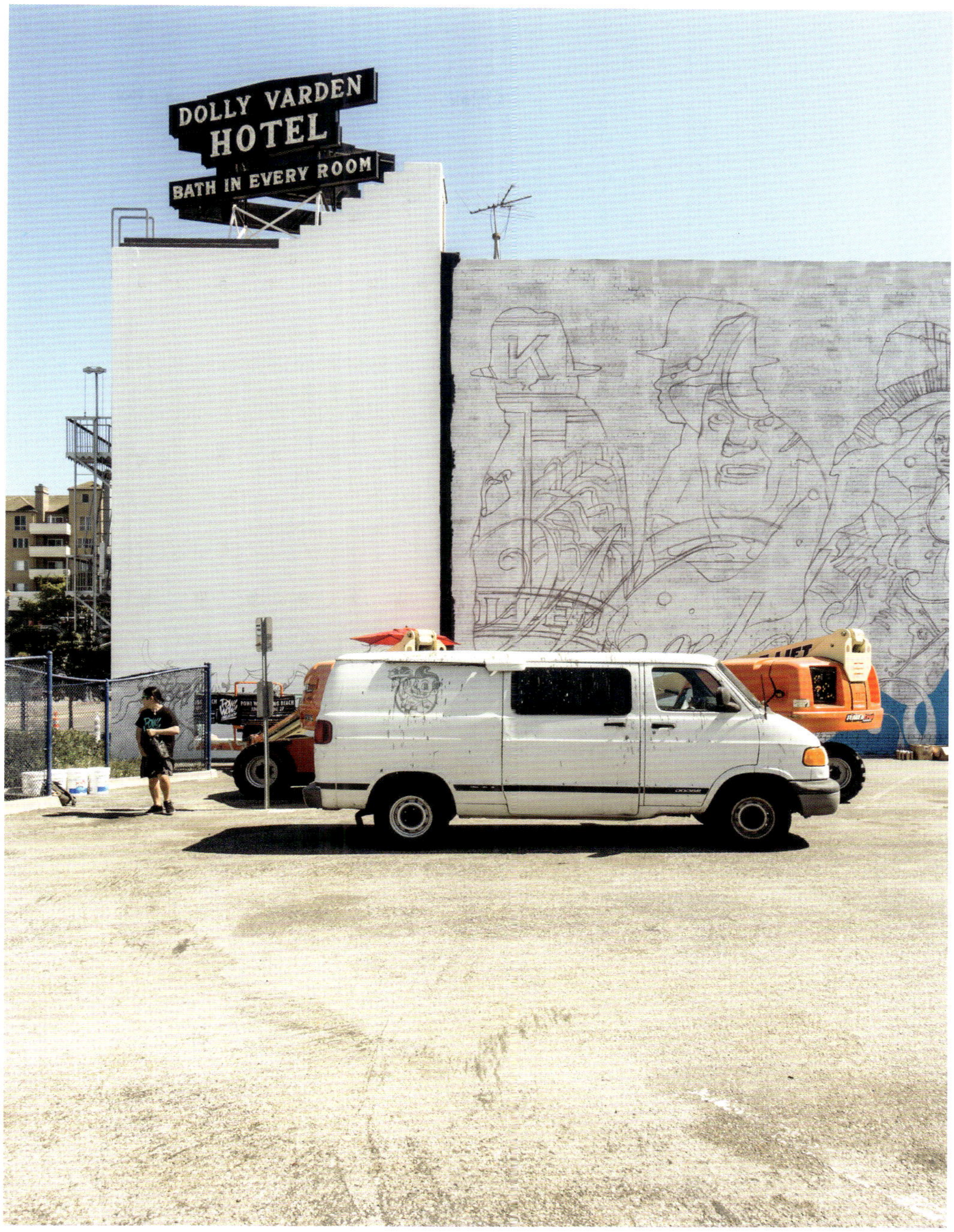
DOLLY VARDEN
HOTEL
BATH IN EVERY ROOM

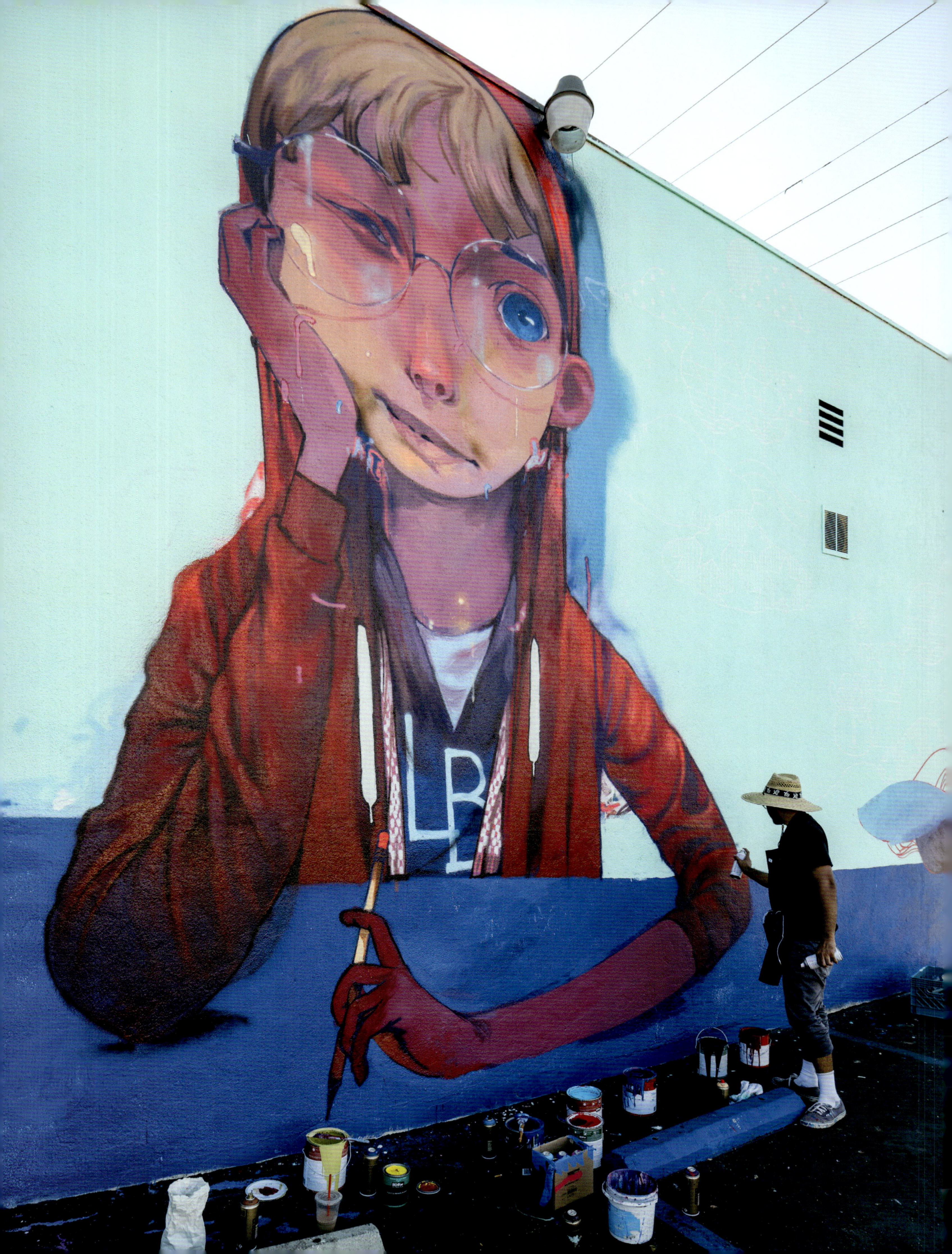
LB

Long Beach
2016

Andrew Hem, Yoskay Yamamoto & Edwin Ushiro

@ANDREWHEM @YOSKAYYAMAMOTO @EDWINUSHIRO

Raised as the child of Cambodian immigrants in Los Angeles, **Andrew Hem's** illustrative paintings bridge disparate aesthetic influences as well as cultural touchstones and sensibilities. Hem's paintings typically highlight an individual within a group of figures, homing in on the one person who is often somberly staring out from the canvas. Using a cool palette in which the colors do not quite match up with the real world, the artist creates somber moods in illusionistic spaces set at a remove from reality. Although his color scheme—with its supernatural rendering of the natural world—elicits comparisons to impressionism, Hem also echoes graffiti art based on his straightforward and illustrative rendering of figures and space, as well as allusions to street culture, art, and fashion.

Born and raised in Toba, Japan, **Yoskay Yamamoto** moved to the United States at the age of 15. A self-trained illustrator, Yamamoto's artistic tastes expanded as he fell in love with the urban culture of the West coast. Yamamoto discovered a way to fuse the two different cultural backgrounds together into his work. Yamamoto nostalgically blends pop iconic characters from his new Western home with traditional and mythical Japanese elements, balancing his Asian heritage with urban pop art.

Edwin Ushiro is an Artist born on Maui and bred in California. Ushiro attended the Art Center College of Design and attained a BFA in Illustration with Honors. Since then, Ushiro has been working in the amazing world of entertainment as a Production Designer, Visual Consultant, Art Director, Storyboard Artist, and Concept Designer.

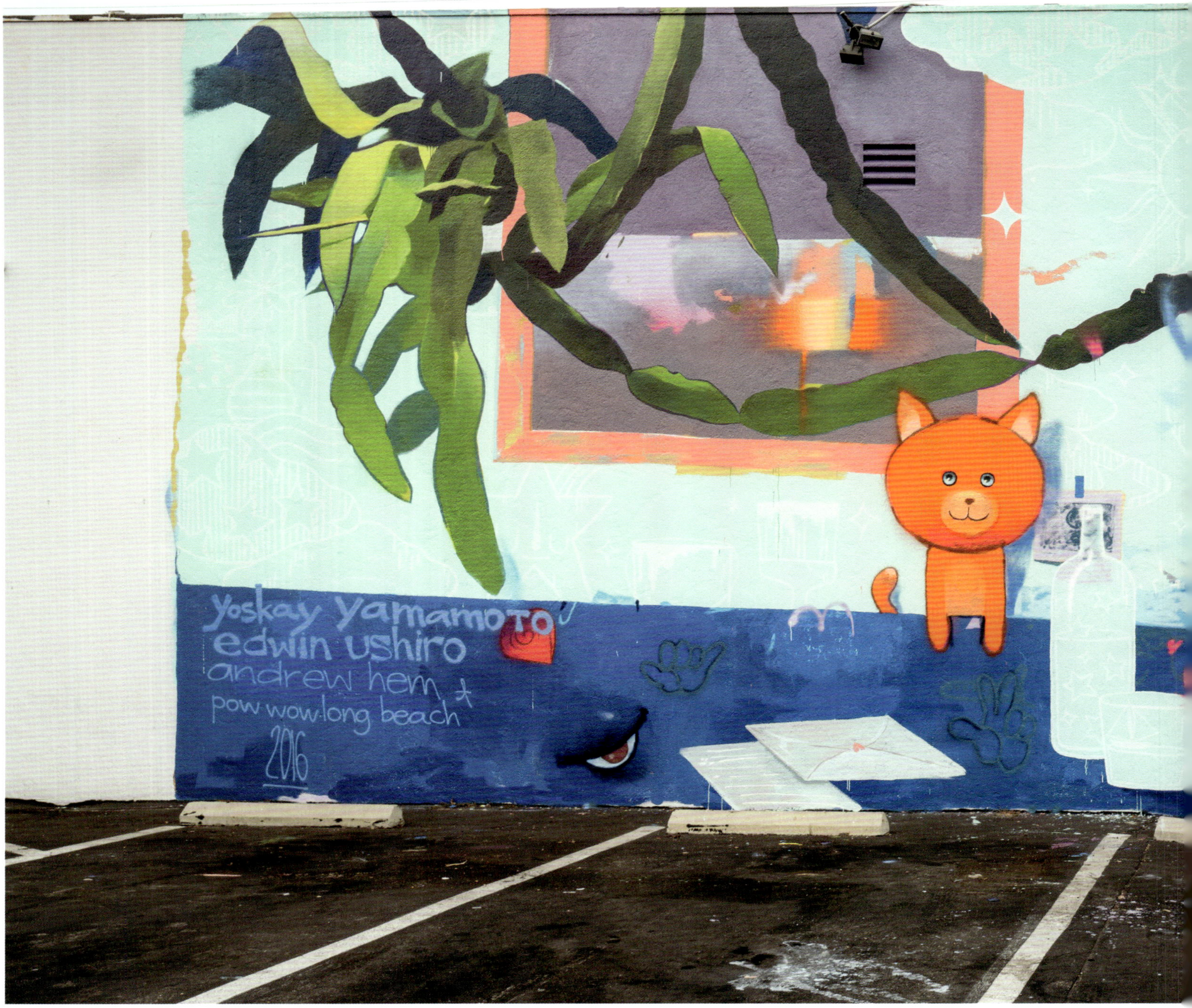
yoskay yamamoto
edwin ushiro
andrew hem +
pow wow long beach
2016

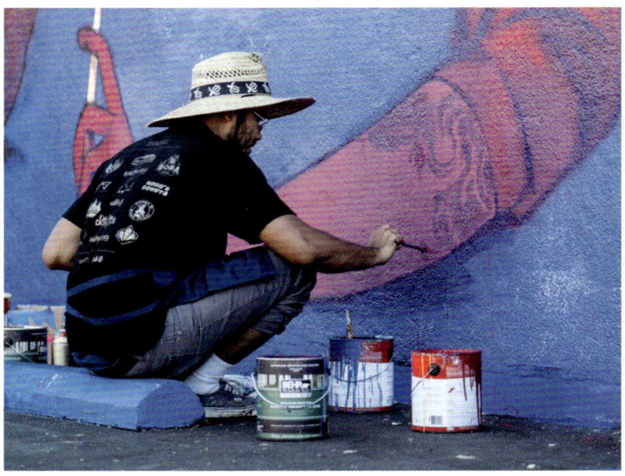

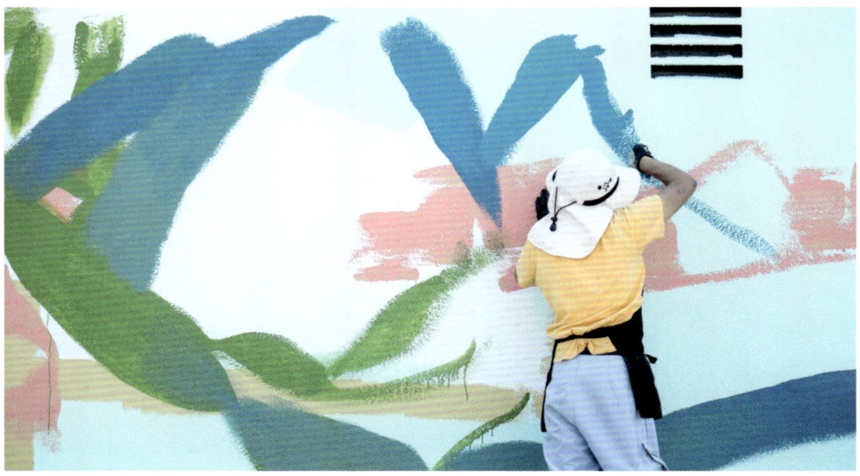

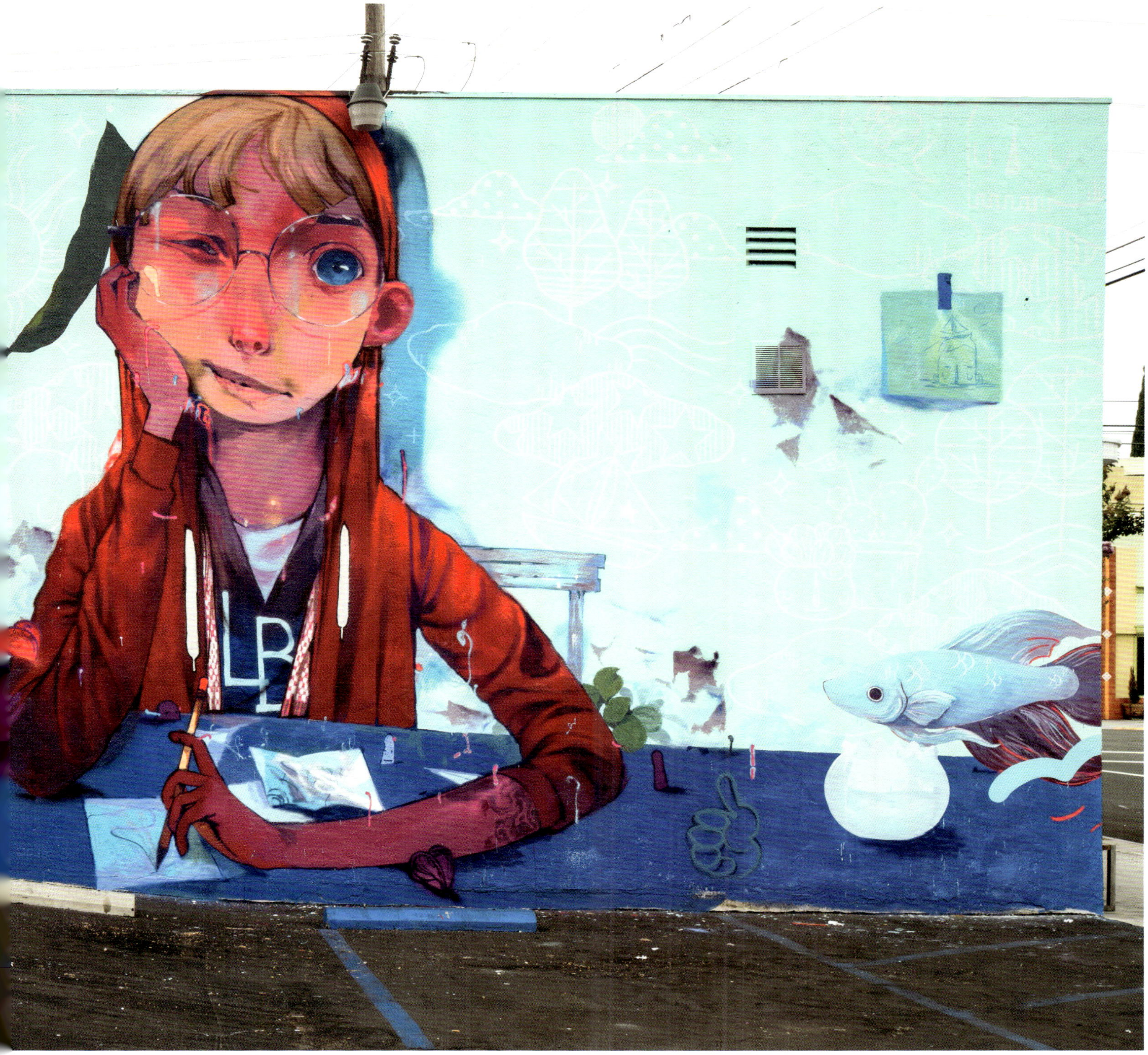

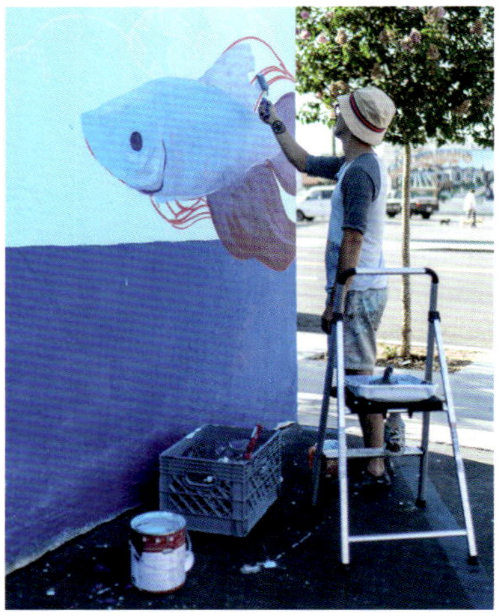

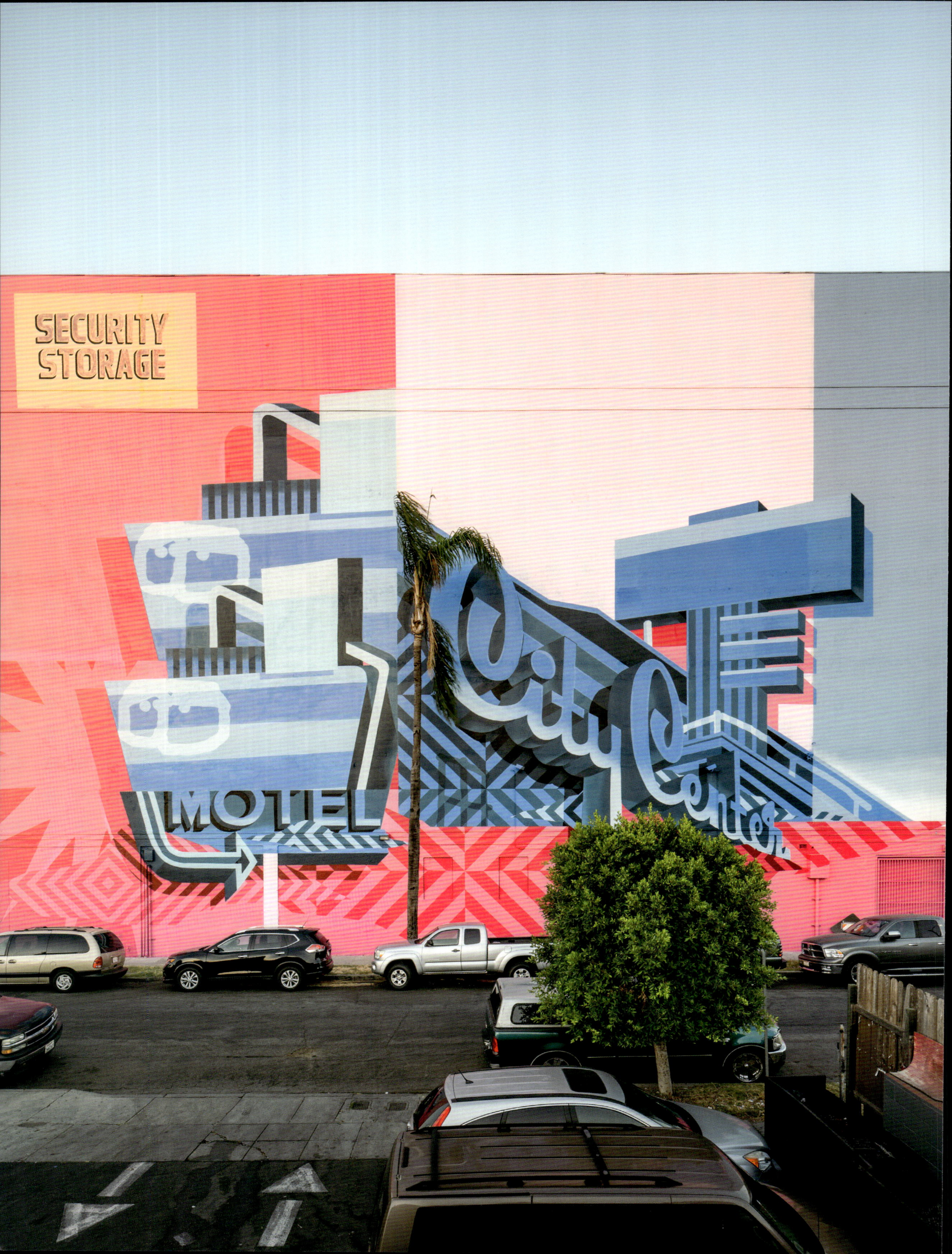
SECURITY
STORAGE
MOTEL
City Center

Long Beach
2017

Trav MSK

@TRAVMSK

TRAV is a Los Angeles-based artist who has made a name for himself painting graffiti on walls and trains throughout the United States. He is an active member of The Seventh Letter and Mad Society Kings Artist Collective.

Trav's work has shifted to document current times in society as we evolve from the physical world and emerge into the digital space.

He pays homage to the craftsmanship of an older generation while embracing current technology to produce his work. Trav has chosen to focus on creating public work around this narrative to give back to the community.

Trav collages photographs of vintage signs and hand crafted typography, then arranges them in various compositions that interact with geometric patterns. He then overlays digital gestures to represent emotion often to resemble eyes or faces.

Trav bounces between studio, public, and commercial work cohesively by staying true to his narrative and true to himself. He believes "living life on your own terms" is essential to his process.

His work stands somewhere between fine art and graffiti. Trav has moved beyond the sphere of traditional graffiti to occupy a more permanent legacy.

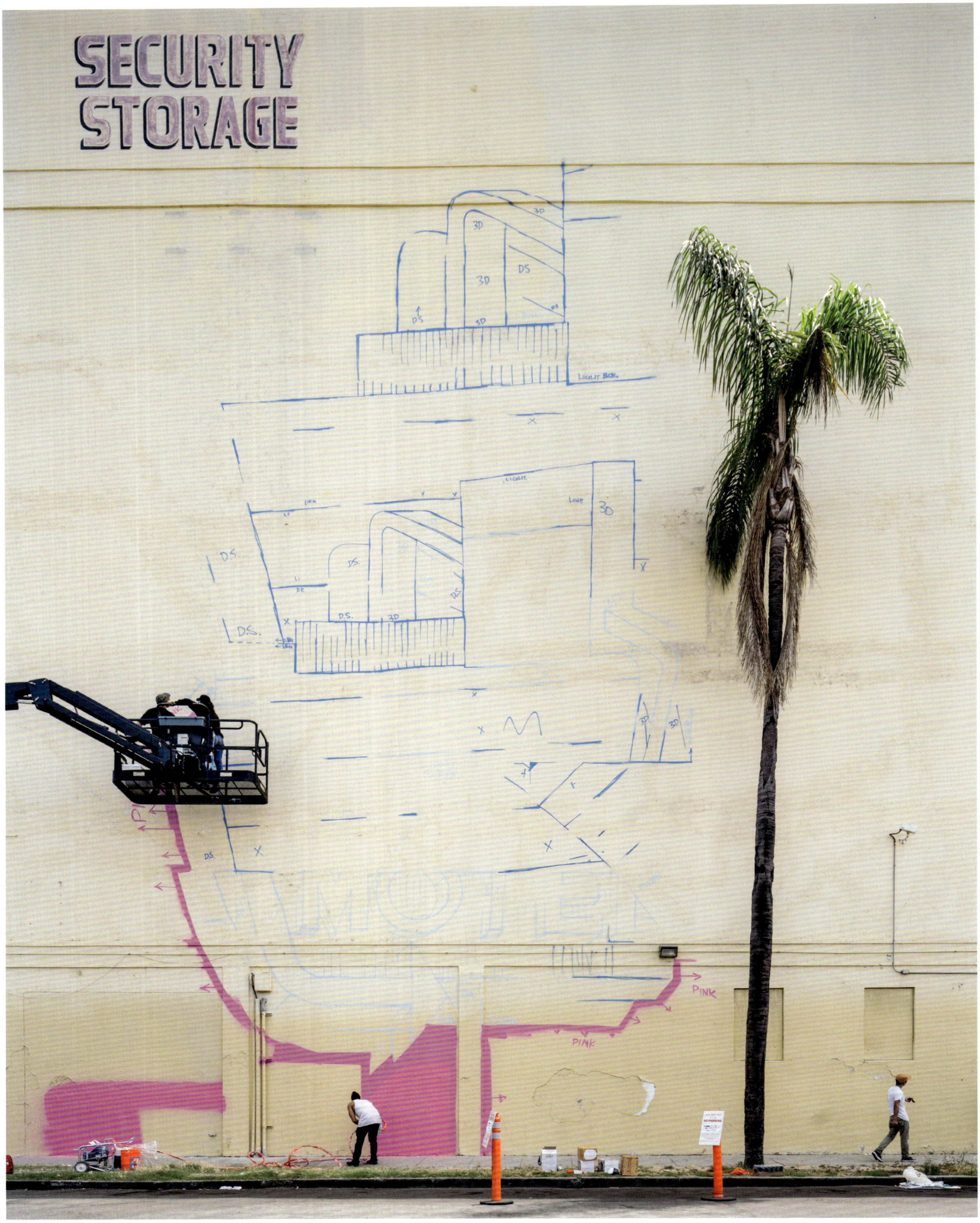
SECURITY
STORAGE
PINK
PINK

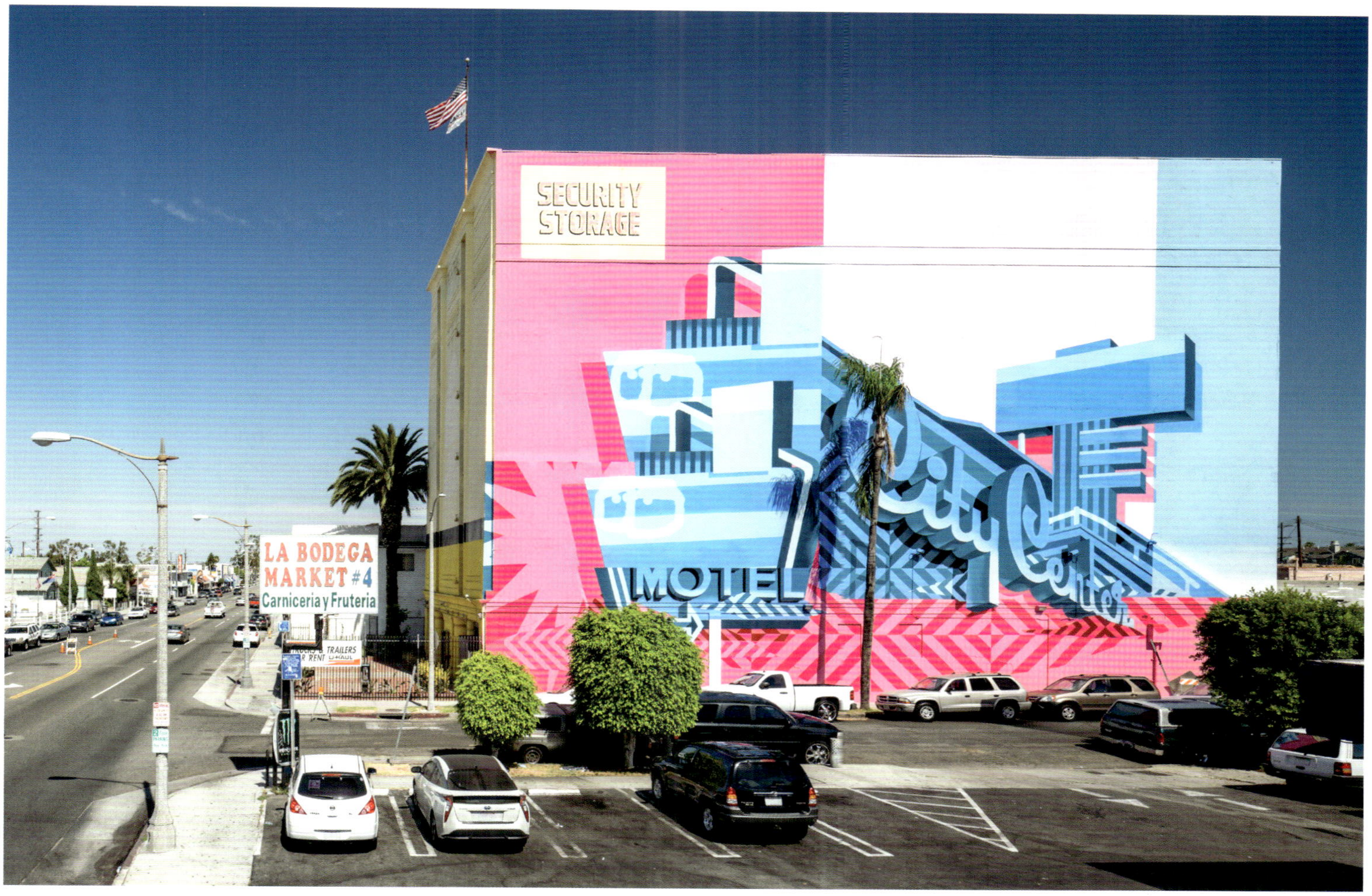
SECURITY
STORAGE
LA BODEGA
MARKET #4
Carniceria y Fruteria
MOTEL

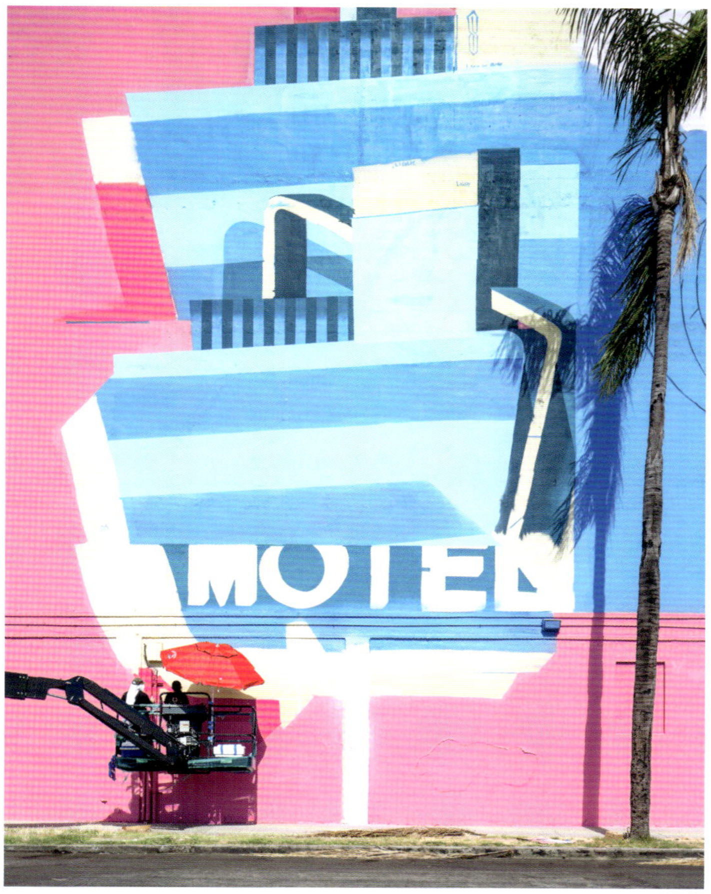
MOTEL

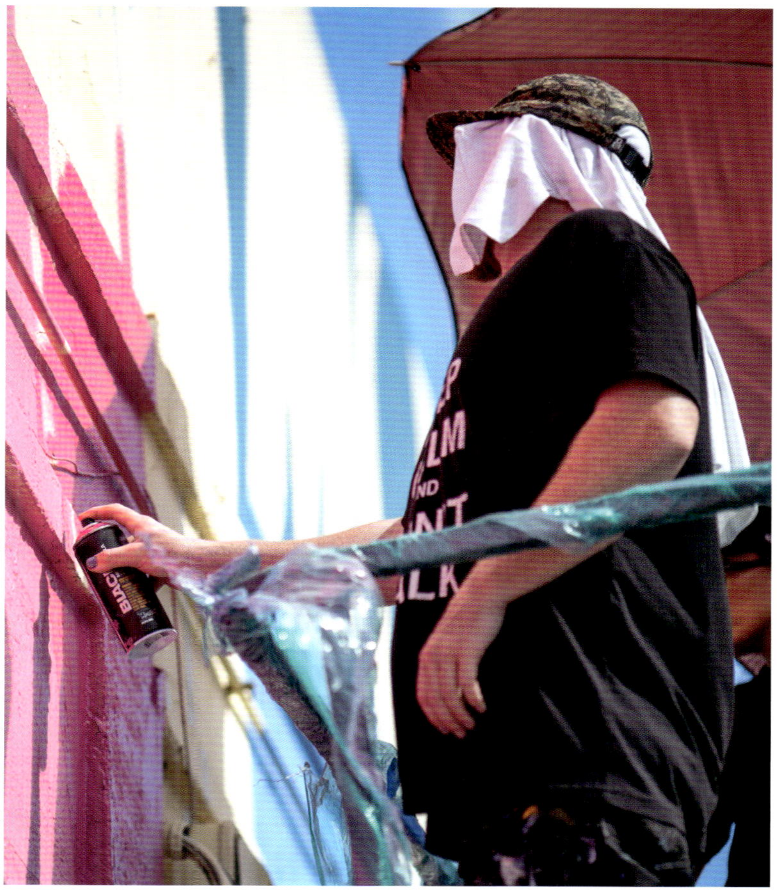

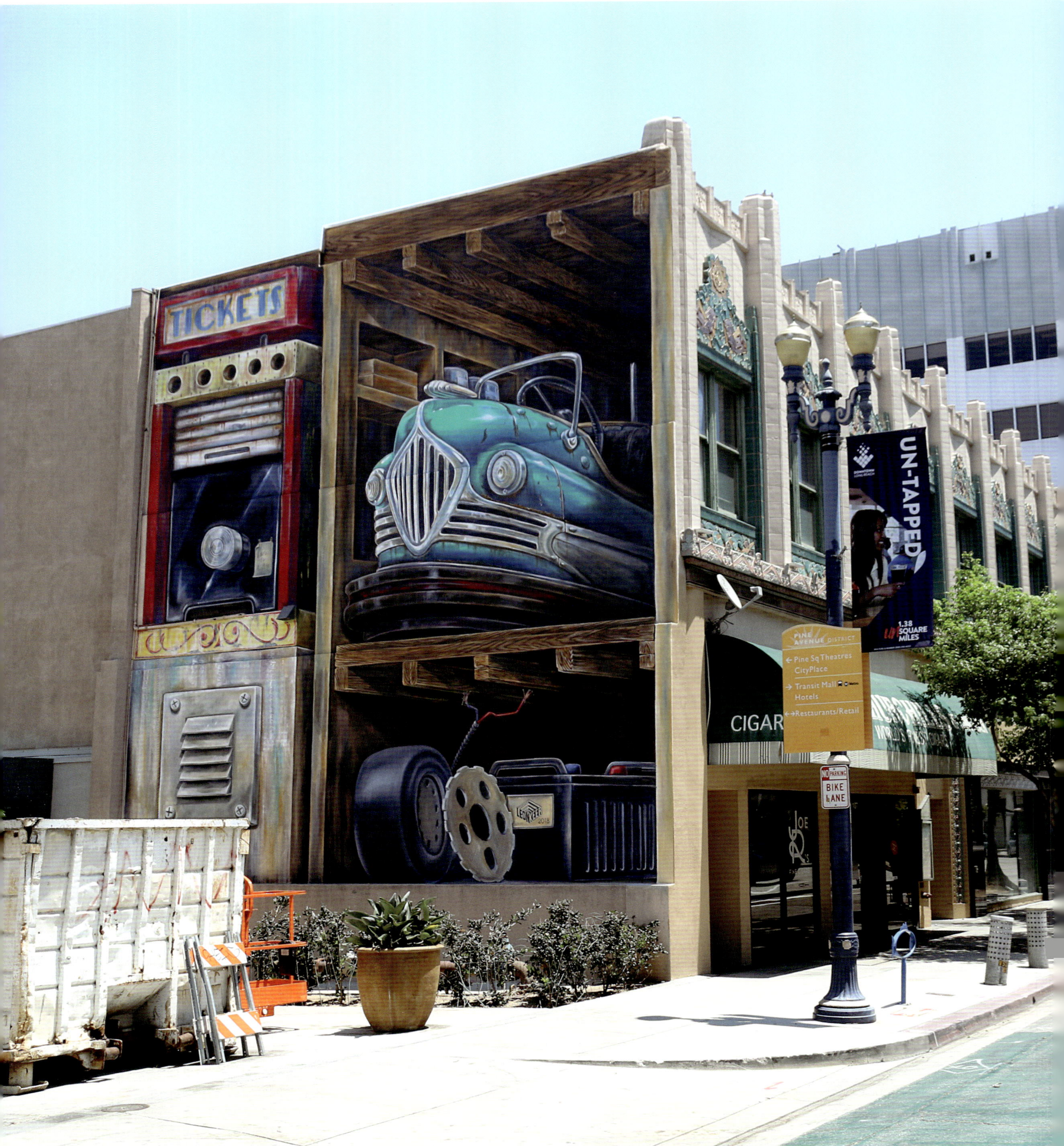
TICKETS
UN-TAPPED
1.38 SQUARE MILES
PINE AVENUE DISTRICT
Pine Sq Theatres
CityPlace
Transit Mall
Hotels
Restaurants/Retail
CIGAR
BIKE LANE

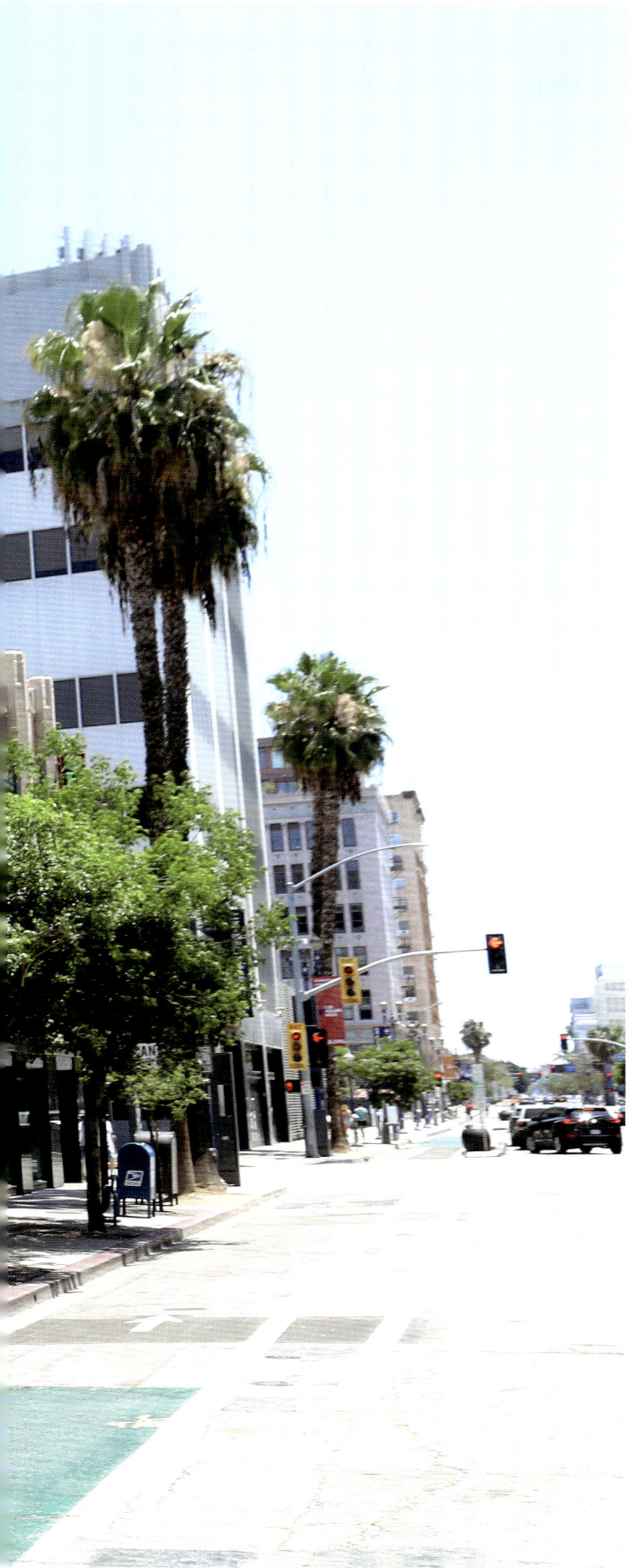

Long Beach
2018

Leon Keer

@LEONKEER

Leon Keer is one of the world's leading artists in anamorphic street art. He has created work on canvas and (3D) artwork on the streets across the world (3D Street Art, 3D Streetpainting, Murals). His art has been showcased in Europe, the United States, Russia, Mexico, the United Arab Emirates, Australia, New Zealand, and several Asian countries. In addition to using optical illusion, he often presents his art by adding new technologies, such as augmented reality and video mapping. The art is temporary, but the images are shared all over the world via social media.

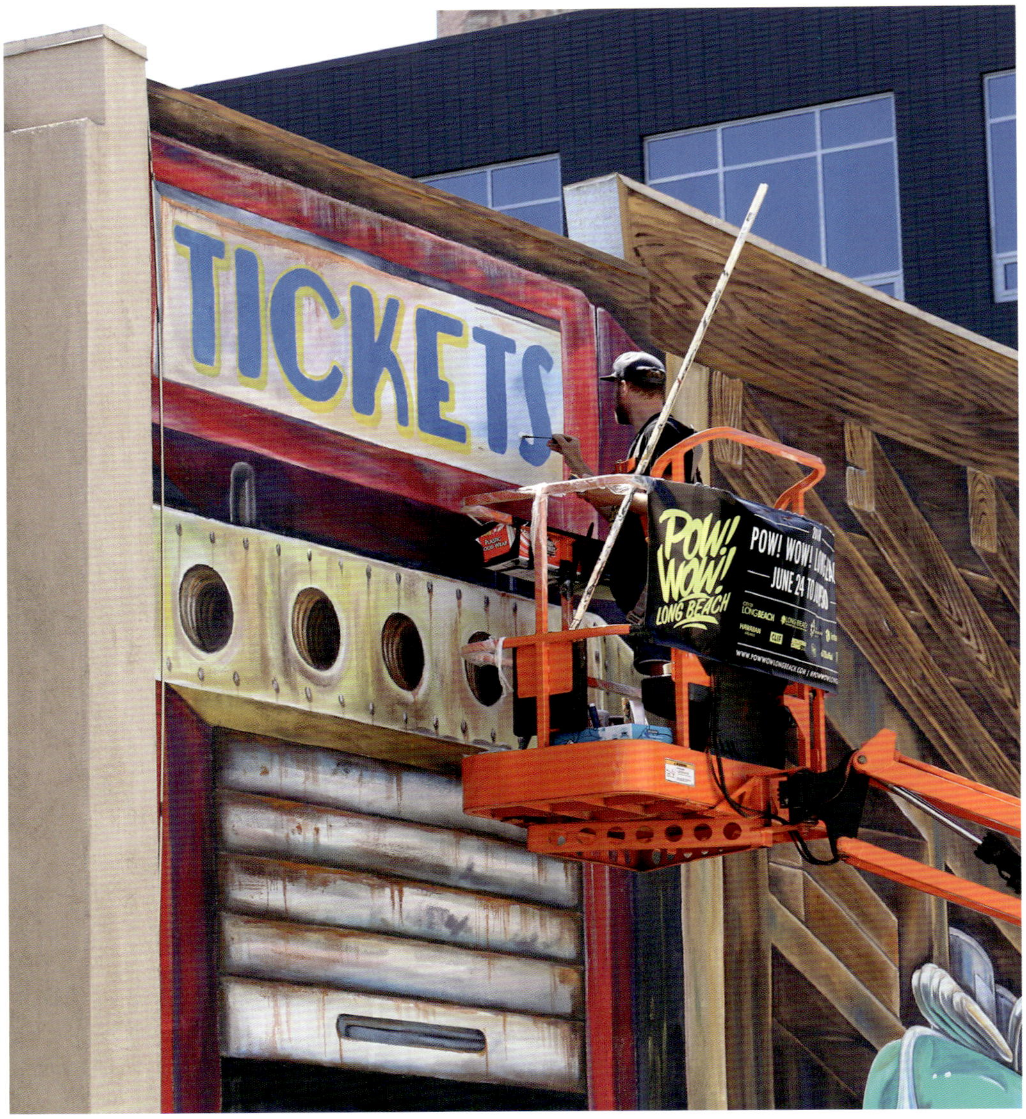
TICKETS
POW! WOW! LONG BEACH

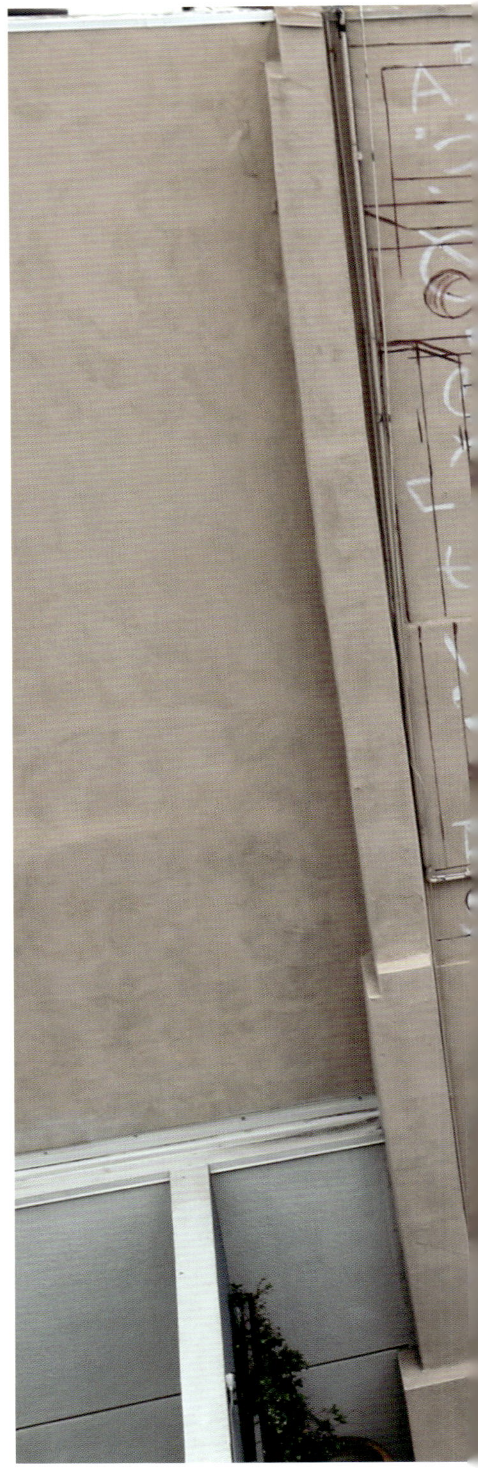

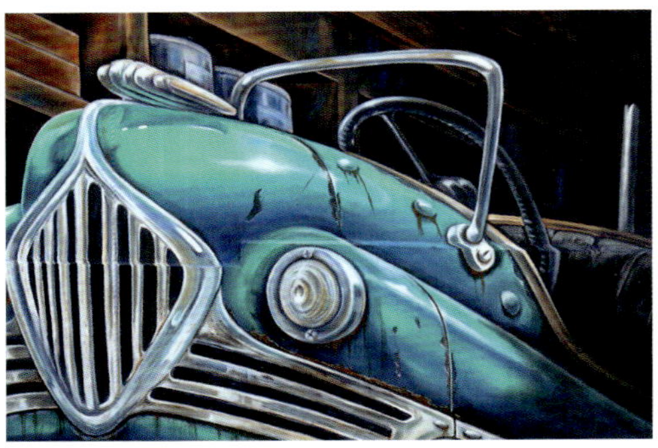

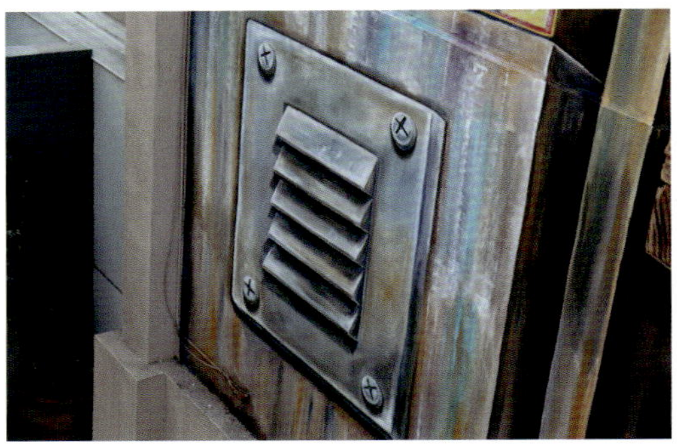

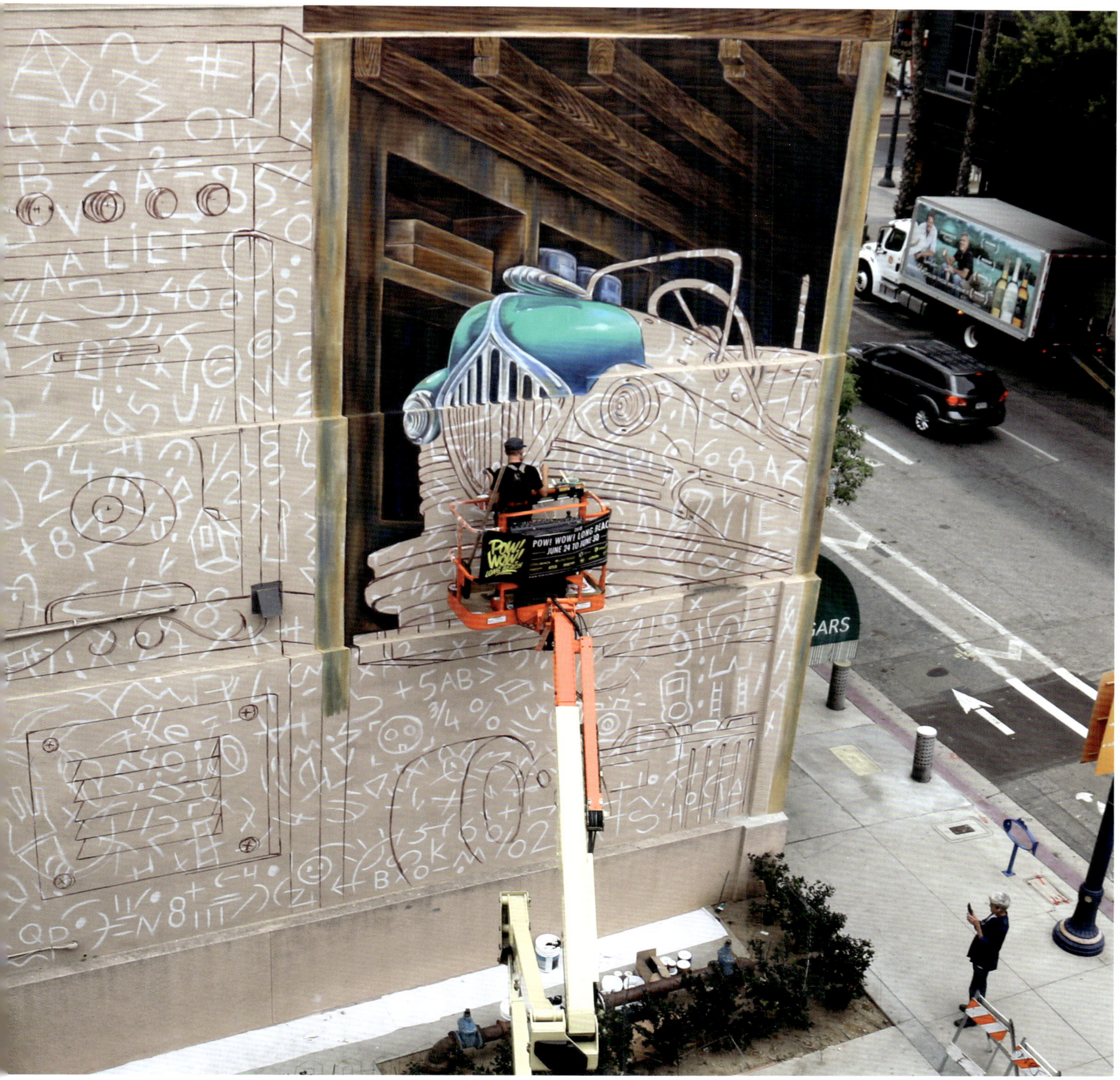
POW! WOW! LONG BEACH
JUNE 24 TO JUNE 30
ARS

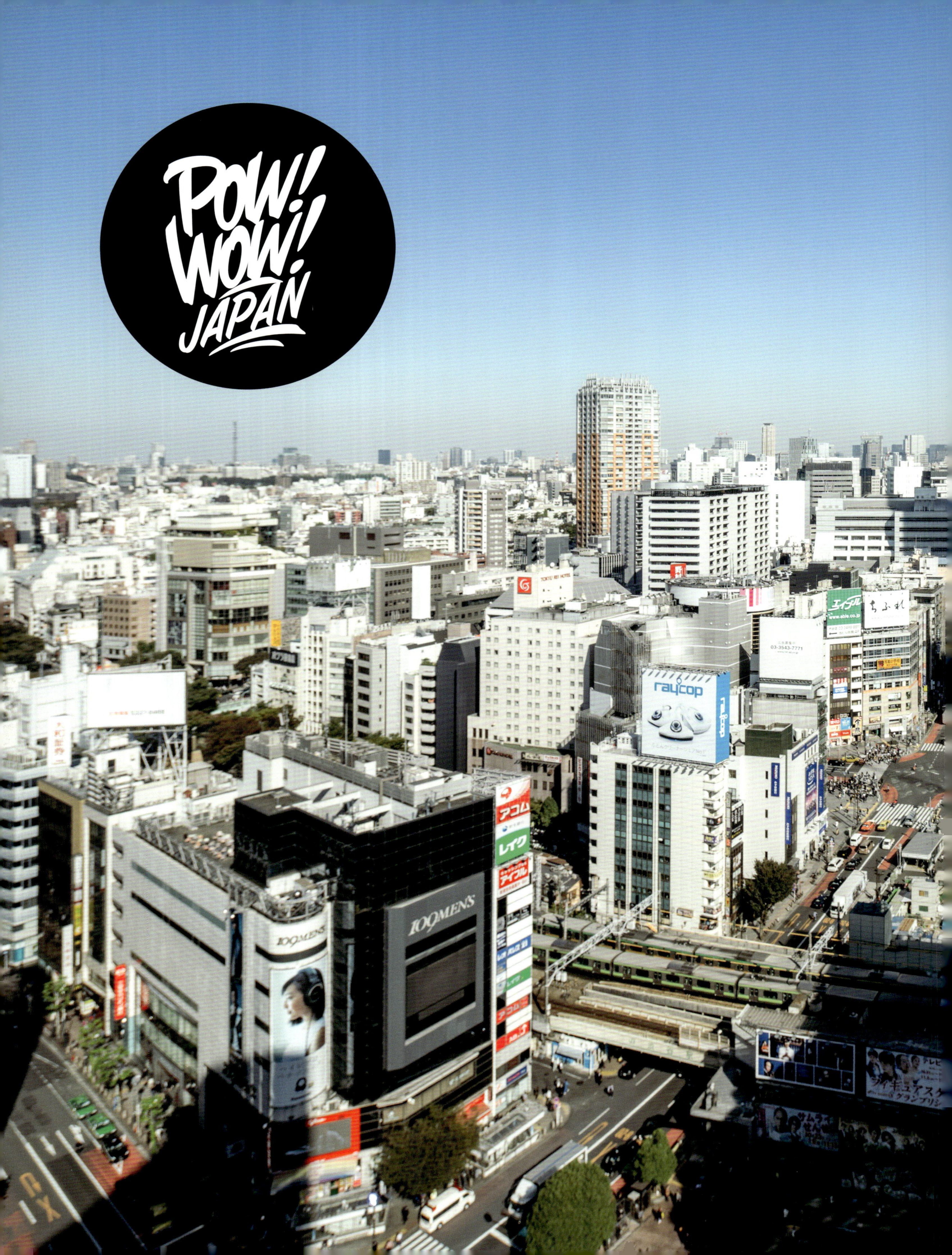
POW! WOW! JAPAN
raycop
109MEN'S
アコム
レイク
アイフル

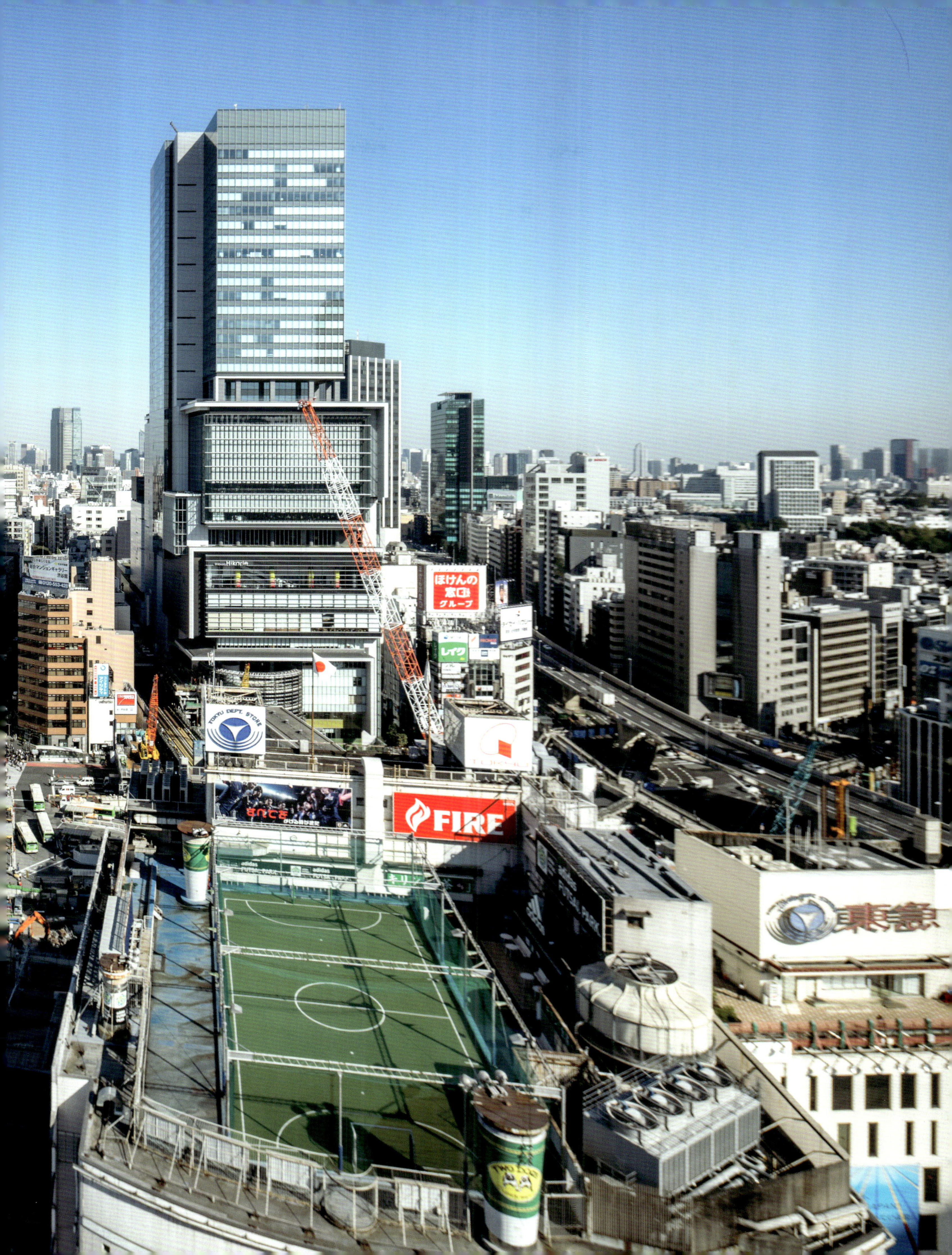

ほけんの
窓口
グループ
TOKYU DEPT. STORE
FIRE
東急

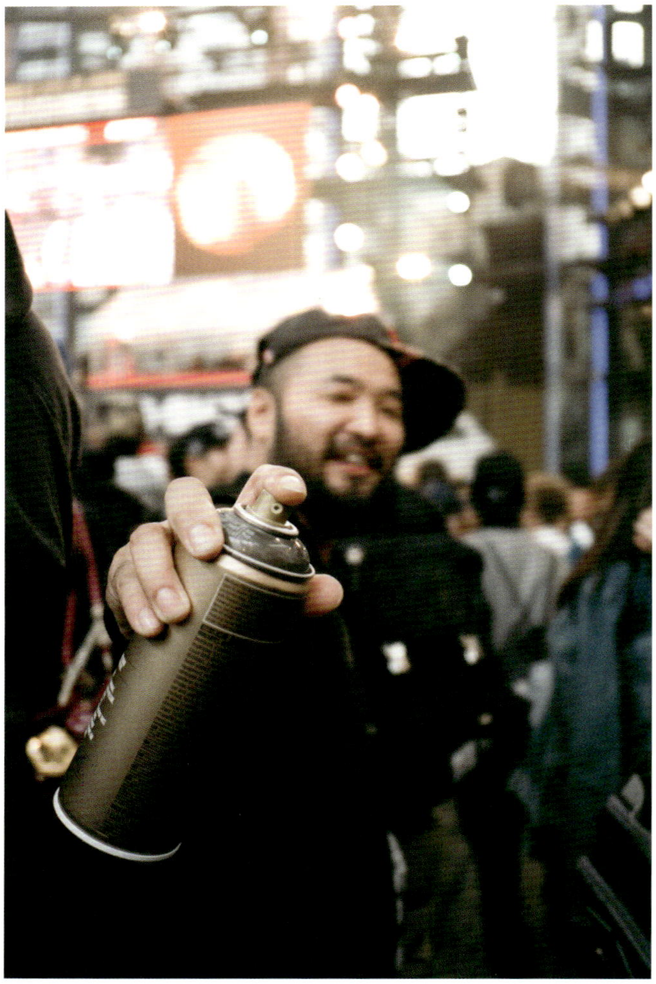

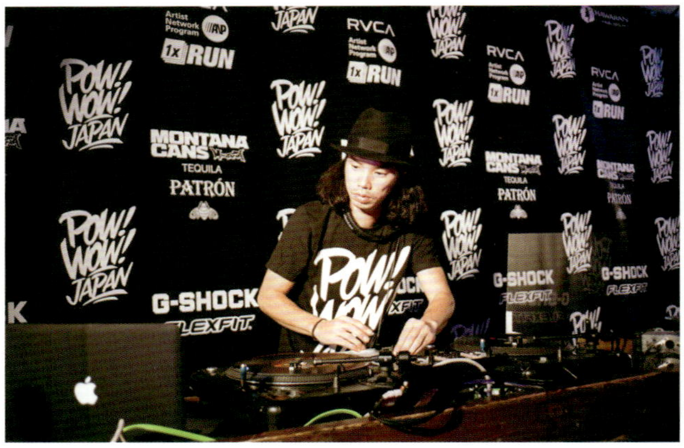

Artist Network Program
1xRUN
RVCA
POW! WOW! JAPAN
MONTANA CANS
TEQUILA
PATRÓN
G-SHOCK
FLEXFIT

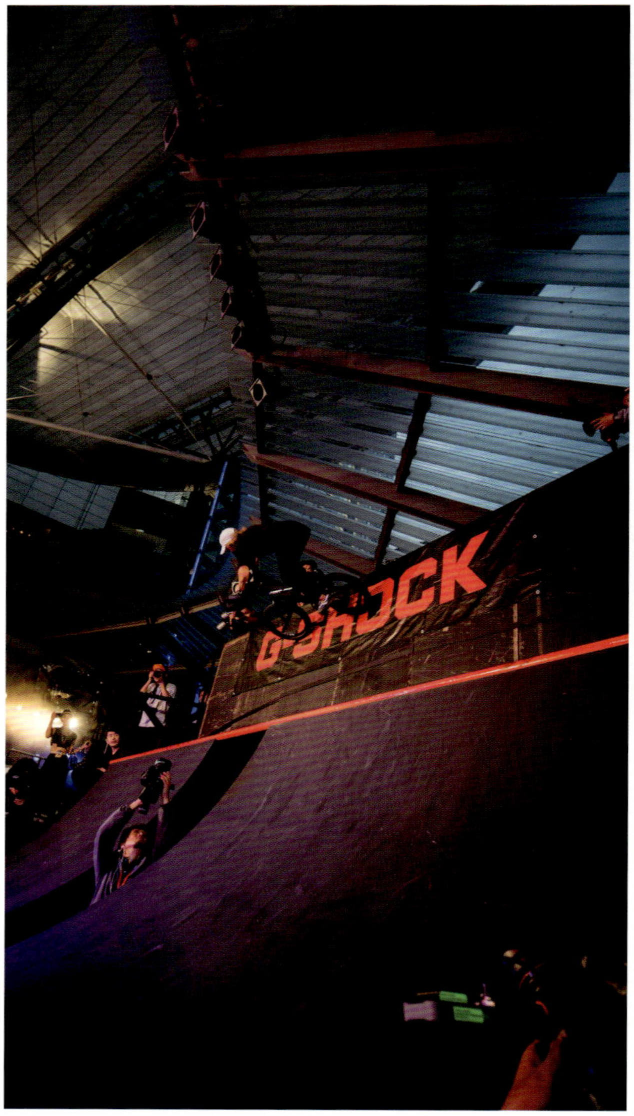

G-SHOCK

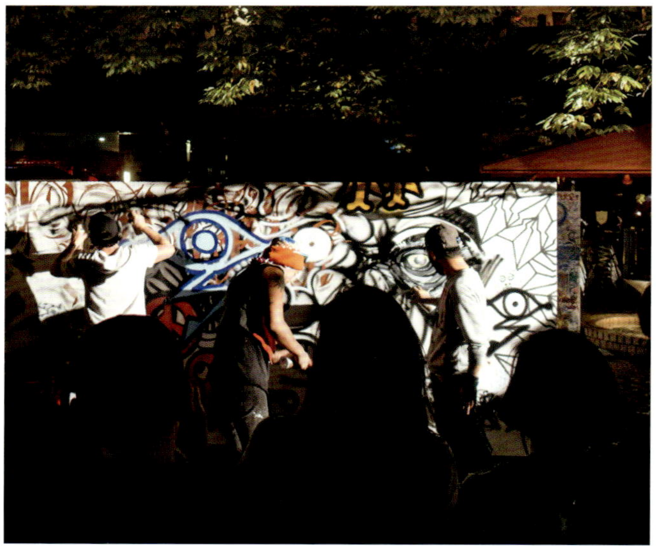

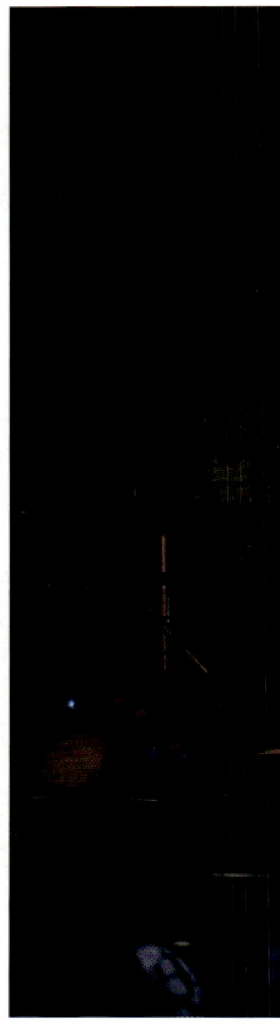

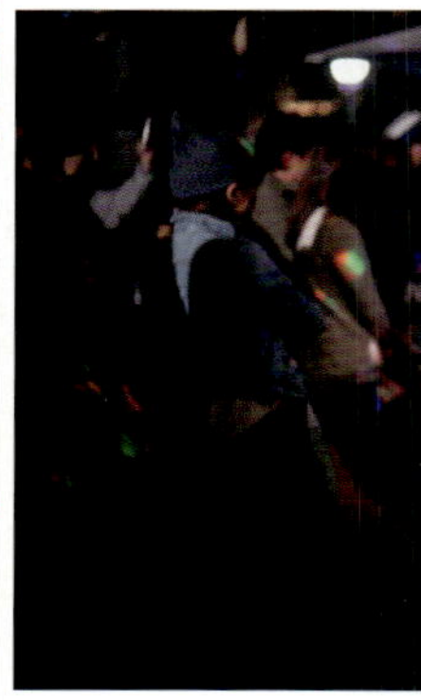

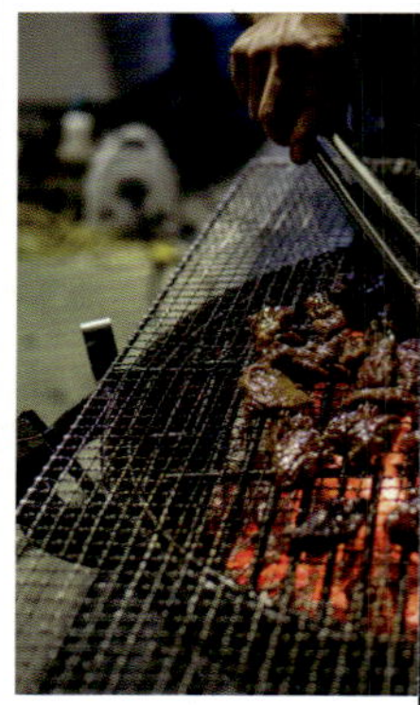

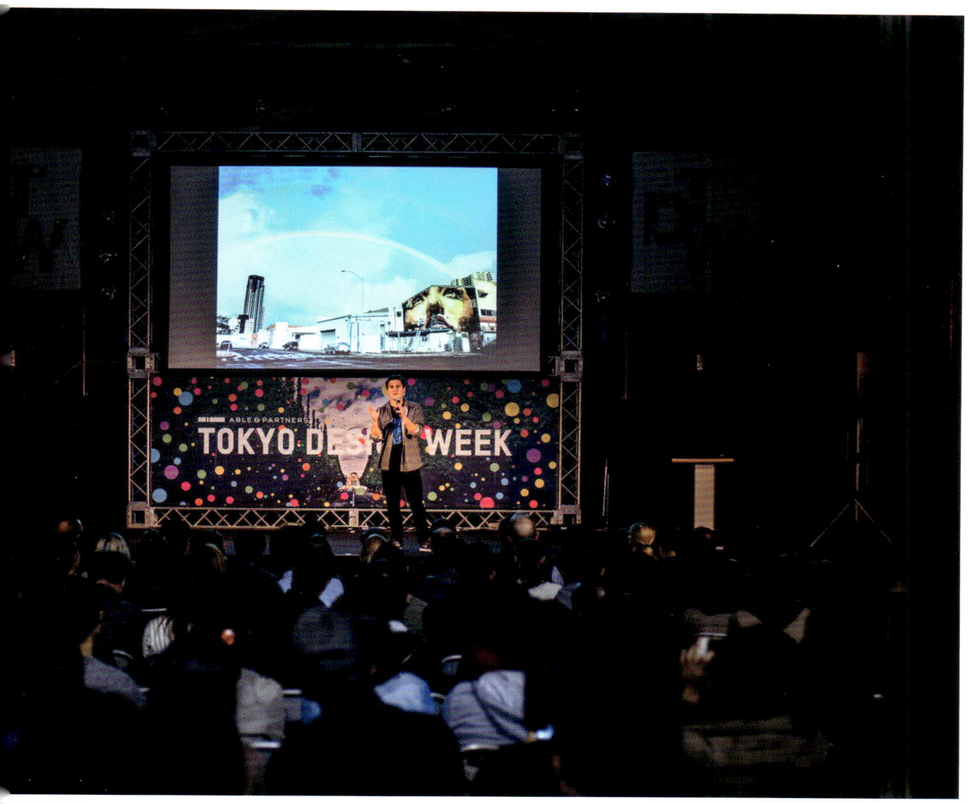

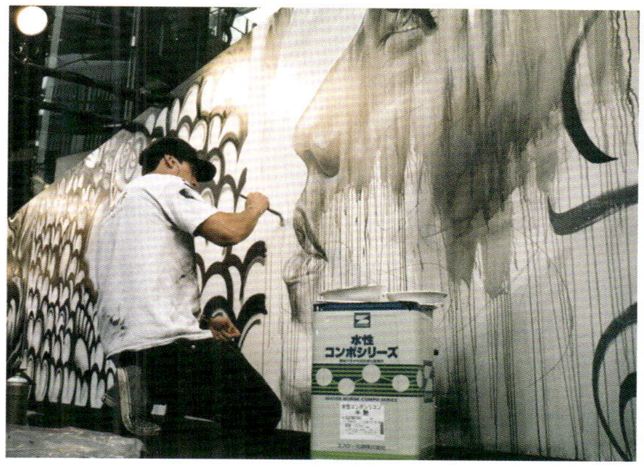
水性
コンポシリーズ

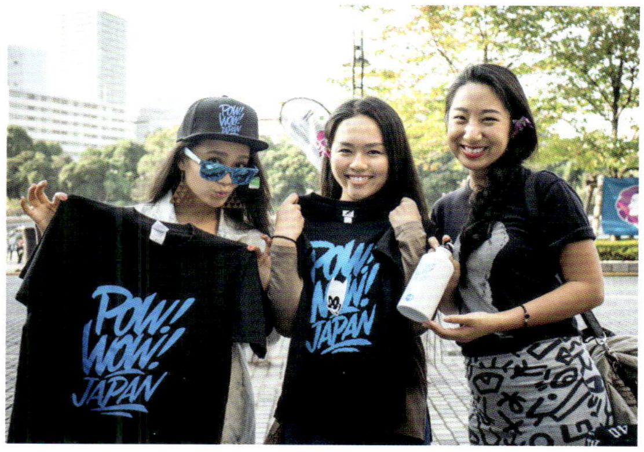
POW! WOW! JAPAN

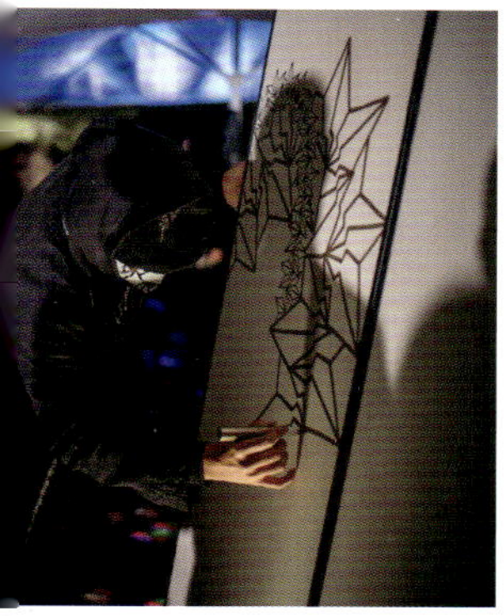

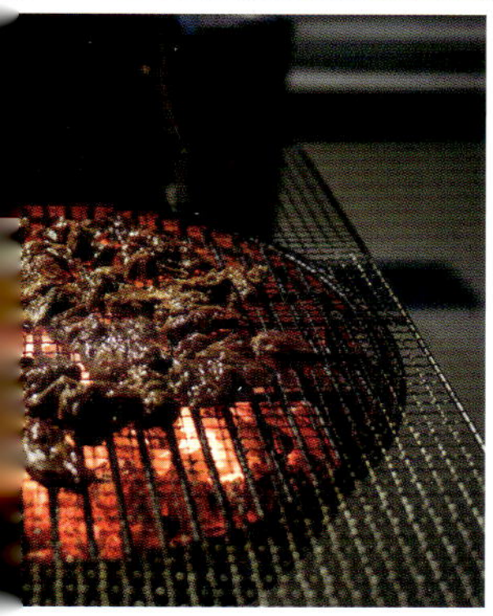

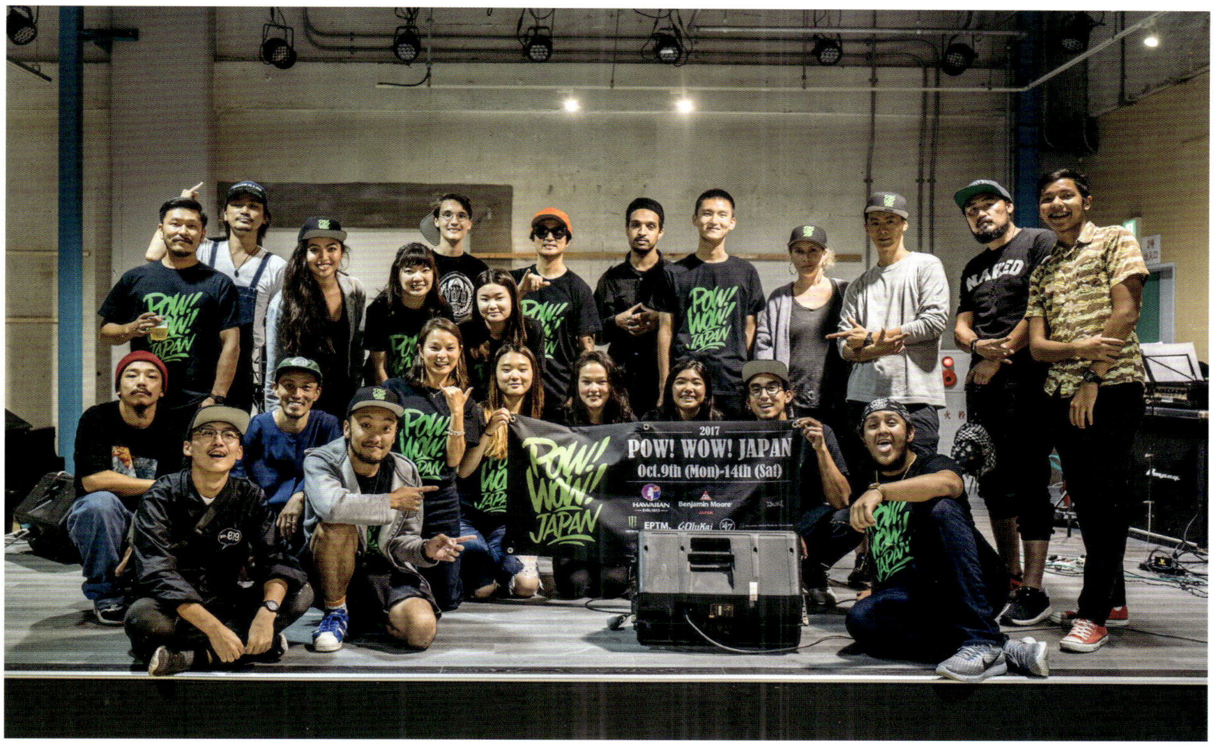
2017
POW! WOW! JAPAN
Oct.9th (Mon)-14th (Sat)
Benjamin Moore
EPTM.
OluKai

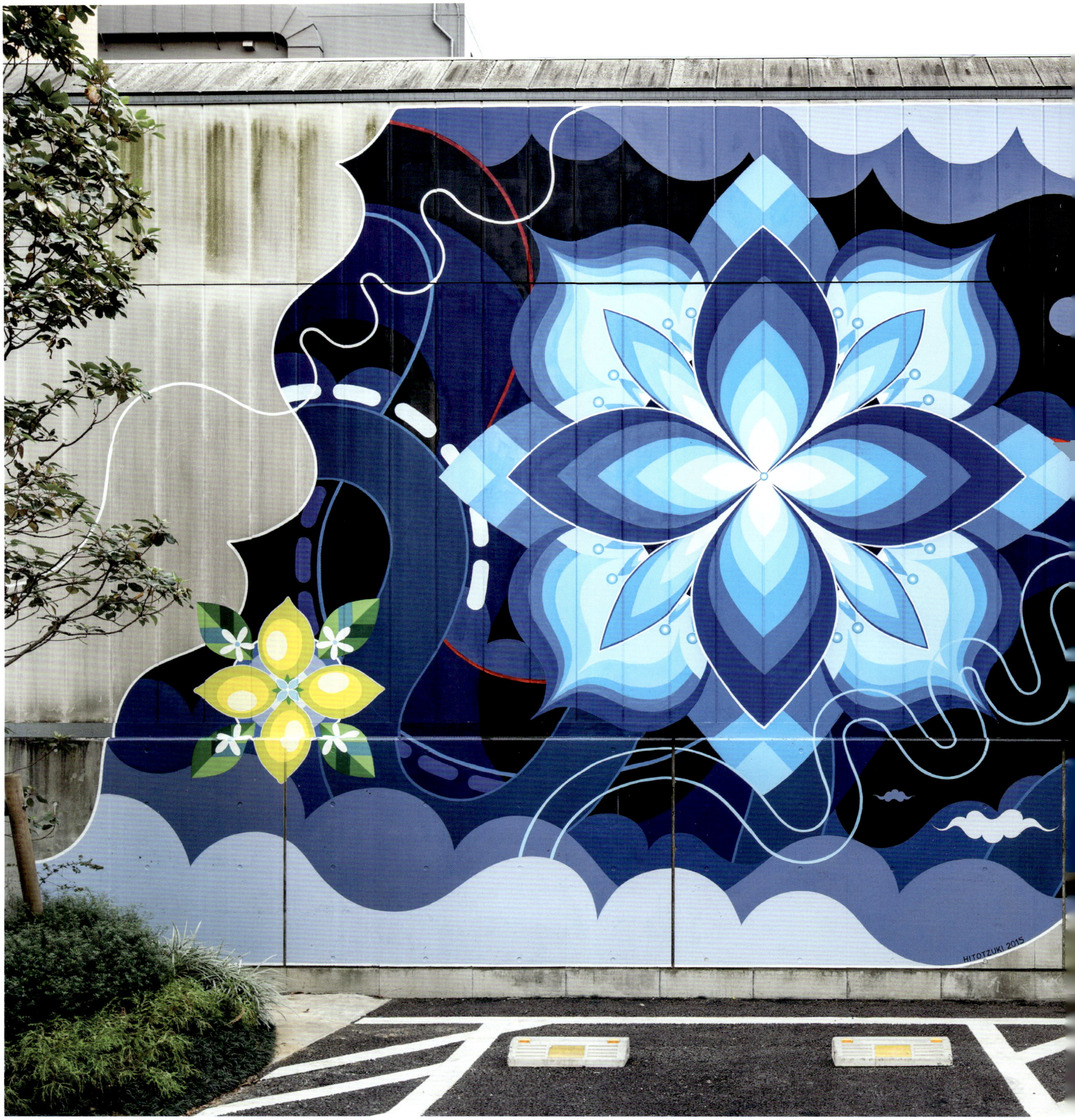
HITOTZUKI 2015

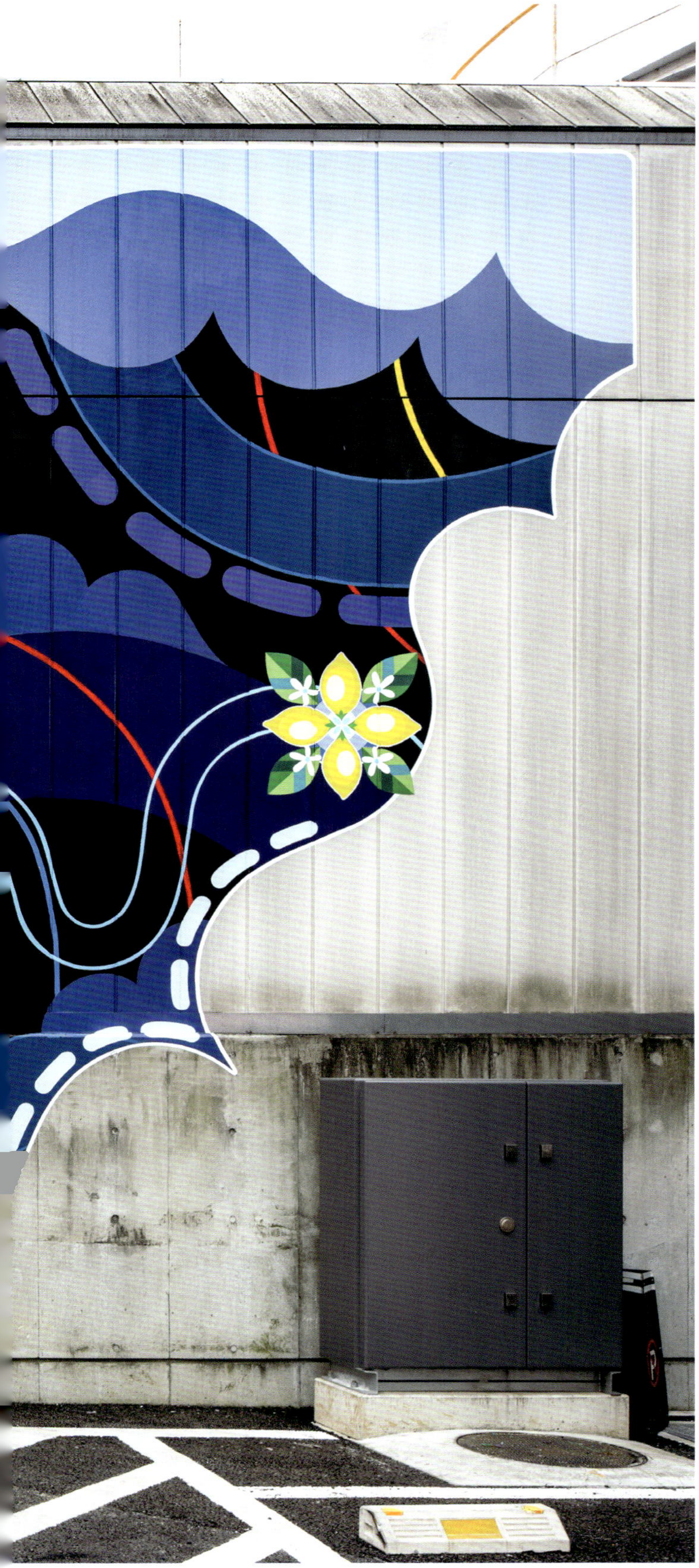

Japan 2015

Hitotzuki

@HTZK

The collaboration work of **KAMI** and **SASU** from 1999, aimed at expanding the stage for creativity rooted in the dimension of street culture.

Their distinctive worldview stems from the fluid interaction between the dynamically flowing curves fashioned by KAMI, and the strong and flamboyant symmetric motifs engineered by SASU.

This vision breaths new life into the sense of beauty derived from the street, and has succeeded in invigorating the era with a steady stream of vivid new landscapes. The pair views art as lying in the domains of their everyday lives, and while based in Tokyo, continues to lead a lifestyle interspersed with creative journeys around Japan and to overseas.

"**HITOTZUKI**", stands for the sun and the moon, being contrary to one another, they differ yet fuse together. Through their ideology, depicting scenery from their lifestyle and feelings.

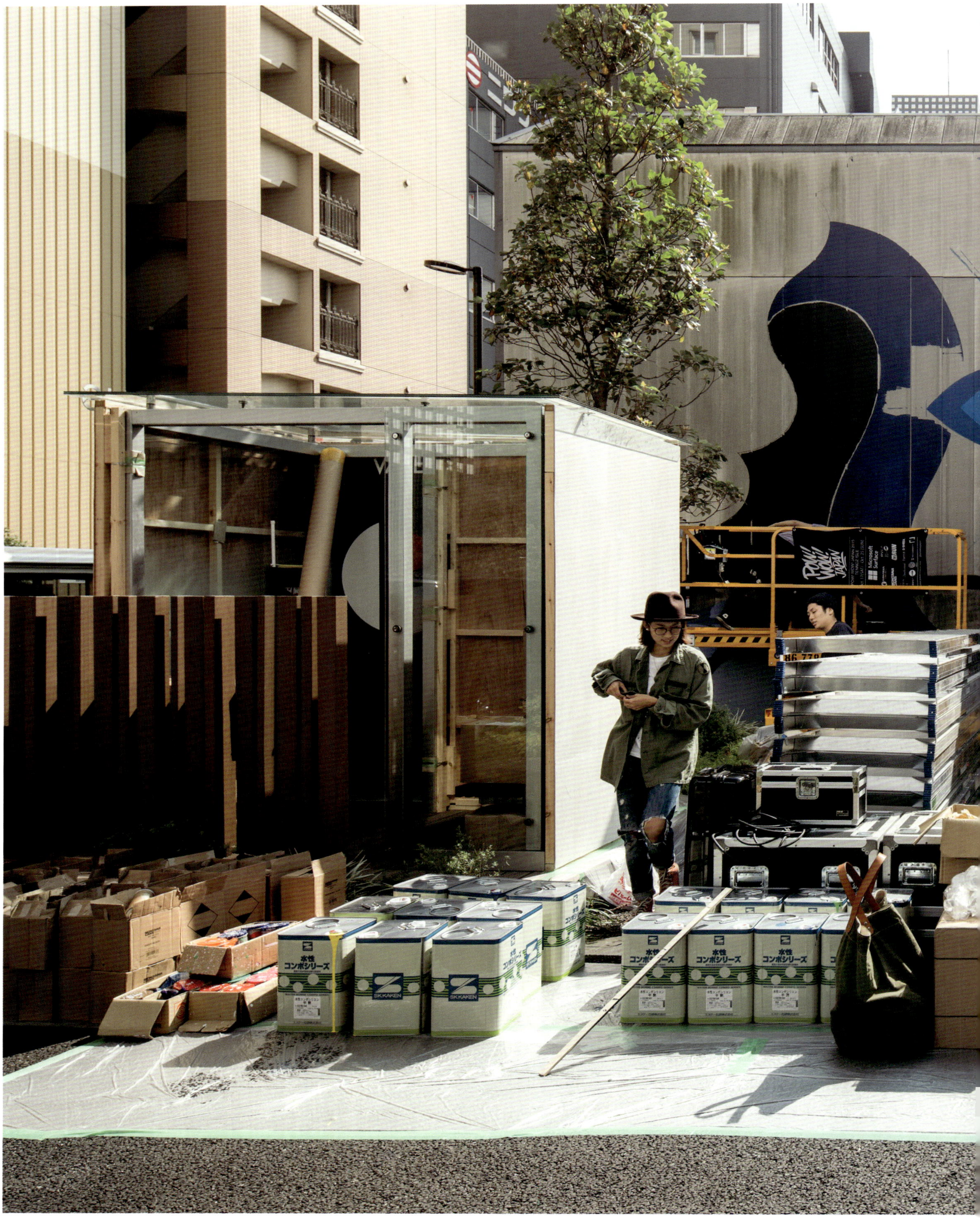
水性
コンポシリーズ
SK KAKEN

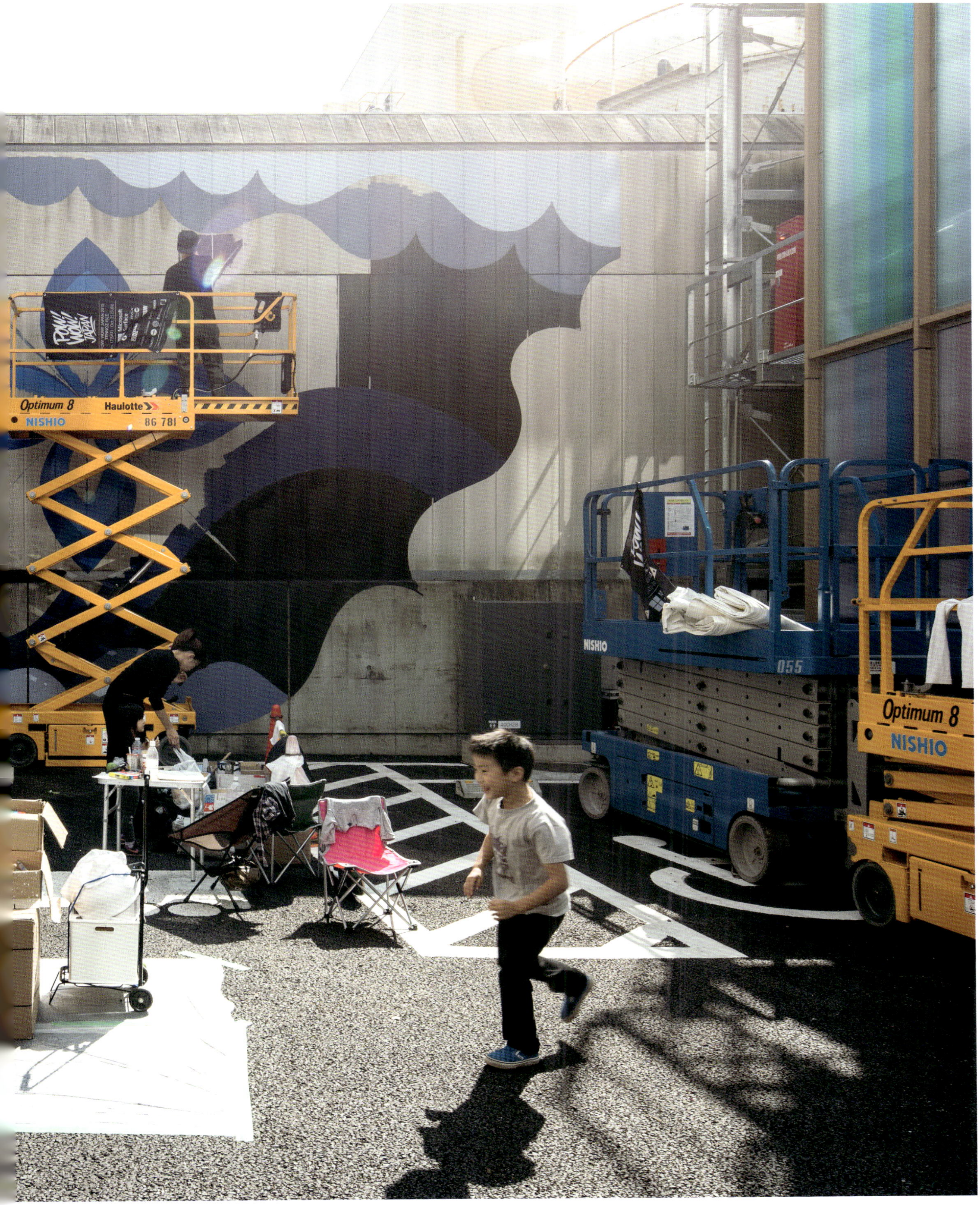
Optimum 8
Haulotte
NISHIO
86 781
NISHIO
055
Optimum 8
NISHIO

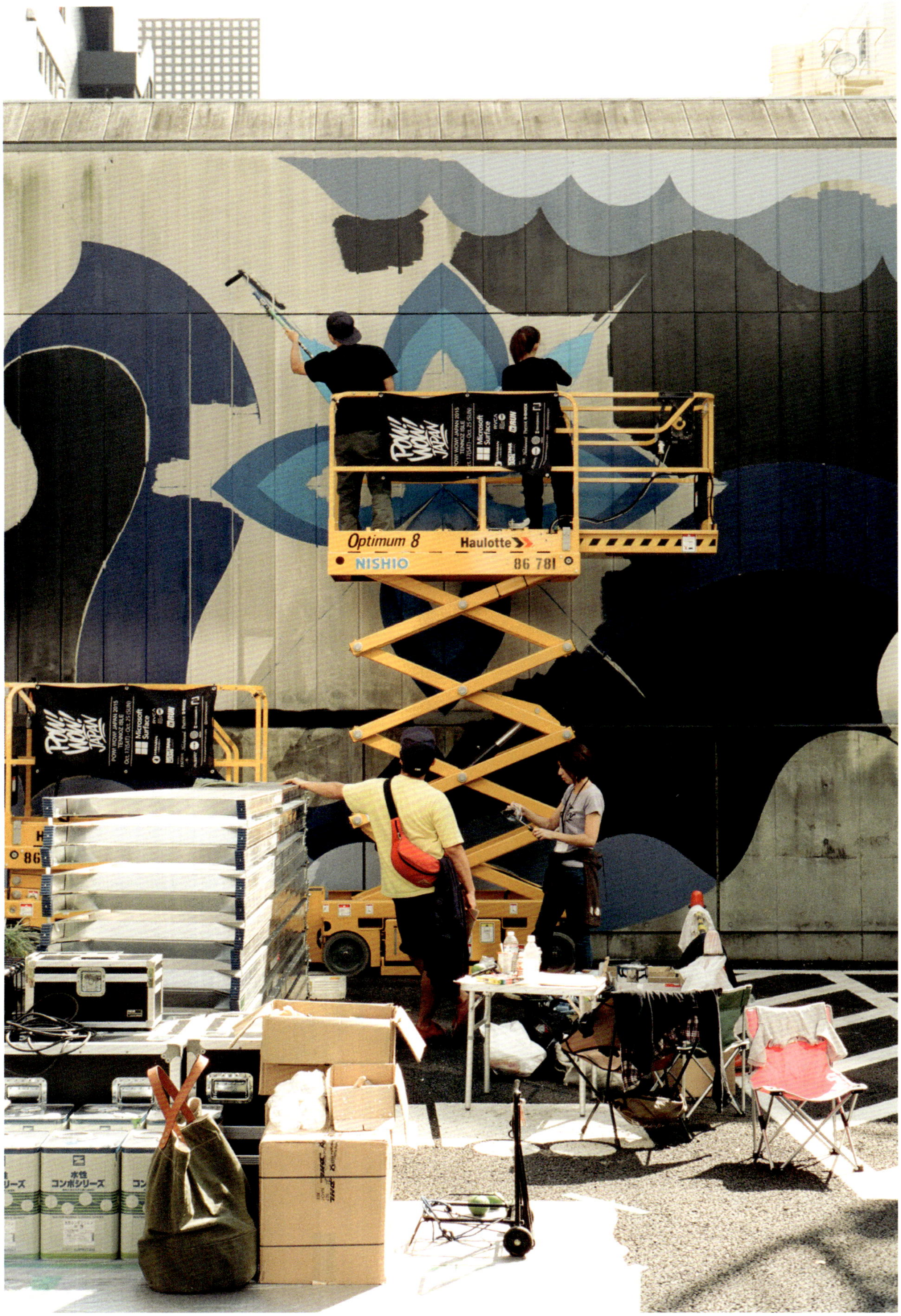
Optimum 8
Haulotte
NISHIO
86 781
POW! WOW! JAPAN
Microsoft Surface
水性
コンポシリーズ

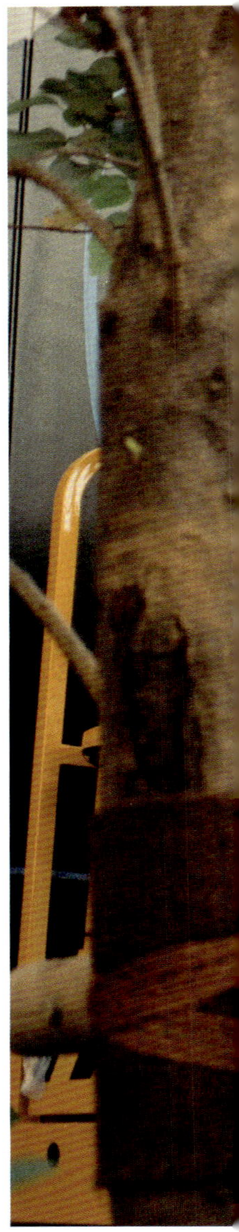

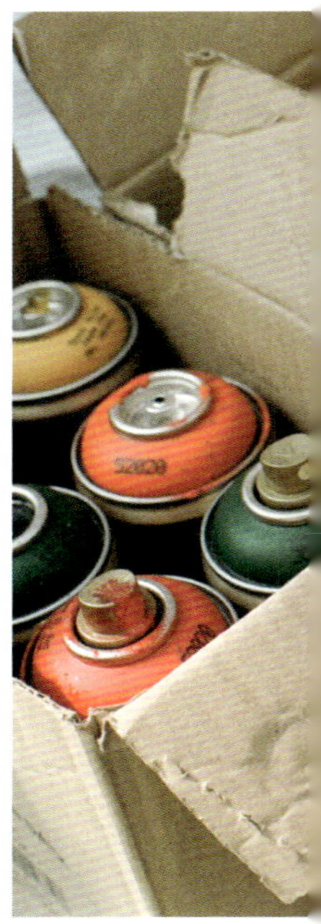

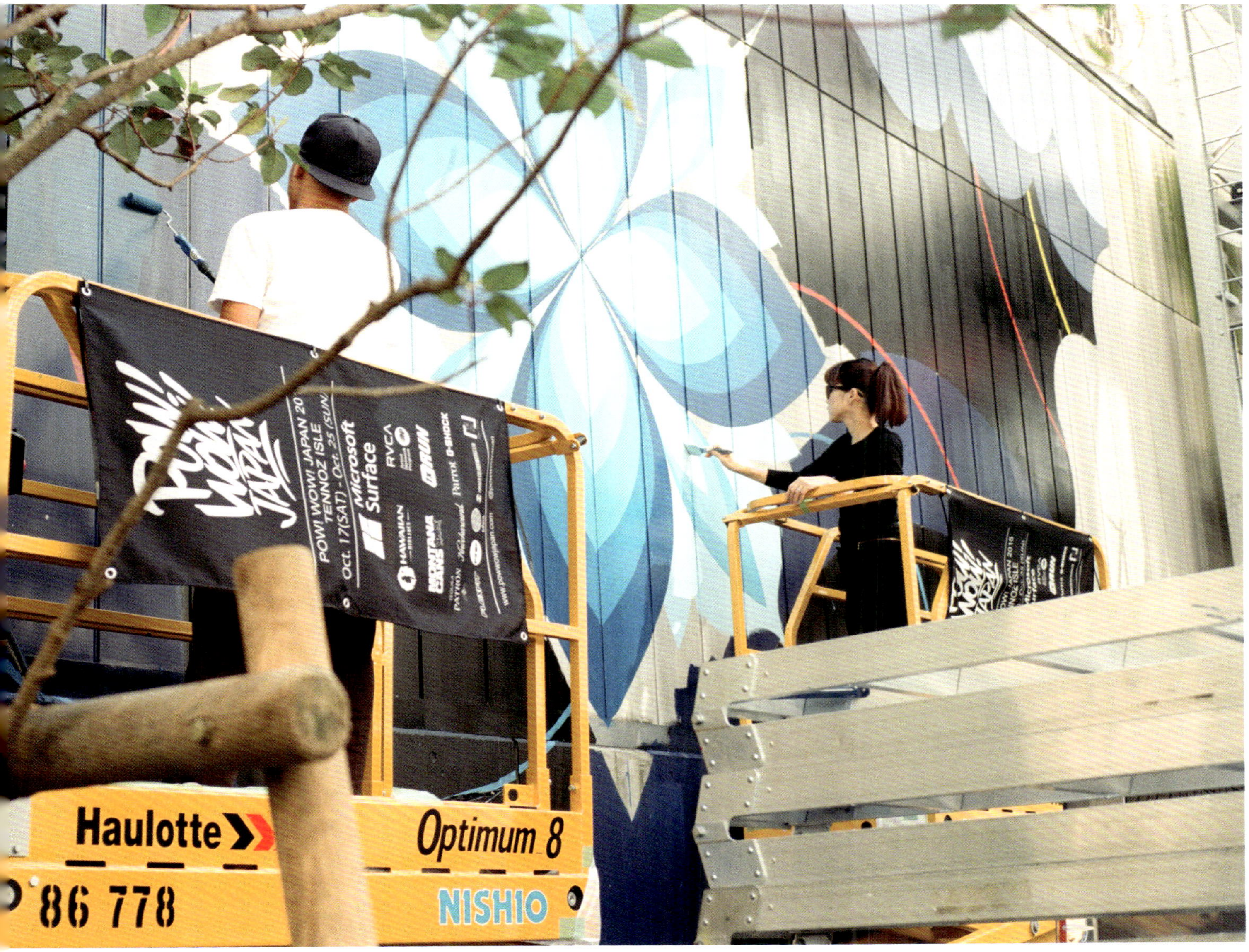
Microsoft Surface
RVCA
Haulotte
Optimum 8
86 778
NISHIO

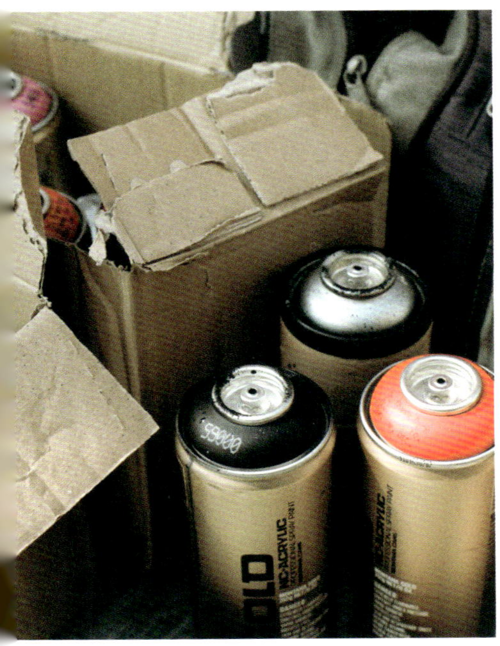

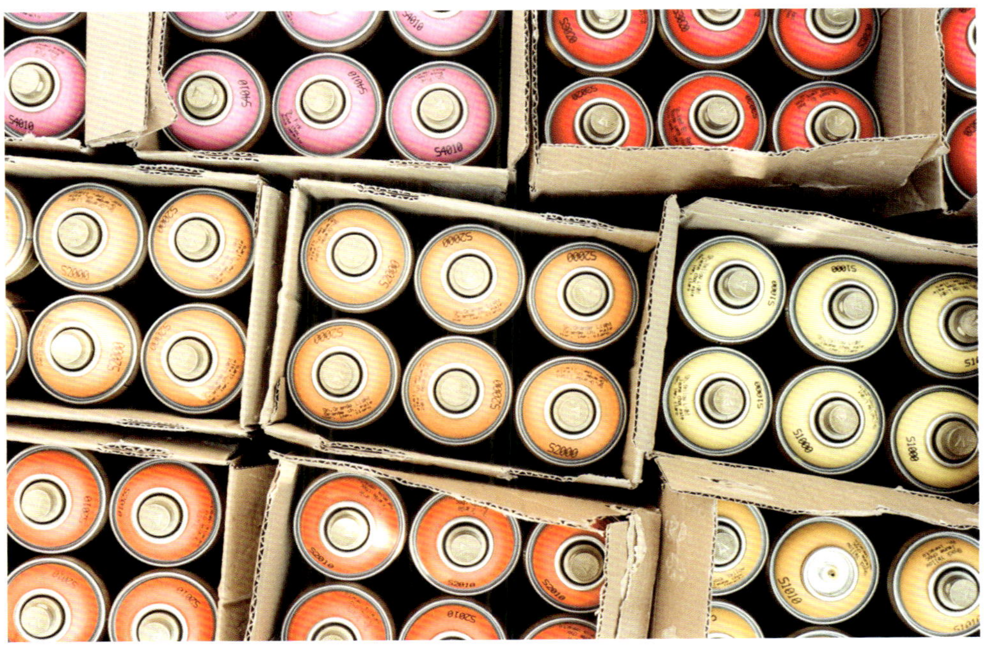

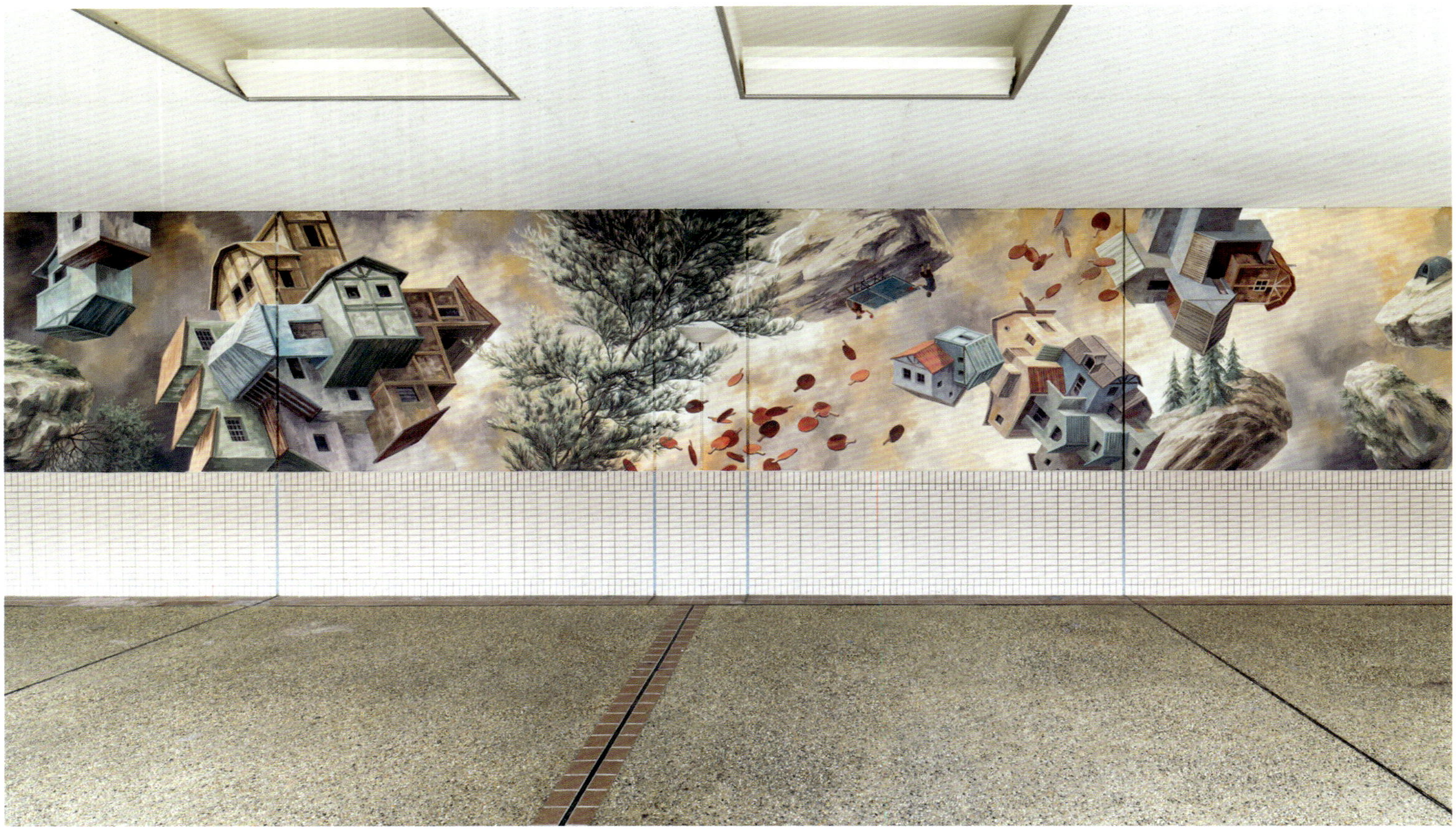

Japan 2016

Cinta Vidal

@CINTA_VIDAL

Cinta Vidal Agulló has been drawing since she was a kid. Vidal studied at Escola Massana in Barcelona and when she was 16, Vidal started working as an apprentice in Taller de Escenografia Castells Planas in St. Agnès de Malanyanes where she learnt from Josep and Jordi Castells to love scenography and the backdrop trade. Vidal has never stopped experimenting with illustration. Vidal worked as a freelancer for various clients and gradually she headed into the world of painting and creating her own work.

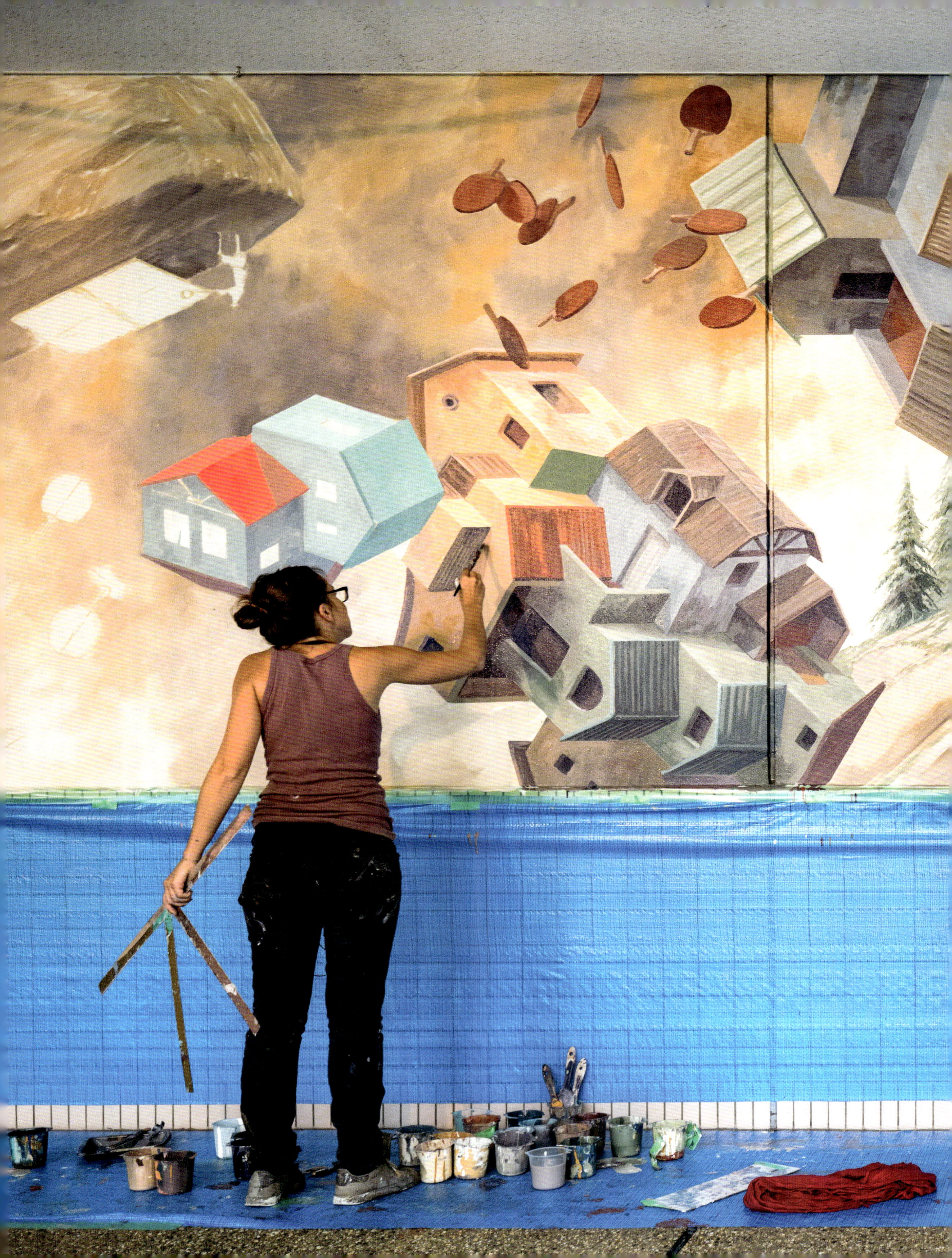

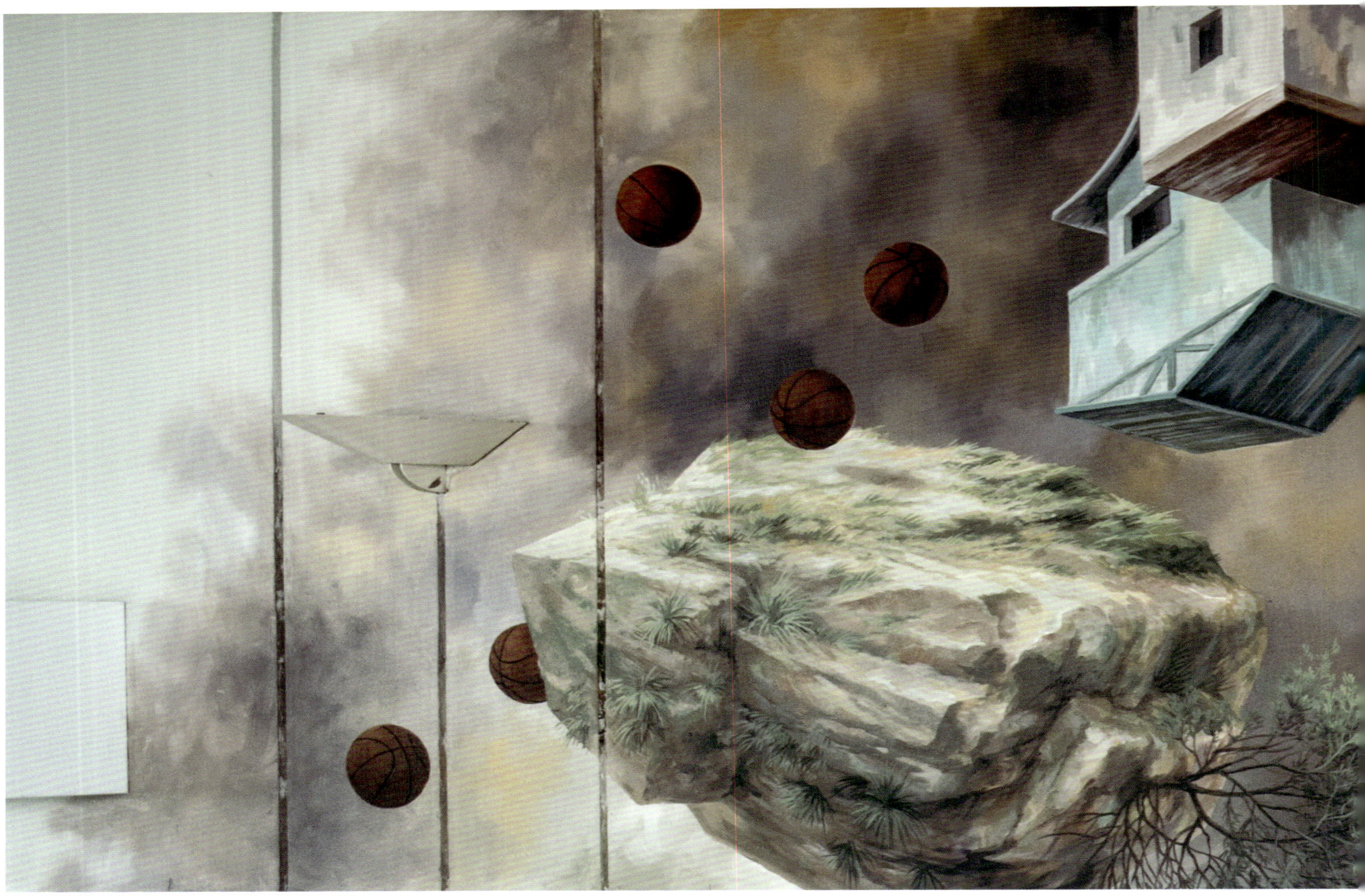

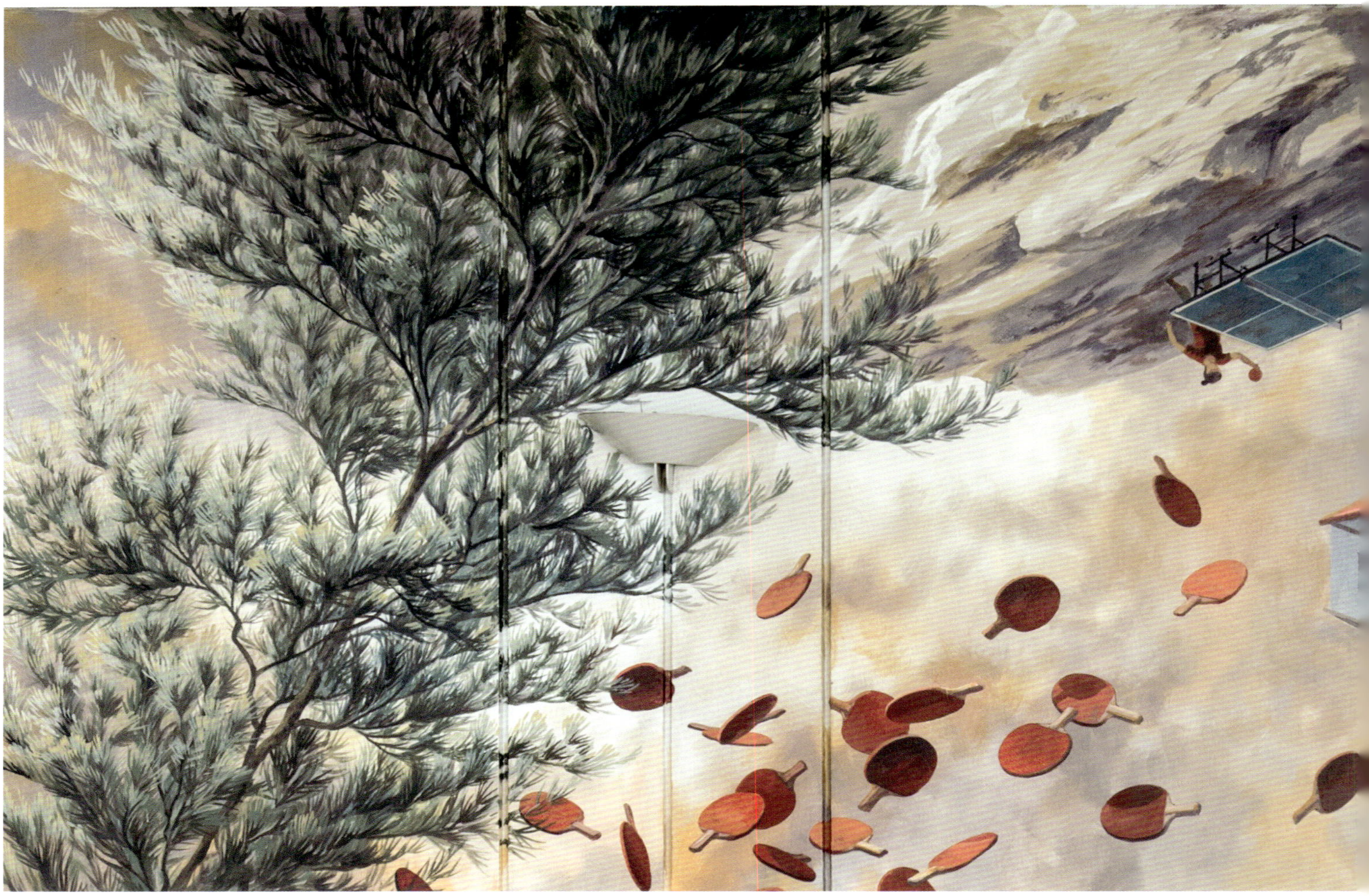

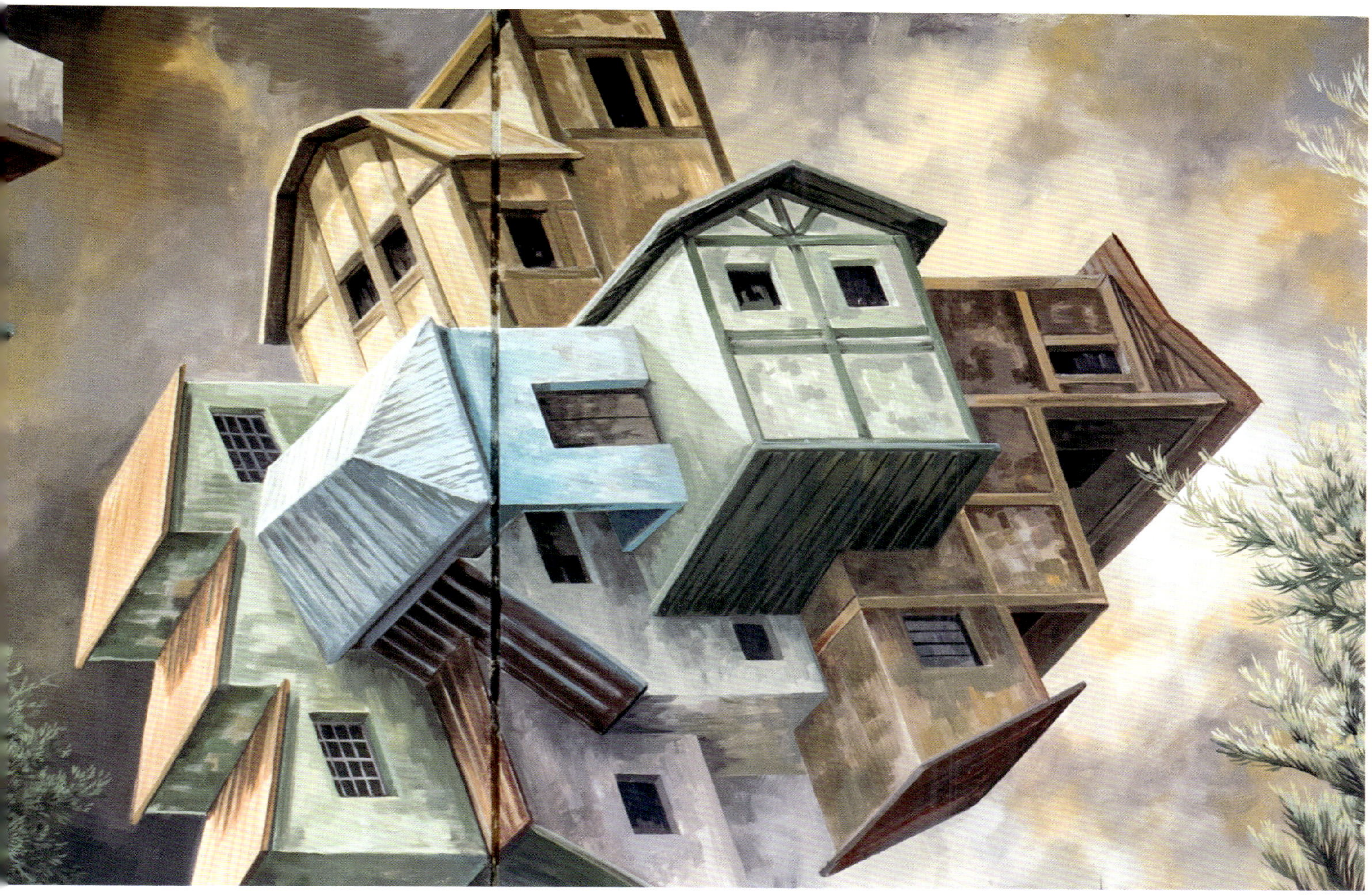

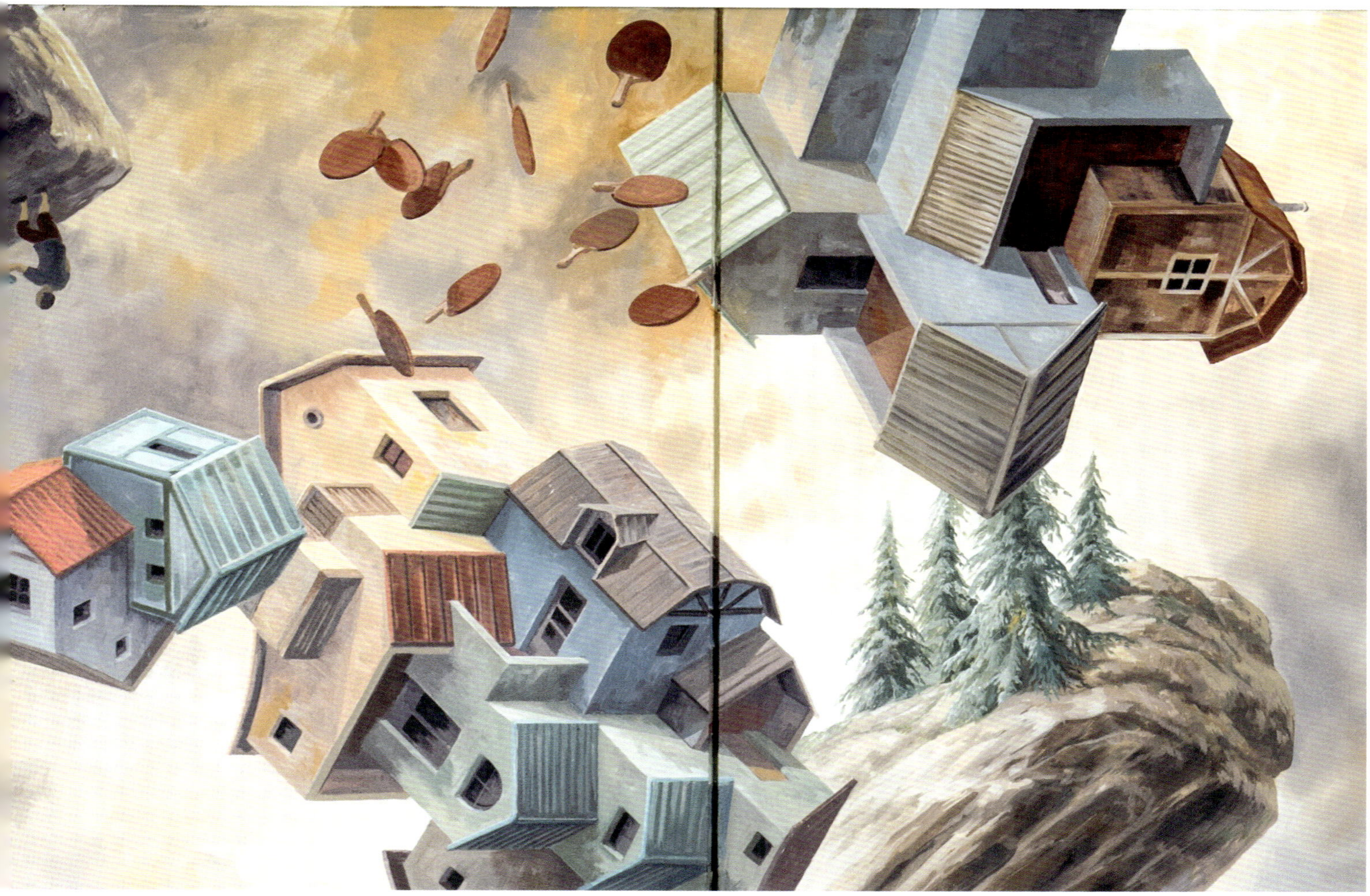

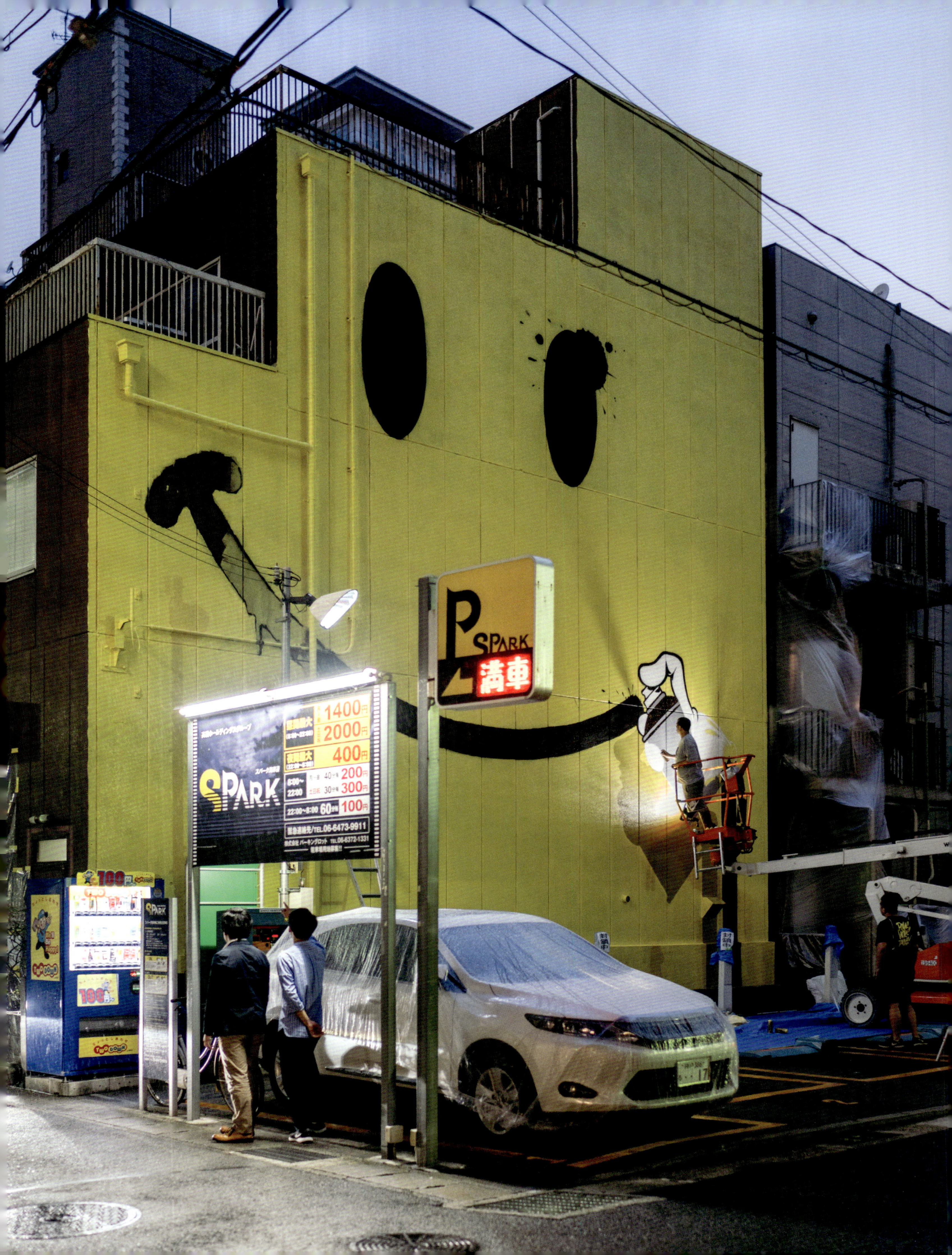

P SPARK
満車
SPARK
1400円
2000円
400円
200円
300円
22:00~8:00 60分毎 100円
TEL.06-6473-9911
TEL.06-6372-1331

OG Slick

@OG_SLICK

Slick's rise to the top can be traced back to the mid '80s, from painting on the streets of Honolulu to the mean streets of Los Angeles. Slick spent his early years attending ArtCenter College Of Design during the day and doing graffiti at night.

The legendary "Slick vs Hex" graffiti battle was pivotal moment in Slick's career. He went from underground hell raiser to garnering worldwide acclaim, forever changing how graffiti characters are painted to this day. The international attention opened the doors for Slick to paint everything from music videos, feature films, album covers to full fledged gallery exhibits. It was during this time, he realized he could reach a larger audience by putting his art on t-shirts. Since his first designs in the late 80's, Slick has designed graphics for the likes of Stussy, X-Large, Adidas, Obey, Disney and the list goes on. His graphic design aesthetic has influenced an entire generation of artists/designers. He pioneered a movement called "street wear" long before the term was even coined.

Slick's main focus nowadays is his clothing brand Dissizit! Over the past 12 years, Dissizit has established itself as a brand not to be taken lightly with their "take no prisoner" attitude on it's assault on pop culture. Slick's "LA Hands" logo icon has become a sort of an anthem and symbol for Los Angeles pride!

Whether it's painting a mural, designing a sneaker, formulating a paint scheme for an automobile, art directing graffiti for a video game, creating an entire collection season after season for Dissizit, or as small as signing his name for a fan, Slick treats each and everything he touches as a work of art that's worthy of being Slick.

25+ years in the game and Slick still has shown no signs of slowing up.

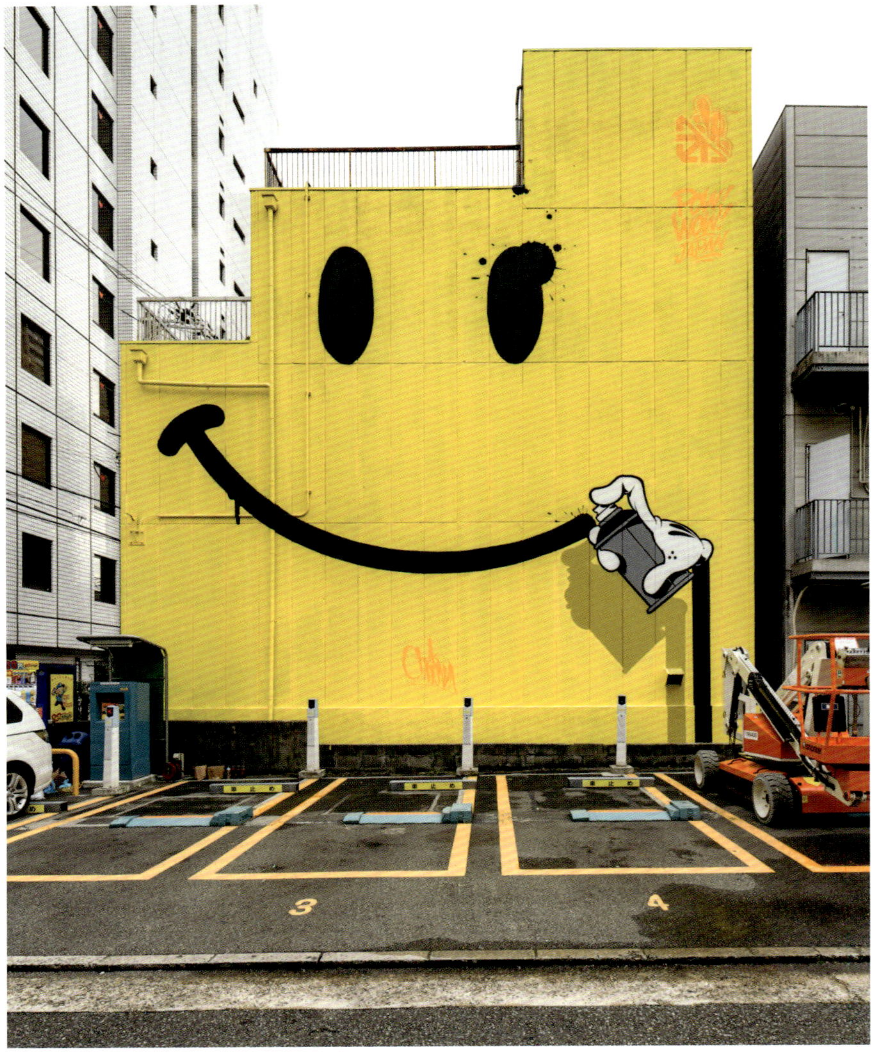

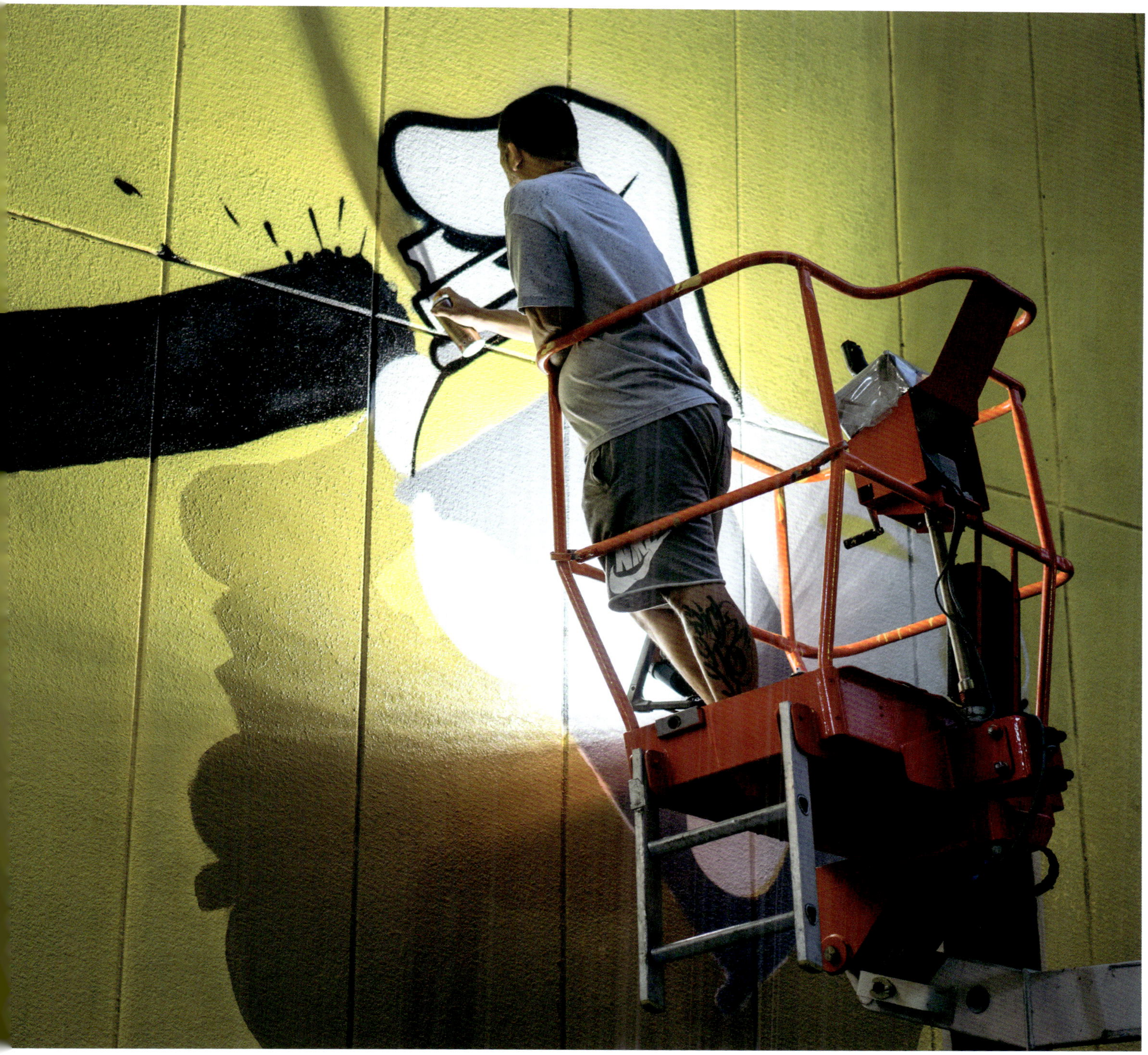

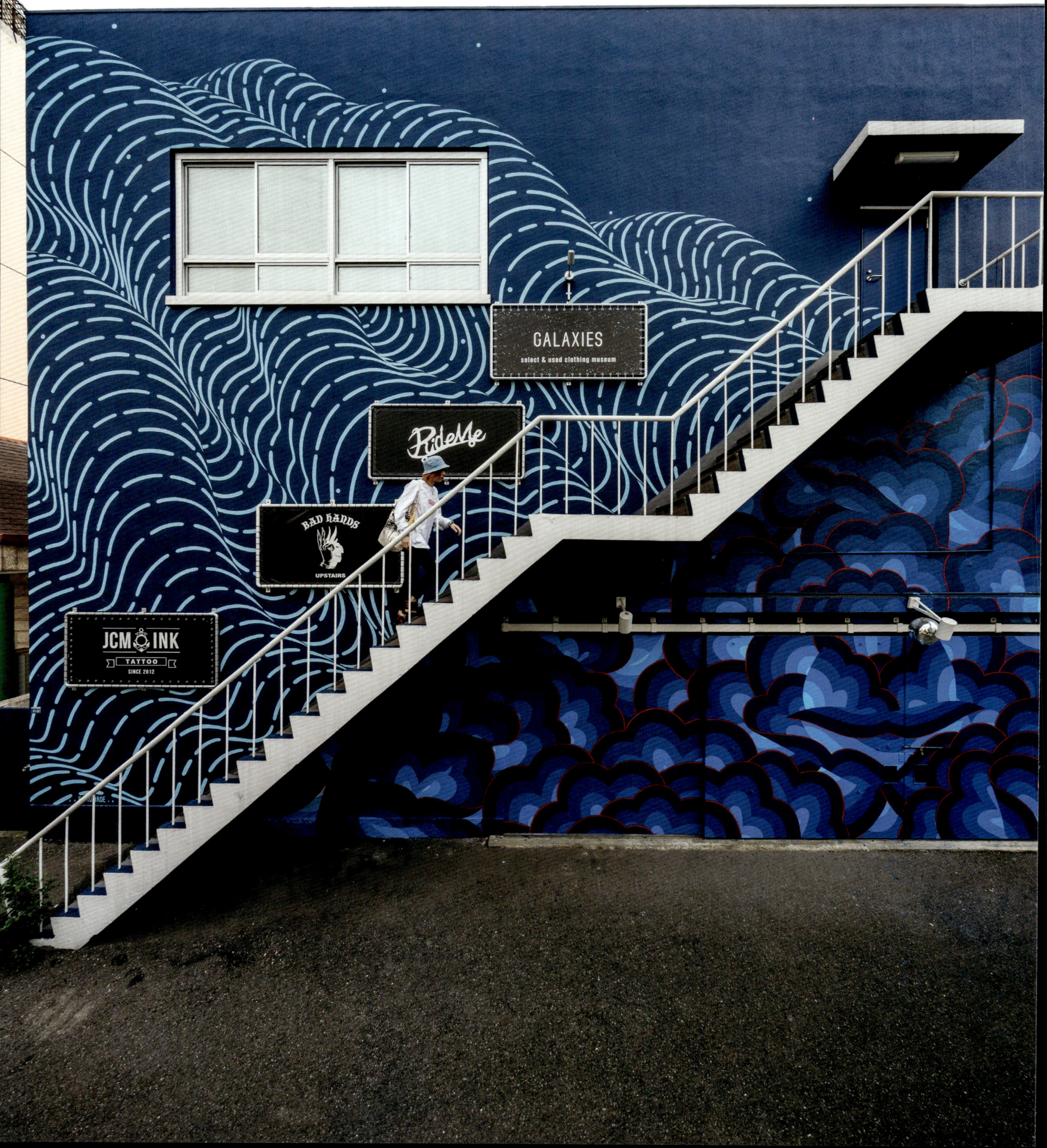
GALAXIES
select & used clothing museum
RideMe
BAD HANDS
UPSTAIRS
JCM INK
TATTOO
SINCE 2012

Brendan Monroe & Jet Martinez

@BRENDANTHEBLOB @JETMAR1

Brendan Monroe (b.1980) studied at ArtCenter College of Design in Pasadena. A sculptor and painter, his work consists of explorations of motion and abstracted matter, translated into a graphic black and white language that plays with perception. It's this dual quality and the tension between the flat surface and form that gives them their power and allure. He also works with clay in his collaboration with Heath Ceramics, where he's experimented with tile murals and hand built sculptures. His murals can be found in cities around the world with a concentration in California where he is based.

Jet Martinez is a full time muralist & painter based in Oakland, California, where he lives with a much beloved and talented wife and two ridiculously energetic children.

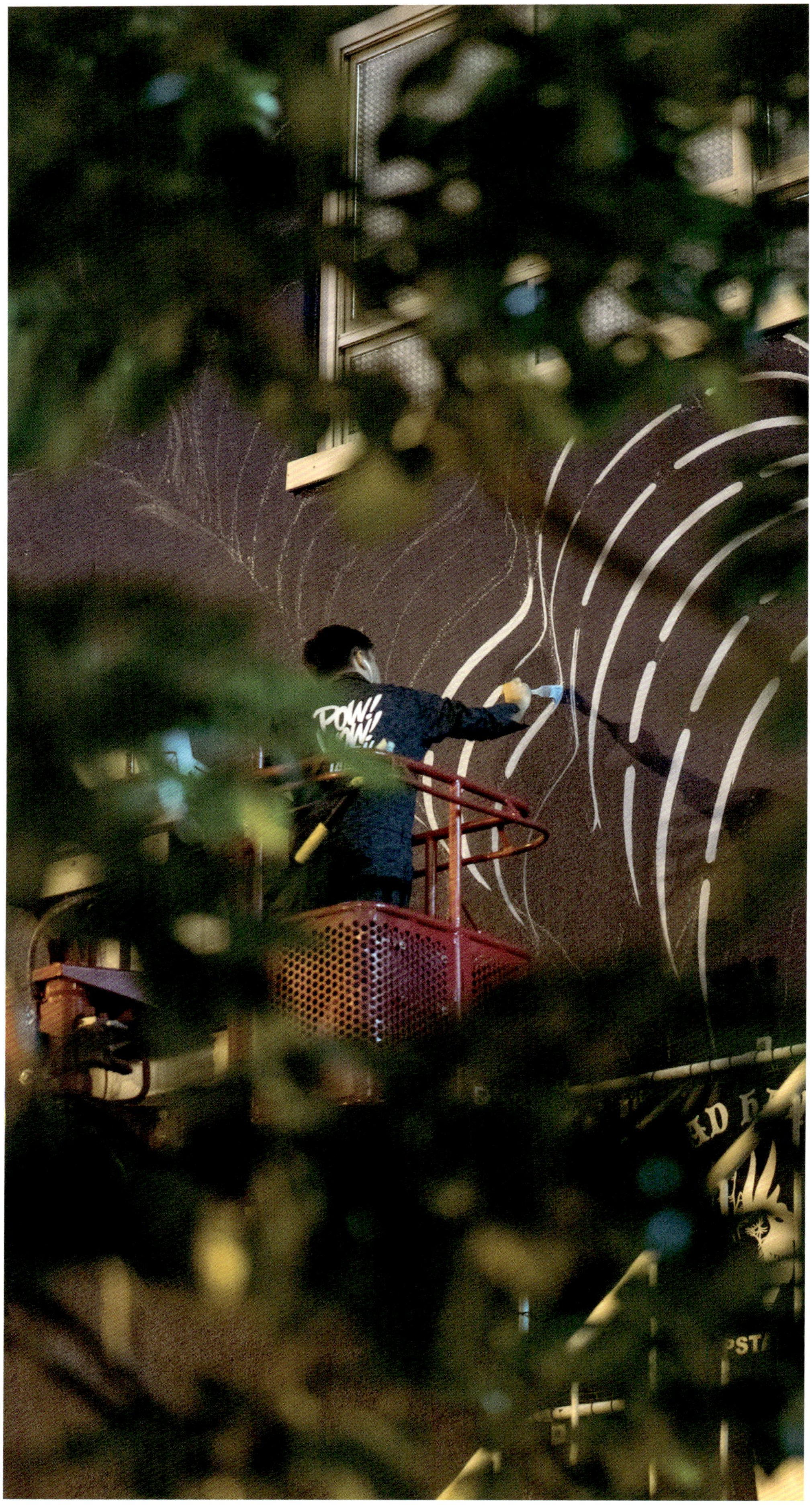

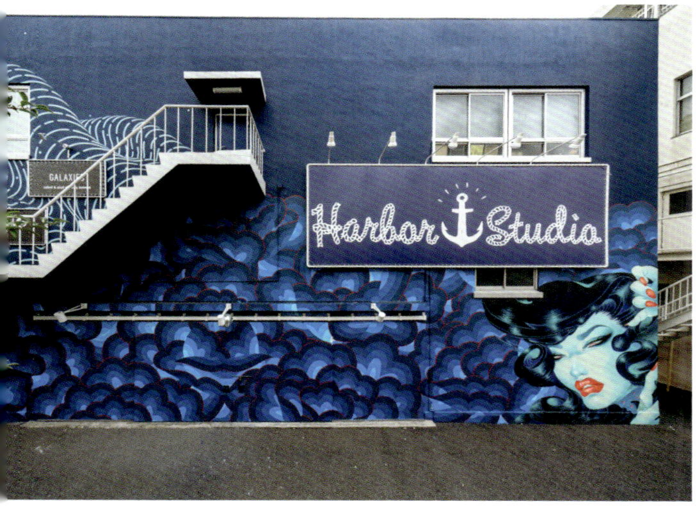
Harbor Studio
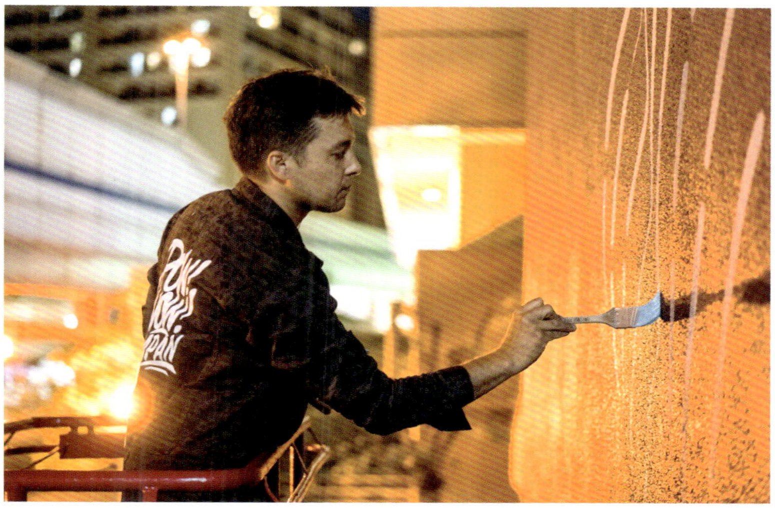
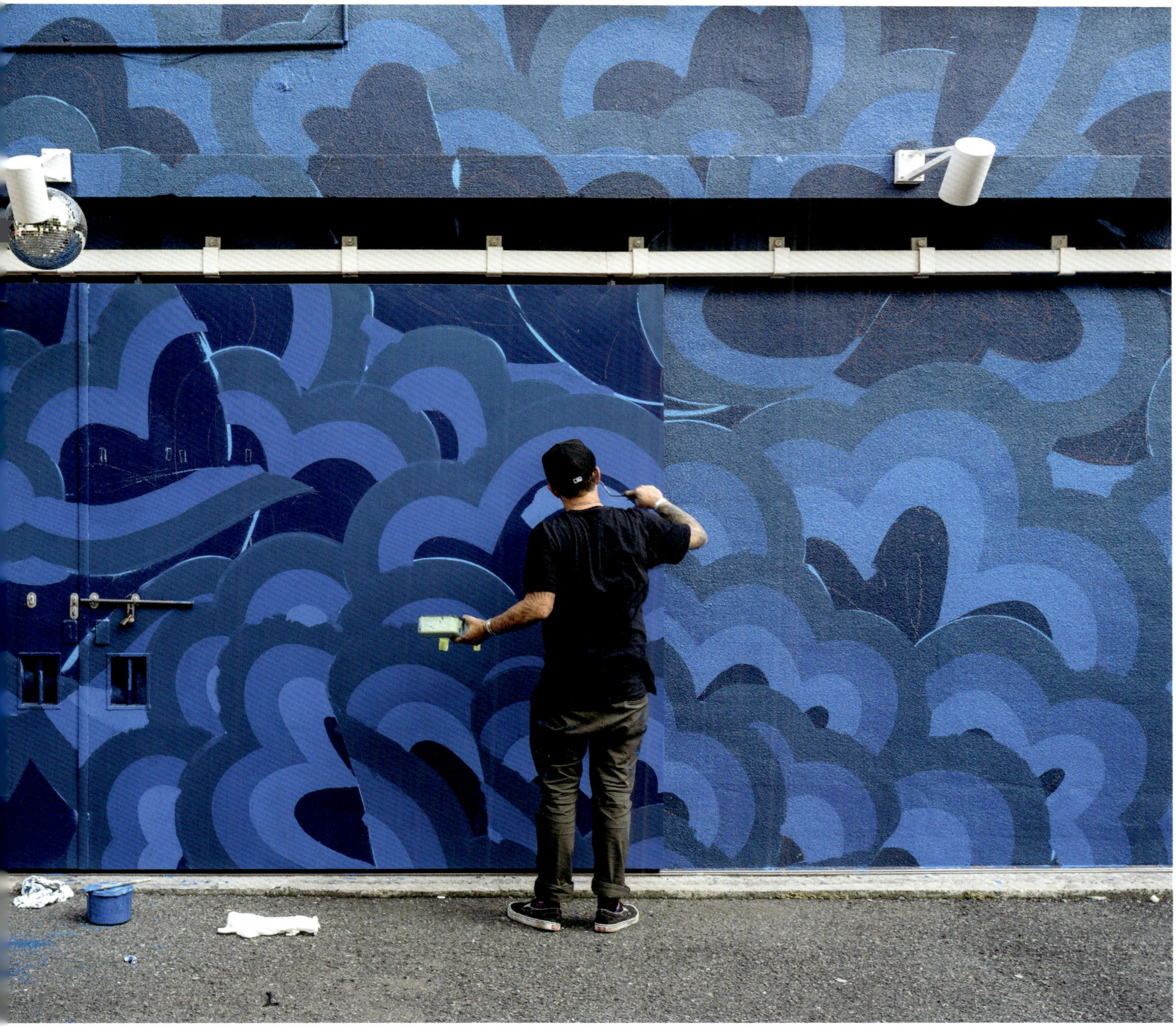

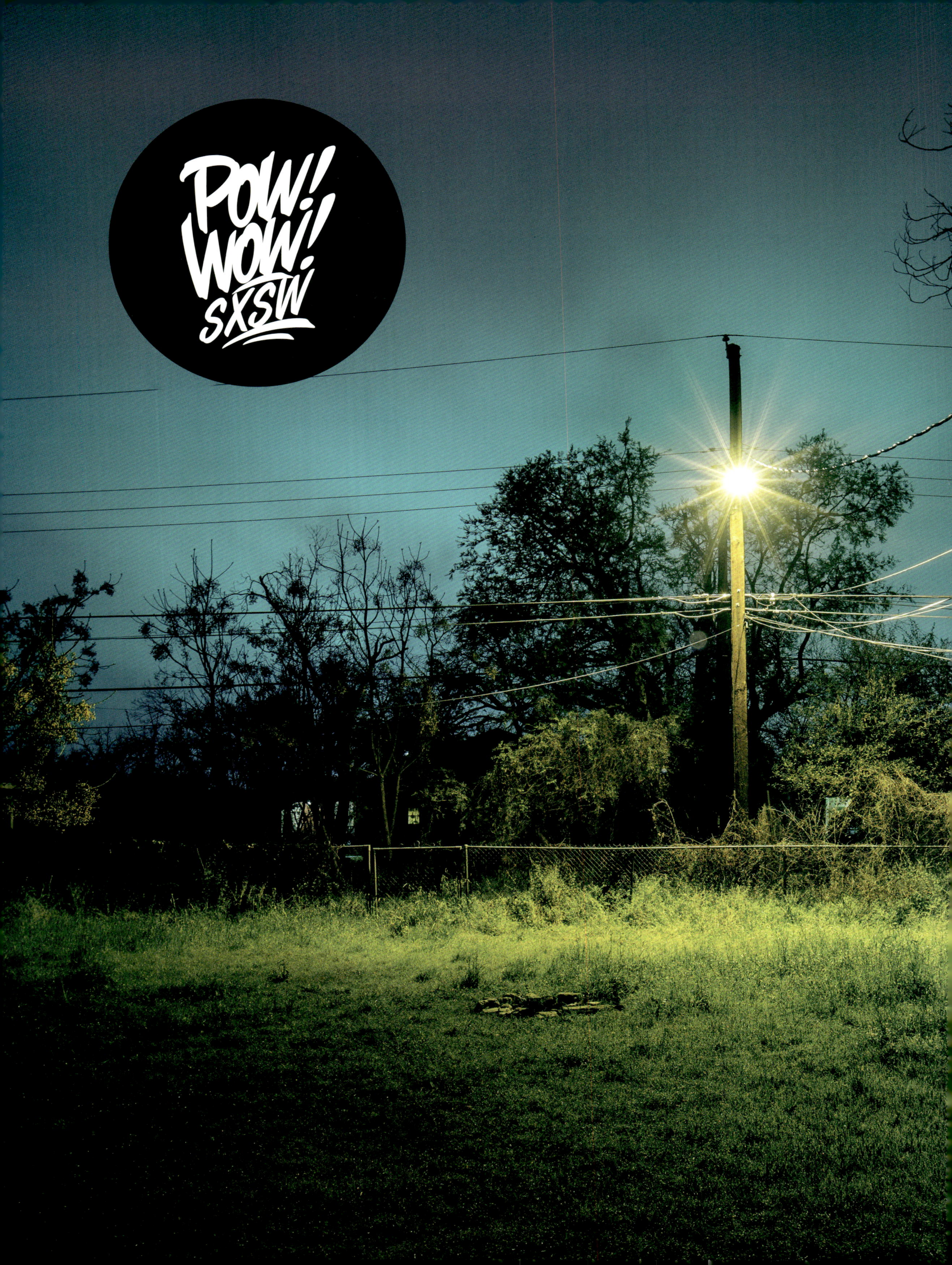
POW!
WOW!
SXSW

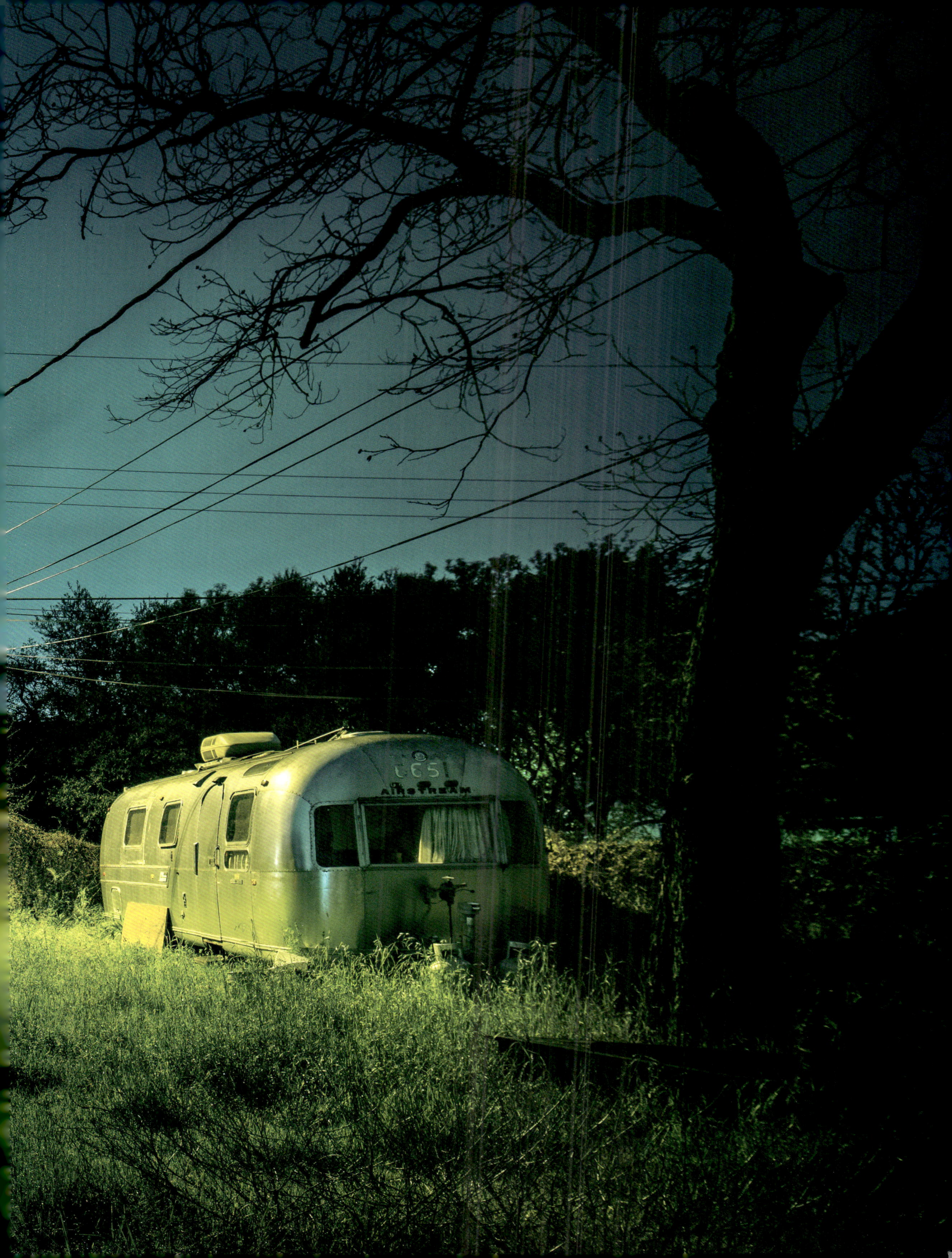
AIRSTREAM

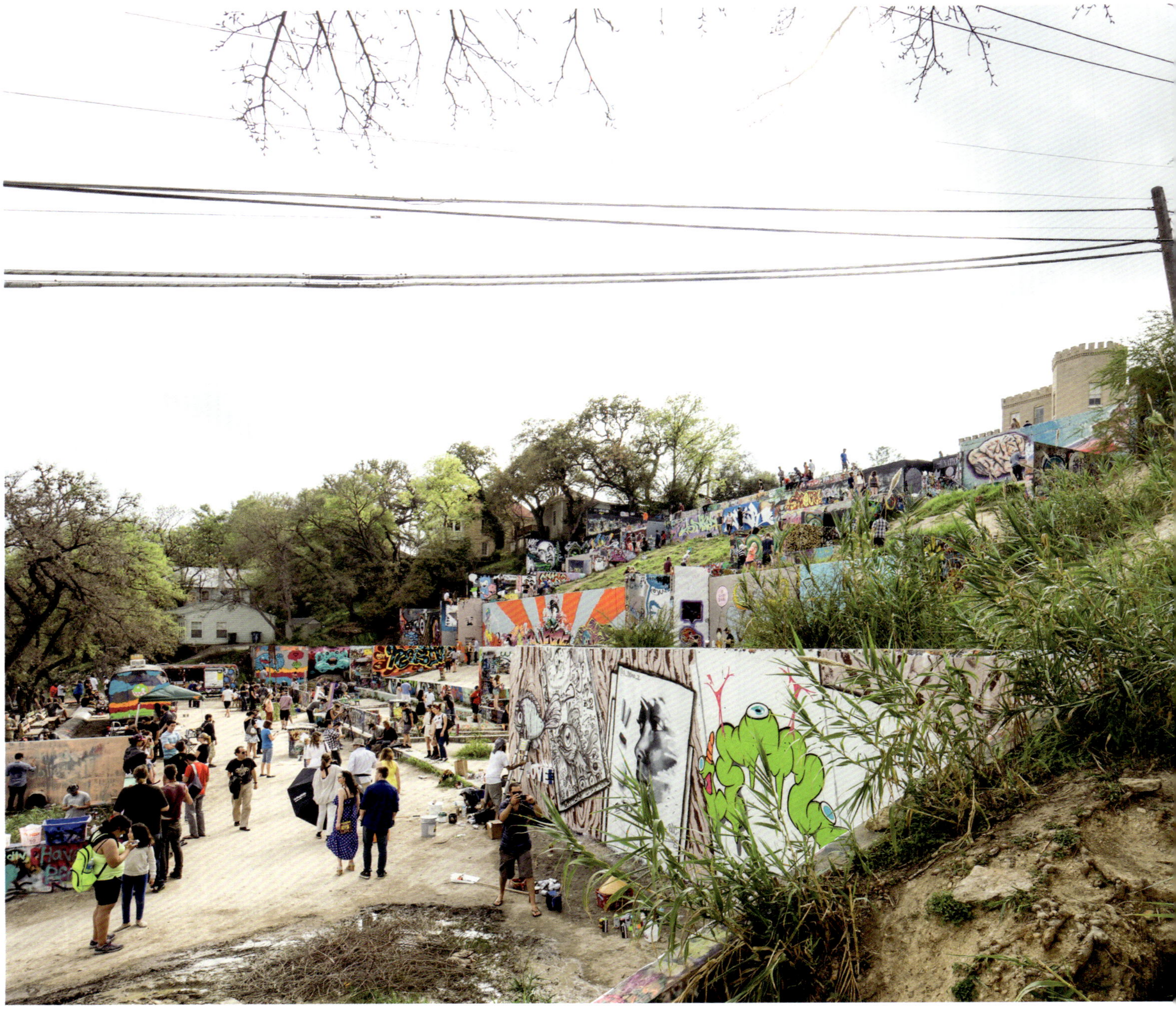

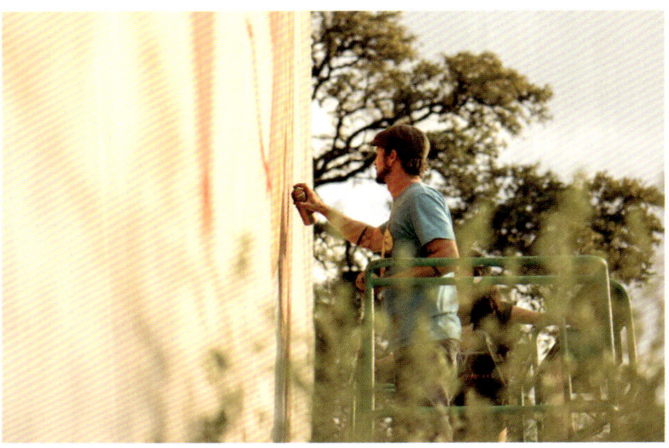

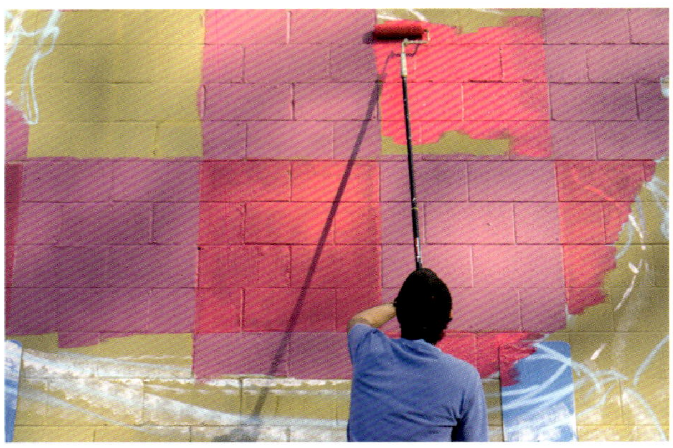

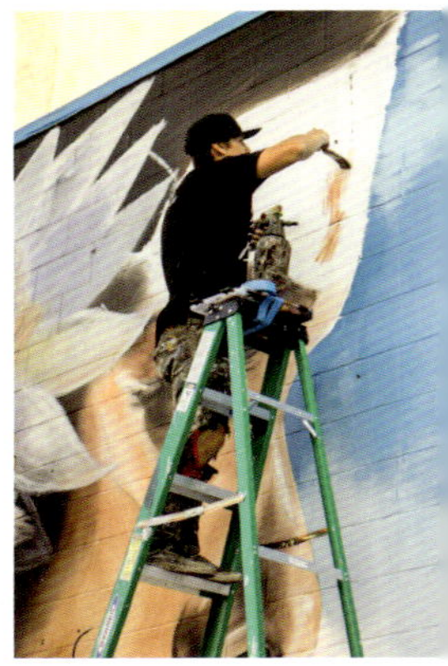

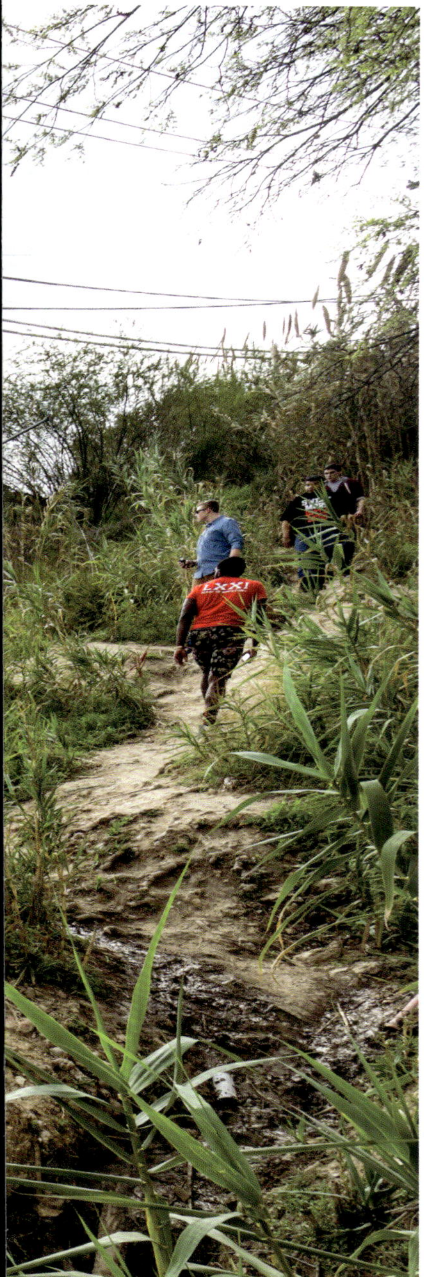

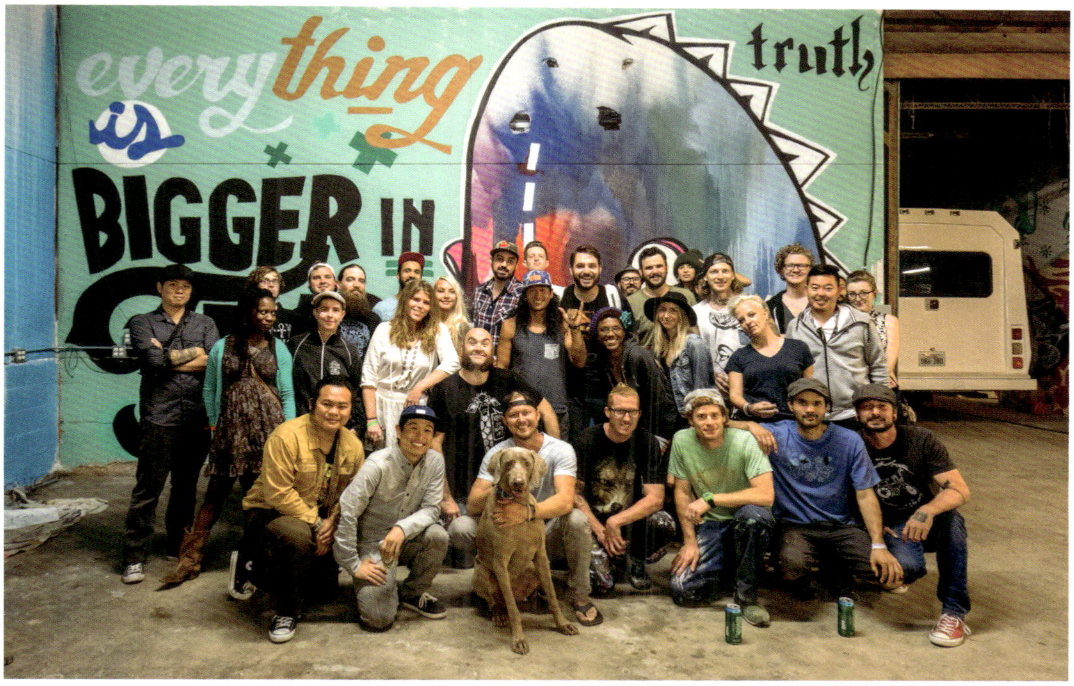
everything
is
BIGGER IN
truth

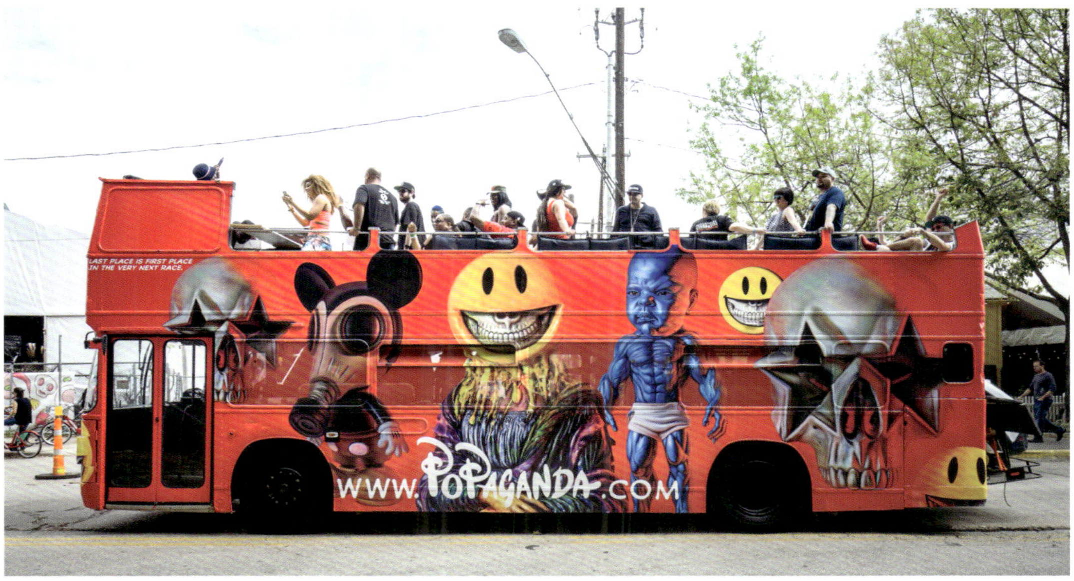
WWW.POPAGANDA.COM

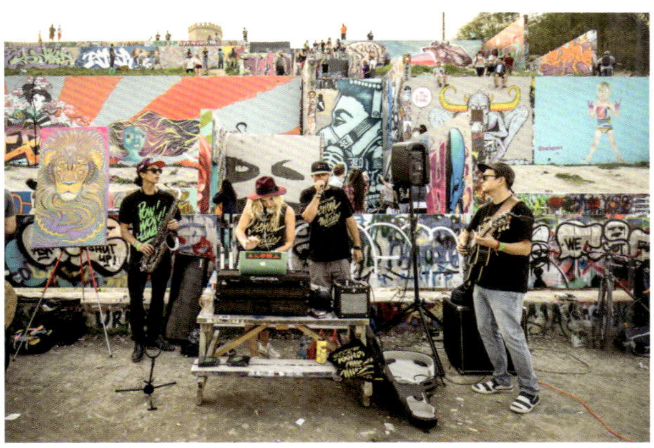

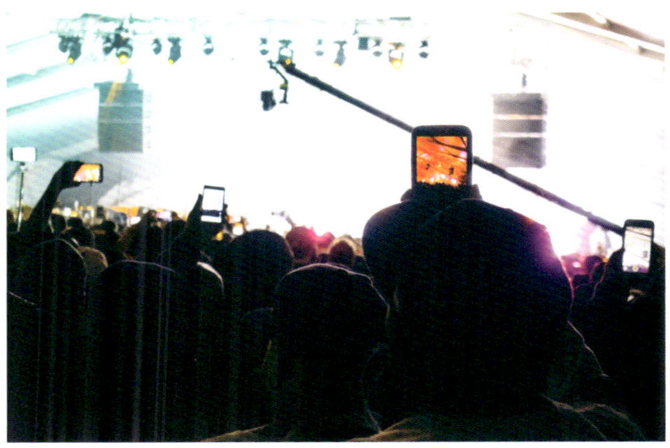

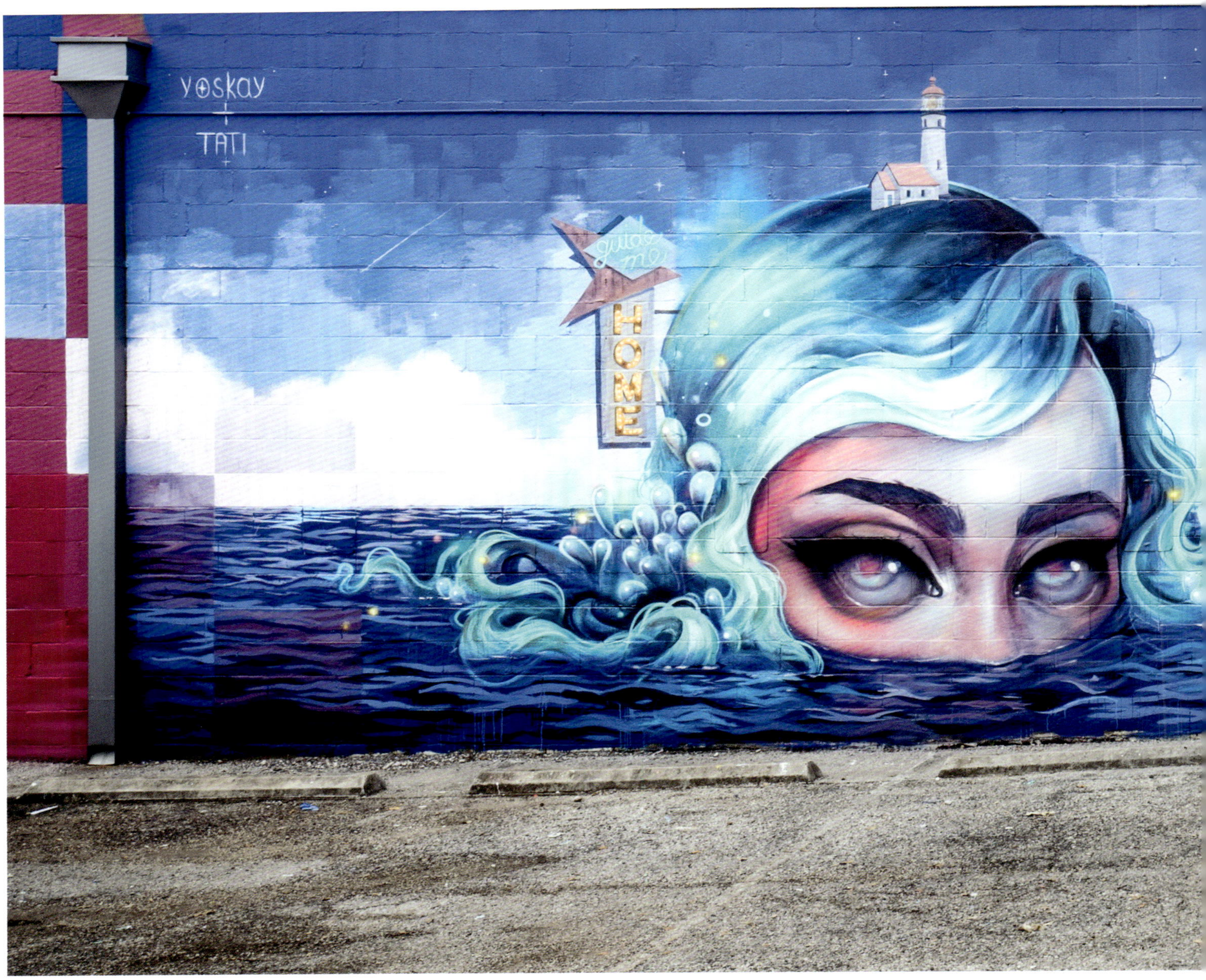

SXSW 2015

Tatiana Suarez & Yoskay Yamamoto

@TATUNGA @YOSKAYYAMAMOTO

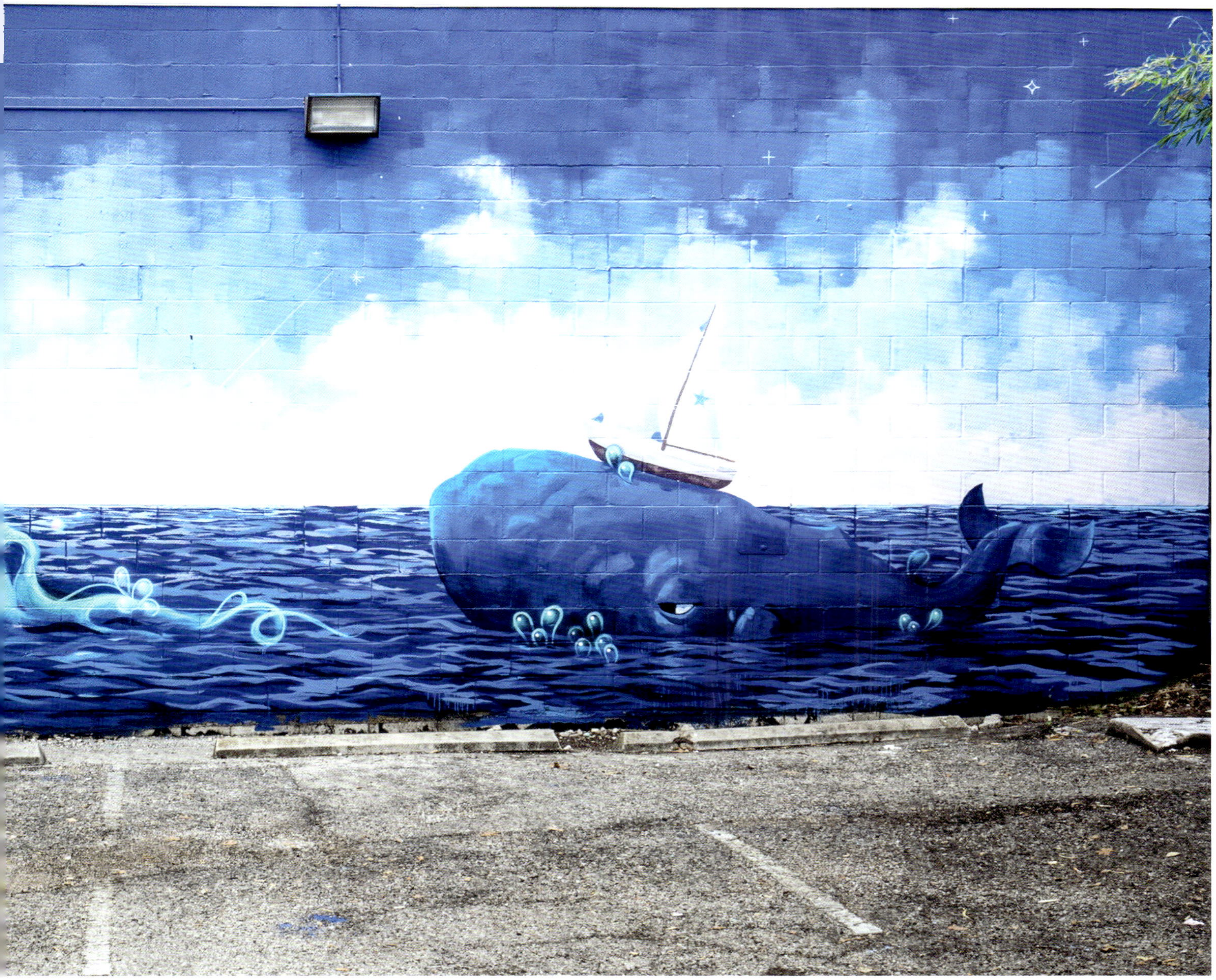

Tatiana Suarez (b. 1983) is a Brooklyn-based Miami native. Her charming style is distinctive—first, the trademark eyes that draw the viewer into a beautiful and surreal world. Suarez takes full advantage of the oil paint's ability to create creamy, soft images on canvas. Rich with symbols that stem from her Brazilian and El Salvadorian heritage, subjects appear as if they are under water, frozen in lovely stillness. The doe-eyed figures look childlike, but also exude sexual overtones, ornamented with plants, insects and other unsettling accompaniments. Beauty is presented concurrently with exotic—even creepy—creatures to create enchanted narratives.

Born and raised in Toba, Japan, **Yoskay Yamamoto** moved to the United States at the age of 15. A self-trained illustrator, Yamamoto's artistic tastes expanded as he fell in love with the urban culture of the West coast. Yamamoto discovered a way to fuse the two different cultural backgrounds together into his work. Yamamoto nostalgically blends pop iconic characters from his new Western home with traditional and mythical Japanese elements, balancing his Asian heritage with urban pop art.

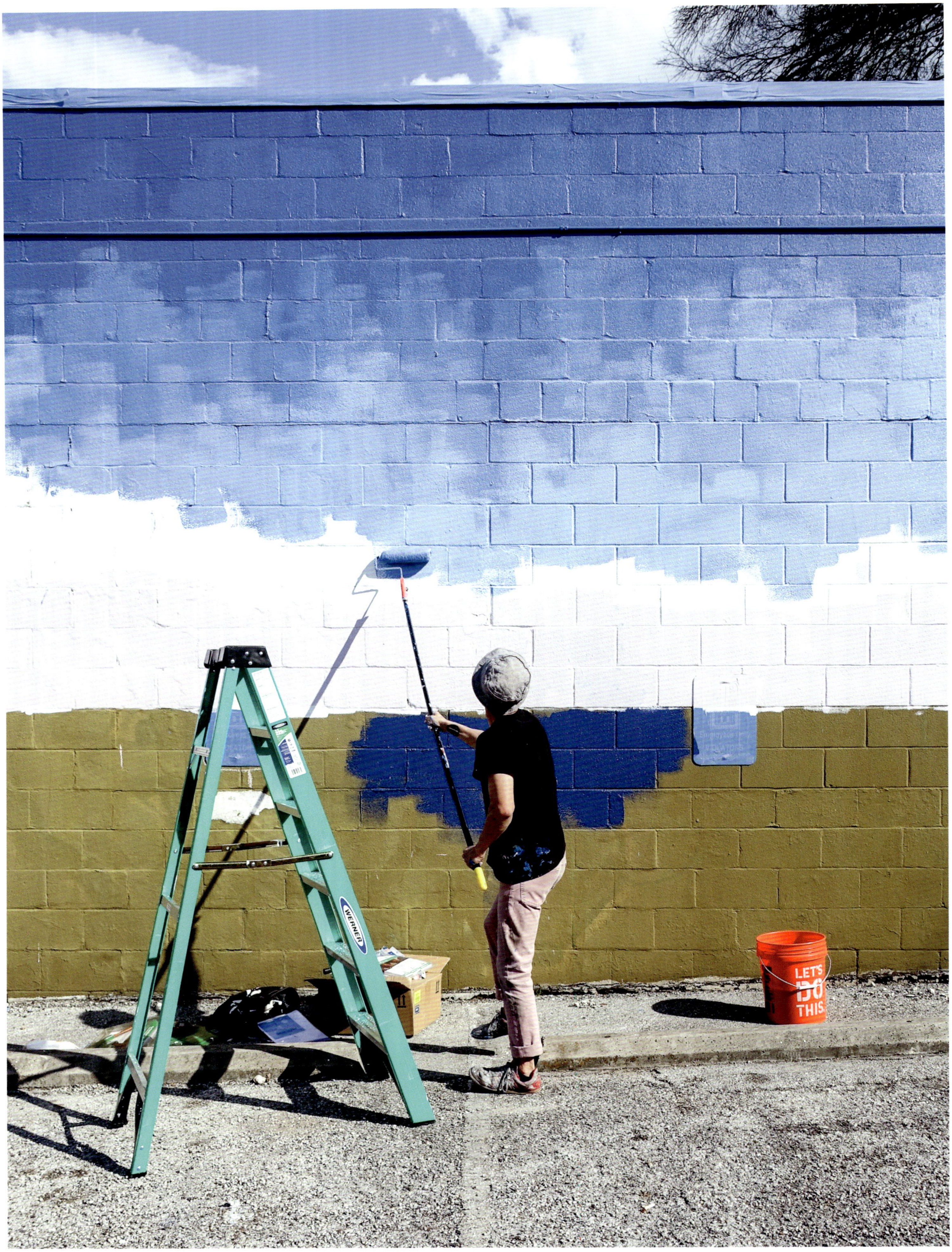
WERNER
LET'S
DO
THIS.

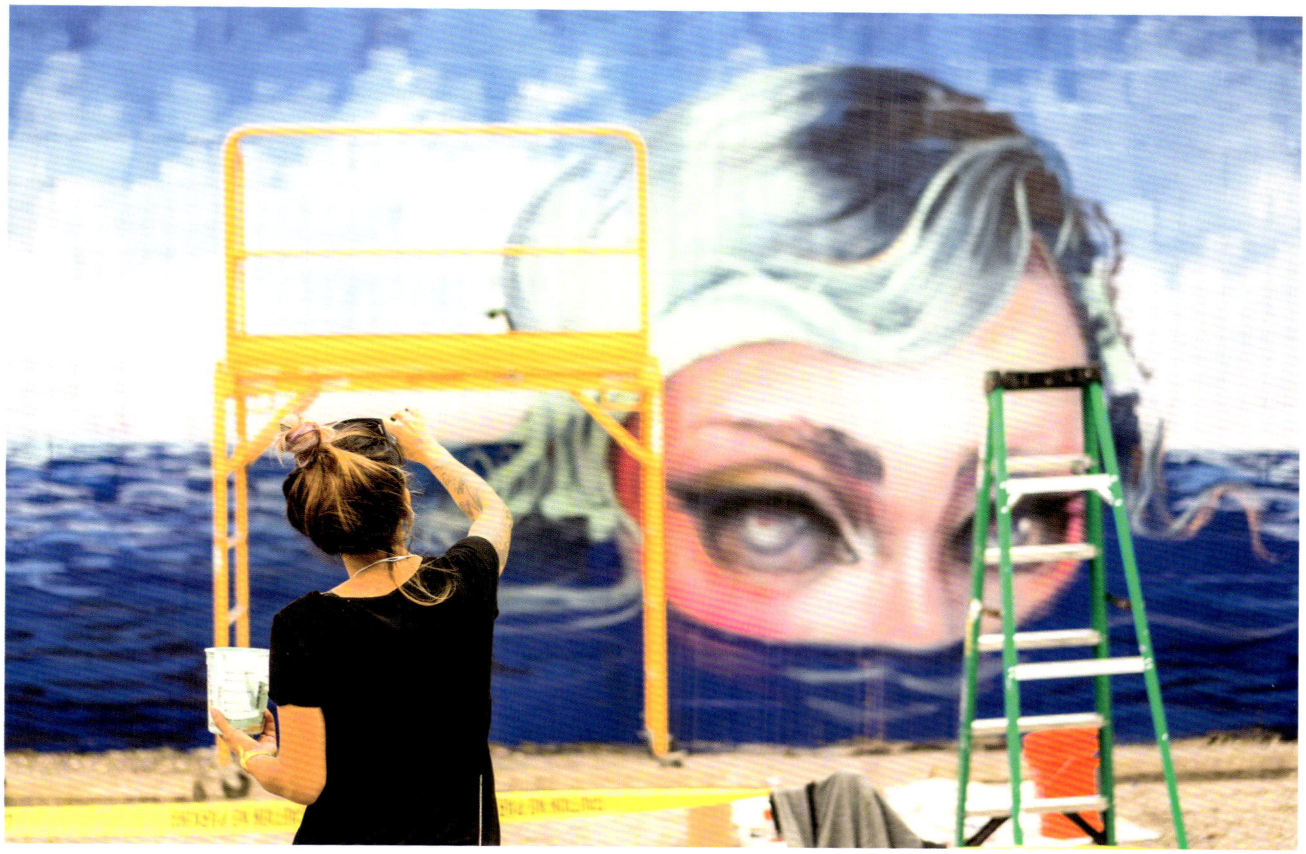

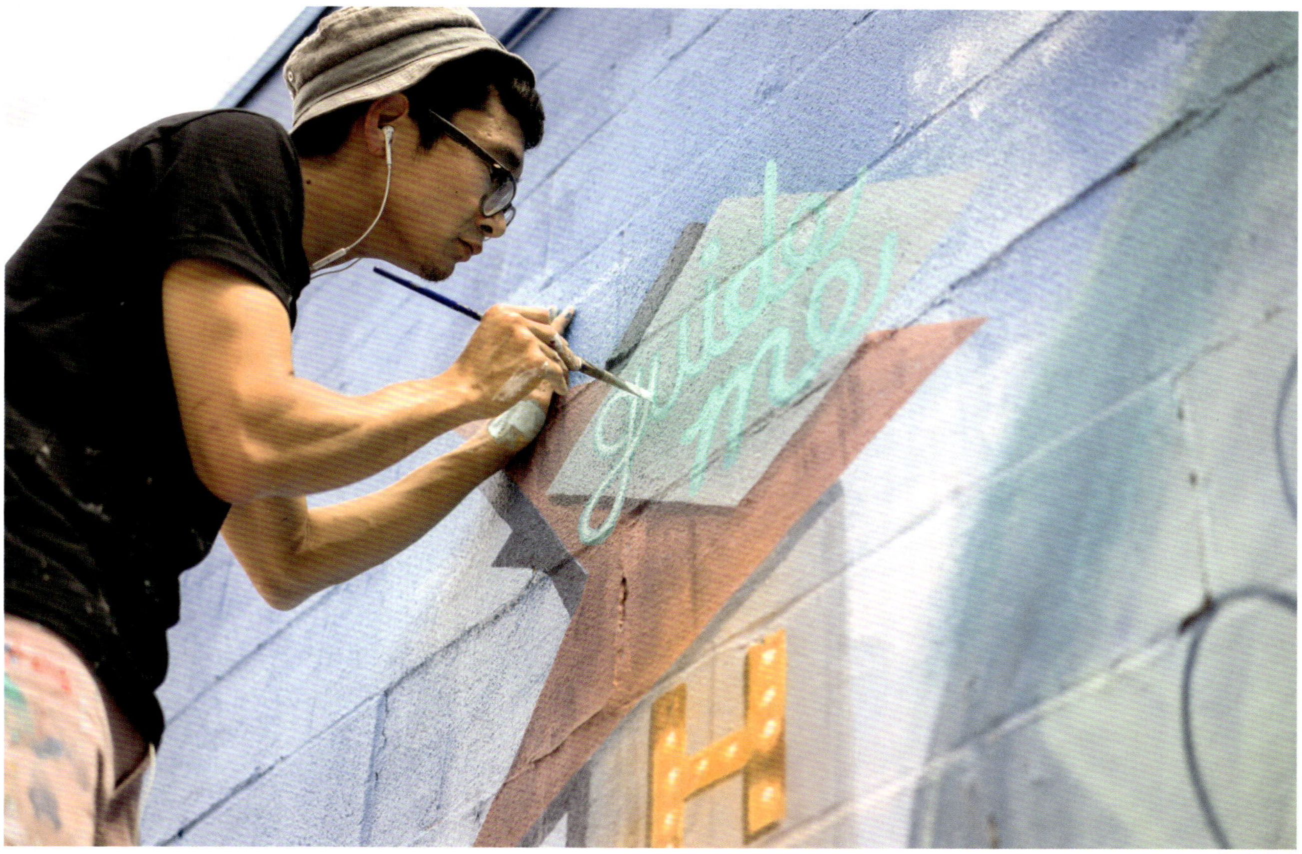

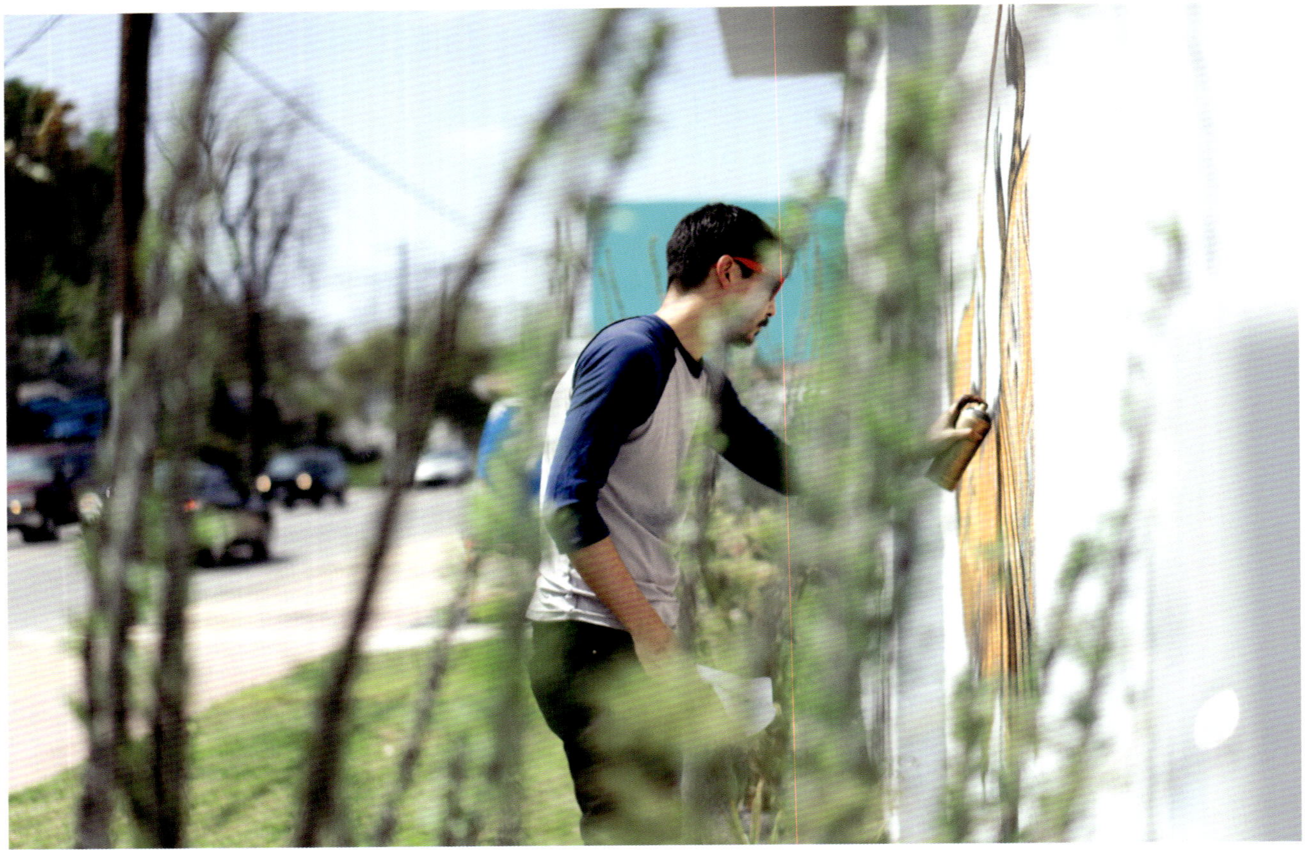

SXSW 2016

Esao Andrews

@ESAO

Esao Andrews (b. 1978) Is a surreal painter who grew up in Mesa, AZ and received his BFA in Illustration from the School of Visual Arts in NYC in 2000. He continues to pursue a life of art-making in sunny Los Angeles, CA.

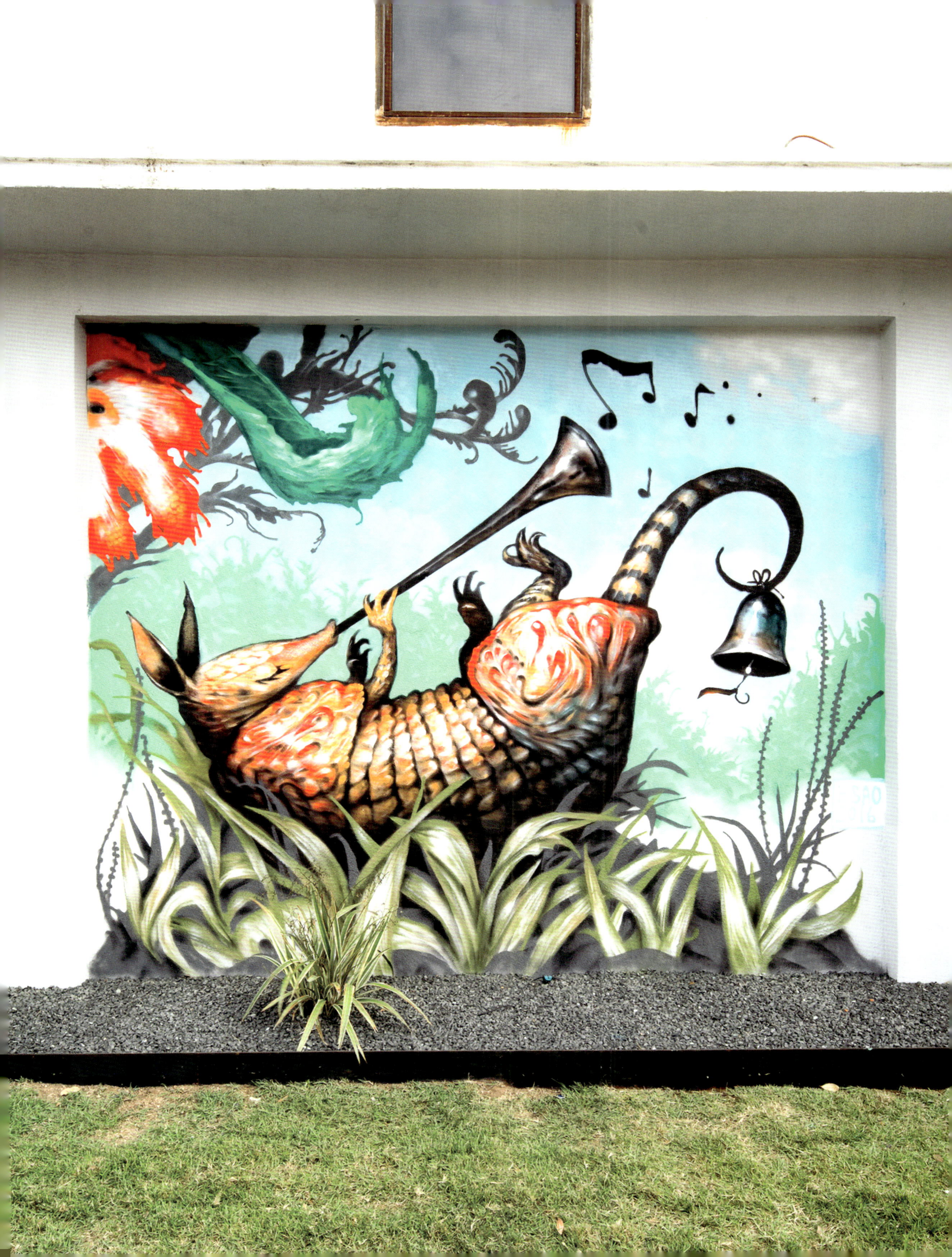

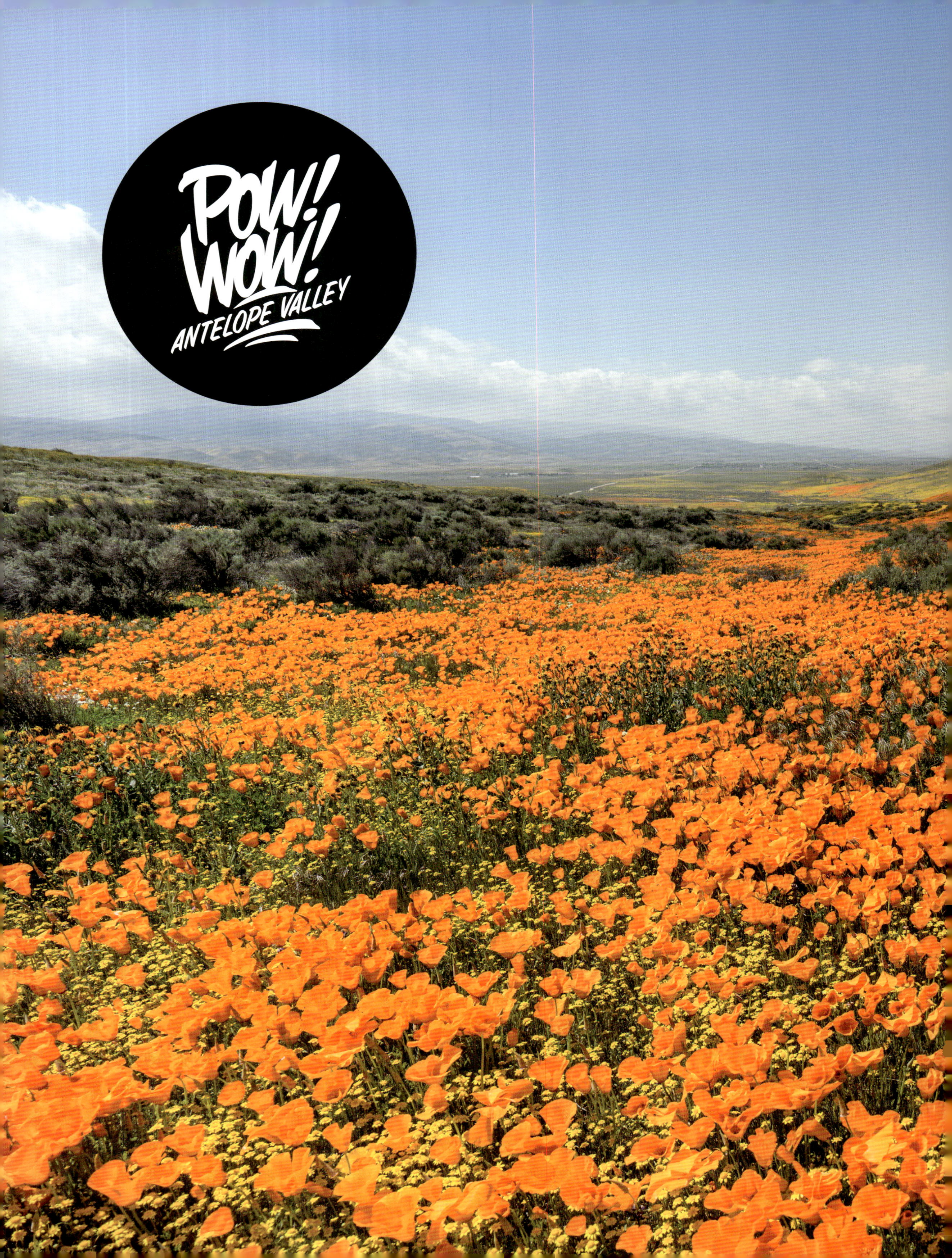
POW!
WOW!
ANTELOPE VALLEY

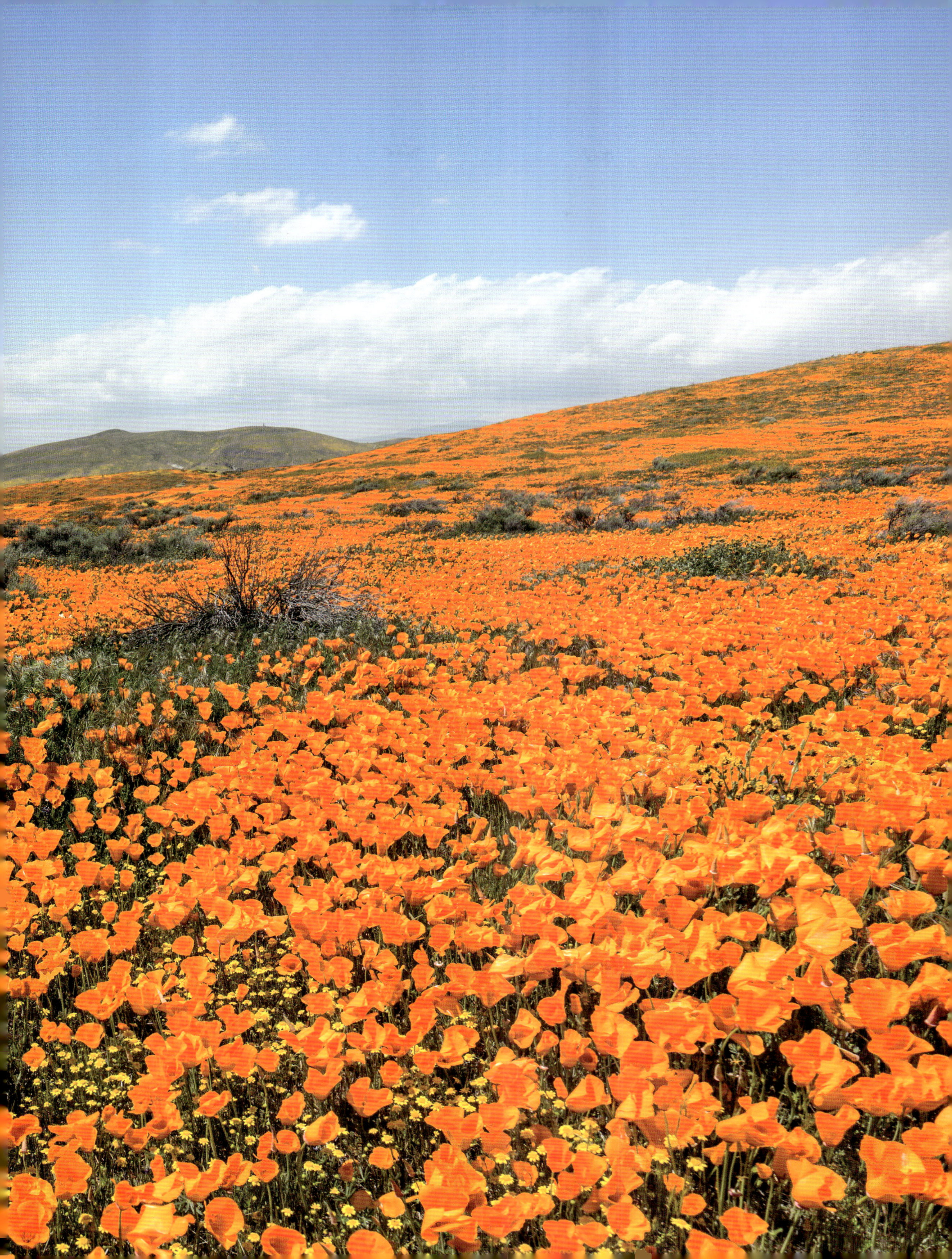

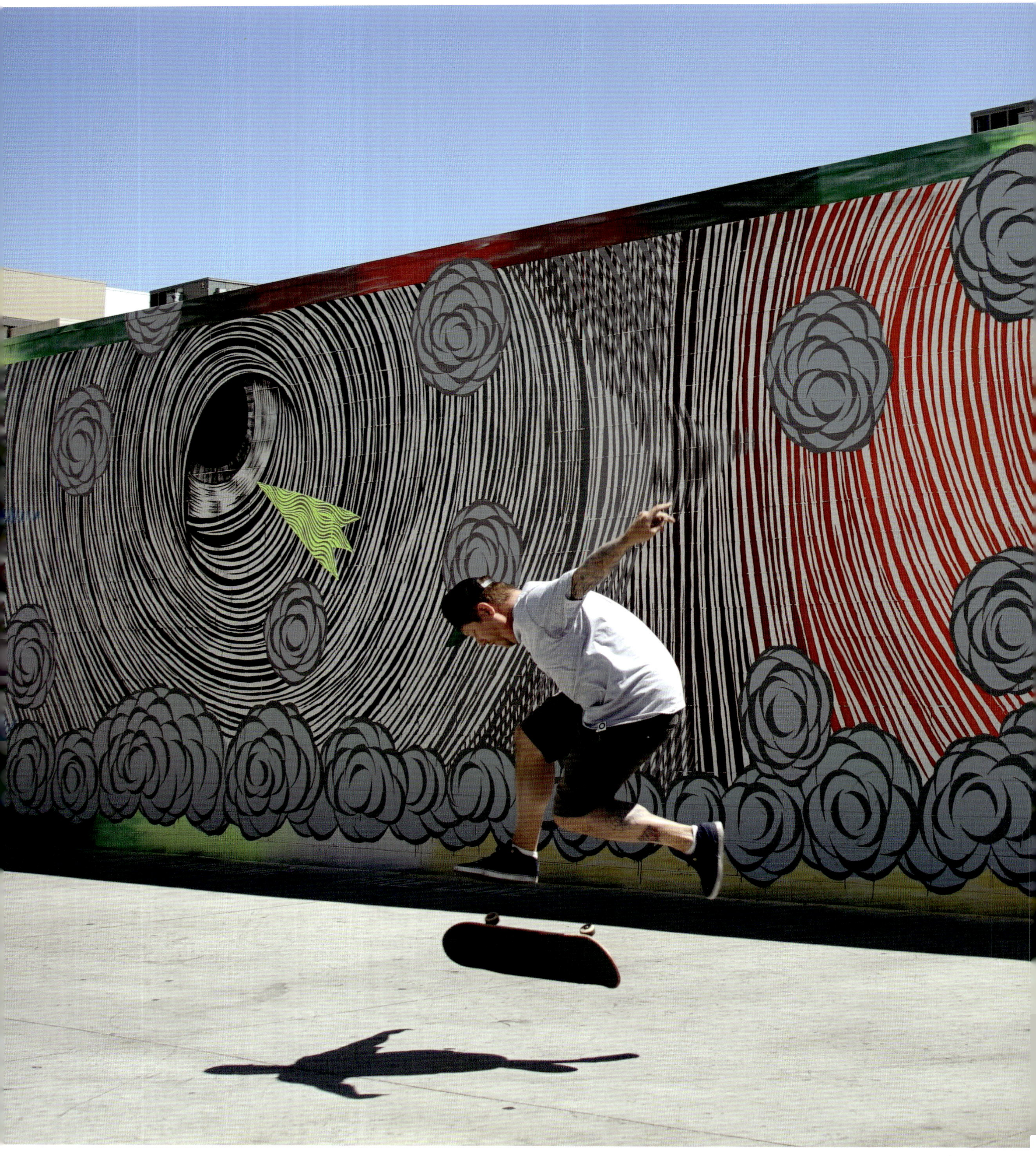

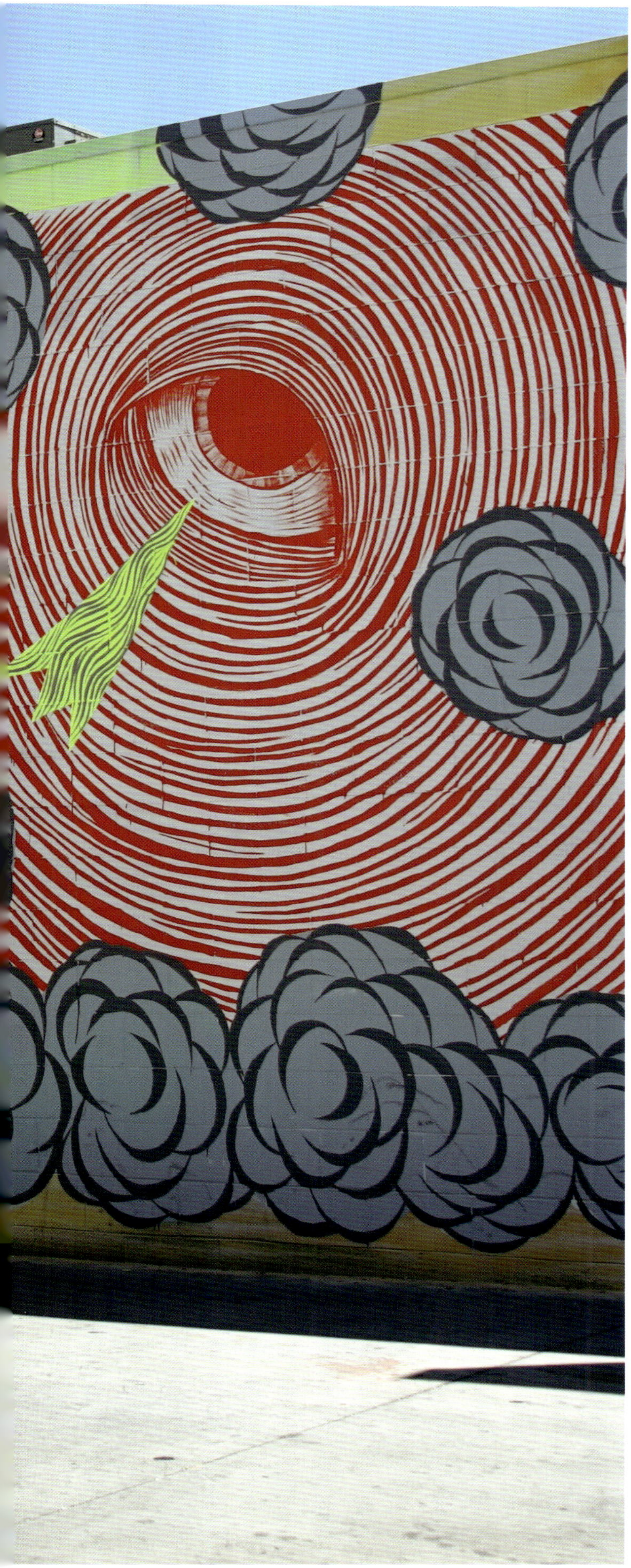

Antelope Valley
2016

Andrew Schoultz

@ASCHOULTZ

Sourcing inspiration from 15th Century German map making and Indian miniature paintings, **Andrew Schoultz's** frenetic imagery depicts an ephemeral history bound to repeat itself. In his mixed-media works, notions of war, spirituality and sociopolitical imperialism are reoccurring themes, which shrewdly parallel an equally repetitive contemporary pursuit of accumulation and power. Intricate line work, painting, metal leaf and collage twist and undulate under Schoultz's meticulous hand, ranging from intimately sized wall works to staggering murals and installations. While his illustrated world seems one of chaos and frenzy, Schoultz also implies a sense of alluring fantasy and whimsy—a crossroads vaguely familiar to the modern world.

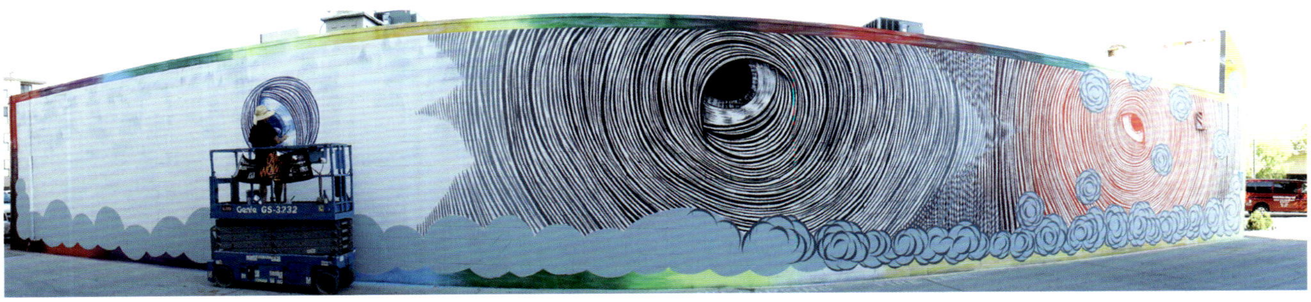
Genie GS-3232

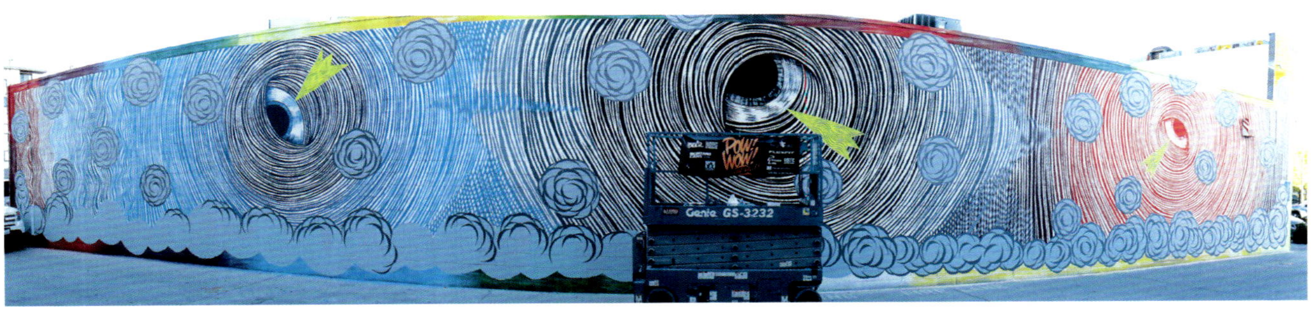
Genie GS-3232

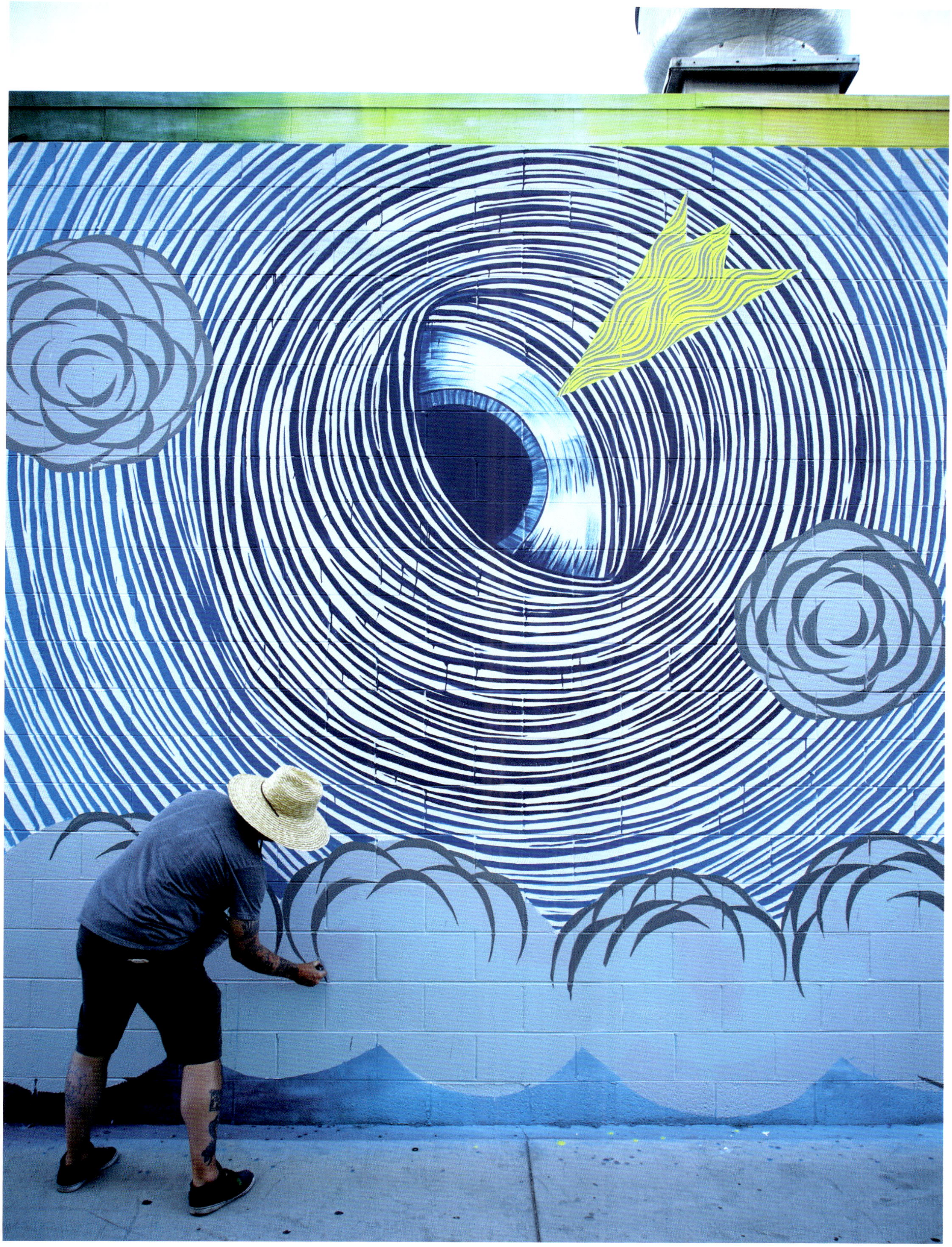

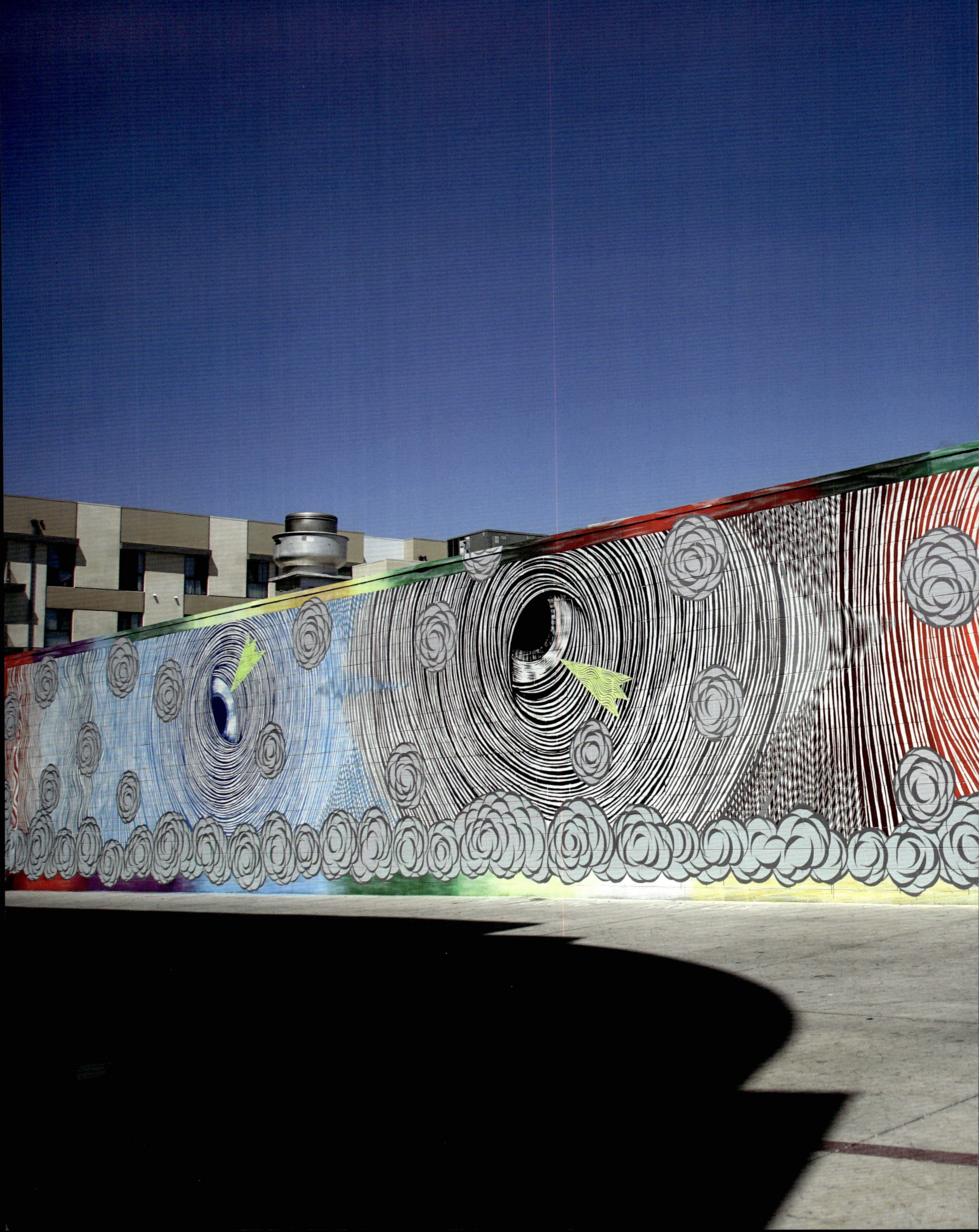

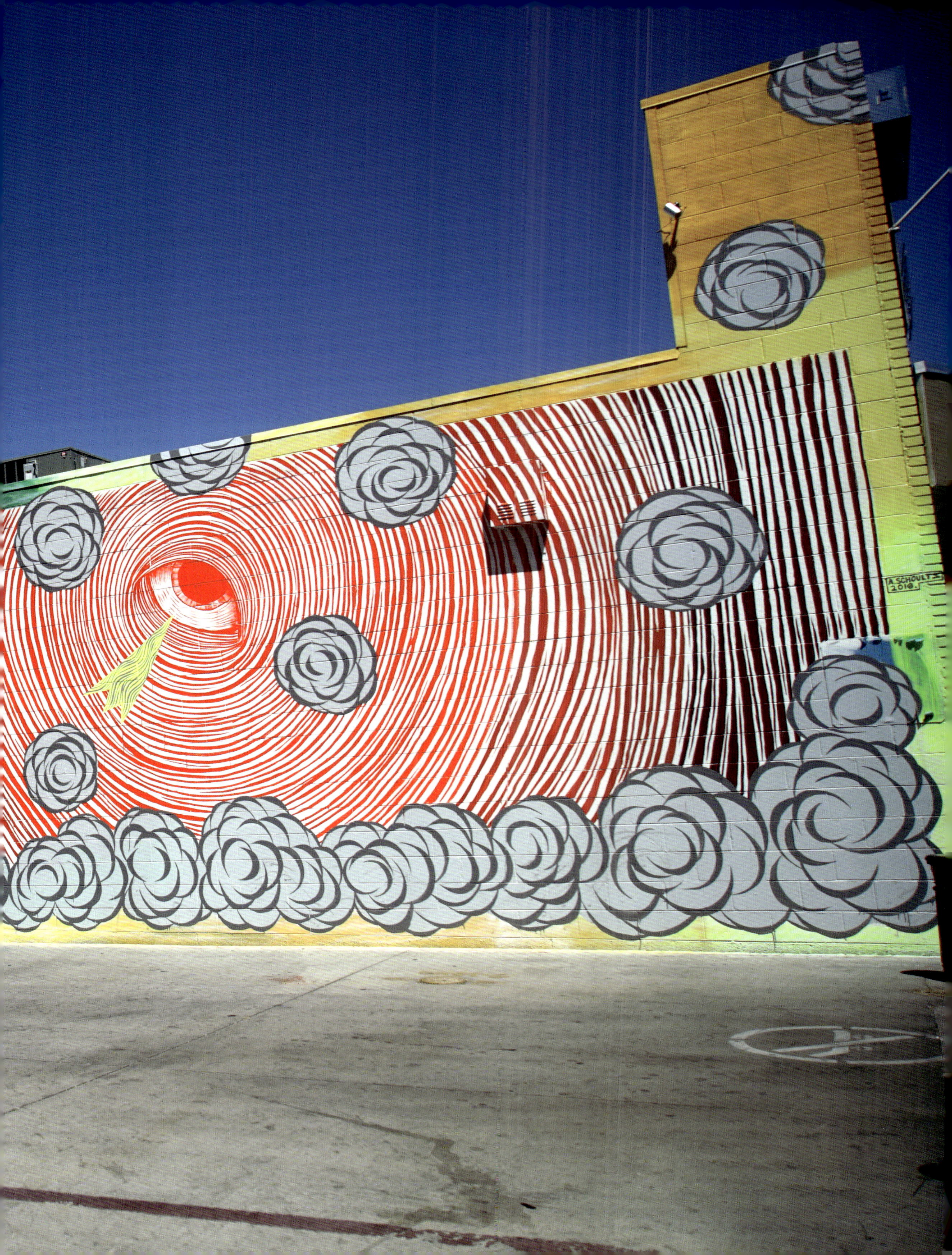
A SCHOULTZ
2016.

Antelope Valley
2018

Tran Nguyen

@MYNAMEISTRAN

Tran Nguyen is an award-winning illustrator and gallery artist. At the age of three, she and her family were given the opportunity to immigrate to the States, escaping their impoverished life in Vietnam. Growing up in a more developed country, she was able to pursue her passion for the arts and is currently working as a freelancer.

Tran's paintings are created with a soft, delicate quality using colored pencil and acrylic on paper. She has worked for clients such as VH1, Tiger Beer, World Wildlife Fund, and has showcased with galleries across the world.

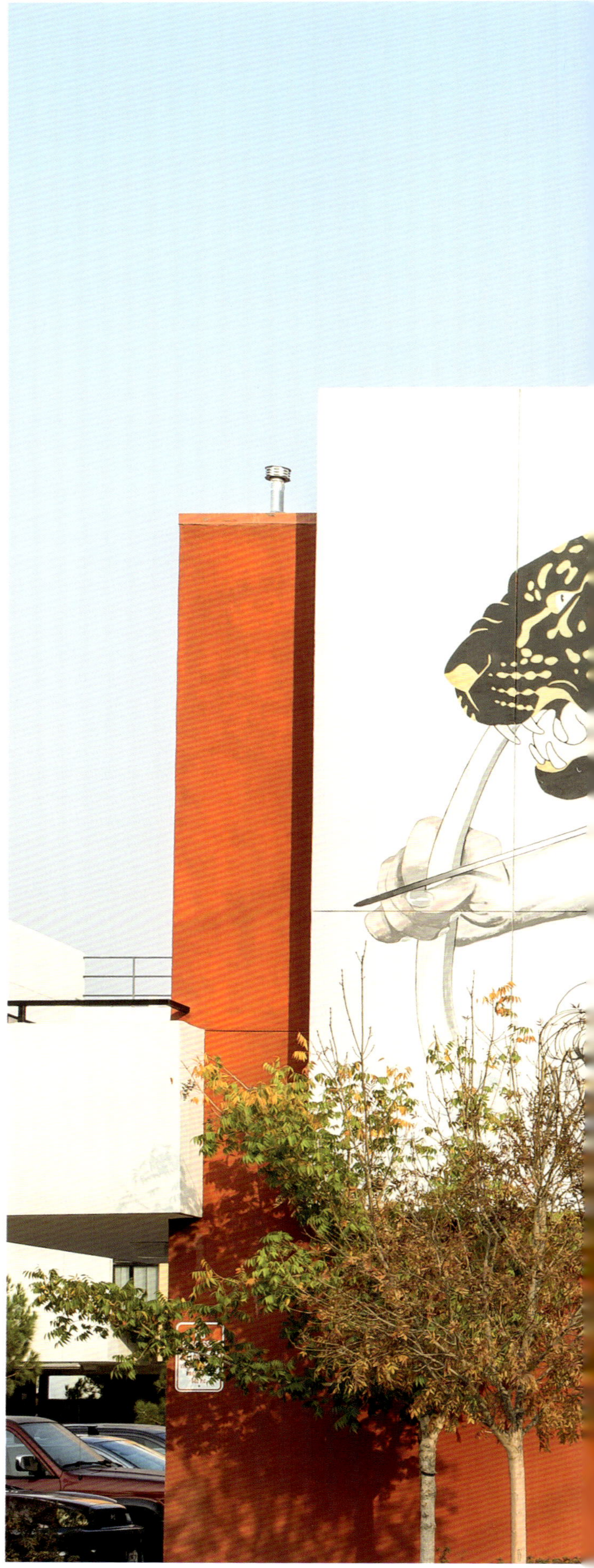

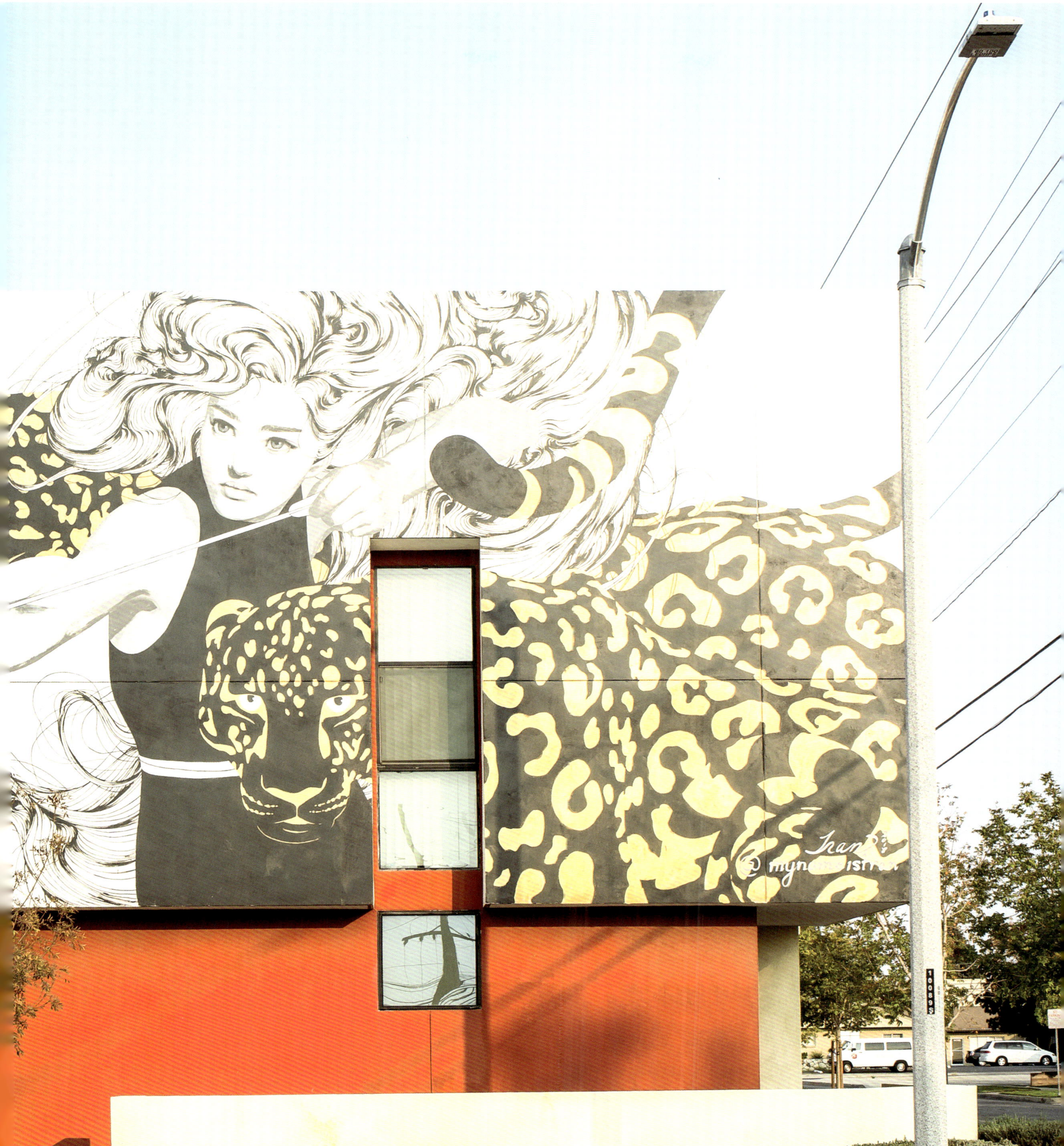

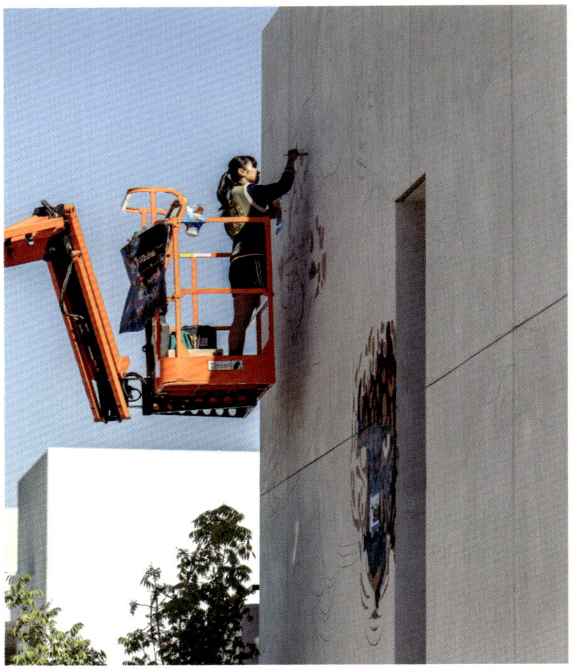

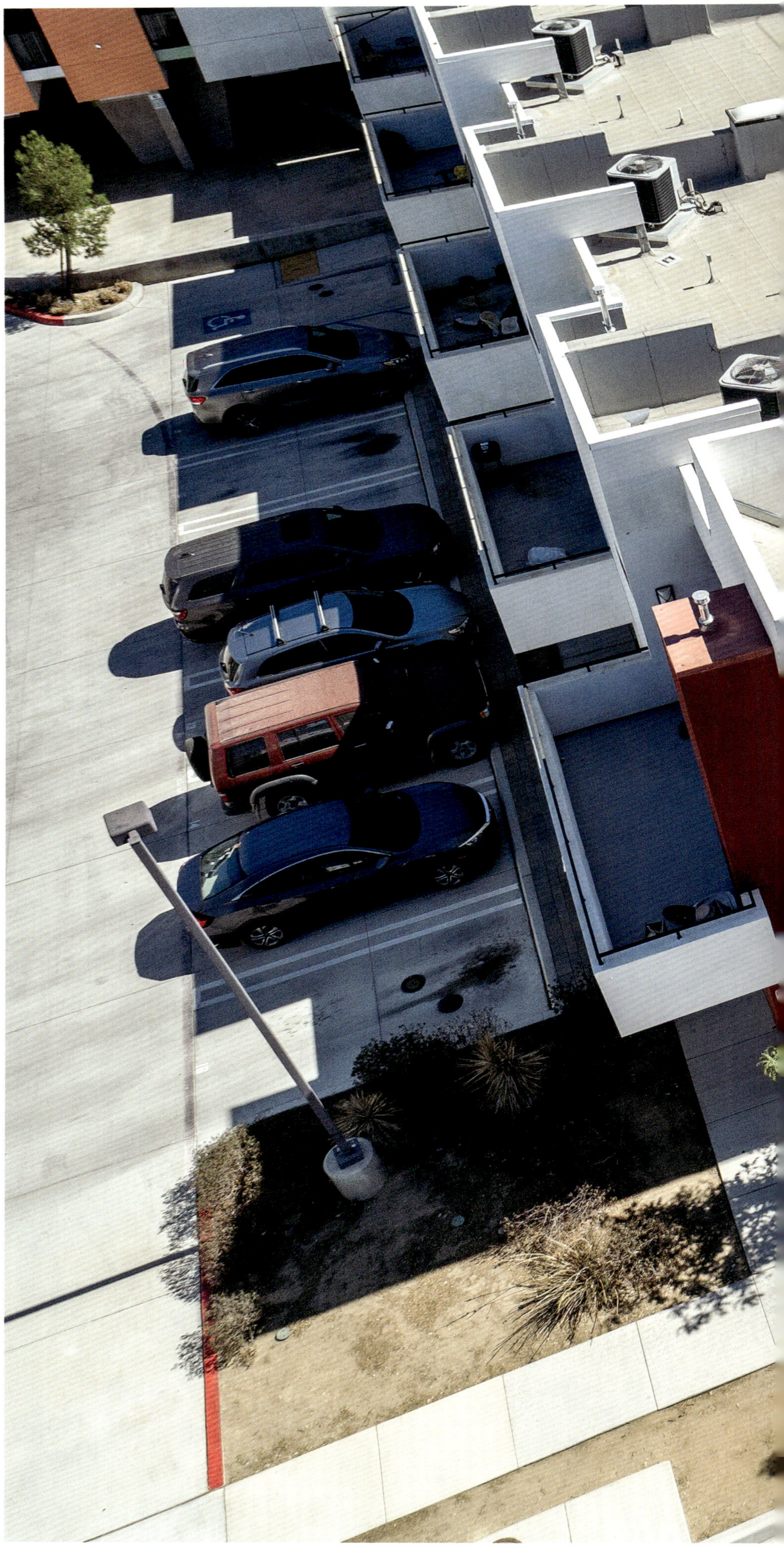

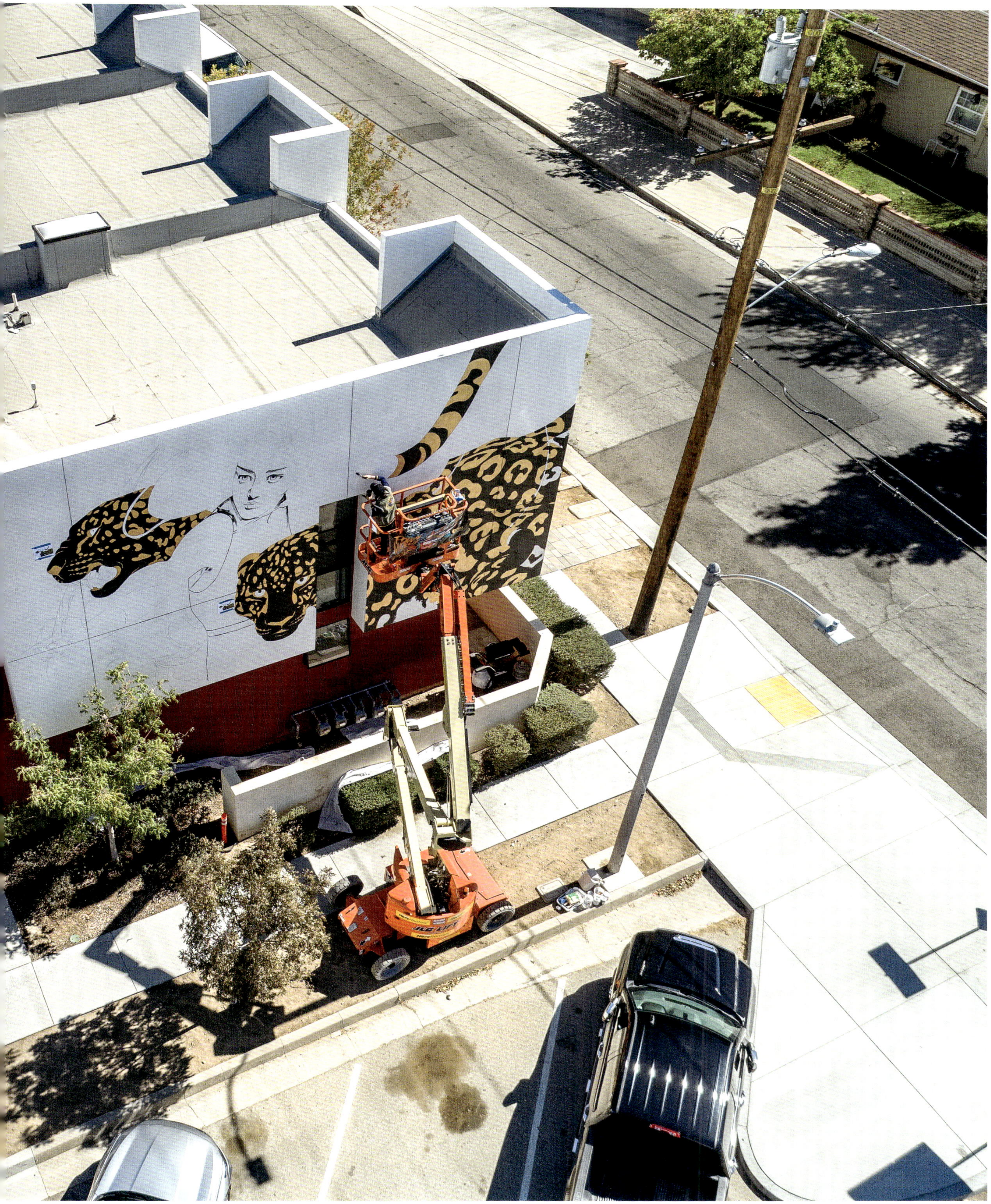

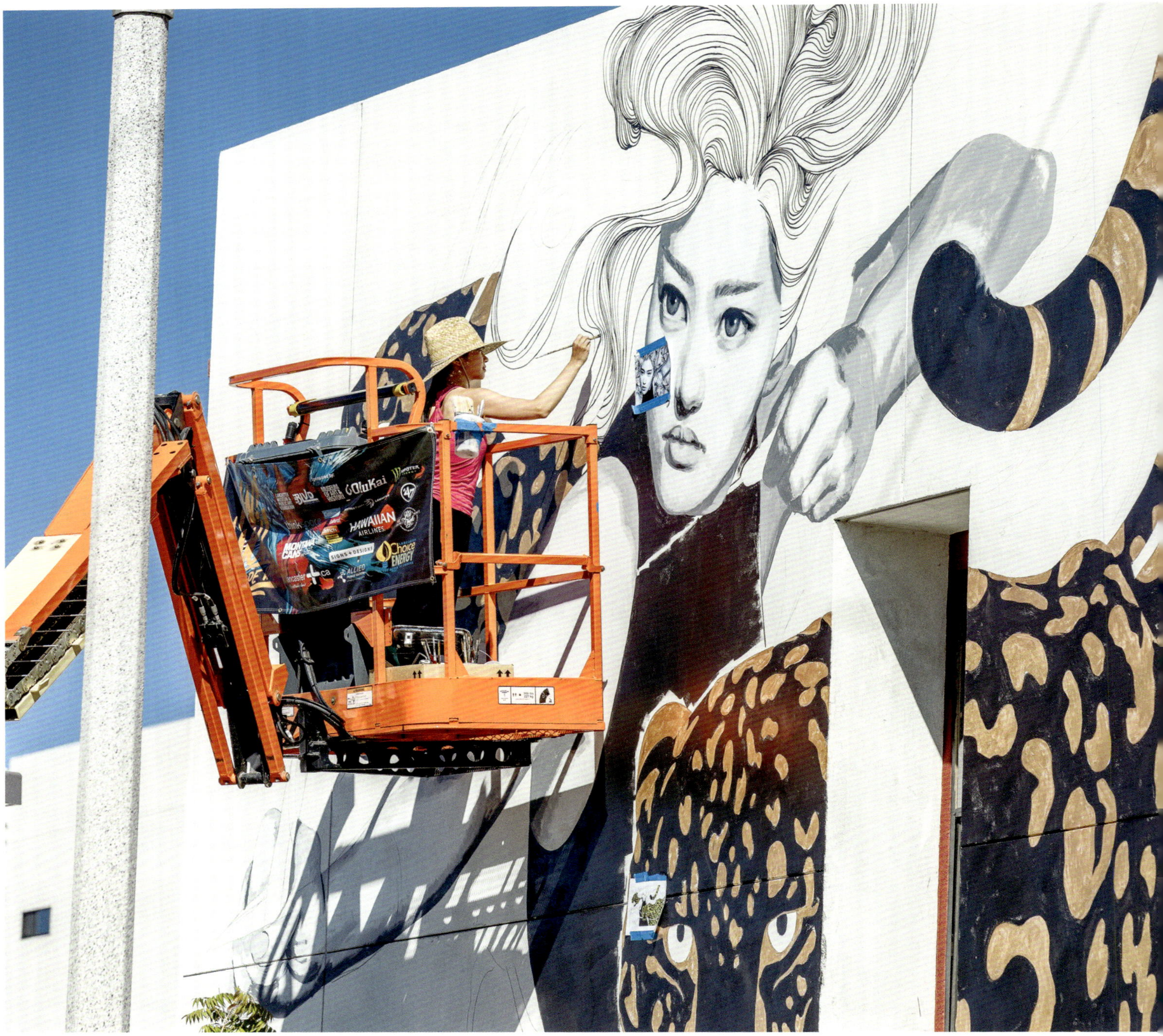
OluKai
BLVD
MUSEUM OF ART & HISTORY
HAWAIIAN AIRLINES
SIGNS + DESIGNS
Choice ENERGY
ALLIED

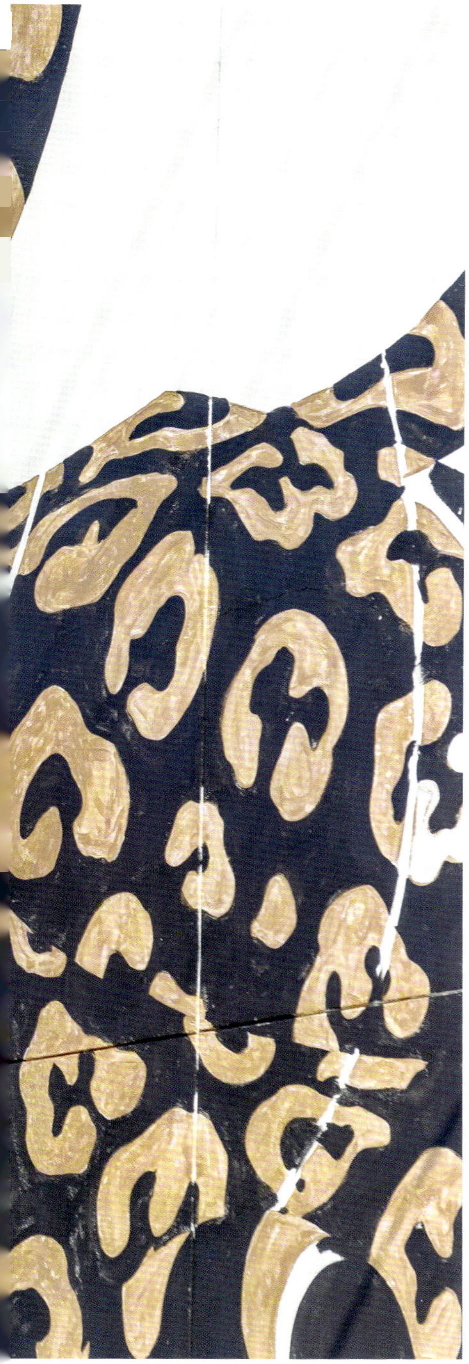

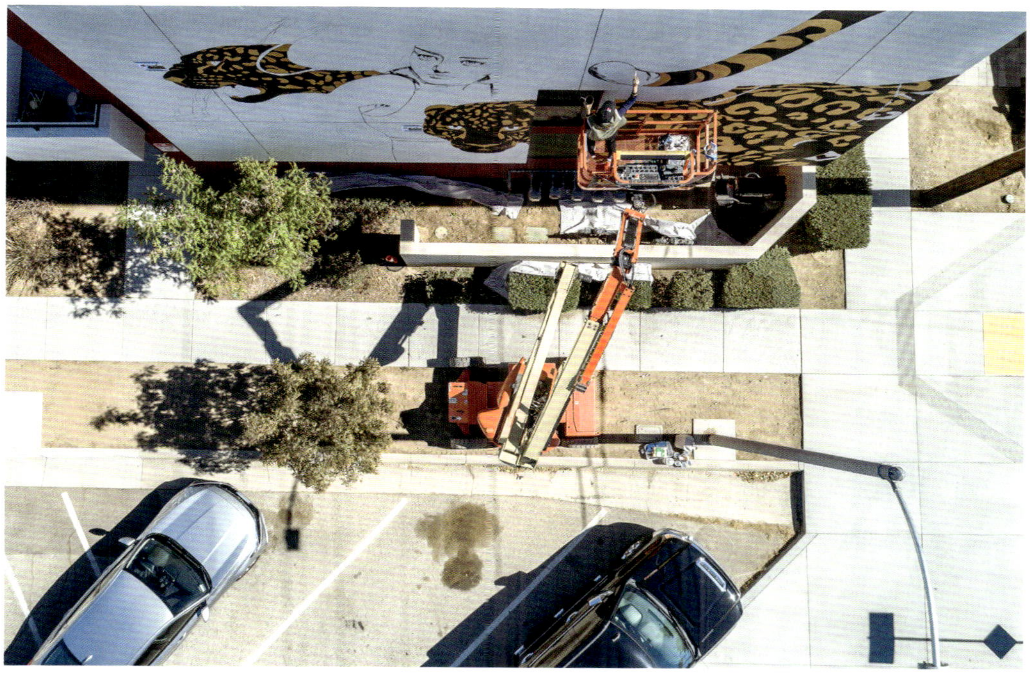

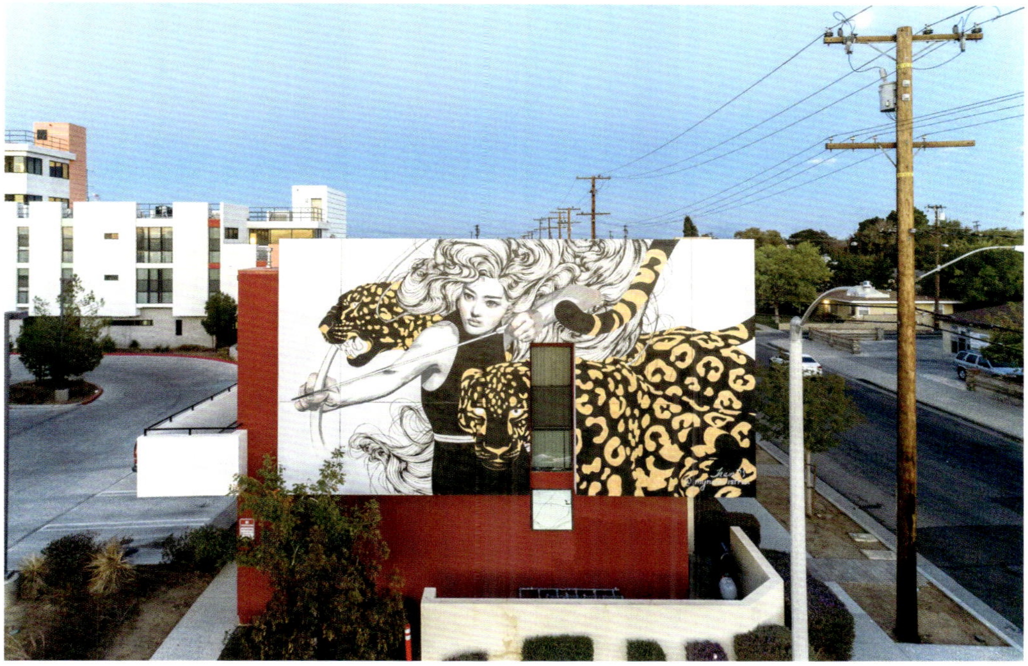

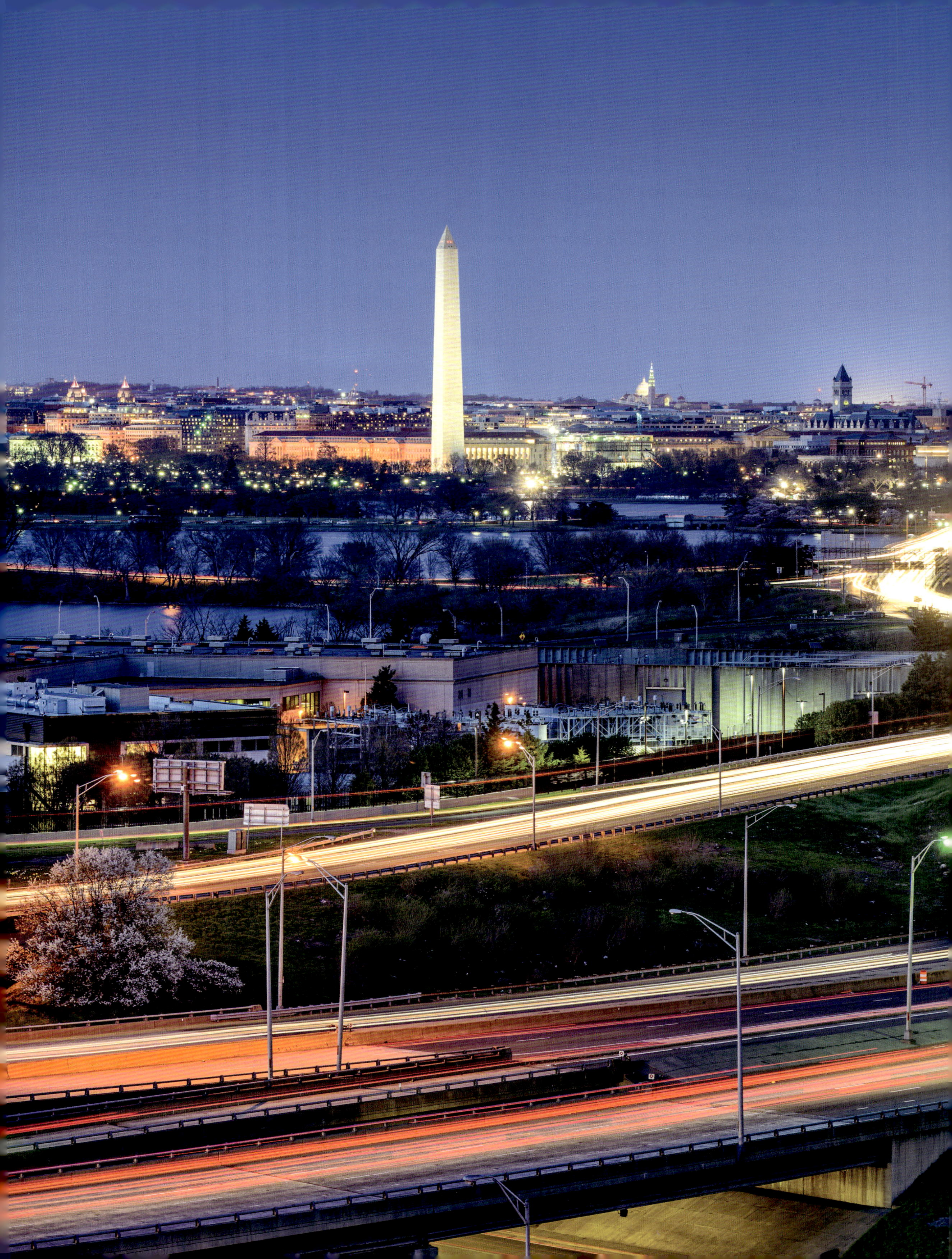

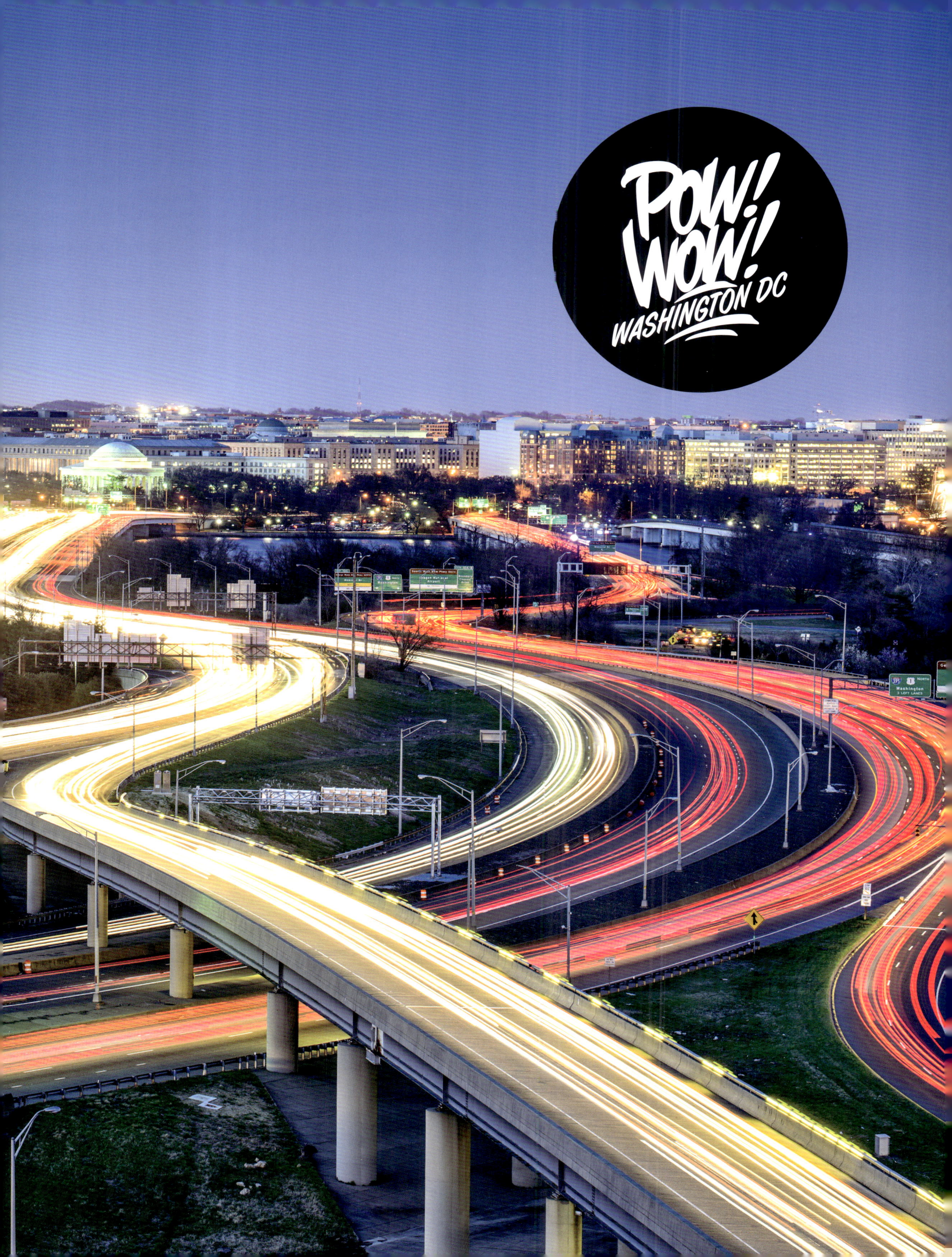
POW! WOW!
WASHINGTON DC

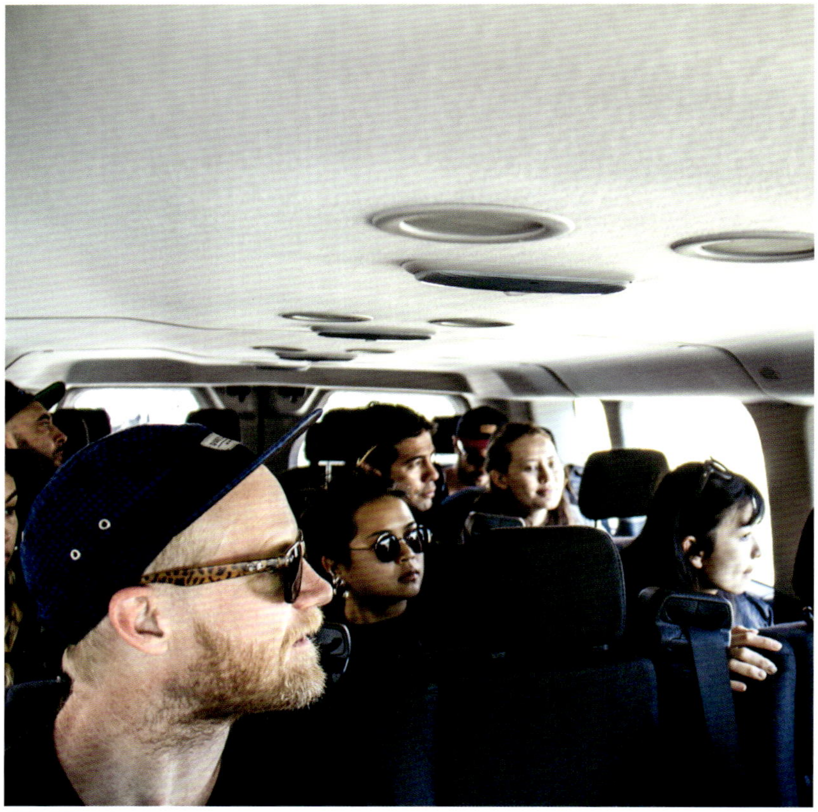
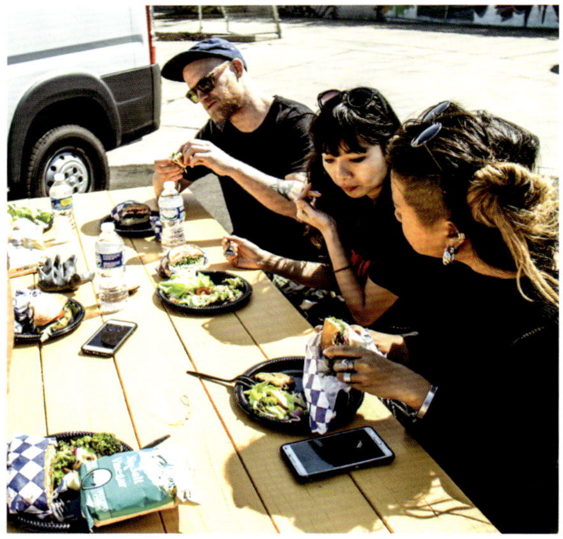
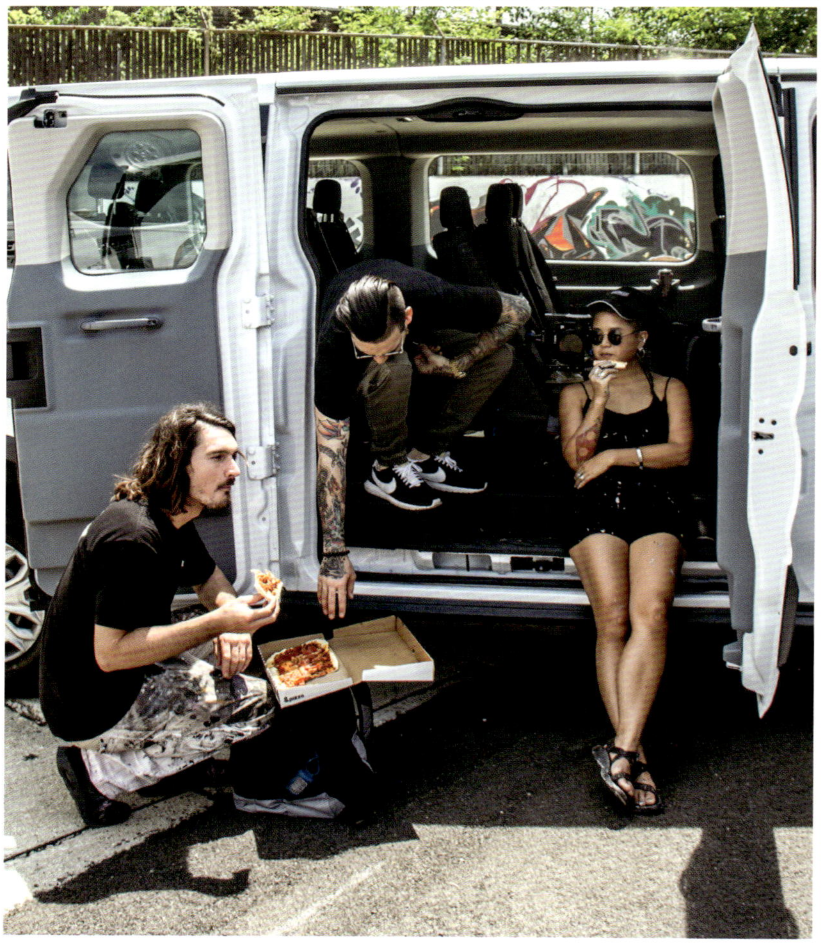
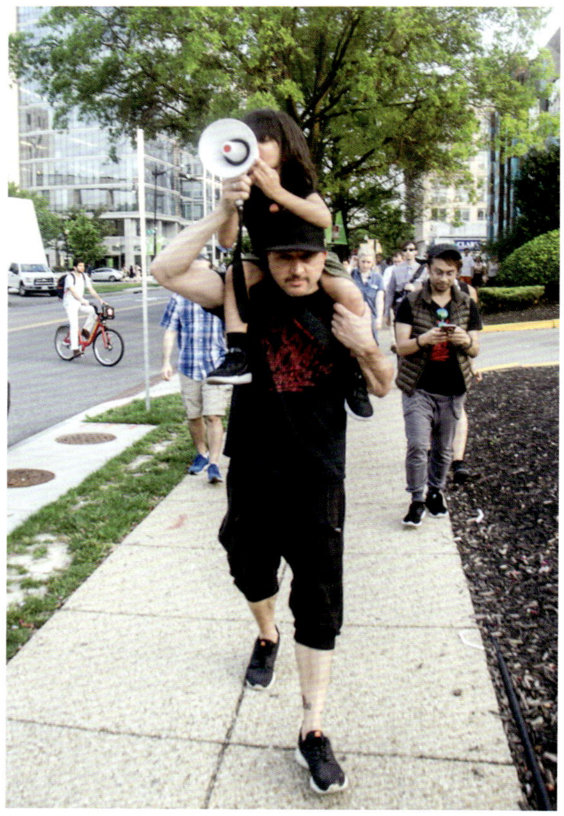
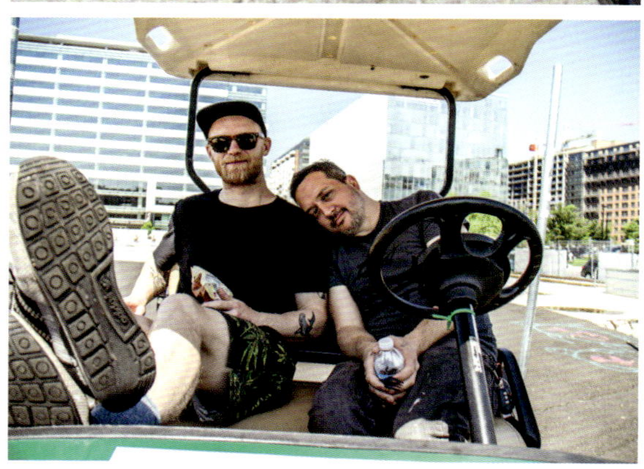
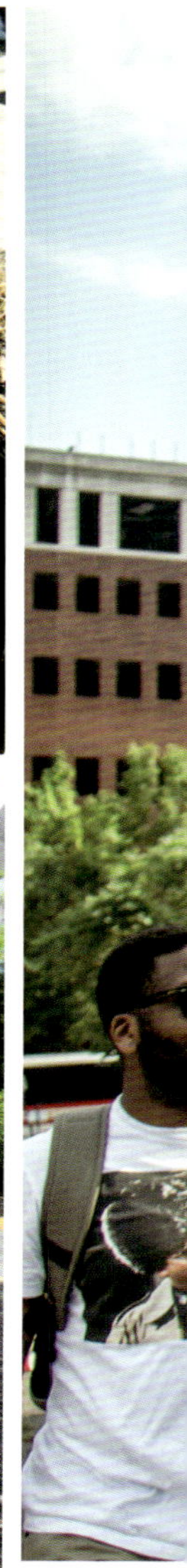
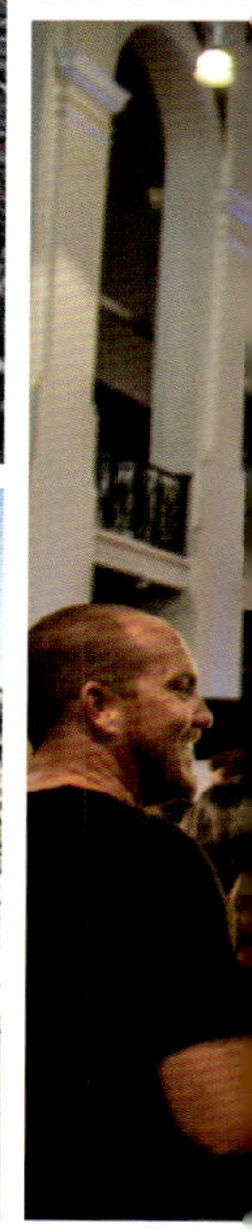

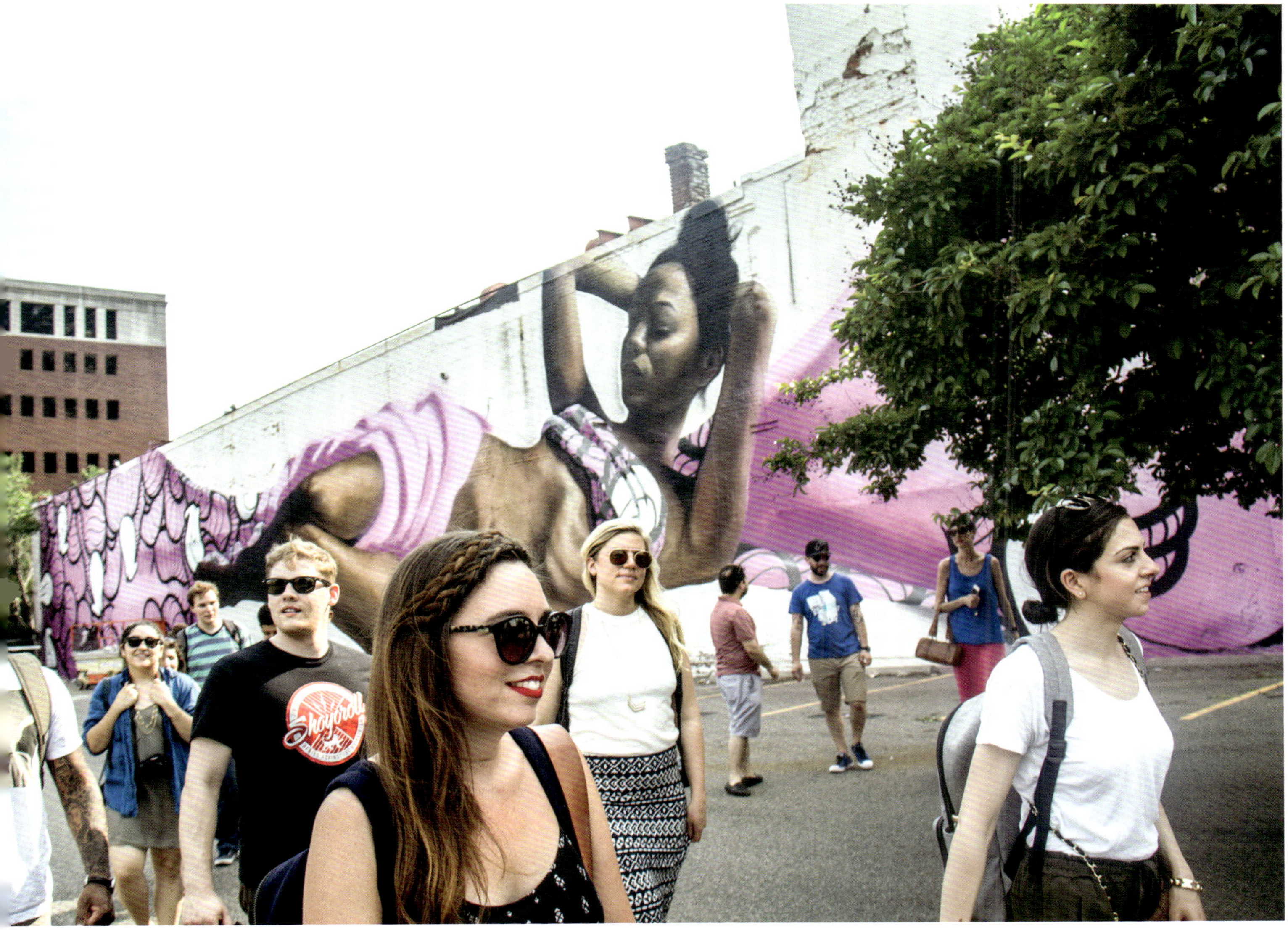

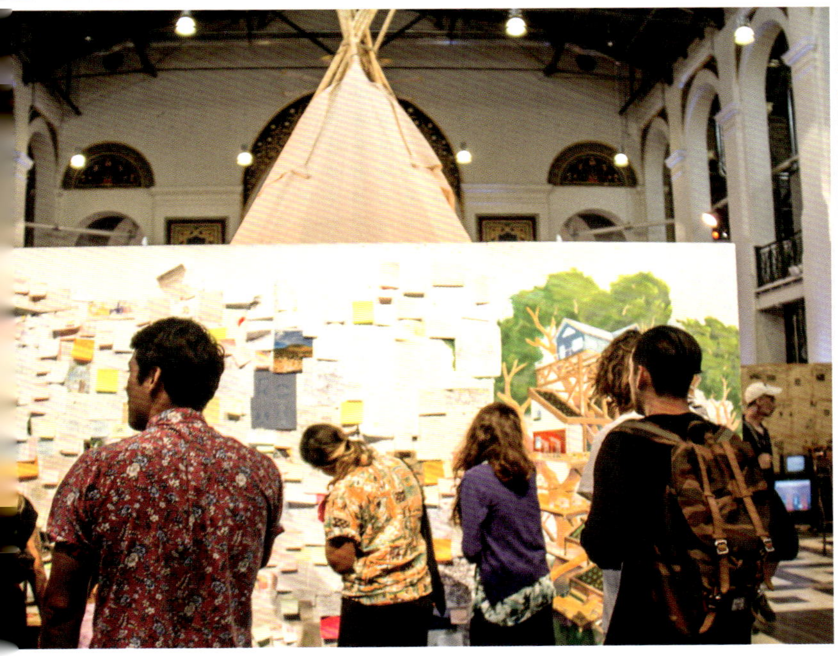

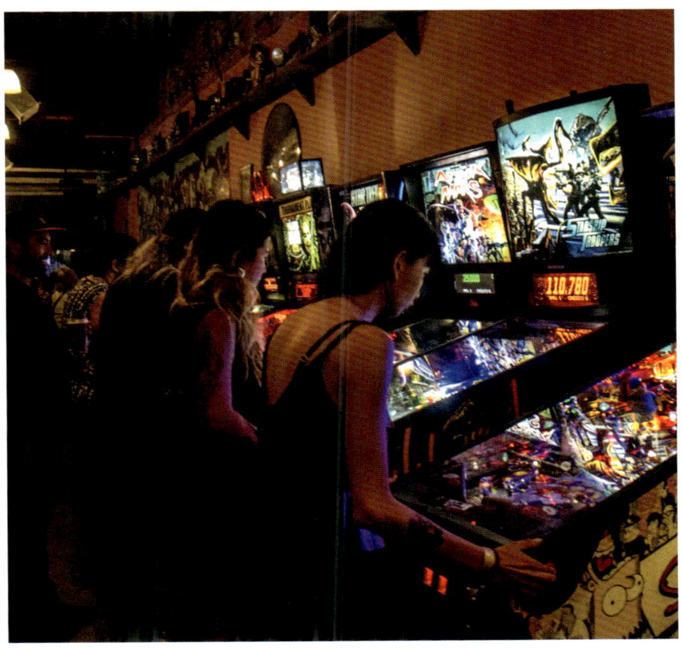

Washington D.C.
2016

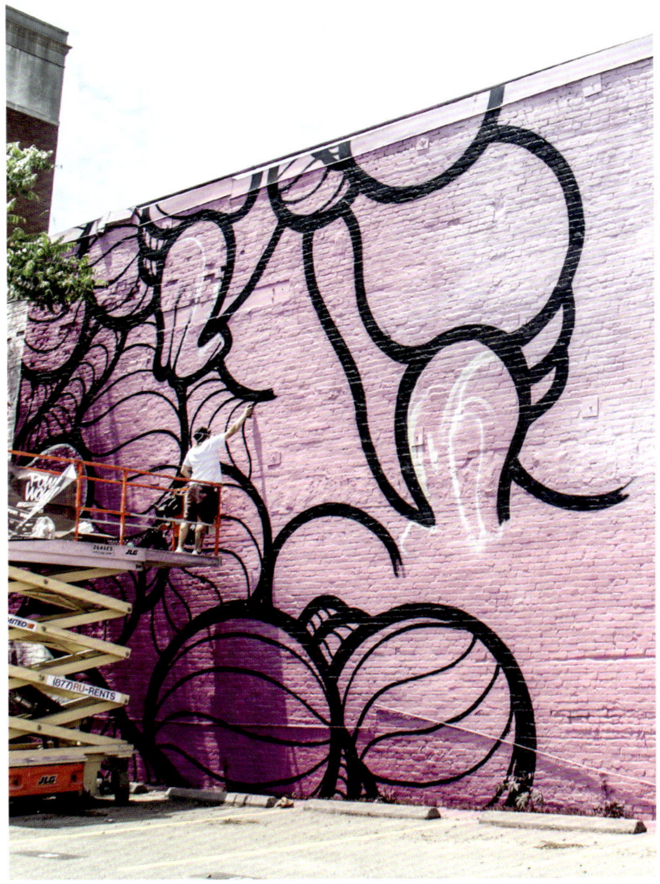

Drew Merritt & INSA

@DREWMERRITT @INSA_GRAM

When **Drew Merritt** was a kid he always painted by himself. Then when he turned 12 or 13, Merritt got really into graffiti. Everybody he would talk to, always say that graffiti got them into art, but for Merritt it was the other way around.

Like other kids, he was arrested and got in trouble for years worth of work. He never considered himself that good at graff anyway. He admitted that he has the worst hand style in the world, but Merritt really liked doing it. When Merritt got in trouble, he tried to pay his attorney fees, but his attorney was like, "Oh don't worry about it, my wife wants to put murals in our kid's room." So that evolved into making money off Art.

Merritt started painting windows for people, script, whatever. When he went to college, his mother and aunt said, "We have all these paintings stacked up in the garage from years ago, since you were little.... What do you want us to do with them?" He advised his family to throw them away, but they said, "No, we're going to try to sell them. We're going to have a show." So they had a show at his aunt's home. Merritt was going through the motion of working a boring job at a department store and trying to balance the college life. Then his paintings sold, he quit his job and pursued Art as a career.

INSA is a fine artist and designer who has established himself from a graffiti background through extensive street level work and gallery shows around the world. Throughout his career, INSA has allowed himself to explore different approaches and outlets for his artistic agenda, including designing signature collections for brands such as Kangol, Kid Robot and Oki-Ni, as well as starting his own heel company 'INSA HEELS'. He has undertaken many private commissions for clients such as Sony and Nike and was recently invited out to Sweden as one of only two British artists to help curate and sculpt the 2008/2009 ICE hotel.

INSA's canvases and installations are often hyper real, finely crafted creations in which sexual desire and commodity-fetishism merge and contrast. Always with a heavy sense of irony, INSA visually exaggerates the notion of objectification meets commodification with graphically depicted oversized body parts that are suspended in the controlled architectural lines of a sneaker or bold black and white graphic patterns. INSA uses these powerful patterns to play with and distort the spaces where his work is installed to entice the viewer into the 'fantasy'; a shallow fantasy of materialistic aspiration where sexual objectification is flaunted as a symbol of wealth and success.

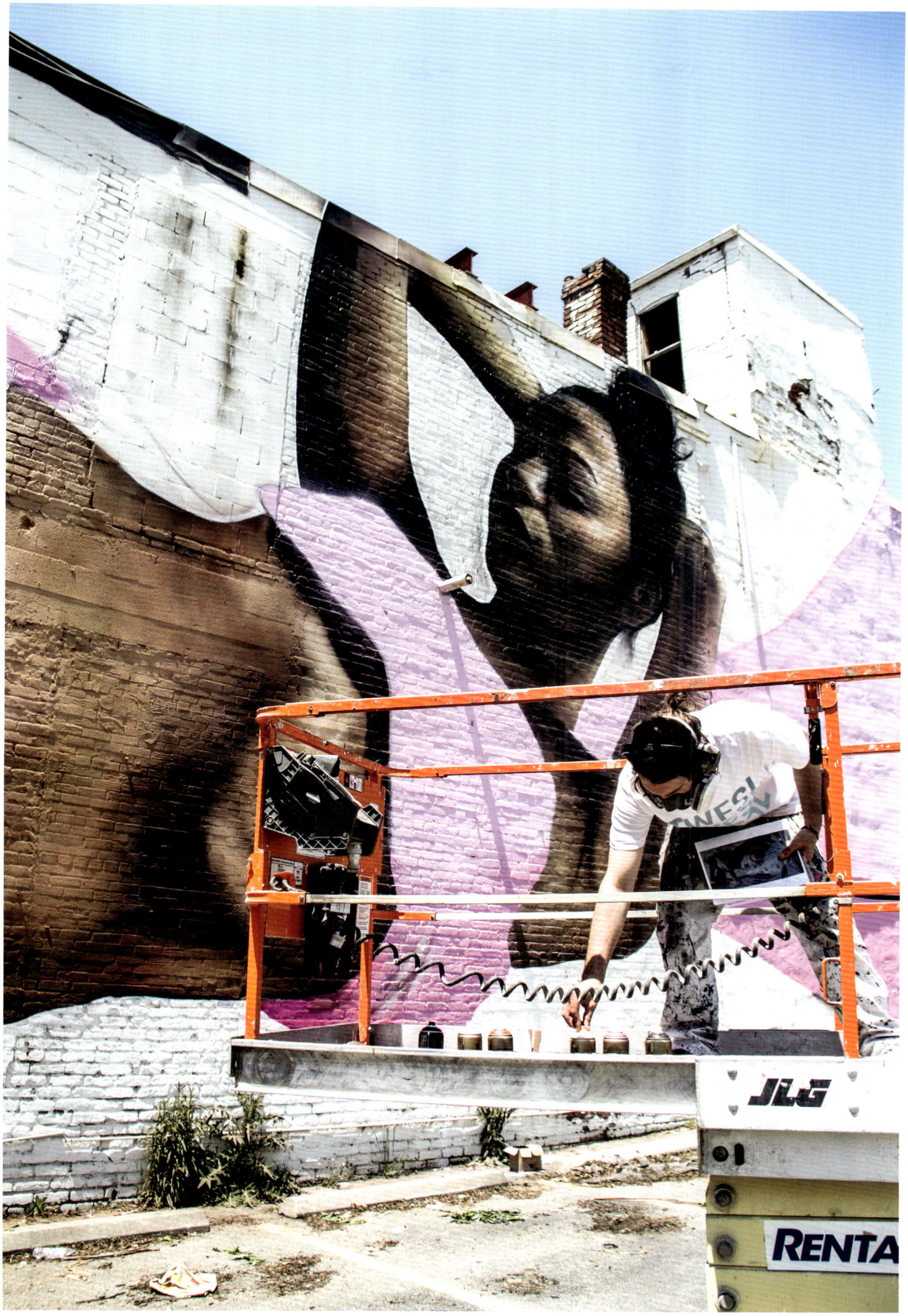
JLG
RENTA

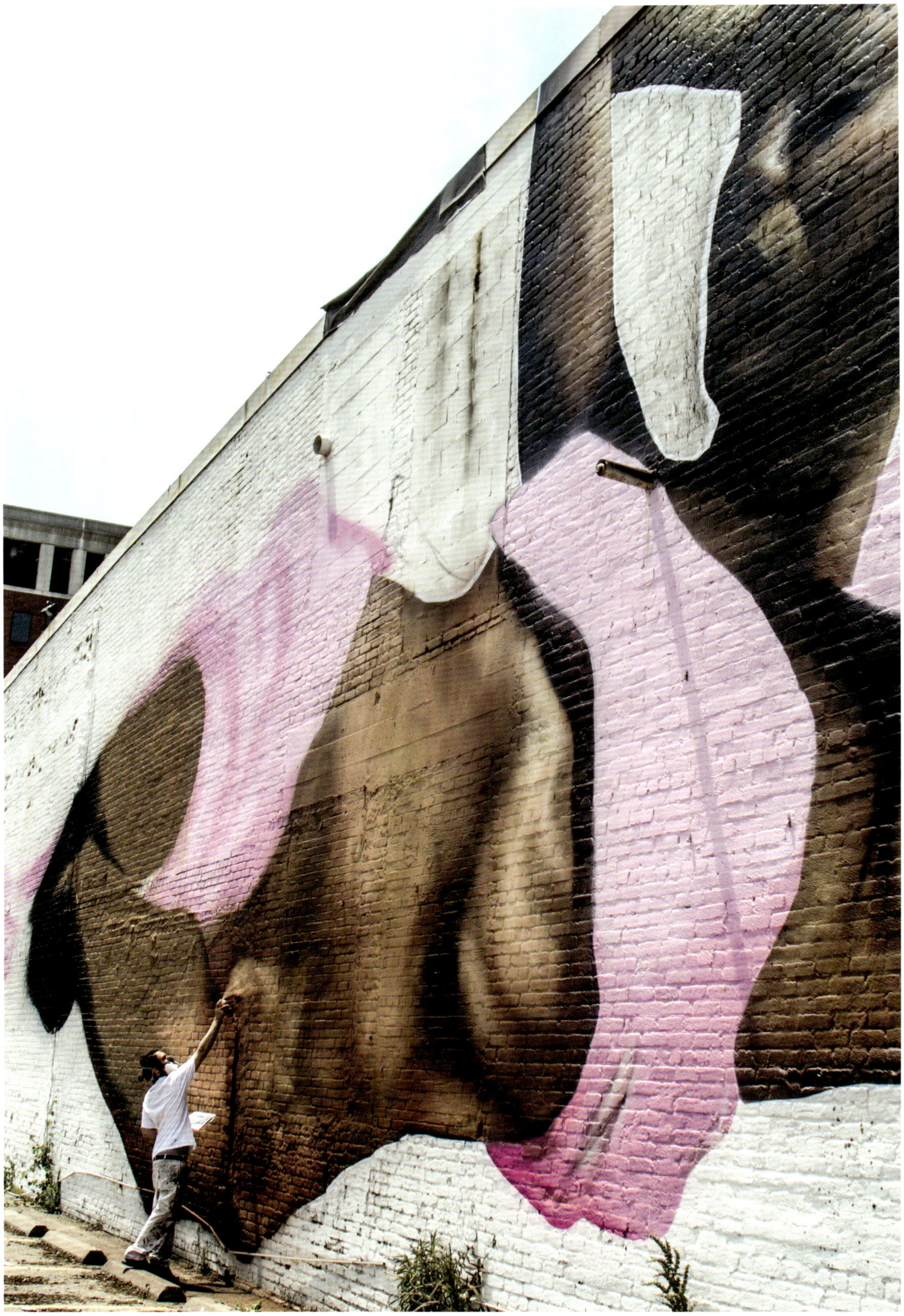

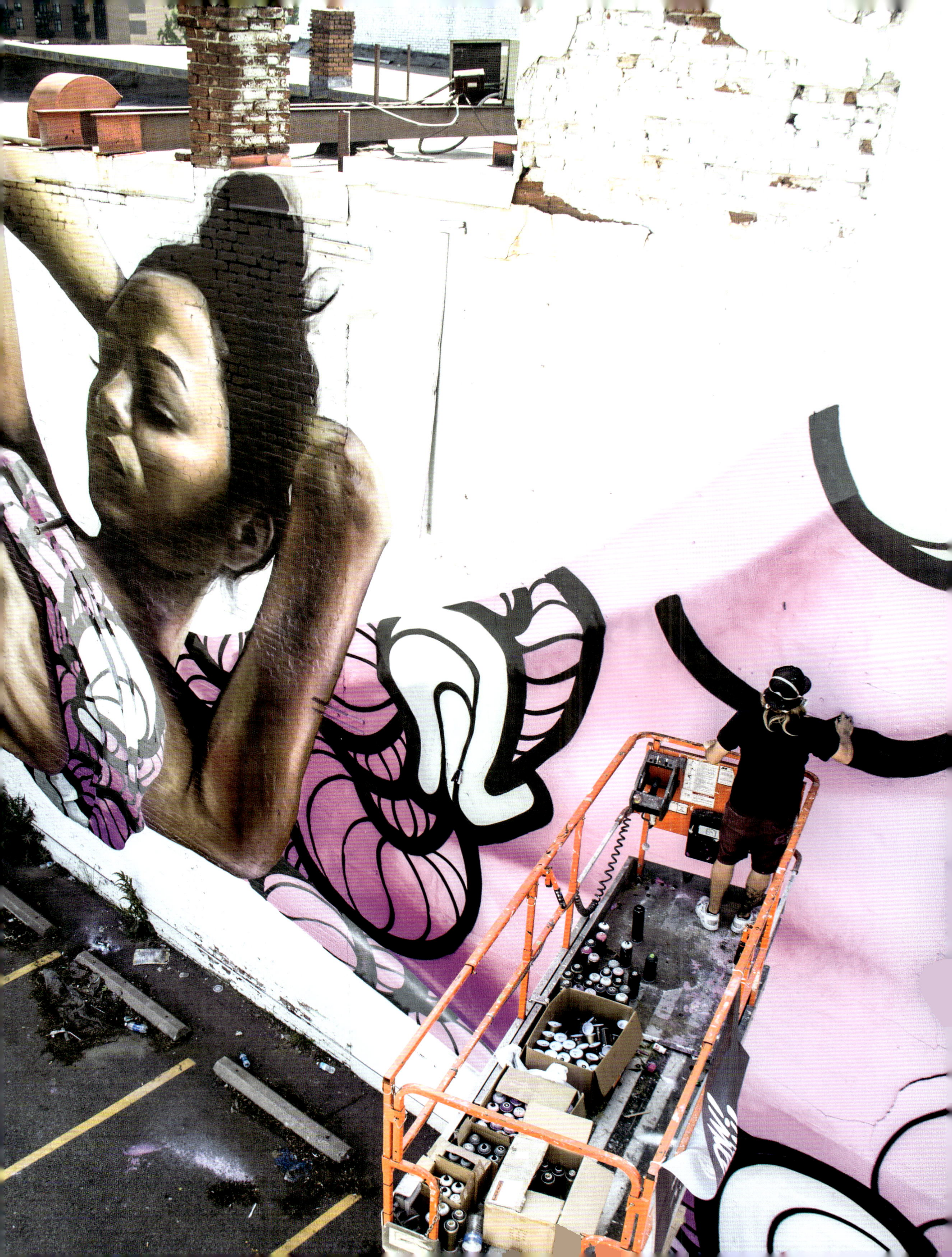

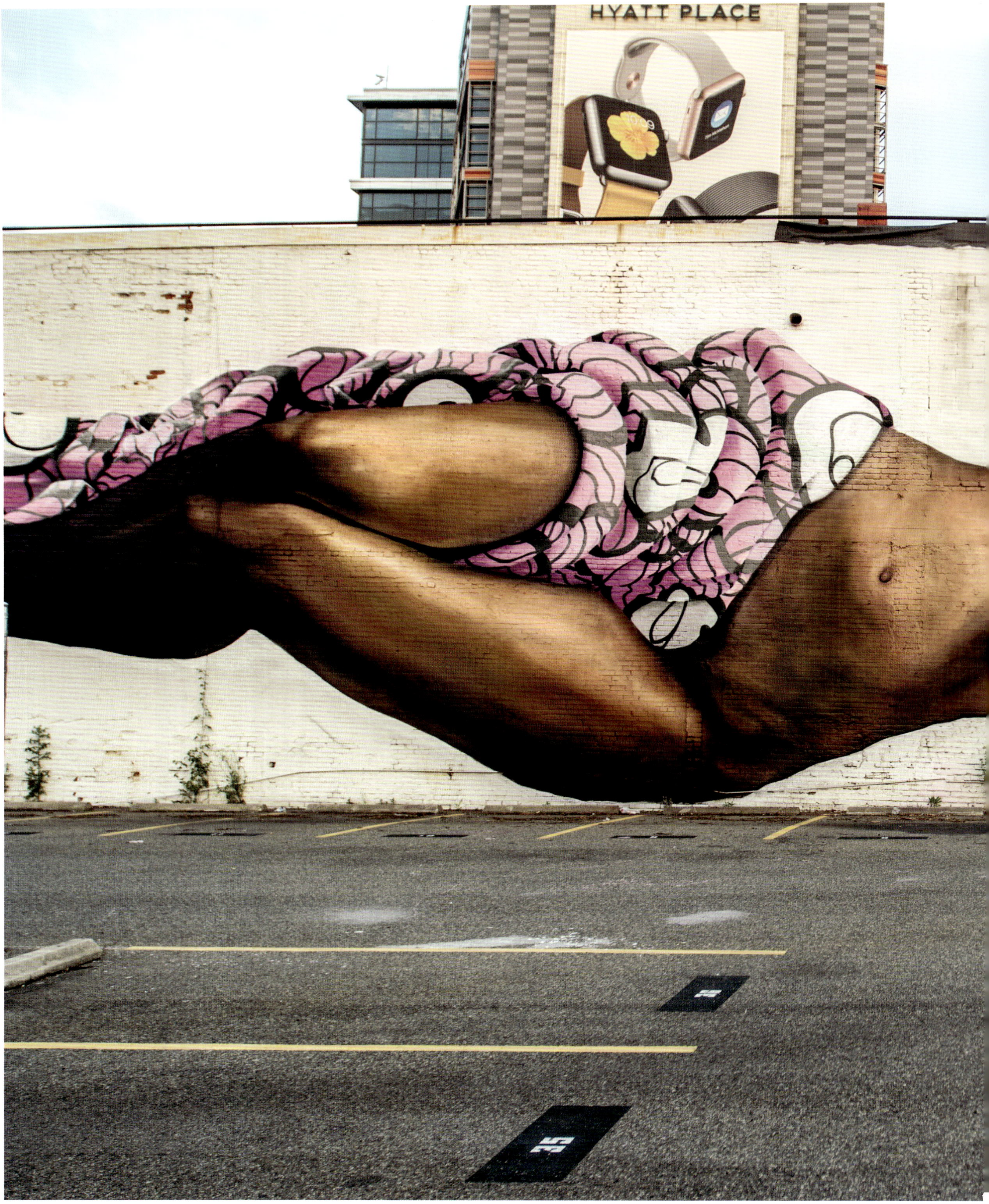
HYATT PLACE

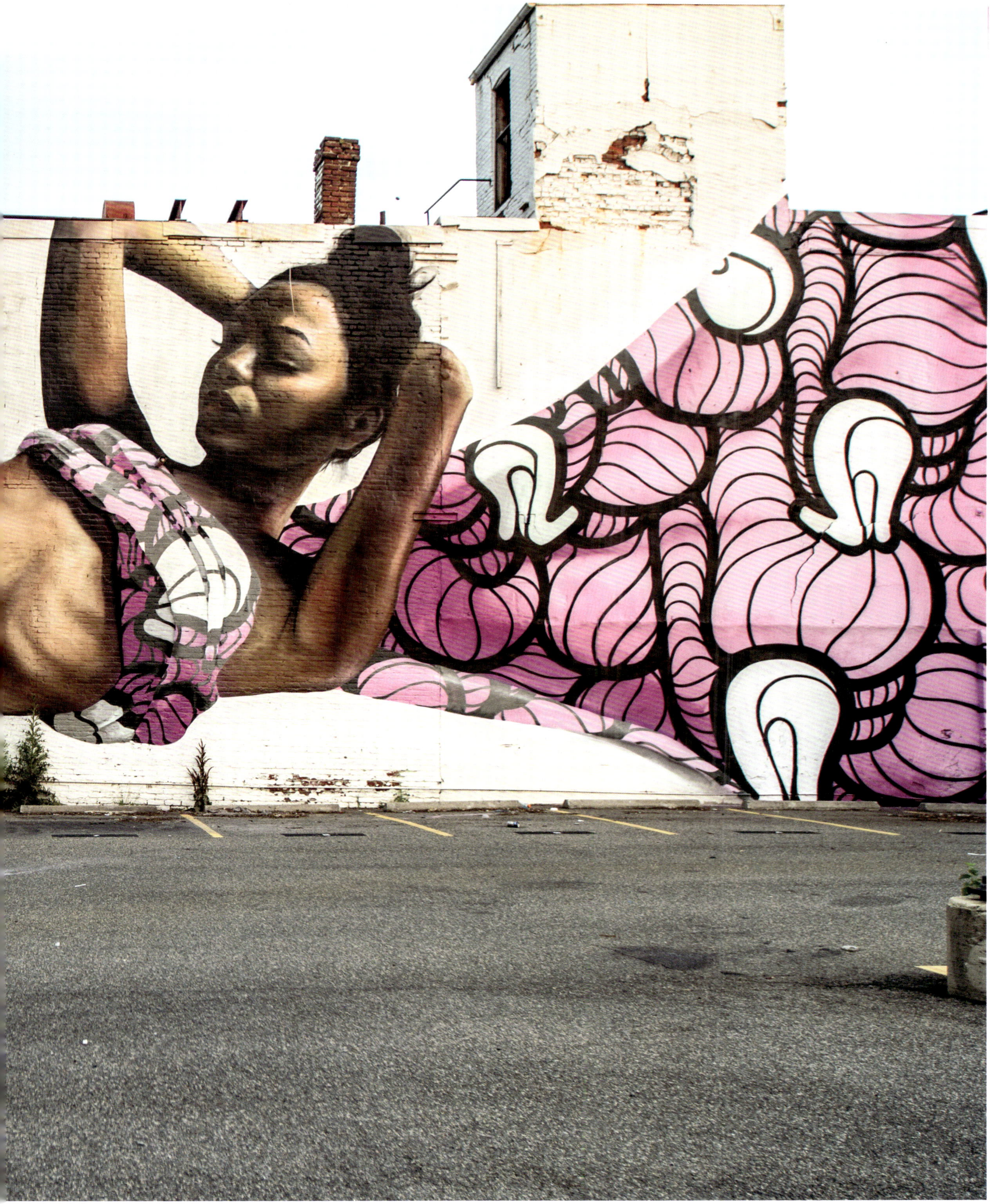

Washington D.C.
2017

Madsteez

@MADSTEEZ

After being born blind in his left eye and given three first names, artist Mark Paul Deren, (aka **MADSTEEZ**) is a human color wheel spinning on overdrive. Currently based in WEENSV!LLE, CA, Deren grew up on the outskirts of Washington DC, surrounded by nicknames and the oh so frequent game of biscuit, where his HEYD!K sense of humor emerged. From his scrappy WEEN!MAL doodles to his larger-than-life pop-soaked paintings and portraits, Deren's vivid creations have caught the eye of an impressive list of commercial collaborators (not to mention Dennis Hopper, who himself has sat for a Deren portrait). His methodical approach to large-scale murals has granted him worldwide appreciation, with accompanying film documentation highlighting his process behind the multi-layered landscapes that transform blank canvases into an acidic voyage and cosmic explosion. In his second decade as a professional artist, Madsteez has been featured in renowned publications like The New York Times and Dazed and Confused, with commissions coming from Nike, Mini Cooper, De La Barracuda, Target, Stussy, and many more.

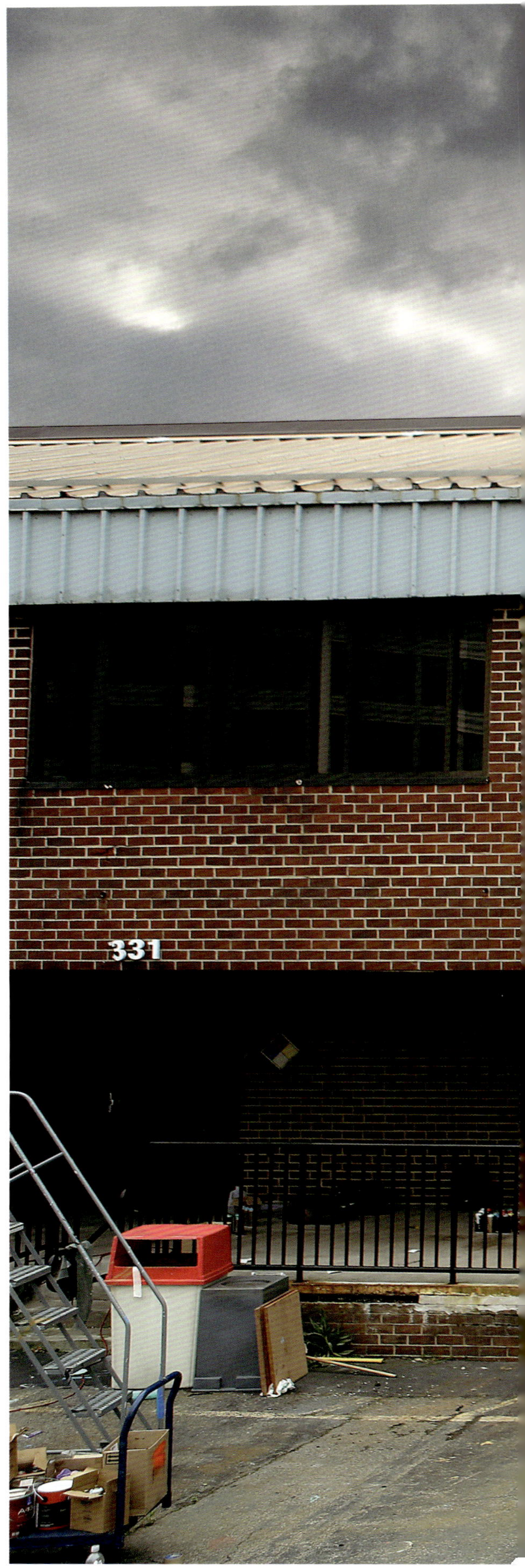

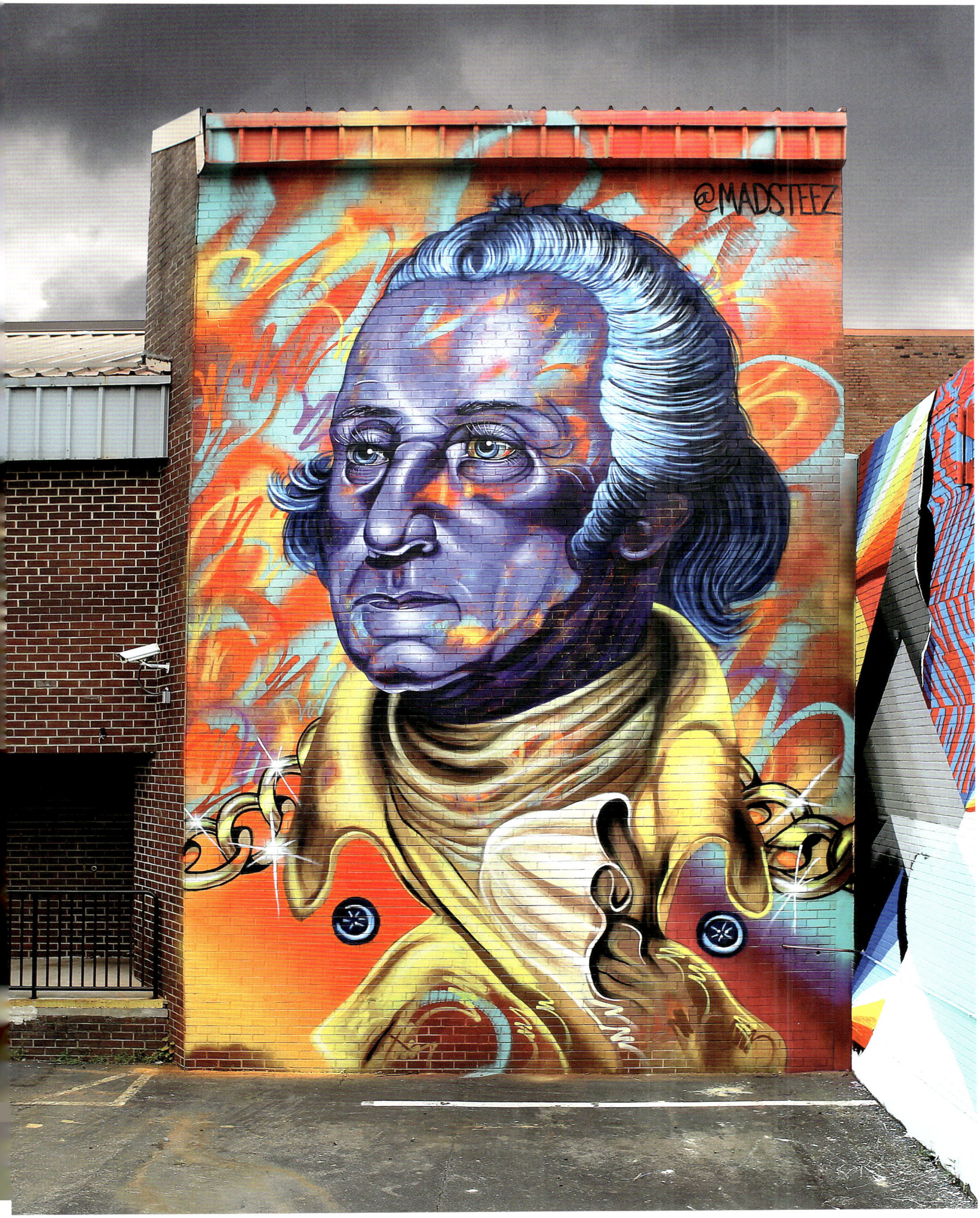
@MADSTEEZ

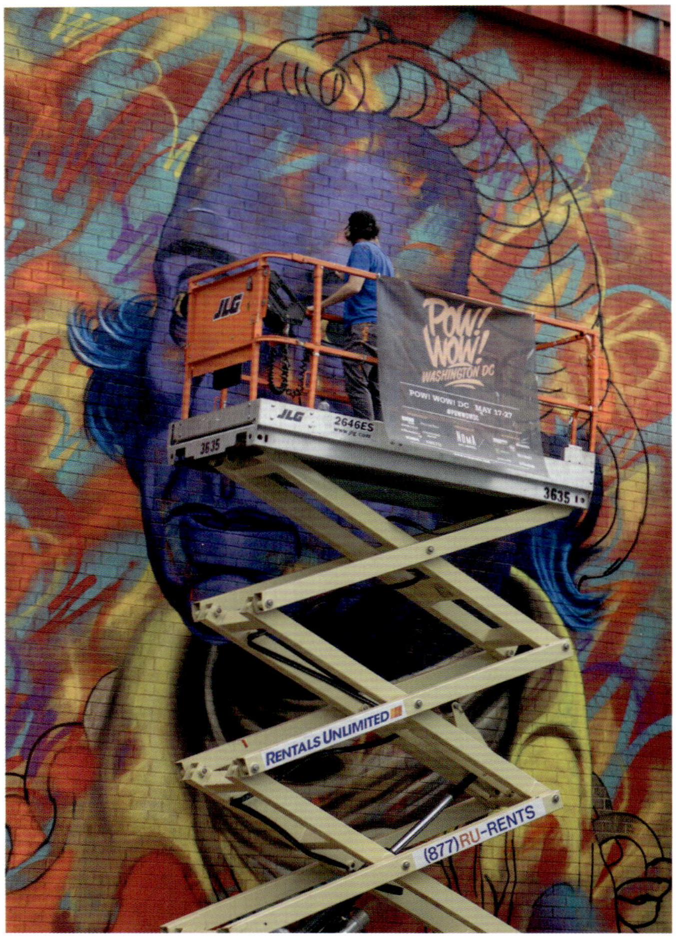
JLG
POW! WOW! WASHINGTON DC
2646ES
3635
RENTALS UNLIMITED
(877)RU-RENTS

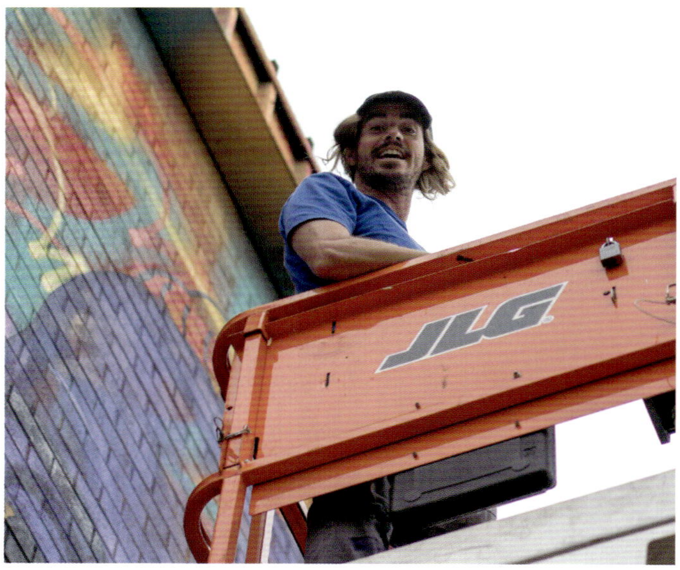
JLG

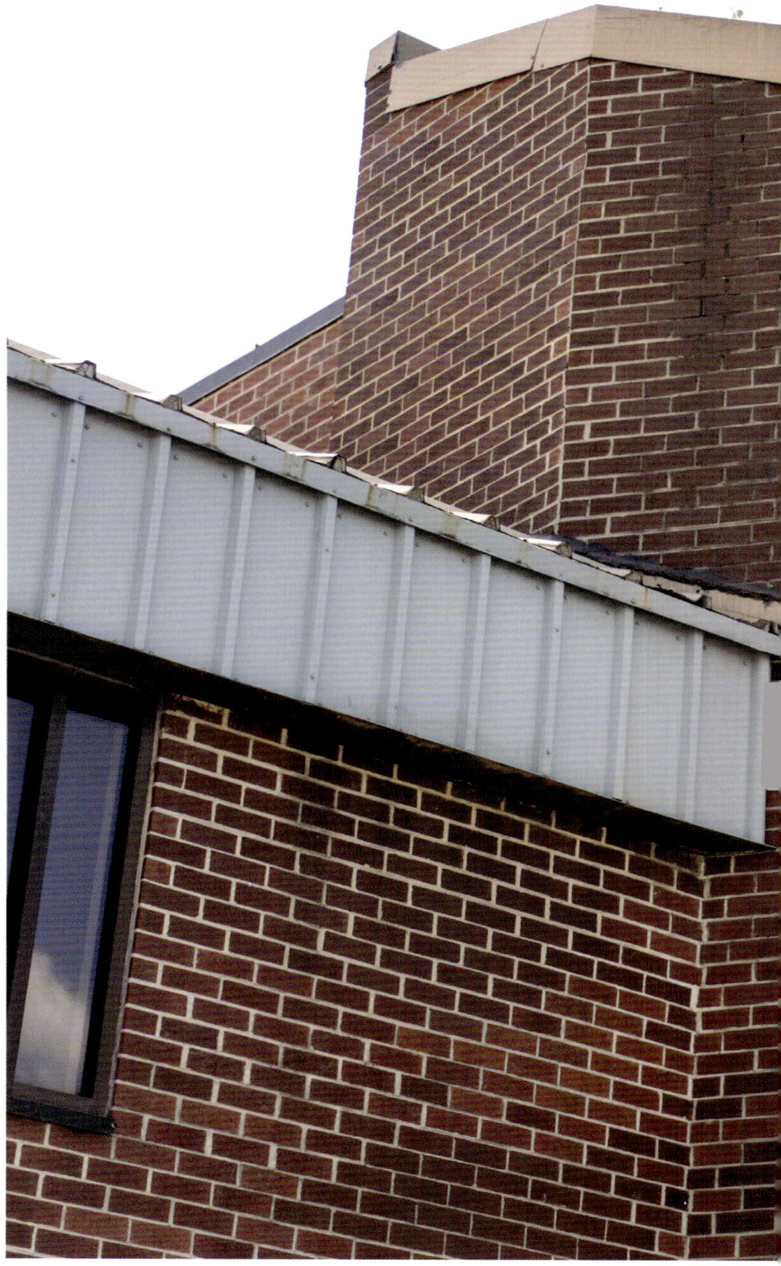

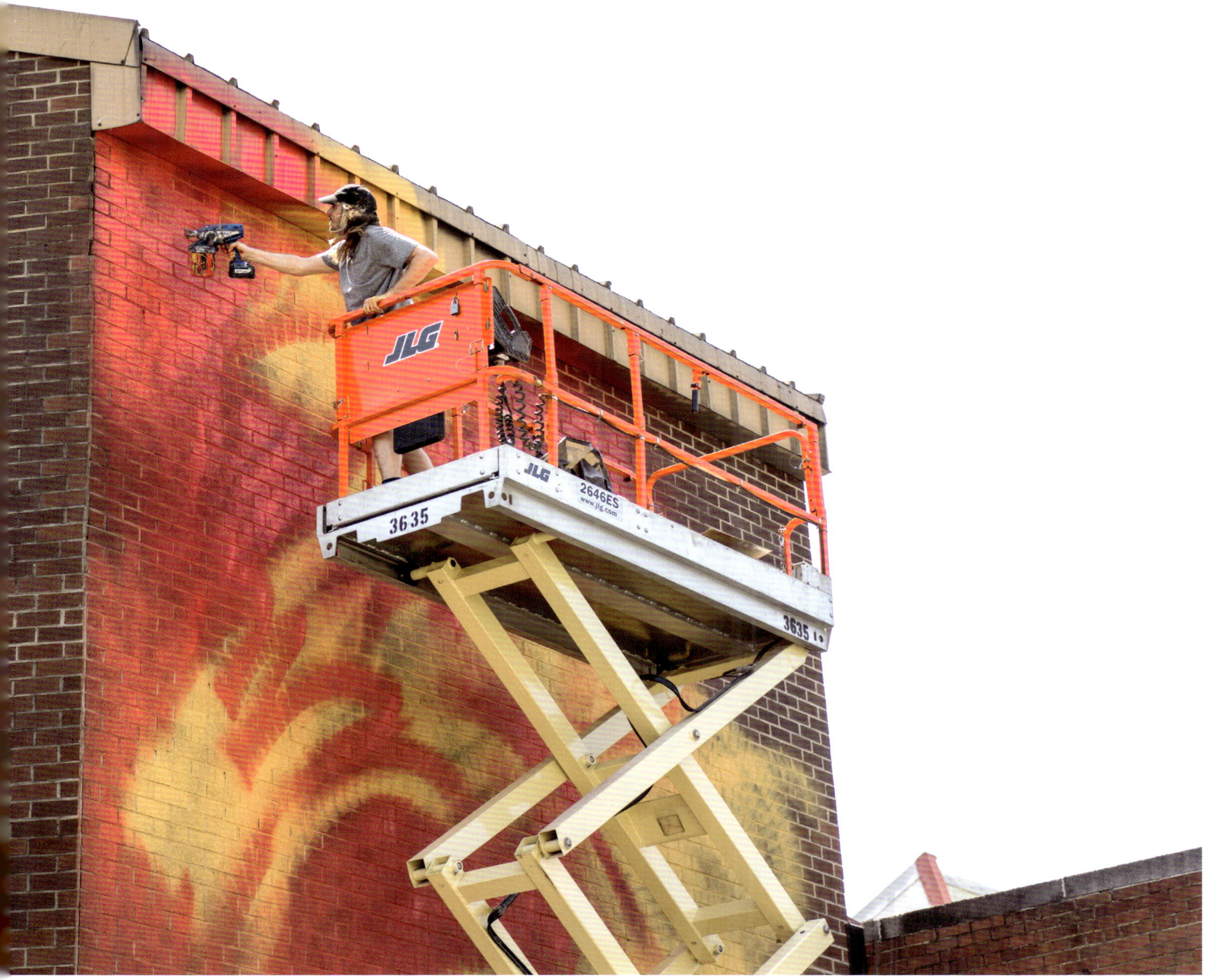
JLG
JLG
2646ES
3635
3635

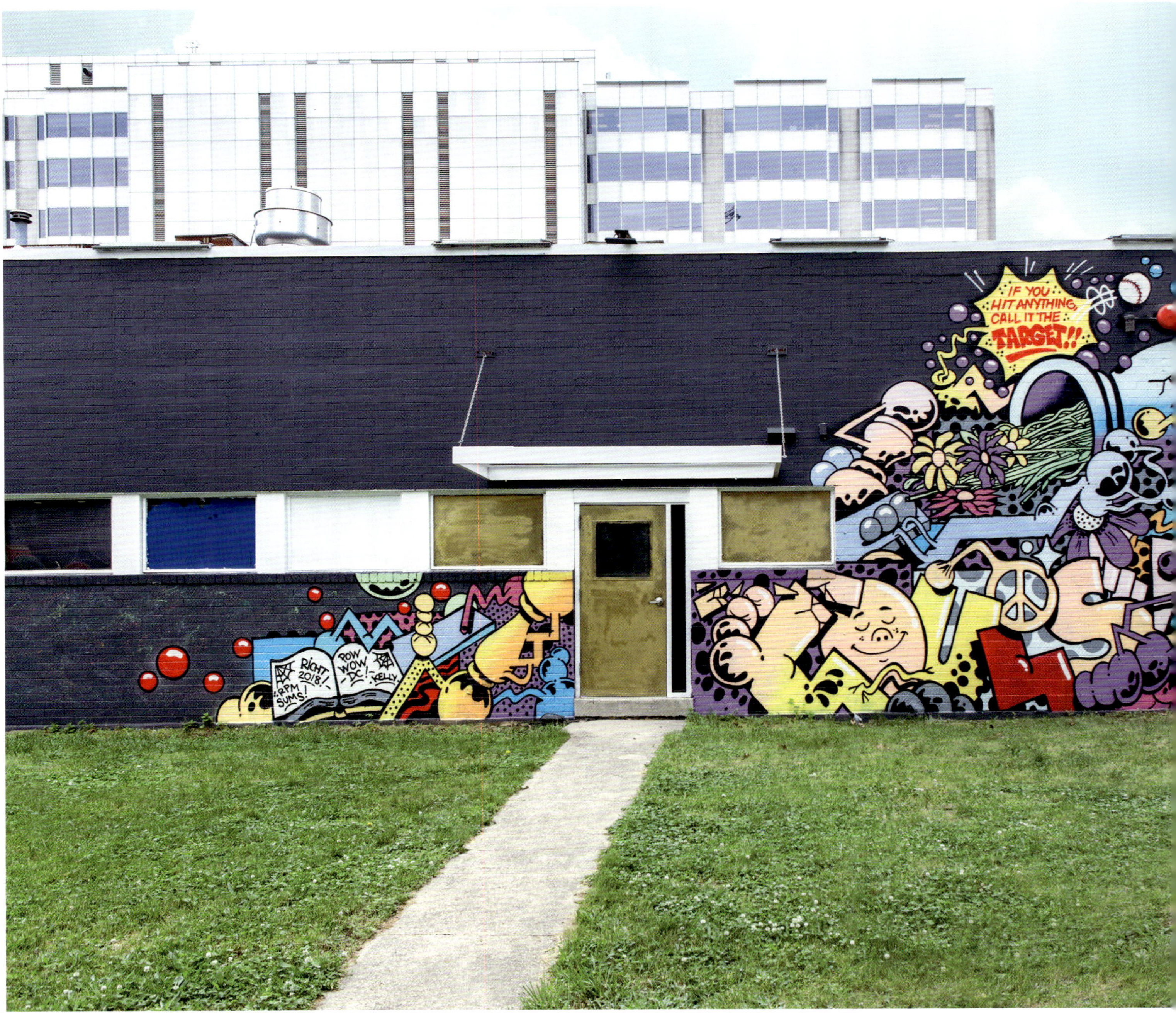

Washington D.C.
2018

Richt

@RICHTPAINT

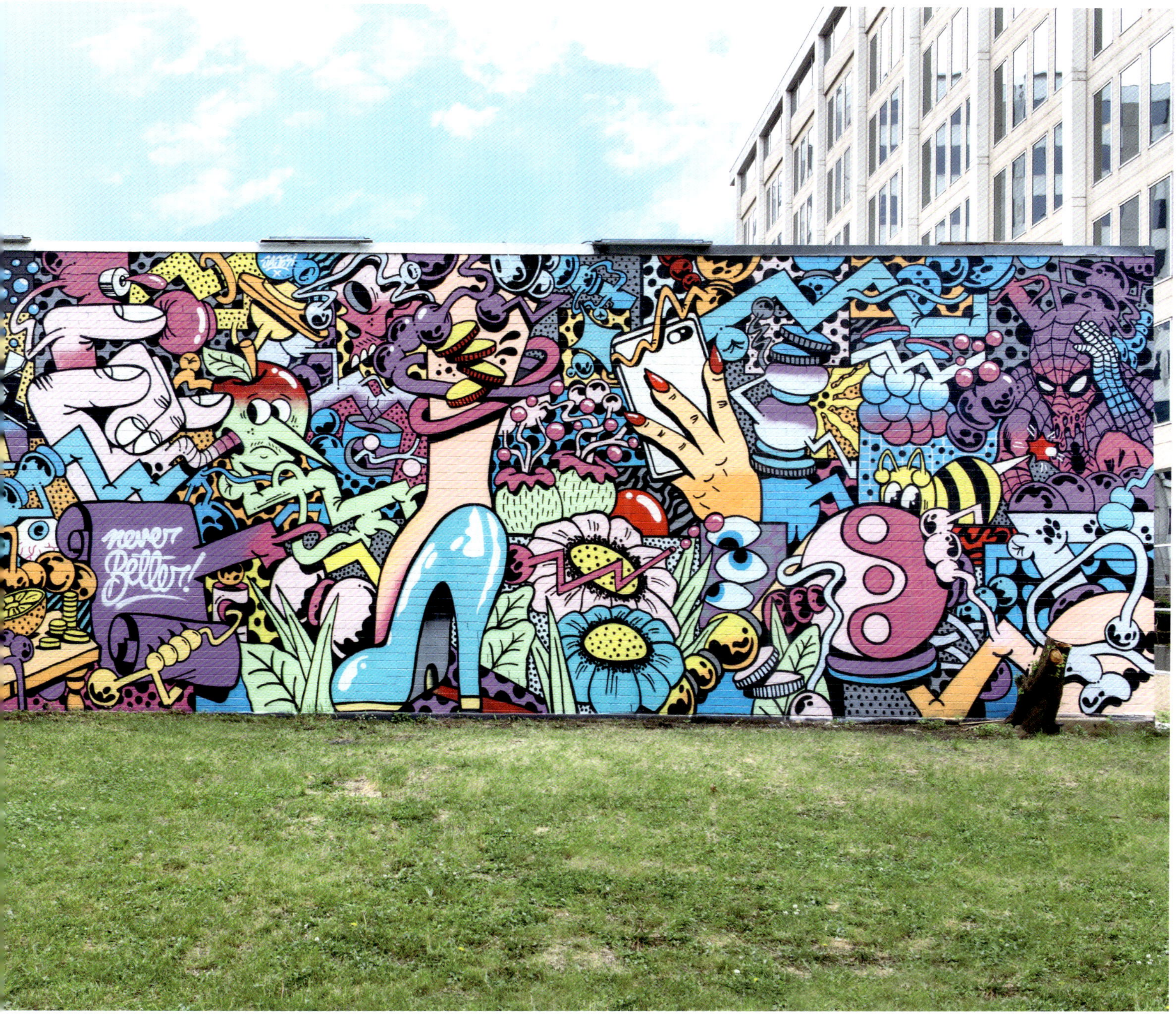

Originally a part of the british street art scene in the early noughties, **Richt** has established himself in both the art scene and illustration world. His work has been featured in magazines and publications across the globe for graffiti and street art including the highly influential "Street Sketchbook" by Tristan Manco (Thames and Hudson, 2007)

Over the past decade, Richt has been focussing on illustration and outdoor painting. Alongside curating and participating in numerous group exhibitions Richt has been working as a creative director and commercial illustrator for animation giants 'Aardman', the BBC, America's got talent, Golden Wolf, Vans and more...

Most recently Richt has been in the States and Europe painting large scale murals and spent a year art directing a europe wide project for Vans.

His recent solo show saw him progress further into the traditional art market with an exhibition of work based on his love for the comic book aesthetic from the early '60s and '70s.

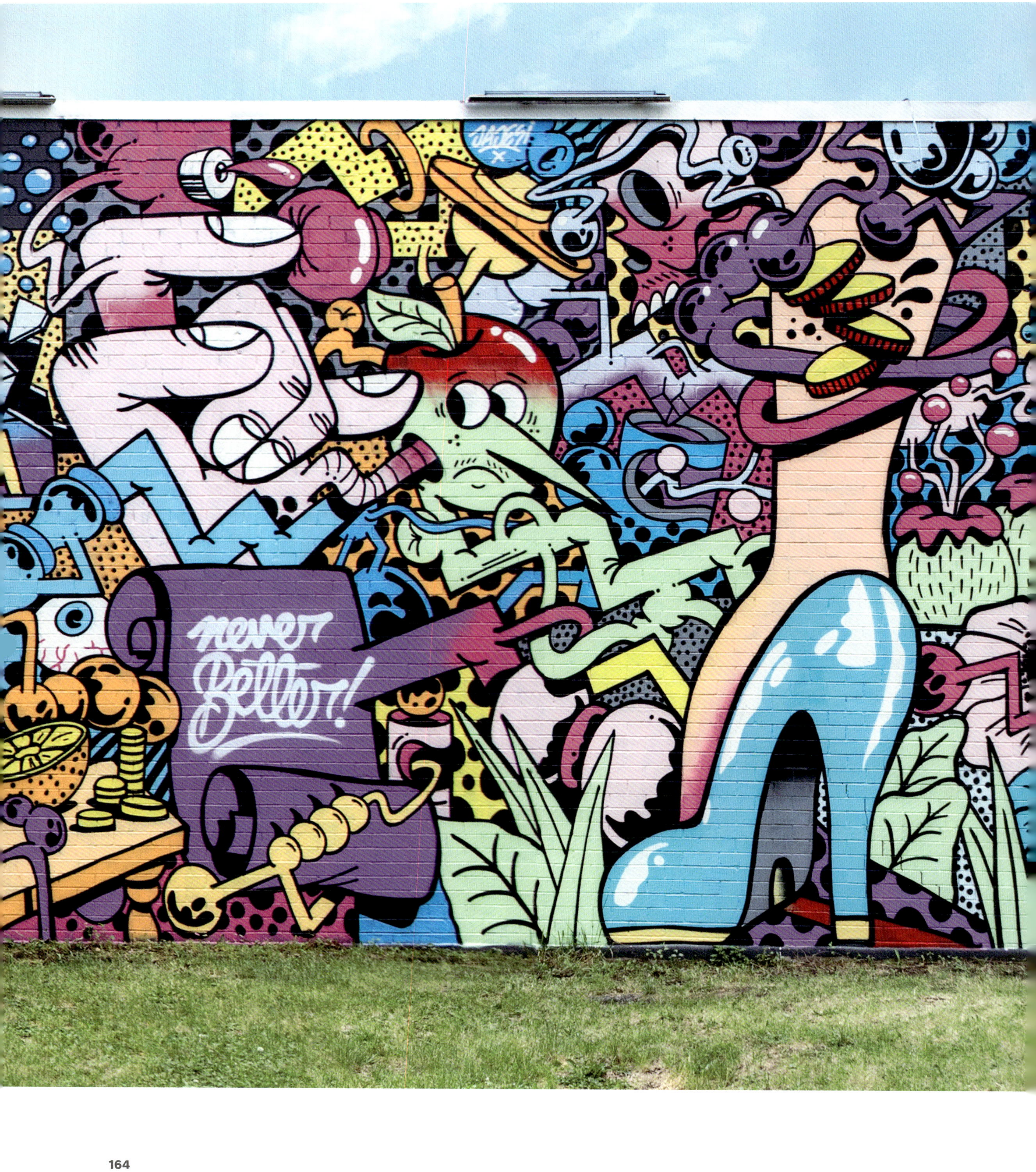
never
Better!

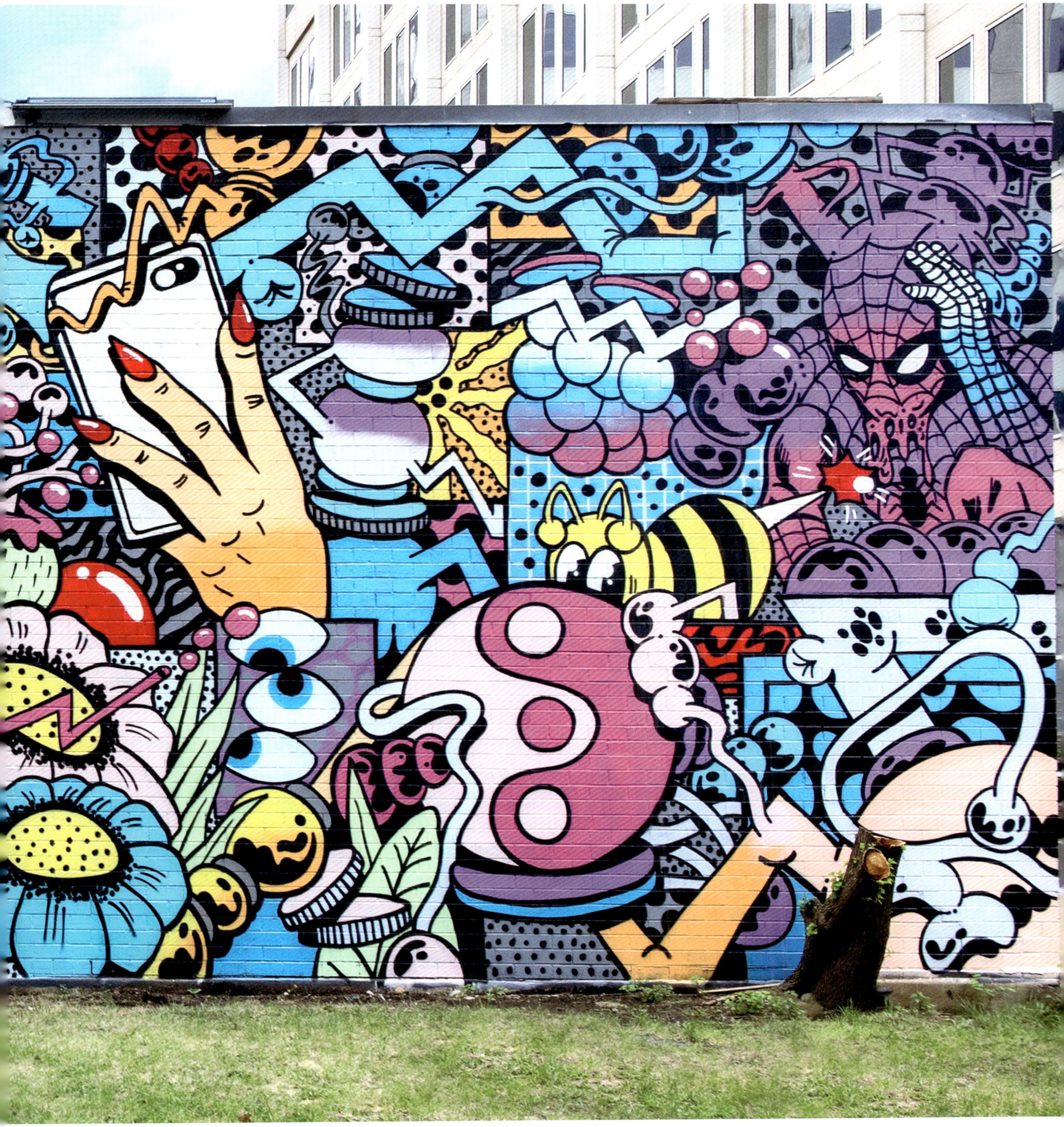

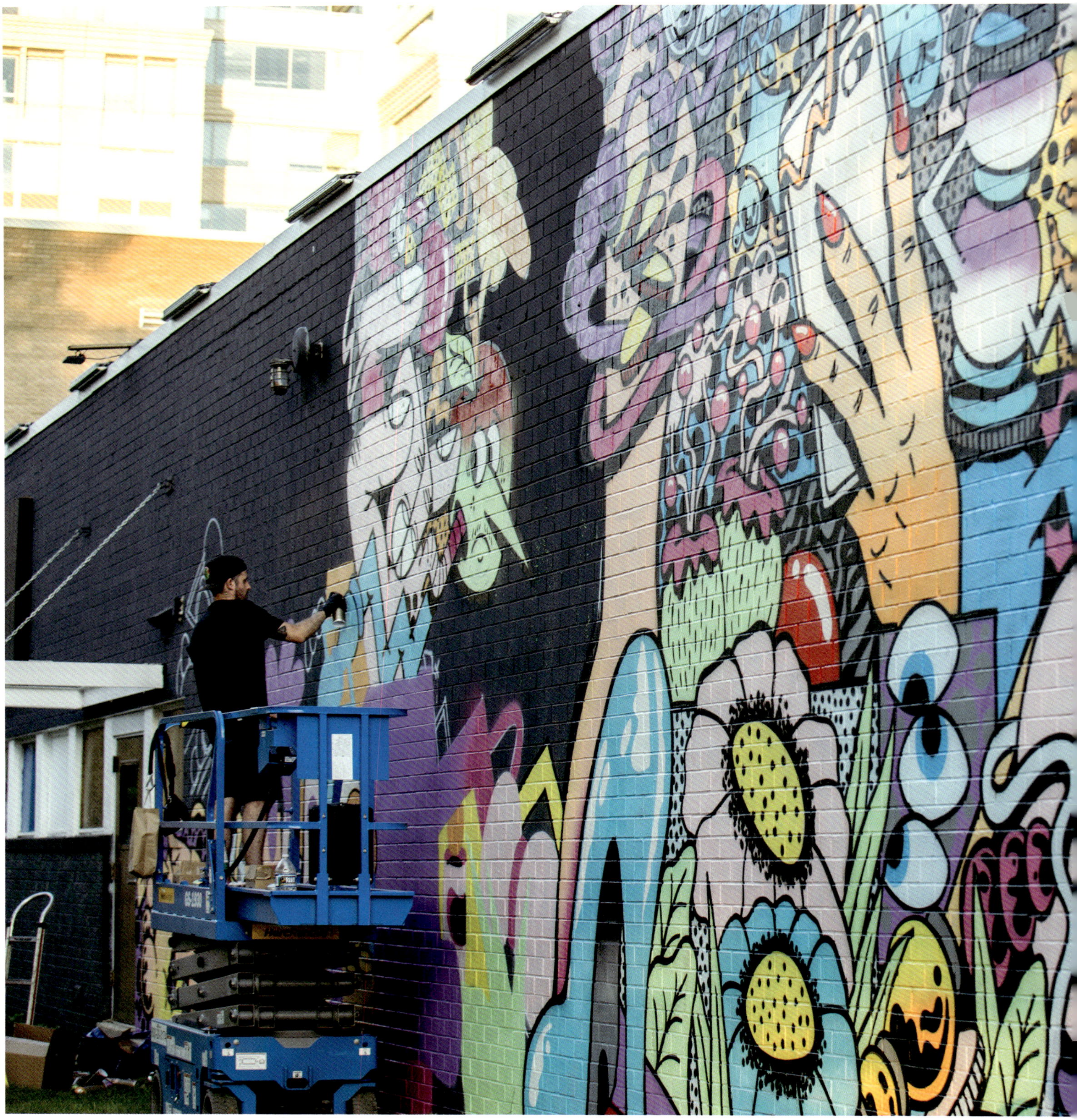

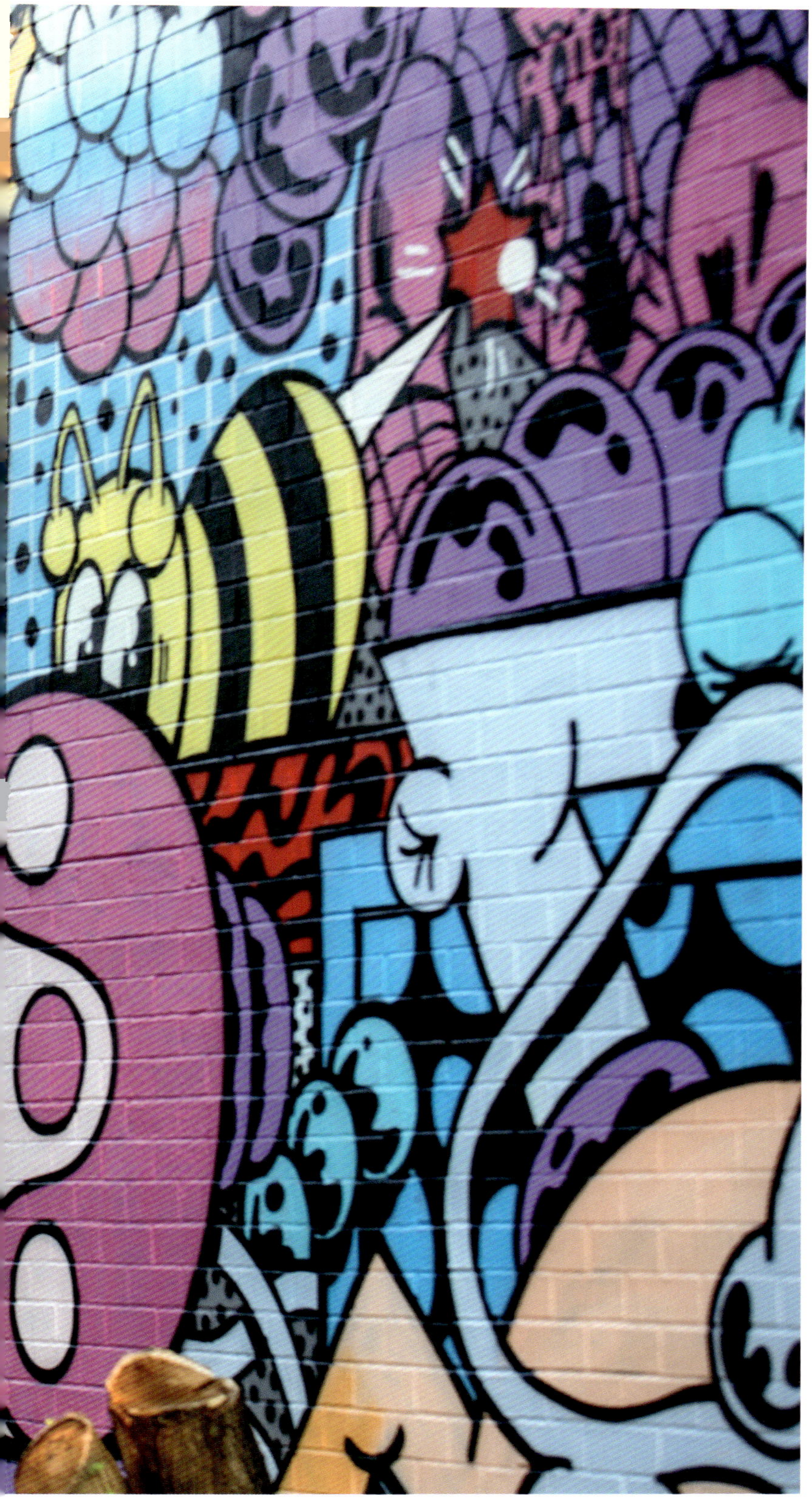

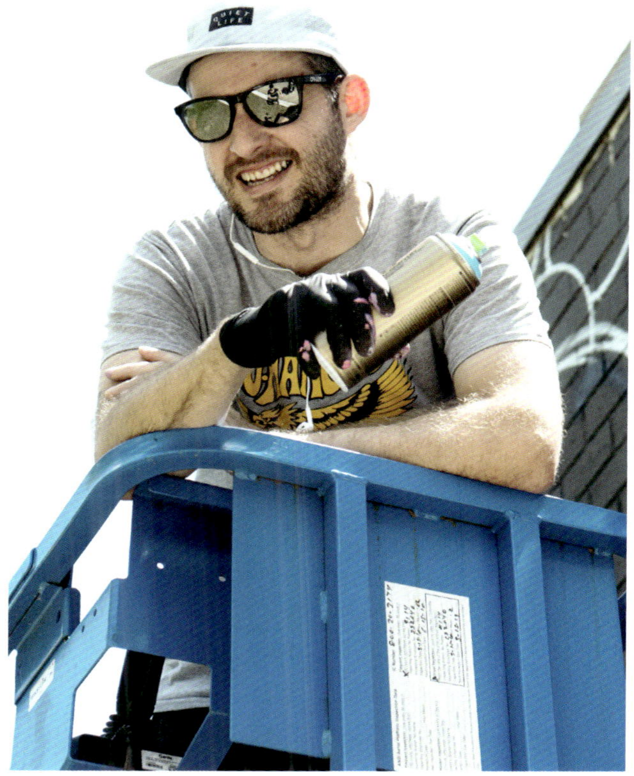

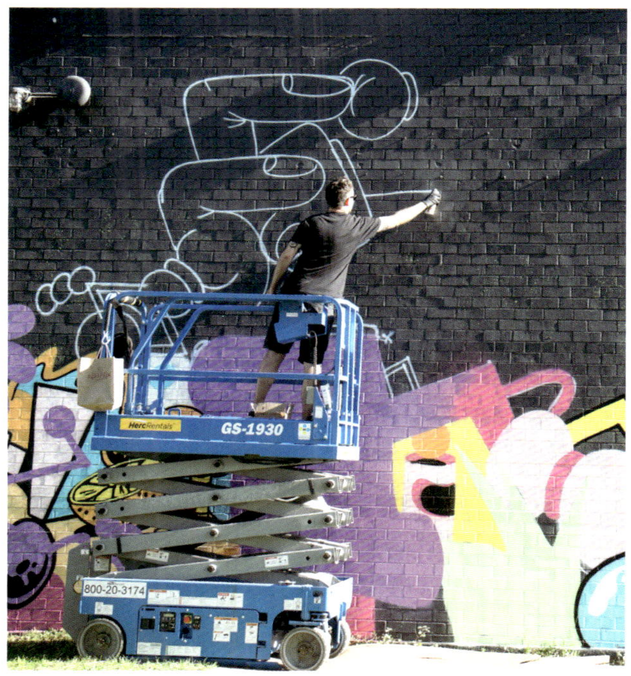
HercRentals
GS-1930
800-20-3174

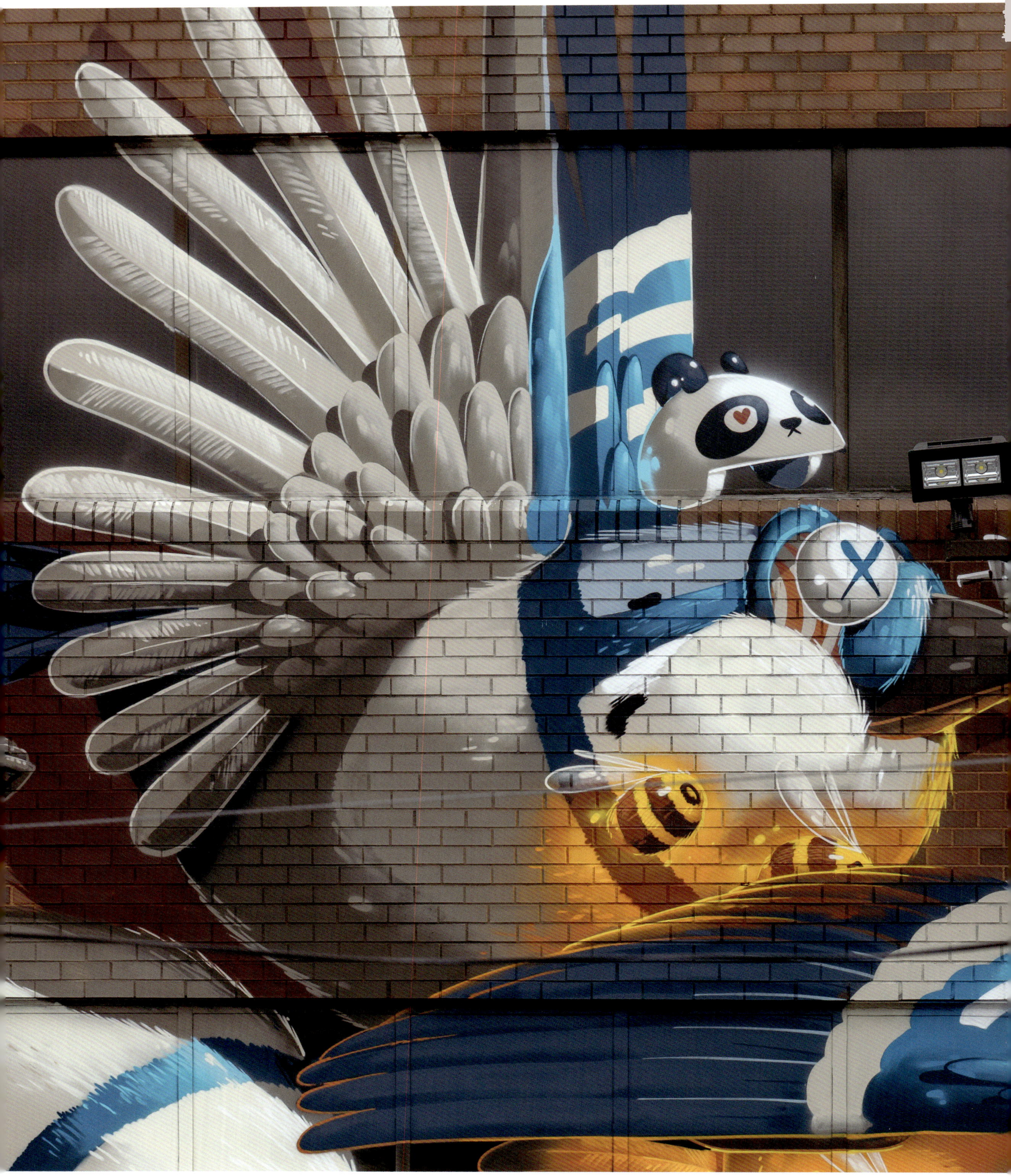

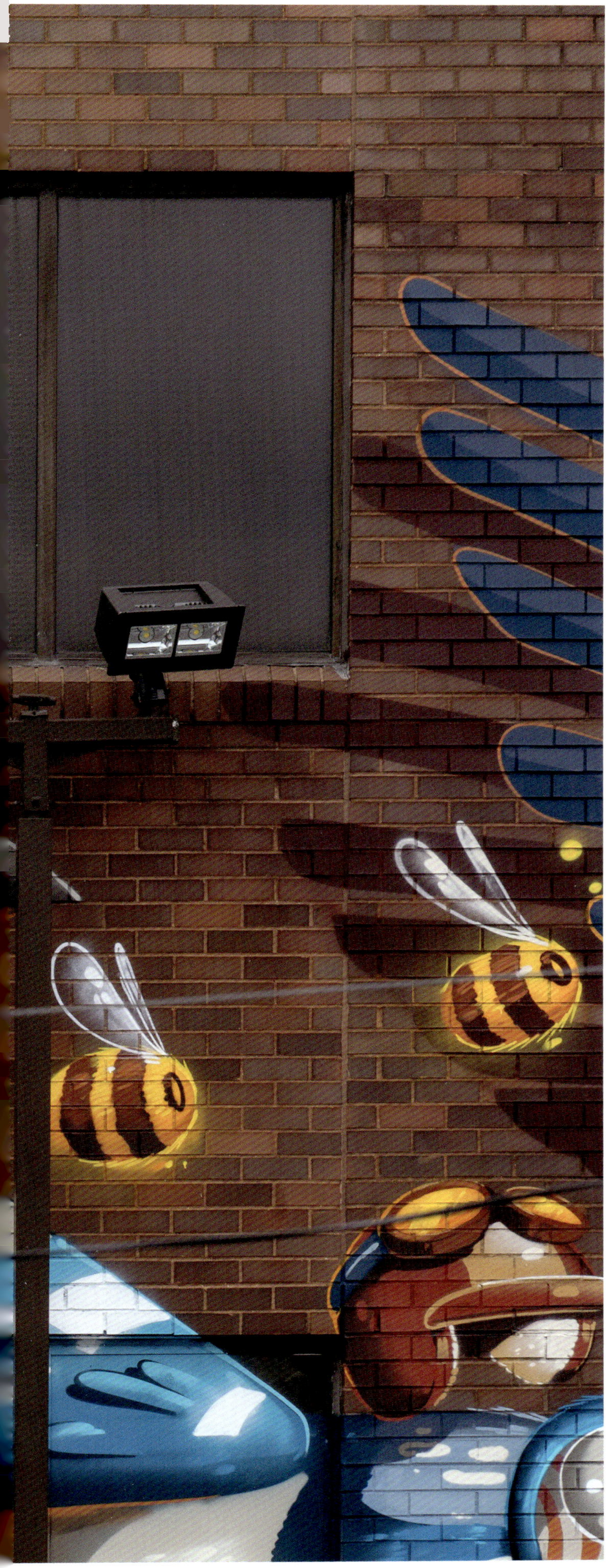

Washington D.C.
2019

Stom500

@STOM500

Cultivating a delirious & humorous universe nourished by the euphoric energy of the cartoons, this self-taught virtuoso, from a village next to the common Swiss of Basel, multiplies his talents.

Trained as a graphic designer, illustrator by vocation and renowned graffiti artist for the past five years, **Stom500** is, as he defines himself with amusement, a true "Swiss Army knife". Spray, posca, acrylic, large murals, or paintings in a smaller format: he uses mediums and styles as diverse as they are varied.

With a predilection for animal themes which, under the varnish of comedy, carry a relevant message, often of a humanistic or ecological nature. Like its whirling bees or its apparently incompatible bestiaries, such as the raven and the fox inspired by the fables of La Fontaine, symbols of living together.

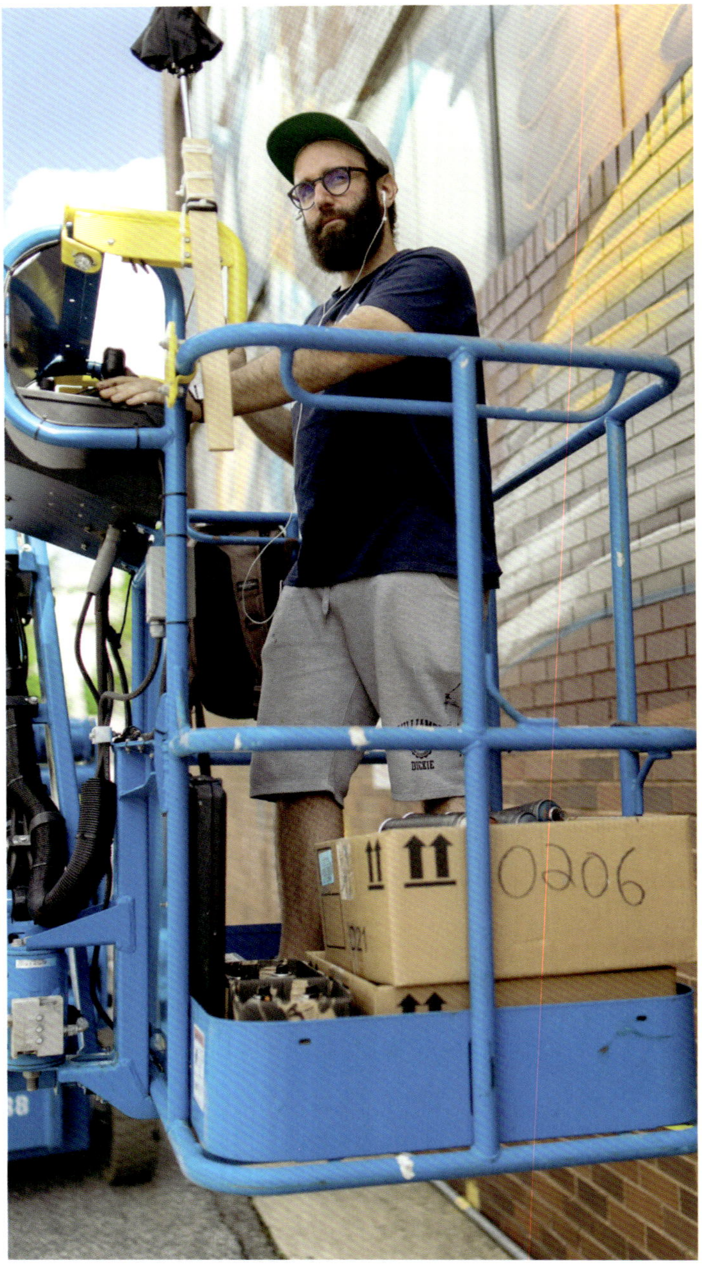
0206

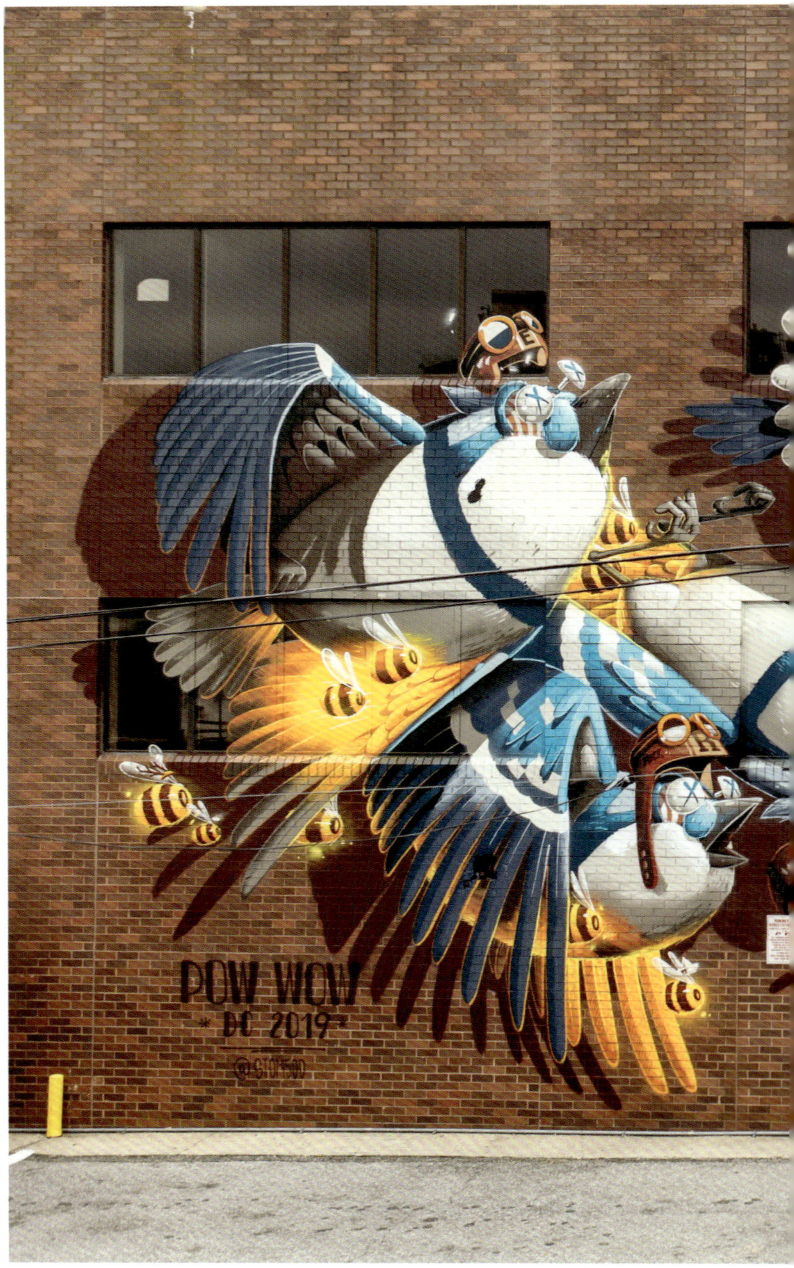
POW WOW
DC 2019

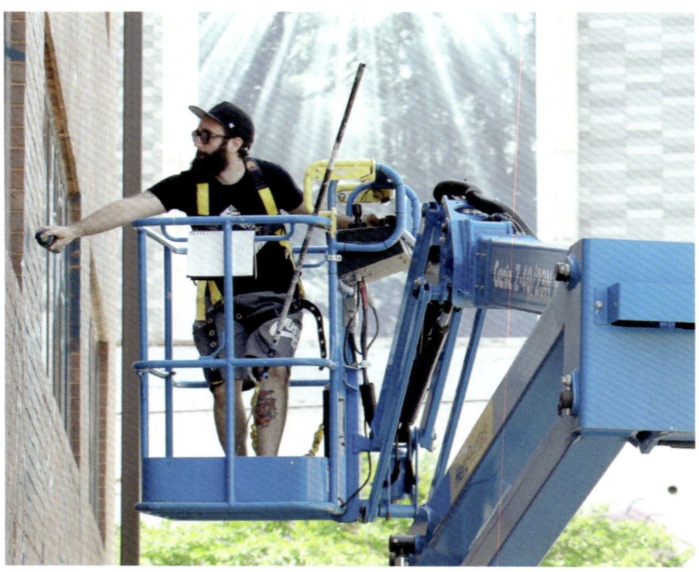

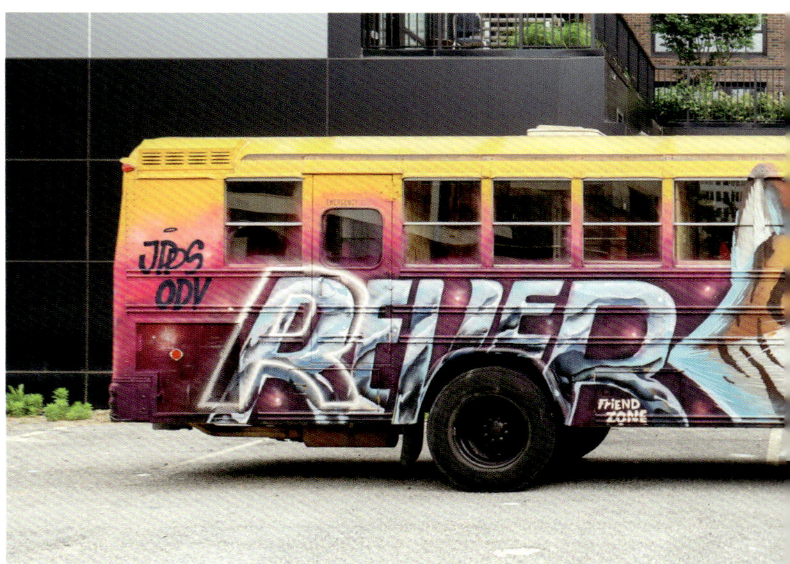

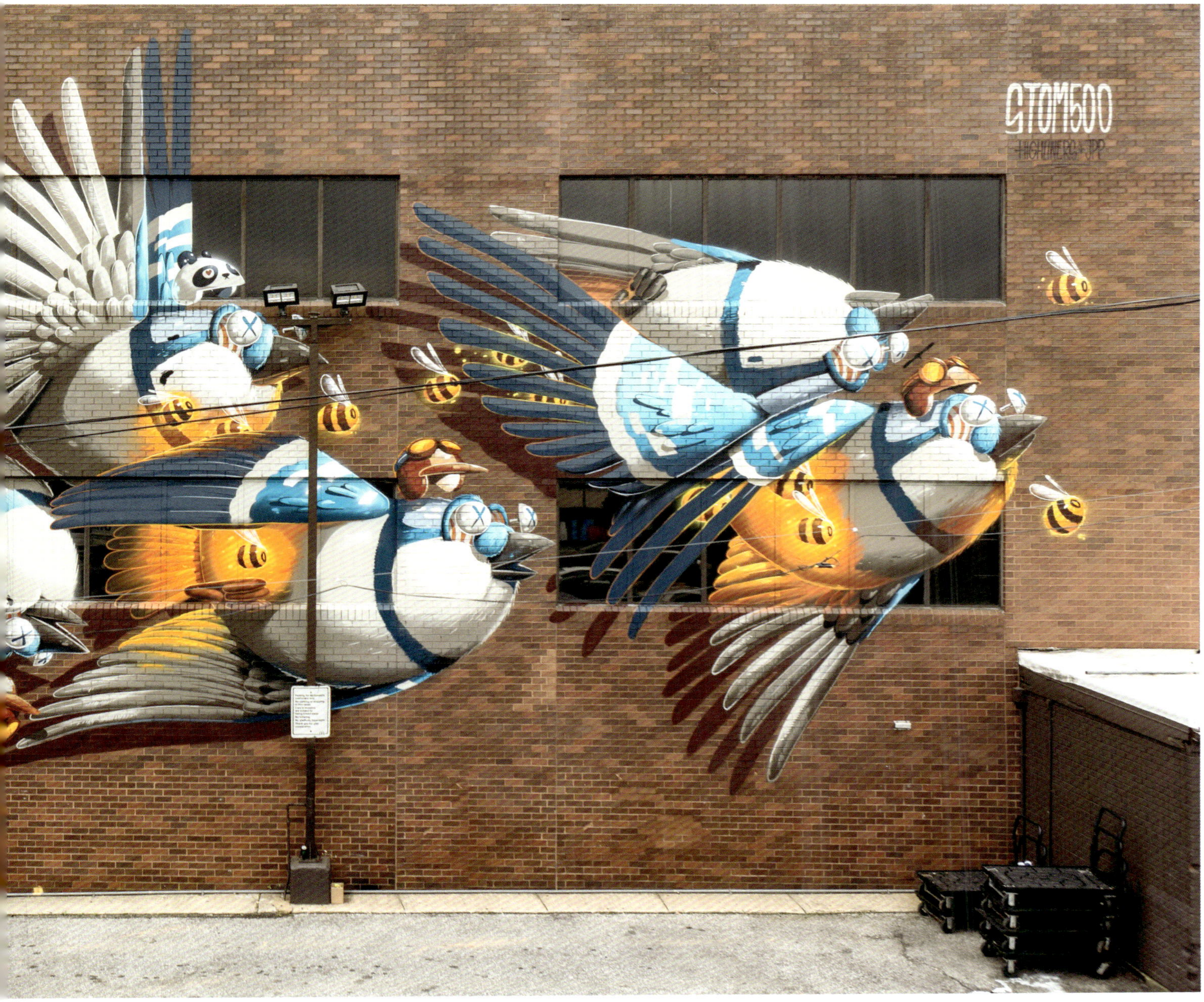
STOM500

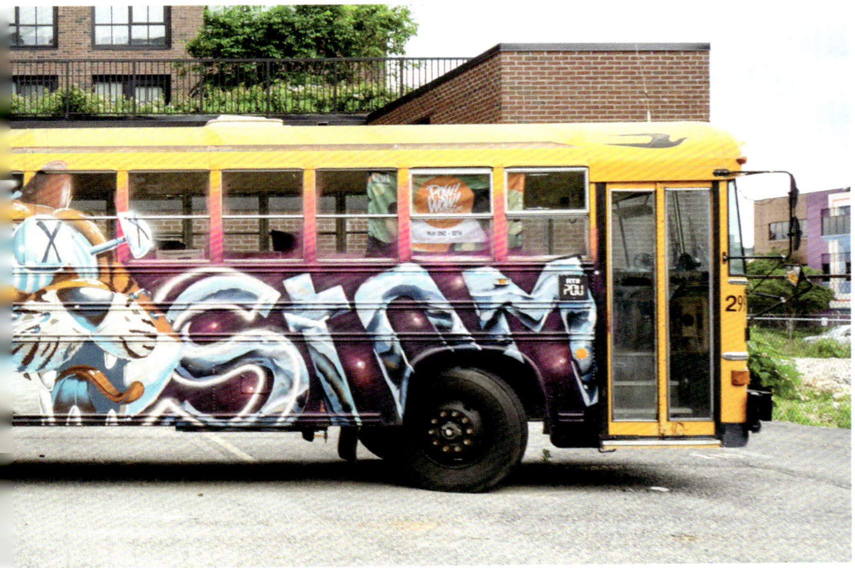

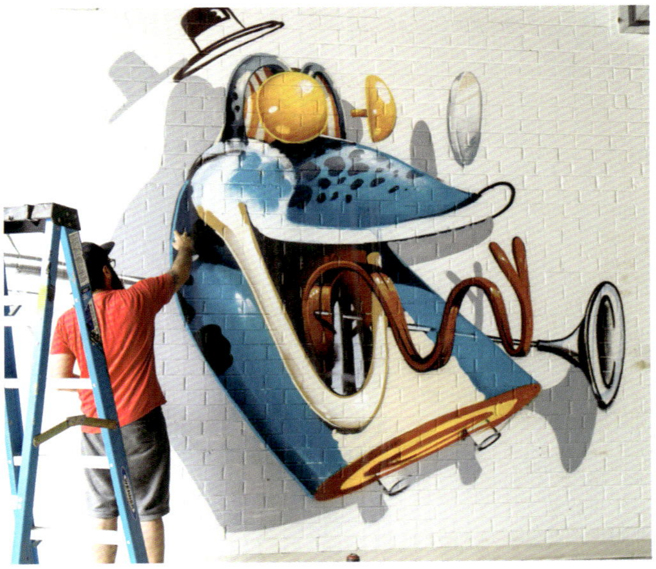

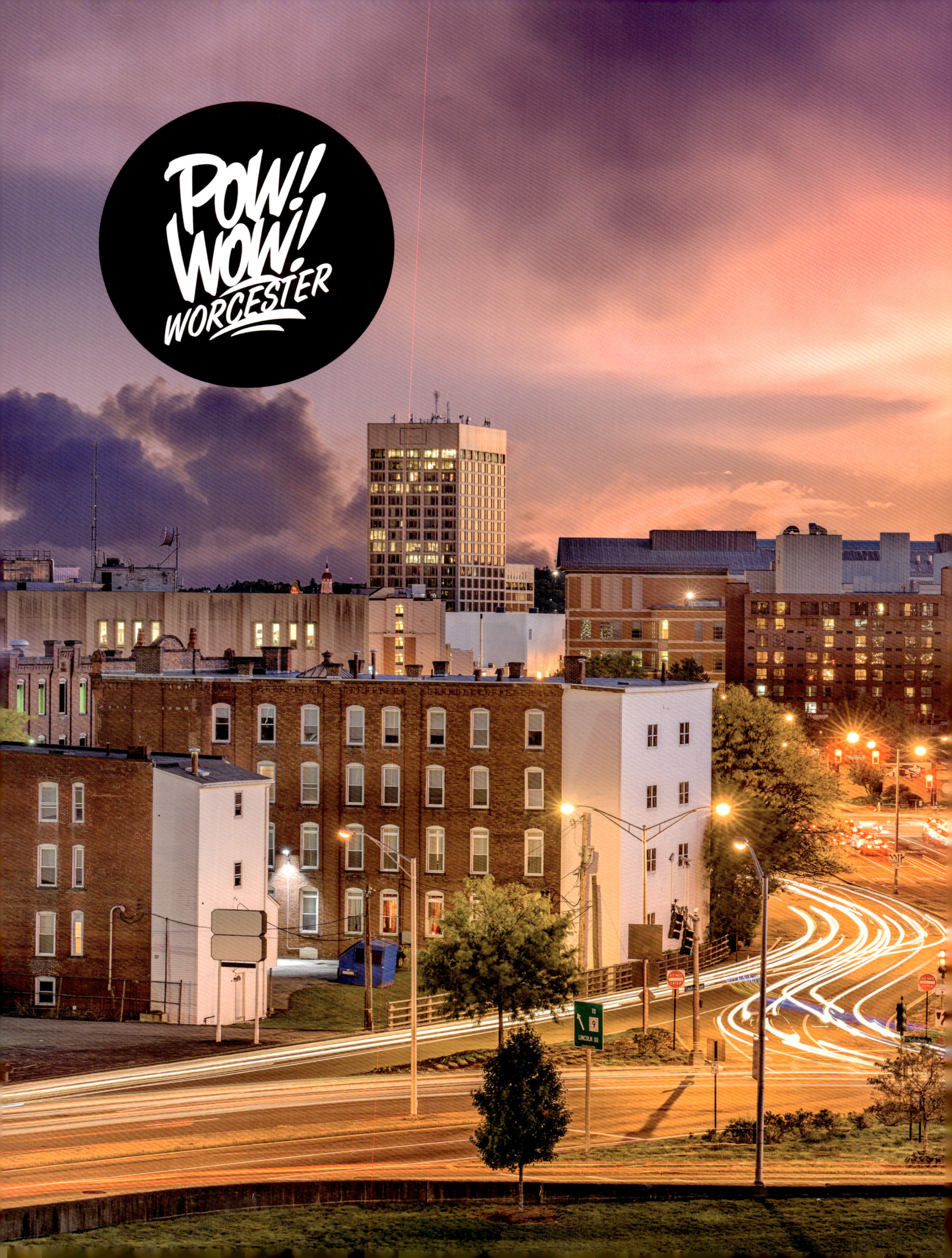
POW!
WOW!
WORCESTER

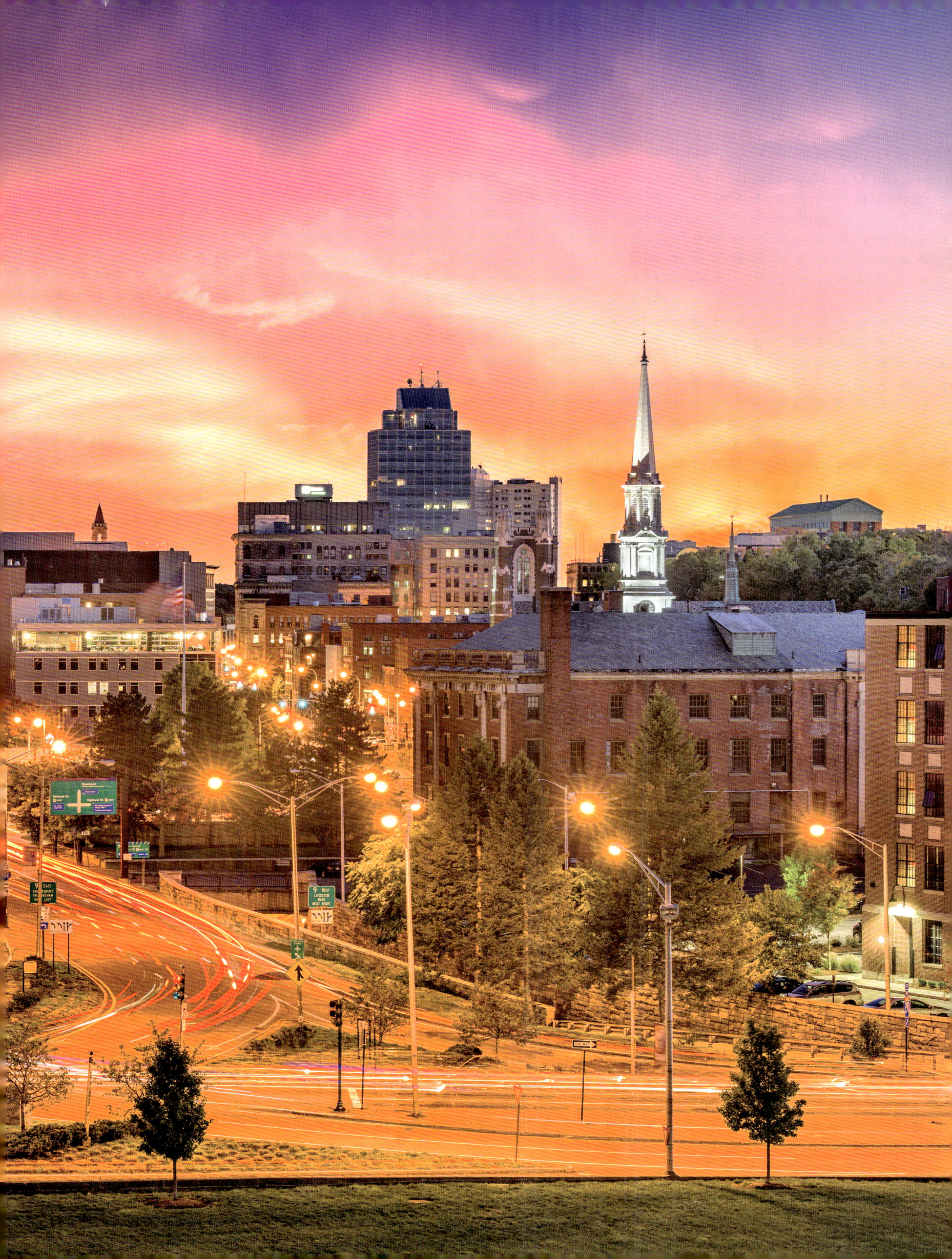

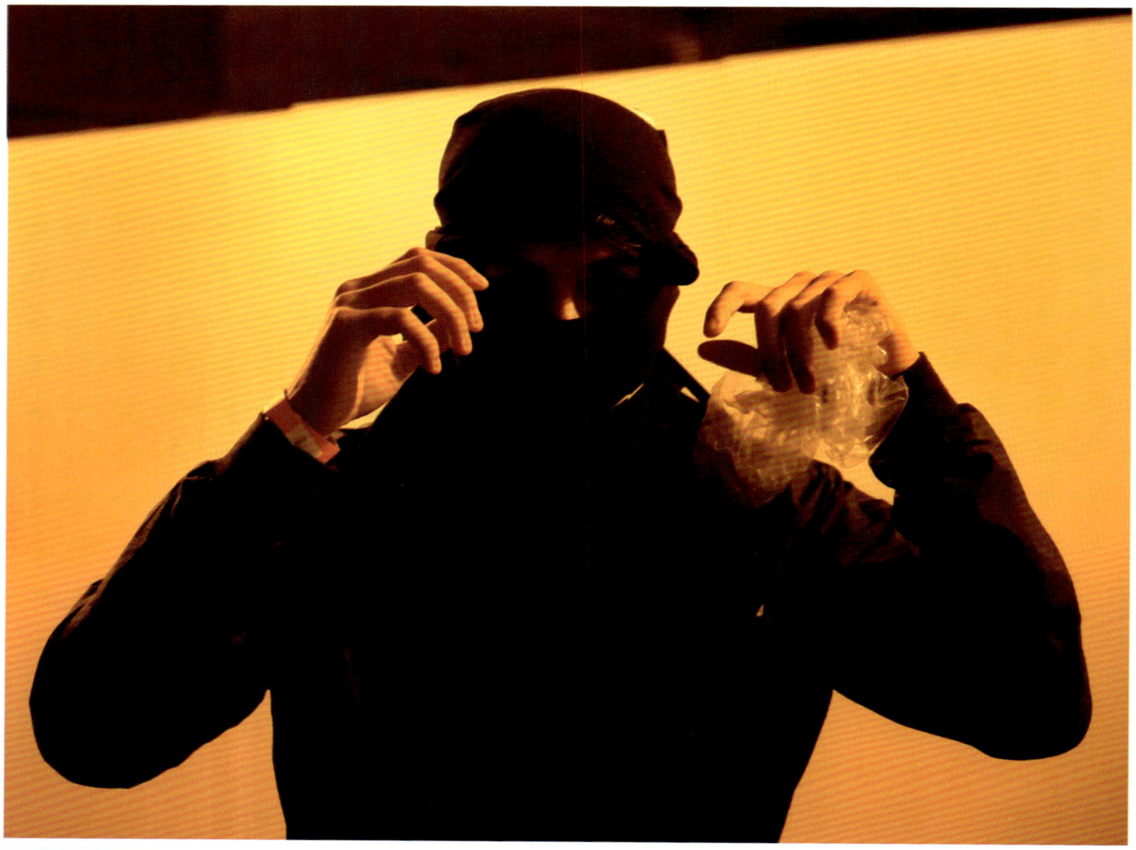

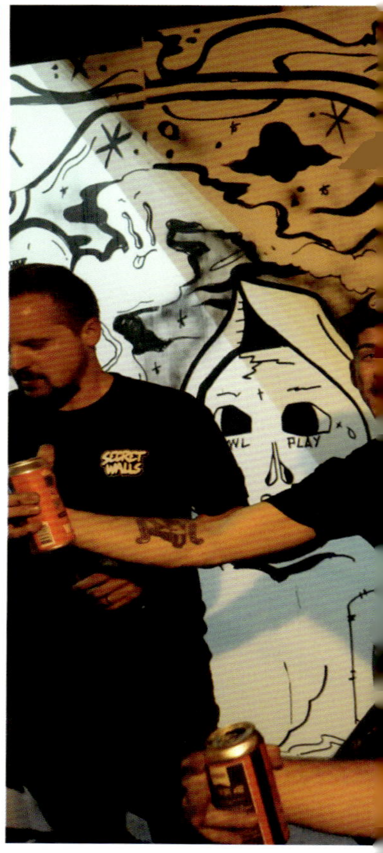
SECRET WALLS
PLAY

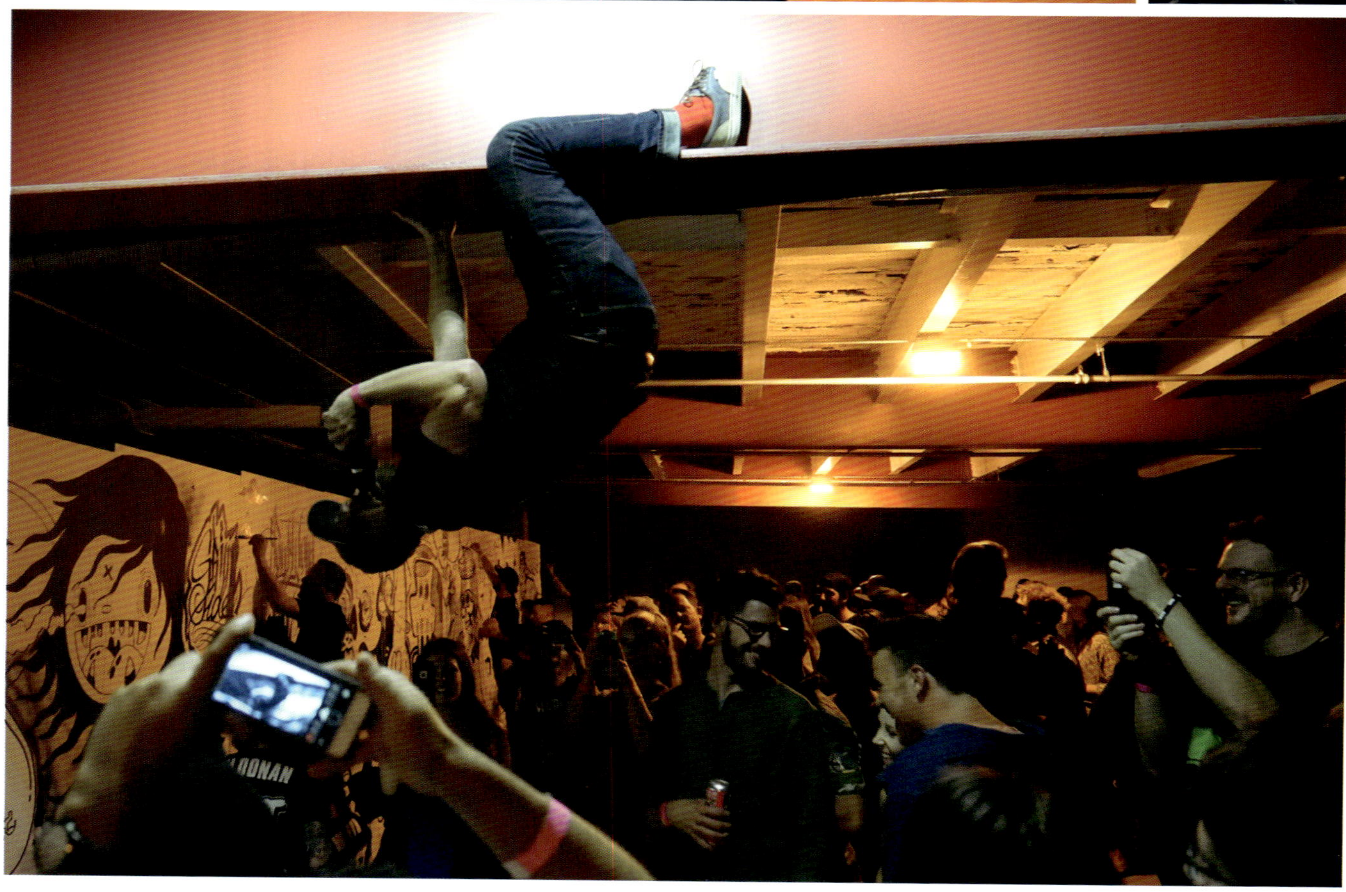

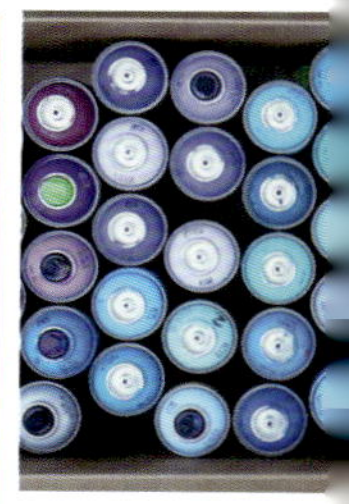

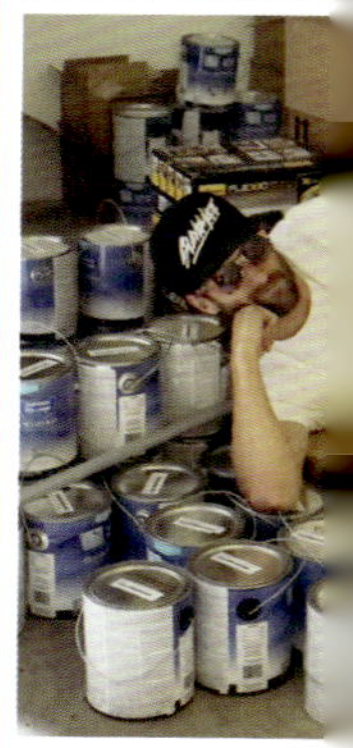

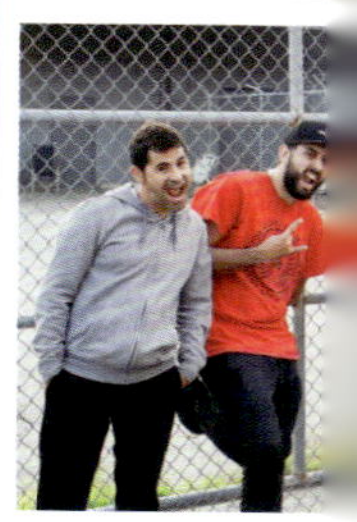

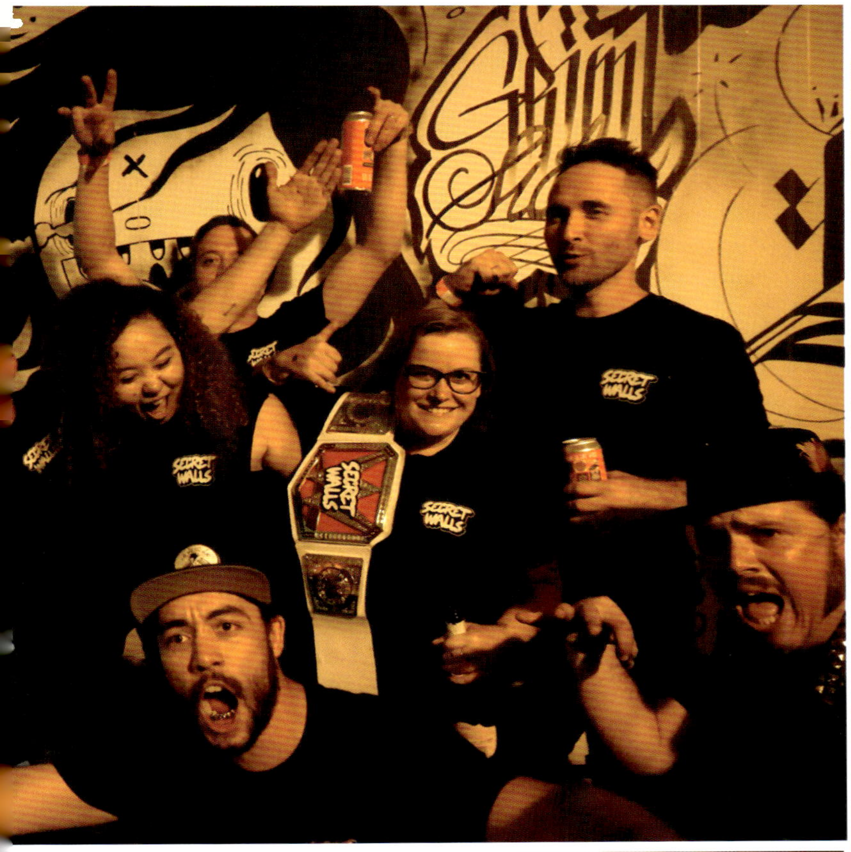
SECRET WALLS

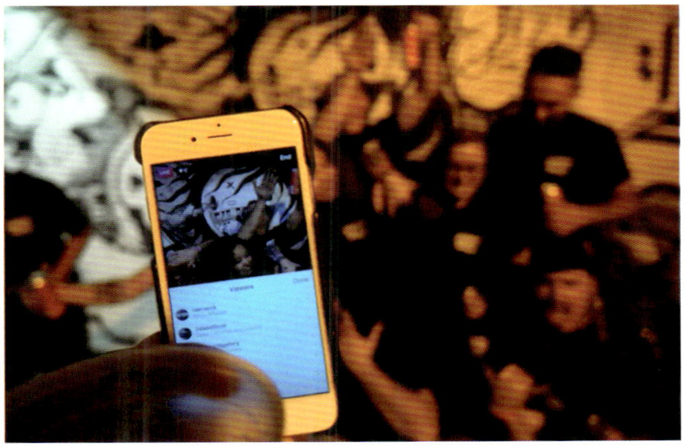

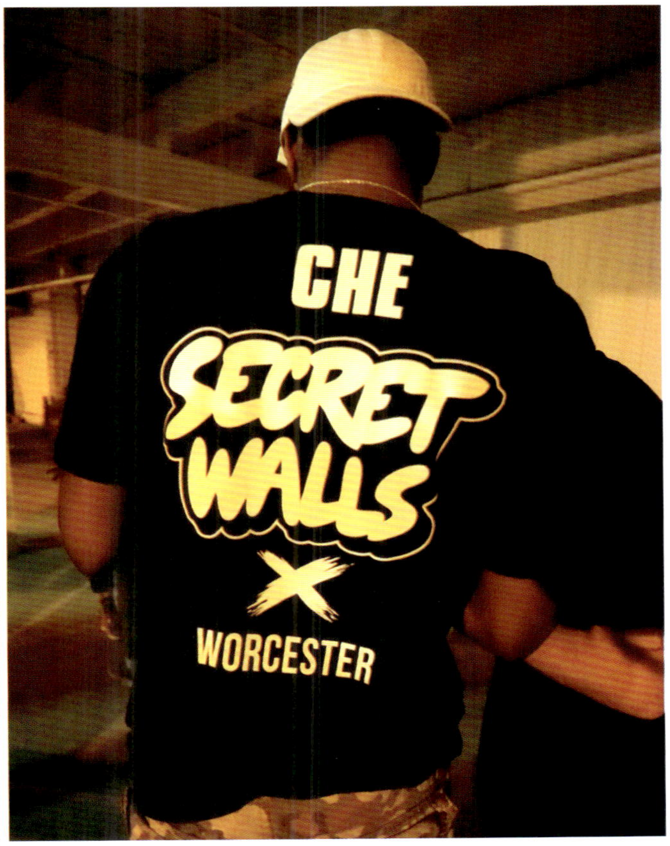
CHE
SECRET WALLS
X
WORCESTER

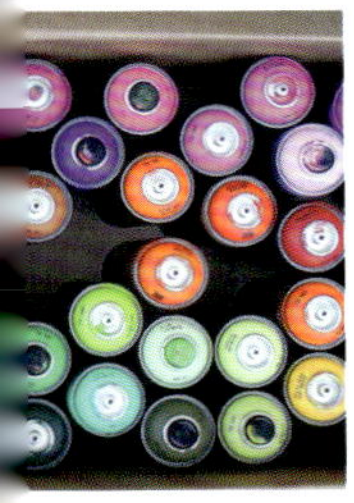

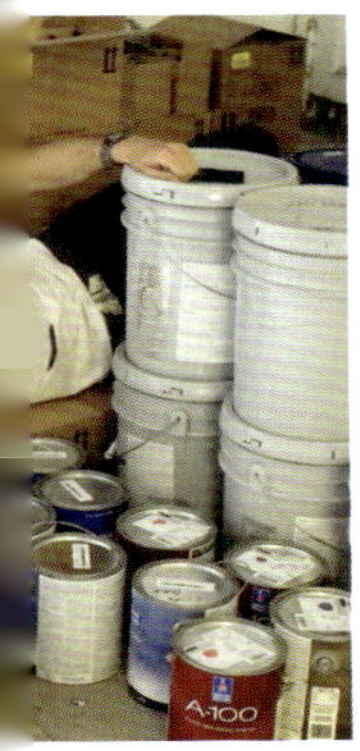

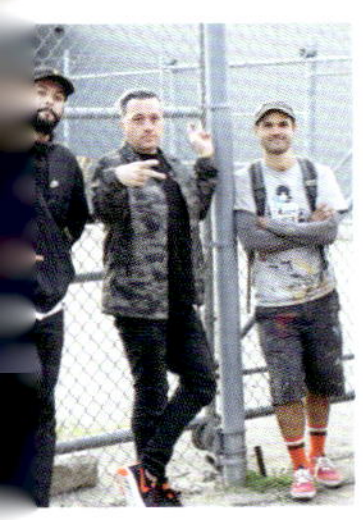

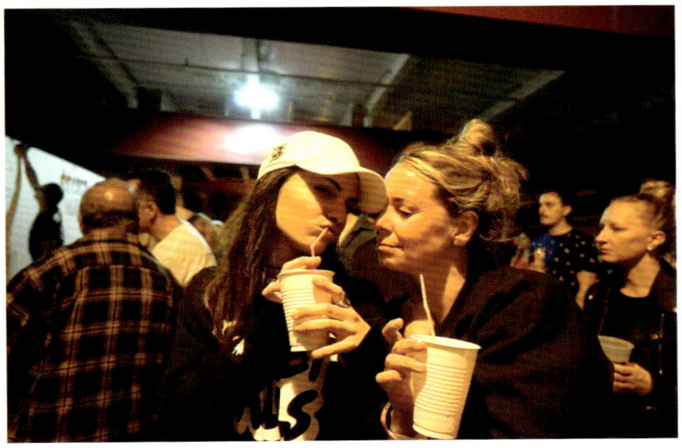

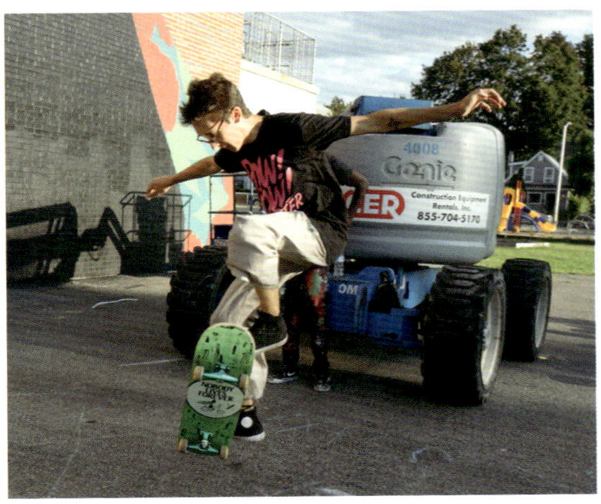
Construction Equipment Rentals, Inc.
855-704-5170

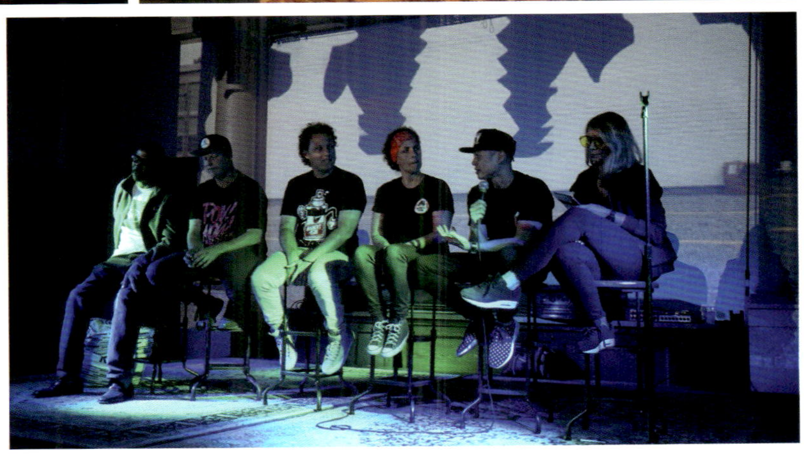

Arlin Graff

@ARLIN_GRAFF

Arlin Graff is Brazilian, based in New York and São Paulo. He is 33 years old and was born in the city of Tatuí, in the countryside of São Paulo. As a child, he loved to play with wood blocks, putting things together and then dismantling them again in a small woodshed where his father passed his time making birdcages and other small objects with wood.

As a teenager, specifically at the end of 1999, Arlin began with graffiti, painting trains in his neighborhood. In 2007, he graduated with a degree in industrial design. A year later, when he moved to São Paulo, he combined this passion for art with design, while he worked as an art director in various advertising agencies.

Quickly, Arlin began to piece together a type of deconstructionism, inspired by his childhood in the little woodshed. He created a very distinct style, giving life to his abstract creations that seem to be emerging from a digital work.

Beyond just painting in the streets, the artist moved toward fine arts and began to study new possibilities. Each time in a more elaborate form, animals are Arlin's principal theme, creating a species of synthetic nature fragmented by the influence of the modern technological world.

Today, in addition to canvasses, his elaborate paintings are executed in large scale around the world, bringing a little more of color to city walls.

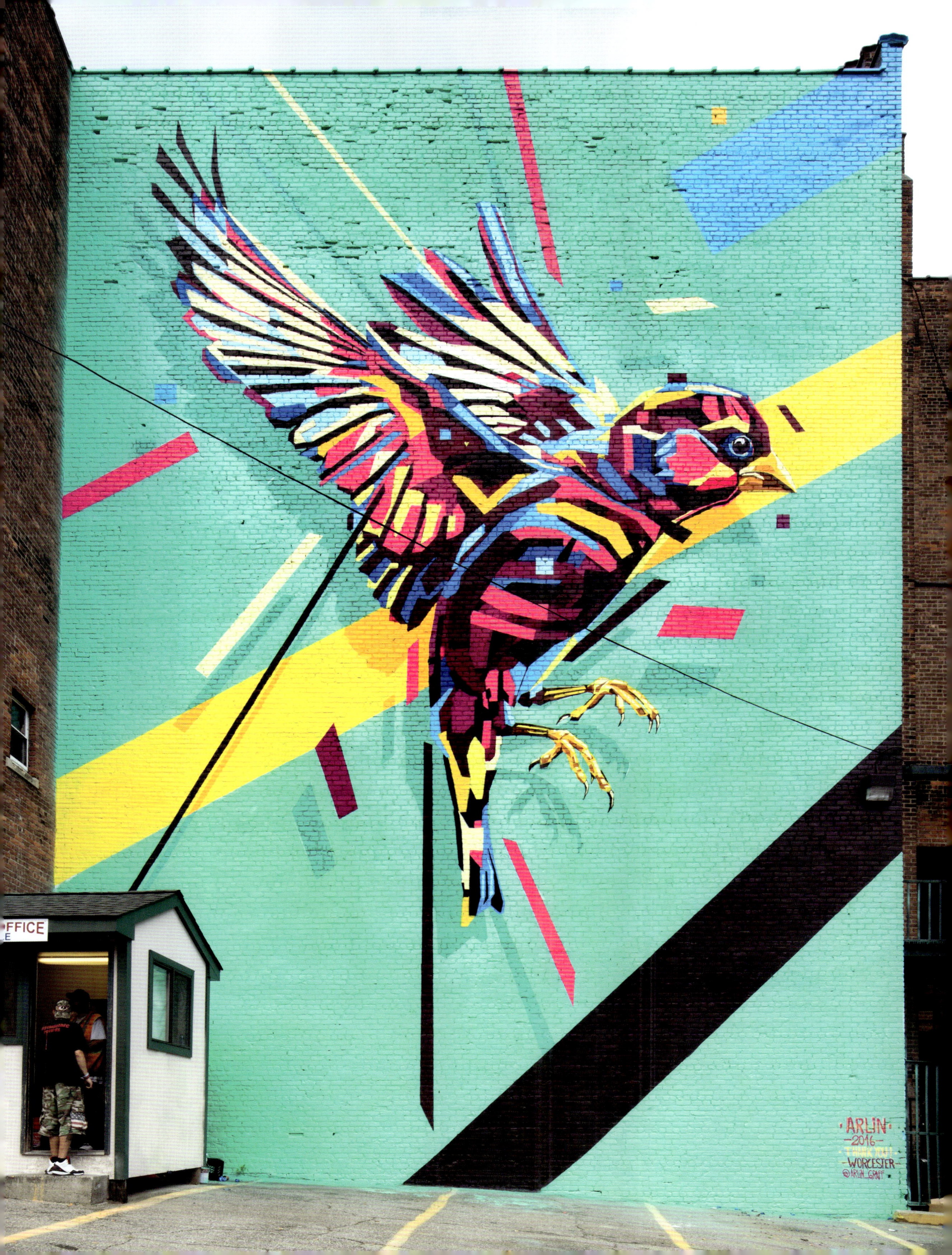
FFICE
ARLIN
2016
THANK YOU!
WORCESTER
@ARLIN_GRAFF

PichiAvo

@PICHIAVO

PichiAvo is Juan Antonio Sánchez Santos (Pichi, b. 1977) and Álvaro Hernández Santaeulalia (Avo, b.1985), a duo of street artists from Valencia (Spain).

Recognised for their skill at creating connections between painting and sculpture in urban settings, they adopt a thoroughly innovative approach in their artistic fusions. A balanced combination of classical art and the most contemporary urban art can be identified in their work. From the outset PichiAvo shunned artistic individuality, joining forces to create an absolutely unique body of work using a conceptually urban idiom, both in the street and in the studio.

They trained in Fine Art and in Design and met on the graffiti art scene in Valencia, forming the PichiAvo duo in 2007. From that moment they worked on developing joint projects, pursuing an unremitting search for a style of their own.

In 2019 they created a monumental 26-metre-high sculpture for the Fallas festival in Valencia and held their first major exhibition in a public art centre. In April 2019 they executed the second largest mural in the world in the city of Porto, in collaboration with the celebrated Portuguese artist Vhils.

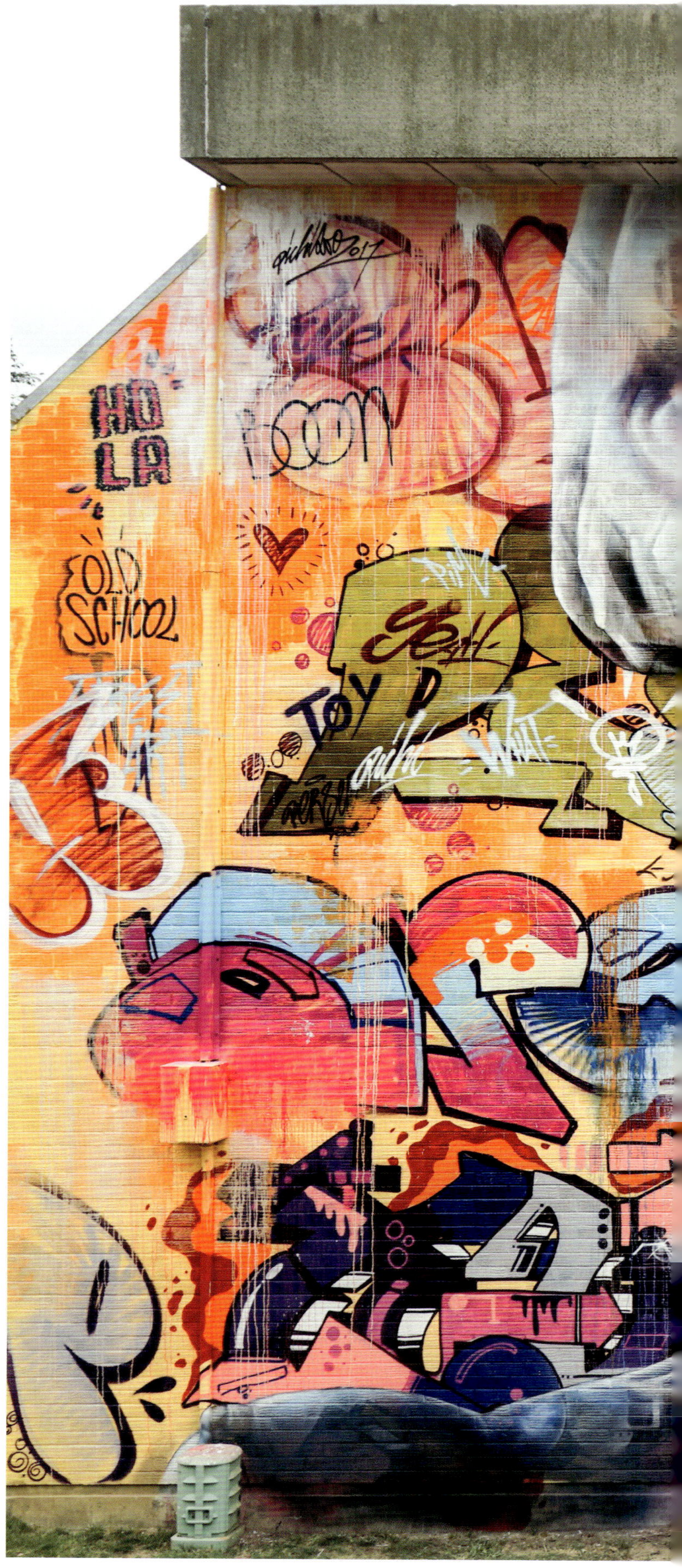

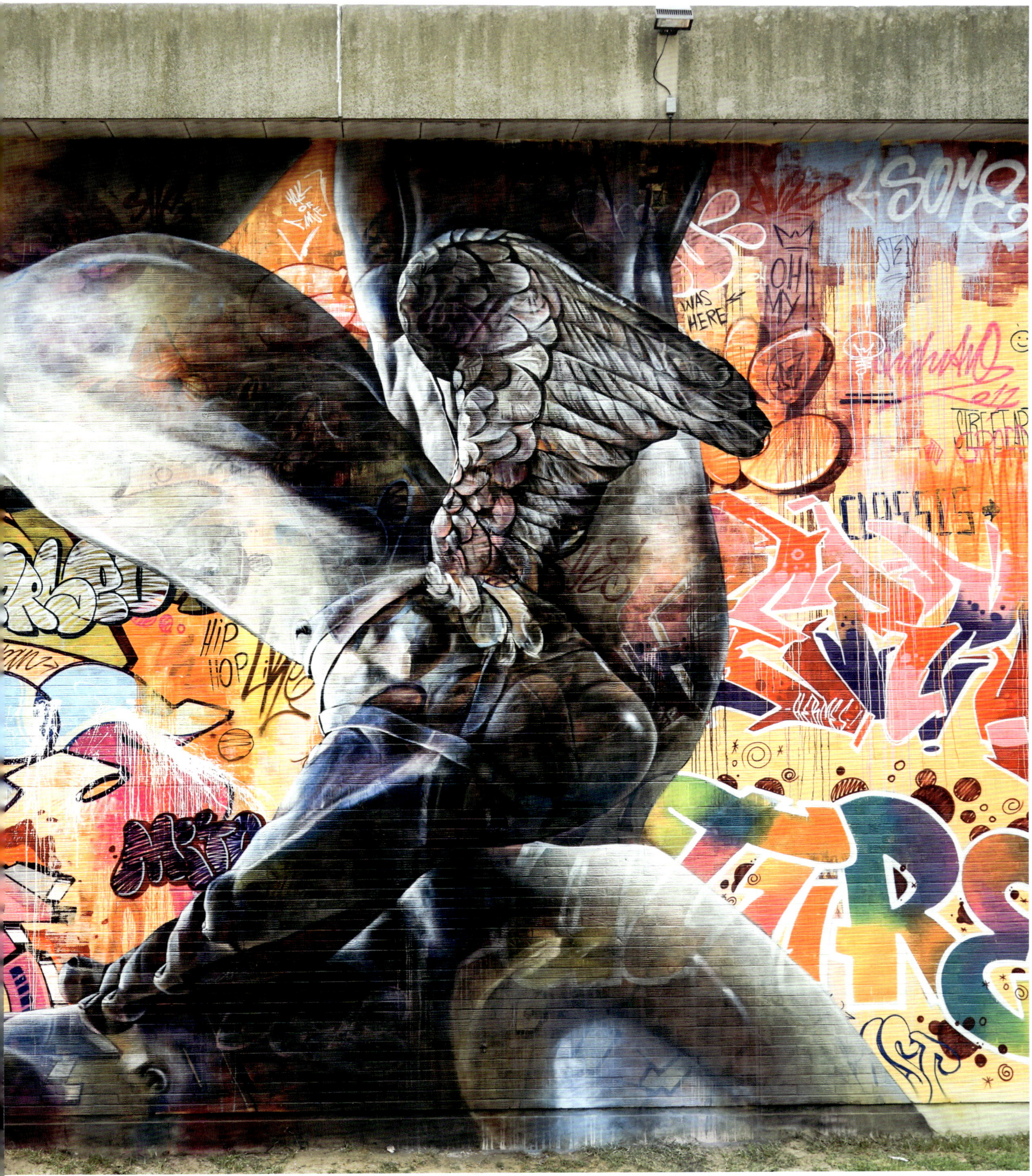
WAS HERE
OH MY
HIP HOP

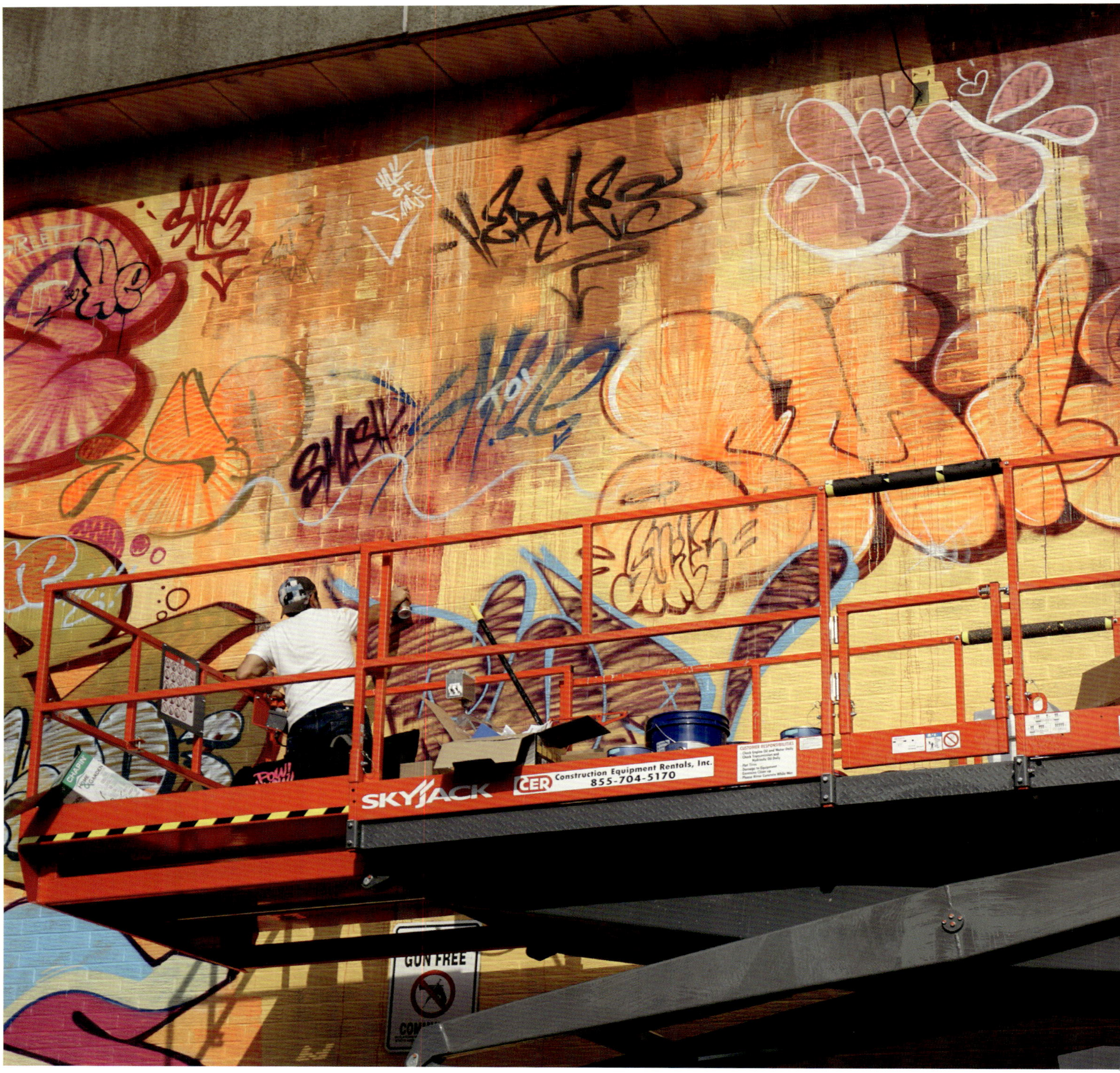
SKYJACK
CER Construction Equipment Rentals, Inc.
855-704-5170
GUN FREE

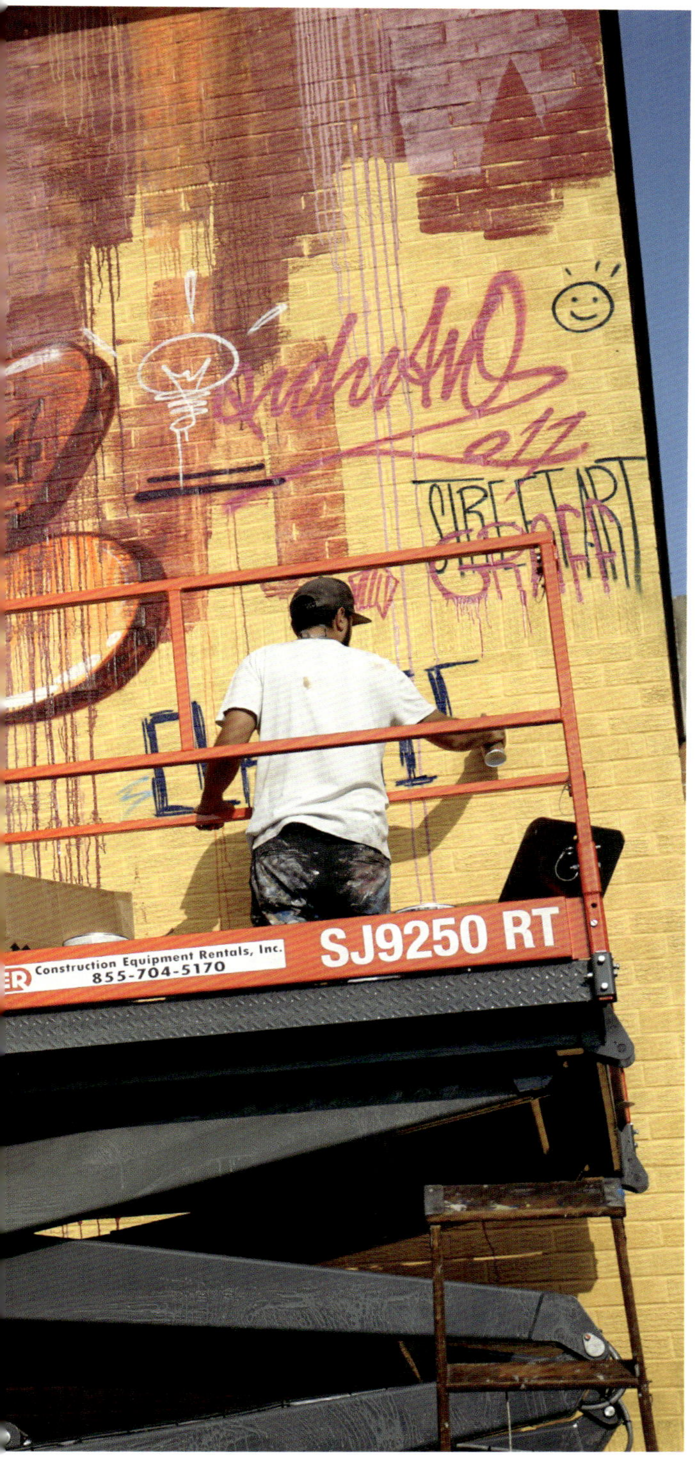
SJ9250 RT
Construction Equipment Rentals, Inc.
855-704-5170

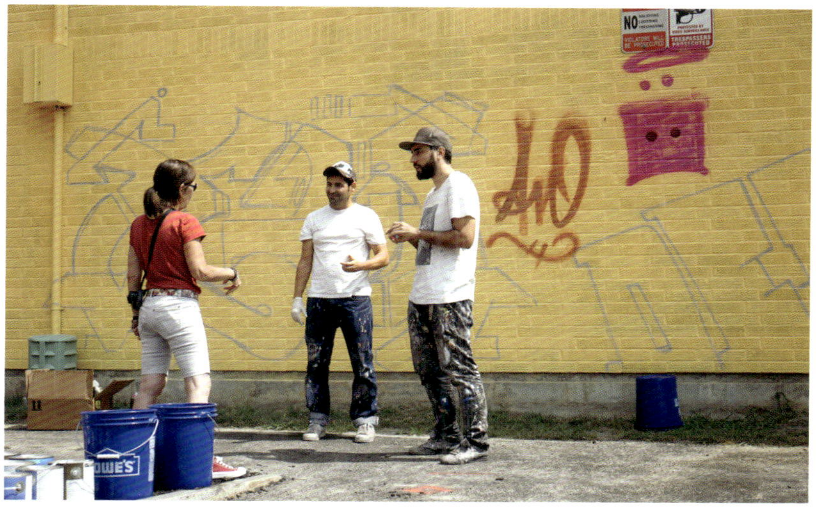

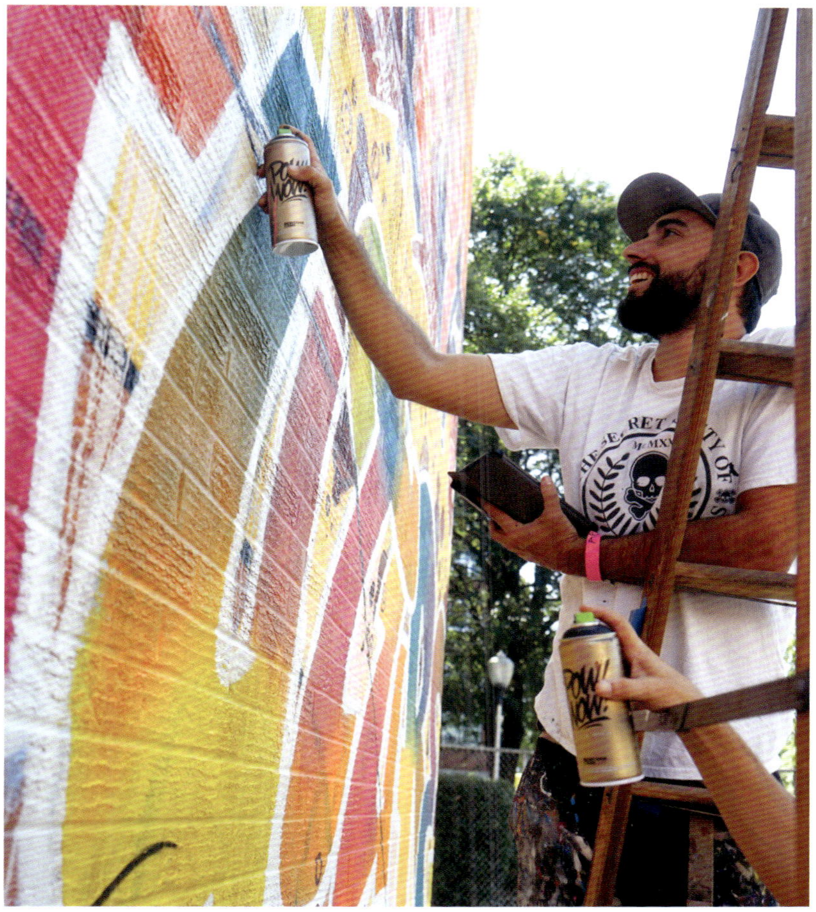

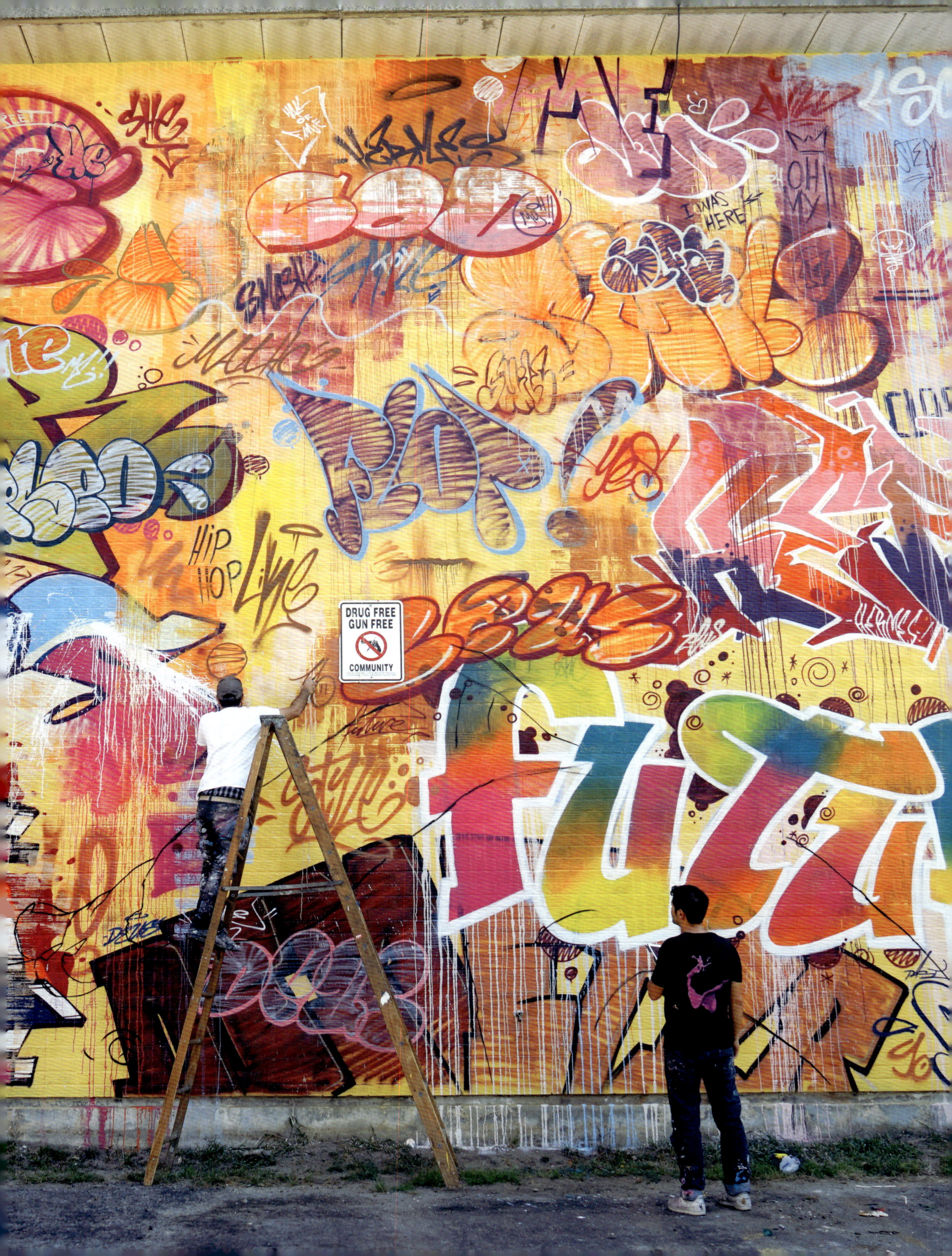
DRUG FREE
GUN FREE
COMMUNITY
HIP HOP
I WAS HERE
OH MY

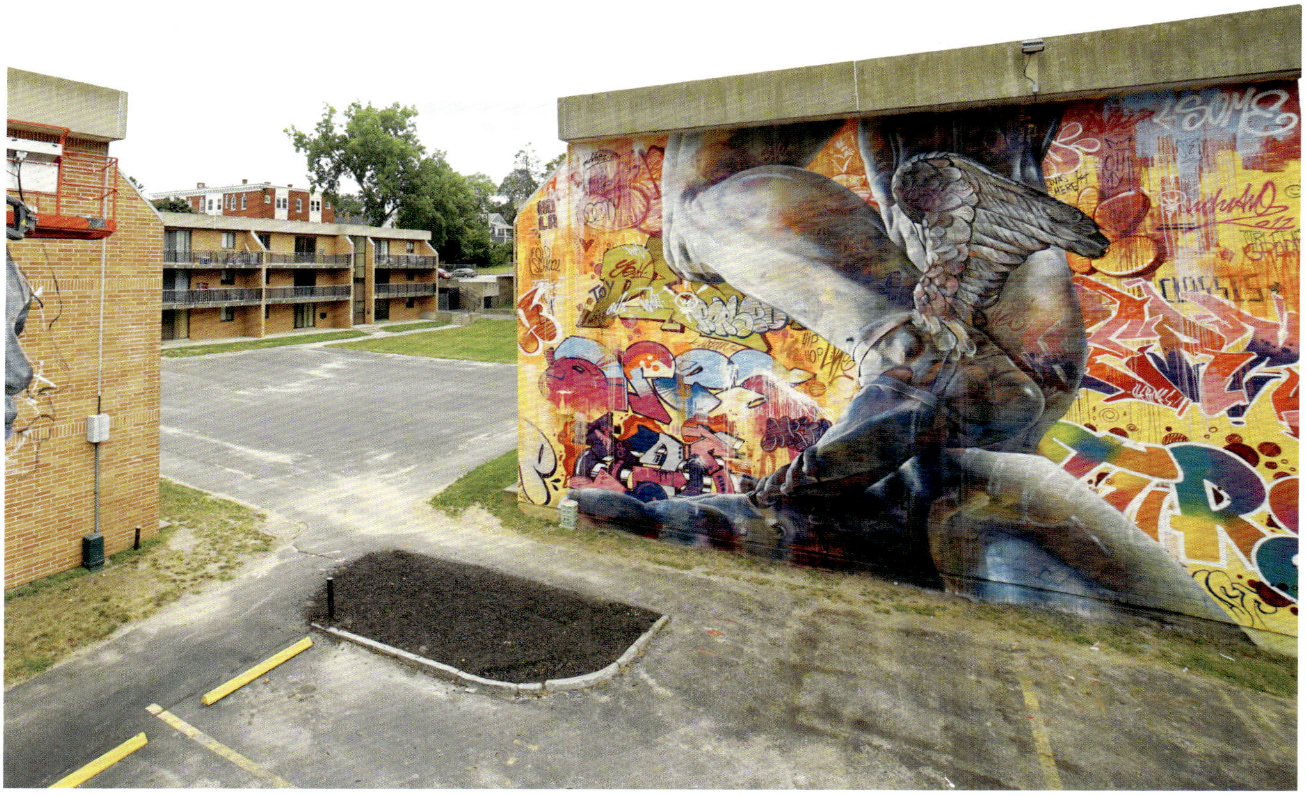

The London Police

@THELONDONPOLICE

The London Police started in 1998 when big english geezers headed to Amsterdam to help rejuvenate the visually disappointing streets of Hollands capital.

They were part of a small group of artists at the end of the last century that helped pioneer a new street art movement.

After a few years of mixing traveling and making art in the street TLP began to receive Worldwide recognition for their contribution to the graffiti/street art movement.

They were included in many of the books documenting the scene and invited for shows and live drawing performances all over the globe.

19 years on TLP have amassed more than 100 shows and events in over 35 countries and their street work continues to pop up everywhere they go.

Since 2009 TLP has concentrated on more intense canvas work, on bigger solo shows and largescale mural projects.

TLP are Chaz Barrisson who draws the iconic 'LADS' characters and Bob Gibson whose tight portrait and architectural illustrations help marry the two styles to create an endearing, exciting fantasy world.

The current duo have managed to form a partnership more cohesive than Han Solo & Chewbacca in Star Wars and are continuing to produce slick artwork that is tighter than a butlers cuff.

Never be scared, don't be a hero and let the good times roll!

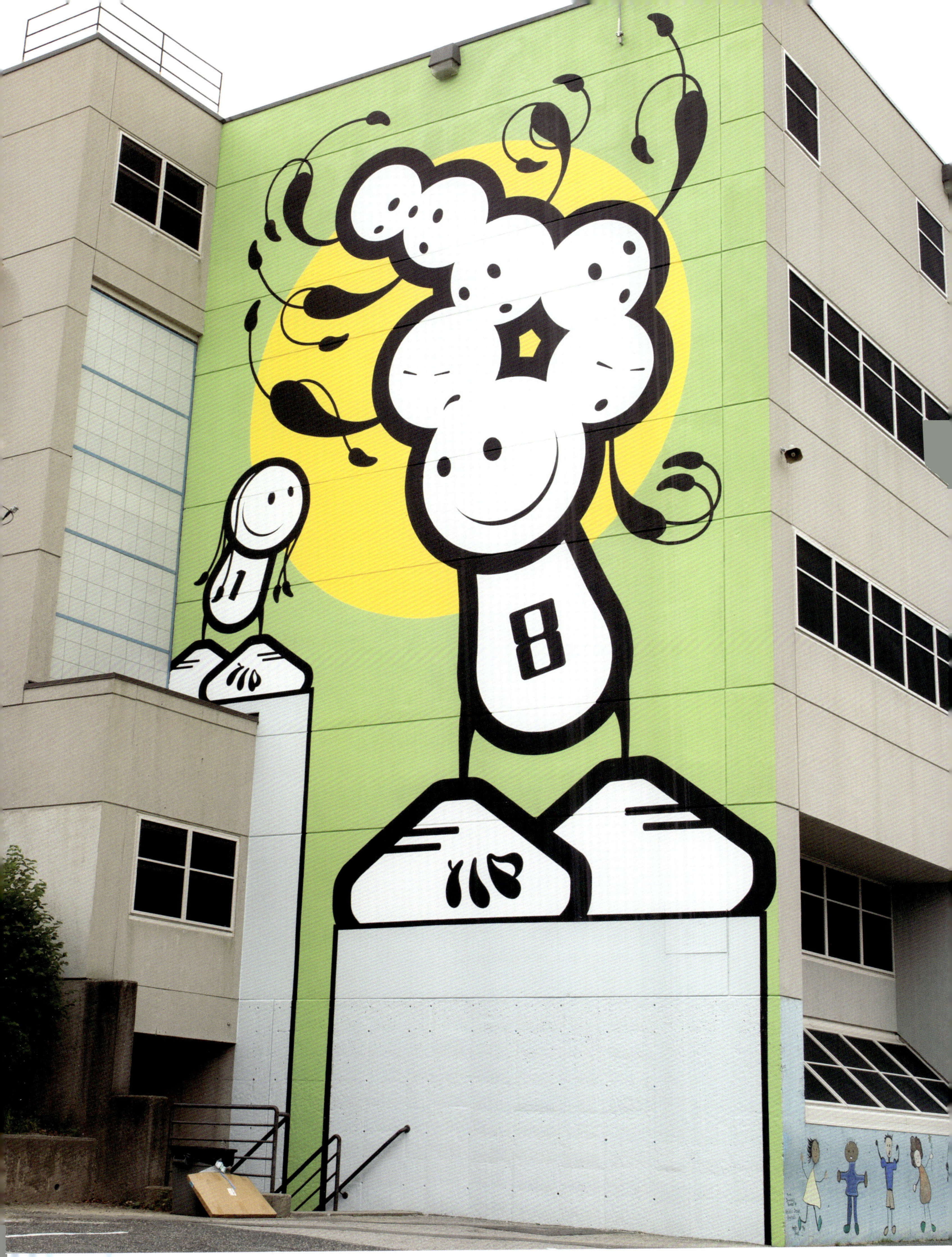

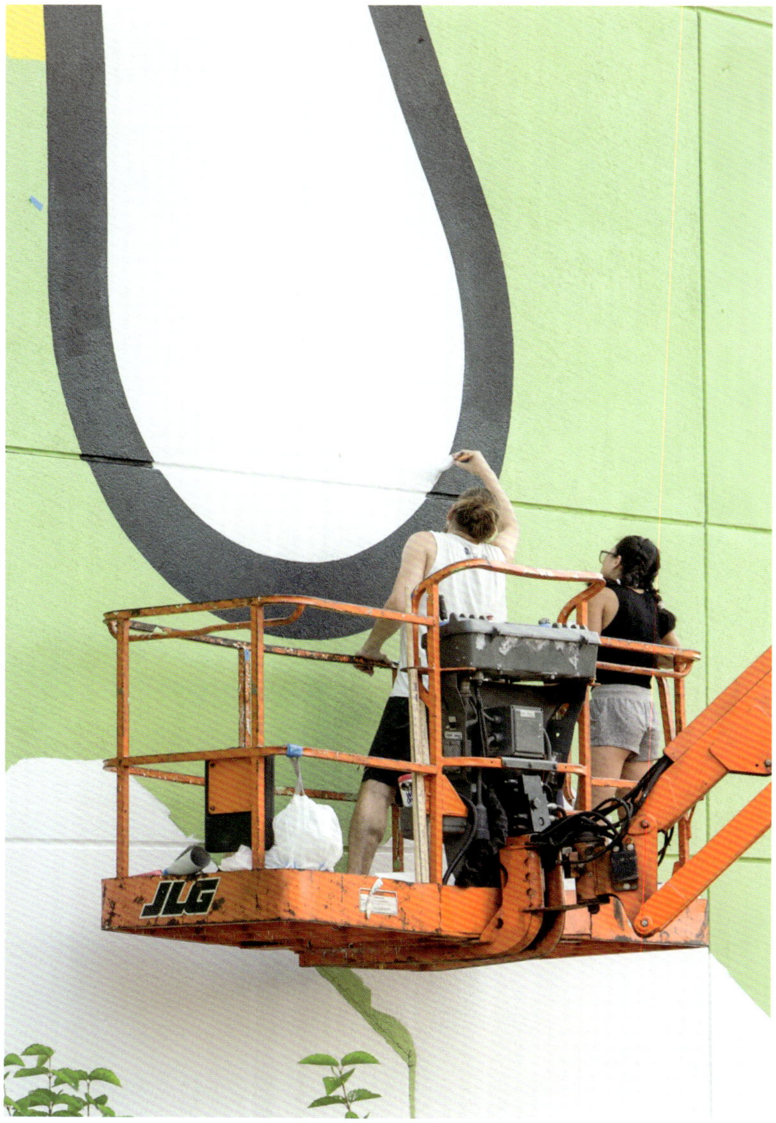

JLG

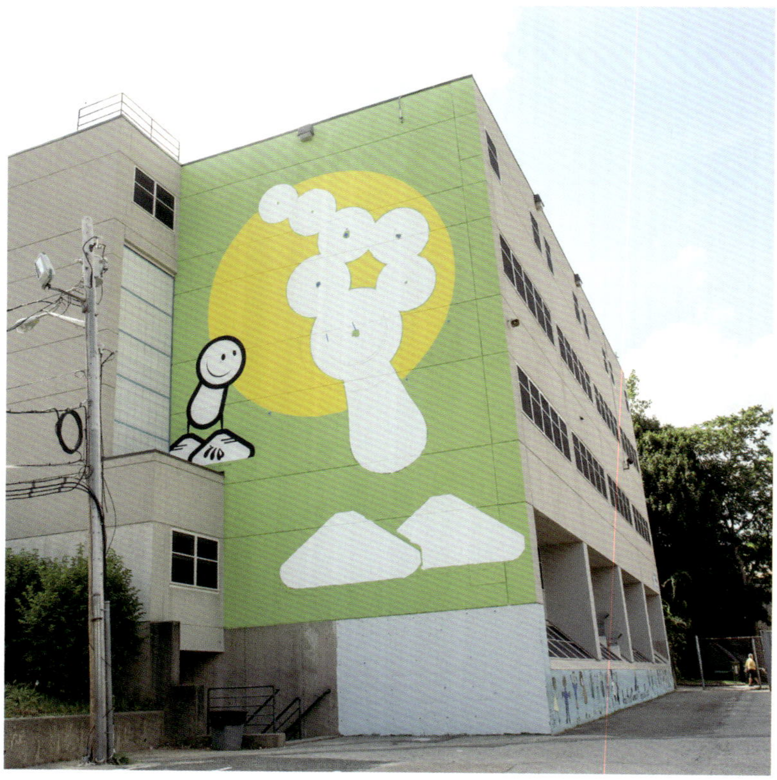

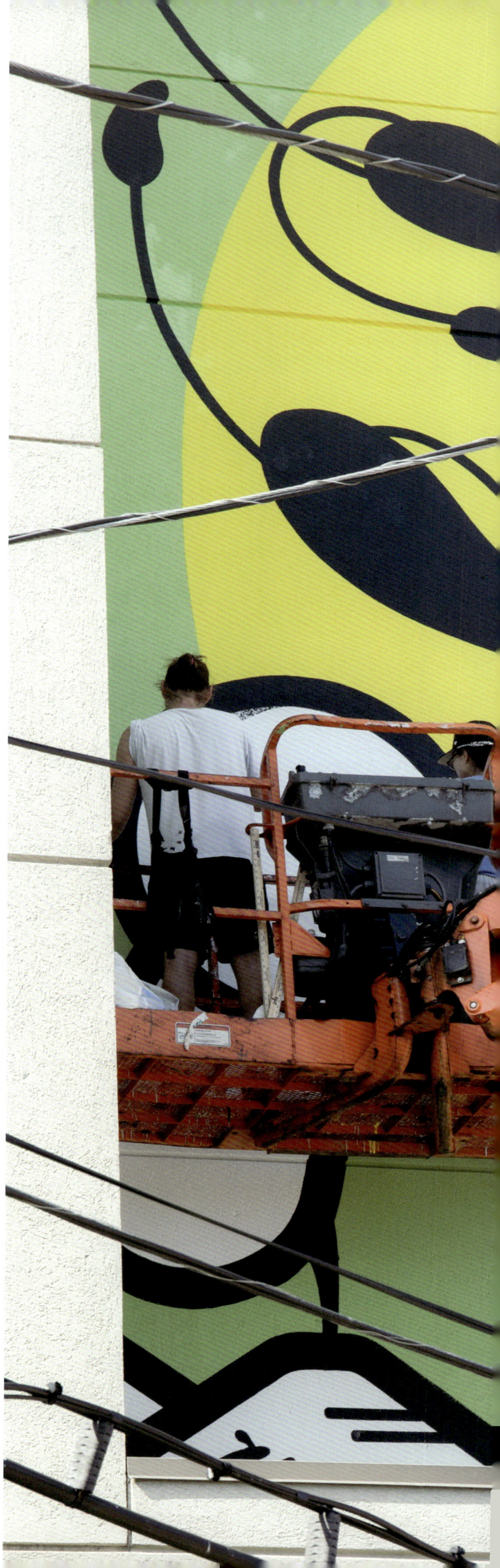

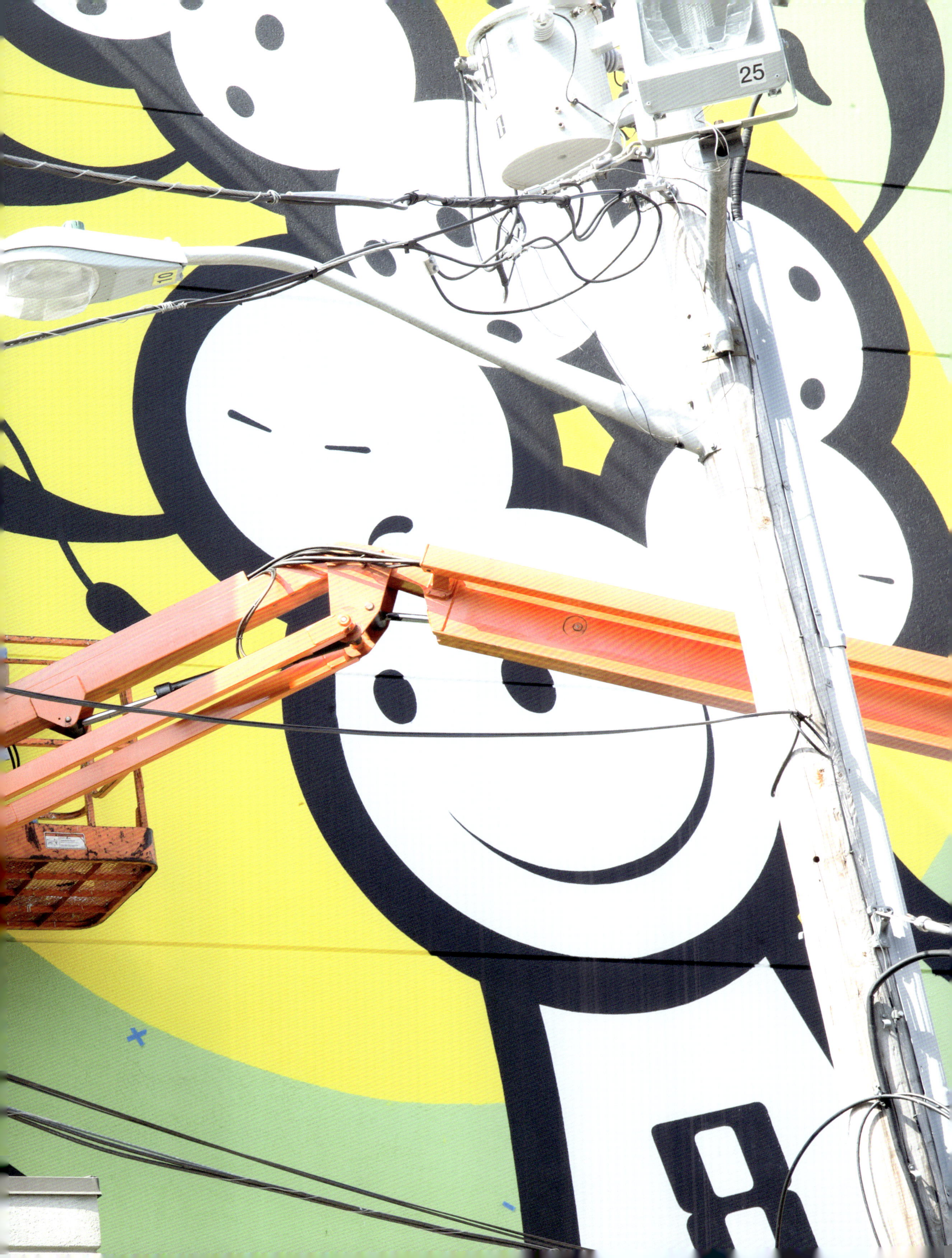
25
10

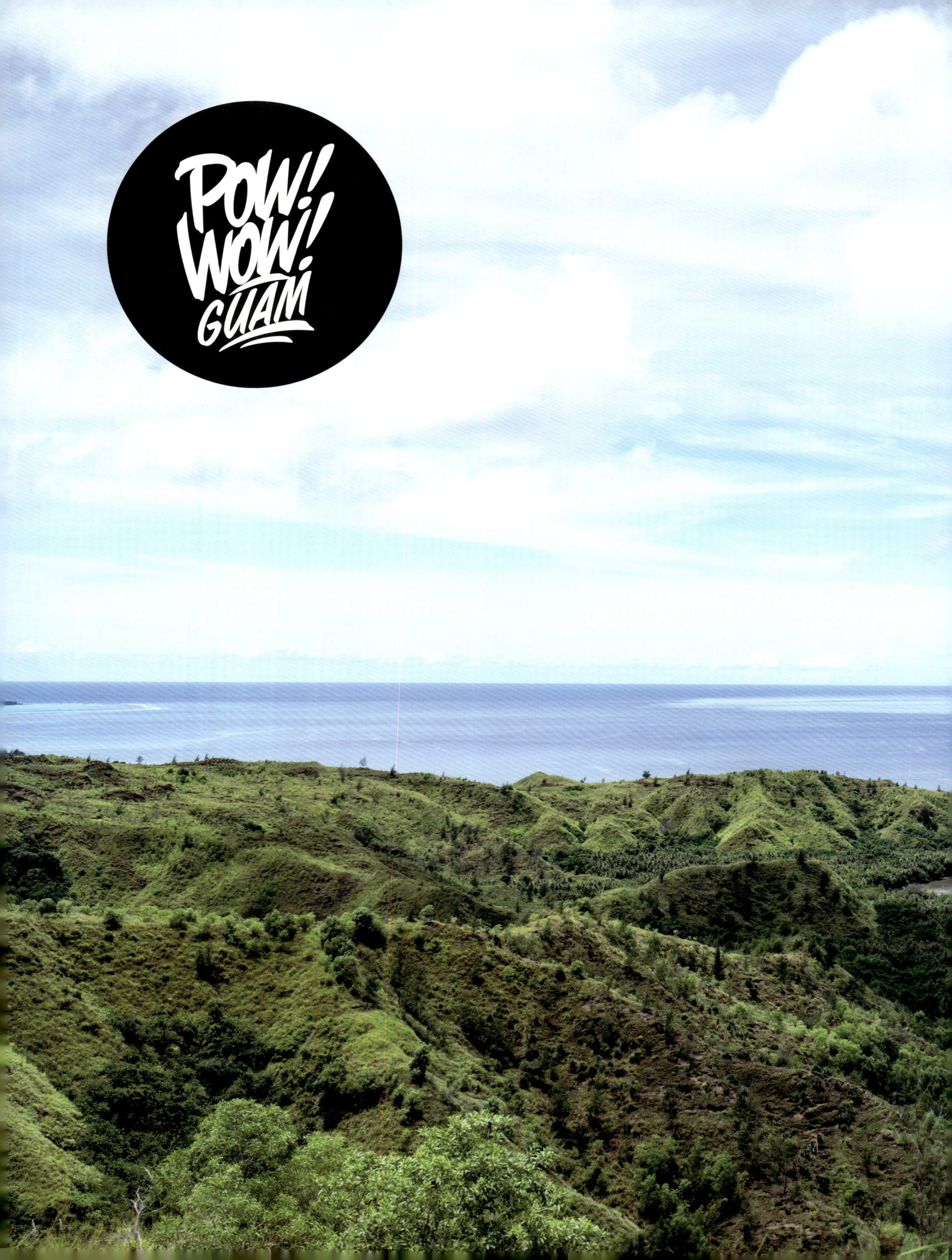
POW!
WOW!
GUAM

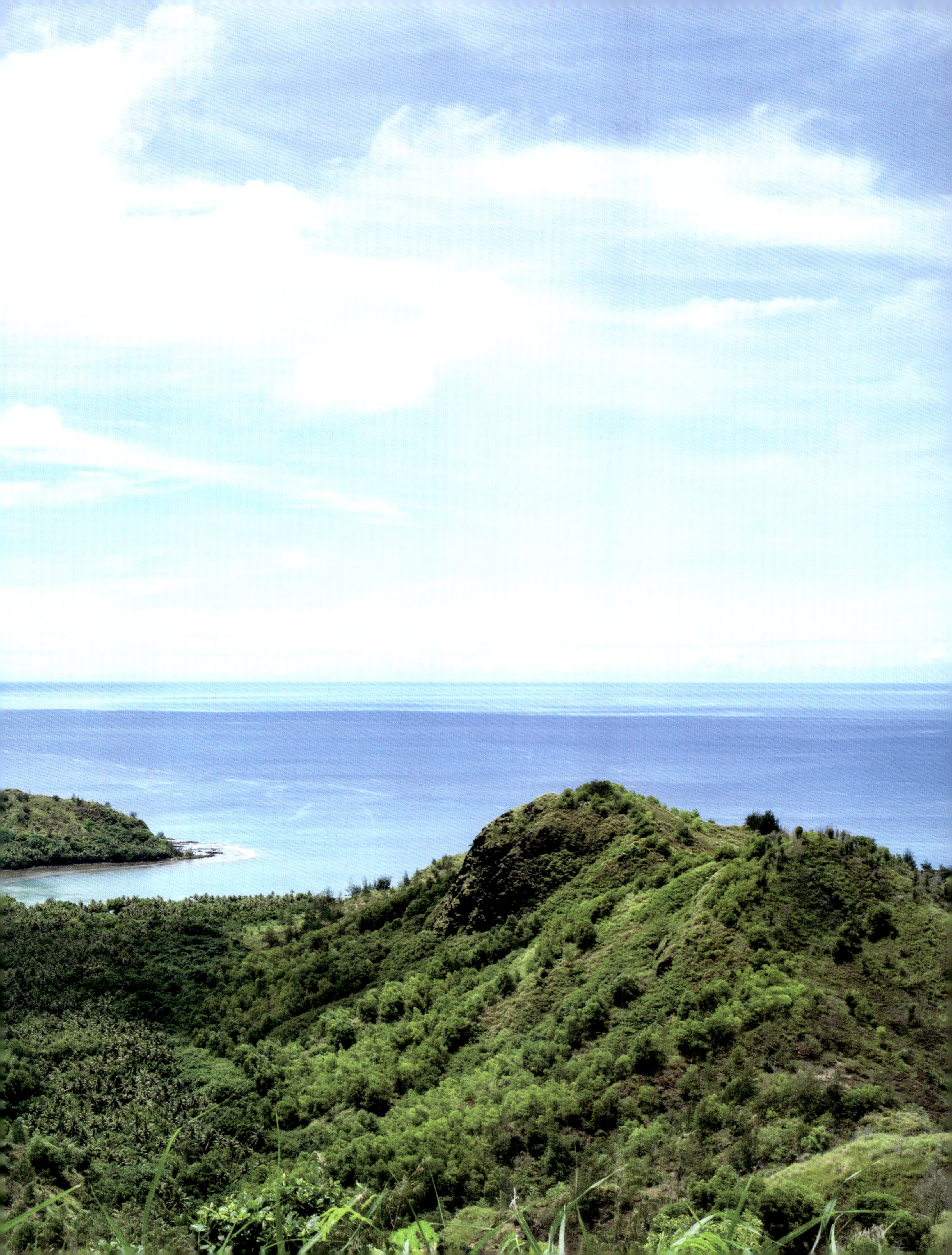

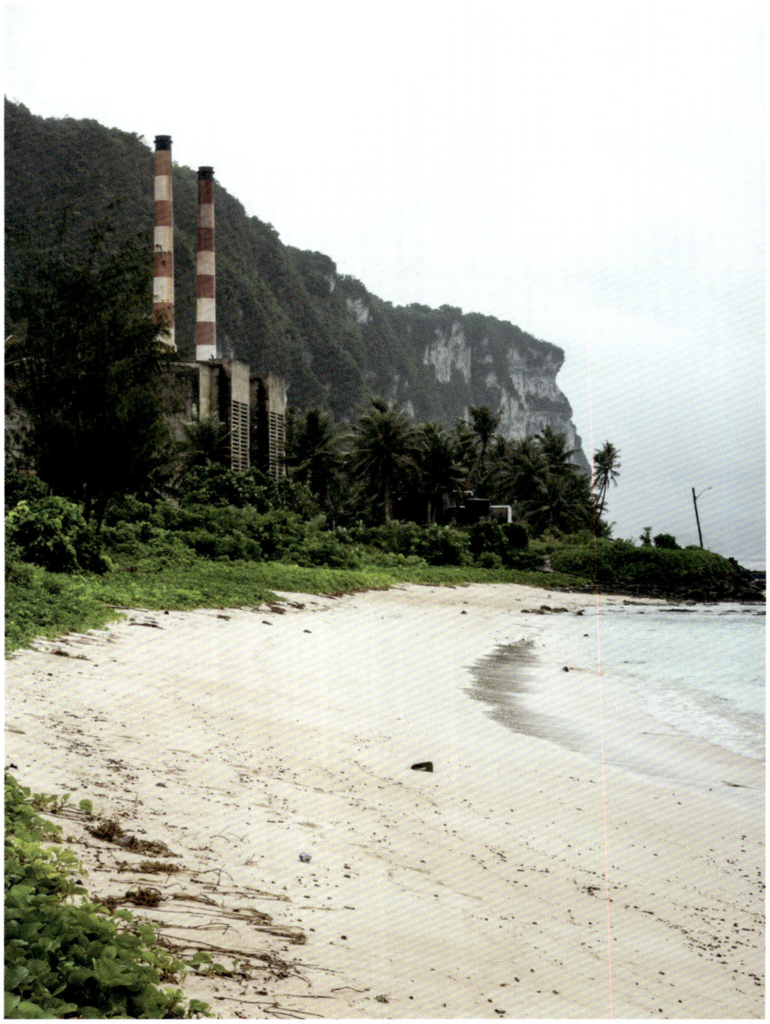

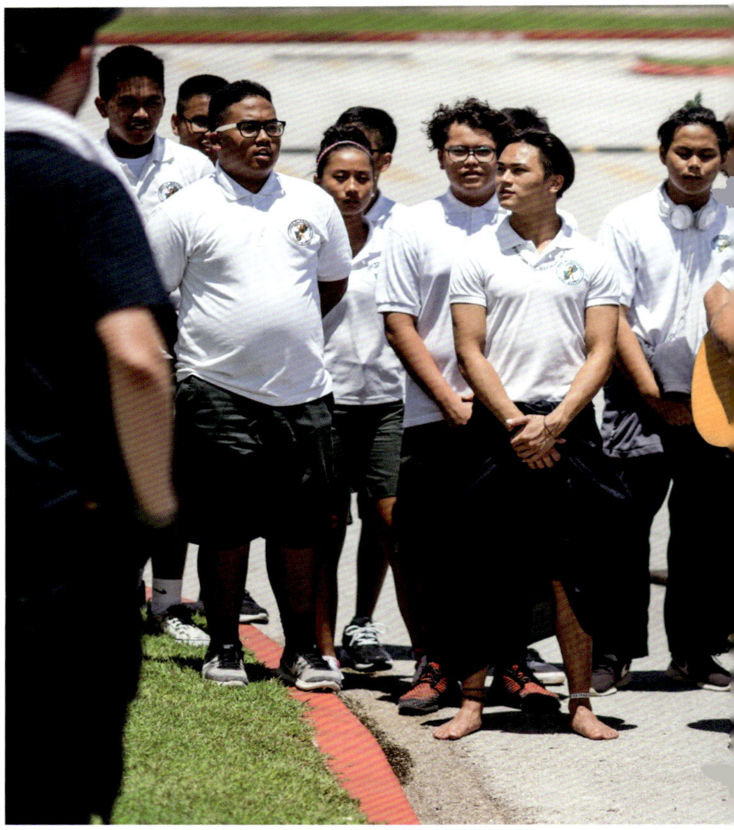

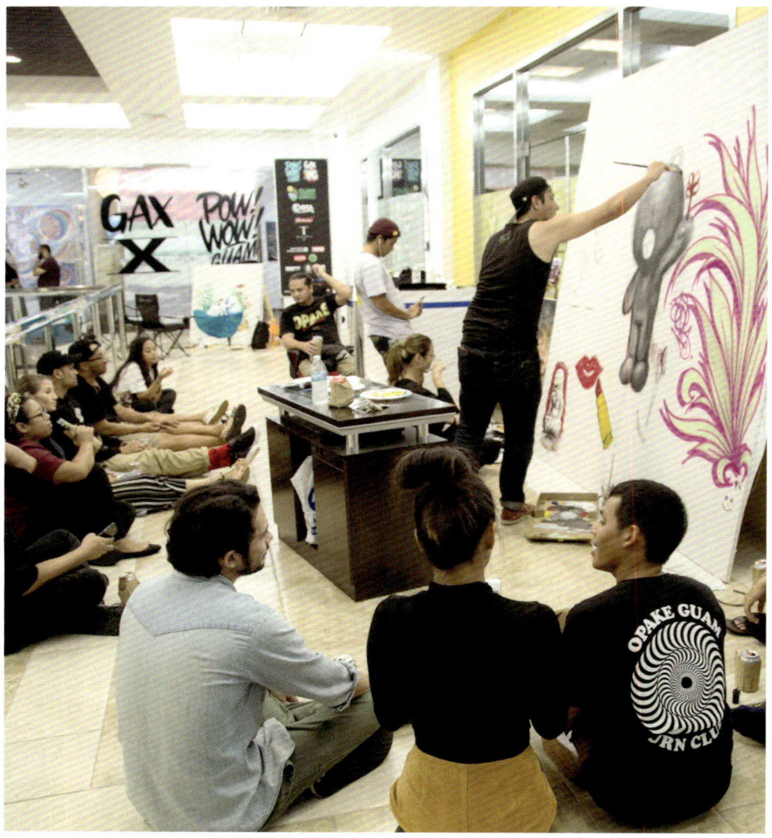
GAX
X
POW! WOW!
OPAKE GUAM

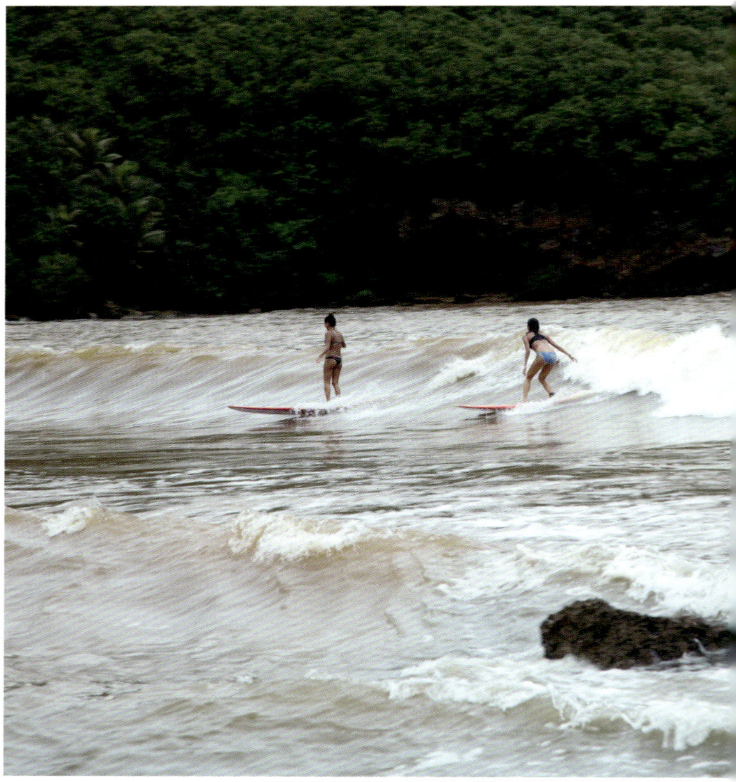

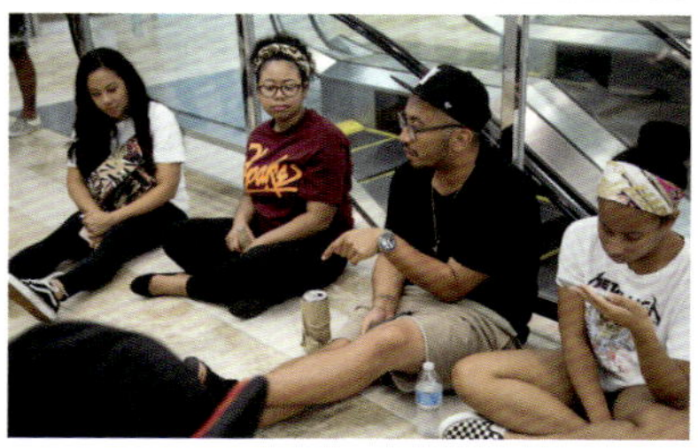

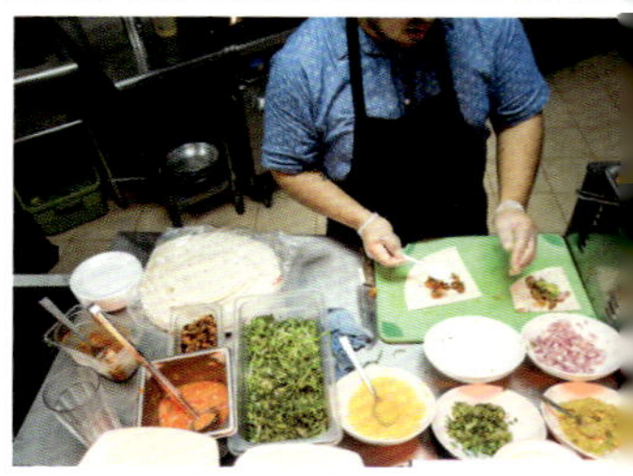

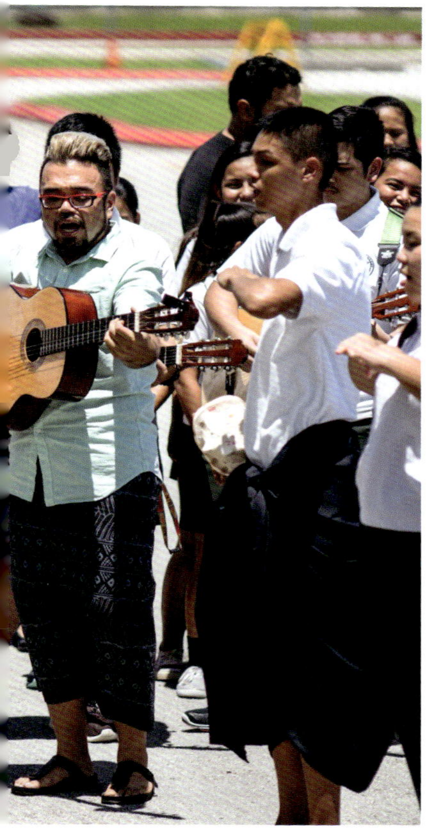

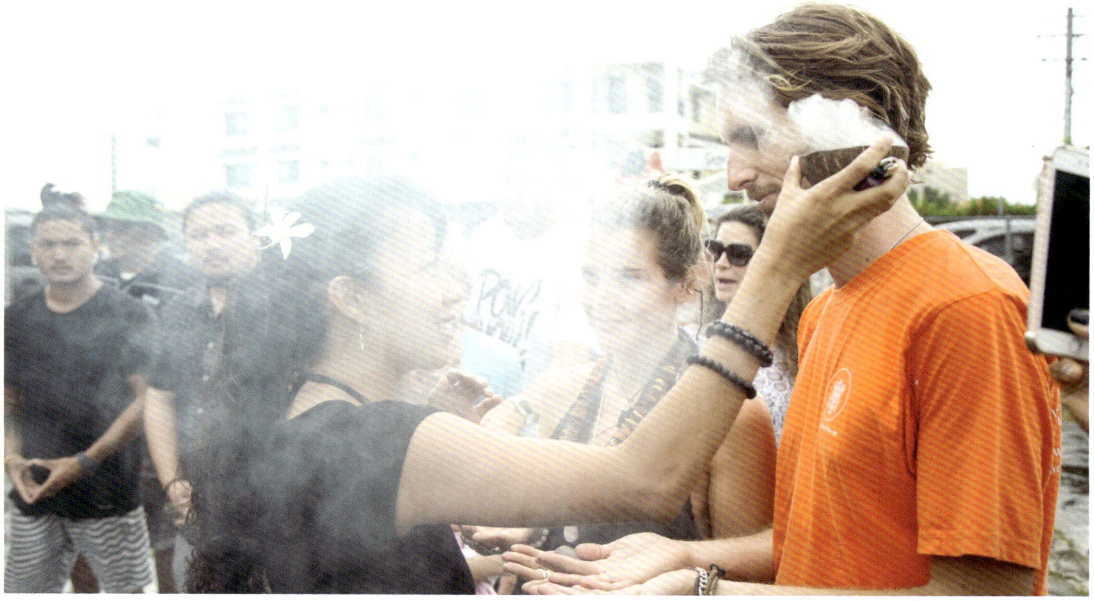

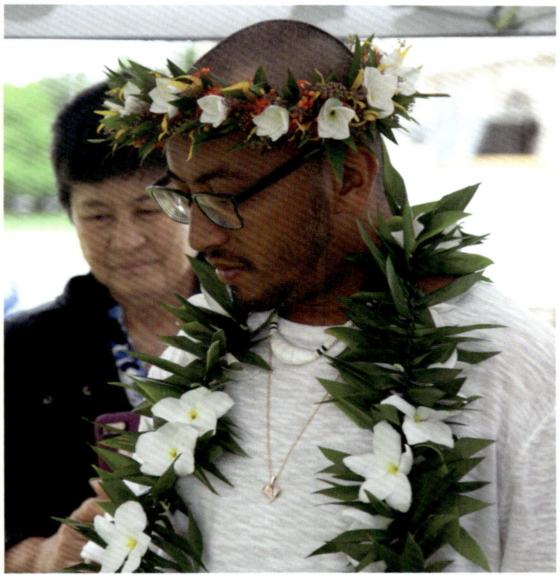

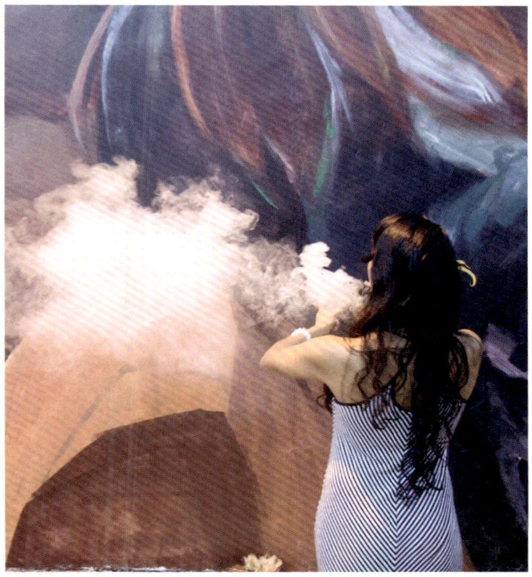

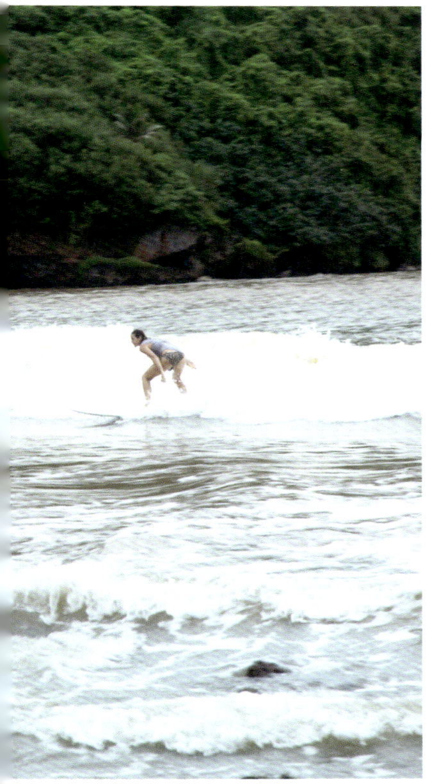

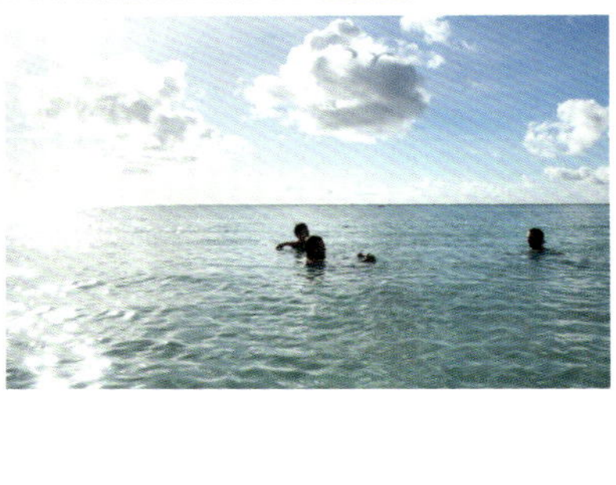

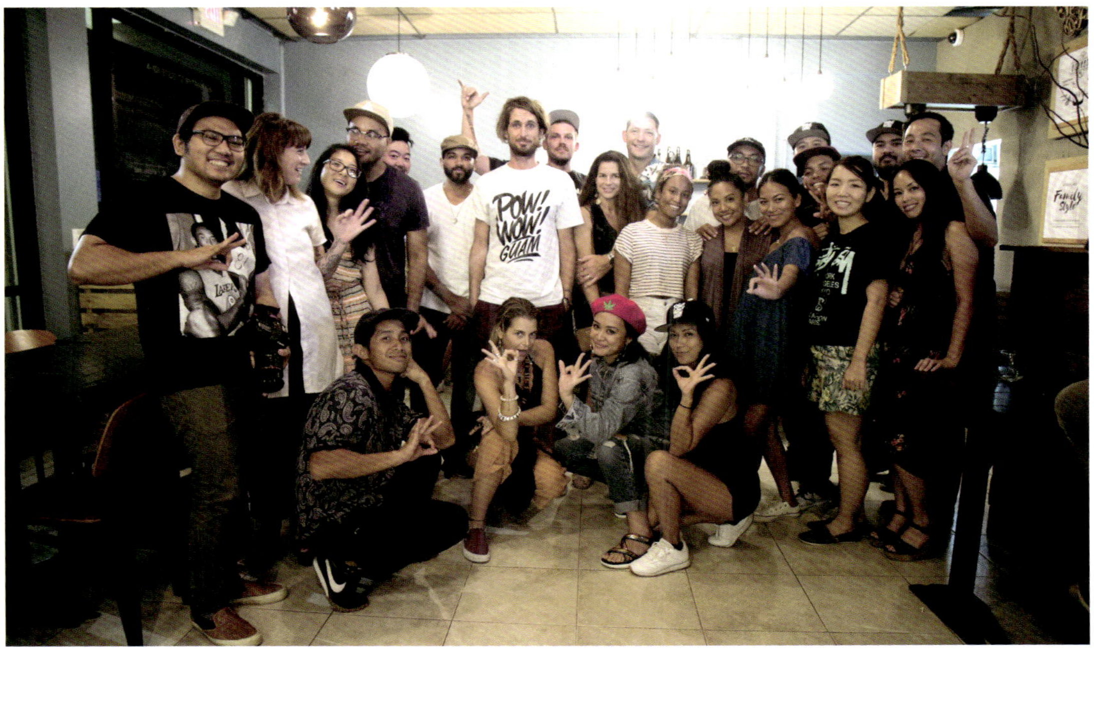
POW! WOW! GUAM

Naturel

@NATUREL

Lawrence "**Naturel**" Atoigue was born in 1983 in Landover, Maryland. Professionally known as Naturel, Atoigue has quickly emerged in today's postmodern scene. His sharp, triangular illustrations are a futuristic blend of pop and cubism, with a surrealist twist. Considered an influencer himself with a massive social media following, his talents have also attracted the eyes and ears of celebrity clients such as Swizz Beatz, Rihanna, Spike Lee, Paul Rosenberg and LeBron James, among many others. Working directly with Jay-Z on iconic apparel designs, he has also served as Creative Director for global campaigns ranging from brands like Crooks & Castles to Levi's, as well as working with multi-national brands like Courvoisier and the NFL.

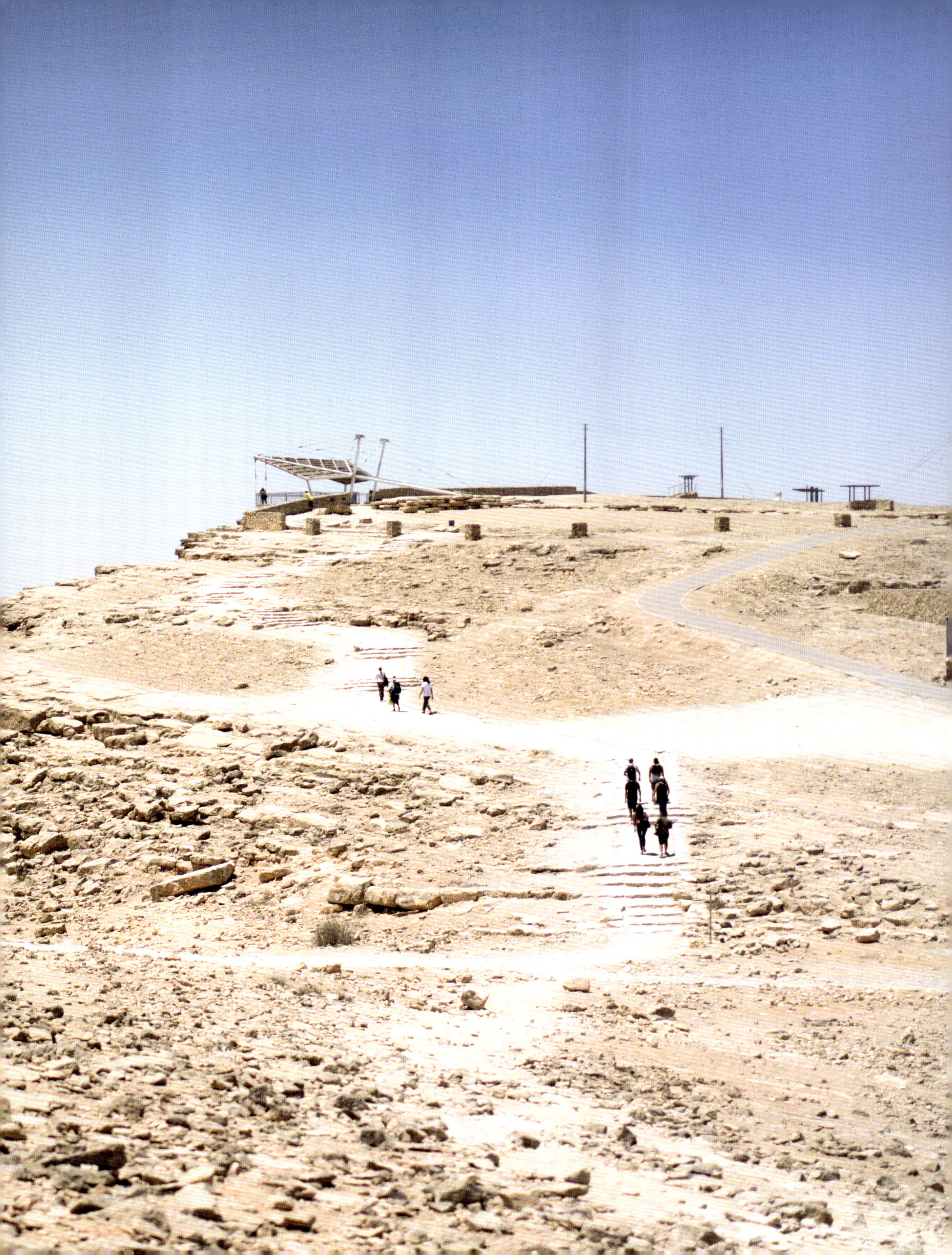

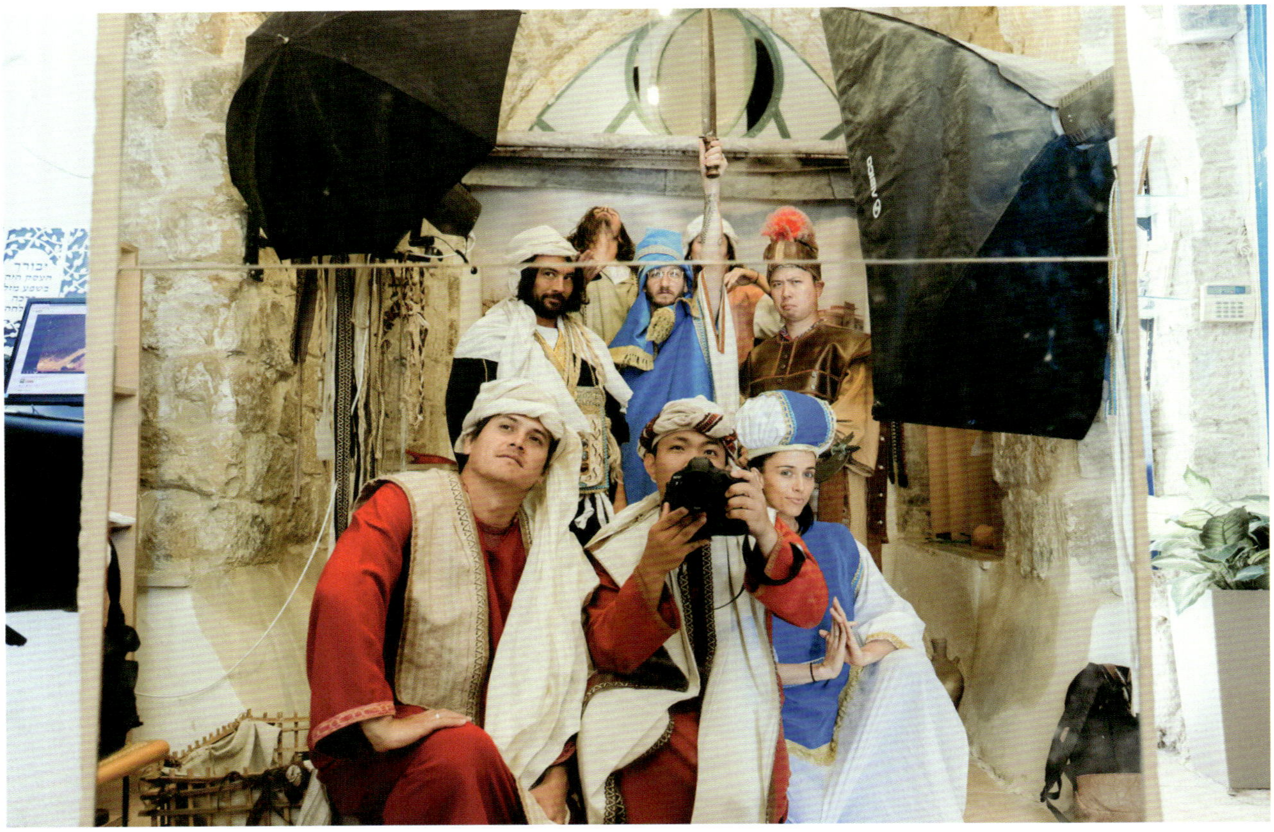

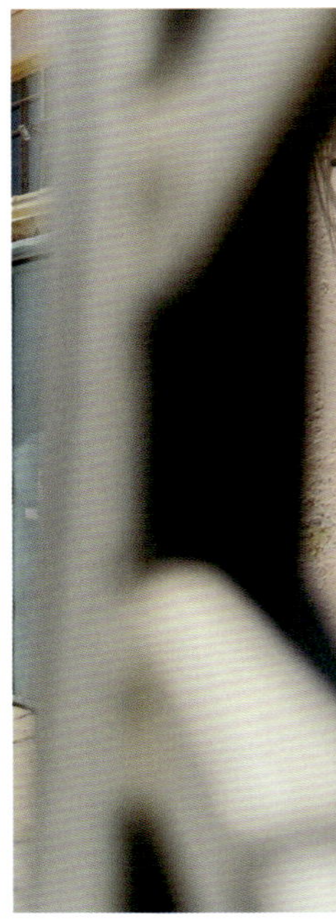
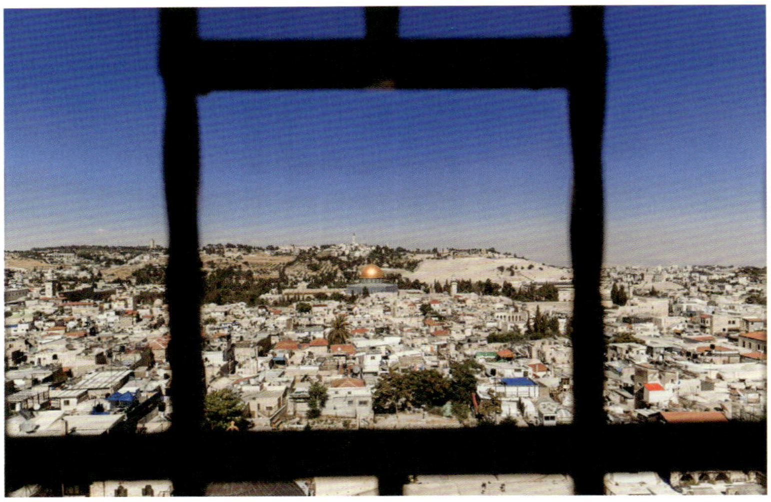
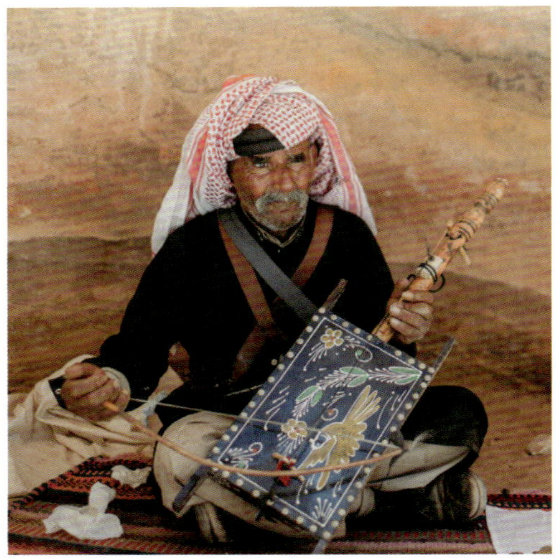
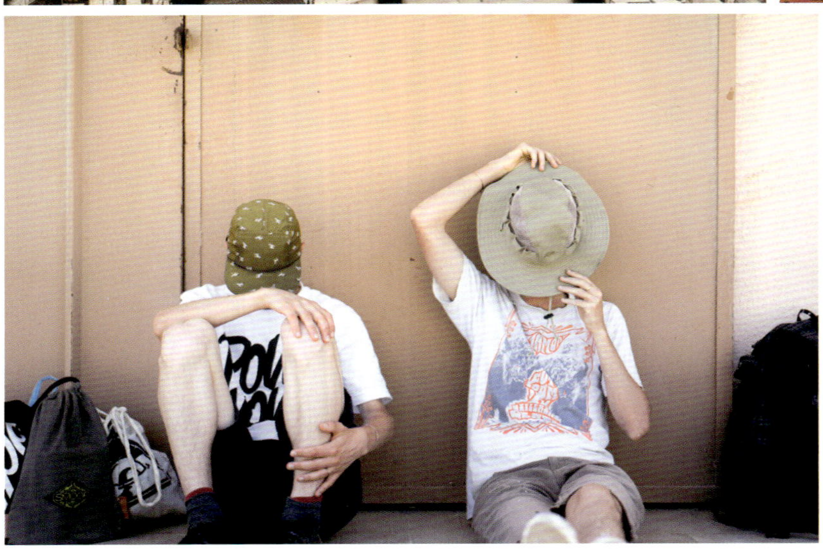
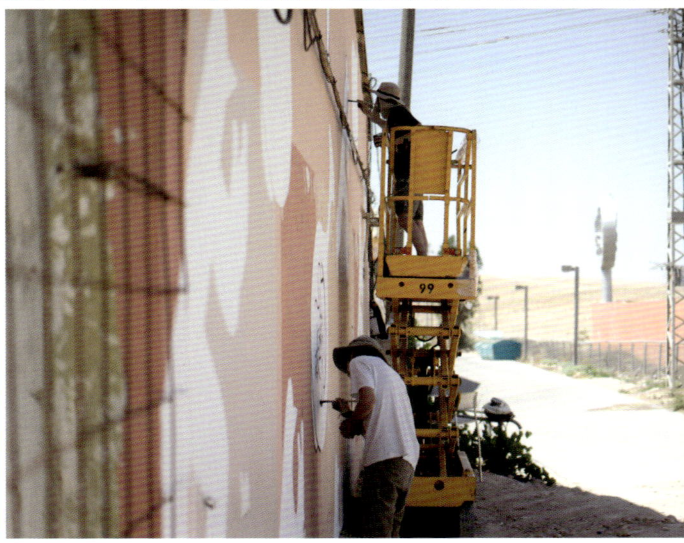

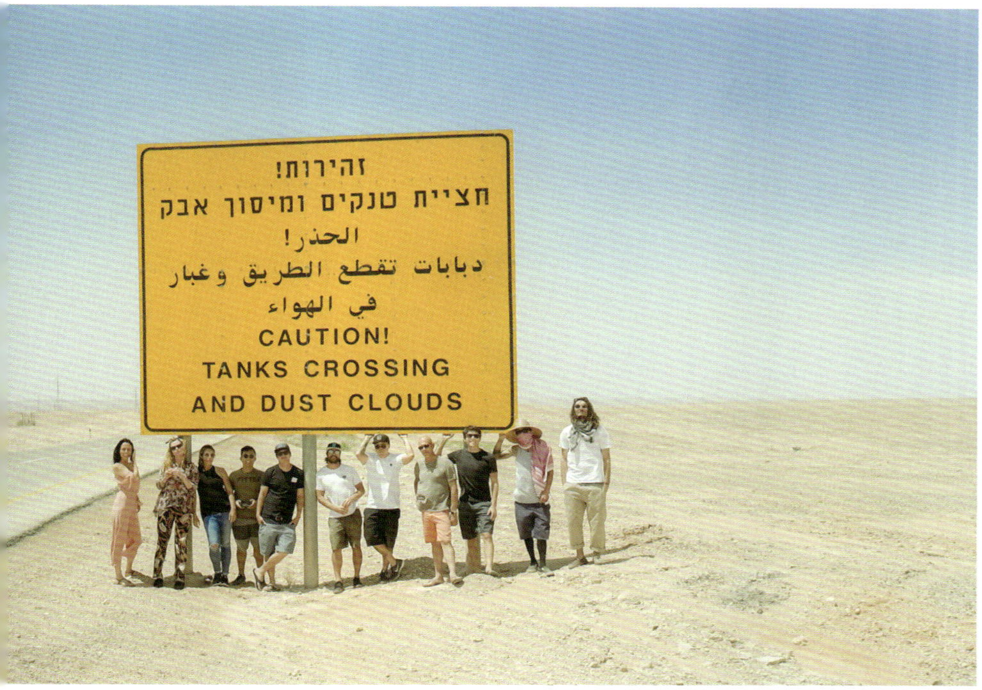

זהירות!
חציית טנקים ומיסוך אבק
الحذر!
دبابات تقطع الطريق وغبار
في الهواء
CAUTION!
TANKS CROSSING
AND DUST CLOUDS

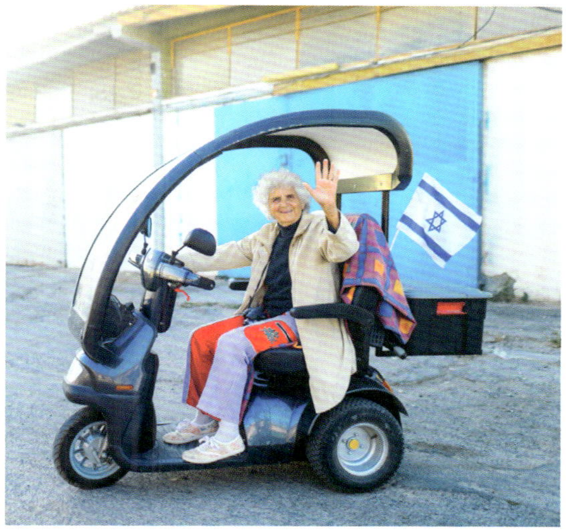

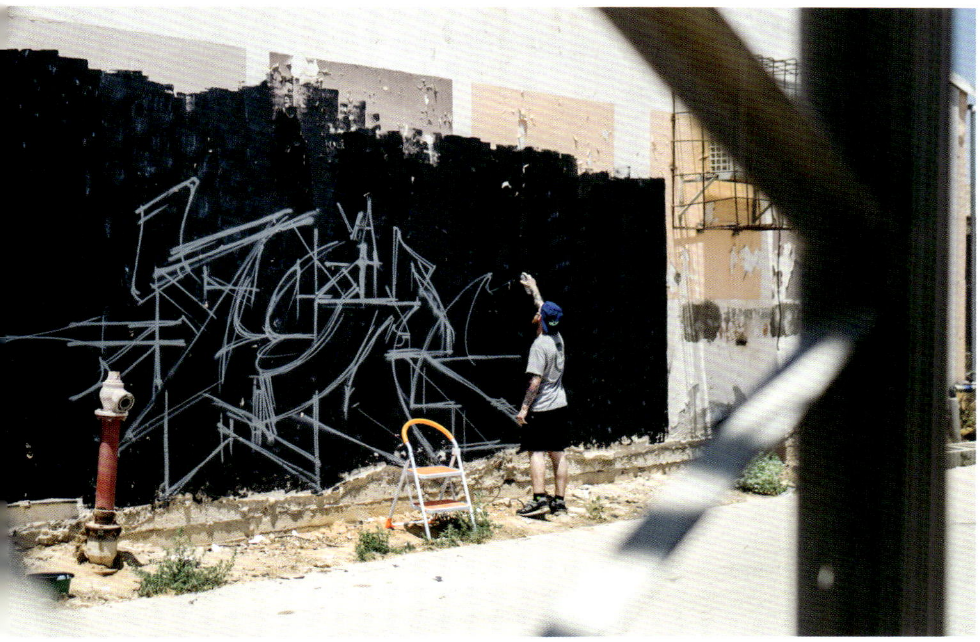

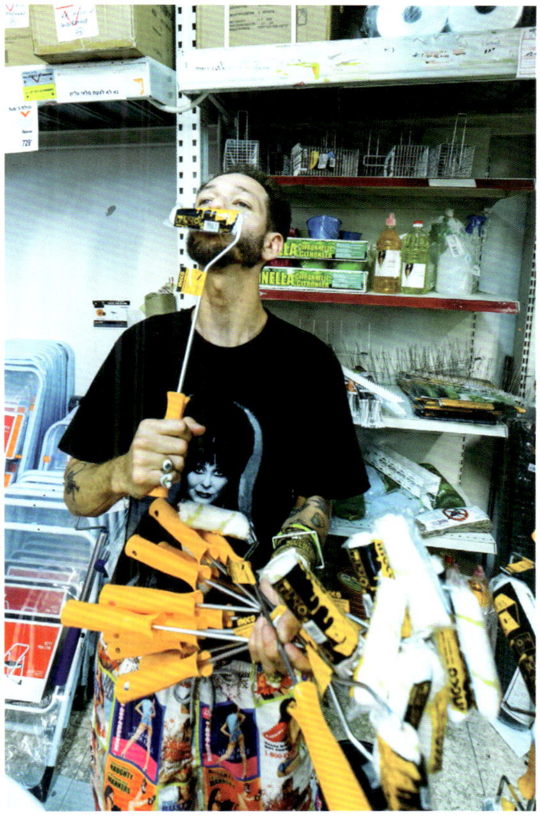

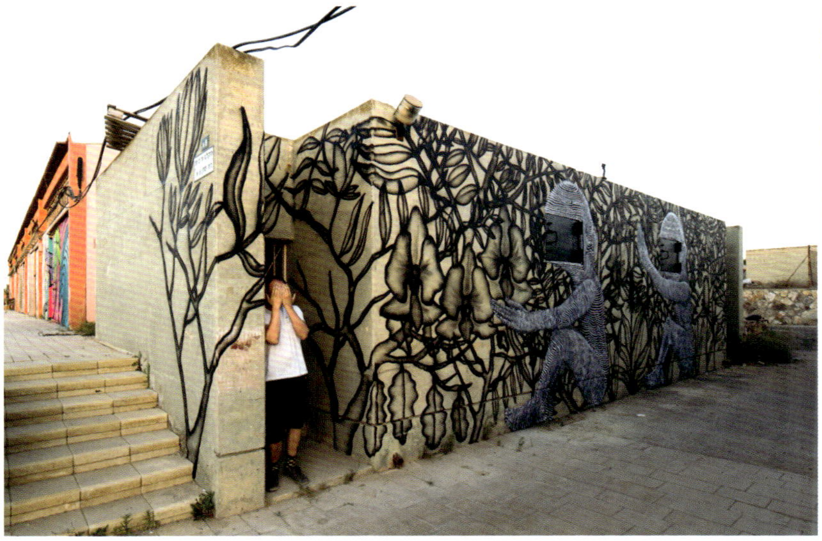

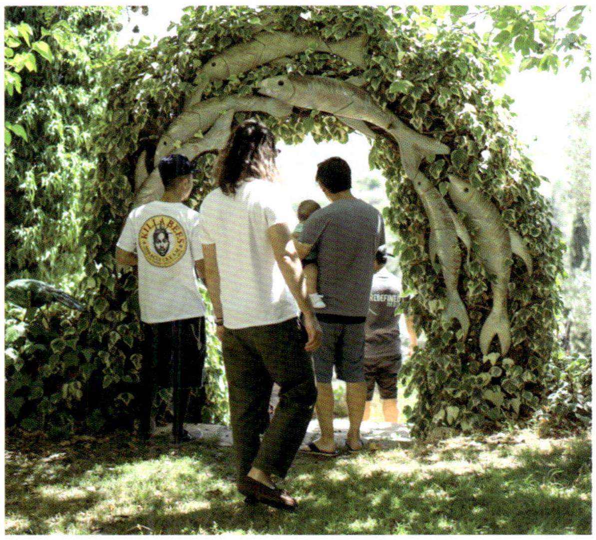

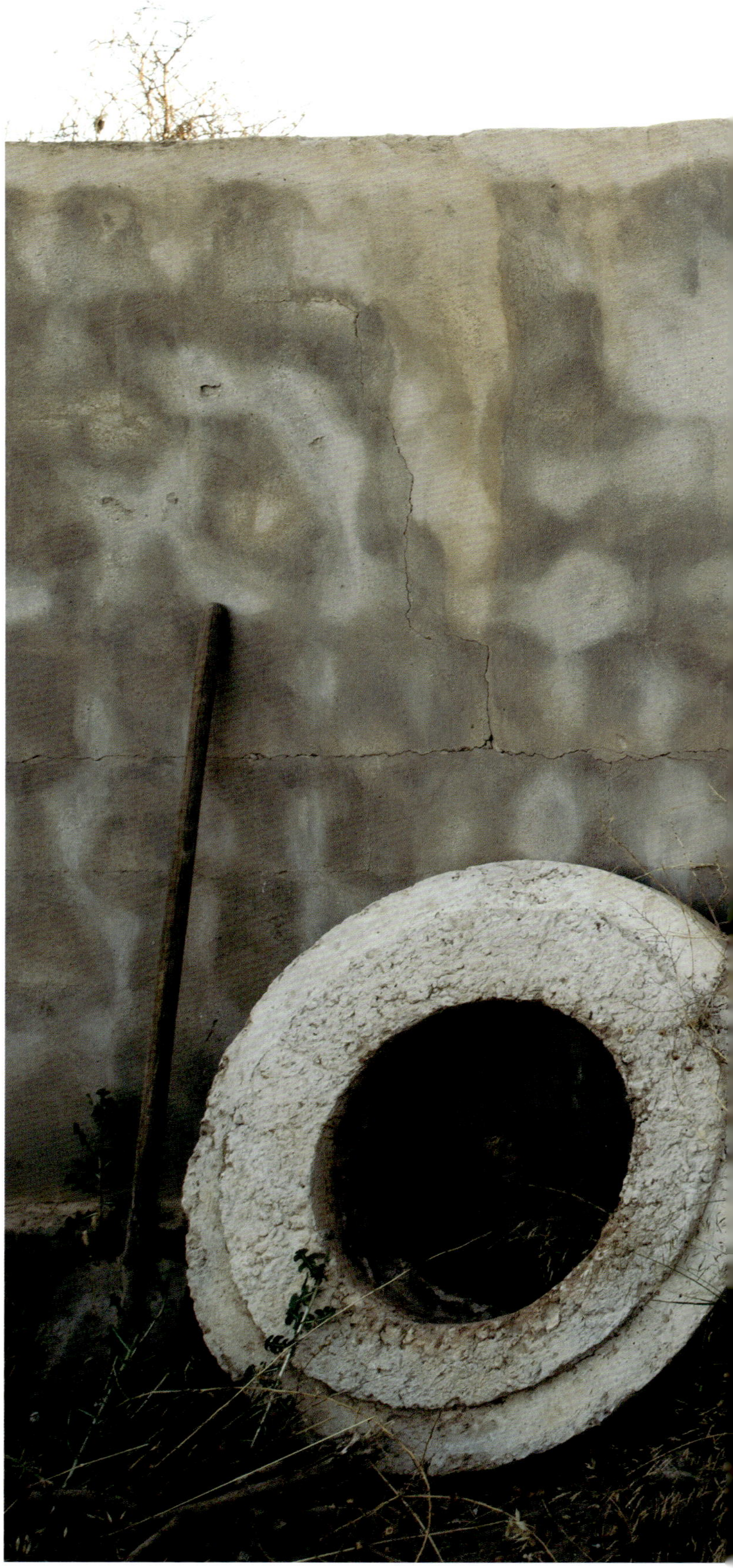

Cryptik

@_CRYPTIK_

The **Cryptik** Movement is a public art campaign dedicated to helping humanity evolve towards greater awareness and understanding through the use of compelling, iconic imagery that demands both scrutiny and reverie. The purpose of this organization is to facilitate the development of a deeper, more meaningful philosophy of life. Our main objective is to challenge people to think of other possibilities and to see a different reality; one that encompasses many ideologies, philosophies, and belief systems in order to help us better understand our place in the universe. The organization is entirely free of any religious or political agendas and, therefore, serves only to provoke wonder and inspire thought. The goal of this organization is to serve as a catalyst for a change in consciousness on a global scale. At this very critical juncture in human history, either we evolve or perish. Join the Movement! The "Great Awakening" is upon us.

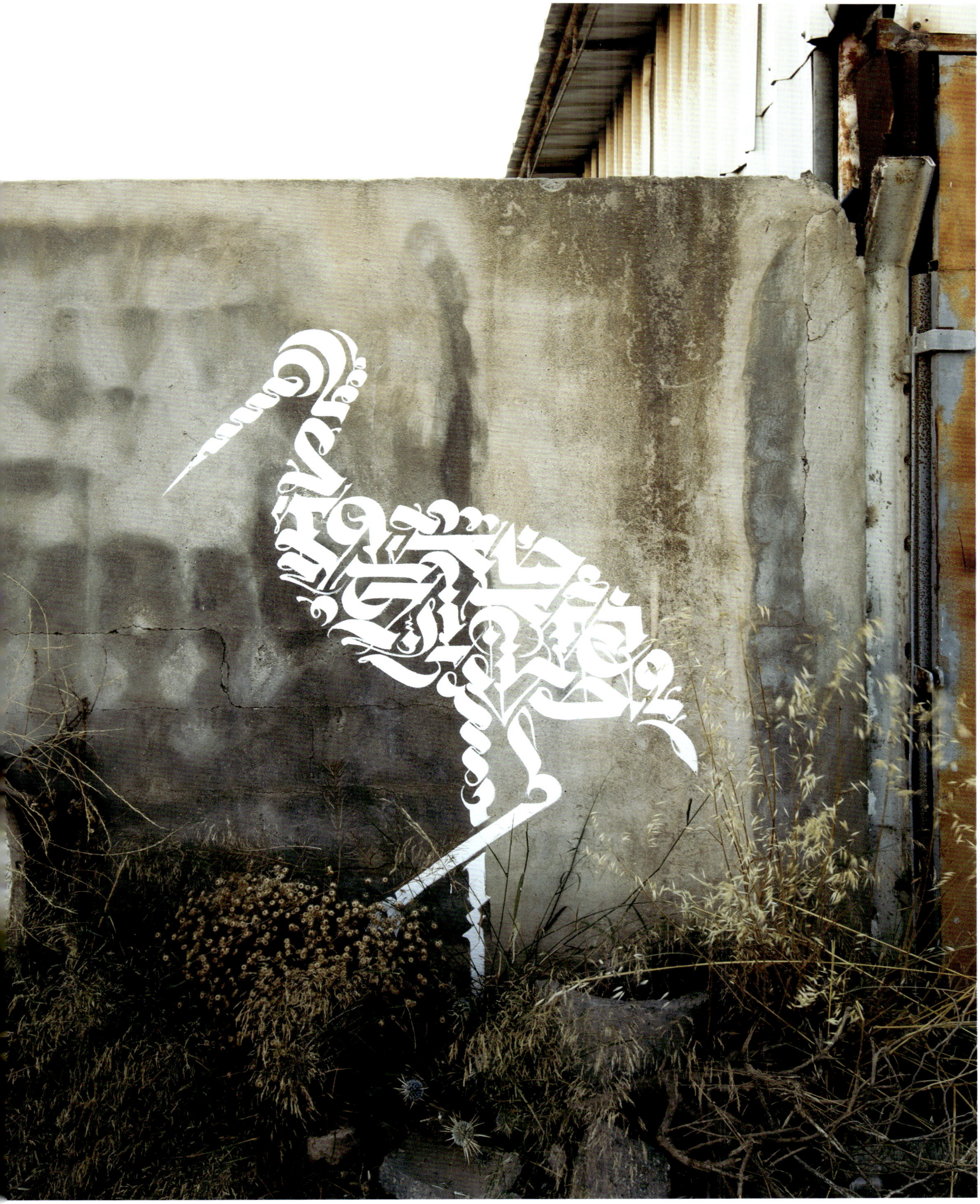

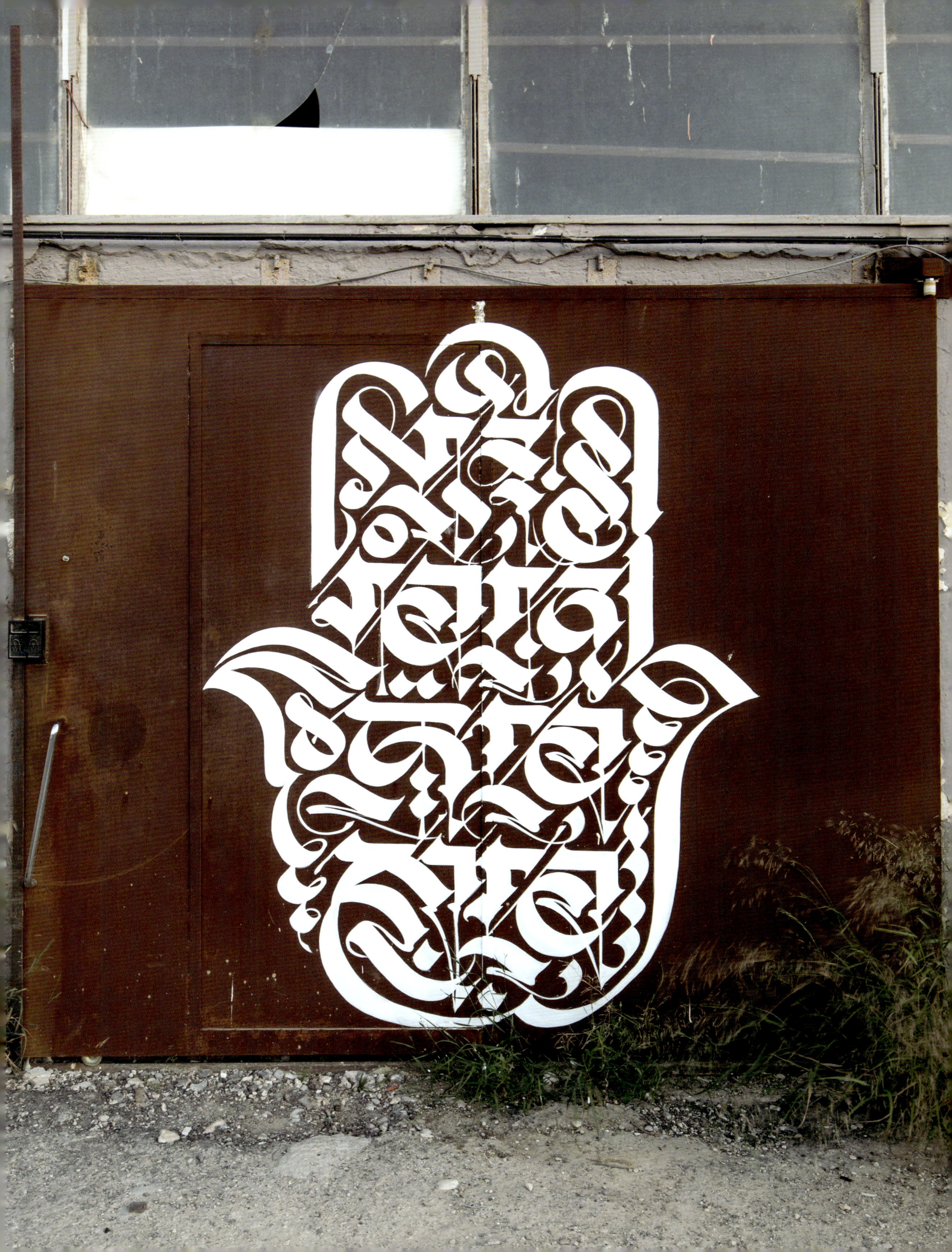

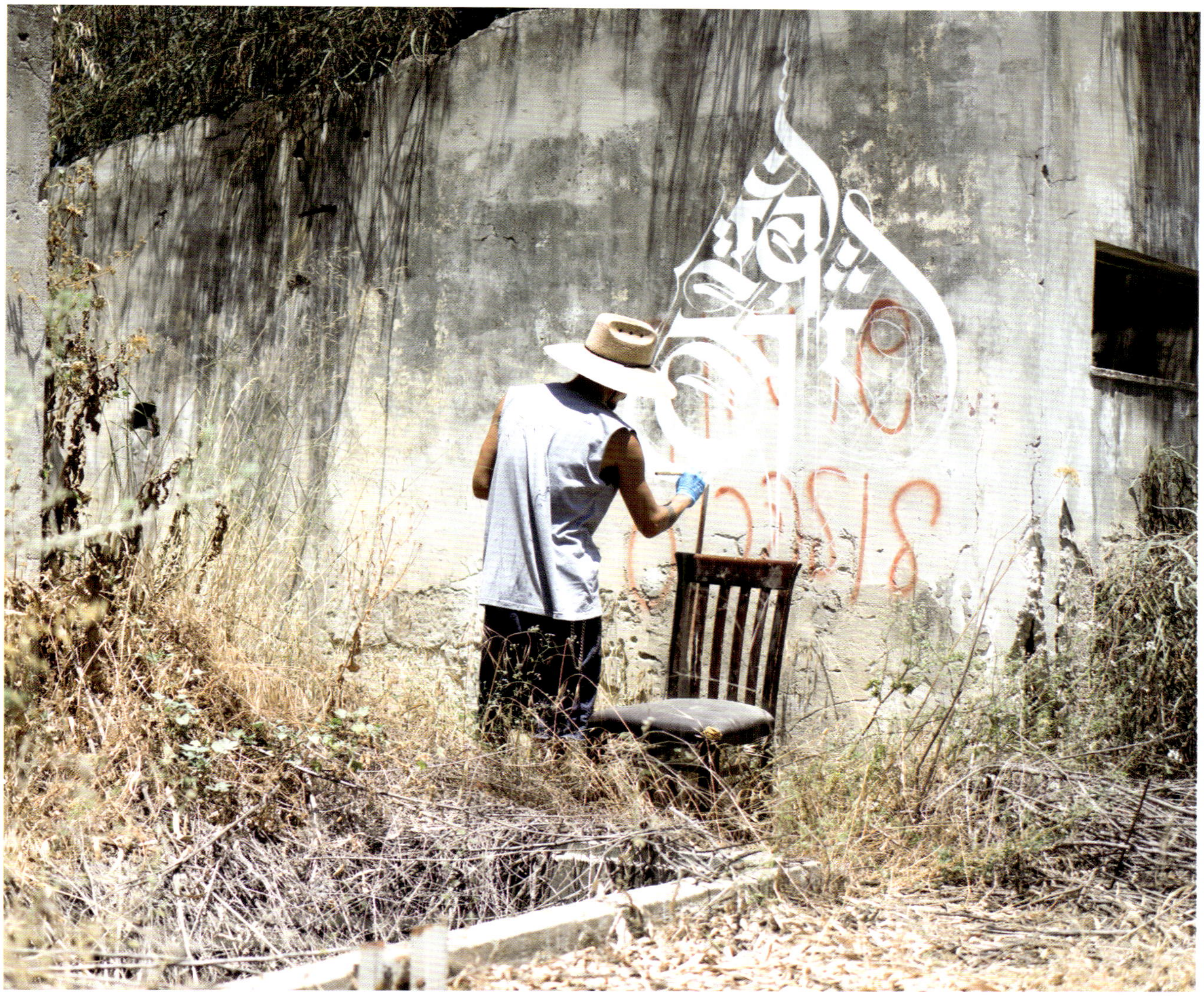

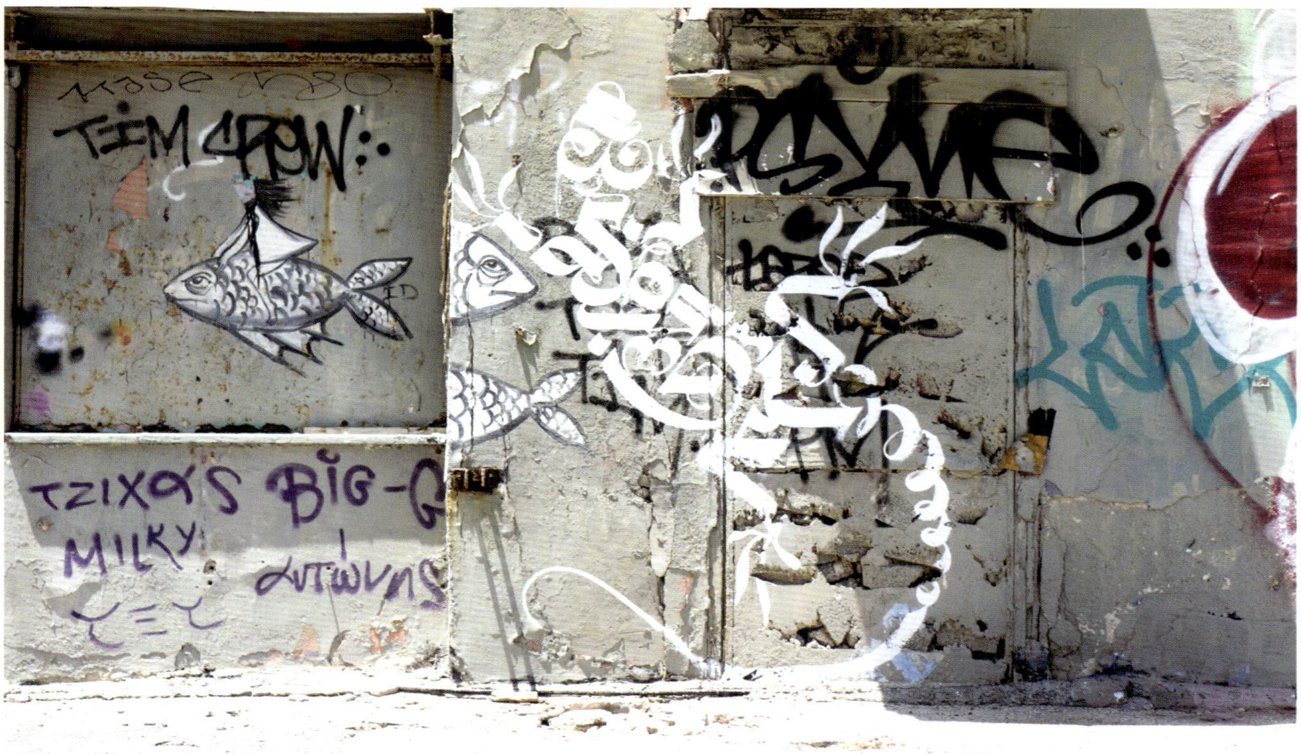
BIG-G
MILKY

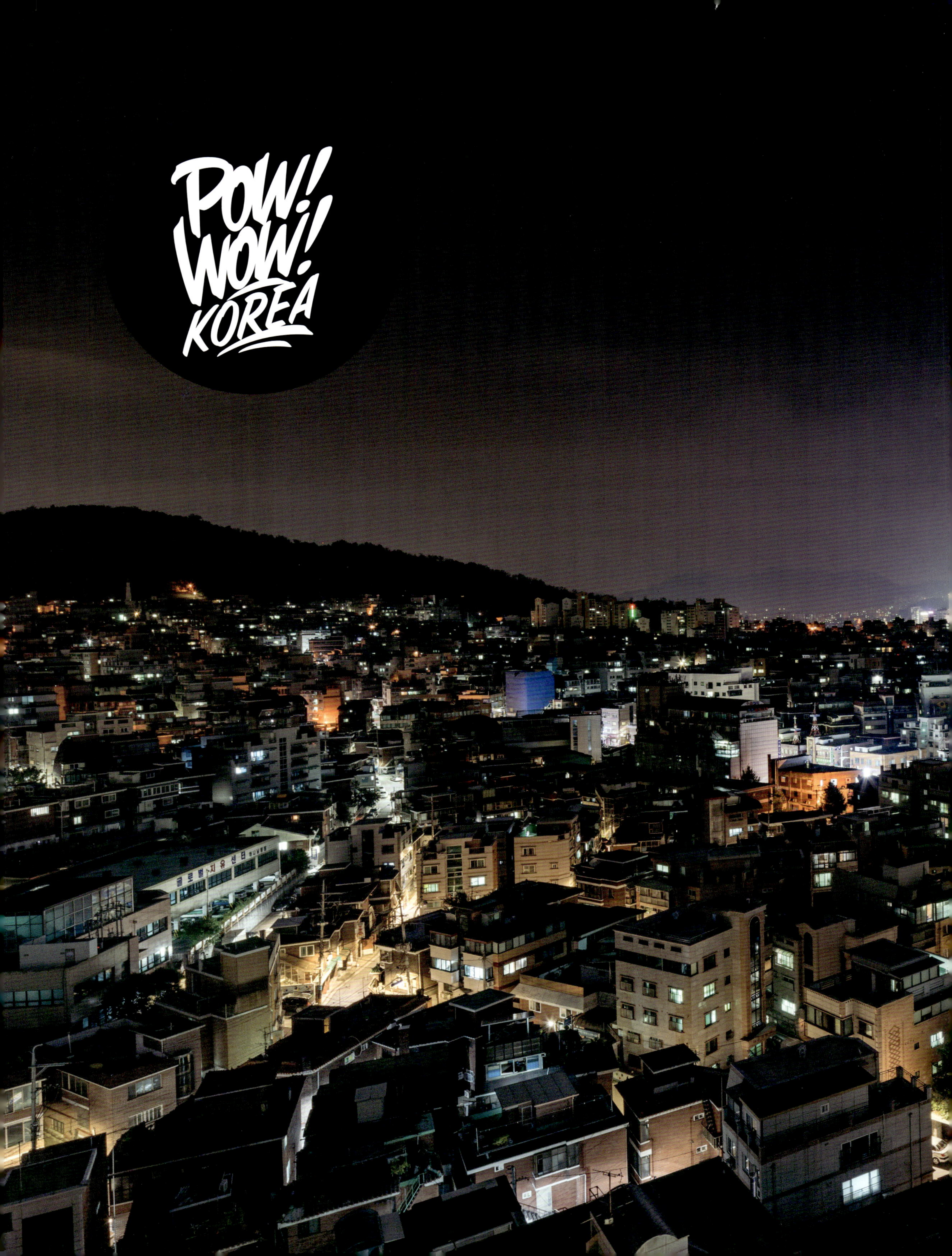
POW!
WOW!
KOREA

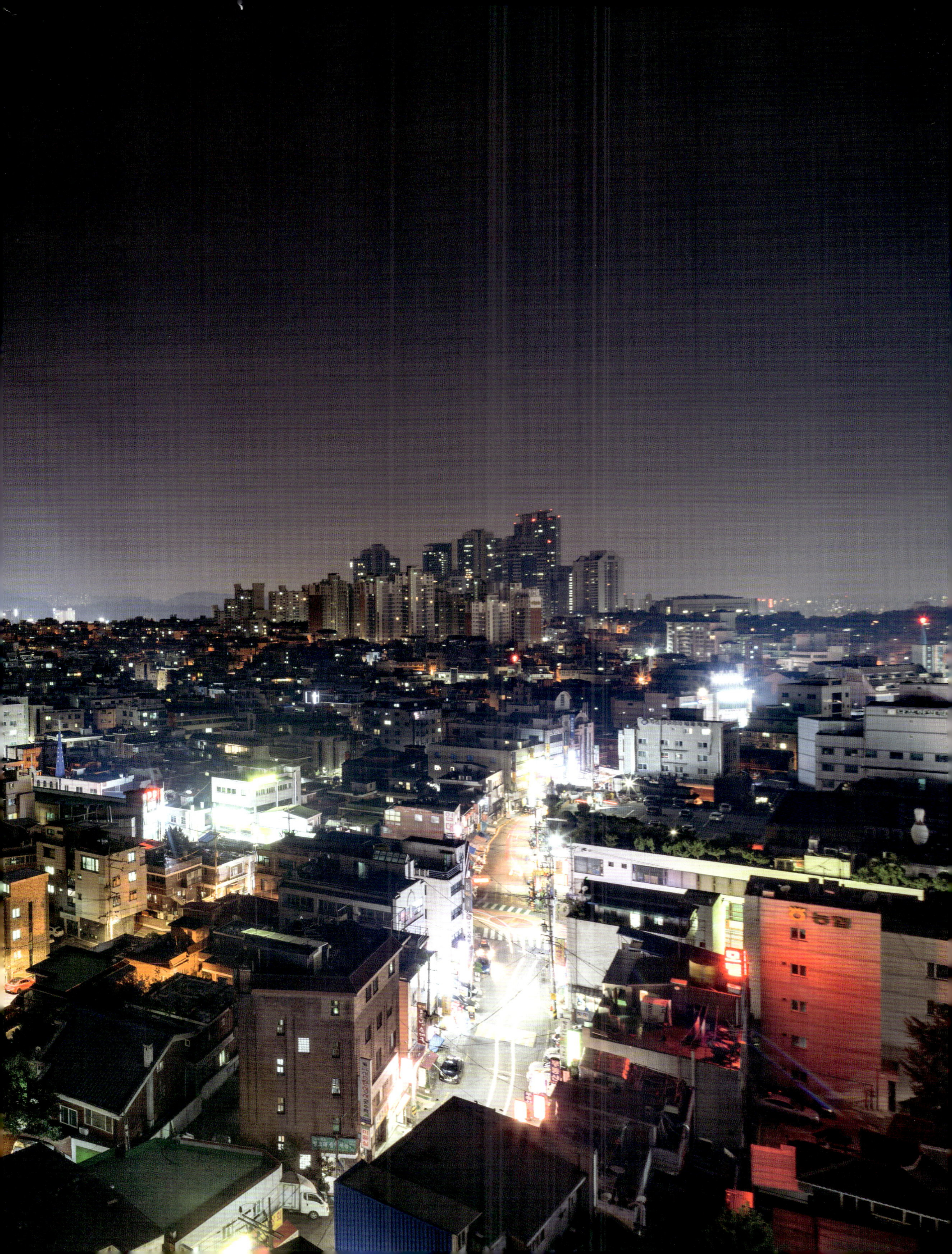
농협

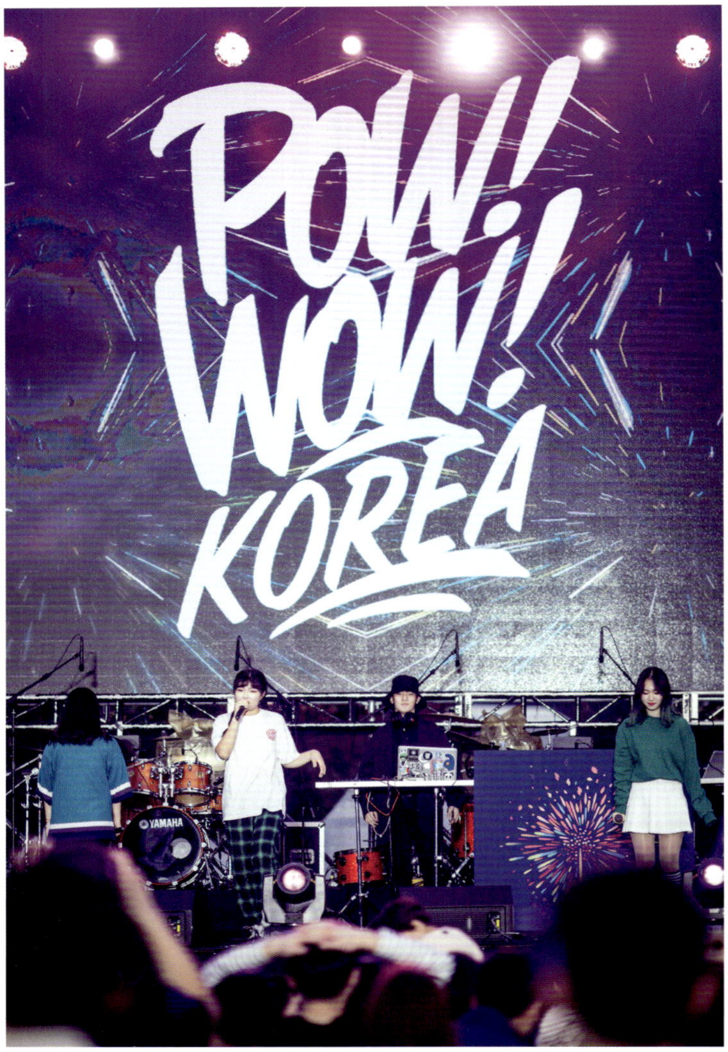
POW!
WOW!
KOREA

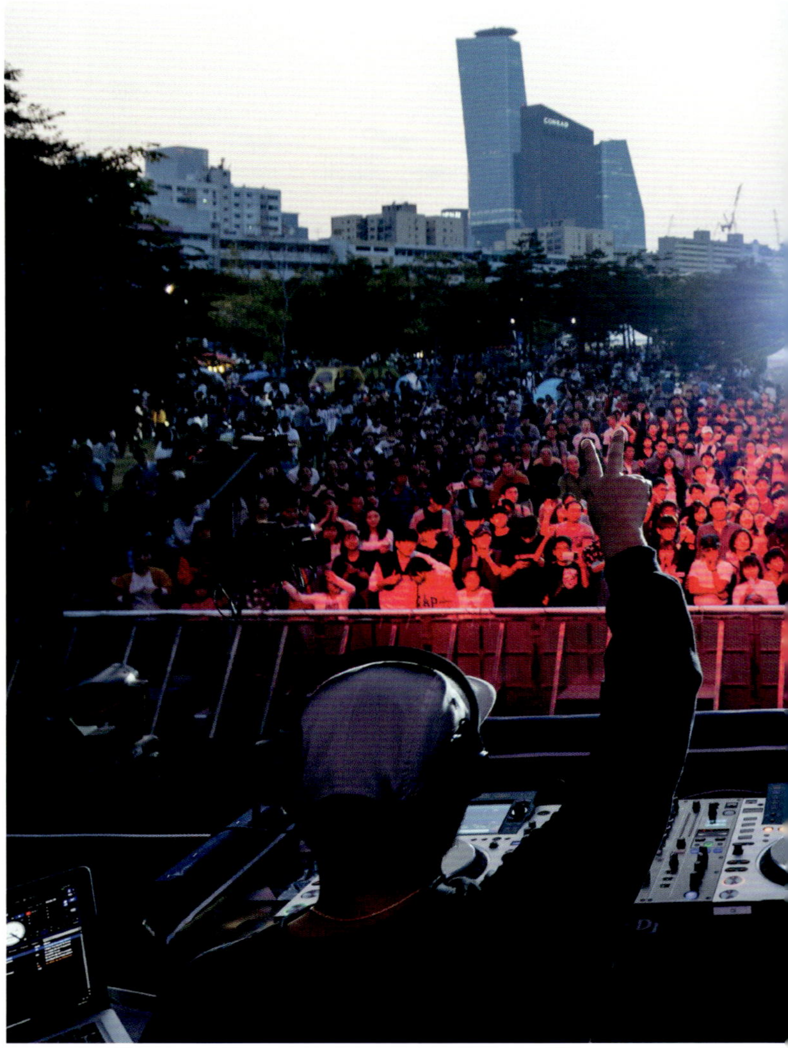

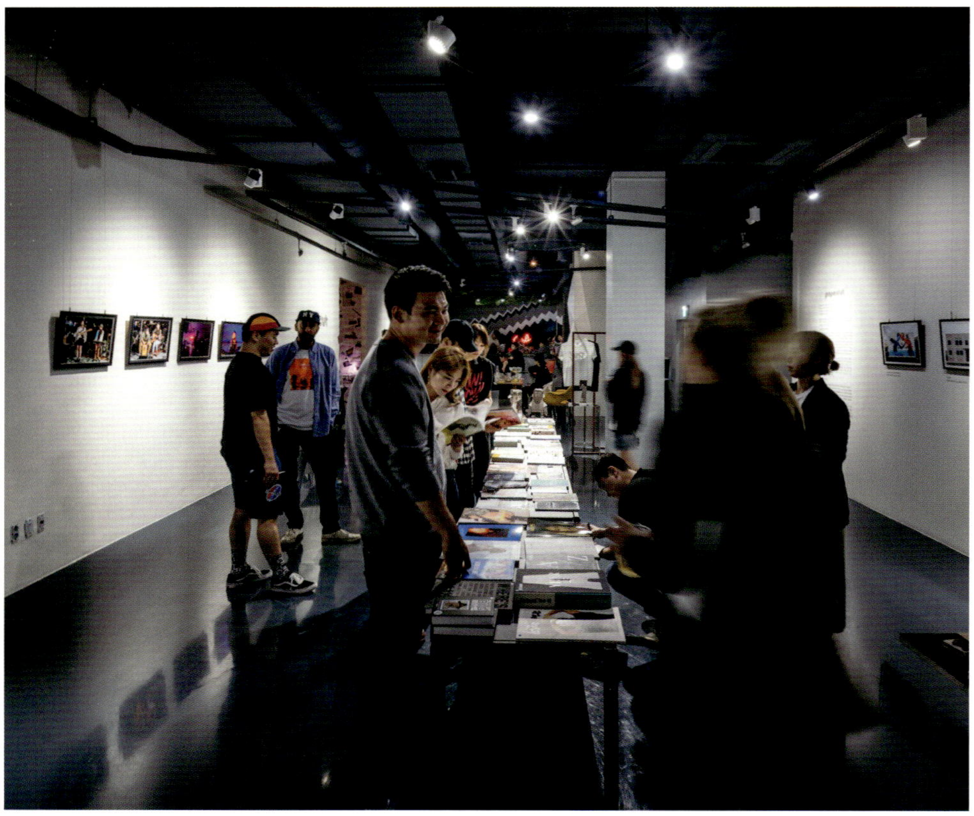

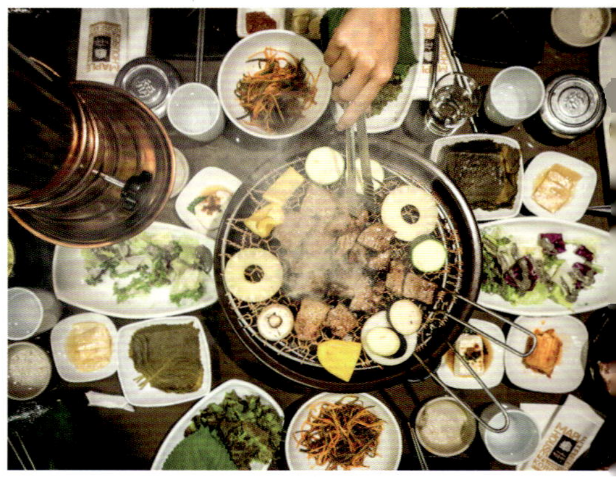

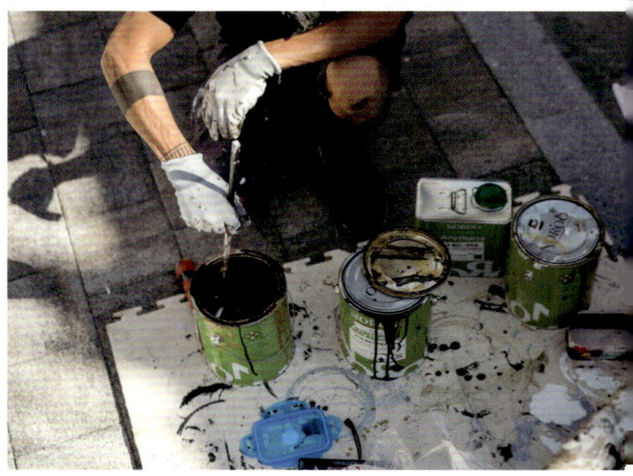

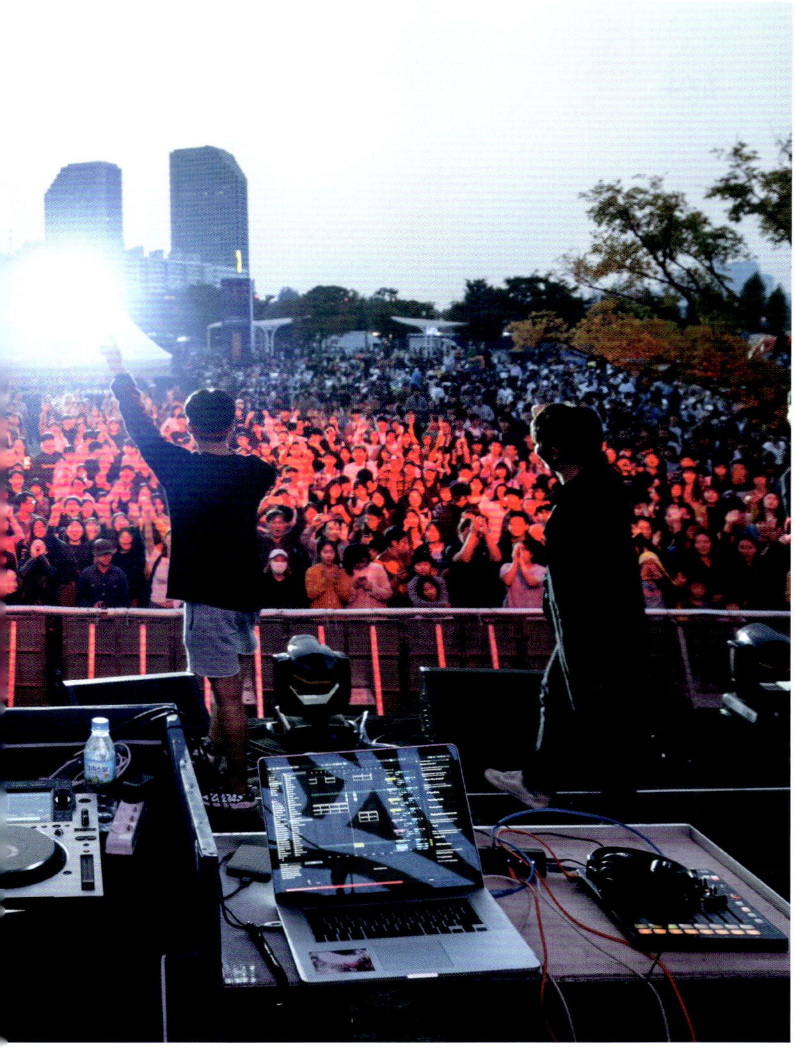

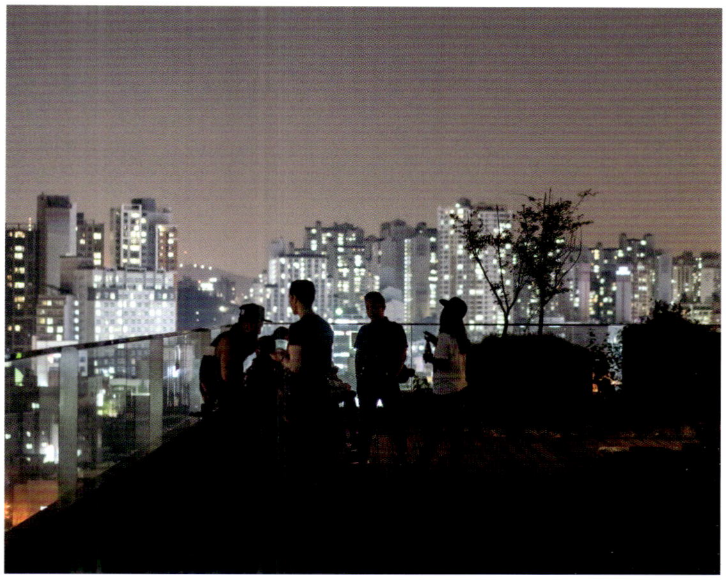

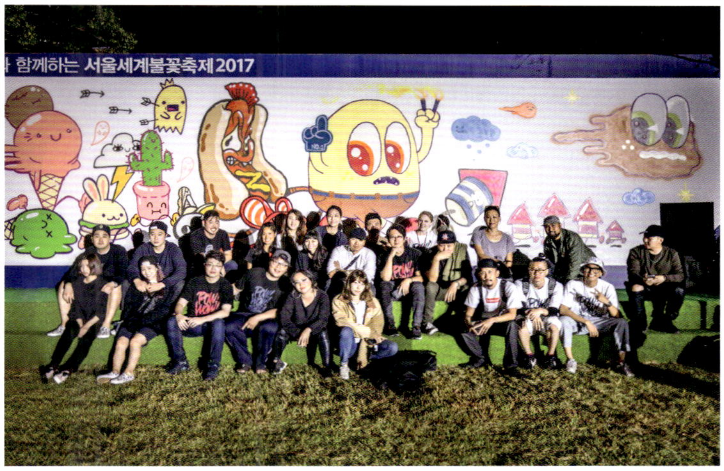
함께하는 서울세계불꽃축제2017

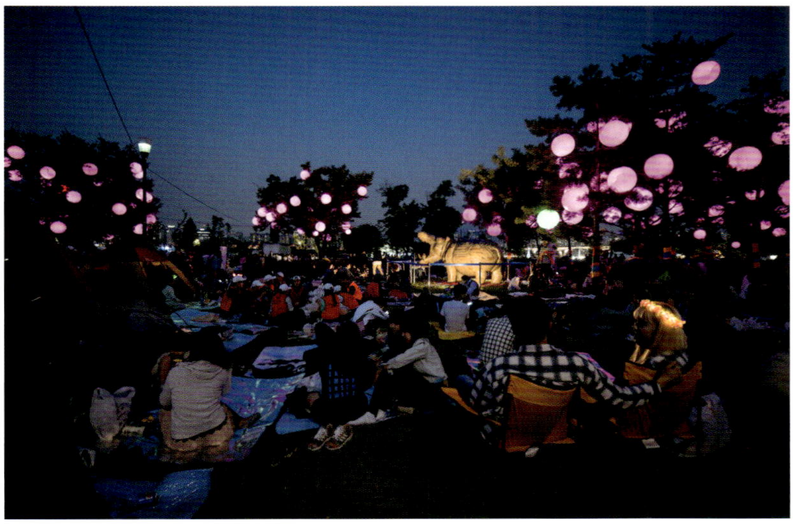

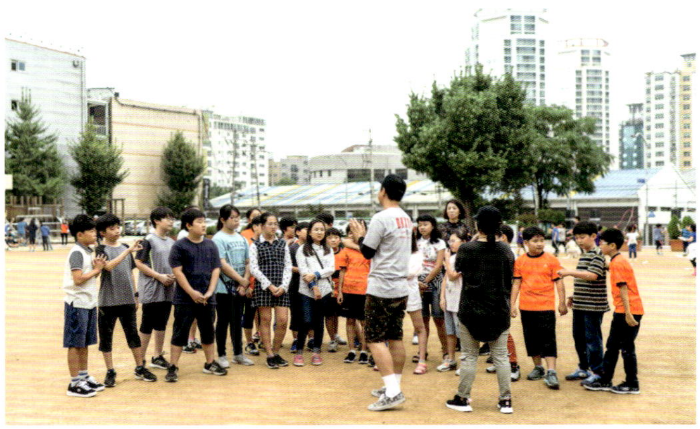

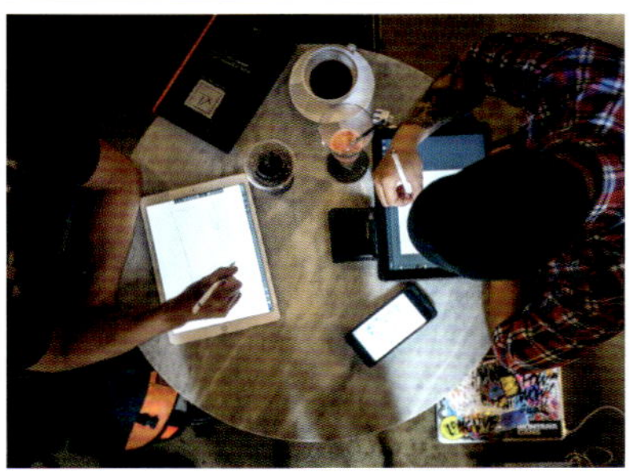

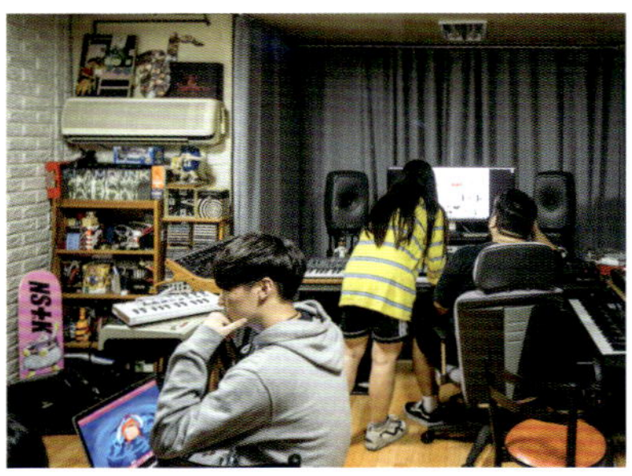

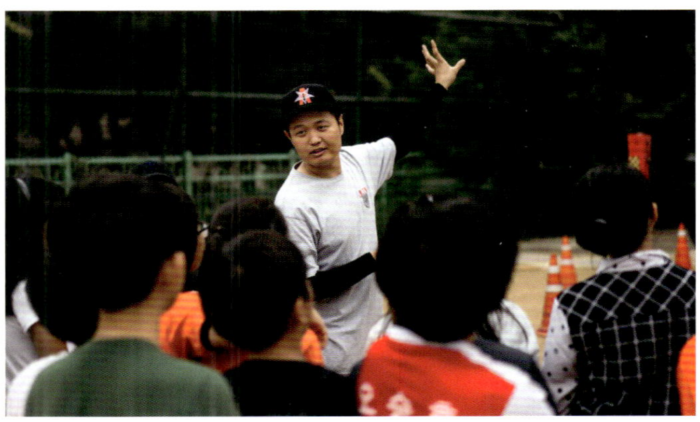

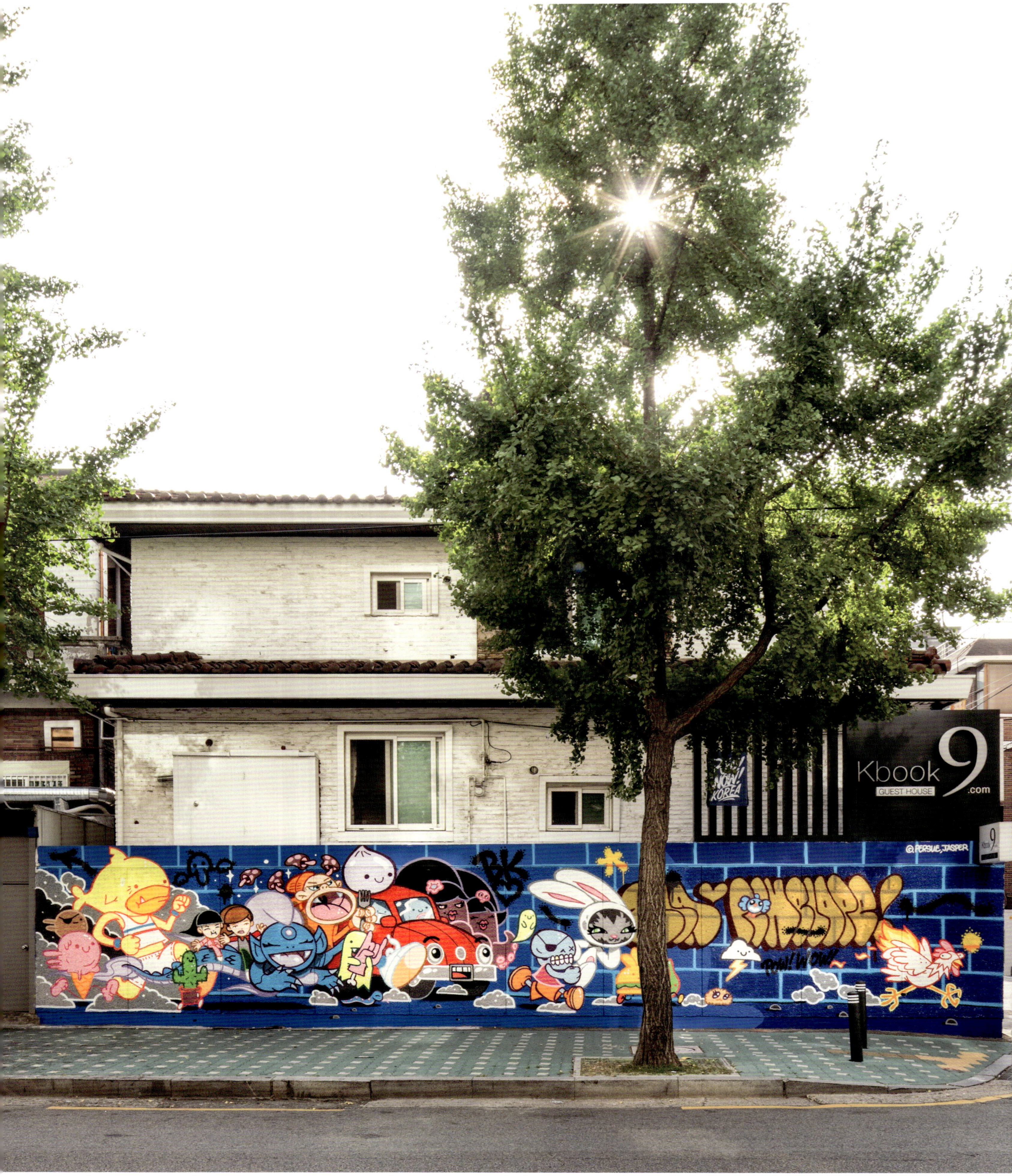
Kbook
GUEST HOUSE
9
.com
NOW! KOREA
@PERSUE_JASPER

Korea 2017

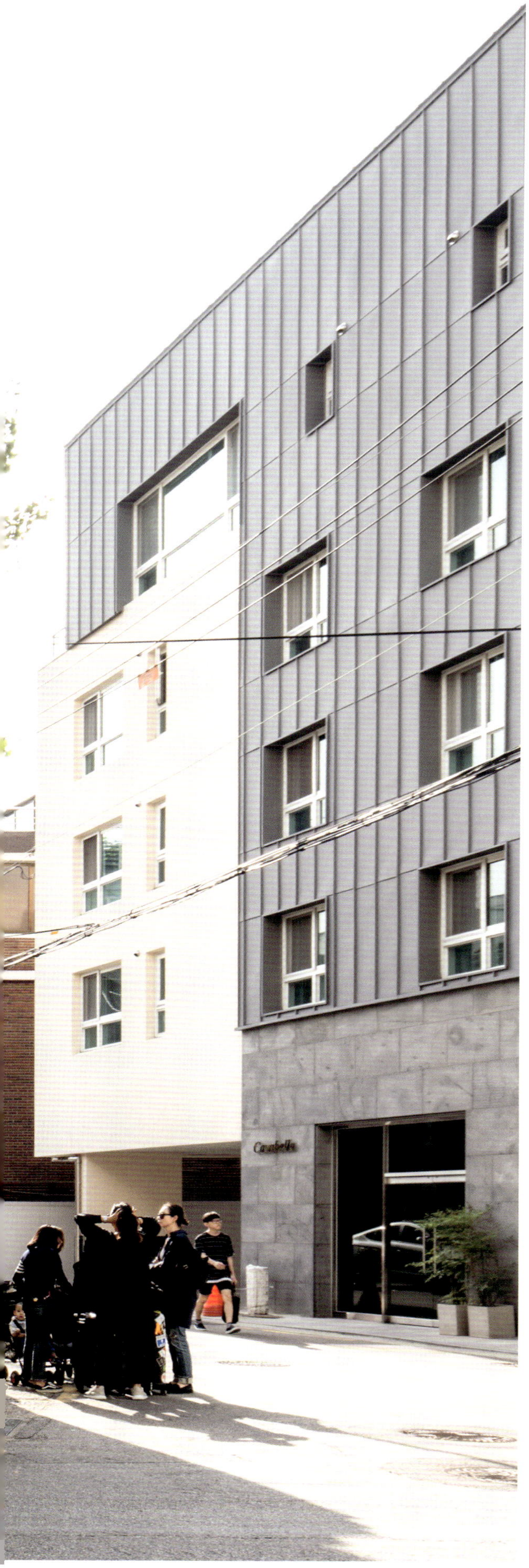

Persue & Jasper Wong

@PERSUE1 @MRJASPERWONG

Persue (pronounced "per-SWAY") is a west coast graffiti and skateboarding pioneer. His design resume pre-dates almost any example of street aesthetics being paired with the skateboarding industry, making his earliest designs the catalyst that created modern day youth culture as we know it. Much of his work is in plain sight and yet his name is rarely attached to it.

However his skill and evident talent in the realm of painting characters and letters–legally or otherwise–put him in the spotlight and he quickly became a household name in the worldwide graffiti community.

Persue eventually started a project for fun that would inadvertently become a phenomenon all its own: Bunny Kitty. His most ambitious and [beloved/coveted] creation to date, Bunny Kitty is a whole world unto itself. Persue has spent the last few years fleshing Bunny Kitty's universe out, whether it is by taking the characters to the street level with elaborate and colorful murals that he has painted the world over, or bringing her to life through plush toys, apparel, and children's books.

Anyone who knows him can tell you that Persue's artwork is a reflection of his personality. His animated and fun-loving demeanor, as well as an intense imaginative way of looking at the world around him, are the building blocks of his work. As a traditionalist, he paints on the streets, but has more recently meshed that background with a rough-edged illustration style to create works for galleries.

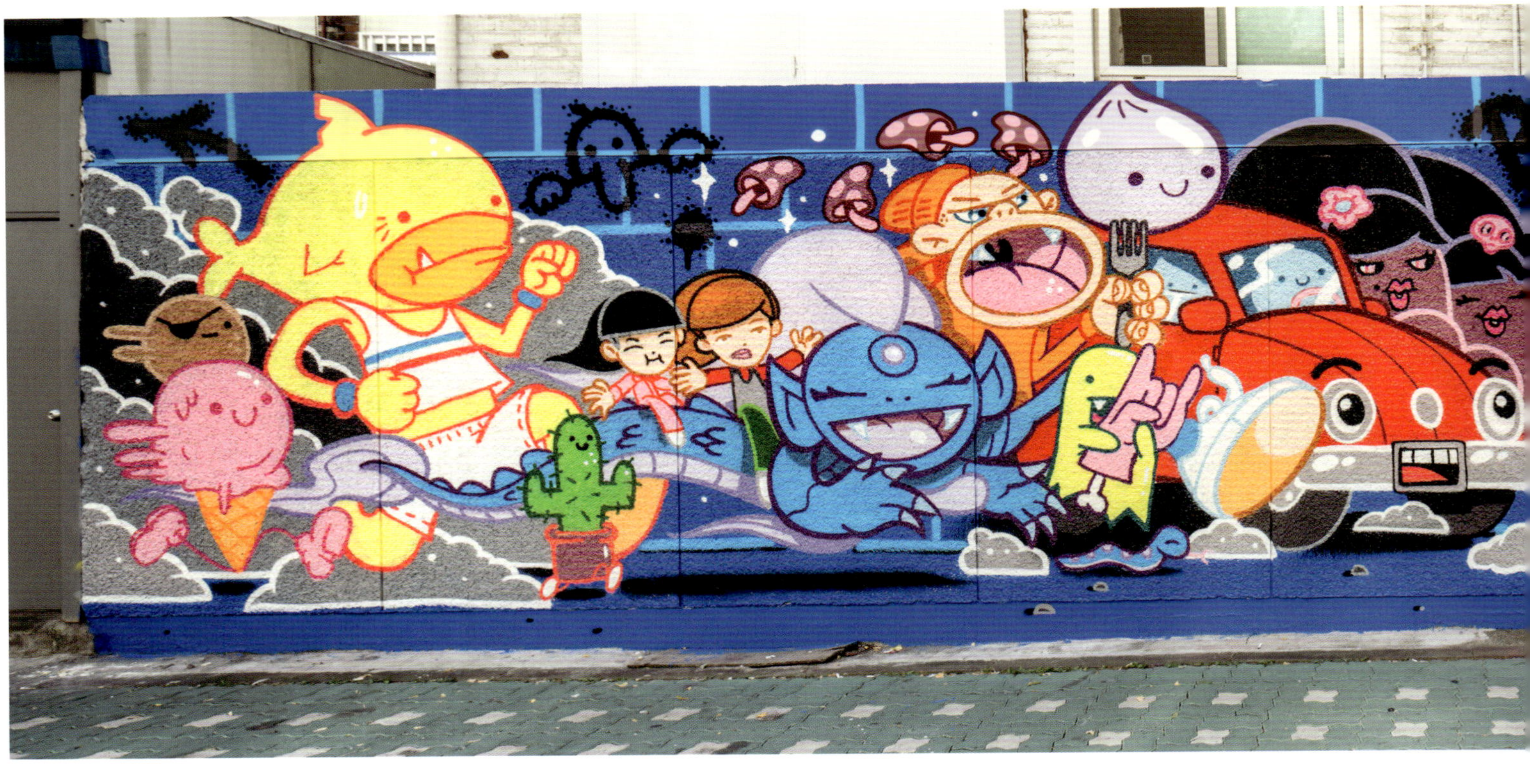

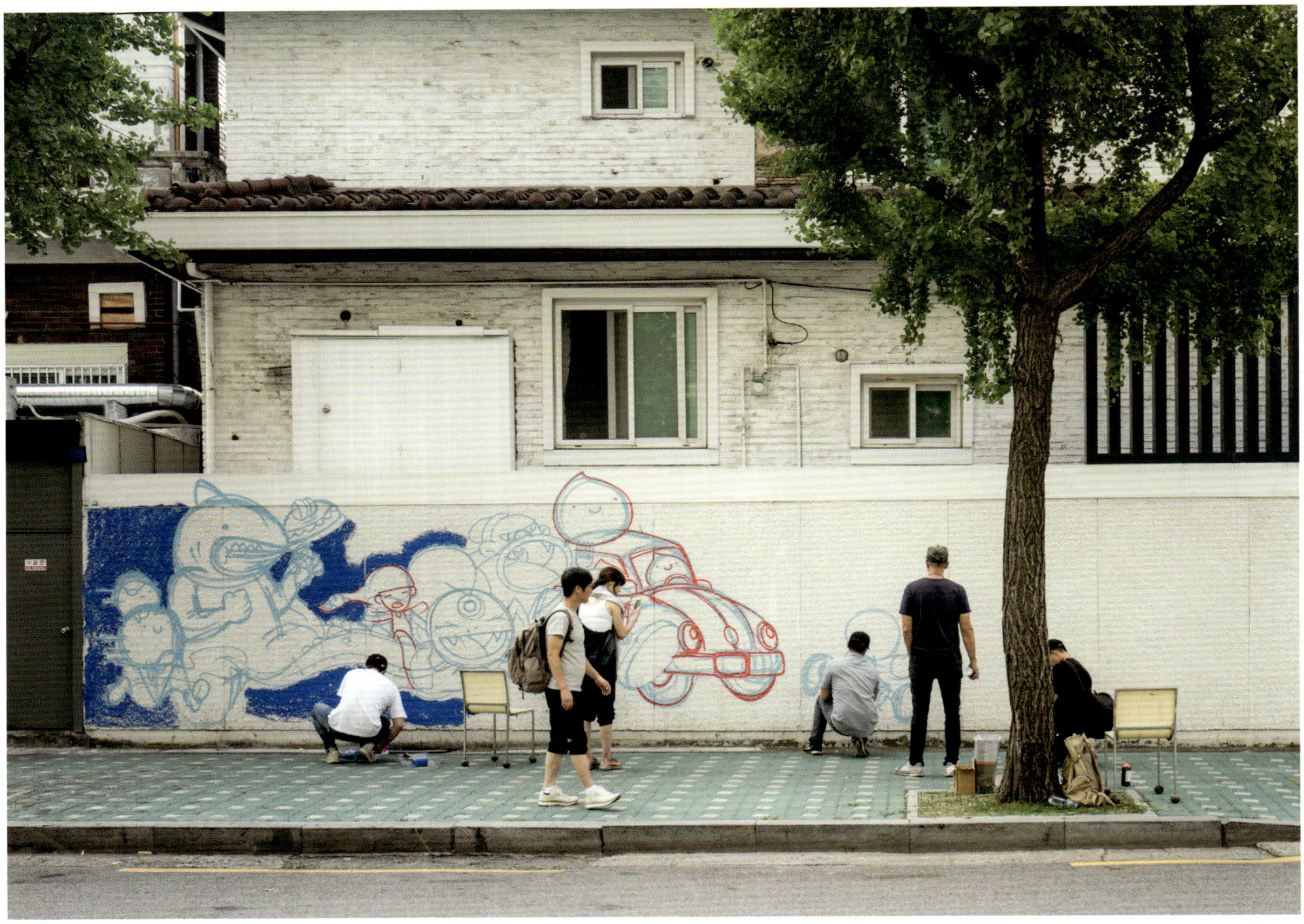

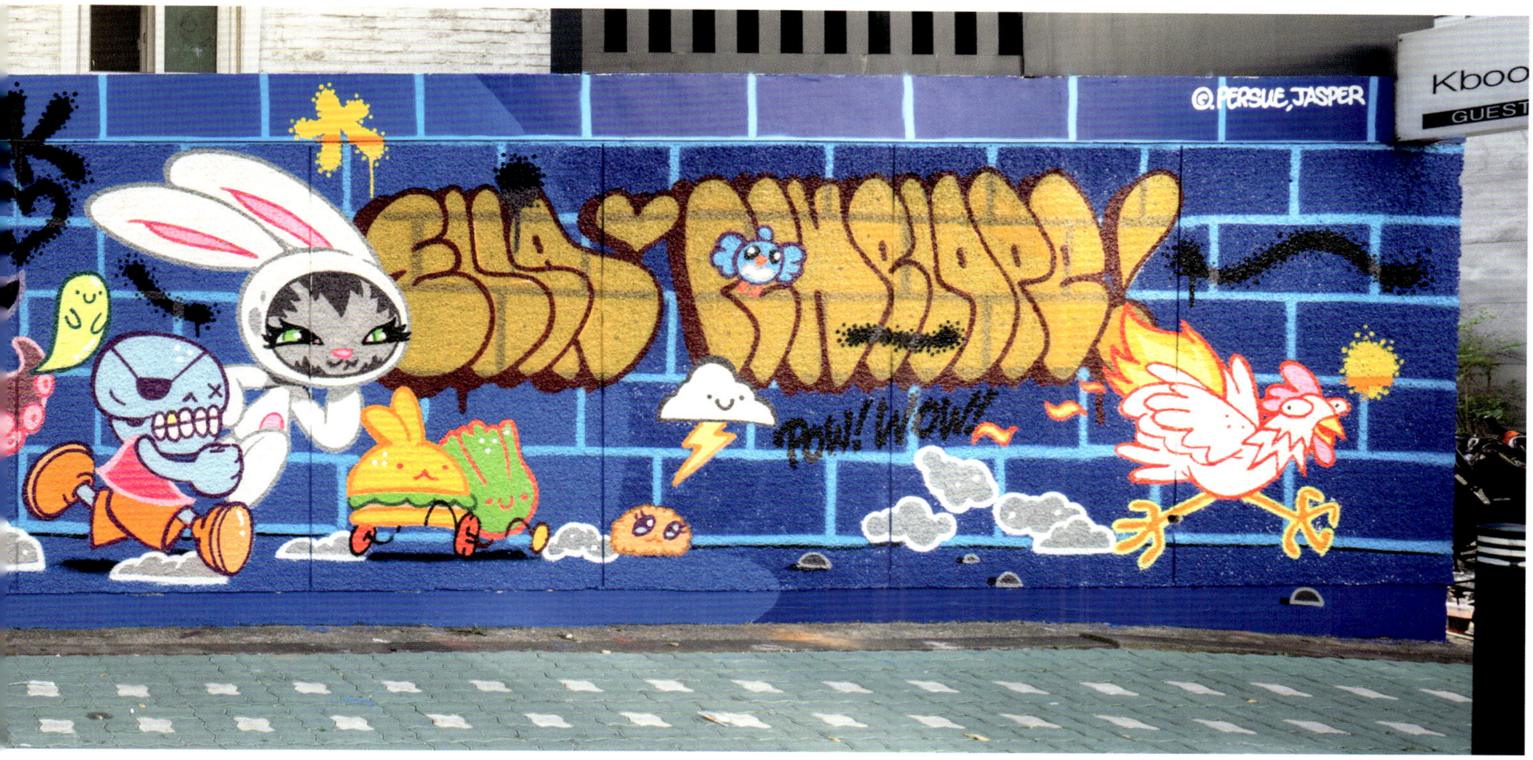

@PERSUE_JASPER
POW! WOW!

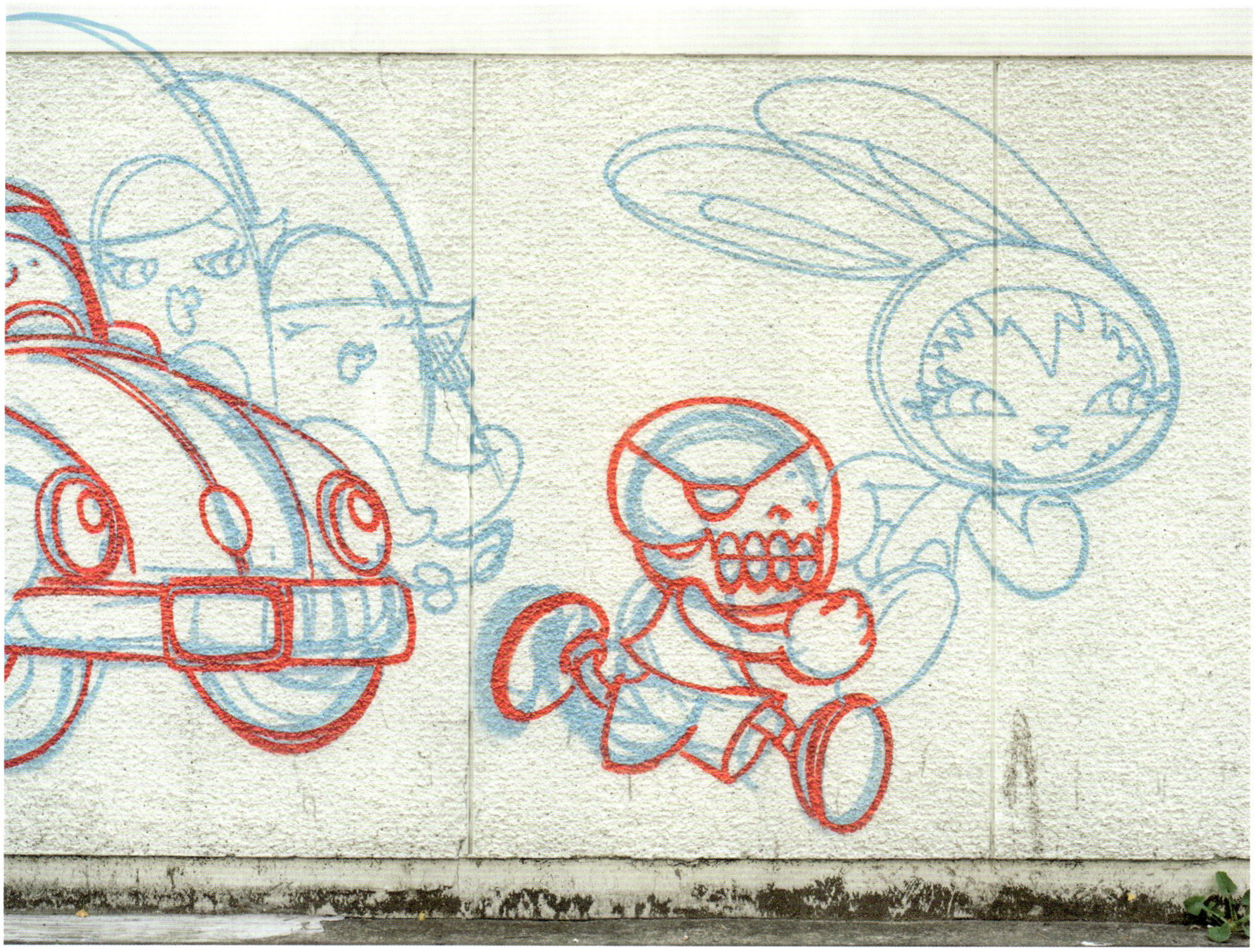

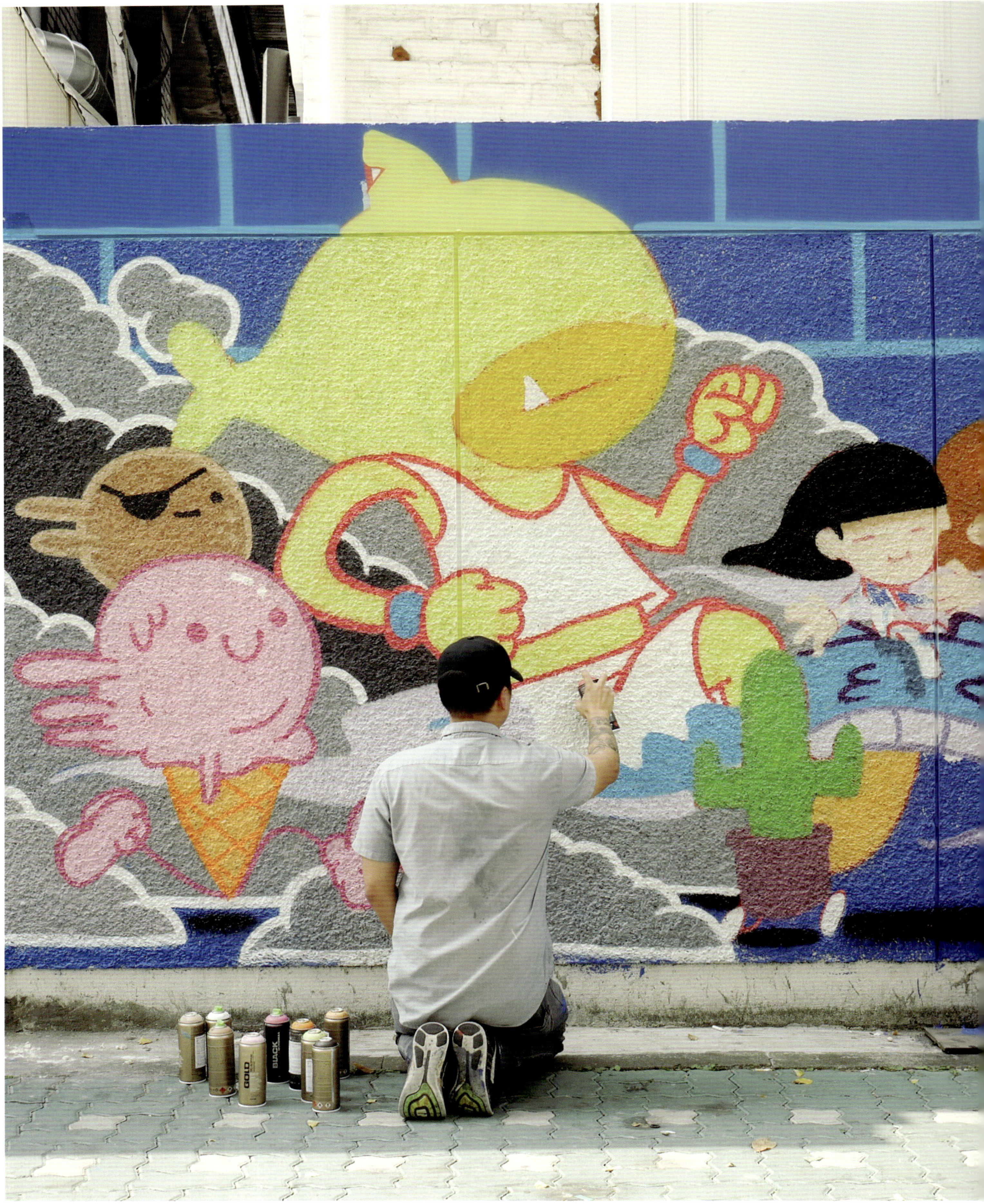
BLACK
GOLD

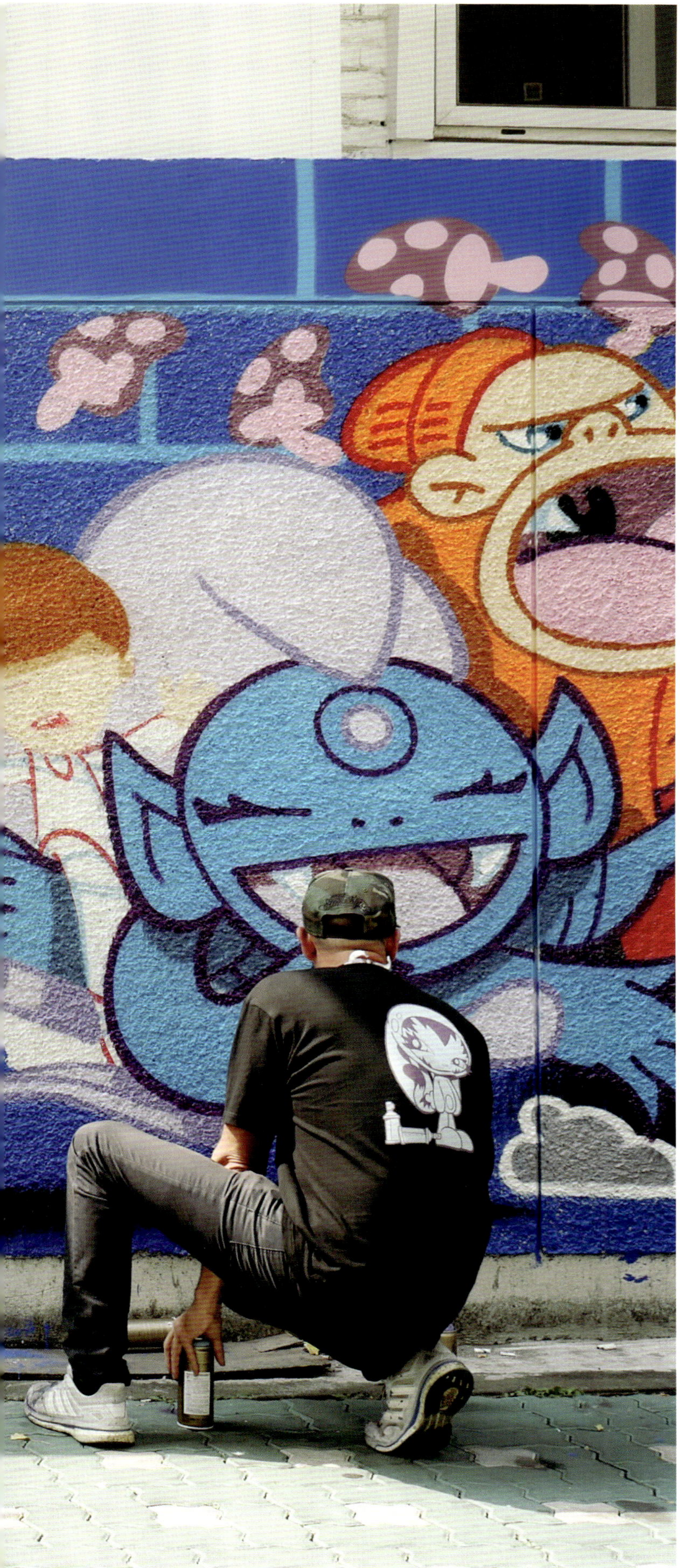

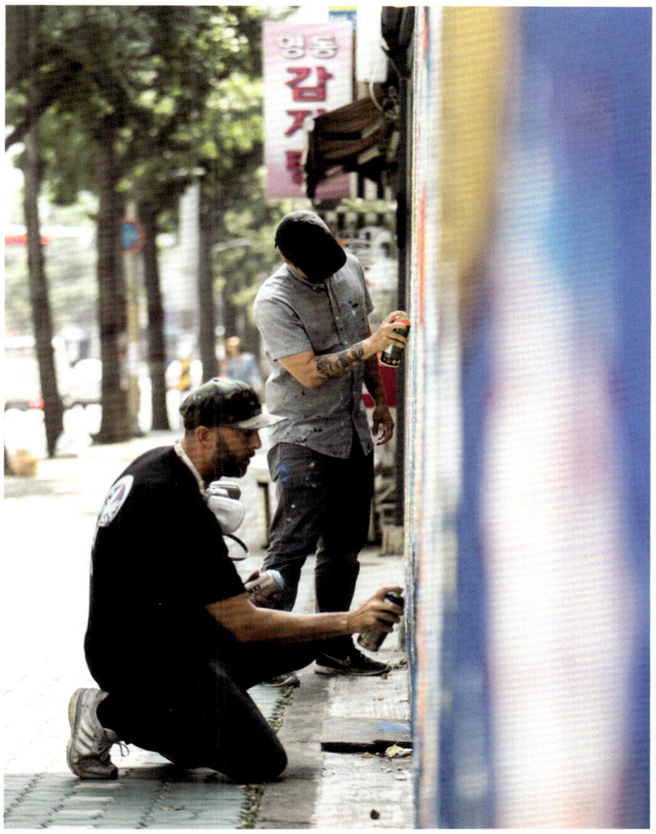

Jasper Wong is an artist, illustrator, and curator. He is a man who wears many hats and best known for his art that is a unique clash of Asian-influenced pop culture on paper. Jasper has exhibited worldwide, in places such as Japan, California, France, London, Mexico, New York, Hong Kong, Chicago, and Australia and he has been selected on multiple occasions by Archive magazine as one of the 200 Best Illustrators worldwide. He has also scored press in publications such as Communication Arts, Society of Illustrators, American Illustration, Taschen's Illustration Now, Hypebeast, Boooooom, Arrested Motion, Hi-Fructose, Acclaim, Complex, Vice, and Juxtapoz.

Jasper is also the creator and lead director of POW WOW, a non-profit organization of contemporary artists committed to community enrichment through the creation of art outreach programs, educational programs and engaging the community in the creation and appreciation of art.

Alongside POW WOW HAWAII, Jasper's newest venture is in the form of a community art center called LANA LANE STUDIOS located in the heart of Honolulu's Kaka'ako district. A repurposed industrial warehouse that has been transformed into progressive 2D/3D creative workspace and center for teaching and learning, it is a place where creative output not only flourishes, but also interacts with and inspires the community. It is a combination of private studio spaces and a fully functional art school for the youth of Hawai'i.

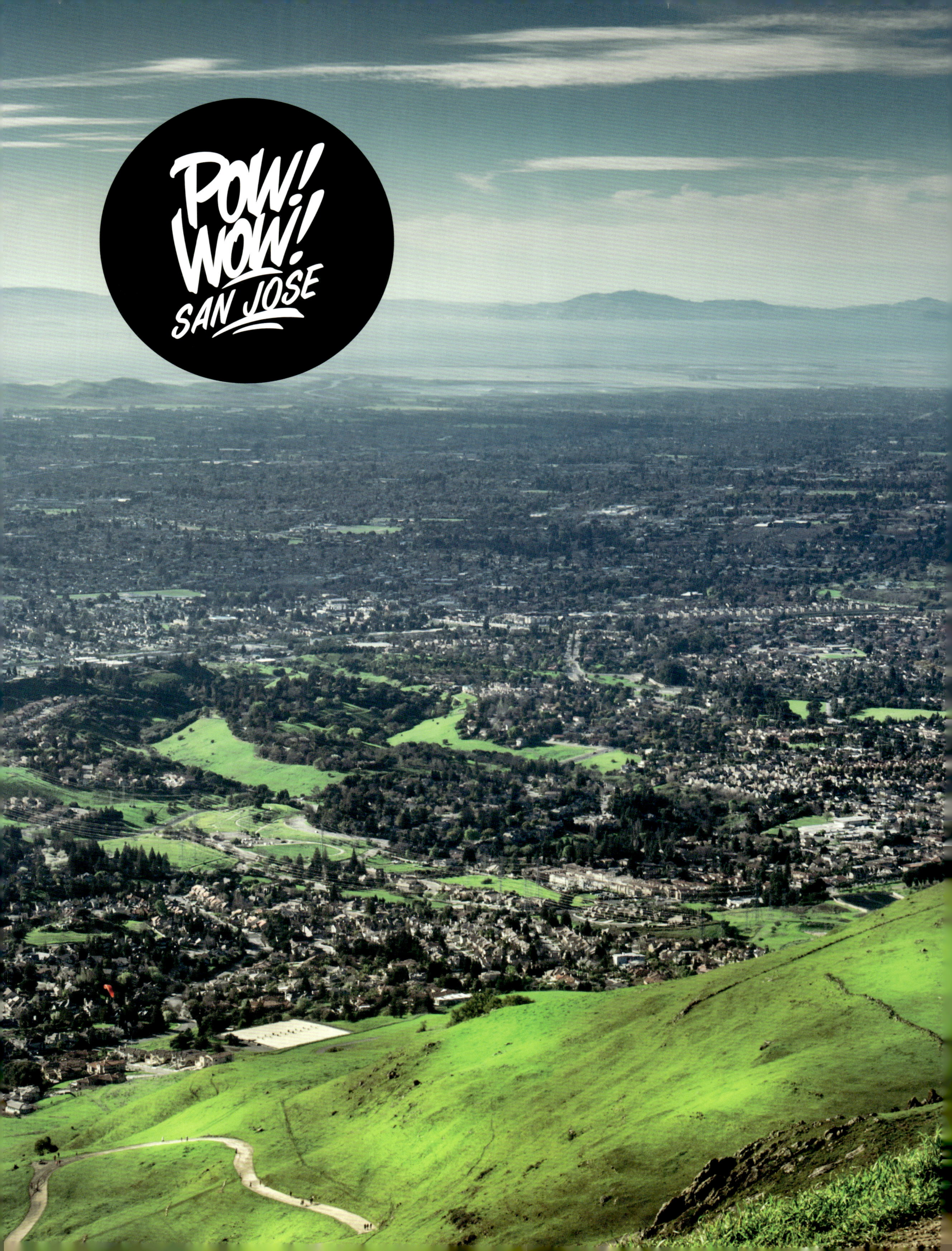
POW!
WOW!
SAN JOSE

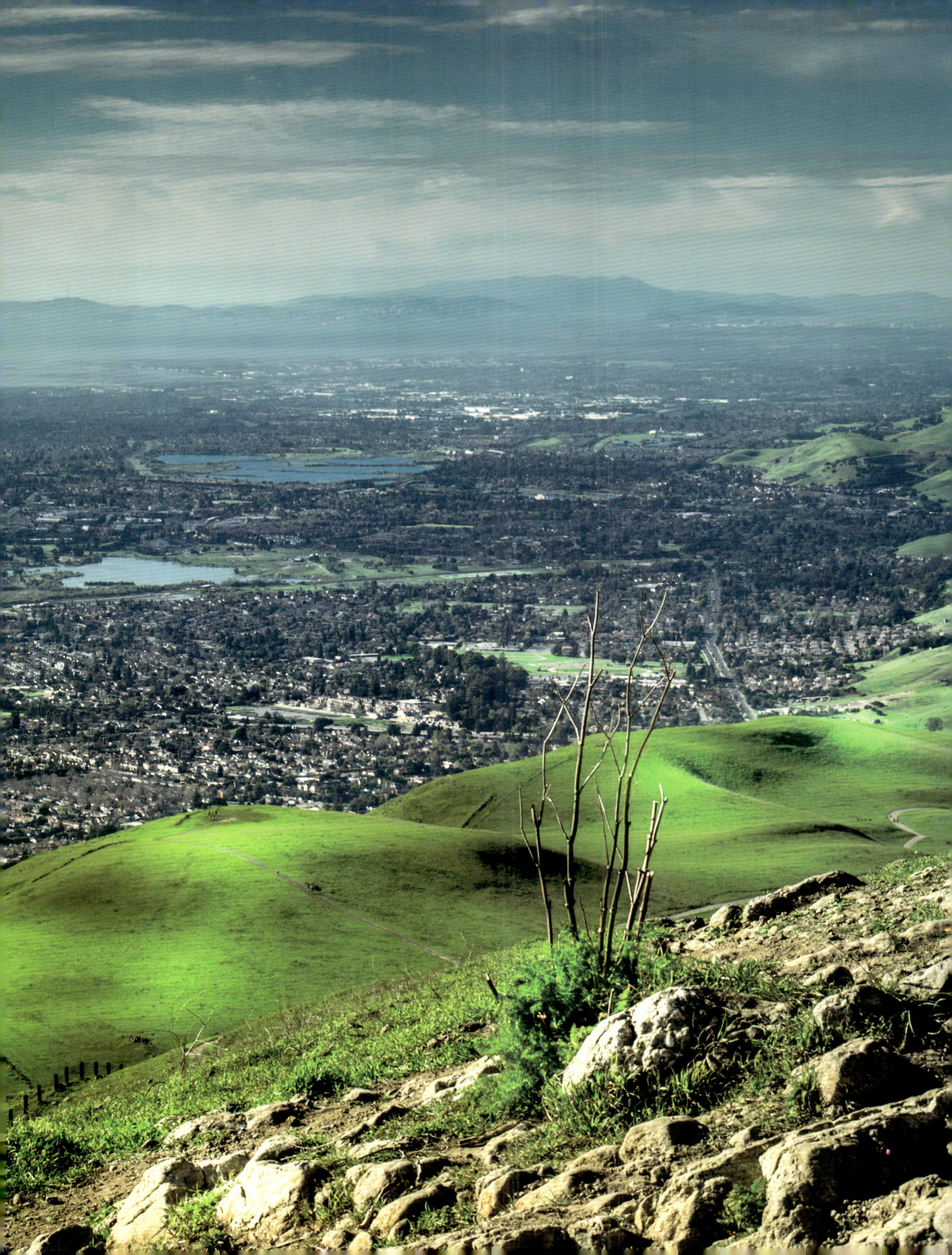

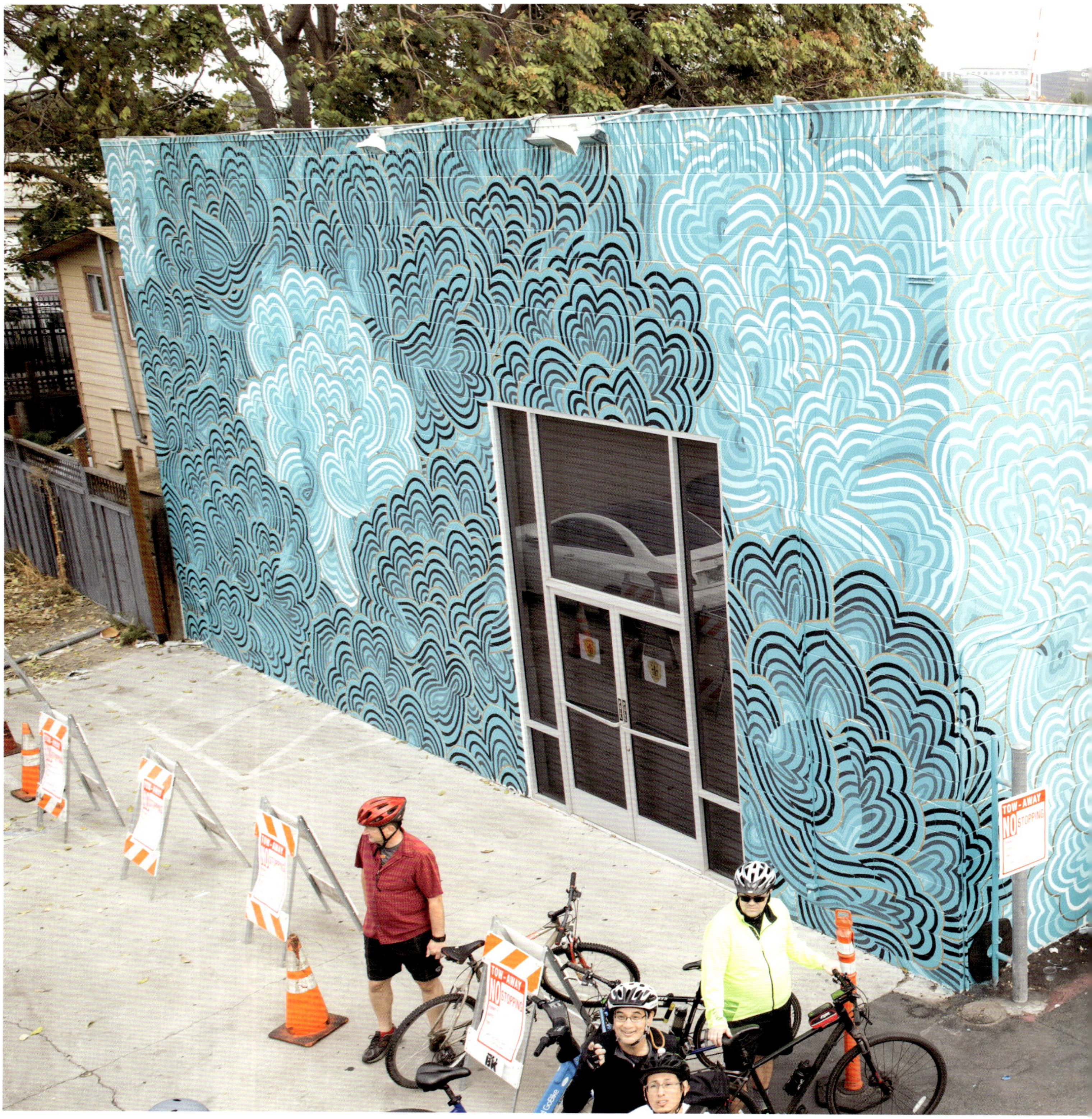

San Jose 2017

Jet Martinez

@JETMAR1

Jet Martinez is a full time muralist and painter based in Oakland, California, where he lives with a much beloved and talented wife and two ridiculously energetic children.

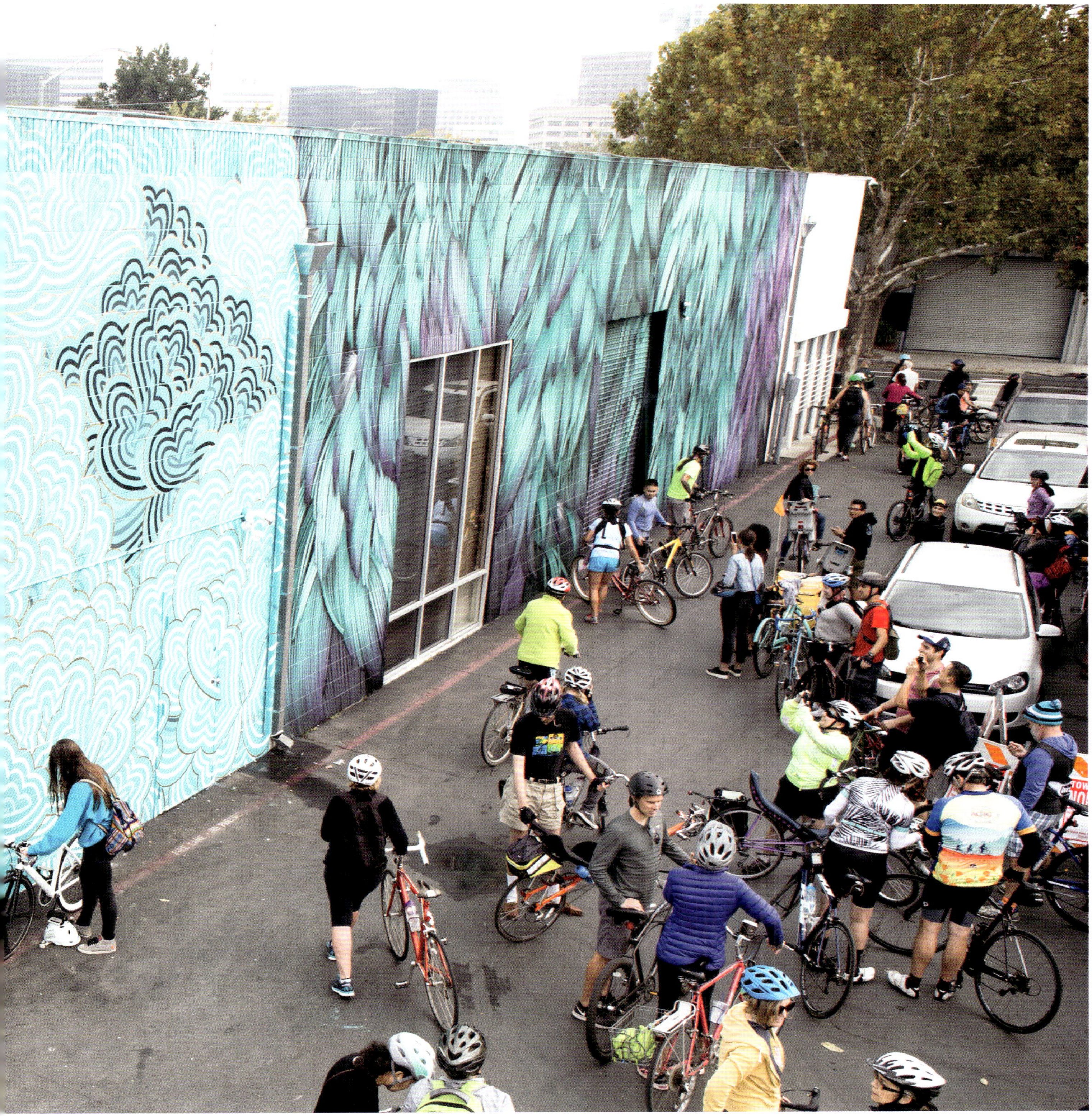

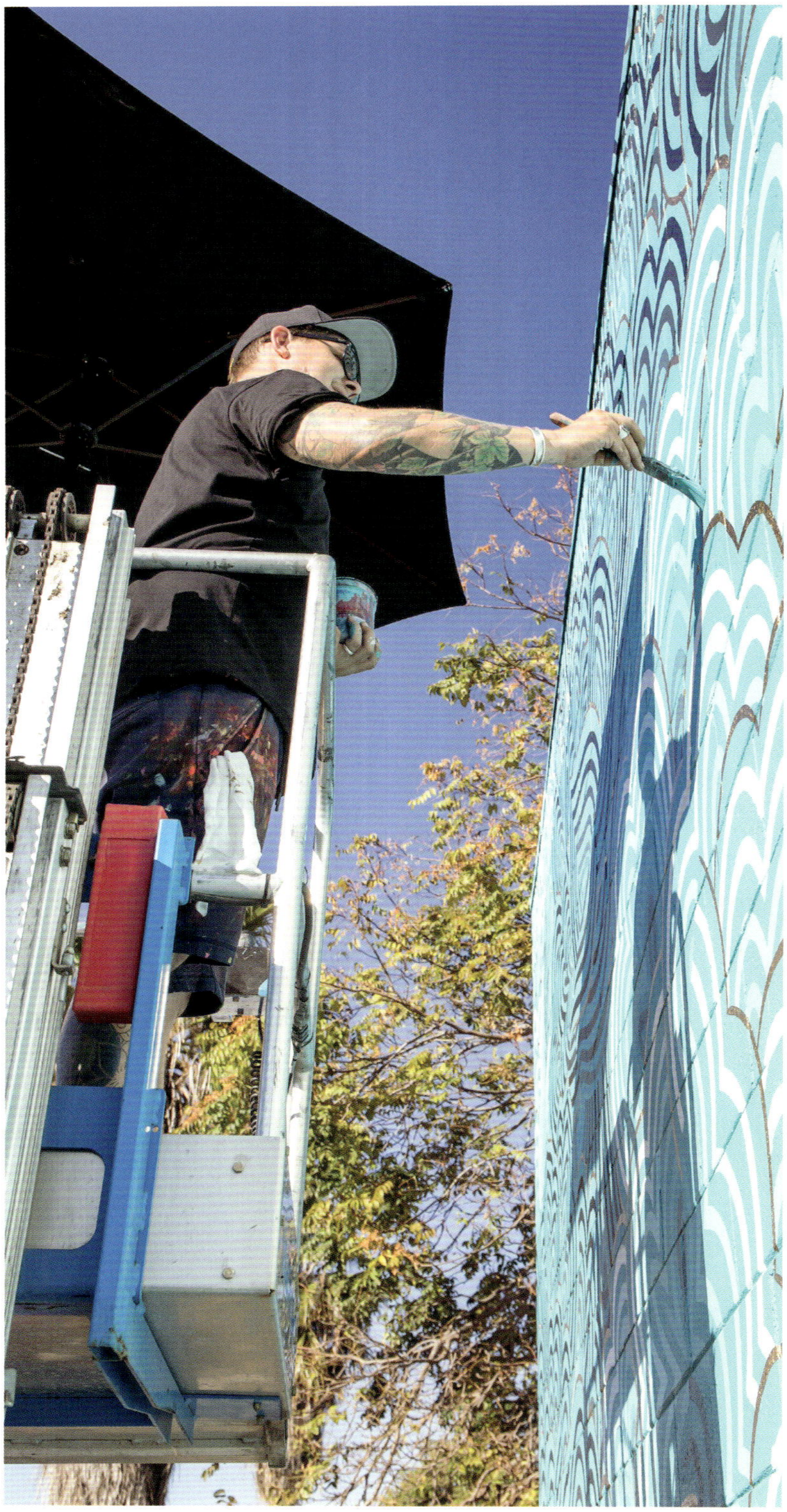

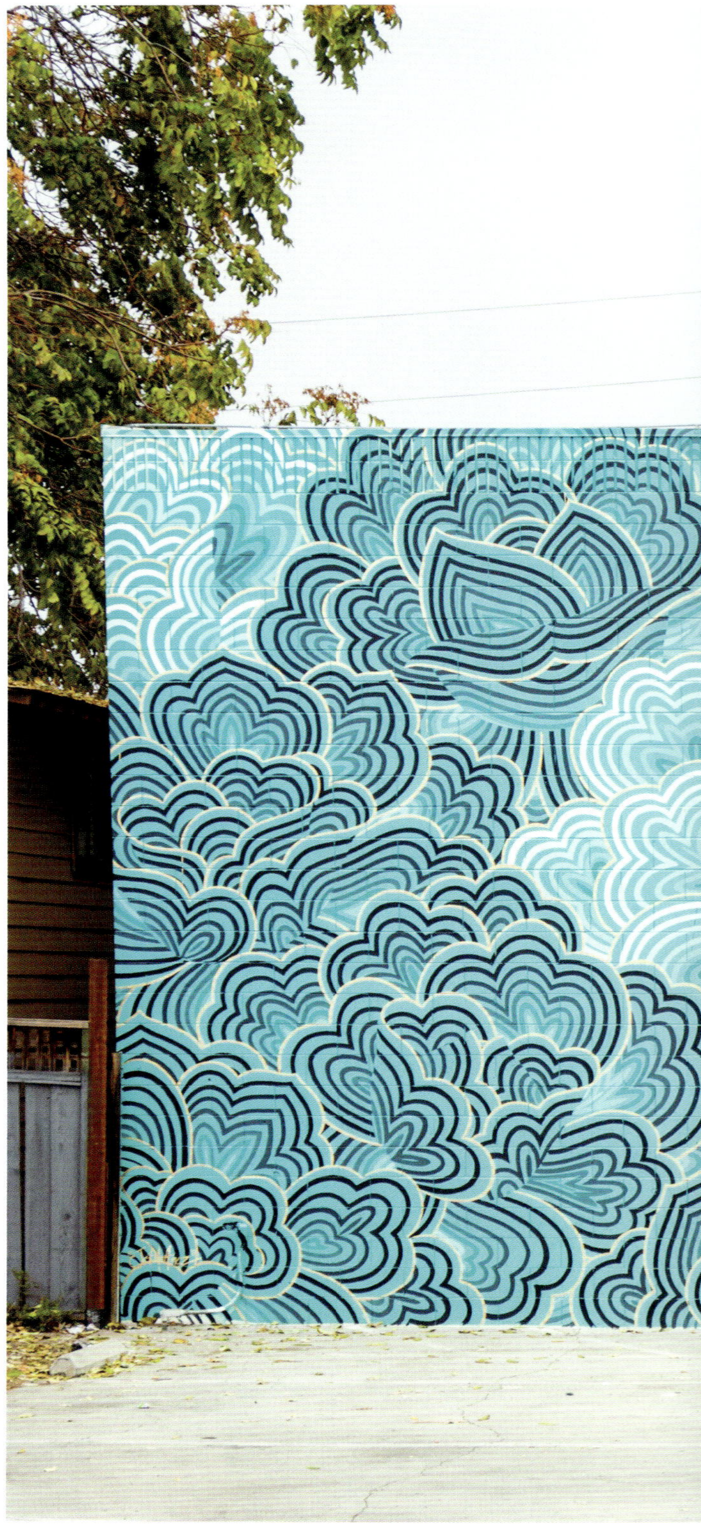

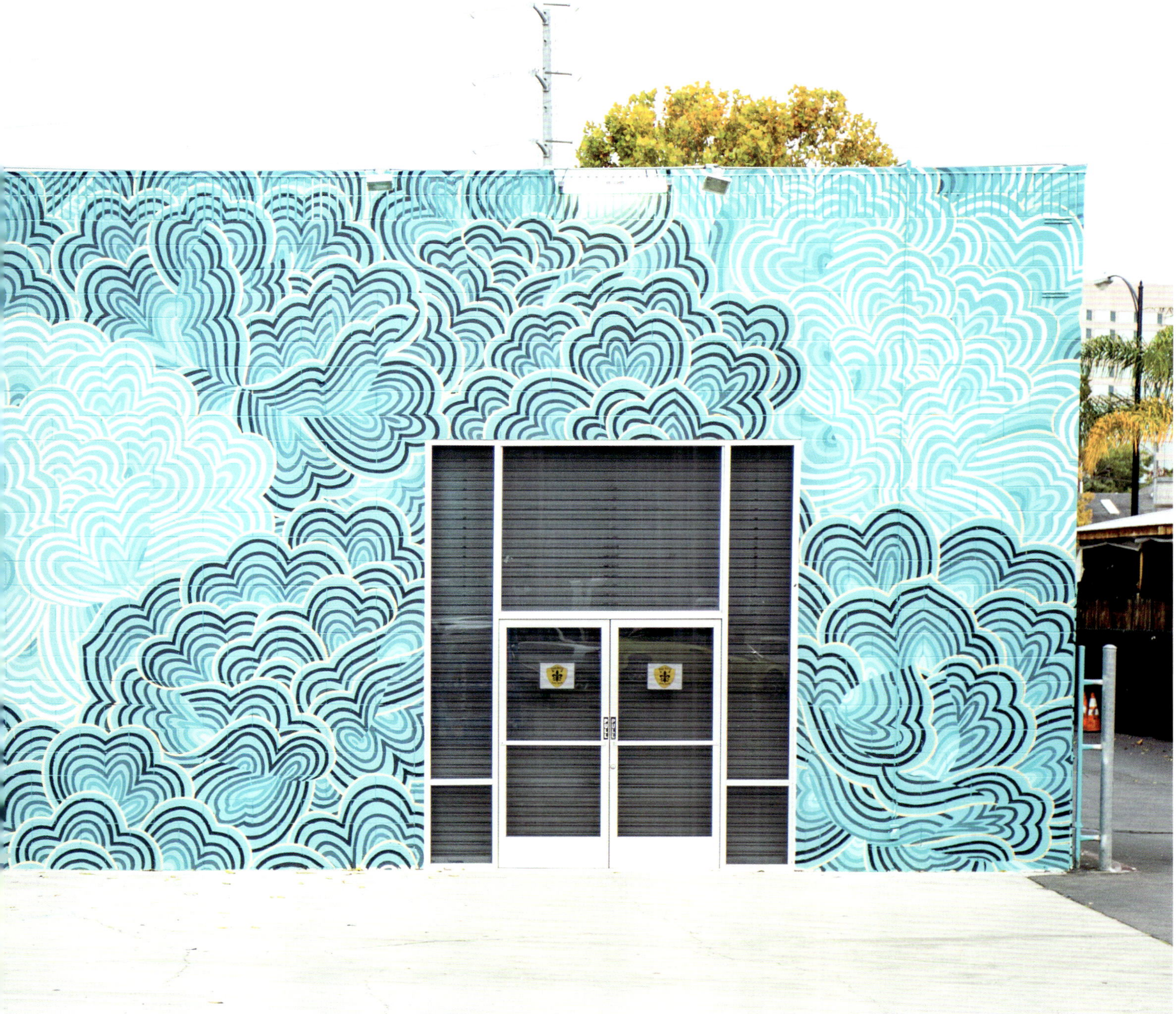

San Jose
2018

How & Nosm

@HOWNOSM

How & Nosm (Raoul and Davide Perre) are identical twin brothers known for their large scale murals that adorn city walls around the globe. The red, black, and white-based imagery with the addition of grey and pink gradients is instantly recognizable and commands attention through the impressive size and the intricate detail.

The closeness between the brothers is inspiring. They finish one another's sentences much like they continue their lines on mural walls and studio work in sync without hesitation. One ends and the other begins, their complicated yet effortless contours twist and turn like a three-dimensional maze. There is a flow present that is part of this process that allows their individuality to merge for a unified statement. Something that seems essential for artists who work on a large scale.

The aerosol can is paramount in all their public works and is the essential ingredient they use to raise this imagery to new levels. Precise execution and determination is what has driven them. Their style is essentially who they are as artists and people as a grittiness is hidden beneath levels of thoughtful design and bold form.

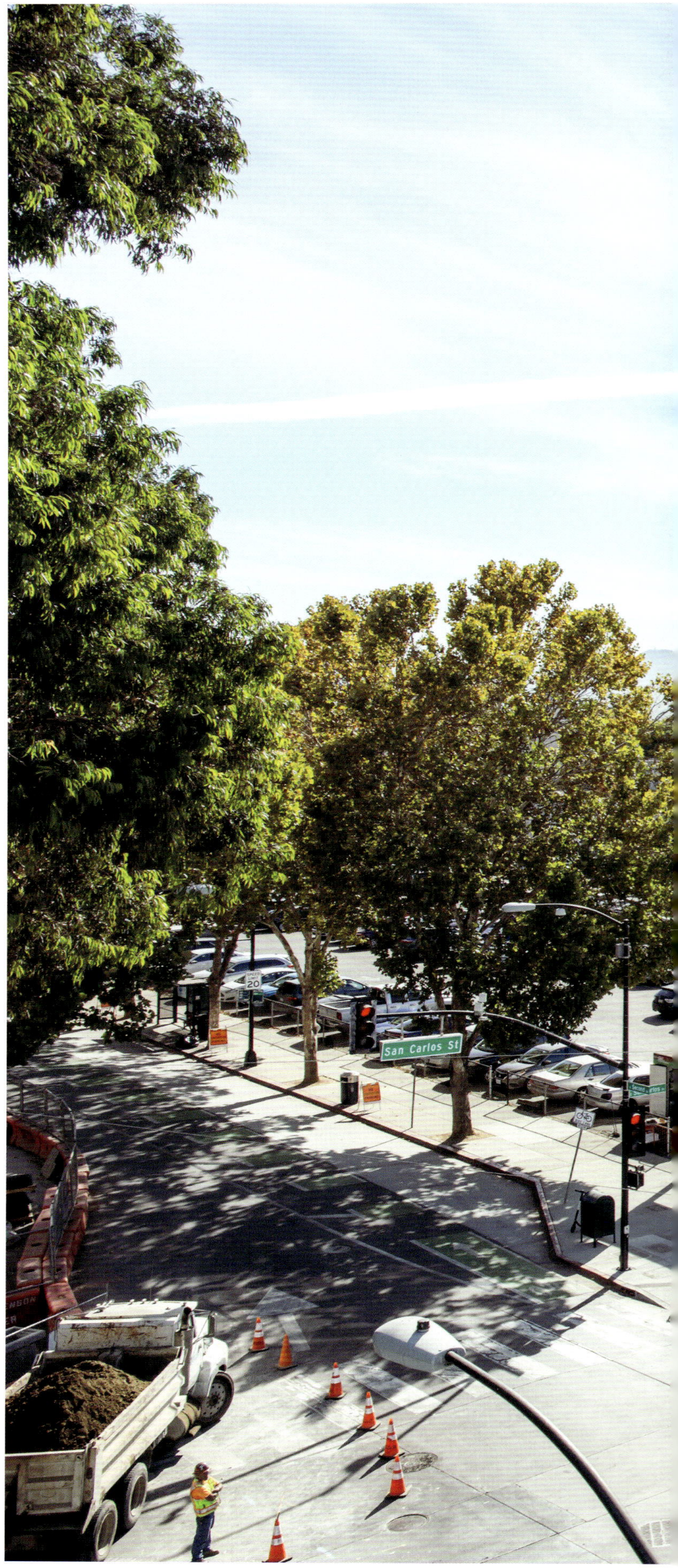

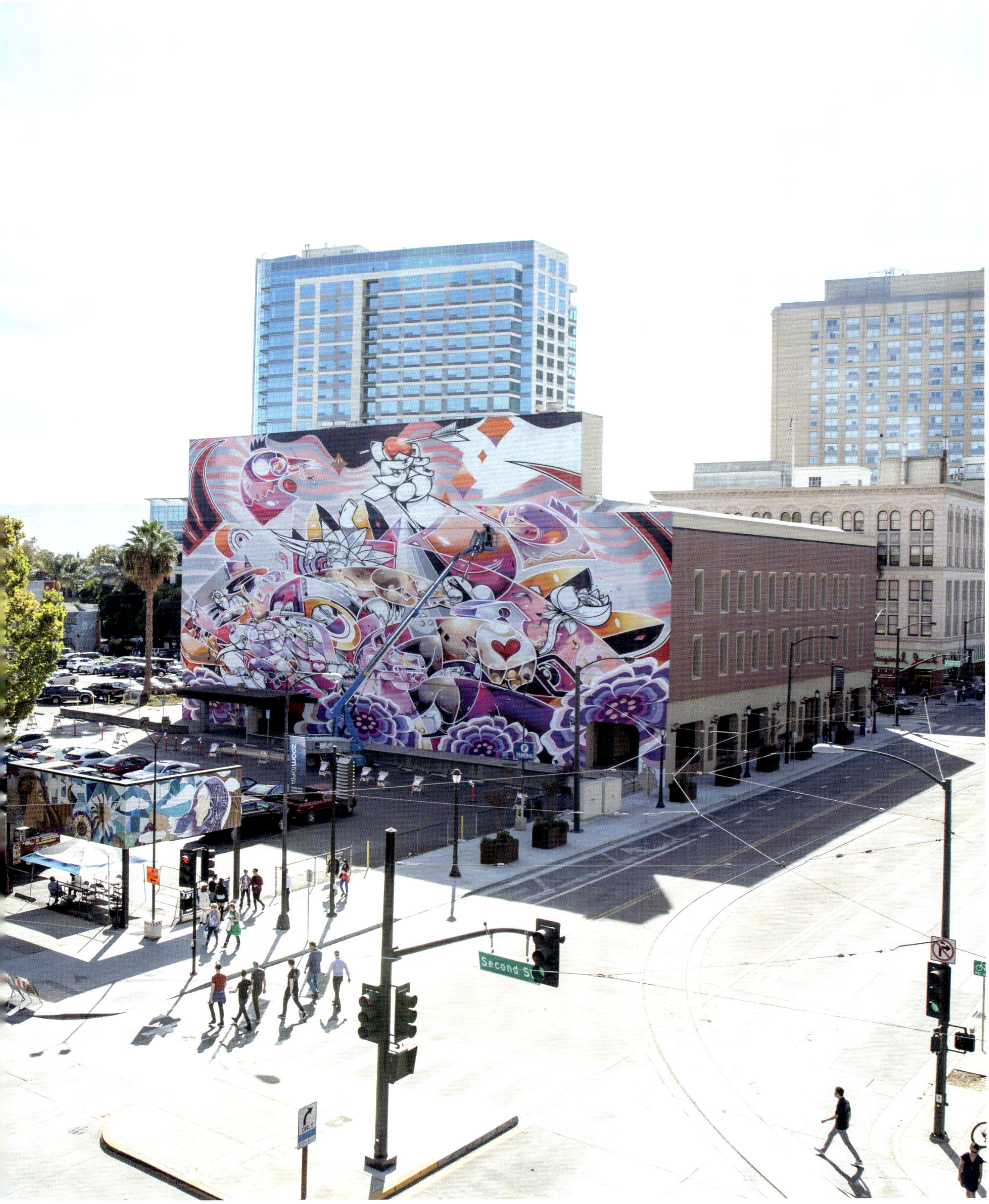

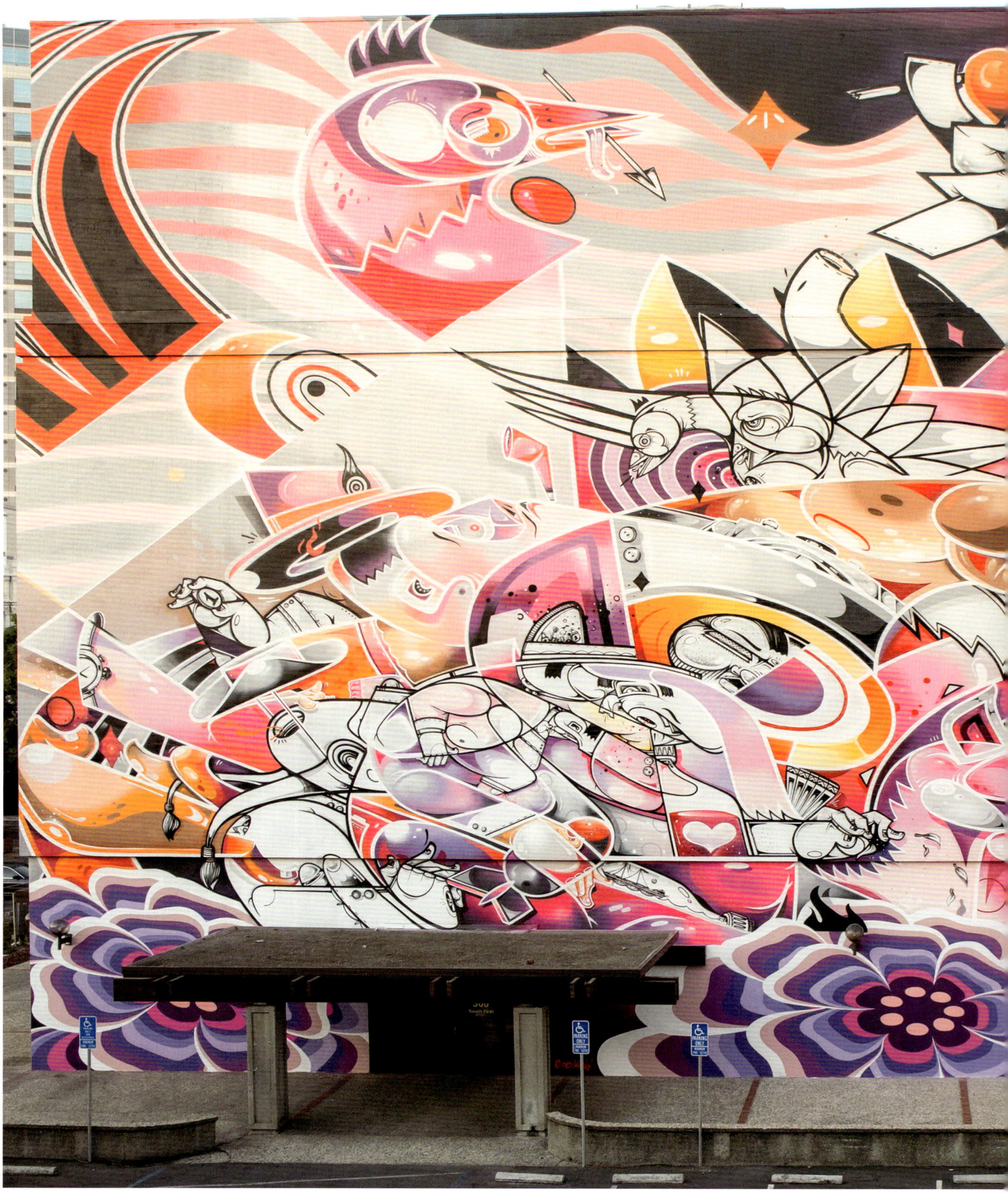

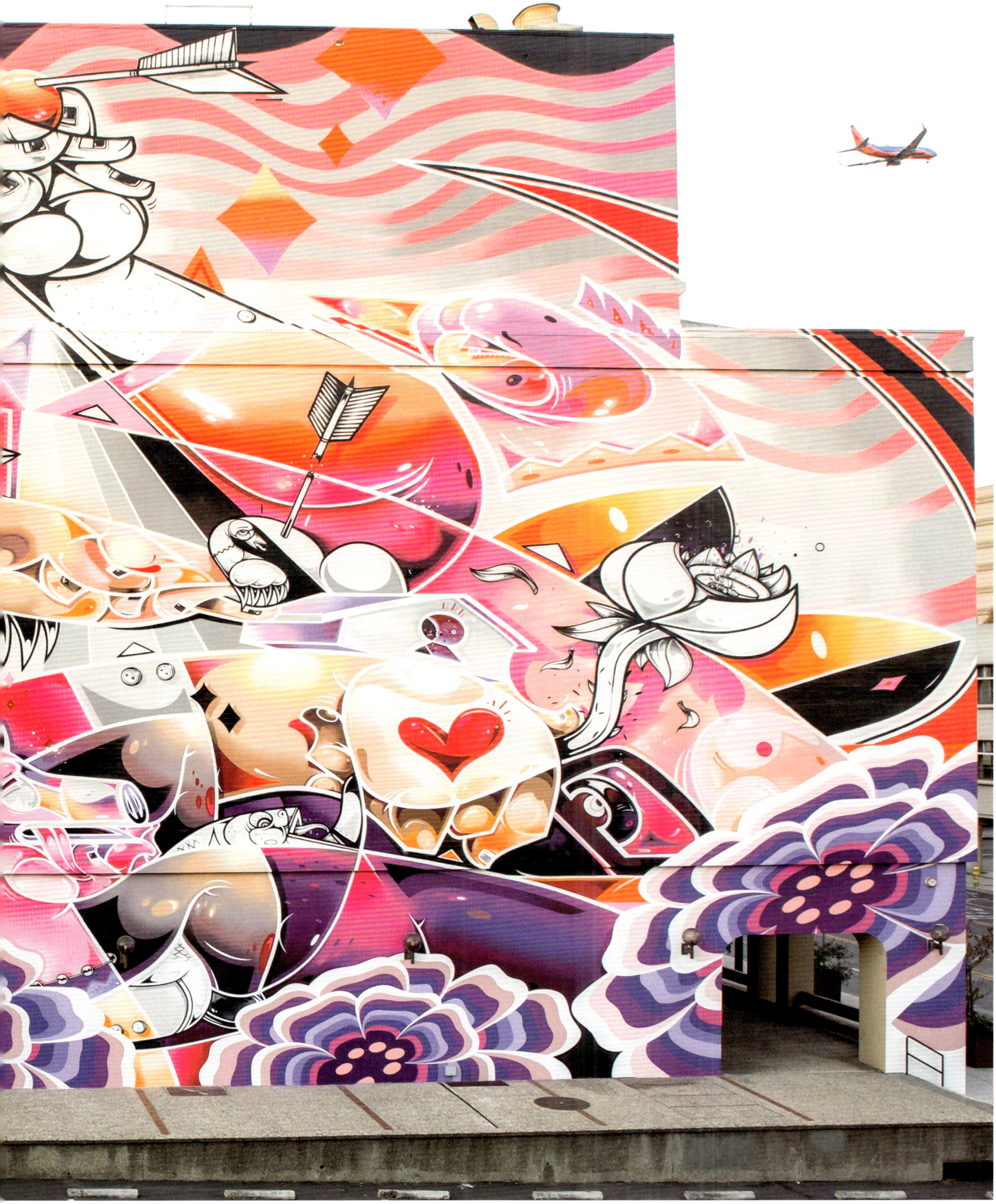

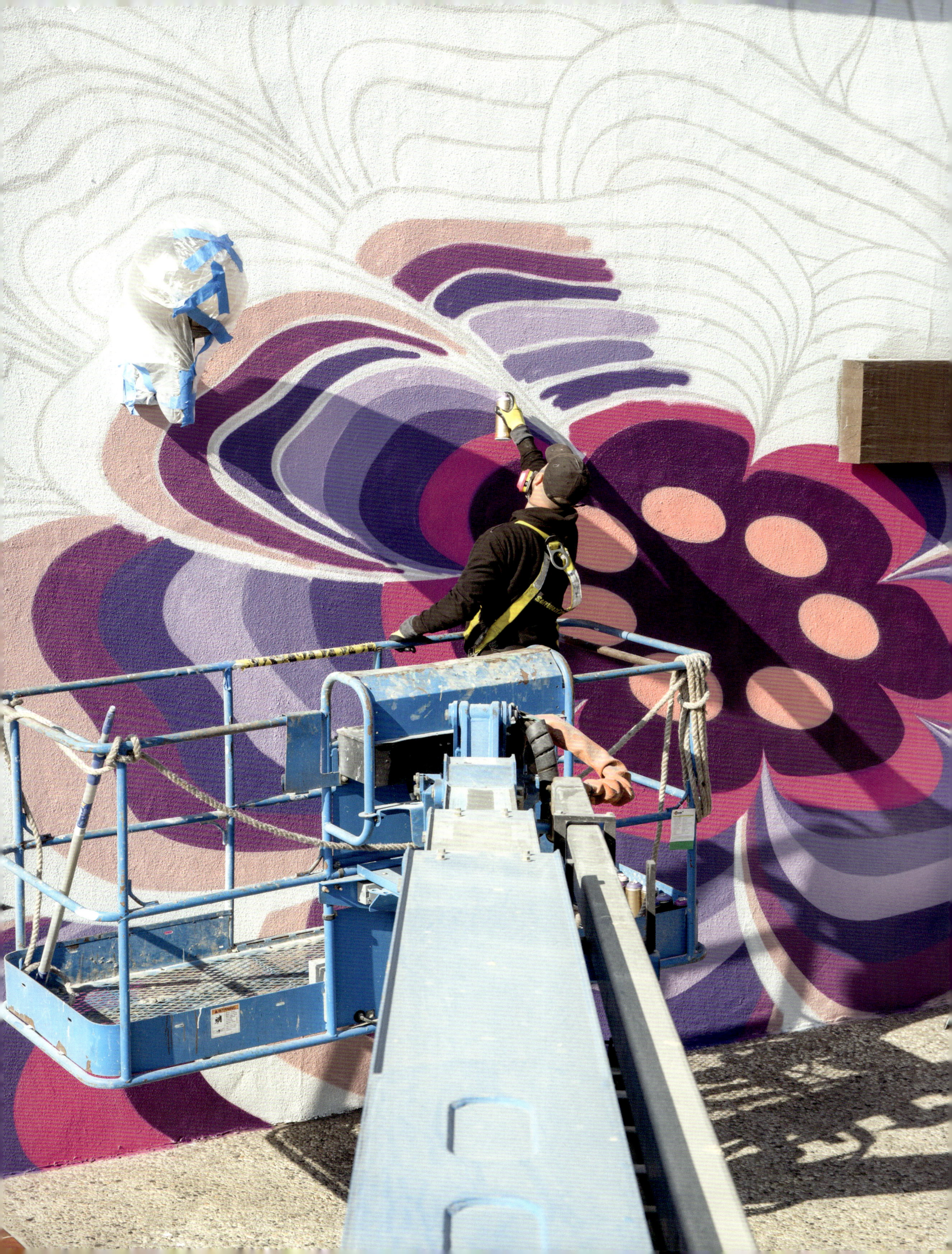

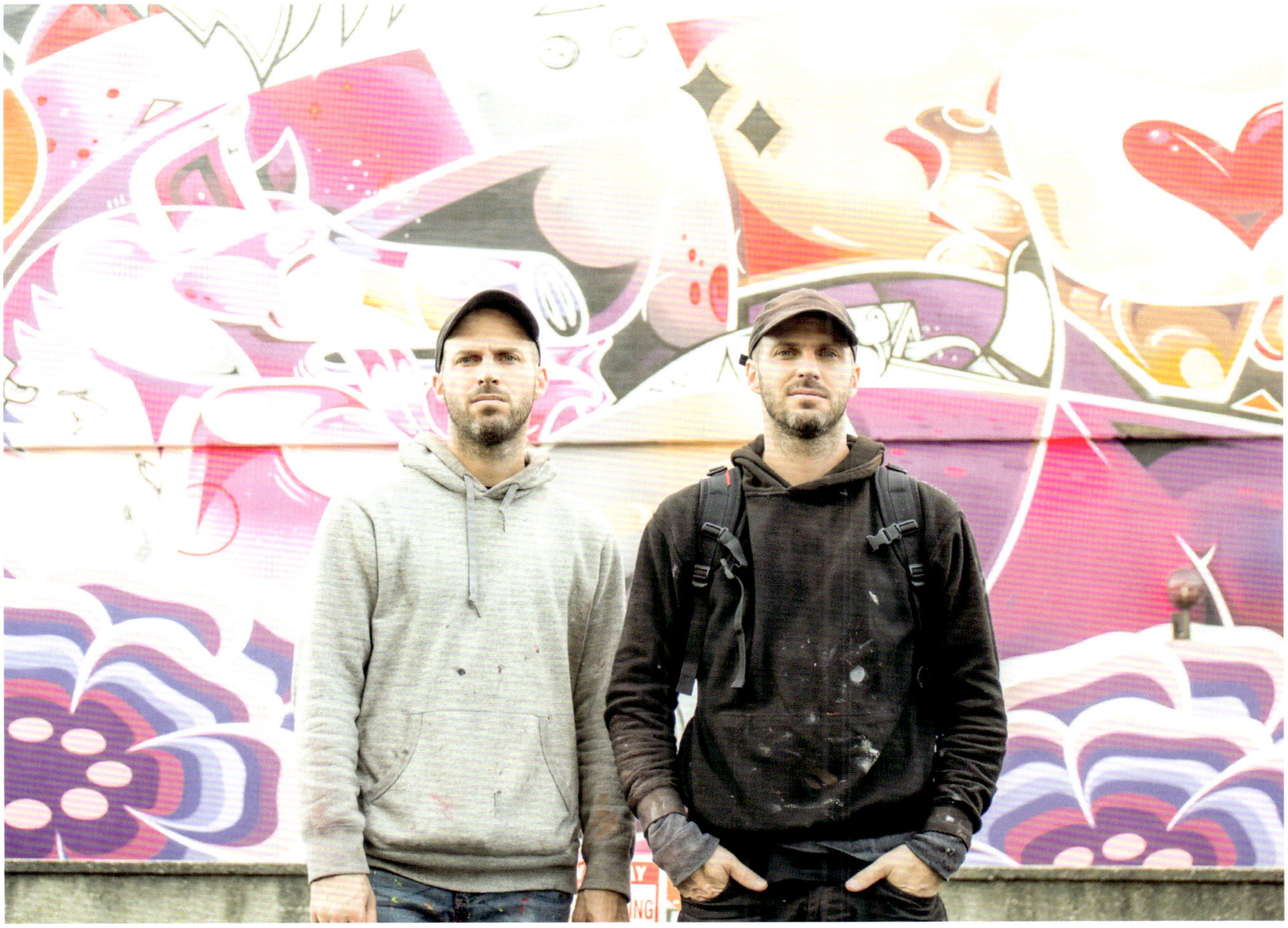

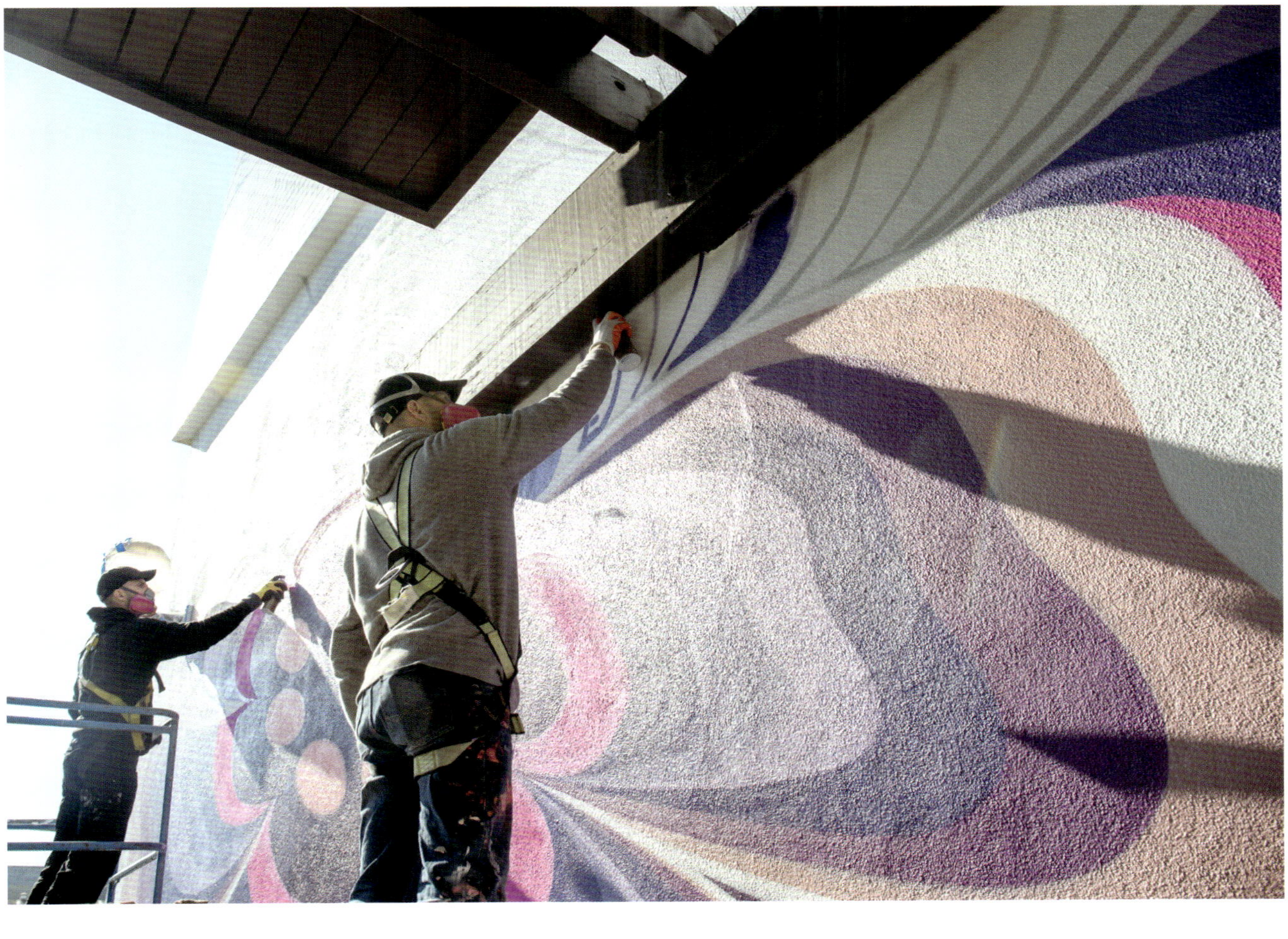

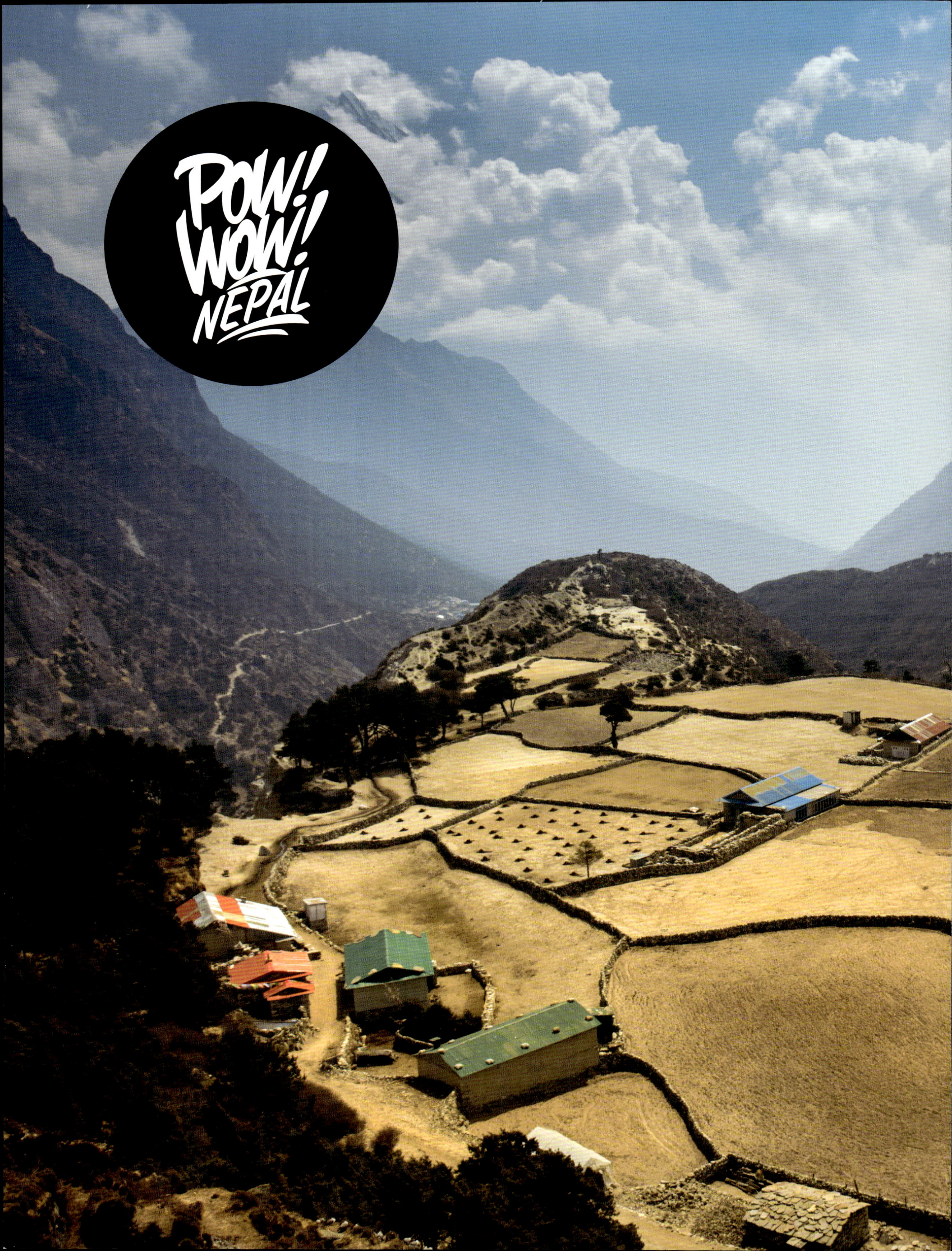
POW!
WOW!
NEPAL

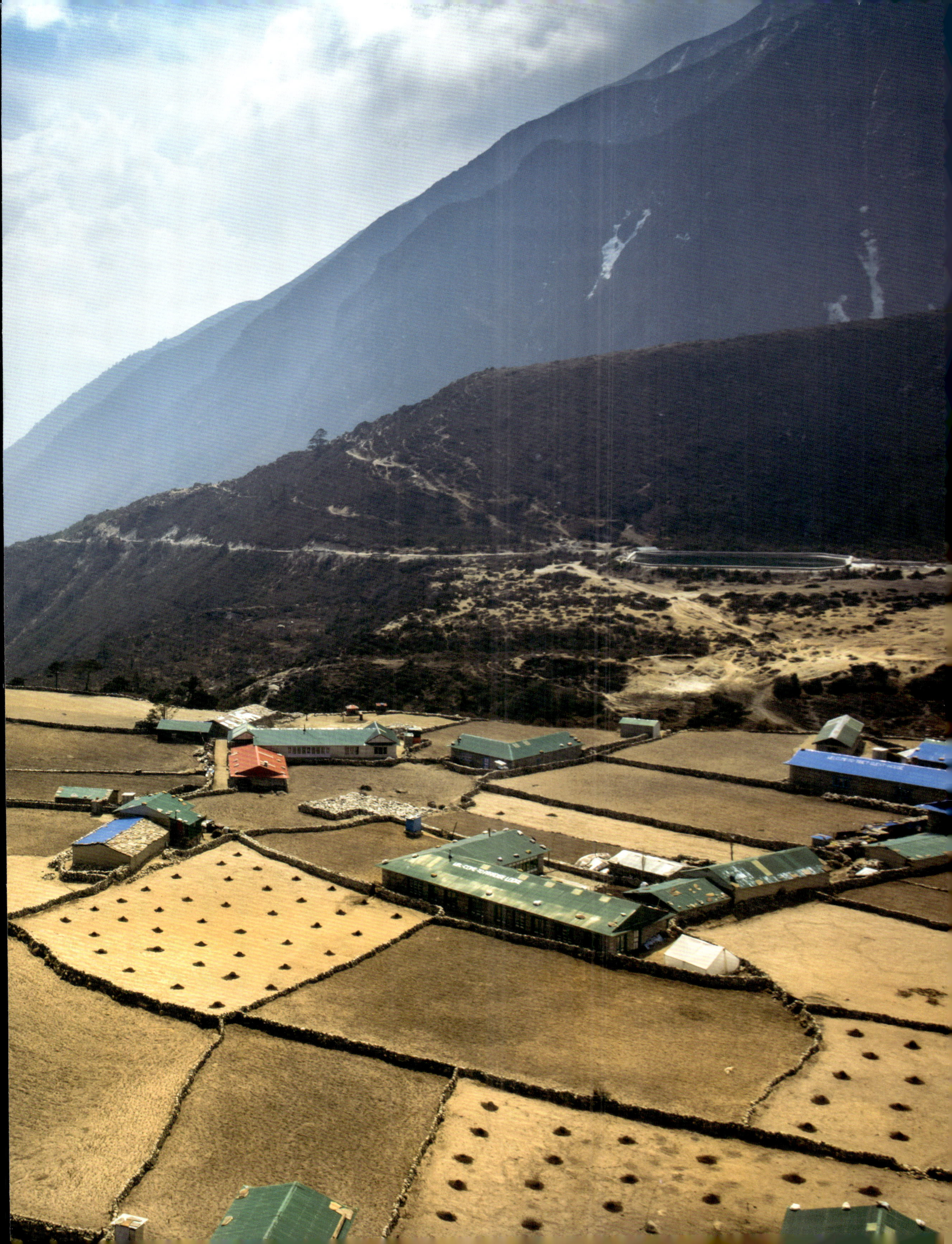

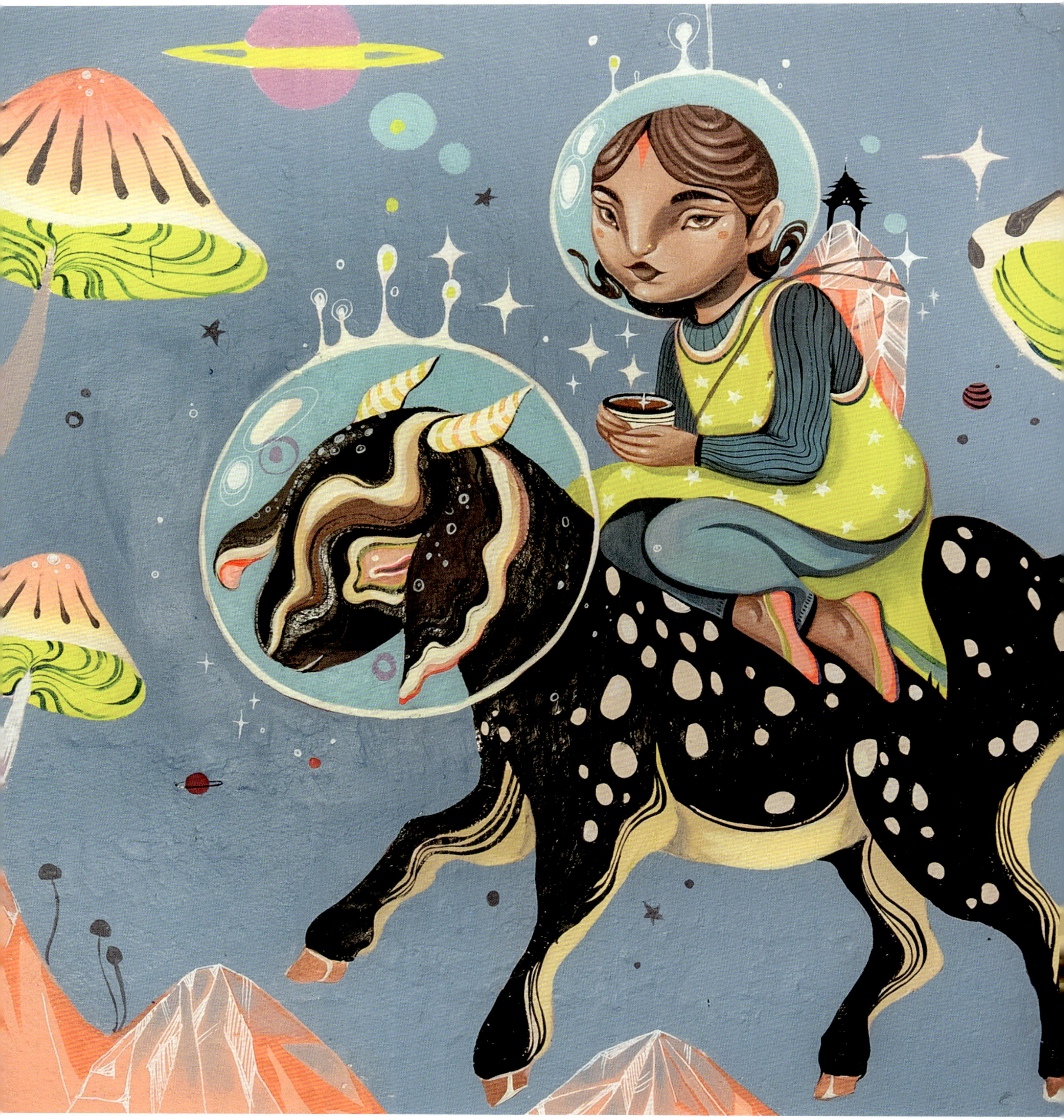

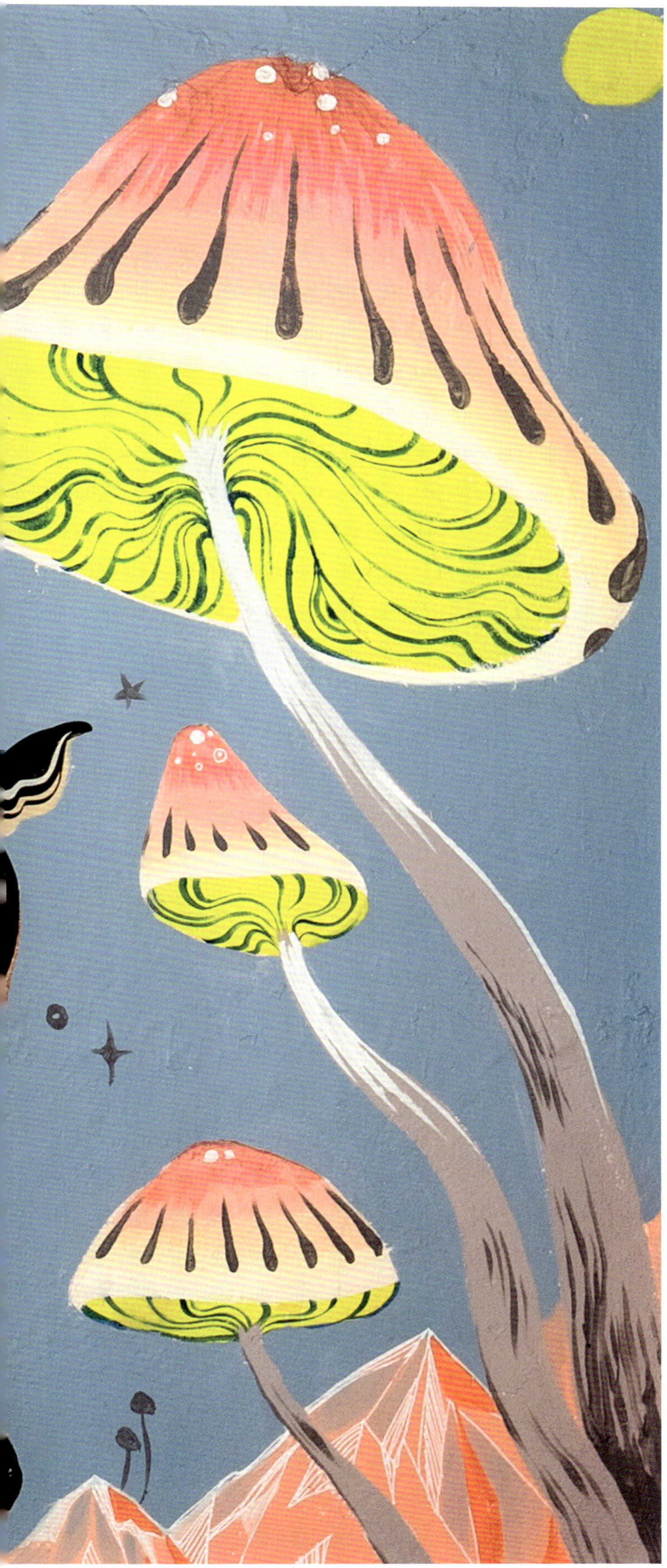

Nepal 2018

Lauren YS

@SQUID.LICKER

Lauren YS is a Bay Area artist whose work is influenced by multiple stages of focus, both geographically and in practice. With dynamic bouts in academics, literature and writing, teaching, illustration, and animation leading up to her arrival in the urban art sphere, the influences of these phases of her own career add up to a robust style of murals and fine art. Since graduating, Lauren has dedicated herself to creating large-scale works of public art that aim to bring a sense of vibrancy and wonder to every community she approaches. Lauren's work aims to create and populate a misfit wonderland in which imaginary heroines can address the absurdities of reality in the confines of a page or a wall. Influenced by dreams, mythology, death, comics, love, sex, psychedelia, animation, nostalgia, and her Asian-American heritage, Lauren's work is often geared towards pushing a narrative undertone and always has a fantastical aesthetic. Lauren has completed a residency and solo show at Nychos' Rabbit Eye Movement studio in Vienna, and has since shown work and live-painted at various international art festivals and institutions. Festivals include Art Basel Miami, Pow!Wow! Hawaii, PangeaSeed SeaWalls (New Zealand), Wander and Wayfare SF, Colorado Crush. Outdoor and indoor mural locations include the World Trade Center in New York. She has shown work in galleries nationwide and in International cities including Vienna, London, Auckland, Melbourne and Sydney.

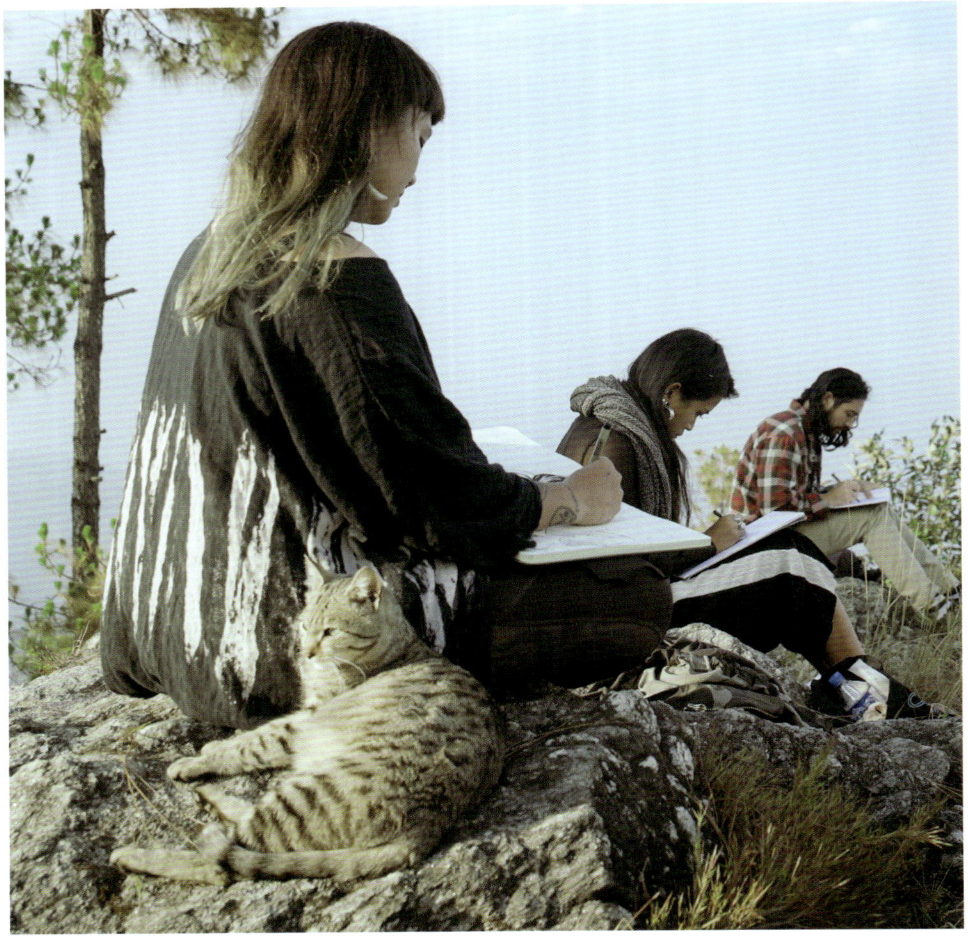

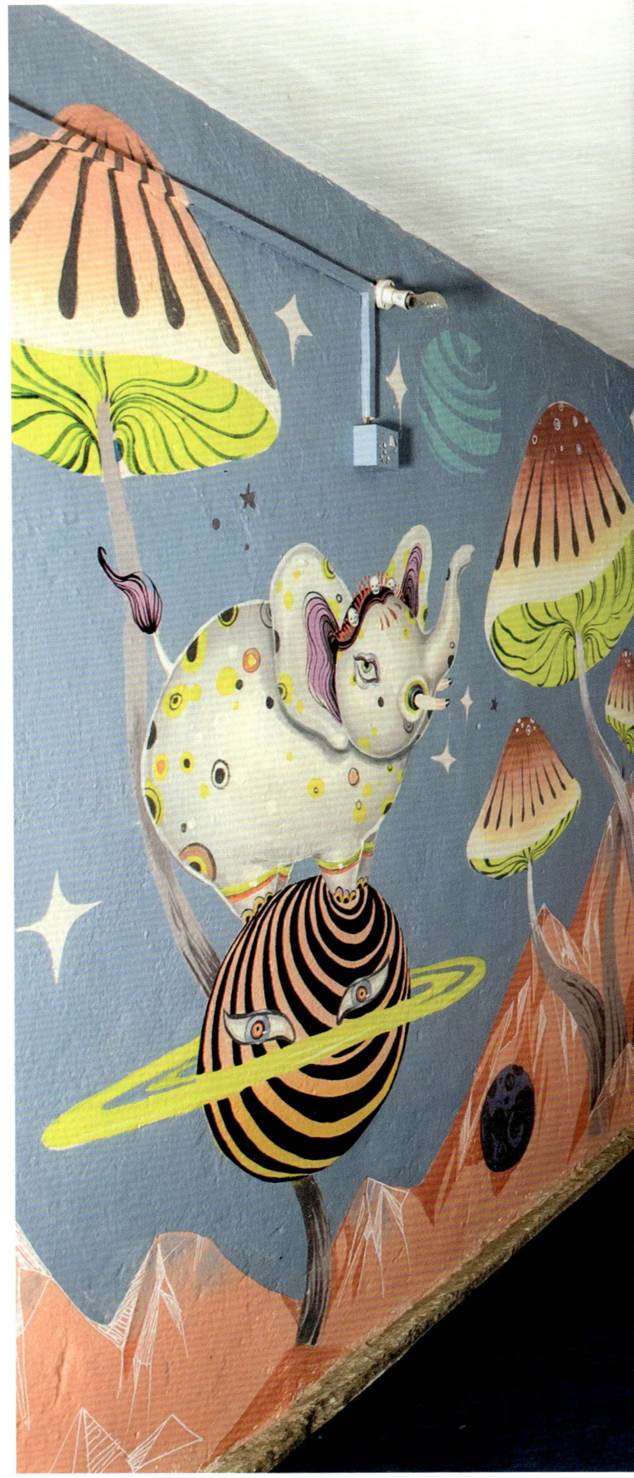

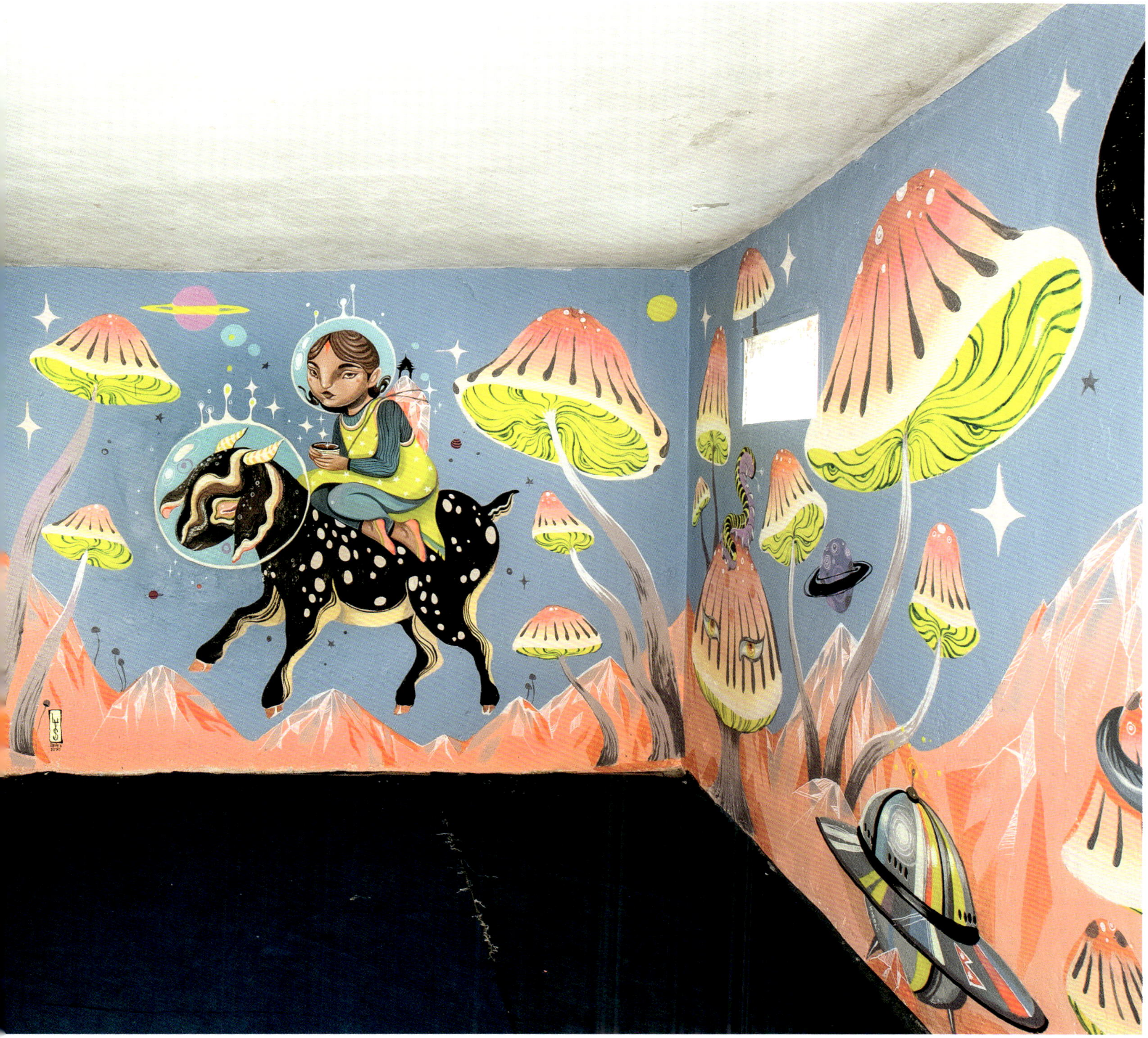

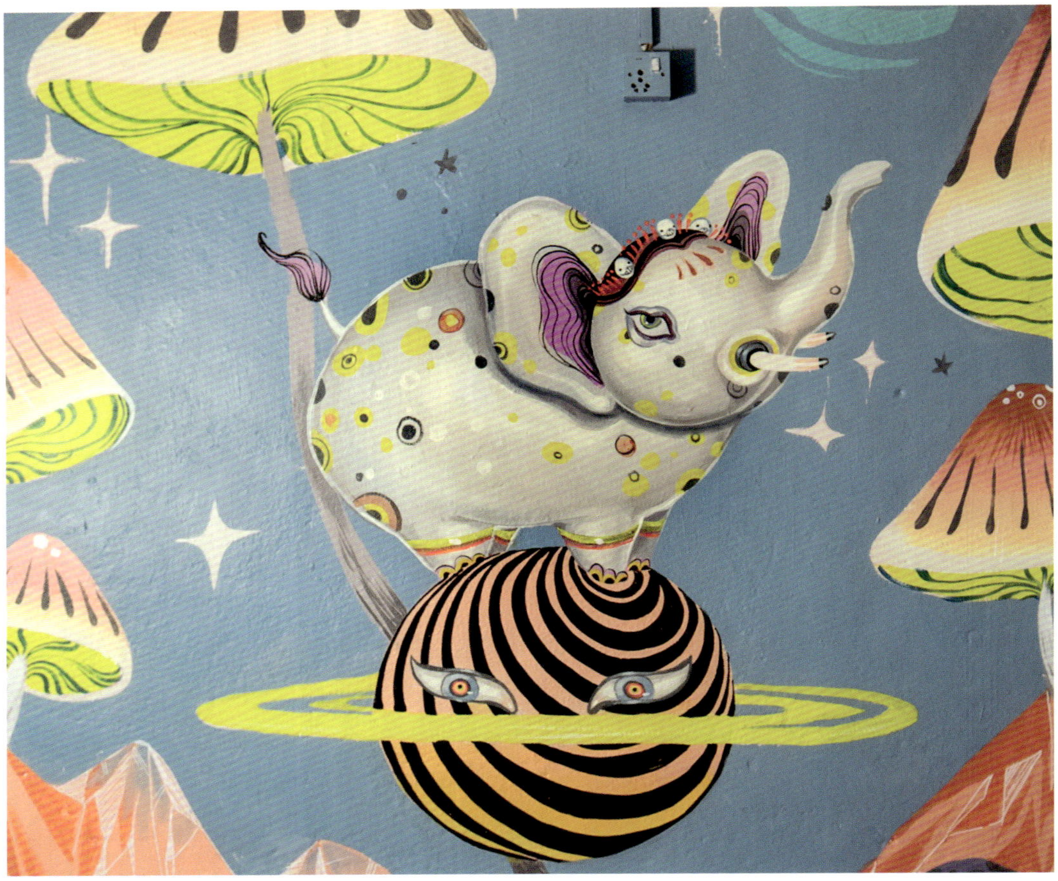

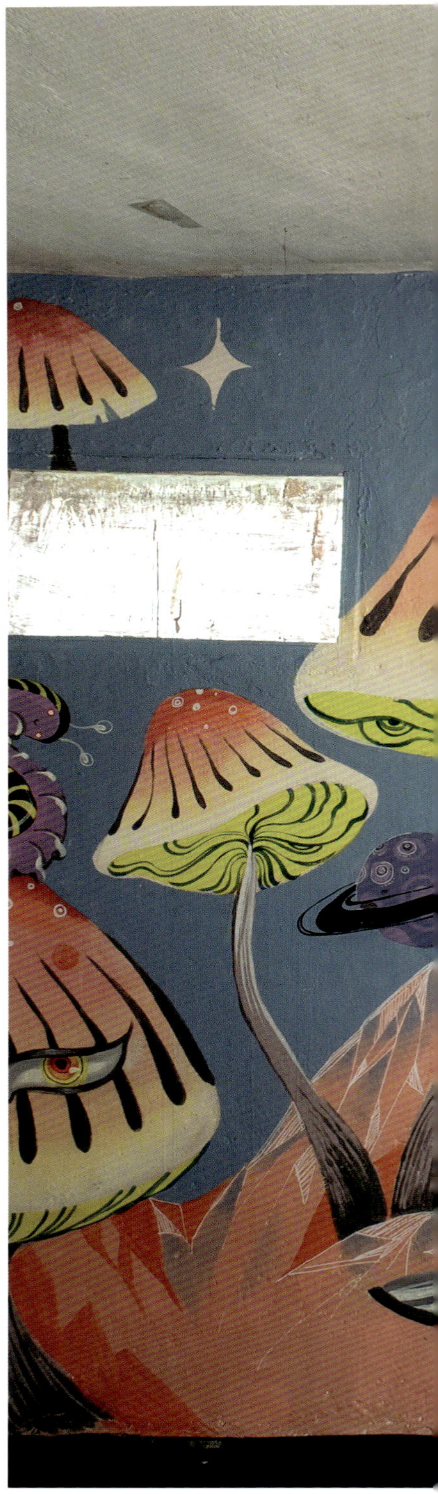

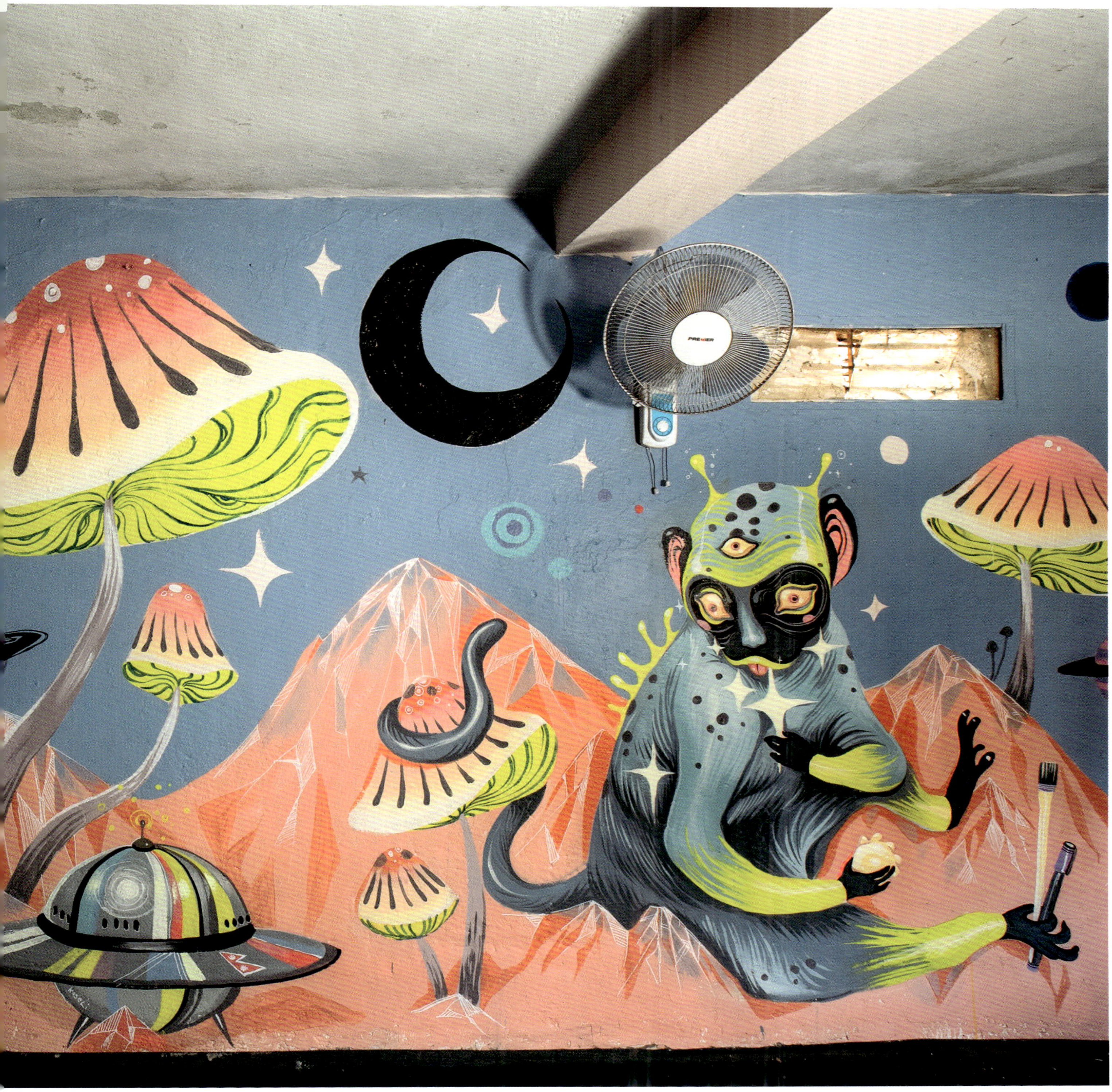

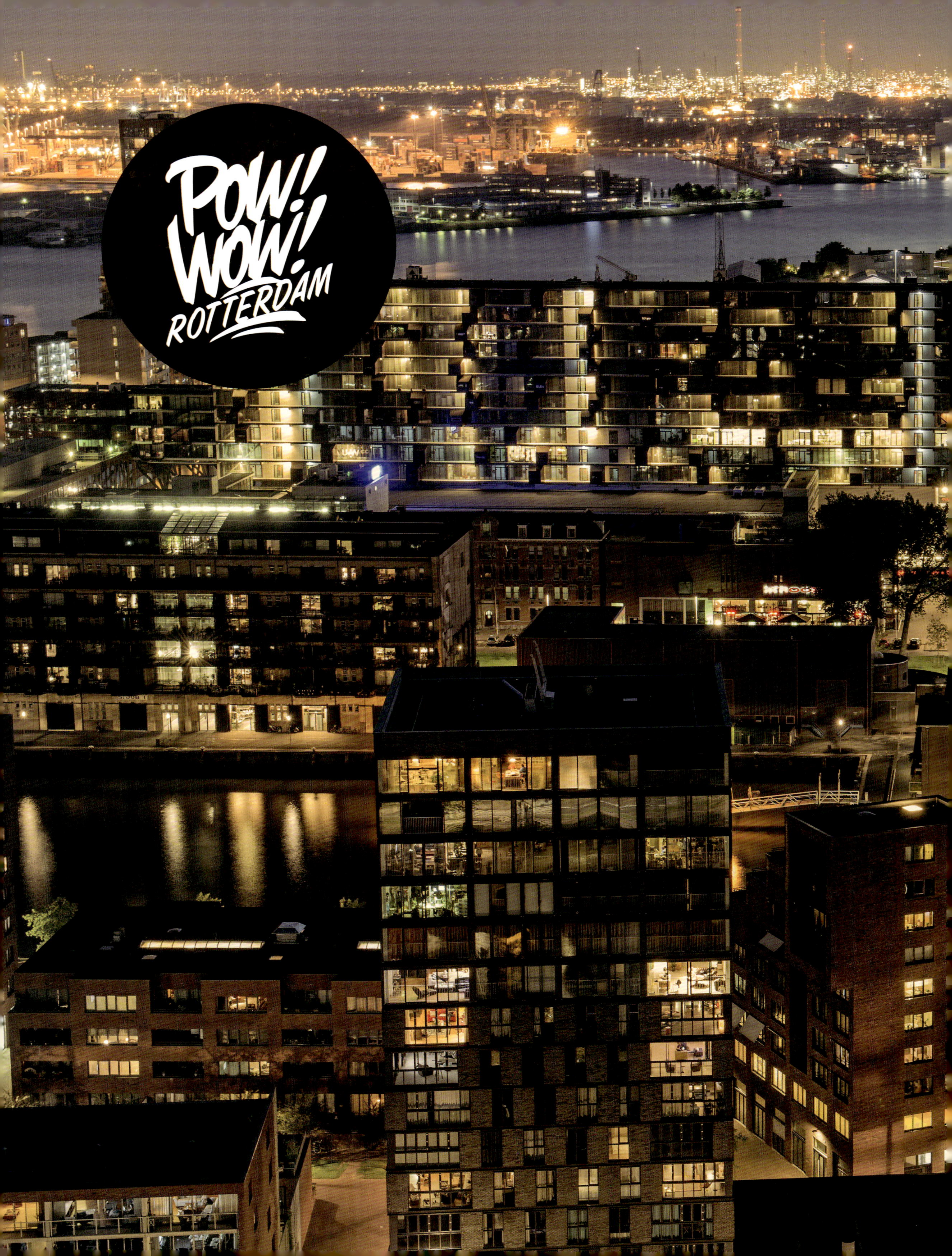
POW!
WOW!
ROTTERDAM

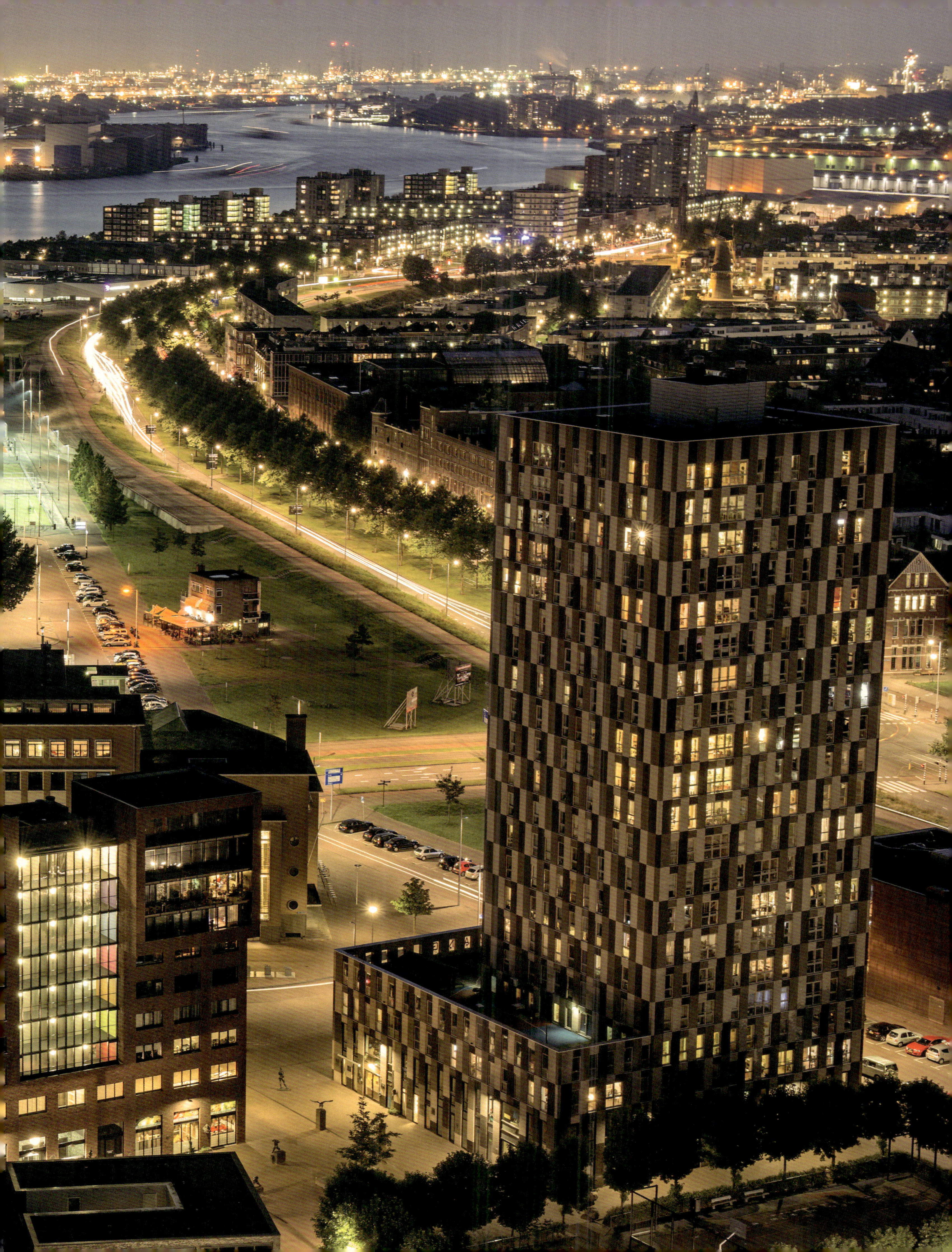

Rotterdam 2018

Super A

@MR.SUPER_A

Stefan Thelen's anti-superhero identity **Super A** is a Dutch artist who uses traditional painting technique and a knack for design to create compositions that manipulate familiar iconography into mind-bending and inquisitive pieces. His alter-ego, Super A is the filter with which the life and observations of Stefan Thelen are distilled down and turn into inspiration. All of his work evolves out of personal experiences or thoughts that grow into concepts which tightrope between fiction and nonfiction. Super A is a mystery that leans on the art doing most of the talking for Stefan Thelen, taking the viewer into a wonderland walking down a yellow brick road in which Thelen's figurative and modern surrealist compositions are providing playful puzzles to decipher.

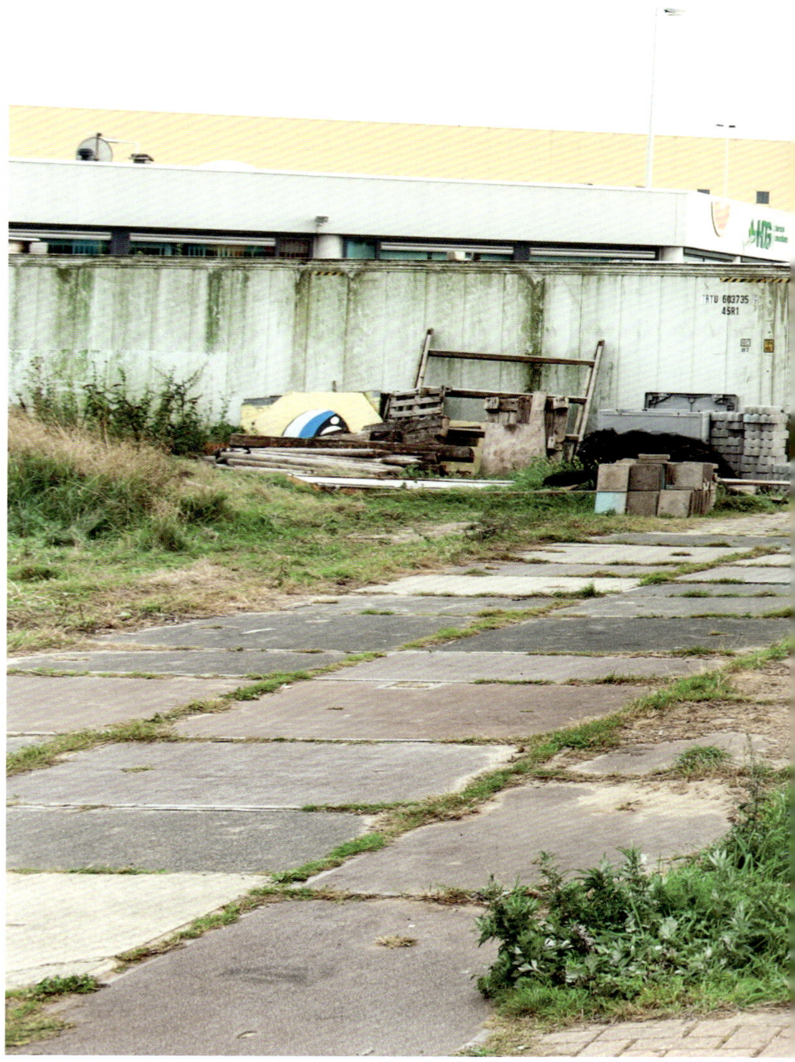

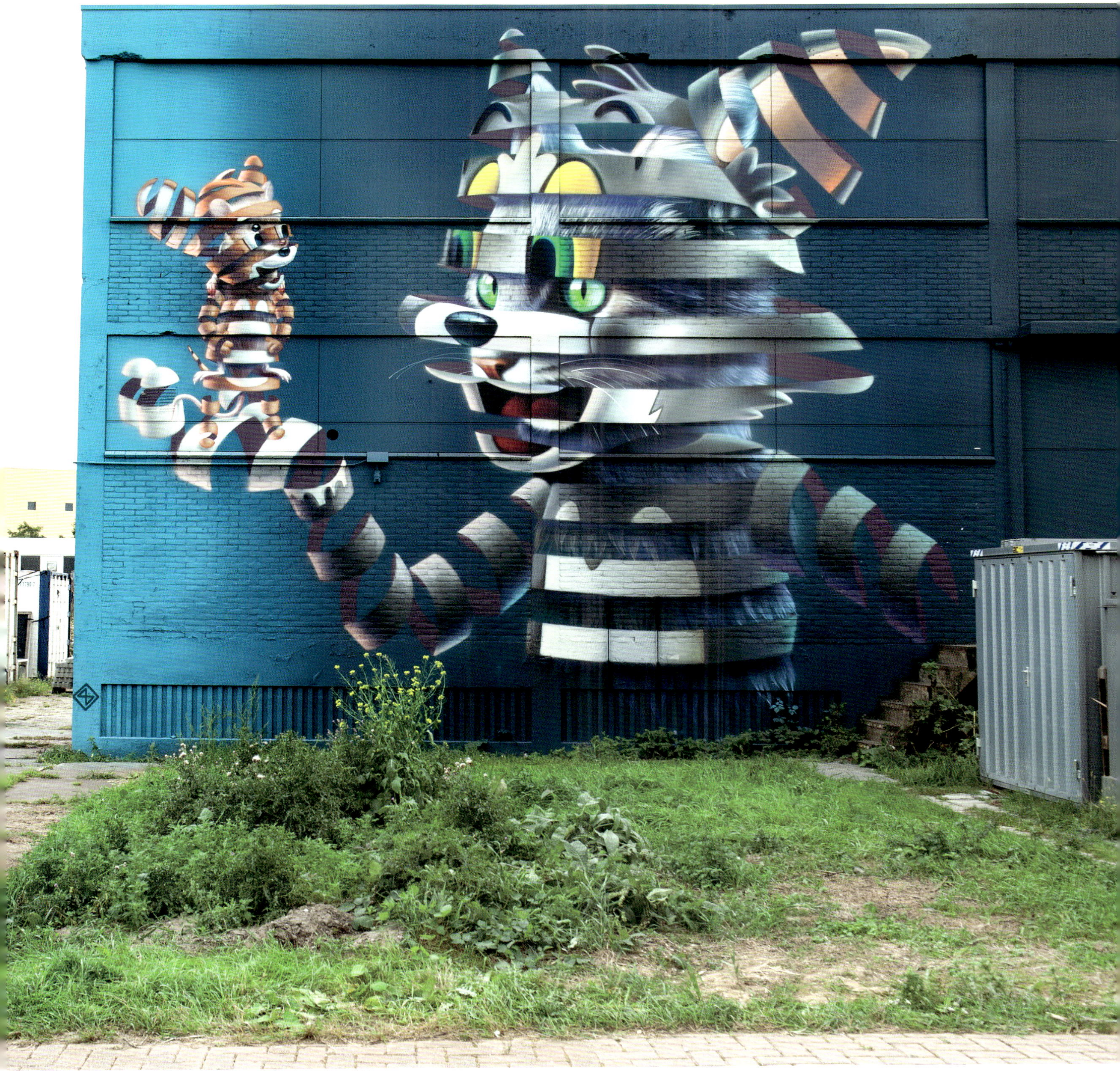

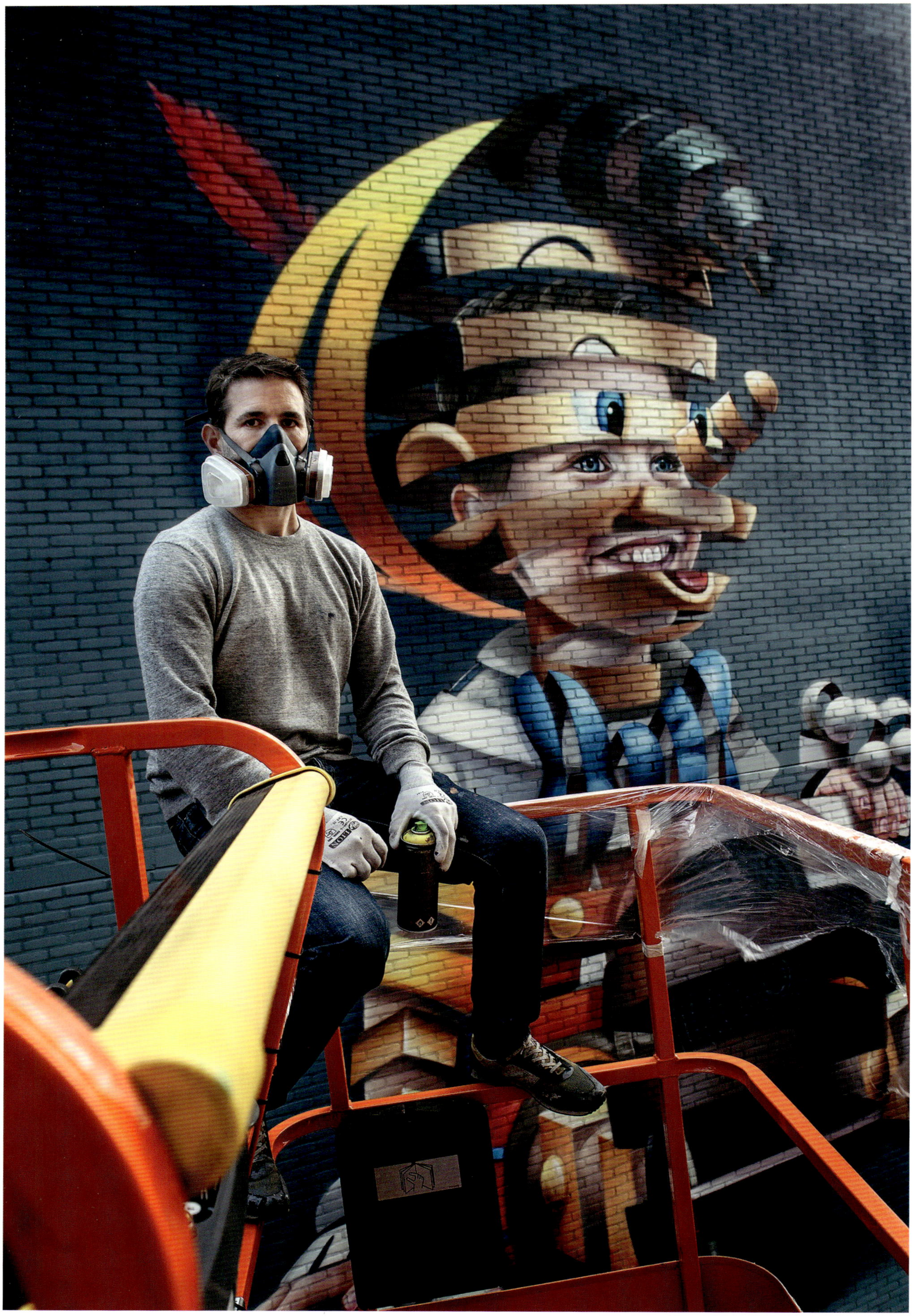

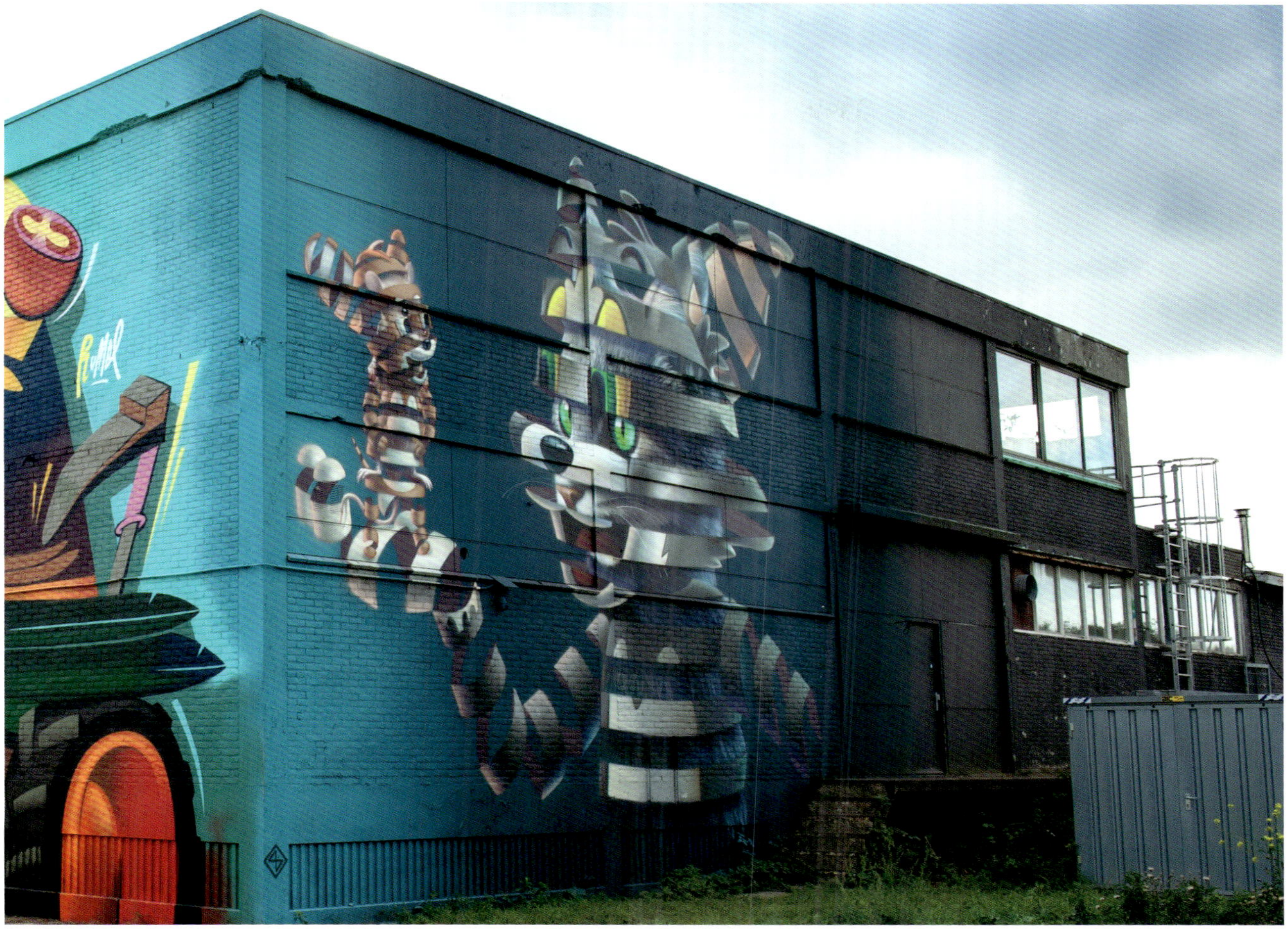

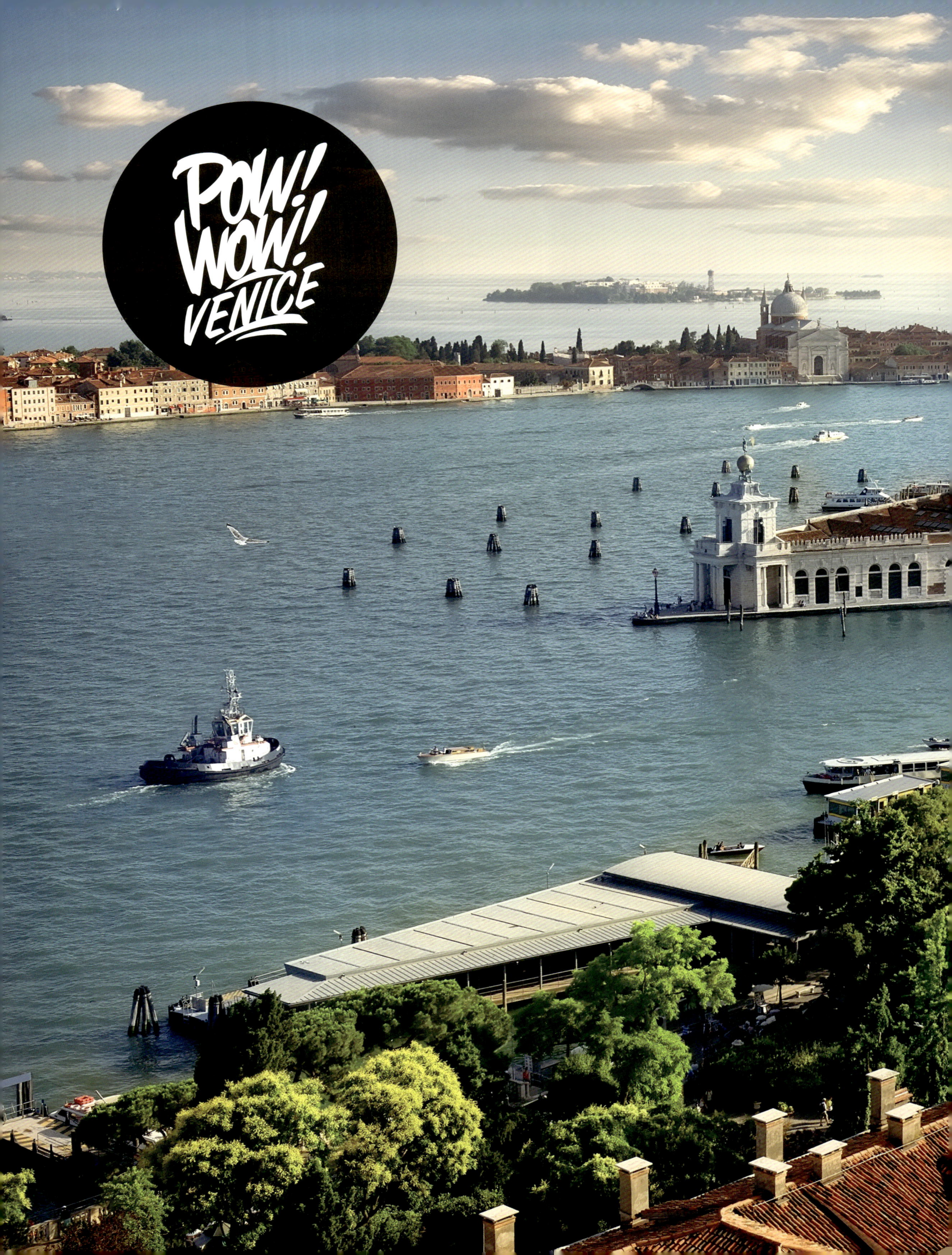
POW!
WOW!
VENICE

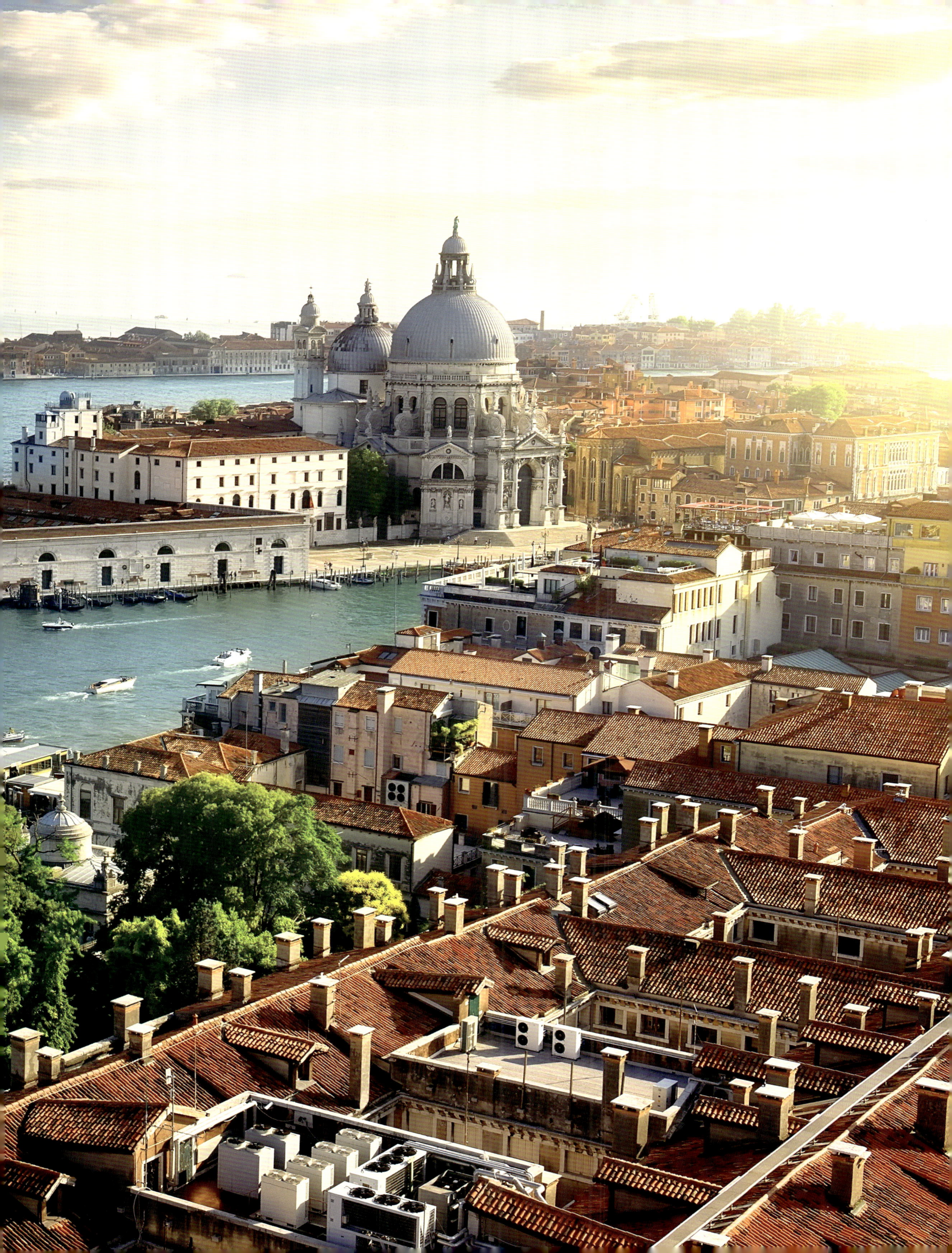

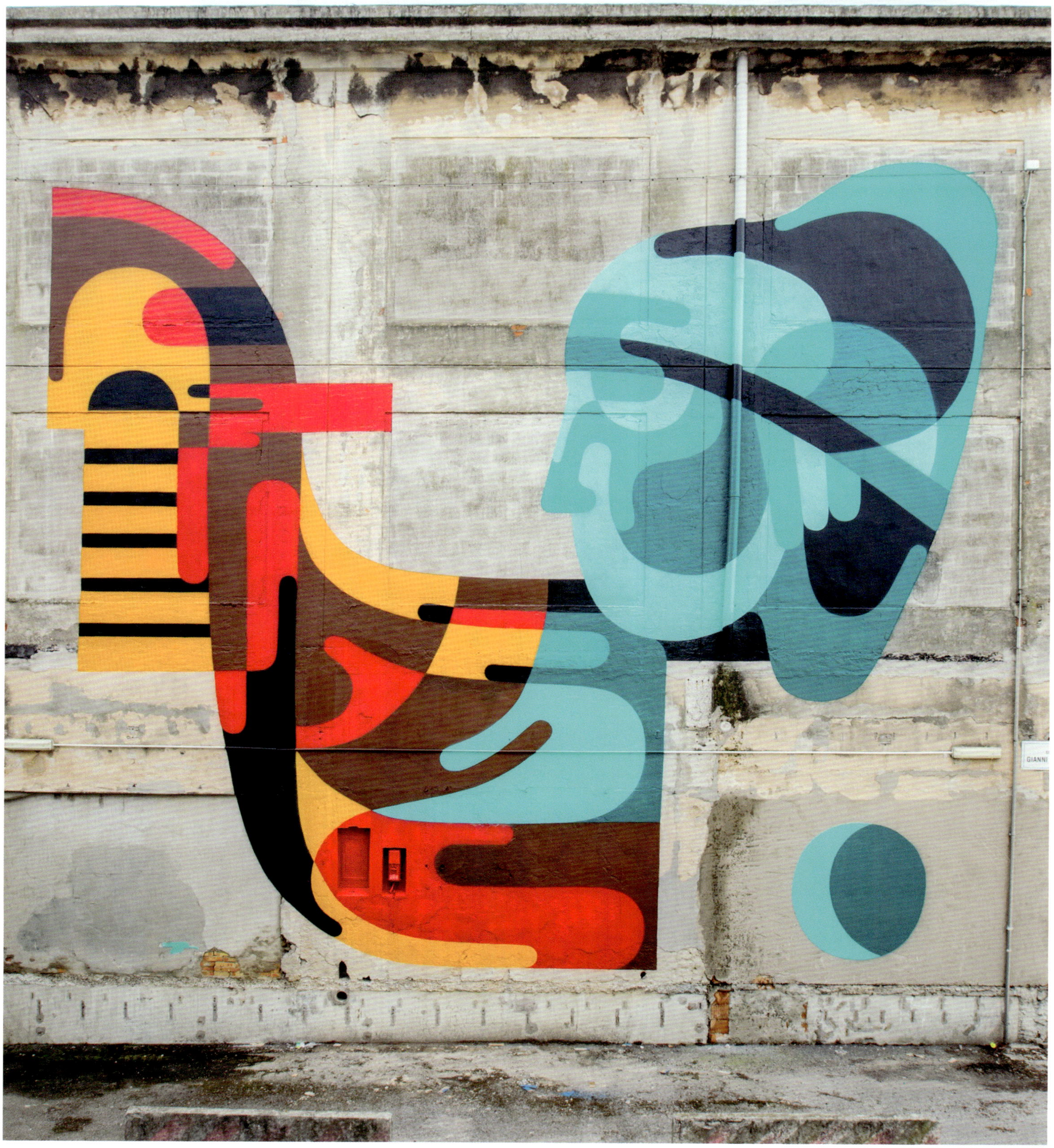
GIANNI

Reka

@REKAONE

James Reka is a young contemporary Australian artist based in Berlin, Germany. His origins lie in the alleyways and train lines of Melbourne's inner-suburbs where he spent over a decade refining his now-emblematic aesthetic. His character work has come to represent the beginnings of a new style of street art: clean, unique and not necessarily on the street (much to his mother's joy). Surrealist, abstracted creatures emerge from the depths of Reka's mind, communicating through strong lines, dynamic movement and bold colors. Theses figures haunt the laneways over three continents, clambering up brick walls and giving the urban environment a literal fresh coat of paint. Their personalities mirror those of their often-decrepit metropolitan context, opening a dialogue between the viewer and their surroundings.

Reka has had solo shows in Denmark and Melbourne, has exhibited at the Royal West of England Academy (RWA) in Bristol and has participated in Stolen Space's 7th Anniversary Group Show in London as well as pieces appearing in New York, Munich, Denver and Cologne exhibitions. On the streets, his characters adorn the walls of cities around the world from Japan to Milan and Paris to Brooklyn. Reka's works have recently been acquisitioned by the National Gallery of Australia for their permanent collection, cementing his place as one of Australia's most respected contemporary street artists.

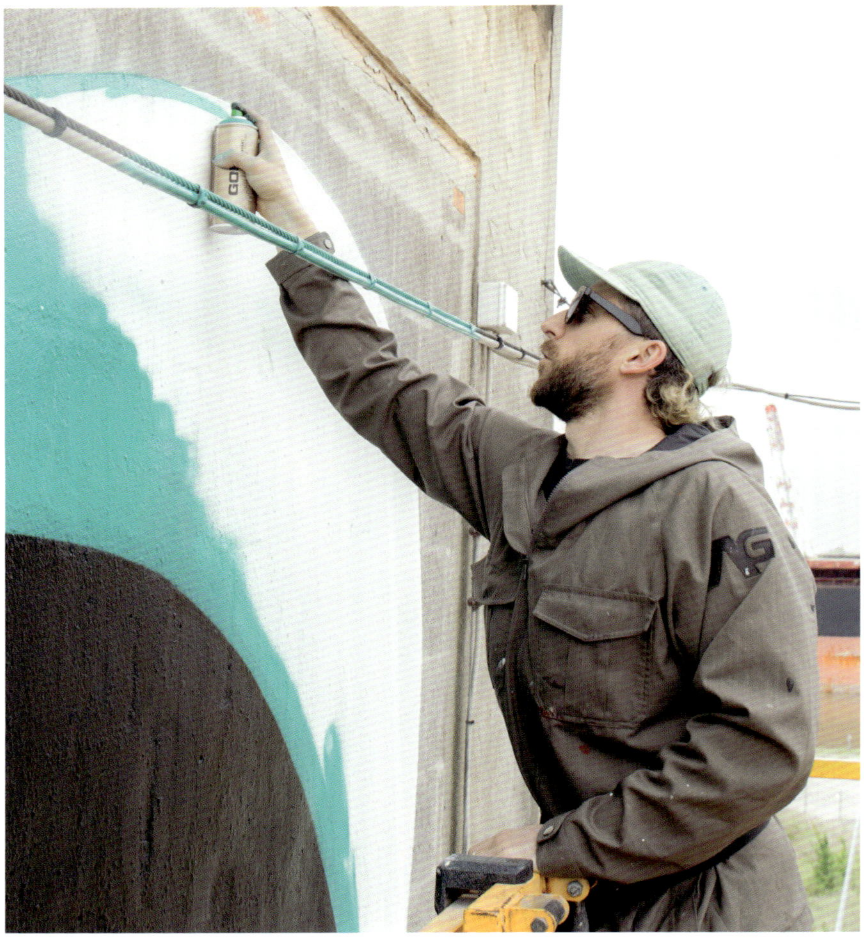

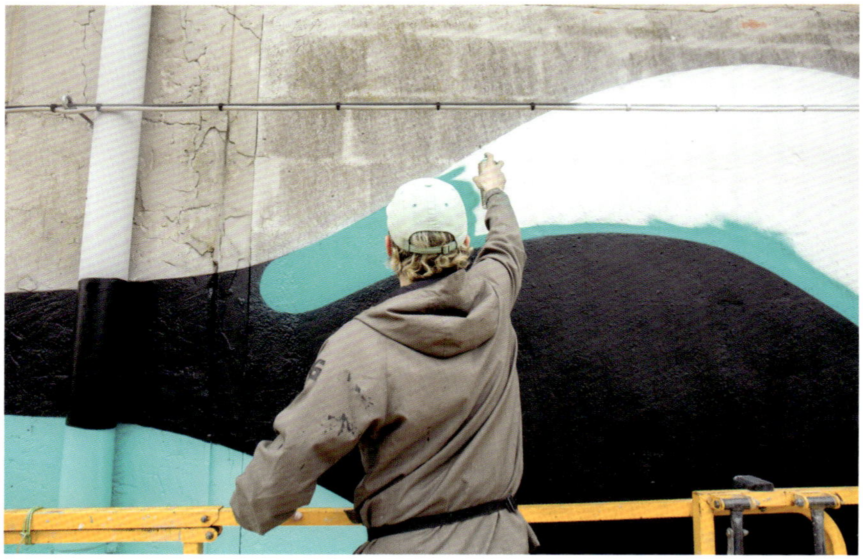

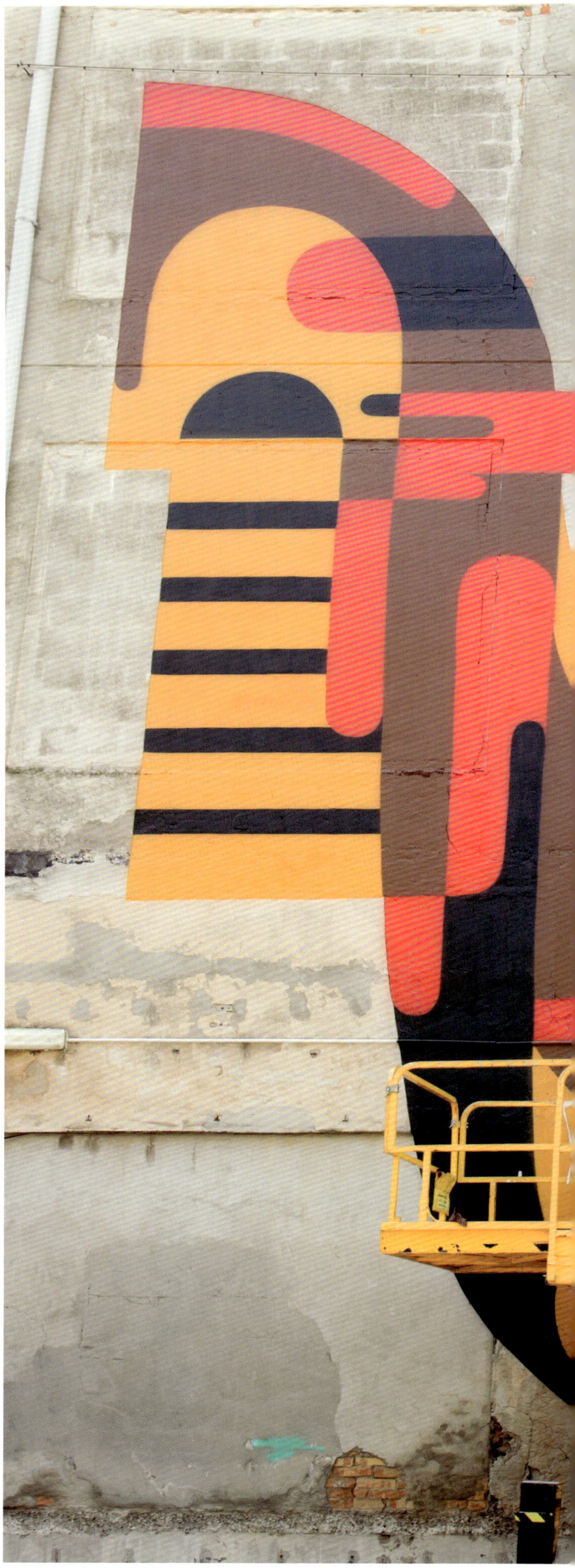

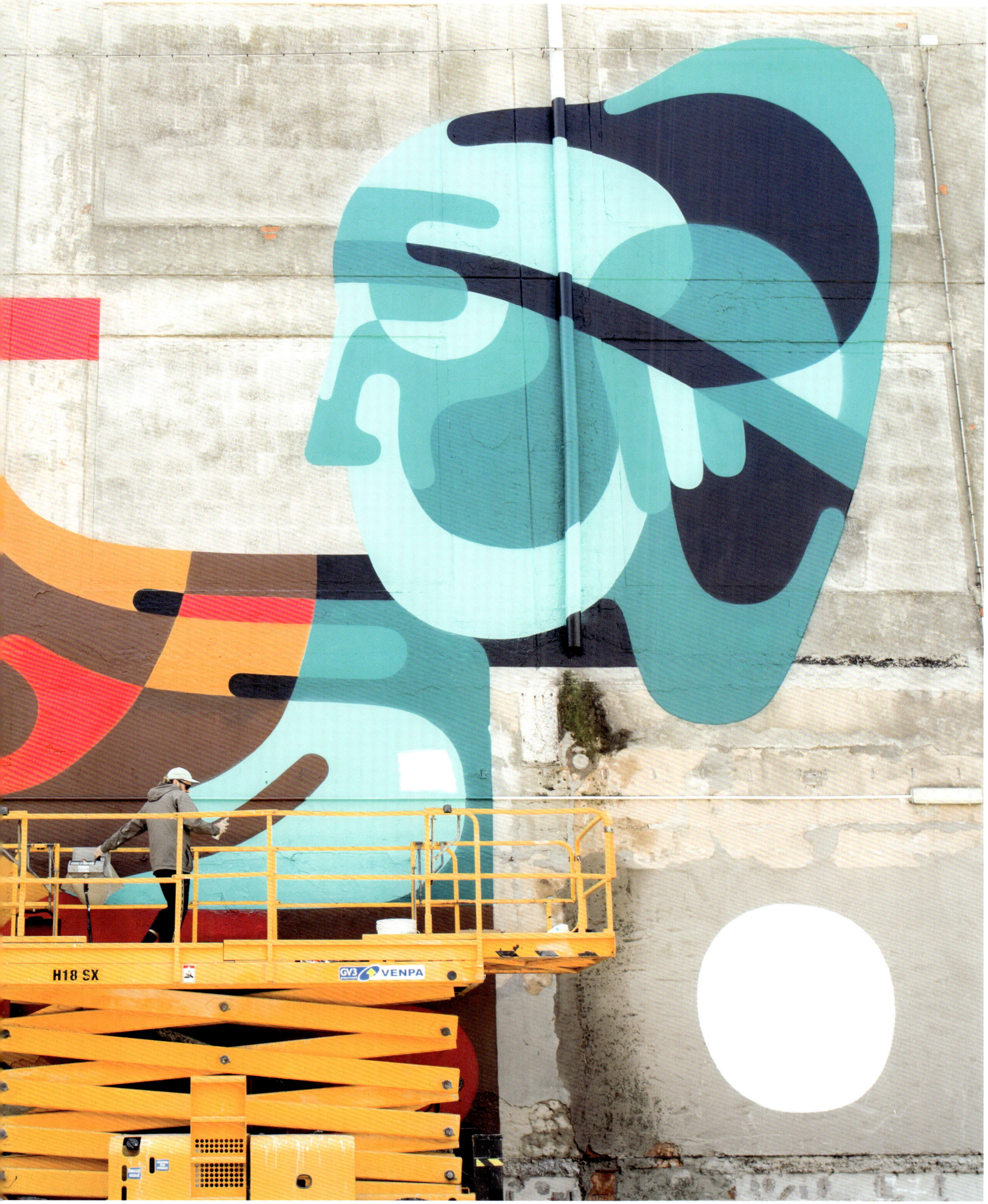
H18 SX
VENPA

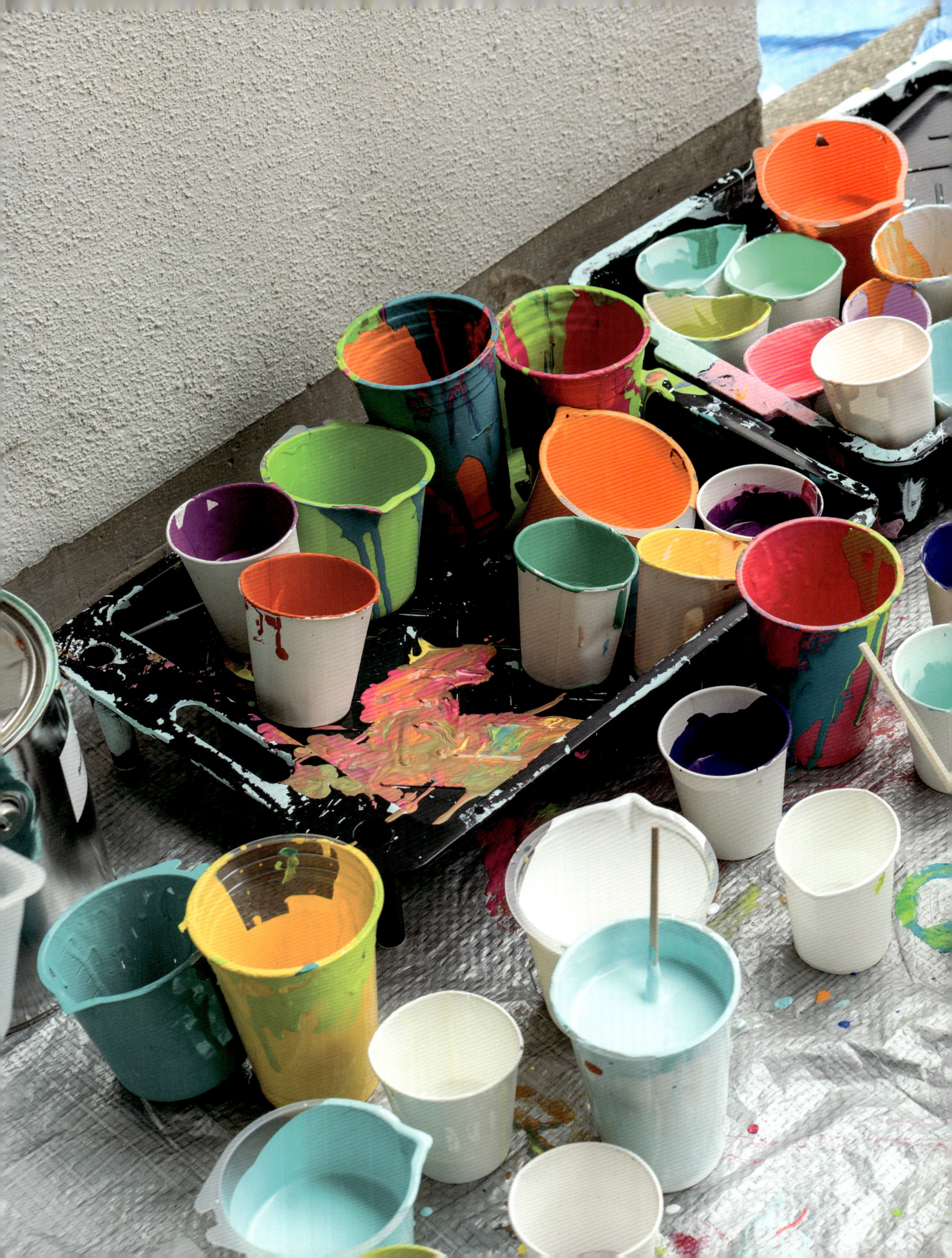

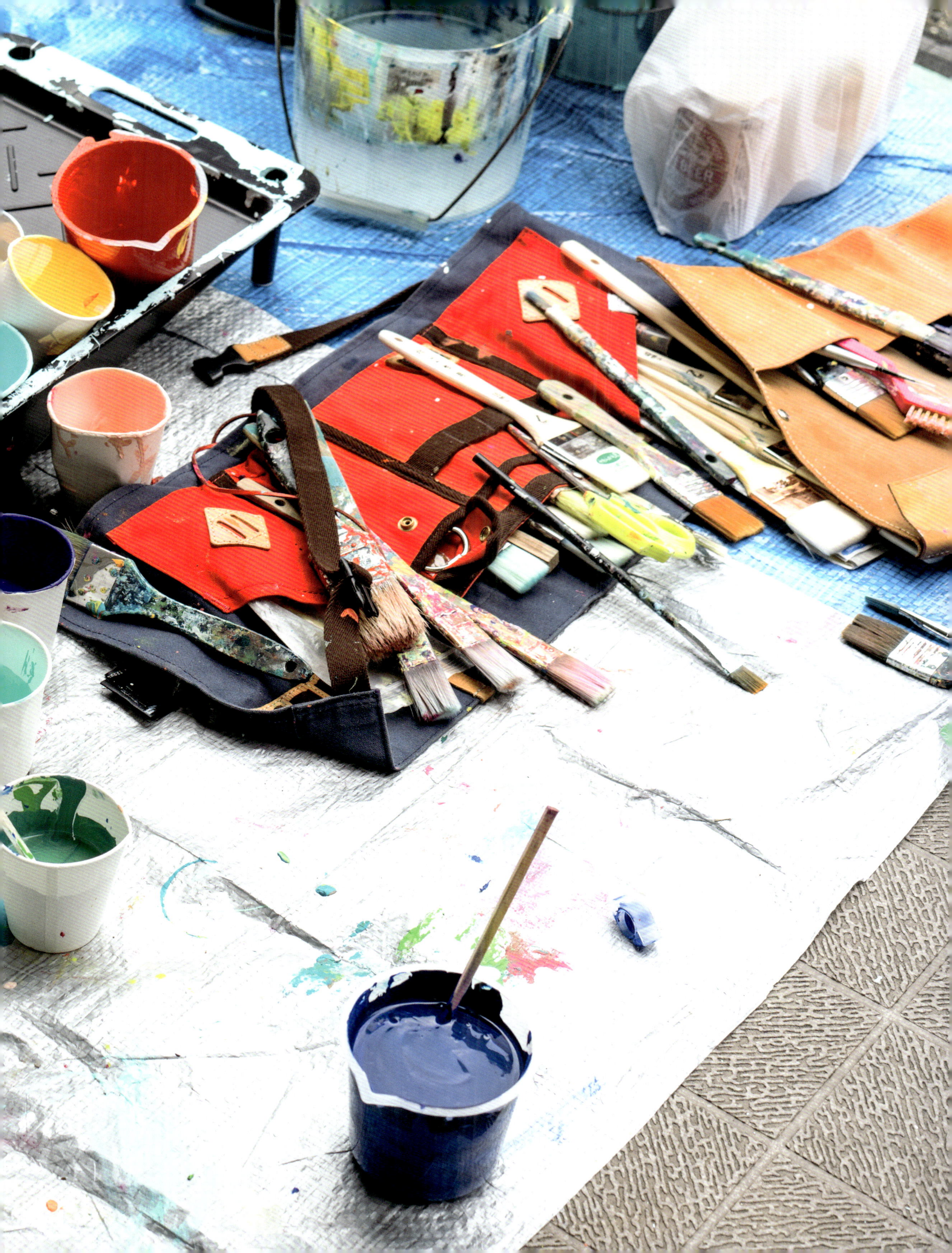

Photography Credits

123KLAN
@123klan

ANDREW TRAN
@weerdnaa

ANTONIO SEGURA
@dulk1

BRADLEY W JOHNSON

BRANDON SHIGETA
@bshigeta

BRYAN "BIRDMAN" MIER
@birdmanphotos

DANIEL WEINTRAUB
@halopigg

EMMA MCALARY
@em_mcalary

ERIC YEN
@hexalis

IAN LUNDIE
@1ill510

IAN ROCHE
@iansmash

JASPER WONG
@mrjasperwong

JEFF SOTO
@jeffsotoart

JEROME THOMAS

JOHN PANGILINAN
@ john_pangilinan

JONAS MAON
@jonasmaon

JOSEPH SONG
@thegyopo

JOSHUA AGERSTRAND
@joshuabarrigada

LAN NGUYEN
@lannycatcheswalls

LEON KEER
@leonkeer

MARINNA JULIAN
@marinn_

MARK KUSHIMI
@markkushimi

MIKEY INOUYE
@minouye

MJAY PHOTOGRAPHY
@mjayphotos

SEAN MARC LEE
@seanmarclee

Hawaii

pp. **10–11**, **16–19**, **34–35**, **40–41**, **50** .. © Brandon Shigeta
p. **51** .... © Jonas Maon

WILL BARRAS
pp. **20–23** .... © Brandon Shigeta

OG SLICK, 123KLAN, & FLYING FORTRESS
pp. **24–25**, **26** (TOP, & BOTTOM-LEFT) ...... Courtesy of 123Klan
pp. **26** (BOTTOM-RIGHT), **27** .... © Brandon Shigeta

NYCHOS & JEFF SOTO
pp. **28–29**, **30** (BOTTOM), **32–33** .... © Brandon Shigeta
pp. **30** (TOP), **31** .... Courtesy of Jeff Soto

JAMES JEAN
pp. **37–39** .... © Brandon Shigeta

D*FACE
pp. **42–43** .... © Brandon Shigeta

AUDREY KAWASAKI
pp. **44–47**, & **49** .... © Jonas Maon
p. **48** .... © Brandon Shigeta

KEVIN LYONS
pp. **52–55** .... © Brandon Shigeta

JAMES BULLOUGH & RICKY WATTS
pp. **56–57** .... © Jasper Wong
pp. **58**, **59** (BOTTOM-LEFT) .... © Ian Lundie
pp. **59** (TOP, MID-LEFT, RIGHT) .... © Lan Nguyen

SHEPARD FAIREY
pp. **60-63** .... © Ian Lundie

Taiwan

pp. **64–67** .... © Brandon Shigeta

RONE & AARON DE LA CRUZ
pp. **68**, **70–71** .... © Brandon Shigeta

CASE MACLAIM
pp. **72–75** .... © Brandon Shigeta

FELIPE PANTONE
p. **76** .... © Sean Marc Lee
p. **77** .... © Eric Yen

DULK
pp. **78**, **80–81** .... Courtesy of Antonio Segura

Long Beach

pp. **84–85** .... © Brandon Shigeta
p. **85** (TOP ROW) .... © John Pangilinan

TRISTAN EATON
pp. **86–89** .... © Brandon Shigeta

HEM, YAMAMOTO, & USHIRO
pp. **90**, **92–93** .... © Brandon Shigeta

TRAV MSK
pp. **94**, **96–97** .... © Brandon Shigeta

LEON KEER
pp. **98–99** .... Courtesy of Leon Keer

Japan

pp. **102–103** .... © Brandon Shigeta
pp. **104** (TOP-LEFT & RIGHT), **105** (TOP-RIGHT) © Mark Kushimi

HITOTZUKI
pp. **106–109** .... © Brandon Shigeta
pp. **110–111** .... © Mark Kushimi

CINTA VIDAL
pp. **112–115** .... © Brandon Shigeta

OG SLICK
pp. **116**, **118–119** .... © Brandon Shigeta

BRENDAN MONROE & JET MARTINEZ
pp. **120**, **122–123** .... © Brandon Shigeta

SXSW

pp. **124–127** .... © Brandon Shigeta

TATIANA SUAREZ & YOSKAY YAMAMOTO
pp. **128–131** .... © Brandon Shigeta

ESAO ANDREWS
pp. **132–133** .... © Jasper Wong

Antelope Valley

ANDREW SCHOULTZ
pp. **136–141** .... © Daniel Weintraub

TRAN NGUYEN
pp. **142–143** .... © Ian Lundie
pp. **144–147** .... © Bryan "Birdman" Mier

Washington D.C.

pp. **150–151** .... © Jasper Wong

DREW MERRIT & INSA
pp. **152–157** .... © Ian Roche

MADSTEEZ
pp. **158–159** .... Courtesy of Madsteez
pp. **160–161** .... © Ian Roche

RICHT
pp. **162–165** .... © Ian Roche
p. **166** .... © Bradley W Johnson
p. **167** .... © Emma McAlary

STOM500
pp. **168–171** .... © Ian Roche
pp. **170** (TOP-LEFT), **171** (BOTTOM-RIGHT) ... © Jerome Thomas

Worcester

pp. **174–175** .... © Daniel Weintraub

ARLIN GRAFF
p. **177** .... © Jasper Wong

PICHIAVO
pp. **178–183** .... © Daniel Weintraub

THE LONDON POLICE
pp. **185–187** .... © Ian Lundie

Guam

pp. **188–189**, **190** (TOP-LEFT, TOP-RIGHT, BOTTOM-RIGHT),
191 (BOTTOM-LEFT) .... © Brandon Shigeta
p. **190** (BOTTOM-LEFT & CENTER, MID-RIGHT) ... © Marinna Julian
p. **191** .... © Joshua Agerstrand

NATUREL
pp. **193**, **194** .... © Brandon Shigeta
p. **195** .... © Joshua Agerstrand

ONEQ
pp. **196–199** .... © Ian Lundie

Israel

pp. **200–201**, **202–203** (TOP ROWS) .... © Andrew Tran
pp. **202–203** (BOTTOMS ROWS) .... © Jasper Wong

CRYPTIK
pp. **204–207** .... © Jasper Wong

Korea

pp. **208–211** .... © Brandon Shigeta

PERSUE & JASPER WONG
pp. **212–215** .... © Brandon Shigeta
p. **216** .... © Joseph Song
p. **217** .... © Andrew Tran

San Jose

JET MARTINEZ
pp. **220–221**, **222** (LEFT) .... © Ian Lundie
pp. **222–223** .... © Lan Nguyen

HOW & NOSM
pp. **224–228**, **229** (BELOW) .... © Ian Lundie
p. **229** (ABOVE) .... © Lan Nguyen

Nepal

LAUREN YS
pp. **232–237** .... © Mikey Inouye

Rotterdam

SUPER A
pp. **240–243** .... © Mjay Photography

Venice

REKA
pp. **246**, **248–249** .... © Lan Nguyen

pp. **250–251** .... © Brandon Shigeta

We are inspired by Native American Pow Wows.

Pow Wows are the Native American people's way of meeting together, to join in dancing, singing, visiting, renewing old friendships, & making new ones. This is a time method to renew Native American culture and preserve the rich heritage of American Indians.

There are several different stories of how the pow wow was started. Some believe that the War dance Societies of the Ponca and other Southern Plains Tribes were the origin of the Pow Wow.

Pow Wow singers are very important figures in the Native American culture. Without them there would be no dancing. The songs are of many varieties, from religious to war to social.

As various tribes gathered together, they would share their songs, often changing the songs so singers of different tribes could join. With these changes came the use of "vocables" to replace the words of the old songs. Thus, some songs today are sung in "vocables" with no words.

Yet they still hold special meaning to those who know the song. Many songs are still sung in Native American Languages either newly composed or revivals of old songs. These songs are reminders to the Indian people of their old ways and rich heritage.

Dances have always been a very important part of the life of the American Indian. Most dances seen at pow wows today are social dances which might have had different meanings in earlier days. Although dance styles and content have changed, their meaning and importance has not. The outfits worn by the dancers, like the styles of clothing today evolve over time, it is not a stagnant culture, but a vibrant and changing way of life.

Gathering of Nations Pow Wows are organized by committees that work for weeks before the event. At the Pow Wow, the MC runs the events. The MC works with the Arena Director to keep the Pow Wow organized and running smoothly. These two individuals along with the committee work hard to bring the people together to dance and fellowship together in the circle.

Learn more about Native American Pow Wows at:
www.powwows.com

PARAGON BOOKS